VICTORIAN LITERATURE AND CULTURE

Volume 21

ADVISORY BOARD

VICTORIAN LITERATURE AND CULTURE

Volume 21

EDITORS

JOHN MAYNARD
ADRIENNE AUSLANDER MUNICH

Associate Editor: Sandra Donaldson

Managing Editor: Abigail Burnham Bloom

Review Editor: Winifred Hughes
Assistant Review Editor: Susan Katz

Special Effects Editor: Jeffrey Spear
Assistant Special Effects Editor: Pearl Hochstadt

AMS PRESS
1993

Copyright © 1994 by AMS Press, Inc.
ISSN 0092-4725
Series ISBN 0-404-64200-4
Vol. 21 ISBN 0-404-64221-7
Library of Congress Catalog Card Number: 73-80684

For current subscription information or back orders for volumes 1–20, write to AMS Press, Inc., 56 East 13th Street, New York, NY 10003, USA

VICTORIAN LITERATURE AND CULTURE is a publication of the Browning Institute, Inc., a nonprofit organization. It is published through the generous support of New York University and the State University of New York at Stony Brook. The editors gratefully acknowledge our indebtedness to our editorial assistants Lisa Golmitz, Catherine Pavlish, and Mary Sullivan.

Manuscripts and editorial correspondence can be addressed to either editor: Adrienne Munich: Department of English, SUNY/Stony Brook, Stony Brook, NY 11794 (516 632 9176; fax: 516 632 6252). John Maynard: Department of English, NYU, 19 University Pl., Room 235, N.Y., NY 10003 (212 998 8835; fax: 212 995 4019).

Please submit two copies of manuscripts; articles should be double-spaced throughout and follow the new MLA style (with a list of Works Cited at the conclusion). Chapters of books submitted for the *Works in Progress* section may follow the author's chosen style in the book project.

Correspondence concerning review essays should be addressed to Winifred Hughes: 50 Wheatsheaf Lane, Princeton, NJ 08540 (609 921 1489).

Suggestions for reprints of Victorian materials, texts or illustrations, should be addressed to Jeffrey Spear, Department of English, NYU, 19 University Pl., Room 200, N.Y., NY 10003 (212 998 8820; fax: 212 995 4019).

All AMS Books are printed on acid-free paper that meets the guidelines for performance and durability of the Committee on Production Guidelines for Book Longevity of the Council on Library Resources.

Manufactured in the United States of America

CONTENTS

Revelations on Pages and Stages   1
    NINA AUERBACH

"Signs of Things Taken'': Testimony, Subjectivity, and the   19
    Nineteenth-Century Mug Shot
    JENNIFER M. GREEN

Under Cover of Sympathy: *Ressentiment* in Gaskell's *Ruth*   51
    AUDREY JAFFE

John Bull and His "Land Ohne Musik"   67
    EMILY AUERBACH

Reform, Rescue, and the Sisterhoods of *Middlemarch*   89
    MICHAEL COHEN

It Thought It Were a Mouse-Trap: The *Sylvie and Bruno* Books   111
    as Archetypal Menippean Satire
    EDMUND MILLER

Family Secrets and the Mysteries of *The Moonstone*   127
    ELISABETH ROSE GRUNER

The Sorrows of Carlyle: Byronism and the Philosophic Critic   147
    ANDREW ELFENBEIN

The Empire as Metaphor: England and the East in *The Mystery*   169
    of Edwin Drood
    JOHN S. DEWIND

Observation and Domination in Hardy's *The Woodlanders*   191
    CATES BALDRIDGE

Sir Walter Besant and the "Shrieking Sisterhood"   211
    EARL A. KNIES

A Cinderella Among the Muses: Barrett Browning and the   233
       Ballad Tradition
    MARJORIE STONE

WORKS IN PROGRESS

E. M. Forster at the End   271
    RICHARD DELLAMORA

Retelling the Story of Science   289
    BARBARA T. GATES

"Certain Learned Ladies": Trollope's *Can You Forgive Her?*   307
       and the Langham Place Circle
    MARGARET F. KING

Muscular Anxiety: Degradation and Appropriation in *Tom*   327
       Brown's Schooldays
    DONALD E. HALL

Looking at Cleopatra: The Expression and Exhibition of Desire   345
       in *Villette*
    JILL L. MATUS

REVIEW ESSAYS

Feminism, History, and the Nineteenth-Century Novel   371
    DEBORAH EPSTEIN NORD

"A Terrible Beauty is Born": Textual Scholarship in the 1990s   379
    JUDITH KENNEDY

Index   389

ILLUSTRATIONS

Page 30–31

1. "The Bashful Model." *Harper's Weekly*.

Page 35

2. Thomas Byrnes, "The Inspector's Model."

Pages 37-40

3. Edward McCarthy, identification card.

4. Edward McCarthy.

5. Isma Martin.

6. J. B. Black.

Pages 43-44

7. Measuring features as part of the Bertillon system.

8. Bertillon system.

Page 76

1. Thomas Rowlandson, "John Bull at the Italian Opera" (111).

Page 81

2. Tables of Contents from *The Musical Herald: A Journal of Music and Musical Literature*.

Pages 349, 351, 352, 353

1. Hans Makart, "The Death of Cleopatra."

2. Eugène Delacroix, "Women of Algiers in their Room."

3. Auguste Renoir, "Odalisque."

4. Edouard De Biefve, "Une Alme."

REVELATIONS ON PAGES AND STAGES

By Nina Auerbach

A FRENCH ACTRESS MAKES A cameo intrusion into the ordinariness of *Middlemarch* to stab her husband onstage. The murder is not important; British domesticity is filled with murders, if less conspicuous ones. What matters in *Middlemarch*, that exactingly scientific anatomy of character, is the theatrical meaning of the murderer. Laure does her best to explain herself to the worthy British doctor who offers to marry her into salvation, but she does so by eluding all explanations novels offer.

> "I will tell you something," she said, in her cooing way, keeping her arms folded. "My foot really slipped."
> "I know, I know," said Lydgate deprecatingly. "It was a fatal accident — a dreadful stroke of calamity that bound me to you the more."
> Again Laure paused a little and then said, slowly, "*I meant to do it.*"
> Lydgate, strong man as he was, turned pale and trembled: moments seemed to pass before he rose and stood at a distance from her.
> "There was a secret, then," he said at last, even vehemently. "He was brutal to you; you hated him."
> "No! he wearied me; he was too fond: he would live in Paris, and not in my country; that was not agreeble to me."
> "Great God!" said Lydgate, in a groan of horror. "And you planned to murder him?"
> "I did not plan; it came to me in the play — *I meant to do it*" (105; ch. 15).

The four main plots of *Middlemarch* linger over their slow self-formation through the gradual accretion of causes and consequences, but no planning or plotting explains this actress's eruption. Laure has no secret motive. She is as far from intelligible a character as another actress, Rachel, "the panther of the stage," is from recognizable humanity in George Henry Lewes's description of her: "with a panther's terrible beauty and undulating grace she moved and stood, glared and sprang. There always seemed something not

1

human about her" (35). Laure too defines herself in unfathomable motion. Melodramatic stage directions punctuate her story without explaining it: she coos, poses, pauses, prompting Lydgate to turn pale, tremble, even groan. Character in *Middlemarch* is constructed as "a process and an unfolding" (102; ch. 15), but Laure's performance unfolds out of nothing and leads nowhere. It "means" the intensity of its moment.

Laure's "I meant to do it" is purely theatrical and, thus, in a realistic novel, deeply chilling. Even comically conventional inhabitants of Middlemarch are made of intricate causal patterns: "metaphorically speaking, a strong lens applied to Mrs. Cadwallader's match–making will show a play of minute causes producing what may be called thought and speech vortices to bring her the sort of food she needed" (39; ch. 6); but no microscope, not even Lydgate's, can penetrate Laure's play. Stage meanings lack the developmental logic of novelistic motivations; with the randomness of lightning, they illuminate the disruptions and inconsistencies of character. A stage murder can be simultaneously accidental and deliberate, motivated and gratuitous. The horrified Lydgate is quick to relegate Laure to "the throng of stupid criminals," but her crime's incongruities allow her to stand alone. "I do not like husbands," she explains cryptically, refusing to shape her taste into a coherent, categorizeable protest (105; ch. 15). George Eliot's contrapuntal case histories of the Casaubon, Lydgate, and Bulstrode marriages scrutinize the "play of minute causes" that can turn wifely organisms toward murder, but this wife has no discernible cause; she simply performs.

From a nineteenth-century medical perspective, the abruptness of Laure's obscurely-motivated act is a symptom of monomania, "a localized but profound break in the unity of the psyche" (During 86). To act out of character is, in this definition, to be insane, but Victorian theatrical characters take their lives from such localized, profound breaks. Galvanized by ontological eruptions clinicians called insanity, they hold audiences by refusing to make sense.

George Eliot's lulling narrative voice tempts readers to respond to the murder (if it is one) as Lydgate does, resisting Laure's performance by categorizing her; it is easier to label than to confront the rifts performers expose in one's own character. Laure, however, ruptures Lydgate's own seeming consistency, exposing him as "incongruous" and therefore, according to his own profession's definition, mad:

> He knew that this was like the sudden impulse of a madman — incongruous even with his habitual foibles. No matter! [Marrying Laure] was the one thing which he was resolved to do. He had two selves within him apparently, and they must learn to accommodate each other and bear reciprocal impediments. Strange, that some of us, with quick alternate vision, see beyond our infatuations, and even while we rave on the heights, behold the wide plain where our habitual self pauses and awaits us. (104; ch. 15)

But which self is Lydgate's real — or at least his habitual — one? The infatuated man is the one we know in the novel, not the calm gazer on the wide plain. The Lydgate we live with is a monomaniac, consumed by a single role, that of helpless consort to Rosamond, another, more refined killer of husbands. The scientific assurance of *Middlemarch*'s narrator, the firmness with which she traces causes that lead to universalizing generalizations ascending from "he" to "some of us" to the inclusive "we" and "us," distract the reader from Lydgate's chronic separation from his "habitual self." The intact observer on the wide plain gazes remotely at a histrionic double who has little in common with the true man.

Laure's melodramatic intrusion into the even rhythms of *Middlemarch* introduces a prospect more threatening even than the marital murder that will dominate the novel: the actress's volatility evokes an answering volatility in one of Eliot's most apparently stable characters. Confronting Laure, Lydgate lives in melodramatic stage directions, leaping and climbing onto the stage (104; ch. 15), turning pale, trembling, groaning in horror. Laure shows us a good doctor who might have a Mr. Hyde capering within him, who might even *be* this capering Hyde, and not the good doctor at all. The advent of the actress dislodges the intricate web of provincial life, exposing fissures in the integrity of character and the meaning of acts. Choices in *Middlemarch* are fraught with portentous, inevitable, and often tragic consequences, but Laure gives her key line, *"I meant to do it,"* all the arbitrary shock of a stage death. The randomness, the contingency, of the murder, its affinity with theatrical improvisation rather than tragic inevitability, call into question the very existence of an integral character defining itself in significant acts. The "habitual self" who "pauses and awaits us" on a "wide plain" becomes, like Beckett's Godot, a self who may never have been.

The energy of Victorian fiction comes from its compulsion to make sense of its own amplitude. *Middlemarch*, with its universalizing commentary, its scientific claims, epitomized the ambition of a form that aimed to rise above its ephemeral journalistic origins, struggling to transcend the part-issue's episodic clutter to rest on the stationary heights of an Arnoldian criticism of life. Like her characters, the narrator of *Middlemarch* experiments on her material to consolidate it, peering through microscopes, changing the lights for us, adding candles that turn random scratches into patterns, "unravelling certain human lots, and seeing how they were woven and interwoven" (96; ch. 15), in order to reveal their common sense. In 1871, with the novel poised on the verge of canonicity after decades of vulgar popularity, *Middlemarch* consolidated its genre's ambition to become literature by yearning, like its protagonists, toward "a binding theory which could . . . give the remotest sources of knowledge some bearing on [its] actions" (58; ch. 10).

But, as the sad self-knowledge of *Middlemarch* acknowledges, binding theories coerce as well as connect. The theatricality with which Laure unravels (if only for a page or two) the fabric of character woven into the assumptions that give *Middlemarch* its magnitude is, as Eliot's narrator might put it, a parable. Laure's capacity to make Lydgate erupt out of the self we are told is his own defines the danger the Victorian theater posed to the humanistic aspirations of its literature. The theater was an embarrassing inspiration to the Victorian novel, one whose centrality few literary scholars acknowledge, even today: critics' own quests for self-ennoblement through binding theories have led many to avoid acquaintance with that apparently primitive, scrappily-documented, but culturally crucial institution, the Victorian theater.[1] In the same spirit, as novelists strove to mature, to be morally and psychologically complex, they regarded the theater with the sort of apologetic obsession Lydgate directs to the women in his life: an increasingly formidable rival, the theater seemed to lure novelists into childlike regression, intoxicating them with lovely surfaces, with sensuality, with silliness, with an expensive incoherence that underlay its supposed moral clarity.

THE LURE OF THIS LIVING theater has little to do with the theatricality that is so pronounced in Victorian novels: fictional theatricality is less a gesture toward the theater than it is a diminution of it into the florid, the overwrought, the meretricious. Such "theatrical" characters as Dickens's Quilp or *Middlemarch*'s Raffles are eccentric enough to die without touching us: by epitomizing the theater's extravagance, they enhance the novel's apparent reality. Even the theatricality of that supposed theater-lover Dickens is fueled by competitive condescension, so that the two performances his novels represent — the antics of the Crummles company in *Nicholas Nickleby* and Wopsle's Hamlet in *Great Expectations* — are a truthtelling narrator's gleeful exposure of performing falsity.

Even critics who claim to relish the theater praise fictional theatricality in novelists' own condescending terms. J. B. Priestley, for example, celebrates the theatrical Dickens by relishing the exuberant excess of Wackford Squeers:

> Perhaps he is trying to make us, the readers, laugh. Perhaps . . . he is not really a horrible schoolmaster: *he is a superb comedian playing a horrible schoolmaster*. And as much might be said of many of the other characters, especially in the earlier novels. Perhaps other superb comedians are playing Sam Weller and his father, Dick Swiveller, Crummles, Mantalini, Pecksniff, and the rest. *They deliberately overdo their characters, making them more and more preposterous but more and more laughable, to entertain us.* (Priestley 27; second emphasis mine)

For Priestley, and for many humanist writers still, to be theatrical is to be safely fake; the theatrical flares Victorian novels send out are similar reassurances of preposterous exaggeration. But such reassuring signals appropriate the surface of theater while shunning its essence: a fluidity, an energy, like that of Eliot's Laure, that can infect an audience or murder a mate with no causes or consequences at all.

The art of theatrical character was concentrated in its murderers. From the ghoulish Sweeney Todd to the demure Lady Audley to the upright Mathias in *The Bells*, stage murderers seemed, on the face of it, more motivated than Laure; moreover, whereas they were always punished, she confesses and vanishes. But the ritual rewards and punishments of theatrical melodrama veiled an energy of violence that transcended motivation and made consequences irrelevant. "The frenzied nature of the homicide and the ensuing excess of the villain's retribution justify each other" (Kalikoff 28). Sinful or retributive, theatrical murder was above all a spectacle, one of the most popular exhibits in a medium whose essence was self-display. In *The Bells*, for instance, a respectable burgomaster's guilty memories of the murder he committed years before arouse all the resources of the stage: the domestic action opens out into an ornate dream sequence involving snowy visions, mesmerism, a trial, and hanging. Murder is the cue for theatrical spectacle, while in novels, it is generally a guarantee of seriousness. Thackeray's Becky Sharp is an alluring mimic until the novel damns her by hinting that she has not only mocked and robbed her fat adorer, she may also have killed him. Authenticating her perdition, Becky vanishes as a spectacle. Even in *Vanity Fair*, that most mobile of Victorian novels, murder fixes the soul. It is too weighty an activity for theatrical play.

Like twentieth-century films, the Victorian theater was memorable less for the sort of self-mocking exaggeration J. B. Priestley praises in Dickens than for intoxicating, surrealistically shifting images that often belied the rigid simplicity of the plays themselves: what was seen generally overwhelmed what was said. The visual profligacy of pantomime, its magic transformations, fluidity of gender and genre, set the tone of actual as opposed to fictional theatricality. "Late Victorian pantomime was the most purely visual, pictorial, and lavish of nineteenth-century theatrical arts and the most spectacular form of theatre in English stage history," claims theater historian Michael R. Booth. "Spectacle existed for its own sake more than in any other sort of theatre, feeding upon itself, growing bigger and bigger, greedily consuming all the resources of technology, money, and manpower it was given. Yet pantomime spectacle was a close relation of other kinds and other uses of spectacle," such as Henry Irving's lofty production of *Faust* at the Lyceum in 1885 (Booth 92). Even when it aspired to high culture, the theater lost itself in dizzying visual play, overwhelming high seriousness with transformations, dreams, and hypnotic nonsense.

Even a less aggressively sensuous theatricality can appear dangerous by definition. Jonas Barish's explication of Platonic antitheatricality speaks for all those who endorse the integrity of a Lydgate in the face of Laure's confusing and thus contaminating play:

> Mimesis, which can place new and unsettling thoughts in the mind, must be treated as a dangerous explosive. Except in rare moments, it works chiefly on the irrational side of us, giving license to our dreams and foul thoughts, to whatever in us is devious, intricate, and disordering. Theater being the quintessentially mimetic art, acting being radically founded in multiplication of roles and transgression of boundaries, all that is urged in suspicion of poetry, music, recitation, and the other arts must apply here with a maximum of force and a minimum of regretful qualification. (26)

Just as Laure functions as a "dangerous explosive" to Lydgate's steady identity, so the theatrical institution disrupted the mighty claims of a literature founded on assumptions of integrity. In the spirit that led Eliot to depict for our inspiration would-be heroes who are too noble for their trivializing age, Matthew Arnold exhorted to transcendence a literature whose mission was the preservation of our "best self" from dispersion into fragmented incoherence. But in the course of the nineteenth century, a literature committed to redeeming the best self from the tyranny of masks and petty roles confronted an increasingly successful rival: a theater that flaunted its mobility, aspiring to neither coherence nor transcendence. Even at its most artistic, when it "realized" supposedly timeless works of art — H. T. Craven's comedy *Meg's Diversion* (1866) contains the typical stage direction, "MEG *places her hand to her heart* — *Music* — *this realizes the picture of* [Philip Calderon's] *'Broken Vows'* " (Meisel 91–92) — these deceptively frozen moments dissolved, unlike paintings on canvas, as soon as the viewer recognized them, mocking by their momentariness the supposed permanence of art.

This medium of gorgeous transformations brought fame to actors who, unlike literary characters, thrived on versatility. Not only were nineteenth-century actors expected to play a wide assortment of ages and generic types as they learned their trade in strenuous provincial tours; they were adept at blending into gorgeous stage environments. Ideally, "a pictorial acting style perfectly suited a pictorial production style" (Booth 157); an accomplished actor could turn into paintings by any number of artists. But even the greatest champions of actors relegated them to a place in the aesthetic hierarchy far below that of artists and authors. Lewes, one of the few literary men to commemorate acting as an art, elevated performers in evocative prose portraits only to dismiss their importance: "He who can make a stage mob bend and sway with his eloquence, what could he do with a real mob, no poet by to prompt him?" (58). The actor is a sham made real only by the author's words. To dispel the mistrust of a self-preserving culture, Victorian actors gradually learned, once they became successful, to subordinate their many identities to the appearance of a best self, simulating the apparent consistency of fictional characters. These "devious, intricate, and disordering" beings, as Barish calls them, learned acceptable selves from novelists.

The rise of the nineteenth-century theater, its ascent out of mid-century disreputability to a fin-de-siècle centrality and chic that eclipsed the increasingly self-reflexive novel, is a wry achievement in an age that wanted its success stories to illustrate moral truths. Lady Macbeth might have supplied the moral of the theater's metamorphosis: "To beguile the time, look like the time" (I.v.61–62). Between 1861 and 1901 (the year Queen Victoria died and Henry Irving lost his regal position as actor-manager of the Lyceum), the theater normalized itself into respectability: it domesticated not only its settings, but its actors, purging itself of the disruptive mobility that threatened to become anything with no warning. The novel had by that time virtually made the leap from subversive popularity to cultural authority; inadvertently, it showed its chief competitor how to win respect. The last half of the nineteenth century brought the theater cultural canonicity when it learned to simulate the integrity of a readerly and middle-class approach to literary character.

Much has been written of the Robertsonian revolution of the early 1860s, in which the Bancrofts' tasteful mounting of Tom Robertson's gentle domestic comedies imported middle-class realism into a phantasmagoric medium (Rowell 75–84); Marie Bancroft's canny eye for new bourgeois norms turned her Prince of Wales's Theater into a simulation of a cozy home.[2] Less has been written about the tempering effect on actors of the Bancrofts' seductively ordinary mise-en-scène. Like their theater, the most successful Victorian performers subdued the versatility that, for most of them, was the pride of their art, embracing a uniformity that limited their repertoire while endearing them to audiences for whom knowable character was an article of faith.

The exemplary career of Henry Irving set the pattern of theatrical development: the knighthood Irving won in 1895 consolidated the respectability of the entire theatrical profession. Self-transformed from the obscure John Brodribb, Irving assumed a multitude of characters before he became the hero audiences imagined him to be. During the long provincial apprenticeship that preceded his London success, Irving played roughly 650 roles, becoming everyone conceived by an eclectic theater, from ugly stepsisters to handsome heroes, comic villains to glowing martyrs. His career turned in 1871, only a few weeks before the serialization of *Middlemarch* began, when he won acclaim for his guilt-stricken murderer Mathias in Leopold Lewis's *The Bells*. Audiences soon identified him solely with anguished repentance, choosing to forget that Mathias was initially only one act in an evening designed to display the performer's versatility, not his integrity: *The Bells* was originally paired with *Jingle*, an adaptation of Dickens's *Pickwick Papers* in which Irving played an irrepressible con man whose deceitful brio subverted Mathias's cathartic contrition. When he understood the nature of his own success, Irving pared away Jingle and the other manifestations of his diabolical comedy, forcing his beloved partner Ellen Terry to do the same in a bereavement from which she never recovered (Auerbach, *Ellen Terry* 175–266).

As he became more eminent and his Lyceum encased itself in high seriousness, Irving became more marmoreally Irvingesque until even admirers like Arthur Symons complained in 1893 that he was unable to sink himself into a part: "Mr. Irving, who is a man of genius, may be justly blamed, from a certain standpoint for the brilliant obtrusion of personality into all the characters which he represents" (qtd. in Stokes 91). Symons blames Irving for his most consummate histrionic achievement: the creation of a personality that destroys his potential to be many people, a personality that turns a player into a character as his age longed to believe in the term.

This amputation of superfluous selves is one of Victorian culture's most adept artistic compromises, one that both elevated the novel and made theatricality officially acceptable. Its legacy clings to performers today. The spurious intimacy of movies and television, whose gigantic close-ups allow us to mistake actors' moles and pores for their souls, and the pseudo-truthtelling imposed by typecasting, talk shows, confessional interviews, and memoirs, force generations of actors to bear witness to their sincerity before the public will accept them as performers. In a recent tribute to Cary Grant, Garson Kanin praised Grant's persona for its very monotony: "If an actor or an actress tries to create a different person, a different personality, for every single role, then the audience doesn't have anything to latch onto *except* the creative talent of that player. . . . They do not want a movie star to be anything but his own or her own self that they have come to admire and to love." Audiences shy away from the "creative talent" that makes a performer many people; an actor is multiple, but a star must be familiar. Our cultural unease with actors *as* actors is a story at least as old as the quests of nineteenth-century novelists for binding theories and Henry Irving's obliging suppression of his own and Ellen Terry's metamorphic play in deference to audiences looking for their souls.

IRVING'S CANNY TRANSFORMATION INTO a man one could claim to know was more than a theatrical trick affecting future actors and even, perhaps, the invention of the new, more apparently intimate theatrical technology of film and television. Irving's self-making was informed by an ideology that determined not only the politics of his profession, but literary assumptions about the integrity and significance of character: to be great was to be legible, even translucent, to suppress discontinuity and surprise. Heroes worthy of commemoration contract into their own best selves. In a sense Irving performed in his person one central compromise of the Victorian novel, whose domestication of performer into character made possible the quasi-religious ardor with which all classes of readers absorbed novels at their peak of cultural authority. Esther Summerson's fluctuating scars in *Bleak House* are a paradigm of the ineffable, ultimately banished theatricality of Victorian literary characters, because, like actors' multiple selves, these scars can be neither fully seen nor fully forgotten.

Esther Summerson carries half the narrative burden of Dickens's account of confusions, obfuscation, and tangled identities. The novel casts her in a healing role: her autobiographical narrative exemplifies the humane virtues of modesty, domestic duty, and kindness, "natural" attributes threatened with extinction by the stunting urban professionalism that infects the rest of *Bleak House*. Esther defines her purity of being by telling us about herself with compulsive precision: "I had always rather a noticing way — not a quick way, O no! — a silent way of noticing what passed before me, and thinking I should like to understand it better" (62–63; ch. 3). Too modest to tell us how good she is, she is a scrupulous if blushing recorder of others' praise: "Well! It was only their love for me, I know very well, and it is a long time ago. I must write it, even if I rub it out again, because it gives me so much pleasure. They said there could be no East wind where Somebody was; they said that wherever Dame Durden went, there was sunshine and summer air" (482; ch. 30). Writing herself and rubbing herself out at the same time, Esther rehearses and revises her character continually, collaborating with her adoring audience to shape the formless Somebody into the adorable Dame Durden.

Everything in *Bleak House* is a mystery except — ostensibly — Esther. Few characters in any novel are so incessantly and authoritatively talked about. But Esther radiates a subterranean fascination because she cannot be so easily labelled, even by her allegorical name: her visual life evades that sunny, summery designation. For one thing, she so uncannily resembles the proud Lady Dedlock, whose illegitimate daughter she will discover she is, as to take on the identity of an avenging ghost. Even to herself, she becomes alien and spectral. Seeing Lady Dedlock for the first time, she sees herself erupt out of her narrative: "*I — I*, little Esther Summerson, the child who lived a life apart, and on whose birthday there was no rejoicing — seemed to arise before my own eyes, evoked out of the past by some power in this fashionable lady" (305; ch. 18). Her specter overwhelms her defining name; the Esther who rises before her own eyes obscures the reassuring Esther in whom the rhetoric of the novel tells us to believe.

Smallpox intensifies this undefined visual intensity. Delirious, she dreams transformations — "Dare I hint at that worse time when, strung together somewhere in great black space, there was a flaming necklace, or ring, or starry circle of some kind, of which *I* was one of the beads!" (544; ch. 35) —

that are harbingers of her transformation once she is healed. The scars that destroy her youth and beauty turn her into the motherly, sexless Dame Durden she has struggled to construct. Esther's visual mutability forces her to become her own persona, obstructing her control over her future — she is less marriageable scarred — while giving her implicit power to question her apparently fixed identity. If her scarred self makes her the Dame Durden those who loved her had always called her, was the loving appellation itself a scar? And if Dame Durden is a mutilation of her true self, who was that authentic Esther *before* she was scarred? Or before she became Esther Summerson?

"Esther Summerson" is itself an assumed name like "Dame Durden" or "Henry Irving": Esther's mother's maiden name is Barbary, and her father is — ominously — "Nemo." Names in *Bleak House* are sinister; their abundance carries the hovering suggestion that Esther is no one. Visually though, there are more Esthers than names can encompass. A novel of preternatural visionary acuteness encourages us to look at Esther incessantly, but since her scars are evoked rather than described, we can never quite see her: she acquires the tantalizing indistinctness of a leading actress in a large nineteenth-century theater, a dominant presence never quite in focus. As with Victorian actresses, who turned themselves into enigmatic visual semaphores, each creating "her own sign conventions through which audiences perceived her" (Stokes, Booth, and Bassnett 4), Esther's haunting, half-visualized image suggests multiple possibilities of being.

At the very end of her story, we learn that there may be no scars; perhaps there never were? Her husband, a doctor more morally authoritative than Lydgate, if less scientifically adept, looks lovingly at an Esther beyond the reader's line of sight:

> "I have been thinking about my old looks — such as they were. . . . I have been thinking, that I thought it was impossible that you *could* have loved me any better, even if I had retained them."
> " 'Such as they were'?" said Allan, laughing.
> "Such as they were, of course."
> "My dear Dame Durden," said Allan, drawing my arm through his, "do you ever look in the glass?" (935; ch. 67)

Since the reader cannot look in Esther's glass, the novel gives no answer to this tender question. Its trick is to make us wonder how many faces that glass might reflect and to sense the inadequacy of verbal labels and even loving names before a play of visual identities whose elusive potential is richer than words.[3]

Within our dear, knowable Esther hover a multitude of possible Esthers, all of them darker, some more sinister, than the offical redeemer of *Bleak House*. In typical Victorian fashion, though, *Bleak House* curtails by its language and plot the multiple possibilities it allows its reader to glimpse. As Esther's genealogy and her illness combine to scatter her into myriad apparitions, her plot circumscribes her utterly. She begins by claiming that her story is "a progress": solitary and abused, she makes a new life, striving "to be industrious, contented, and kind-hearted, and to do some good to some one, and win some love to myself if I could" (65; ch. 3). But by the end, her progress is taken out of her hands: her narrative is resolved when she becomes a pawn in others' plots. Inspector Bucket untangles her genealogical narrative by whirling her off on a surreal midnight chase through the labyrinth of London; his helpless passenger is so bemused that she loses the threads, the characters, the settings, of her own story. The philanthropic John Jarndyce resolves her love story in his magnanimous present of her to Woodcourt, along with a new Bleak House the domestic virtuoso Esther is not even allowed to furnish. As Esther's fluid identities threaten to escape narrative definition, Dickens locks her in a plot that deprives her of narrative agency. Her destiny and identity are determined and defined by authorizing men. The many Esthers we cannot see in the mirror are overwhelmed by an Esther whose story is so consummately finished that we forget the stories she might have told.

At the end, singleness of being encases Esther and dissipates her scars; her tender doctor assures us that she is, after all, the "dear Dame Durden" we were always assured we knew. A scarred stage heroine, Isabel Vane in T. A. Palmer's dramatization of Ellen Wood's *East Lynne*, is less easily restored. This runaway wife returns to East Lynne, her former home, maimed by suffering and a railroad accident. She claims to be Madame Vine, her own children's governess. Her husband and children accept Madame Vine, though marginal household figures — a servant, a dependent comic spinster — recognize Isabel to no avail. Weeping hungrily over her son's deathbed, Isabel Vane/Madame Vine remains impenetrable to those she loves. Dying little William longs to meet his "very own mama" in Heaven but senses that knowledge is impossible even there: "Do you think we shall know everybody there, or only our own relations? . . . And shall I know her, I have quite forgotten what she was like; shall I know her?" (389).

Since Heaven is far from the Victorian stage, Willie dies unknowing, cuing his mother's celebrated curtain line, one of Victorian England's most famous and resonant laments: "Oh, Willie, my child dead, dead, dead! and *he never knew me*, never called me mother!" (390; emphasis mine). The transforming power of Isabel's scars is the climax of her theatrical fate; stage convention allows her to metamorphose out of domestic familiarity forever. No diagnosing husband overlooks Isabel's scars to tell her who she is. Mystery, opacity, and discontinuity determine the action even of this most moralistic of popular melodramas.

Ellen Wood's original novel gave the play its plot, but the novel dwells on the known and knowable, muffling the shock of Isabel's transformation as *Bleak House* does Esther's. Wood makes of transformation a universal principle by philosophizing windily about change; she hints at the domestic apathy of Isabel's noble husband and his second wife Barbara; she enumerates in clinical detail the injuries that make Isabel's transformation appear plausible; she connects wife and governess by focusing on Isabel's agony, her perpetual condition in the novel. Above all, Wood uses East Lynne itself as a principle of permanence that heals the breach between Isabel Vane and Madame Vine: "Mr. Carlyle was in the room, this very room, and he had soothed her sorrow, her almost childish sorrow, with kisses sweet. Ah me! poor thing! I think our hands would have shaken as hers did. The ornament and the kisses were Barbara's now" (464; ch. 17). Ellen Wood does her best to consolidate Isabel Vane's scarred identity around the omnipresence of the house that holds her memories, while the stage Isabel Vane undergoes a metamorphosis no home can heal.

The case of these scarred heroines, all of whom are more or less successfully transported out of their lovable selves, is, in little, that of Victorian character at its most potent and potentially disruptive. Even the characters who consolidate such apparently seamless masterpieces as *Middlemarch* are prone to fissures and discontinuities that trouble omniscient authorities, for the life of all Victorian characters springs from an amorphous energy that goes beyond defining boundaries to share the performer's immeasurable suggestiveness. The metamorphic intensity of the Victorian theater threatens to swamp the redemptive moral coherence that justifies the existence of characters in novels.

In the second half of the twentieth century, academic critics have taken Victorian novels at their own monolithic valuation, stressing the unity, even uniformity, within their surface abundance. Mid-century formalist critics appreciated, not amplitude, but image patterns.[4] While for a later critical generation confusion is more alluring, its leaders — George Levine, for example — find heroism in insistent sense–making: "The Victorians, surely, did write with the awareness of the possibilities of indeterminate meaning and of solipsism, but they wrote *against* the very indeterminacy they tended to reveal. Their narratives . . . reconstruct a world out of a world deconstructing, like modernist texts, all around them" (4).

Even critics who make a profession out of resistance assume the single-mindedness of Victorian fiction. Feminist revisions like Gilbert and Gubar's *The Madwoman in the Attic* and its progeny find within the variety and versatility of novels by women a single story, re-told obsessively. Foucauldian critics try to fight free of the uniformity they assume is Victorian, accusing the novel of policing itself virtually out of existence in its adherence to "a linear, cumulative time of evolution" that "secures duration against the dispersive tendencies that are literally 'brought into line' by it. Once on this line, character or event may be successively placed and coherently evaluated" (Miller 26).

But this "line" is always about to be broken by the many things coherence cannot contain. Such readings of fiction suffer from the cultural parochialism they set out to expose, ignoring the disparate, half-acknowledged ideologies and genres that compose apparent hegemony. Victorian character is irresistibly dynamic because it is the site of an incessant struggle between the theatrical and the literary, the impulse to spill over boundaries and the will to confine. If we understand the values of a rival art form, the Victorian theater, we may appreciate the dynamic turbulence that keeps Victorian novels alive.

GEORGE HENRY LEWES, WHO bridged, ambivalently, the worlds of page and stage, defined this turbulence in his powerful appreciations of the Romantic actor Edmund Kean. Kean was spotty and unpredictable, but his intensity makes him the archetypal performing genius of Lewes's pantheon. Lewes commemorated Kean's greatness by repeating Coleridge's evocative tribute: "seeing Kean act was reading Shakespeare by flashes of lightning" (Lewes 14).

This paradoxical activity defines the mixed nature of Victorian performance. To Victorian bardolators, Shakespeare was so elevated a hero that he was virtually immobile; serene and still, "out-topping knowledge" in Matthew Arnold's reverent sonnet, England's literary emblem of greatness was nothing if not consistent (Auerbach, *Private Theatricals* 4–8). But lightning brings mystery, mobility, discontinuity, fracturing the Bard's wisdom into a message no longer entirely comprehensible, turning the placid receptiveness of reading to struggle and uncertainty. Shakespeare on the page is an untroubled seer whom the stage can electrify into shapes as strange as those of another creature: Frankenstein's, who is also animated by lightning. The contesting lives of Shakespearean characters in the nineteenth century embody the discordant vitality of constructions of character itself.

His Ophelia is neither a monumental actor like Henry Irving nor a fictional narrator like Esther Summerson: she is somewhere between them, at once narrative cipher and visual icon, whose potential for autonomous existence took on, in the nineteenth century, the authority of myth. Ophelia begins her undefined life in Shakespeare's *Hamlet*, but her nineteenth-century incarnations in various narrative genres make her a site of the age's tension between mobility and domestication. Fully at home neither in novels nor onstage, haunting both, but hinting at stories foreign to both, Ophelia is the nebulous essence of Victorian character.

She is a cipher in Shakespeare. Ellen Terry, whose Ophelia made her the poignant darling of late Victorian audiences, scrawled impatiently in one of her *Hamlet* scripts that Ophelia is "Nothing on a stick!" (Auerbach, *Ellen Terry* 214). Her sparse lines, her lack of poetry or initiative, her indeterminate motivation, place Ophelia among Shakespeare's most vacuous women, but visually, in the nineteenth century, she alone in *Hamlet* claimed the canvas; whereas Hamlet, in his few representations, emerges monotonously as the same darkly-clad brooder, Ophelia's drowning and death animate a medley of powerful, preternatural female figures.[5]

As a living painting, Ophelia transcended the sketchiness of her role in the text. Her visual presence was so potent that it galvanized theatrical representation. Indelibly identified with Ophelia, Ellen Terry became the prisoner of her own pictorial plenitude. Michael R. Booth describes her power over artists and theirs over her performance:

> her Ophelia created a pictorial as well as a theatrical stir. The Pre-Raphaelite qualities of her portrait of the character are evident in Henry James's description of "a somewhat angular maiden of the Gothic ages," and Hiatt's comparison with a Pre-Raphaelite saint or a madonna by Giovanni Bellini — a clear pictorialization of the innocence and purity in Ophelia. George Bernard Shaw took the view that a picture had come to life; the actress had added what she learnt in the studio [in her year as G. F. Watts's wife and model, when she posed for his Ophelia paintings] to what she learnt on the stage so successfully that "it was exactly as if the powers of a beautiful picture of Ophelia had been extended to speaking and singing." (Stokes, Booth, and Bassnett 83–84)

This Ophelia is the creature of so many disparate artists that she becomes, it seems, *any* picture by any number of painters. Her visual authority infiltrates even the majestic objectivity of Victorian science: Ophelia engravings illustrated medical types of female insanity, allowing doctors to "explain" their patients by dressing them up to be photographed in the conventional Ophelia garb of garlands, weeds, and white draperies (Showalter 80, 86). The escape of character from character's confines could go no further. As spectacle, Ophelia gains an authority — aesthetic, religious, political, and scientific — utterly foreign to her literary role. No words on a page can encompass the Ophelias spectators saw.

In literature, though, Ophelia's parallel story is one of overdetermination and constraint. The literary appropriation of Shakespeare begun by the Shakespearean narratives of Coleridge, Lamb, and Hazlitt and extending into our own century was at odds with the multiple suggestiveness of visual imagery and with the speaking silences possible in the theater. Coleridge, for example, recreates Ophelia as absence, expatiating on Hamlet's reference in the nunnery scene to "the faults of the sex from which Ophelia is so characteristically free that the freedom therefrom constitutes her character. Here again Shakespeare's charm of constituting female character by absence of characters, [of] outjuttings.'' Coleridge's approval relegates Ophelia from multiplicity to negation; she is what she is not: ''The soliloquy of Ophelia is the perfection of love! — so exquisitely unselfish!'' (Coleridge 1:27). ''This antitheatrical understanding of Shakespeare,'' as Jonathan Arac calls it, commemorated a version of character that was coherent, consistent, and above all, explicable in words and reducible to them (323). Its Ophelia modulates accordingly from a demi-divinity exuding undefined powers to the suffering star of a case history whose motives are translucent. Like Lydgate confronting the disruptive surprises of Laure, literature classifies Ophelia when it considers her at all, turning her into a type amenable to explication.

Ophelia makes cameo appearances in various novels, doubling at key moments for broken, maddened women like Maggie Tulliver or Catherine Linton: at their grandest and most doomed, mid-Victorian heroines take on the contours of painters' mad Ophelia icon. But her most powerful and sustained appearance comes in a work that is now unfairly derided: Mary Cowden Clarke's popular series of novelistic case histories, *The Girlhood of Shakespeare's Heroines*. With great ingenuity, Clarke ''explains'' each heroine by providing her with a minutely realized and vivid childhood development, forming her character and elaborating her motivations so carefully that her behavior in her play becomes a mere coda to the drama of her girlhood. Clarke's *Girlhood* is the Victorian novel's most consummate and compelling capture of the stage: Shakespeare's sketchily-realized heroines, who can be played in any number of ways, are exhaustively interpreted in a series of novels of development. ''The Rose of Elsinore,'' Clarke's account of the successive traumas that form Ophelia, locks the heroine into so harrowing a series of events that there is no room in her character for disruptive ambiguities.

Clarke's Ophelia begins life as a vacancy:

> The babe lay on the nurse's knee. *Could any impression have been received* through those wide–stretched eyes, that stared as wonderingly *as if* they were in fact beholding amazed the new existence upon which they had so lately opened, the child *would have seen* that it lay in a spacious apartment, furnished with all the tokens of wealth and magnificence, which those ruder ages could command. (2: 183, emphasis added)

The babe has no character; her eyes are sightless. Bringing nothing to her world, she grows up to take the shape of the terrible events that happen to her. These events are initiated by a group of women who have no place in Shakespeare's kingdom.

Her loving mother Auodra must leave the child with her nurse to travel to Paris with the clownish Polonius — an ancillary figure in Clarke's revision. Ophelia's stay among peasants is a cadenza of sexual traumas. Jutha, her young companion and protector, is seduced by Eric, a careless and cruel aristocrat; she dies when he abandons her. Simultaneously, Ophelia is pursued by the bear–like simpleton Ulf, a personification of brutal male sexuality. Auodra returns in the nick of time as Ulf is about to molest the child, but the girl's return to her family and station — the happy ending that would bring closure to most Victorian novels — holds only further abuse: at Court, Ophelia's new friend Thyra is seduced and abandoned by the same Eric who betrayed Jutha. In consequence the court woman dies still more horribly than the peasant girl.

In the climax of this carnage among women, Auodra dies as well. On her deathbed, she warns Ophelia — as if the preceding events were not warning enough — of the unknown Hamlet's capacity to betray her. Auodra is so authoritative and beloved that Polonius's later warning against Hamlet becomes superfluous, as, in fact, does all *Hamlet*'s ensuing violence. Ophelia's destiny and her madness are determined before the play begins. In case we doubt the power of one trauma to form her conclusively, the same trauma recurs with only slight variations. The heroine has no space for surprises. Anyone, under these circumstances, would become Ophelia.

Even Ophelia's silence, that theatrical virtue of her defective role, is naturalized out of mystery: it is an inevitable consequence of her transplantation. "Among these rough cottage people, more and more did the child feel herself alone and apart. Her shyness and sparing speech grew upon her. She was not unhappy; but she became grave, strangely quiet and reserved for a little creature of her years, and so confirmed in her habit of silence, that she might almost have passed for dumb" (2: 205). Everything is explained. Like Esther Summerson in the final chapters of *Bleak House*, Clarke's Ophelia is the consummate creature of events. She loses her variety to become her plot.

This discrepancy among Ophelias defines an age that could not stop telling stories, while insisting on controlling the stories it told. The visual energy of Victorian performance fought with a narrative ideology avid to define, to place, to understand, to explain. This tension between what we see and what is said, between the theatrical and the diagnostic imaginations, accounts for the uncanny life of nineteenth-century characters. Generated from warring ideologies, haunting, as Ophelia does, mighty opposites, they simultaneously played and evaded all the incompatible needs cultural imperatives demanded they fulfill.

University of Pennsylvania

NOTES

1. Some exceptions, to which this essay is greatly indebted, are Meisel, Woodring, and Eigner, who have begun to weave coherent cultural statements out of the apparently intractable empiricism of Victorian theater history. See also my *Ellen Terry* and *Private Theatricals*.

   In order to dispel the vexed academic distinction between "drama" (plays studied as literary texts) and "theater" (attention to the elusive conditions within which plays are seen and heard), I quote a theater historian's stirring definition of his enterprise: "The miracle of theatre is that a community, an audience, has agreed to let drama happen" (Styan 3). This essay asks the reader to imagine the sketchy texts of Victorian drama "happening" before audiences whose senses were more responsive than their official ideology.

2. In 1898, Arthur Wing Pinero's nostalgic *Trelawney of the "Wells"* celebrated the marriage between theatricality and middle-class respectability that the new domestic realism made possible, thus formulating a metatheatrical myth of a union that was in fact an unresolved, if fruitful, antagonism in the world beyond the stage.

3. Esther's scars forced a recent BBC serialization into laborious ingenuity. A doctor was dragged in to explain that smallpox scars sometimes faded; they did so accordingly, with predictable regularity from episode to episode, as the actress's face evolved from near-leprous disfigurement to perfect clarity in the end. In Dickens's novel, though, the mobile scars are emblems of a play forbidden by conventional characterization, making us see out of the corner of our eye a medley of Esthers beyond the boundaries of her official identity. The theatrical suggestiveness of *Bleak House* may be too delicately subversive for theatrical adaptation.

4. See, for instance, Barbara Hardy's influential account of George Eliot's covert coherence:

   The novel may be described in terms of the outline — the disposition of its trunk and limbs — but it must also be recognized as depending on the presence of a pattern in every unit, like the pattern within the pattern of a Chinese puzzle or of any bit of matter. . . . George Eliot's organization, like Shakespeare's, extends, for instance, to her imagery. Her irony, her continuity, and her presentation of change and collision, depend to some extent on repetitions, more or less prominent, of phrases and images which may make a casual first appearance. (8–9)

5. Auerbach, *Ellen Terry* 106–11, 240–47, analyzes the variety of Victorian Ophelia paintings.

WORKS CITED

Arac, Jonathan, "*Hamlet, Little Dorrit*, and the History of Character." *South Atlantic Quarterly* 87 (Spring 1988): 311–28.

Auerbach, Nina. *Ellen Terry, Player in Her Time.* New York: Norton, 1987.

———. *Private Theatricals: The Lives of the Victorians.* Cambridge, MA: Harvard UP, 1990.

Barish, Jonas. *The Antitheatrical Prejudice.* Berkeley: U of California P, 1981.

Booth, Michael R. *Victorian Spectacular Theatre, 1850–1910.* London: Routledge, 1981.

Cary Grant: The Leading Man. PBS. October 23, 1989.

Coleridge, Samuel Taylor. *Shakespearean Criticism*. Ed. T. M. Raysor. 2 vols. London: Dent, 1960.

Cowden Clarke, Mary. *The Girlhood of Shakespeare's Heroines*. 3 vols. 1851. New York: AMS P, 1974.

Dickens, Charles. *Bleak House*. 1853. Harmondsworth: Penguin, 1971.

During, Simon. "The Strange Case of Monomania: Patriarchy in Literature, Murder in *Middlemarch*, Drowning in *Daniel Deronda*." *Representations* 23 (Summer 1988): 86–104.

Eigner, Edwin M. *The Dickens Pantomime*. Berkeley: U of California P, 1989.

Eliot, George. *Middlemarch*. 1871–72. New York: Norton, 1977.

Gilbert, Sandra M., and Susan Gubar. *The Madwoman in the Attic: The Woman Writer and the Nineteenth-Century Literary Imagination*. New Haven: Yale UP, 1979.

Hardy, Barbara. *The Novels of George Eliot: A Study in Form*. 1959. New York: Oxford UP, 1967.

Kalikoff, Beth. *Murder and Moral Decay in Victorian Popular Literature*. Ann Arbor: UMI Research P, 1986.

Levine, George. *The Realistic Imagination: English Fiction from Frankenstein to Lady Chatterley*. Chicago: U of Chicago P, 1981.

Lewes, George Henry. *On Actors and the Art of Acting*. New York: Brentano's, 1875.

Meisel, Martin. *Realizations: Narrative, Pictorial, and Theatrical Arts in Nineteenth-Century England*. Princeton: Princeton UP, 1983.

Miller, D. A. *The Novel and the Police*. Berkeley: U of California P, 1988.

Palmer, T. A. *East Lynne*. 1874. *Nineteenth-Century British Drama*. Ed. Leonard R. N. Ashley. Glenview, IL: Scott, Foresman, 1967, 353–96.

Priestley, J. B. "The Great Inimitable." *Charles Dickens, 1812–1870*. Ed. E. W. F. Tomlin. New York: Simon and Schuster, 1969. 13–31.

Rowell, George. *The Victorian Theatre, 1792–1914*. 2nd ed. Cambridge: Cambridge UP, 1978.

Showalter, Elaine. "Representing Ophelia: Women, Madness, and the Responsibilities of Feminist Criticism." *Shakespeare and the Question of Theory*. Ed. Patricia Parker and Geoffrey Hartman. New York: Methuen, 1985. 77–94.

Stokes, John. *In the Nineties*. Chicago: U of Chicago P, 1989.

Stokes, John, Michael R. Booth, and Susan Bassnett. *Bernhardt, Terry, Duse: The Actress in her Time*. Cambridge UP, 1988.

Styan, J. L. *Drama, Stage and Audience*. Cambridge: Cambridge UP, 1975.

Wood, Ellen. *East Lynne*. 1861. New Jersey: Rutgers UP, 1984.

Woodring, Carl. *Nature into Art: Cultural Transformations in Nineteenth–Century Britain*. Cambridge, MA: Harvard UP, 1989.

"SIGNS OF THE THINGS TAKEN": TESTIMONY, SUBJECTIVITY, AND THE NINETEENTH-CENTURY MUG SHOT

By Jennifer M. Green

IN 1911, IN ILLINOIS, a man named Jennings was convicted of murder upon the evidence of photographs that were introduced into court. The photographs were of a freshly painted fence on which Jennings had left his fingerprints during his escape from the site of the murder. Eyewitness accounts of the occurrence had been deemed inadmissible owing to their uncertainty; the photographs, however, were admitted, and were solely responsible for Jennings's conviction. In its record the court stated:

> A great deal has been written and said in the past concerning the doubtful nature of testimony identifying persons. Men's faces, like their handwriting, may be so similar that the keenest observer may be baffled in seeking to discover differences. "The witness," says Wharton['s book on Criminal Evidence], "is asked how he knows that the prisoner at the bar is the person who fired the fatal shot, and his answer is, 'I infer it from a similarity of eyes, of hair, of height, of manner, of expression, of dress.' Human identity, therefore, is an inference drawn from a series of facts, some of them veiled, it may be, by disguise and all of them more or less varied by circumstances." (*People v. Jennings*, 1081)

The court was correct in acknowledging that, for its purposes at least, identity is cumulative, the result of repetition, either in the individual (in having a sufficient number of similarities between him or herself and the person s/he is supposed to be) or of evidentiary signs (in pointing repeatedly to the same individual human source). The similarities between Jennings in court and the figure spotted leaping over the fence were insufficient to allow the testimonies of three eyewitnesses to be convincing, but the evidentiary signs of his fingerprints on the wet paint were so convincing that they alone were held

19

sufficient to convict. The case, unusual only in its precocious use of fingerprints as evidence, illustrates the fallibility of human testimony: although
three persons were witness to Jennings leaping the fence, none of their testimonies was admissible. The agentless camera, on the other hand, was pre-
sumed infallible.

Although testimony may falter because of the testifier's poor memory,
nervousness, or deliberate lies, it is obviously central to the process of a trial.
Black's Law Dictionary defines it as "evidence given by a competent witness
under oath or affirmation; as distinguished from evidence derived from writings, and other sources." While, as *Black's* says, "in common parlance,
'testimony' and 'evidence' are synonymous[; t]estimony properly means only
such evidence as is delivered by a witness on the trial of a cause, either orally
or in the form of affidavits or depositions" (1324). Testimony, then, begins
life as the spoken word and is, in its legal use at least, distinguished from
evidence, which may include writings and other artifacts. In its more general
use, W. V. Quine describes the mechanism of testimony as "an extension
of our senses. It was the first and greatest human device for stepping up the
observational intake. Telescopes, microscopes, radar, and radio-astronomy
are later devices to the same end" (51). The testimony of these instruments
has been deemed sufficiently reliable to allow the world to be represented
according to their evidence. In court the testifier presents certain pieces of
information which may or may not be deemed to be relevant. The function
of the jury, assisted by counsel, is to reassemble the pieces and decide whether
the narrative they are able to fashion from these bits of testimony is credible.

Ideal testimony, then, would logically be that from which only limited
narratives are possible, so that juries would necessarily believe the same
story. It would consist of what Quine calls "observational sentences" —
sentences which require no external information in order to bring one to the
conclusions of the testifier, sentences that make, in other words, no assumption of additional information other than what anyone would see were the
object of the sentence before one. Ideal testimony, of course, is an impossibility — the nature of the subjective experience will not allow otherwise — but
as a model it shares the same place in the courtroom as the ideal photograph,
which is self-explanatory, self-evident, and in consequence, undeniably true.
The difference between ideal testimony and the ideal photograph lies in the
fact that where the former is recognized to be an impossibility, the latter is
frequently produced in evidence.

During photography's early decades, the distinction made in the courts
between it and other forms of evidence lent credence to the theory that a
photograph might function as an observational sentence, that it could be
a self-evident and self-explanatory truth. Even into the twentieth century
photographs were described by the courts as "light printed pictures produced

by the operation of natural laws and not by the hand of man" (*Porter v. Buckley*, 142–43. Scott 2: 294); as "inerrant map[s] . . . drawn by the subtile forces of sunlight" (*State v. Clark*, 371. Scott 2: 294). More than sixty years after the invention of photography, human agency was still denied or overlooked, in the interests of empowering the scientifically "true" photograph.

Despite their figuration by courts as images produced "not by the hand of man," photographs have, in particular circumstances, been held to constitute "written evidence."[1] The word "writing" as used in Article one, section eight, of the Constitution, which secures to authors and inventors "the exclusive right to their respective *writings* and discoveries," has been construed to mean photographs (Scott 2: 304). This infers (by its grouping of the photographer with the author and the inventor) that photography does indeed involve human artistry and that it can produce not only something to which it is worth having exclusive rights but something to which it is *possible* to have exclusive rights.

The nineteenth-century photograph's status as non-writing, or more precisely as non-verbal artifact, was significant to the disagreement over whether photography was testimony, or merely testimonial in nature. A photograph appears to make ideal testimony by virtue of the fact that it does not consist of words and seems (therefore) to be more easily understood and more immediately effective through the apparently simpler relation which it has to the object that it represents; yet technically, and ironically, a photograph was not admissible as testimony in court precisely *because* it was not verbal.

Photographs were admissible as illustrations of oral testimony. If a wound, for example, were being described by a doctor, it was acceptable to use a photograph to illustrate the description. One such case inspired the court to offer its opinion that photographs were indeed preferable to oral testimony:

> we cannot conceive of a more impartial and truthful witness than the sun, as its light stamps and seals the similitude of the wound on the photograph put before the jury; it would be more accurate than the memory of witnesses, and as the object of all evidence is to show the truth, why should not this *dumb witness* show it? (*Franklin v. State*, 43. Scott 2: 297)

The language of the opinion reveals what was well before the eighteen-eighties part of the cultural baggage accompanying photography: its products, metaphorically, spoke. Although a photograph was denied the stature of true testimony in court, it was nonetheless figured as an "impartial and truthful witness" (albeit dumb), an image which suggests the photograph itself to be cognizant. As a matter of law, however, the photograph could not — and cannot — stand alone. The photographs of the fingerprints on the painted fence in *Jenkins* were introduced in addition to oral testimony, and actual pieces of the fence itself were exhibited. These photographs apparently were able to reveal the fingerprints more clearly than the naked eye could perceive them and were admissible as verification of the fact that Jenkins did indeed leave his prints upon the fence.

In order for any photograph to be admissible, accompanying testimony must be supplied by a witness who can state that what the photograph shows is an accurate representation of its subject. In the early years that testimony came from the photographer, but owing to the rapid widespread use of photography, expert witness was not long considered necessary. Any reliable person might testify that the photograph was an accurate picture of its subject. A photograph could not, despite the implications of popular language, stand alone as a witness.[2]

The conflict over whether or not a photograph should be permitted to serve as a witness, and in that sense give testimony, was fuelled by an emergent need for distinction between public and personal affairs. Although a photograph was not admissible as testimony in the courts, in instances which involved the forced making of identity photographs in the jails and police stations, it functioned as such. By photographing a man's body against his will, after all, one forced him to testify against himself. But in response to the grey areas surrounding one's rights to refuse to be photographed, the courts established that, as one's appearance is not a private concern but in effect belongs to the public domain, photographing a defendant against his or her will was (and is) "sometimes considered as non-testimonial and therefore not within the privilege against self-incrimination" (Scott 2: 307).[3] In such instances the photograph was viewed, in other words, as non-testimonial — although in function it was used as testimony to bear witness against its subject. The use of the photograph against its subject both inside and outside the courts thus urged a redefinition of notions of privacy. Deciding a case in 1902, Judge Gray concluded that "taking photographs without the previous consent of the subject . . . [had] the characteristics of 'a species of aggression,' " but he asserted that such aggression was in fact "an irremediable and irrepressible feature of the social evolution" (*Robertson v. Rochester Folding Box Co.*, 450. Wagner 199). The face was, and continued to be, held by the courts as not personal but rather public property, so that forcing individuals to have their photograph taken could not violate their privacy.[4]

Testimony in the courtroom was matched outside by a wider interest in personal reflection and autobiography. Most especially during the last decades of the nineteenth century, prisoners and other social deviants were encouraged to record their life histories as a contribution to the study of criminal motivation (Tagg 1: 47). As Michel Foucault has remarked, this "turning of real lives into writing . . . functions as a procedure of objectification and subjection," in which the life of the individual becomes the subject for study at the moment in which (and because) the subject is marked off as objectively different, aberrant, Other'' (191–92).

To the number of persons recording their own histories, we can add the many detectives and police officers who began to write down their experiences of dealing with criminals, as well as those individuals who were responsible for pseudo-autobiographies, such as *The Autobiography of a Thief* (1903), a text "recorded" by its "editor," Hutchins Hapgood, who assumes the voice of "ex-pickpocket and burglar," Jim, in order to tell the story of his downfall. Hapgood's apparently willing subject begins his recitation with the unlikely statement that "I shall tell my story with entire frankness. I shall not try to defend myself. I shall try merely to tell the truth. Perhaps in so doing I shall explain myself" (15). The emphasis in this and other such works of confessional ventriloquism is clearly on diagnosis, which proceeded according to the principle that what could be narrated or shown could be controlled and, ultimately, solved.

I

THE TASKS OF CONTROL AND solution were early assigned to photography in the public imagination. In act four of Dion Boucicault's Victorian melodrama *The Octoroon*, an American Indian, Chief Wahnotee, is accused of the murder of a young slave boy. At the scene of the crime is a broken camera belonging to the overseer, Salem Scudder; he, assorted bystanders, and the true murderer, Jacob M'Closky, hold an impromptu trial. Scudder believes Wahnotee to be innocent, but he has no proof. Then Pete, a slave, finds sticking out of the "telescopic machine" (the camera) a photographic plate. There in the picture is the image of M'Closky in the act of murder. Scudder is triumphant in his accusation:

> You slew him with that tomahawk; and as you stood over his body . . . you thought that no witness saw the deed, that no eye was on you — but there was, Jacob M'Closky, there was. The eye of the Eternal was on you — the blessed sun in heaven, that, looking down, struck upon this plate the image of the deed. Here you are, in the very attitude of your crime!

M'Closky of course repudiates the image, but his verbal denial, observes Scudder, is meaningless against the photographic plate before him: " 'Tis true! the apparatus can't lie. Look there . . . Look there. O, you wanted evidence — you called for proof — Heaven has answered and convicted you" (32). But "what court of law," says M'Closky, "would receive such evidence?"

The answer to his question ("*this* would") hints that the practice of using photographs in court, if not yet commonplace, at least was well on the way to becoming standard. By 1859, the year of *The Octoroon*'s first performance,[5] the inability of "the apparatus" to lie had been acknowledged by both American and British legal systems, which recognized in photography a new kind of documentary evidence. The courts perceived the value of the photograph as a substitute for a less compact or more fragile original.

One of the earliest appellate court cases in the United States which involved photographic evidence (and was tried in the same year *The Octoroon* was written) arose out of a claim for a land grant in which the government's defense was that a document of title was a forgery. Original documents were used in the trial court, but in the appellate court photographs were used, and the counsel stated in his brief:

> By the employment of the beautiful art of photography, this tribunal can examine the assailed title, and contrast it with papers of undoubted genuineness, with the same certainty as if all the originals were present, and with even more convenience and satisfaction. . . . These photographs are now presented, that the members of the court may apply the evidence to them, and observe for themselves not only the differences pointed out, but others, that each eye will soon detect for itself. (*Luco v. United States*, 530. Scott 1: 3)

The satisfaction which photography offered the courts was conclusive; the photograph as evidence admitted no ambiguity. The testimonial value of photography was thus regarded, even more than twenty years after *Luco v. United States* was decided, as symbolic of the sophistication of the society which employed it:

> [A]ll civilized communities rely upon photographic pictures for taking and presenting resemblances of persons and animals, of scenery and all natural objects, of buildings and other artificial objects. It is of frequent occurrence, that fugitives from justice are arrested on the identification given by them. "The Rogues' Gallery" is the practical judgment of the executive officers of the law on their efficiency and accuracy. They are signs of the things taken. (*Cowley v. People*, 477. Chernoff 123)

The things taken by the camera — people, for the most part — became in turn things taken by the courts as true and convincing; their referents, or original subjects, might in consequence of the making of these signs be themselves the more easily "taken."

Photographic portraiture in the courts, jails, and police stations, was by mid-century commonly used as a means of criminal identification. Photography helped identify recidivists, but it also offered a method of classifying them as a physically distinct group. Used in this way, it defined, Allan Sekula writes, "both the *generalized look* . . . and the *contingent instance*" (7); it was endowed with implicitly prophetic powers. The identification photograph was a simple personal portrait, in its early form frequently hard to distinguish from the drawing room pose or the *carte de visite*; but in this new context of law it was made to be read differently, in some instances by behavioral scientists whose interests lay in understanding the generalized behavior, rather than the individual character of the subject, and who read the subject's face as symptomatic rather than expressive. To such an audience, the identification photograph spoke of tendencies and allegiances, of potentials and histories. The nineteenth-century resurgence of interest in corporal "testimony" thus not only had consequences for the history of relations between photography and psychiatry, but affected the reading of photographs in other areas.

Clearly, the powers of photography in legal contexts depended absolutely upon the objectivity of each individual photograph; the value of a photograph as evidence was necessarily directly contingent upon its true value. Ostensibly without artistry or human intervention, identification and evidentiary photographs promoted the myth of authorial absence. Further, in the context of nineteenth-century law, the discourses surrounding photography or generated by it reveal a widespread distrust of the power of photographic testimony and, specifically, a dislike of being forced to be the subject of that testimony.

Early court cases employing photographs as evidence do not fall into any immediately identifiable category but include patent cases, real property cases, and cases which involve, as with *Luco*, the production of forged documents; but its critics and enthusiasts early predicted that photography's greatest potential lay in the recording of personal identities. As early as November 1839, German newspapers published reports of a husband "who had succeeded in photographing his wife during a tryst without being discovered and winning a divorce when the daguerrotype was presented as evidence" (Scott 1: 2; Stenger 106). The necessity for long exposure times (twenty to thirty minutes would not be unusual), the required immobility of the subject for the duration of the exposure, and the unwieldy and hopelessly indiscreet apparatus necessary to make a daguerrotype in 1839 suggest this story to be far from credible; but it does reveal some apprehension from photography's very beginning of the ways in which pictures might be used *against* their subjects.

In the United States the earliest appellate case which recognized photography's power in in-court identification was decided in 1871. By means of a photograph witnesses identified the corpses of two men removed from a river (*Ruloff v. People* 224. Scott 1: 4). The photograph of the dead was thus suggestively used as a substitute for the exhibition of the corpses and did not itself testify to anything other than that the subjects of the photographs were recognized by witnesses. The photograph did not affect the court's decision in any more complex way than to establish the identity of the dead. In a murder case decided three years later, however, photographs were introduced of the victim when alive. The court upheld their admissibility, stating:

> There seems to be no reason why a photograph, proved to be taken from life and to resemble the person photographed, should not fill the same measure of evidence [as a painting]. It is true that the photographs we see are not the original likenesses; their lines are not traced by the hand of the artist, nor can the artist be called to testify that he faithfully limned the portrait. They are but paper copies taken from the original plate, called the negative, made sensitive by chemicals, and printed by the sunlight through the camera. It is the result of art, guided by certain principles of science.

The court went on to add that

> the competency of the evidence in such a case depends on the reliability of the photograph as a work of art, and this, in the case before us, in which no proof was made by experts of this reliability, must depend upon the judicial cognisance we may take of photographs as an established means of producing a correct likeness. . . . [P]hotography, of which we have had nearly a generation's experience, . . . has become a customary and a common mode of taking and preserving views as well as the likeness of persons, and has obtained universal assent to the correctness of its delineations. We know that its principles are derived from science; that the images on the plate, made by the rays of light through the camera, are dependent on the same general laws which produce the images of outward forms upon the retina through the lenses of the eye. The process has become one in general use, so common that we cannot refuse to take judicial cognisance of it as a proper means of producing correct likenesses. (*Udderzook v. Commonwealth*, 353. Scott 1: 4)

Producing photographs of the victim when living was in this instance deemed relevant and did not interfere with the jury's ability to do its duty, although the pictures doubtless served to emphasize the fact that as much as the victim had once been truly living, he was now, as the result of the defendant's action, well and truly dead.

The court's justification here for the use of the photographs is rather ambiguous. It argues first that a photograph should be admissible on the same grounds as those on which paintings may be admissible — that is, so far as they are representative of their subjects. The fact that a photograph is not "traced by the hand of the artist," however, is cause not for satisfaction, as one might expect, but rather for apology. The admissibility of the photograph does not depend upon its scientific value but instead upon its value as a "work of art." The court then adds that the photograph is widely used as art, and therefore such general use should permit its use in court; and in confusion, it appears to conclude that, after all, the photograph is significant because "its principles are derived from science": the camera works like the eye, so it must reflect what it sees. Yet it was apparently with the notion of usage that the court felt most comfortable, for finally the opinion side-steps the issue of science or art altogether, returning to the appeal to photography's generality: the process is commonly used outside the court, so it should be acceptable within it.[6]

Whether or not in this particular case the photographs met evidentiary requirements, the court's observations concerning the widespread use of photography to record personal likeness were correct; indeed, by the date of this decision, photography was commonly used within both American and British penal institutions as a method of recording inmates. In England, Phillip Thurmond Smith sets the "adaptation [of photography] to police purposes" at 1854, when the governor of Bristol Jail began a collection of daguerrotypes of the prisoners (121); during the fifties and sixties Birmingham prisoners were photographed (Tagg 1: 23); and in 1868 the Home Secretary gave approval of the setting up of photographic equipment in Scotland Yard (Smith 121).

The histories of photography and the organized police are closely connected. Tagg observes that the beginnings of photography were coincident with the beginnings of a police service in Britain (1: 23). He implies, indeed, that the need and desire for photography grew out of a rapidly expanding and government-controlled police force. Foucault's documentation of the nineteenth-century institutionalization of surveillance in France has made it something of a commonplace to observe the emergent relationships in that country between various kinds of realisms and systems of monitoring human behavior. While America's public surveillance operations were organized rather differently, they too gave rise to a heightened awareness of the powers of imagistic and literary realism.

Subject identification was the most important and primary step in the work of surveillance, and photography was an effective means of retaining records of those subjects for future use. By the 1870s, one of the largest criminal photograph collections in the United States had been amassed by Allan Pinkerton, who, himself originally a fugitive from Scotland, founded his detective agency in 1850. Like other private agencies, Pinkerton's allegiances were to employers who desired, for reasons which ranged from labor unrest to theft in the workplace, detective supervision of their employees. Detective work in general was thus very closely bound up with safeguarding the status quo and its referent, property.

As a result of these associations, Pinkerton's trademark, a large and open eye, and its accompanying phrase, "We Never Sleep," came "to embody a meaning that transcended mere professional competence" (Voss 8). The eye was the eye of the invasive and unregulated private police, the eye of repressive supervision. It was also the symbol of the individual, the self or "I" whose rights to privacy were being redefined in the act of their erosion. The court's opinion that the photograph was a true vision legitimized an already powerful relationship in the public imagination between the camera and the eye. It was inevitable that the camera should become the most potent symbol of the detective's two functions: surveillance and representation. As J. H. Harris notes in his introduction to Lafayette Baker's account of his work as a spy during the Civil War, "Doubtless, the principal reason for the general disfavor toward the police department, arises from the *espionage* inseparable from it. People do not like to be watched" (Baker 21).

At stake was the precious but never-defined threshold of private space, which photographic study of the personal appearance might be perceived as violating. Perhaps suggesting an intuition of this violation, certainly arguing a belief in the camera's powers of surveillance, there was vigorous resistance to enforced photographing. In his article "Crime and the Camera," Arthur Bowes noted of criminal portraits that "it is surprising, at first, to see the evident objection to the process raised by these sitters. They refuse to pose in graceful attitudes, and decline in spite of all entreaty to 'look pleasant' . . ." (649). The violence occasionally involved in the taking of the identification photograph emerged in popular terminology that labelled such pictures "mug" shots, originally implying the ugliness of the subject (from the tradition of drinking mugs bearing grimacing faces) but suggesting also that the subject is being "mugged," or assaulted, by the camera.

The mug shot was conceived almost as soon as daguerrotypy became a known process. Charles Scott cites an article apparently published by the *Muenchener Morgenblatt* in November 1841, which reads:

> The Paris Police now have daguerreotypes of the features of all criminals passing through its hands and attaches these portraits to the respective reports. When set free and suspected of a new crime, the portrait is shown to all police officers, who soon seek out their man. Daguerre certainly never dreamed that his art would be used for such a purpose. (Scott 1: 2)

In the same month (and presumably from the same source) the *Philadelphia Public Ledger* noted on its front page with apparent approval:

> When a discovery has been made in science there is no telling at the time to what useful purpose it may afterwards be applied. The beautiful process invented by Daguerre, of painting with sunbeams, has been recently applied to aid the police in suppressing crime. When any suspicious person or criminal is arrested in France, the officers have him immediately daguerrotyped and he is likewise placed in the criminal cabinet for future reference. The rogues, to defeat this object, resort to contortions of the visage and horrible grimaces. (30 November 1841. Scott 1: 2)

The subjects of these pictures did indeed try to make unrecognizable their features, unwilling to have true likenesses of themselves stowed in the "criminal cabinet." Frequently, however, the mug shot reveals enough of an authoritative presence in the shape of an iron clamp holding the subject's head, or a hand grasping the hair, to suggest that the grimaces are a response to physical violence outside the frame of the photograph. Illustrations in detective histories as well as novels and popular magazines display the force apparently necessary to make a subject submit to having the photograph taken [fig. 1]; in 1882 Marks recorded how photographs — "These useful works of art" — were procured for the most part after the police succeeded "in tiring their man out" after a struggle during which the subject sought to avoid having a true likeness made "by closing his eyes, [and] distorting his features" (53).

By 1888 the science of photography was able to overcome the problem of resistance to the camera as George W. Walling, former chief of the New York Police, testified:

> First-class "professionals" undergo the process of having their faces handed down to infamy with bad grace. Not infrequently they resist the taking of their photograph in a most vigorous manner. Under the old method, such a prisoner was difficult to photograph. Even when force was used it was found impossible to obtain other than distorted features for the gallery. Now-a-days, however, by means of the instantaneous process, and by catching the reluctant sitter at an unguarded moment, portraits sufficiently correct for the required purpose are always obtained. (Walling 193)

By the time Walling wrote, photographic collections of criminals had been established in every major city across the country; the extensive collection of the New York Police had itself been swelling for thirty years. The photographs were intended to arm not only the police detective with a means of identifying his subjects, but the supposed possible future victim, the private citizen. In 1857, police sergeant William H. Lefferts had suggested that an ambrotype gallery be founded in the detective office of the New York City Police. The gallery would be open to the public, particularly to victims of crime who would come to make identifications (Costello 403). The gallery would remind visitors that the individual should be vigilant in the crowds of the city. The public would thus become its own detective.

II

SEVERAL PUBLICATIONS OF THE late-nineteenth century stressed the need for personal awareness of crime, implicitly urging the possibility of retaining

1. "The Bashful Model." *Harper's Weekly* (1873) Vol 17.

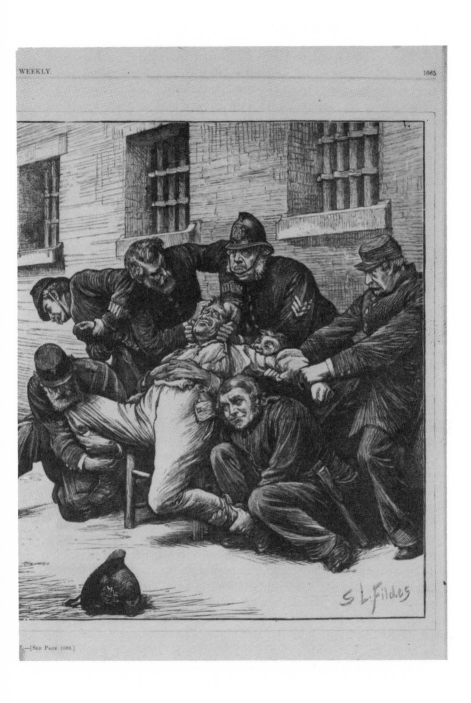

authority over one's personal life by becoming in a sense the guardian of it. Clearly the appeal of such works was more powerful than their superficial claims that by being a watchful and alert citizen one could assist the police in its work. The books in fact were offered largely as a defense *against* the police, or, more precisely, against the need for the police, and the unsophisticated precautions they recommended were intended to protect individual liberty not just from a burgeoning criminal population but from the similarly expanding police force.

The physiognomy-based methods of self-protection involved learning to read human beings in terms of types. The popular text *Seymour's Key to Character or Everybody Their Own Detective* (1894) includes an essay on the classification of the human race, as well as one on palmistry, physiognomical expressions of character, modes of talking, grades of character, the chin, the mouth, the nose, and so on. For devotees, there is even a chapter on how to select a husband or wife. Consistent with the text's imperative throughout to make standard the various different types of human being, and assuming that the purpose of selecting a mate is to produce the best possible offspring, the chapter's advice is oriented toward creating the illusory but scientifically desirable mean, the average human being; thus, Seymour instructs women in search of husbands:

> If you are fair in color of complexion and hair, then select one who is dark. If you are medium in color of complexion and hair, then medium may be chosen in the opposite sex. If your eyes are blue, select one who has dark eyes. If yours are gray, then you can select either light or dark. . . . (120–21)

Some detective guides offered themselves as designed specifically for the professional criminal hunter, though it is probable that with popular interest in detective work, they were actually intended for a wider audience. The emphasis of the guide lay, as in regular detective work, in reading and identifying certain signs, and illustration was an important feature. *Grannan's Pocket Gallery of Noted Criminals of the Present Day Containing Portraits of Noted and Dangerous Criminals, Pickpockets, Burglars, Bank Sneaks, Safe Blowers and All-Round Thieves* consists of a collection of engravings of certain criminals made from photographs. Accompanying each picture is a small narrative of personal exploits and revealing mannerisms. The detective agency which put together this useful guide noted the special work of tracking down both information and photographs: ''The photos from which these fine engraved likenesses have been made, with the descriptions, have been obtained by special effort, from the authorities of States Prisons, Chiefs of Police of the larger cities, from the U.S. Secret Service Department and from our own Gallery'' (5). The miniature collection (the book is smaller than pocket size) had an ostensibly professional purpose: "No Detective, of course, will think of being without it" (6). A more telling observation by its authors is that, although the criminal might speed all over the country thanks to the luxury of modern transportation systems, still "he cannot evade his own likeness" (4). The image itself would police its own subject as though it were connected like a shadow.

In 1880, five years before George Walling retired as Chief of Police, Inspector Thomas Byrnes was made head of the New York detective office. Like Walling, Byrnes was a great proponent of criminal photography and continued to build up the department's collection, in 1886 publishing his *Professional Criminals of America*, not, however, as a handy pocket book, but rather as an exhaustive, expensive, and weighty work, notable for the high quality of its photographic prints. Sharing the professed purpose of the smaller manuals, its promise was of self-help, of protection against dangerous individuals. To this end, Byrnes believed, as he explains in his preface, that photographs were not only useful, but, coupled with short histories of their subjects' activities, they might actually put an end to crime altogether:

> Aware of the fact that there is nothing that professional criminals fear so much as identification and exposure, it is my belief that if men and women who make a practice of preying upon society were known to others besides detectives and frequenters of the courts, a check, if not a complete stop, would be put to their exploits. While the photographs of burglars, forgers, sneak thieves, and robbers of lesser degree are kept in police albums, many offenders are still able to operate successfully. But with their likenesses within reach of all, their vocation would soon become risky and unprofitable. (v)

Following this assertion of the amateur market at which his book is aimed, however, Byrnes validates the volume's status as a serious tool in crime prevention by noting that it will be invaluable to the *professional* detective and will, therefore, be useful in the active pursuit of criminals, in addition to offering protection from them. The dual aims of the book, like those of other detective publications, and Byrnes's gestures toward both aims, encapsulate the tension of the public attitude toward criminal photography, with its desire for social order and personal safety tempered by fears of photography's authority and its policing eye.

The protection from crime which Byrnes offers his readers is the opportunity to arm themselves with the "facts." To this end a collection of measurements, histories, and general apocrypha accompany and indeed themselves illustrate the photographs:

> In the following pages will be found a vast collection of facts illustrative of the doings of celebrated robbers, and pains have been taken to secure, regardless

of expense, excellent reproductions of their photographs, so that the law-break-
ers can be recognized at a glance. By consulting this book prosecuting officers
and other officials will be able to save much time and expense in the identification of criminals who may fall into their hands. (v)

The work thus offers convenience as one of its many benefits — it will speed
up the process of identification and minimize costs — but more significant
than this boast is Byrne's implied claim, the unspoken assurance which provides the basis for the entire book, that its contents are reliable and worth
consulting: the histories are true; the photographs look like their subjects.
Obviously, without the assumption that it is reliable, Byrnes's book loses its
claim to being an aid to the fight against crime in the real world. Yet in fact
the several and diverse chapters which accompany the photographs and which
describe aspects and methods of a life of crime do little to assure the reader
of the reliability — or even the identity — of their narrators. Byrnes published
the book, and one assumes therefore that the text is his creation; yet for some
reason he felt it necessary to couch his own narratives of crime in voices
other than his own. Some chapters function as testimonials, such as the two
which describe in the first person their authors' introduction to and struggles
with opium addiction (of their identities the reader must remain ignorant).
In the chapter entitled "Why Thieves Are Photographed," Byrnes uses a
complicated narrative frame to tell the story of a reporter who, after spotting
a well-dressed thief in elegant surroundings, discusses with a police inspector
the facial characteristics of thieves. The police inspector is identified halfway
through the narrative as Byrnes himself, who then holds forth upon the value
of his Rogues' Gallery in the identification of the criminal. The story is told
in such a way as to make it seem deliberately fictional: Byrnes, as omniscient
narrator, sets the scene in a particularly melodramatic style; by using the
third person he avoids the immediacy of first-person testimony and allows
the reader to interpret the text as though it is romantic fiction; but most
intriguingly, he reinvents his own persona in the process, self-consciously
promoting his image as omnipresent, omnipotent detective — as a personification, in short, of "the eye that never sleeps."

The picture illustrating this chapter further indicates Byrnes's awareness
of the potential to dramatize and thus play off standard fictional and romantic
notions about the powers of the police. The photograph, ambiguously titled
"The Inspector's Model," reveals a man held by four police officers, to
whose framing points he is the center, in the act of having his photograph
taken [fig. 2]. There is no indication either of photographer or of photographic
apparatus within the frame of the picture. Instead of showing us merely the
individual's face, however, this mug shot is intended to display the structure
within which the picture had meaning. Thus, to one side of the officers'

THE · INSPECTOR'S MODEL.

2. Thomas Byrnes, "The Inspector's Model." *Professional Criminals of America* (New York: 1886). This photograph was published in the 1895 edition of *Professional Criminals* under the title "Photographing a Rogue."

frame, and quietly balancing the violence of the five men, stands Thomas Byrnes himself. The contortions of the one who must have his picture taken contrast with the dispassionate gaze of the Inspector, who, a model for the reader, figures the way in which we are urged to regard the ostensive subject of the picture. The Inspector's very power lies in his passivity, in his ability and need to do nothing but observe. The hierarchical relation between the police and the single aberrant individual is thus both expressed and distilled here in a picture which records not the facial features of the captive, but his status as subject of the authorial and authoritative gaze.

Byrnes's choice of illustration for the chapter (the copyright belongs to him; the pose of the picture we may asume to be his own production) in fact illuminates the real meaning of the chapter. Falling rather short of answering satisfactorily its own title question ("Why Thieves Are Photographed"), the chapter's residual impression is that any individual is helpless before the camera's superior powers of recording detail, no matter how distorted the details may be. "The very men" says the fictional, self-created Byrnes, "who have gone to the most trouble to make their pictures useless have been betrayed by them" (53). The chapter is as much a warning of the power of the policing eye as it is a celebration of it. Concerning the photograph's power to reveal the psychic characteristics of the criminal, however, Byrnes is surprisingly cynical. "Is physiognomy any guide?" asks the reporter, to which Byrnes replies that it is "A very poor one. Judge for yourself. Look through the pictures in the Rogues' Gallery and see how many rascals you find there who resemble the best people in the country" (Byrnes 55). The conclusion, despite the invitation of the book itself to peruse and know the criminal through a study of his or her features, is that "it is a bad thing to judge by appearances, and it is not always safe to judge against them" (55).

The Inspector's emphasis upon visual records was remarked by Augustine Costello, who undertook a history of the New York Police at the time of Byrnes's management of the detective department. Like Pinkerton, claimed Costello, Byrnes "lifted the prosaic and plodding life of a Detective into the realms of romance [by being] a consummate judge of human nature, [able to] 'size a man for all he's worth' with an unerring judgment that is intuitive" (Costello 410). Lincoln Steffens, an admirer of Byrnes and most likely the reporter of the chapter described above, wrote that, more than lifting his life into the realms of romance, Byrnes actually created the circumstances within which romantic fictions appeared to play themselves out. The stylized devices of the various chapters of *Professional Criminals of America* may indeed have had their sources in art rather than life; Steffens claimed to have discovered a secret hoard of detective stories belonging to Byrnes and "recognized in them the source of his best narratives. Thus I discovered that instead of detectives' posing for and inspiring the writers of detective fiction, it was the authors

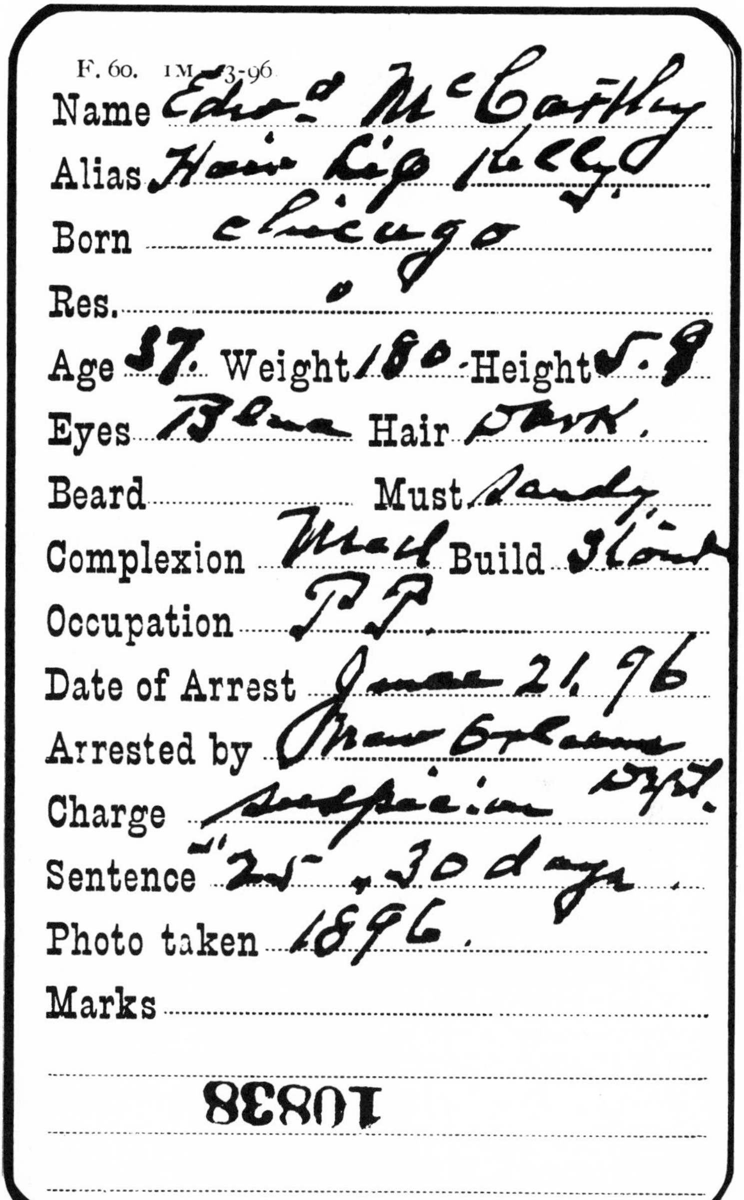

F. 6o. 1 M 3-96

Name *Edwd McCarthy*

Alias *Hair Lip Kelly*

Born *Chicago*

Res.

Age *37.* Weight *180* Height *5.8*

Eyes *Blue* Hair *Dark.*

Beard   Must *Sandy*

Complexion *Med* Build *Stout*

Occupation *P.P.*

Date of Arrest *June 21, 96*

Arrested by *New Orleans*

Charge *suspicion Dpt.*

Sentence *"25" 30 days.*

Photo taken *1896.*

Marks

10838

3. Edward McCarthy, identification card. Bain Collection. Library of Congress.

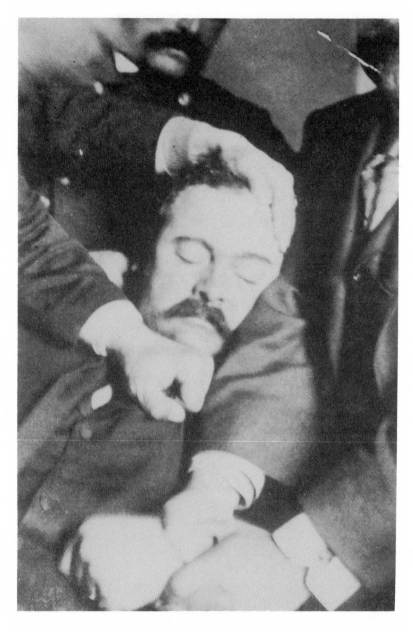

4. Edward McCarthy. Bain Collection. Library of Congress.

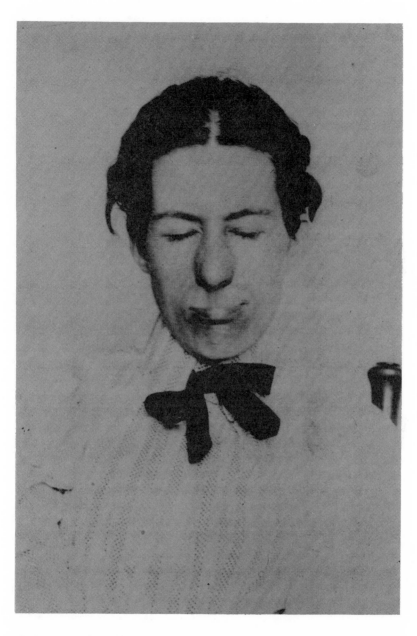

5. Isma Martin. Bain Collection. Library of Congress.

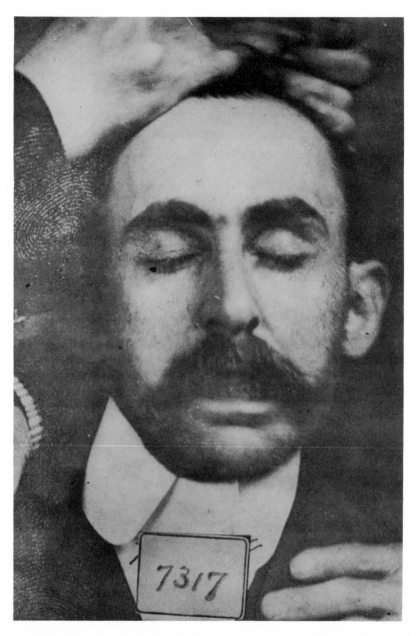

6. J. B. Black. Bain Collection. Library of Congress. Bain's letter from the Cincinnati police states that Black "was arrested at San Francisco, Cal. June 17, 1902, for forgery and designated by the San Francisco department as a 'forger' and 'Bogus check man.' "

who inspired the detectives'' (qtd. by Arthur Schlesinger in Byrnes xix). After one arrest, wrote Steffens, Byrnes apparently described the adventures leading to it ''so perfectly modelled upon the forms of the conventional detective story, that the cynical police reporters would not write it'' (xix). Byrnes was not alone in his fondness for the romance of detective work; the publisher confessed in the preface to Harry Marks's volume of true crime stories to having, in some instances, ''slightly modified the stiffness of stereotyped newspaper phraseology'' (although otherwise the tales are ''statements of verified facts'' [3]), while George Walling revealed his understanding of the work to be colored by his vision of the detective as actor and hero:

> In describing not so much a perfect detective as the peculiarities of his calling, I should be doing an injustice if I did not state that there is a certain element of romance about his work. The detective must have, at times, histrionic traits, and must be able not only to wear a disguise, but to enact the personage he assumes to be. (519)

Byrnes's accumulation of criminal photographs was paralleled in the private sphere by collections such as that of George Grantham Bain, whose news agency, over a course of years in the late nineteenth and into the early twentieth centuries, gathered photographs of police activities, including mug shots. Judging by a letter addressed to him on 23 March 1908 from the Cincinnati, Ohio Police, Bain habitually requested selections of photographs from police files, in this particular instance of ''local'' individuals. The six photographs sent to Bain with this letter are remarkably similar in quality and design to the *carte-de-visite* and were accompanied by short descriptions of their subjects, as, for example,

> 1. Edward McCarthy, alias ''Hair Lip'' Kelly. He is a dangerous pickpocket and has a record running back to before 1896, when he came under our knowledge. He operated successfully in Chattanooga, Tenn. and Chicago, Ill., this latter named city being his home. He there shot and killed a police officer and was sent to the penitentiary at Joliet for four years. He is regarded as desperate.

On the back of each card is a standardized form to be filled out by the officer, detailing name, alias, coloring, crime and so on [figs. 3–6]. The photographs themselves are remarkable for the violence that they reveal: in three of the six pictures, the subject is being forcibly restrained by police. Number five, Isma Martin, alias Irma Martin, though apparently passively seated before the camera, has firmly closed her eyes to its lens. ''It will be observed,'' the accompanying letter notes,

> that Irma has distorted her features; whether or not she attempted to cheat the picture or cover an extraordinary physical defect of the face, will remain a

mystery, except with herself, for in opening her eyes and looking steadily at one object, both eyes would reveal a convergent strabismus, making the face more hideous than the puckering up of the lower lip and closing of the eyes.

The police commentary betrays a curiosity concerning motivations that is unrelated to Martin's crime of mail fraud but intuitively focuses on her refusal to have her picture taken. Is it an effort to "cheat the picture" (as she attempted to cheat, we are told, several Kentucky families) that causes the grimace, or a personal vanity to hide a "hideous" defect? The answer to the "mystery" is located in the individual who, an unlocked code, gives up no answers and indeed deliberately resists allowing herself to become the subject of police scrutiny and interpretation. The photograph itself is useless as an identification card. Moreover, since Martin had already served her eighteen months in a house of correction at least eight years earlier (during which lapse of time she might have changed in appearance, reformed, or simply moved), it is unlikely that Bain's reason for requesting a selection of mug shots was to guard against their subjects.

The pictures within the context of Bain's photographic collection are perhaps supposed to be instructive about the very generalized class of persons known as criminals. Collecting photographic likenesses was part of a more or less organized study of human nature in which the captive subject revealed traits about its species as a whole; as a hobby it grew out of a wider colonial drive to make collections of human beings and their cultures. Such collections, if they were to be of practical use, required a simple but ruthless separation between subject and object, in which the viewer was absolutely dissociated from the viewed. Collectors of criminals' faces in fact sought to extend the distance between themselves and their subjects in order to guarantee their personal dissociation from the criminal.

Of course the very reason for the existence of these photographs was guarantee of their subjects' identification as Other. The criminal action of the subjects caused them to be set off from society through incarceration and various other ways in which the criminal's body is differentiated from that of a non-criminal; but through their photographs their features were identified as belonging to a group of humans who, even after punishment, would be forever different — as they were even before they committed their crime. The impetus of physiognomy and phrenology which informed the readers of criminal collections was not toward therapy and rehabilitation but rather to their polar opposite, fatalism. Its advocates were well aware of the charge that physiognomy could lead only to the abdication of personal moral responsibility, but if there were truth to this "sentimental objection," argued Caleb Weeks in one of the many phrenological studies of the period, then "so be it" (44). The overriding goal of this method of policing humankind was the

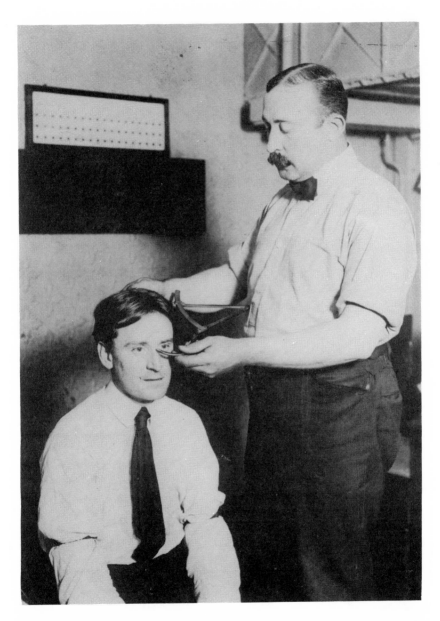

7. Measuring features as part of the Bertillon system. Bain Collection. Library of Congress.

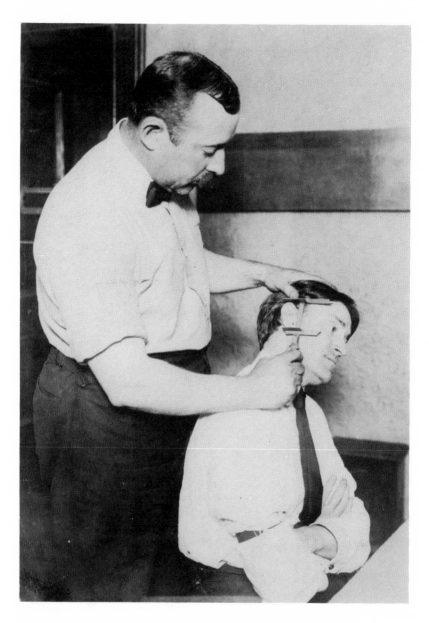

8. Bertillon system. Bain Collection. Library of Congress.

early recognition of tendencies articulated in figures of flesh, which inescapably determined from birth what path the mind could take.[7]

III

THE POLICE, LIKE THE PUBLIC, greatly overestimated the efficiency of the photograph as a means of tracking down fugitive identities. The main reason that the photograph proved an unwieldy clue was the sheer volume of albums that was rapidly built up throughout the fifties and sixties, a symptom of the growing criminal population in America and reflective also of the growing number of police forces. Photography was a useful addition to such complex ways of recording details of identity as the Bertillon system,[8] which involved the painstaking measuring of body parts in order to reduce the subject to a number of statistics that might the more easily be filed away. Bain's collection includes several posed photographs of police officers taking measurements according to the Bertillon system. The function of these pictures seems to be similar to that of Byrnes's "The Inspector's Model" in that the photographs display a method, rather than an individual instance; it is the system, rather than the subject, which defines the picture [figs. 7 & 8].

Photographs were soon perceived to be useless, however, without some organizational method. One problem was the sheer exhaustion of witnesses asked to make an identification from several hundred photographs. Another problem was how to store such volumes of pictures in albums in such a way as to be able to cross-reference subjects. Ironically, as a result of photography's astonishing growth, the usefulness of criminal photographs — their portability, their two-dimensional reduction of unwieldy humanity — was undercut by the sheer enormity of their collections. Photography had appeared to offer a method for controlling and making transportable data which was previously uncontrollable and untransportable, but this reduction and organization of materials now resulted in the need for a new science to classify and reduce photography itself.

Meanwhile the classification or systematized analysis of human features permitted through the agency of photography inevitably had widespread effects upon notions of personal appearance generally and on human type theories specifically. Photography's testimony concerning the human race was distinctively different from other kinds of records of experience in that it was both visual and non-consensual, but this served only to accentuate its assertions. The camera recorded despite the objections of what it recorded, and as it did so, it divided the world into viewers and viewed. It took personal appearance into the public domain and there performed its analysis.

Photography depends heavily for its significance upon a shared understanding of the world, and being thus a social form of representation it is at its most effective in the public space of exhibition. What realist photography there both reflects and determines is a social reality to which everyone who is "real" belongs. The vision of a lunatic or criminal world displayed by nineteenth-century photographs in spaces of varying sizes — the exhibition hall, the police station, the courtroom, and even the page of a book — created a bond between viewers who saw themselves to be unlike the unreal or abnormal subjects of the photographs. The differentiation between viewer and viewed is ultimately unifying, for as it separates the aberrant subject of the photograph from the normal world, so it unites the viewers in the face of aberrancy.

As many of the court writings suggest, even fifty years after their invention photographs used in the service of realism were empowered by their apparent lack of human agency. The metaphors which shaped their meaning in law figured photographs not as creations of individual genius, skill, or mere involvement but instead as the products of the natural workings of a science which had been discovered, not invented. The light rays passing through the camera were "dependent on the same general laws" as those of vision (*Udderzook v. Commonwealth*); they were "produced by the operation of natural laws and not by the hand of man" (*Porter v. Buckley*); they were "drawn by the subtile forces of sunlight" (*State v. Clark*). The laws to which photography was subject were held to be those of nature, as opposed to those of convention.

Not only were photographs depicted to be agentless, but they were self-explanatory. Like physiognomy, and contributing to its authority, photographs appeared to provide their own self-contained meaning, to offer no room for error in interpretation. The photographic sign, like its physiognomic counterpart, had a limited number of referents; its testimony was therefore as ideal as testimony could possibly be. There was no language to obscure issues or create ambiguities. And in its limited interpretive space and despite its anti-narrative aspirations, testimonial photography — photography used as proof of someone or something — had its literary partner in autobiography and journalism which taught its writers to subdue or even extinguish the narratological "I" in favor of the more inclusive eye of realism.

Of course, as Michael Schudson points out, there was nothing new in the realists' belief that art should be mimetic; what was important, he claims, was that "realists identified 'reality' with external phenomena which, they believed, were subject to laws of physical causality as natural science revealed them and as social science might reveal them" (73–74). The detective's work to write truthful accounts of his dealings with crime was complemented by his work with the camera to give similarly truthful accounts. Ironically, the truthfulness of both was frequently undercut by the intrusion of narrators into their own written and photographic texts. In the case of memoirs, detective-authors romanticized their work, mimicking not life but art by turning their recollections into parodies of popular thriller fiction. In the case of photographs, the police often intruded into the pictures, creating not just images of an aberrant individual but pictures in which the power of the police over that individual was also charted.

The divergent public attitudes toward the use of photography in police work (sometimes divergent even within the individual's own understanding of photography) express what are profound tensions at the heart of nineteenth-century American and European culture — the pull between romance and realism, between fact and fiction, between the governing of society and the private freedoms of the individual — so much so that the criminal photograph itself offers an unusually rich site for mapping those tensions or double-pulls. Photography's policing eye was officially welcomed as a method of recording, as a visual shorthand easier to comprehend and recall than Bertillon's system of measurements. But the essence of the criminal photograph, and the fundamental cause for public distrust of photography's use in police work, is that not only is the photograph taken regardless of the consent of its subject, but in order to serve its purpose it must be made public. When Foucault talks of the procedure of objectification and subjection called for in turning life into art — translating intangible experience into tangible documentation — no instance can illuminate his claims quite so well as that of the nineteenth-century police photograph, which took the image into the public domain so that it might be matched with its live subject. The public and reproducible "signs of the thing taken" there policed the private self with photography's apparently irrefutable testimony.

George Washington University

NOTES

My thanks to Craig Lewis for his patient assistance with legal sources.
1. The Uniform Rules of Evidence, rule 1, subsection 13, define writing as follows: " 'Writing' means handwriting, typewriting, printing, photostating, photographing and every other means of recording upon any tangible thing any form of communication or representation, including letters, words, pictures, sound or symbols or combinations thereof" (Scott 2: 305–6). There is contradictory authority, however: see, for example, McCormick, 705–6.
2. Current use of photography in court is given much wider range. Photographs are admitted under two theories, the pictorial testimony theory and the silent witness theory. In the first instance, the photograph illustrates testimony; in the second, most recent category, no percipient witness is necessary for the photograph to be admissible as testimony against an individual. An example of this would be

the film or photograph made of the midnight bankrobber whose image is recorded by automatic camera.

Admissibility of silent witness photographs became necessary at the turn of the century with the invention of the X-ray, which produces independent testimony of a state of affairs which the human eye cannot hope to confirm. Now, according to Charles Scott, photographs are admissible as evidence ''not merely as diagrams or maps representing things about which a witness testifies from his independent observation, but as direct evidence of things which have not been described by any witness as being within his observation. . . . [A] photograph is just as much substantive evidence as the testimony of a witness describing the features of a scene or object without a photograph would be'' (2: 298–99). For a consideration of the implications of this contemporary reliance on photography in legal affairs, see Benjamin V. Madison and Steven I. Bergel.

3. See *Williams v. State*, 837: the case of a man whose chest was photographed with a burn mark of a flat iron which the victim had been using when she was raped. ''A photograph of the scar was held to be admissible over the objection that it violated [the] defendant's privilege against self-incrimination'' (Scott 2: 307–8).

4. The same principle holds for the fingerprints, of course, and, interestingly, for the voice.

5. In New York, at the Winter Garden Theater on 6 December 1859.

6. Similar vaguenesses of language and logic abound wherever photographs were deemed worthy of comment in court opinions. The primary reason for the admissibility of photographs appears to have been their common general application. One court wrote that there was no good reason *not* to regard the photograph as evidence:

If they are relied upon as agencies for accurate mathematical results in mensuration and astronomy there is no reason why they should be deemed unreliable in matters of evidence. Wherever what they disclose can aid or elucidate the just determination of legal controversies, there can be no well formed objection to resorting to them. (*Frank v. Chemical Nat. Bank*, Osborn 62)

The conclusion here is that where the court decides that the photograph may be employed to reveal the truth, then it is to be admitted. The loophole, presumably, would be that the photograph was inadmissible if it did not ''fit'' the desired outcome of the case in question.

7. Allan Sekula makes the point that one goal of physiognomy and phrenology was ''to legitimate on organic grounds the dominion of intellectual over manual labor'' contributing to ''the ideological hegemony of a capitalism that increasingly relied upon a hierarchical division of labor'' (12). This observation is especially interesting as applied to the work of crime, which may be intellectual as well as manual.

8. The system devised by Alphonse Bertillon was the most widely-used method of classifying the apprehended convict. Bertillon first explained the method in an address to the International Penitentiary Congress at Rome in 1885, and it was later published under the title *The Identification of Criminal Classes by the Anthropometrical Method* (London, 1889). For a study of the wider implications of Bertillon's system, see Sekula.

WORKS CITED

Baker, La Fayette C. *History of the United States Secret Service.* Philadelphia, 1868. London: AMS Press, 1973.

Bergel, Steven I. "Evidence — 'Silent Witness Theory' Adopted to Admit Photographs without Percipient Witness Testimony — *State v. Pulphus*, 464 A.2d 153 (R.I. 1983)." *Suffolk University Law Review* 19 (1985): 353–59.

Black, Henry Campbell. *Black's Law Dictionary.* St. Paul, MN: West, 1979.

Boucicault, Dion. *The Octoroon, or Life in Louisiana.* 1859. Miami, FL: Mnemosyne, 1969.

Bowes, Arthur. "Crime and the Camera." *Photography: The Journal of the Amateur, the Professional, and the Trade.* 1.54 (21 Nov. 1889): 648–49.

Byrnes, Thomas. *Professional Criminals of America.* 1886. New York: Chelsea House, 1969.

Chernoff, George, and Hershel Sarbin. *Photography and the Law.* 4th edn. New York: Chilton Books, 1971.

Cincinnati (Ohio) Police. Letter to George Grantham Bain. 23 March 1908. George Bain Collection. Library of Congress, Prints and Photographs, Washington, D.C.

Costello, Augustine E. *Our Police Protectors: A History of the New York Police.* 1885. Rpt. of 3rd ed. Montclair, NJ: Patterson Smith, 1972.

Cowley v. People, 83 N.Y. 464 (1881).

Foucault, Michel. *Discipline and Punish: The Birth of the Prison.* Trans. Alan Sheridan. New York: Vintage Books, 1979.

Frank v. Chemical National Bank, 26 N.Y. Sup. Ct. (1874), *aff'd*, 84 N.Y. 209 (1874).

Franklin v. State, 69 Ga. 36 (1882).

Grannan, Joseph C. *Grannan's Pocket Gallery of Noted Criminals of the Present Day Containing Portraits of Noted and Dangerous Criminals, Pickpockets, Burglars, Bank Sneaks, Safe Blowers, Confidence Men and All-Round Thieves.* 4th edn. Cincinnati, 1892.

Hapgood, Hutchins, ed. *The Autobiography of a Thief.* New York: Fox, Duffield, 1903.

Luco v. United States, 64 U.S. (23 How.) 515 (1859).

Madison, Benjamin V. "Seeing Can Be Deceiving: Photographic Evidence in a Visual Age — How Much Weight Does It Deserve?" *William and Mary Law Review* 25 (1984): 705–42.

Marks, Harry H. *Small Change; or, Lights and Shades of New York.* New York, 1882.

McCormick, Charles T. *McCormick on Evidence.* St. Paul, MN: West, 1984.

Osborn, Albert S. *Questioned Documents.* Albany, N.Y.: Boyd, 1929.

People v. Jennings, 96 N.E. 1077 (Ill. 1911).

Porter v. Buckley, 147 F. 140 (3d. Cir. 1906).

Quine, W. V., and J. S. Ullian. *The Web of Belief.* New York: Random, 1978.

Robertson v. Rochester Folding Box Co., 64 N.E. 442 (N.Y. 1902). (Gray, J. dissenting).

Ruloff v. People, 45 N.Y. 213 (1871).

Schudson, Michael. *Discovering the News: A Social History of American Newspapers.* New York: Basic Books, 1978.

Scott, Charles C. *Photographic Evidence.* 3 vols. St. Paul, MN: West, 1969.

Sekula, Allan. "The Body and the Archive." *October* 39 (1987): 3–64.

Seymour, William. *Seymour's Key to Character; or Everybody Their Own Detective*. Philadelphia, 1894.

Smith, Phillip Thurmond. *Policing Victorian London*. Westport: Greenwood, 1985.

State v. Clark, 196 P. 360 (Or. 1921).

Stenger, Erich. *The History of Photography: Its Relation to Civilization and Practice*. Trans. Edward Epstean. Easton, Pa.: Mack, 1939.

Tagg, John. "Power and Photography: Part One. A Means of Surveillance: The Photograph as Evidence in Law." *Screen Education* 36 (1980): 17–56.

Udderzook v. Commonwealth, 76 Pa. 340 (1874).

Voss, Frederick, and James Barber. *"We Never Sleep": The First Fifty Years of the Pinkertons* (catalogue). National Portrait Gallery. Washington, D.C.: Smithsonian, 1981.

Wagner, W. J. "Photography and the Right to Privacy: The French and American Approaches." *The Catholic Lawyer* 25 (1980): 195–227.

Walling, George W. *Recollections of a New York Chief of Police*. 1888. Montclair, NJ: Patterson Smith, 1972.

Weeks, Caleb S. *Human Nature Considered in the Light of Physical Science, including Phrenology*. New York, 1893.

Williams v. State, 396 S.W. 2d 834 (Ark. 1965).

UNDER COVER OF SYMPATHY:
RESSENTIMENT IN GASKELL'S *RUTH*

By Audrey Jaffe

> Under the cover of sympathy with the dismissed labourers, Mr.
> Preston indulged his own private pique very pleasantly.
>
> *Wives and Daughters*

ELIZABETH GASKELL'S DELIBERATE GOAL in *Ruth* (1853) was to elicit sympathy
for the figure of the fallen woman by means of the detailed representation of
an individual case. As many have noted, the attempt proved problematic both
for some readers and for the author herself: the novel is troubled by its
ambiguous treatment of the category, and the character, with which it is most
concerned. Maintaining that Ruth is "unconscious" of social norms and
naturally good, and critical of the social barriers that would bar her from
respectable society, Gaskell at the same time devises a heroine whose claim
on readers' sympathy has less to do with the insupportability of the idea of
fallenness than with her status as not "really" fallen. And yet, insisting on
her heroine's natural virtue, Gaskell requires Ruth to redeem herself; the novel
remains unable to reconcile her supposed innocence with her ineradicable
transgressiveness, and she dies at its end.[1]

Criticism of the novel has, understandably, been unable to leave the topic
of the fallen woman behind. But in addition to being concerned with the
fate of fallen women, *Ruth* expresses Gaskell's general interest in individual
sympathy as a solution to divisive social problems. In *Mary Barton* and
North and South, for instance, Gaskell offers the sympathy of middle-class
individuals for the poor or the socially or morally "other" as an answer to
class conflict. Rather than adequately solving the complex social issues the
novels raise, however, in those novels sympathy points away from the general
toward the particular, covering and displacing anxieties about class with
individual and emotional conflicts. But in *Ruth*, individual sympathy devised
to resolve the fact of social difference serves as a means of expressing the
social tensions that difference evokes.

51

Sympathy, many readers feel, was Gaskell's own "cover story," the fiction that enabled her to write; disavowing "masculine" knowledge, she claimed the authority of feeling.[2] But, having made this suggestion, Gaskell's critics have neglected what is perhaps one of the most peculiar sympathetic gestures in fiction — one, moreover in which sympathy manifests itself as cover. In *Ruth*, the Bensons — the minister and his sister who sympathize with Ruth and take her into their home — invent a false identity for her, ostensibly to shield her from censure. Ruth becomes known as the respectable widow Mrs. Denbigh, and her eventual exposure causes outrage in the community and especially in Mr. Bradshaw, the wealthy manufacturer and stern Puritan who has employed her as a governess.

That sympathy should manifest itself as disguise brings out, not least, the way both sympathy and disguise involve an imaginative transgression of boundaries — in this case, of the boundaries of social identity. The deceit shifts the novel's focus from Ruth's fall to the Bensons' lie, and to what becomes the novel's insistent concern: the inability of its middle-class characters to reconcile their own transgressive impulses with the moral imperatives they claim to uphold. Focusing not on the alleged crime but on the cover-up — creating transgression where she insists none had existed before — Gaskell links Ruth's situation with, subordinates it to, and makes it appear no less than a displacement of the situations of those respectable members of the community whose identities are fundamentally involved with forms of covering up.

The common critical view of the novel — that Gaskell attempted to construct an innocent character but could not escape her belief in that character's sexual guilt — thus misconstrues the nature of Gaskell's ambivalence. Like the Bensons, Gaskell attempts to protect Ruth's identity by distracting attention from it, moving away from the idea of sexual transgression as if to mitigate it by creating another kind of transgression on which to focus. But the movement away from sexuality produces more rather than less transgressive energy; the shift enables us to see that Gaskell's attempt to elicit sympathy for the fallen woman covers a pervasive uneasiness about the nature of middle-class identity in nineteenth-century England.[3]

Ruth is only one of many divided and uneasy identities in the novel. Thurstan Benson and his sister Faith are at odds with the conventional society dominated by the wealthy manufacturer Bradshaw, who patronizes them; the brother, in particular, suffers from a vague emotional distress that ultimately takes shape as a struggle of conscience over his role in the deceit. Bradshaw, who expresses his own status anxiety in his treatment of the Bensons, has a troubled conscience as well: embarked on a scheme to bribe voters to elect his candidate for Parliament (the candidate, Donne, is the former Bellingham, Ruth's seducer), he warns himself to take care that "the slack-principled Mr.

Bradshaw of one month of ferment and excitement, might not be confounded with the highly-conscientious and deeply–religious Mr. Bradshaw, who went to chapel twice a day'' (307). Farquhar, the man Bradshaw's daughter Jemima is to marry, seems to Jemima to possess "two characters": "the old one . . . a man acting up to a high standard of lofty principle . . . [and] the new one . . . cold and calculating in all he did" (228). And Jemima is also caught between "awe" at her father's demands and a desire to follow her own passionate impulses (211).

Bradshaw's relationship to Donne suggests a cause for this nearly universal condition of self-division. The politician's aristocratic manner makes Bradshaw aware of the "incontestable difference of rank and standard that there was, in every respect, between his guest and his own family. . . . [I]t was something indescribable — a quiet being at ease, and expecting every one else to be so — an attention to women, which was so habitual as to be unconsciously exercised . . . a happy choice of simple and expressive words" (261–62). "In fact," it seems to Bradshaw,

> Mr. Donne had been born and cradled in all that wealth could purchase, and so had his ancestors before him for so many generations, that refinement and luxury seemed the natural condition of man, and they that dwelt without were in the position of monsters. (265)

The difference between Donne and Bradshaw, as the latter sees it, is one of consciousness versus unconsciousness; the natural versus the forced ("His mode of living, though strained to a high pitch just at this time . . . was no more than Mr. Donne was accustomed to every day of his life" [265]), and aristocratic identity versus "monstrous" and self-conscious self creation. But Bradshaw's sense of "straining," of moral and economic uneasiness, is merely one manifestation of a moral and economic discontent that affects almost all of the novel's characters: an awareness of and uneasiness about identity constructed and maintained rather than assumed as natural. In particular, the novel's characters are tormented by the way in which a rigid adherence to the conventions of middle-class behavior seems inevitably to create a transgressive identity determined to deviate from those conventions.[4]

If the character of Ruth has traditionally been regarded as the occasion for an impulse that leads the Bensons outside conventional moral boundaries, then, that character may also be seen as the form such an impulse takes. A social outcast — requiring, as Faith Benson decides, a new identity — Ruth provides the Bensons with a blank slate on which to write. And what they write projects both a desire for natural identity (which here, as in Donne's case, manifests itself in aristocratic form: "she might be a Percy or a Howard for the grandeur of her grace!" thinks Donne/Bellingham [278]), and an identity constructed as a tension between an illicit self and its respectable cover. "Mrs. Denbigh," that is, crystallizes the problem Gaskell raises for all *Ruth*'s characters. Situated undecidably between a transgressiveness defined in terms of both sexuality and class, and a respectability presented as both natural and artificial, Ruth embodies anxieties constitutive of Victorian middle–class identity: the fear that respectability is a masquerade, that the individual self is already and inevitably fallen, and that, as Peter Stallybrass and Allon White have put it, in the construction of bourgeois identity, an "underground self" has "the upper hand" (5). *Ruth*'s primary concern is with middle-class identity as it takes shape in, and as, a tension between what Marjorie Levinson has called "the mythologically antagonistic upper and lower classes" (176–77), and Stallybrass and White have described as an opposition between "high" and "low" central to the construction of bourgeois identity in the nineteenth century.

Ruth's divided identity is transgressive in another sense as well: it serves as a conduit for the Bensons' *ressentiment*. Like a number of Gaskell's heroines, and like Gaskell herself, the Bensons fictionalize in the name of sympathy. But when Bradshaw, taken in by Ruth's disguise, takes her into his home, the lie implicates the Bensons in what is essentially an act of aggression against their wealthy neighbor. Disrupting and confusing social boundaries in their transformation of Ruth's identity, and demonstrating the ease with which a woman from one social background may blend in with another, the Bensons — or more correctly, Gaskell — play on commonplace Victorian anxieties about the fallen woman's ability to rise in society, and in particular to penetrate the protected boundaries of the bourgeois household. And the use to which the fiction of Ruth's identity is put, as well as the urgency of the Bensons' desire to erase its alienating effects once it is discovered, recall Max Scheler's description of *ressentiment* as anger against the rigid categories of identity against which the socially disaffected struggle yet to which they remain bound.[5] The social boundaries that would exclude the fallen woman from the community also define the Bensons' own powerlessness in relation to Bradshaw; disguising Ruth, the Bensons construct a plot that expresses in disguised form their own social discontent. What we might call social sympathy — the imaginative crossing of class boundaries — is violently literalized here in the Bensons' violation of class boundaries.

The sympathetic object, like the fallen woman, is a figure so charged with social significance and emotional resonance for Victorian middle-class novelists and their readers that it is difficult for such a character to be anything but a projective screen. And Ruth's function as sympathetic object is complicated by womens' general role in Victorian culture as conduits for either salutary or transgressive feeling. From the novel's beginning, Ruth is remarkable for her possession of both an unusual receptivity and for her ability to communicate feeling to others. When she arrives at the Bensons', their servant Sally declares her sorrowful feeling unacceptable since it threatens to "infect" others: Sally and Miss Benson "each had kind sympathies, and felt depressed when they saw anyone near them depressed" (173). And Sally takes Ruth's baby out of her arms when, while looking at his mother's face she sees "his little lip begin to quiver, and his open blue eye to grow over-clouded, as with some mysterious sympathy with the sorrowful face bent over him" (173). (In the novel, the term "infection" or the idea of infectiousness is frequently used to refer to feeling. Ruth is "infected" by Bellingham's amusement [15]; Mr. Davis suggests that his wife has "infected" him with a desire for children [437]. Leonard, Ruth's son, at one point develops a tendency to lie, the implication being that he has caught duplicity from his mother; he also "catches" her bravery later on [427].) Because the object of sympathy in this novel is a fallen woman, the eliciting of sympathy *for* her is inevitably bound up with anxiety about sympathy *with* her: with nervousness about the possible communicability of her feeling.

But Sally's anxiety about the "infectiousness" of Ruth's feeling may be seen not only as evoking the fear of contamination conventionally associated with fallen women, but also as amplifying an anxiety about the power of the sympathetic object discussed by Adam Smith and others: a concern about whether the other's feeling — if one takes it on — will displace one's own. These scenes dramatize not Smith's general idea of sympathy — the representation of another's feeling in an observer's mind — but rather what might be termed its opposite: a transformation of the sufferer's feeling in an effort to keep distressful feeling at bay. When, in an effort to assist in her disguise, Sally abruptly cuts Ruth's hair, what is ostensibly done to make her resemble a widow resembles a test of submissiveness: a dramatization of the giving up of identity in exchange for sympathy.

Ruth's disguise — the covering of one identity by another — is in fact an attempt to transform one kind of feeling into another; as the novel progresses, Ruth becomes an instrument for allaying the disruptive feelings she herself embodies. After Sally's warning, Ruth's potential to "infect" others is transformed into what the novel calls an "unconscious power of enchantment" (179): an ability to communicate, without effort or volition, serene and harmonious feeling. (Significantly, the warning is delivered by a female servant who has undergone a similar transformation; Sally has learned to discipline resentful feelings and accept her "station" [176].) With this transformation, Gaskell implicitly defines as the novel's task not so much the alteration of characters' and readers' feeling about Ruth but rather Ruth's ability to alter characters' and readers' feelings about themselves and one another — an ability reminiscent of the kind of reparation for past transgressions one of Gaskell's early critics described as necessary for the fallen woman: "[T]he sin of unchastity in the woman is, above all, a breaking up or a loosening of the family bond — a treason against the family order of God's world — so the restoration of the sinner consists mainly in the renewal of that bond, in the realization of that order, both by and through and around herself'' (*North British Review* 155.) ''[B]y and through and around herself'' — but not *for* herself — Ruth radiates feelings of serenity and cheerfulness; without intention, ''with no thought of self tainting it'' (366), she disseminates familial harmony. Through tensions within the identities of Benson, Bradshaw, Farquhar, and Jemima, Gaskell displaces the issue of sympathy for the social or moral other onto the problem of unifying middle-class identity. And the reformation of character in which she assists within the novel resembles the reformation of identity her author wished to effect outside it: with her peculiar power to transform the feelings of others, Ruth embodies the transformative power Gaskell hoped her novel would possess.

Ruth's influence comes to bear most significantly on the character who possesses an ''impulse'' and passion reminiscent of conventional anxiety about fallen women: Bradshaw's daughter, Jemima. Resisting her father's desire to control her choice of a husband, Jemima is described as being in ''silent rebellion'' against him. In a central episode, Bradshaw asks Ruth to encourage Jemima to soften her behavior toward Mr. Farquhar, the man he wishes her to marry. Though Ruth never consents to Bradshaw's plan, and indeed disapproves of it, it works despite her: ''by simply banishing unpleasant subjects, and throwing a wholesome natural sunlit tone over others, Ruth had insensibly drawn Jemima out of her gloom'' (234). Dissolving ill feeling, Ruth reconciles unruly impulse with patriarchal design; what Jemima later describes, resentfully, as ''admirable management'' (241) is accomplished by Ruth's unconscious role in Bradshaw's plan.

When Jemima learns of her father's request, she is outraged at this attempt at management, and the novel seems to endorse her outrage. But it goes on to manipulate Ruth's feeling to achieve the same end. Farquhar subsequently becomes attracted to Ruth as ''the very type of what a woman should be'' (308), and both through the influence that makes Jemima behave according to her father's wishes, and through Farquhar's attraction to herself, Ruth encourages the marriage the father desires. Described as ''one who always thought before she spoke (as Mr. Farquhar used to bid Jemima to do) — who never was tempted by sudden impulse, but walked the world calm and self-governed'' (242), Ruth is a model for, and an unconscious influence on, Jemima, causing Jemima to focus her feeling and tame her impulse. But — in a manner that connects the novel's authorial consciousness to Ruth's ''unconscious'' — the greater portion of that work is done by the plot of the novel itself.

Jemima's story, and Jemima's impulsiveness, are clearly a muted version of Ruth's: a warning about impulse that leads away from the family. The episode stages the solidification of Victorian middle-class feminine identity as a function of the recognition and externalization of a fallen other: "standing," the narrator comments, "[Jemima] had learnt to take heed lest she fell" (370). Sympathy mediates Jemima's internal conflict between passion and authority; Jemima's resentment toward her father finds just cause in her sympathy for Ruth. And that sympathy simultaneously enables her to come to terms with Farquhar, thus fulfilling her father's wish: "the unacknowledged bond between them now was their grief, and sympathy, and pity for Ruth" (370). In a displacement similar to the Bensons', threatening identification is transformed into sympathetic difference. Redefining the nature of Jemima's passion, differentiating it from the unruly feeling it might seem to resemble, Gaskell both exposes the novel's undercurrent of disruptive feeling, and "solves" the conflict such feeling causes. And by means of this solution — and in suggesting that the unconscious dissemination of feeling and the deliberate attempt to manipulate it amount to the same thing (that the novel's plot is the same as the father's plot) — Gaskell puts Ruth's affective power in the service of a strengthened familial order.

Throughout the novel, Gaskell spells out details of economic and emotional debt. That insistent detailing, along with her careful recounting of the discomforts of the Bensons' poverty and the Bradshaws' ostentatious wealth, reinforces the link between the Bensons' fiction and their resentment; even more suggestive is the way in which Ruth's presence in Bradshaw's home disturbs the manufacturer's desire to maintain legible social boundaries. Breaking through social and economic barriers, the Bensons' deception constitutes their own "silent rebellion," expressing both a frustration at the fixedness of social boundaries and a resentment against Bradshaw's power in the community. Only a few things circulate between the Benson and Bradshaw households: money in the form of pew-rents, gifts from Bradshaw, and Ruth. "Unconscious," Ruth might be seen as the Bensons' gift to Bradshaw: their answer to his patronage. Both as Mrs. Denbigh, a character invented by Faith, and as Bradshaw's employee, she exposes the vulnerability of the home on whose security Bradshaw stakes his identity and that of his family, the home that would place her irretrievably outside it and define her as incapable of redemption.[6] A conduit for the feelings of others and a figure of "silent rebellion" herself, Ruth enables the expression of class feeling whose existence the Bensons cannot own.

Gaskell has been praised for her own transgression of middle-class norms in her representation of the unconventional Benson household: the feminized minister, the strong sister, and the hearty servant represent social and moral alternatives to the Bradshaws, unhappy in their prescribed roles (Jemima rages against her father's dominance; Mrs. Bradshaw looks "as if she was thoroughly broken into submission" [153]). But in suggesting that Faith uses Ruth to express feelings of resentment on which the novel relies yet which it never explicitly acknowledges, this analysis relies on the ways in which the Bensons feel themselves to be outsiders in their own community, and proposes that their sympathy for Ruth expresses that shared status. (Sympathy, the novel explicitly suggests, depends on secret likeness; late in the novel, Mr. Davis offers to raise Ruth's son in just such terms: "I knew Leonard was illegitimate . . . it was being so myself that first made me sympathize with him" [441].) The line Faith's lie draws between the Bensons and the rest of the community expresses their unconventionality, but it also suggests that unconventionality's alienating quality. Benson is deformed, his sister unmarried, and Gaskell repeatedly associates them with an older way of life now in ideological competition with the prosperous mercantile classes. Despite their function as the moral center of the book, they lack the vitality of the less scrupulous, more financially successful Bradshaw. Women — particularly unmarried women — and priests are among the figures Scheler singles out as likely candidates for feelings of *ressentiment*. In particular, Benson recalls Scheler's discussion of the priest, whose role requires that he "always represent the image and principle of 'peacefulness' " (66). Old age is an explicit concern for Faith and her brother, physical weakness for him; Benson saves Ruth from suicide when he falls while pursuing her. Thus, if Benson's fall is primarily social and economic, and Ruth's moral, the two characters are nevertheless linked symbolically, each drawn to the other's powerlessness. Feeling for Ruth is for the Bensons a way of feeling — and not feeling — for themselves. In contradistinction to the usual sense in which sympathy is thought to express feeling for another, for the Bensons sympathy becomes a way of expressing feelings about, and gaining distance from, an unstable social position. Rather than expressing what Barbara Ehrenreich has termed the middle class's "fear of falling," sympathy here acknowledges in displaced form — and expresses in disguised form — the marginality those with limited social power perceive in themselves.

As manifested here, then, sympathy is identified with a threatened disturbance in, and subversion of, the rigid categories of identity — particularly feminine identity — that would exclude Ruth from respectable society. And that subversion is possible only if Ruth's identity retains its transgressive force. It thus makes sense that the transgressive energy Gaskell attempts to eliminate by constructing Ruth as innocent returns via the mechanism of disguise. By displacing the novel's focus from Ruth's fall to Faith's lie, Gaskell alters the stakes of sympathizing with Ruth (and with *Ruth*) to include not just sympathizing, but fictionalizing, which is to say, in the novel's terms, lying: there is no mistaking the analogy between Faith's pleasure in manufacturing details of Ruth's identity and Gaskell's own activity. For while Benson might be said to identify with Ruth's placelessness and vulnerability, or with her unconscious deviation from moral behavior, Faith seizes upon her as an opportunity for transgression, saying "I do think I've a talent for fiction, it is so pleasant to invent, and make the incidents dovetail together . . . I am afraid I enjoy not being fettered by truth" (150). Through her fictionalizing, Faith strikes a blow against the rigid roles that keep the Ruths and the Mrs. Bradshaws of the world "broken into submission"; she disrupts the home organized around the assertion of Puritanical values, and deceives the patriarch, Bradshaw, whose outrage anticipates that of Gaskell's outraged male readers — and ultimately chastens Faith's pleasure in the production of narrative. The analogy between Faith's fictionalizing and Gaskell's — the sense in which getting Ruth into the Bradshaw home is analogous to getting *Ruth* into the homes of Gaskell's readers — affirms the inseparability of Gaskell's plea for sympathy from the social discontent that plea expresses.[7]

II

> "I want to know how I am to keep remembering how old I am,
> so as to prevent myself from feeling so young?" — Faith Benson,
> looking in the mirror.

LIKE HER AUTHOR, Faith Benson transforms resentment into fiction; inventing character to gain authority, she effectively exposes social identities — and hence social authority — as nothing more than fiction. But Faith's fictionalizing ultimately alters the balance of social power in a community in which Benson's moral concerns had been increasingly marginalized, and his financial dependence on Bradshaw had problematized his moral position. Sympathy in *Ruth* depends upon an identification with the marginal: the falling that links Benson with Ruth, the disguise wherein he and his sister reproduce their own conflicted identities. But it is also, finally, a mechanism for eliding that identification, one that enables the novel's characters to assume their proper places in the social order and forget the *ressentiment* Ruth embodies.

As we have seen, Gaskell insists upon Ruth's unconsciousness: her ignorance of social convention saves her from participation in her fall; the lack of deliberateness in her subsequent behavior underscores her essential value (both Benson and Bradshaw admire "the complete unconsciousness of uncommon power, or unusual progress" in Ruth; the fact that "she did not think of herself at all" [187]). Her unconsciousness, I have suggested, defines her as a figure of *ressentiment*: one who cannot act on her own behalf, and for whom others are invited to feel, she embodies the anger the Bensons cannot express directly.

But the novel also associates unconsciousness with a desire to escape the self and its inevitable transgressions. When Ruth first meets Benson, she is about to drown herself — in the novel's words, to "seek forgetfulness" (97). Benson saves her by enabling her to replace one form of self-forgetfulness with another; he falls, and his fall "did what no remonstrance could have done; it called her out of herself" (97). That initial meeting connects the capacity for sympathy with self-forgetfulness, and throughout the novel, Ruth identifies redemption with the possibility of forgetting her former self. She is most herself when most "out of herself," helping the poor and the sick in an effort "to forget what had gone before this last twelve months" (191). (Benson too strives "to leave his life in the hands of God, and to forget himself" [142].) It is as if the absence of consciousness Ruth exemplifies, and for which Benson longs, expresses a desire for relief from consciousness, identified in the novel with an almost unbearable sense of self-division.

As Ruth takes on the fallen woman's traditional role and moves toward death, she does "forget" herself, and her forgetfulness suggests the emptiness of her social identity. On her deathbed, as she becomes literally unconscious, she also becomes literally selfless: lying ill, "She could not remember the present time, or where she was . . . she was stretched on the bed in utter helplessness, softly gazing at vacancy with her open, unconscious eyes, from which all the depth of their meaning had fled" (444, 448). Lying "in utter helplessness, softly gazing at vacancy," Ruth becomes an emblem both of the vacancy of the ideal sympathetic observer, who forgets herself in her devotion to others, and of sympathy's ideal object: the vessel devoid of consciousness and subjectivity that the novel has suggested she was all along. "[S]he could not remember who she was now, nor where she was" (444). Mrs. Denbigh, the novel seems to reassure us, was never anything more than a fantasy about social mobility; moving easily from one social position to another, she gave up the hold on identity she would have possessed had she stayed in one place. As Faith's comment suggests, being someone has some-thing importantly to do with remembering who it is you are supposed to be.

Ruth's exposure — the discovery of her "true" identity — thus coincides with the emptying out of her consciousness. Unable to occupy a legitimate social place, she is left with no "self" in the terms the novel's characters could conceive of one. And the revelation of her emptiness serves to legitimate and solidify the identities of the novel's other characters. As we have seen, the novel initially establishes social and moral uncertainty as a norm of middle-class identity: its characters are perpetually self-divided, guilt-ridden about the moral laxness and social uncertainty they seem unable to avoid. But the narrative works to efface such uncertainty; though it rejects Brads-haw's desire for firm principles ("She has turned right into wrong, and wrong into right, and taught you all to be uncertain whether there be any such thing as Vice in the world'' [339]), somehow events transpire so as to leave no uncertainty about everyone's feelings toward Ruth.

The novel's plot demands the working out of the conflict between Benson and Bradshaw, and the breach Ruth's discovery causes between them — Bradshaw had refused to continue attending Benson's chapel (hence denying him his pew-rents) — immediately effects a transmutation of ''class feelings'' into personal ones:

> He [Benson] felt acutely the severance of the tie which Mr. Bradshaw had just announced to him. He had experienced many mortifications in his intercourse with that gentleman, but they had fallen off from his meek spirit like drops of water from a bird's plumage; and now he only remembered the acts of substantial kindness. . . . [H]e had never recognised Mr. Bradshaw as an old familiar friend so completely as now when they were severed. (352)

But Benson's guilt about his failure to recognize Bradshaw merely suggests guilt about his own *ressentiment*; rather than dissolving class boundaries, the novel's plot allows characters to forget that such boundaries ever disturbed them. Reconciliation in fact demands another fall: Bradshaw's son is revealed to be a forger and then injured in a coach accident.[8] And when Bradshaw sits in Benson's church with his head ''bowed down low in prayer'' where once ''he had stood erect, with an air of conscious righteousness,'' it is his particular demeanor that convinces Benson that ''the old friendly feeling existed once more between them'' (422). The restoration of friendship depends upon an assertion of the priority of the moral and emotional that erases the awareness of social and economic inequities.

But, as these scenes suggest, the novel ''remembers'' everywhere what it claims its characters can forget; Gaskell's language continues to invoke the hierarchical structure it insists has disappeared. The novel's end finds Benson at the ''apex'' of the community: preaching about Ruth after her death, he surveys around him ''one and all — the well-filled Bradshaw pew — all in deep mourning, Mr. Bradshaw conspicuously so . . . the Farquhars — the many strangers — the still more numerous poor — one or two wild-looking outcasts, who stood afar off, but wept silently and continually'' (456–57).[9] Moving from center to margins, high to low, the minister's eye defines the congregation as an idealized microcosm of the social whole, its ability to share the same feelings unaffected by social difference. Finally, the novel's model for the circulation of feeling is no longer an infectious blurring of boundaries but an assertion of harmony in social differences, of personal relationships disturbed by no feelings arising from social inequities. Sympathy provides a way out of immediate social conflicts and produces a fiction of both individual and communal unity here not because it resolves conflict, but rather because it enables the evacuation or forgetting of conflict — and of

the transgressive self — through the projection of that self onto an external
object.

THE INVENTION OF MRS. DENBIGH might be read as a sign of Gaskell's awareness
of the difficulty, even impossibility, of gaining sympathy for her heroine —
an implicit acknowledgement that sympathy for the fallen woman *as* fallen
woman is impossible to achieve. The disguise might be considered a strategic
ploy, an attempt to encourage readers — in on the knowledge of Ruth's
"true" identity — to position themselves in opposition to the narrow-minded
Mr. Bradshaws of the world. In either case, the Bensons' lie raises the same
suspicion as Ruth's death: that, if she is to win sympathy, Ruth cannot be
"herself." For in what would such a self consist? In Ruth, Gaskell describes
an identity so enmeshed in the projections of others, and in literary convention
(her name tells us her story), that it becomes a kind of exposure of the force
of the type to annihilate any sense of identity altogether. In this novel, as in
other fallen woman novels, unconsciousness is the author's way of protecting
her heroine from sexual knowledge. But, as I have argued, unconsciousness
in *Ruth* exceeds the matter of sexuality, becoming a metaphor for a passivity
and absence of character that link sympathy to the appropriation of identity,
and making it not at all surprising that, on her deathbed, Ruth "could not
remember who she was now." Signifying a condition in which feeling flows
through her without her volition (just as Bellingham infects her with his
disease, causing her death), Ruth's unconsciousness defines her as a token
in an emotional drama not her own.

EARLY IN THE NOVEL, Gaskell foregrounds the naturalness of Ruth's identity:
her responsiveness to nature, lack of self-consciousness and ignorance of the
social world. When Bellingham beckons her to look at her image in a pond,
"She obeyed, and could not help seeing her own loveliness; it gave her a
sense of satisfaction for an instant, as the sight of any other beautiful object,
would have done, but she never thought of associating it with herself" (74).
Ruth's inability to associate her image with herself, and the tension between
what she "could not help" and what she "never thought" — between the
natural and the social — appear again in a similar set-piece at the novel's
end. When Bellingham returns, Ruth finds herself in church being observed
by him, and "in this extreme tension of mind to hold in her bewildered
agony" focuses on a gargoyle in one corner of the room.

> The face was beautiful . . . but it was not the features that were the most
> striking part. There was a half-open mouth, not in any way distorted out of its
> exquisite beauty by the intense expression of suffering it conveyed. Any distor-
> tion of the face by mental agony implies that a struggle with circumstance is

going on. But in this face, if such a struggle had been, it was over now. Circumstance had conquered . . . And though the parted lips seemed ready to quiver with agony, yet the expression of the whole face, owing to these strange, stony, and yet spiritual eyes, was high and consoling. . . . Who could have imagined such a look? Who could have witnessed — perhaps felt — such infinite sorrow and yet dared to lift it up by Faith into a peace so pure? . . . Human art was ended — human life done — human suffering over; but this remained; it stilled Ruth's heart to look on it. (282–83)

The gargoyle is an image of the peace Ruth wishes to attain. A projection of her own struggle into the future, it suggests at the same time the future the novel has in store for her: the fulfillment of her objectification in death. And, a vision of suffering transmuted — lifted up ("by Faith") — into art, it also crystallizes the aestheticizing process in which the novel is engaged, and recapitulates the structure of sympathy on which the novel depends. In this scene, Ruth reflects upon an external image she nowhere explicitly names as a reflection — an image that embodies an emotional history reminiscent of her own. Moving beyond Ruth's consciousness to seek the "look" that transformed hers into art, Gaskell's narrator locates understanding of the gargoyle's significance in the consciousness of the novel's readers, in effect unifying the consciousness of those readers around the doubled image of Ruth. The effect is to create a kind of theater in which the sympathetic object assists in the formation of a subjectivity she herself is not permitted fully to possess.

Ohio State University

NOTES

1. For a useful review of *Ruth* criticism, see Helsinger (113–22). Easson discusses the protestations that make Gaskell seem unconvinced of Ruth's innocence in *Elizabeth Gaskell*.
2. As Lovell writes, Gaskell claimed "the right to speak not from knowledge of 'the facts' but from an identification with the feelings of an oppressed and suffering workforce" (87). See also Schor (21–22). The phrase "cover story" comes from Gilbert and Gubar, Ch. 5.
3. The fallen woman is, of course, traditionally regarded as a site of dangerous feeling, particularly feeling perceived as disruptive to the family. Staves argues that eighteenth- and nineteenth-century "seduced maiden" novels express anxiety about what Stone has termed "affective individualism": the shift from an assumed traditional, patriarchal continuity and familial order to an emphasis on individual will and desire.
4. See Kucich for a discussion of the role of transgression in the formation of Victorian middle-class identity.
5. In his introduction, Lewis A. Coser writes: "*Ressentiment* is apt to thrive among those who are alienated from the social order. . . . These persons . . . hate the

existing institutional arrangement but at the same time feel unable to act out this hatred because they are bound to the existing scheme of things'' (Scheler 29). The basic account of *ressentiment* is Nietzsche's. I have used the terms ''resentment'' and ''*ressentiment*'' somewhat interchangeably, but the latter refers to what is explicitly a social emotion, one that exists within a social context in which mobility (the ability not just to identify with the other, but to occupy the other's place) is simultaneously offered and denied. As Scheler's work suggests, similarities between sympathy and *ressentiment* are not irrelevant: each depends upon social inequity and a theoretical possibility of ''becoming'' the other.

6. Note the resemblance between Gaskell's metaphor for the fallen woman's fate and that of Craik in *A Woman's Thoughts* (1858): ''Respectability shuts the door upon her.'' Quoted by Fryckstedt (138). See Todd (100) on woman as mediator between inside and outside.

7. Gaskell connected her own feelings about the novel with the idea of sexual transgression, identifying with her heroine. In her letters, she describes herself as being in pain from the things people are saying about *Ruth*; she is ill, and says she believes she must be ill with a ''Ruth fever'' (222). And in a comment reminiscent of Ruth's ''unconscious'' fall, she writes, ''I think I must be an improper woman without knowing it'' (223). Letter 150 (1853).

8. The elimination of uncertainty — of differences in feeling — requires a certain violence. For Bradshaw to be made part of the community — part, spiritually, of Gaskell's middle class — he must fall; it is not enough that his son turns out to be a forger, but the son must suffer a serious accident to awaken the father's ''humanity.'' (Indeed, the novel's obsessive literalization of the ''falling'' metaphor suggests the violence with which Gaskell imagines the social or moral fall. Benson's deformity is ''owing to a fall he had had'' [135]; Richard Bradshaw is seriously injured in his coach accident. The latter case in particular literalizes Bradshaw's unspoken fear: that self-forgery will lead to a fall.)

9. In 1849, Miall described the way old parish churches, and in particular the pew system, reproduced social inequalities: ''The poor man is made to feel that he is a poor man, the rich is reminded that he is rich, in the great majority of our churches and chapels. . . . the arrangements are generally such as to preclude in their [the poor's] bosoms any momentary feeling of essential equality. We have no negro pews, for we have no prejudice against colour — but we have distinct places for the pennyless, for we have a morbid horror of poverty.'' Quoted in Fryckstedt (58–59).

WORKS CITED

Craik, Dinah Maria. *A Woman's Thoughts about Women*. 1858; rpt. Leipzig, 1860.

Easson, Angus. *Elizabeth Gaskell*. London: Routledge and Kegan Paul, 1979.

Ehrenreich, Barbara. *Fear of Falling: The Inner Life of the Middle Class*. New York: Pantheon, 1989.

Fryckstedt, Monica. *Elizabeth Gaskell's* Mary Barton *and* Ruth: *A Challenge to Christian England*. Uppsala, 1982.

Gaskell, Elizabeth. *The Letters of Mrs. Gaskell*, ed. J. A. V. Chapple and Arthur Pollard. Cambridge: Harvard UP, 1967.

——— *Ruth*. New York: Oxford UP, 1985.

——— *Wives and Daughters*. Harmondsworth: Penguin, 1987.

Gilbert, Sandra, and Susan Gubar. *The Madwoman in the Attic: The Woman Writer and the Nineteenth-Century Literary Imagination*. New Haven: Yale UP, 1979.

Helsinger, Elizabeth K., Robin Sheets, and William Veeder, eds. *The Woman Question Literary Issues, 1837–1883*, vol. 3. Chicago: U of Chicago P, 1983.

Kucich, John. "Transgression in Trollope: Dishonesty and the Antibourgeois Elite." *ELH* 56 (1989), 593–618.

Levinson, Marjorie. *Keats's Life of Allegory: The Origins of a Style*. Oxford: Blackwell, 1988.

Lovell, Terry. *Consuming Fiction*. London: Verso, 1987.

Miall, Edward. *The British Churches in Relation to the British People*. London, 1849.

Nietzsche, Friedrich. *On the Genealogy of Morals*, trans. Walter Kaufmann. New York: Vintage, 1969.

"*Ruth*: A Novel by the Author of *Mary Barton*." *North British Review* 19 (1853), 151–74.

Scheler, Max. *Ressentiment*, trans. William W. Holdheim. New York: Free Press, 1969.

Schor, Hilary. *Scheherezade in the Marketplace: Elizabeth Gaskell and the Victorian Novel*. New York: Oxford UP, 1992.

Smith, Adam. *The Theory of Moral Sentiments*. Indianapolis: Liberty, 1976.

Stallybrass, Peter, and Allon White. *The Politics and Poetics of Transgression*. Ithaca: Cornell UP, 1969.

Staves, Susan. "British Seduced Maidens." *Eighteenth-Century Studies* 14 (1980–81), 109–34.

Stone, Lawrence. *The Family, Sex, and Marriage in England, 1500–1800*. New York: Harper, 1977.

Todd, Janet. *Sensibility: An Introduction*. London: Methuen, 1986.

JOHN BULL AND HIS "LAND OHNE MUSIK"

By Emily Auerbach

IN HIS PROLOGUE to *John Bull; or The Englishman's Fireside*, a comedy performed in London in 1803, T. Dibdin celebrated the sturdy, resolute emblem of his country:

> JOHN BULL is — *British Character* at large;
> 'Tis he, or he, — where'er you mark a wight
> Revering law, yet resolute for right;
> Plain, blunt, his heart with feeling, justice full,
> That is a Briton, that's (thank heaven!) JOHN BULL.
> (Colman, Prologue)

Dibdin drew on John Arbuthnot's portrayal of John Bull in the 1700s as a hearty, choleric, and honest farmer, a figure that rapidly became the popular symbol of Britain. Englishmen proudly ascribed to John Bull manliness, sound sense, and determination, qualities that helped transform his country into the world's leading commercial and industrial power.

Yet as the nineteenth century progressed, many Englishmen began to sense that something was lacking in John Bull — or "*British Character* at large." Although practical, he lacked soul. Nowhere was this fact more obvious than in John Bull's singular lack of musical talent and appreciation.

While nineteenth-century Europe could boast of towering composers such as Beethoven, Brahms, Berlioz, Schumann, Schubert, Wagner, Verdi, Rossini, Chopin, Mendelssohn, and others, John Bull's England could offer nothing better than Sir Sterndale Bennett and M. W. Balfe. Foreign virtuosi such as Paganini, Liszt, and Jenny Lind seemed to have no equivalent English counterparts, and foreign conductors touring England complained of its out-of-tune orchestras and uneducated audiences. Nineteenth-century pianist Anton Rubinstein concluded, "among the English — the least musical of people — not more than two percent can be found who have any knowledge of music. . . . their ignorance of music is only exceeded by their lack of appreciation'' (118). Europe scornfully labelled England "das Land ohne Musik,'' the country without music.

At first Englishmen did not resist this unflattering assessment. In fact, argues Nicholas Temperley, Victorians may have perpetuated the prejudice against their own music and accepted too easily the condemnation of continental Europe. Writes Temperley, "Much of this [prejudice against serious Victorian music] stems from the Victorians themselves. . . . The sobriquet 'Das Land ohne Musik' . . . was founded squarely on the Victorians' estimation of themselves'' (19).[1] But despite Temperley's valiant efforts to redeem Victorian music from its low repute, the fact remains incontrovertible that nineteenth-century England lagged behind continental Europe in musical composition, performance, and theory.

Throughout nineteenth-century periodical literature and other publications, writers acknowledged this abysmal state of music in England. The *John Bull Magazine and Literary Recorder* remarked that "an artist in this country is like a fish out of its element" (July 1824) and admitted that contemporary English composers deserved European laughter (October 1824).[2] *The Musical World*, conceding that "England, the most commercial country of modern Europe, is by all accounts the least musical,'' printed an article entitled "Our Musical Wants'' on 2 June 1837:

> Notwithstanding the many really great names adorning the history of music in England, and the various meritorious efforts which are made from time to time to rescue from foreign contempt our character for musical ability, no one in his senses will think of asserting that we have produced a Bach, a Handel, or a Mozart. It will be allowed that our country grows no such men — that they are, so far, a distinct race of beings.

Henry Chorley, musician and close friend of Charles Dickens, concluded his lectures on "The National Music of the World'' with the observation that England has "never produced a great instrumental composer, neither a towering player on any instrument'' (221); another Victorian music critic sadly acknowledged, "The English are not a Musical People'' (Haweis, *Music and Morals* 409) and "I blush for my country'' (*My Musical Life* 209).

Why, in a country teeming with distinguished authors, politicians, lawyers, and philosophers, were there no musical geniuses who could rank with the talents of Europe? Why was John Bull a musical philistine — a man who prided himself on his tone-deafness, regarded musicians as effeminate "fiddlers,'' and "preferred Pop-goes-the-Weasel to Beethoven'' (Ruskin 437)? Writing of Victorian amusicality, D. J. Smith concludes, "The Victorians cultivated music. . . . but in reality it eluded them. The root of the difficulty was lack of taste'' (517). Temperley reasons, "The problem surely lay in the lack of encouragement for English composers'' (14). These answers only lead to further questions: Why the lack of taste? Why the lack of encouragement? Why was John Bull pictured with a heavy knob stick rather than a violin case, a man more interested in his pork chops than in Mozart's symphonies?

Surprisingly, the best answers come from the Victorians themselves. As *Douglas Jerrold's Shilling Magazine* observed in December 1845, "The English have a sturdy sort of magnanimity in discussing their own character, and John Bull seldom hesitates to admit his own faults." England's amusicality provoked lively debate in its periodicals, where writers turned their country's poverty of music into a wealth of essays probing the strengths and shortcomings of John Bull.

John Bull had not always been unmusical, noted *The Musical World* of 3 January 1839:

> Who was not [an ardent lover of music], till puritanism came and found that one of the loveliest of God's gifts was to be despised? . . . Puritanism helped to effect a great good, but did much evil by the way. . . . We live within the fume of many of its dreary clouds still, and one of the voices which that shadow has comparatively silenced is the prevalence of singing and playing musical instruments among the male sex.

Under Oliver Cromwell's Protectorate, Puritans had ended the use of organ playing and choir music in English churches, allowing only plain psalm tunes sung in unison.

Victorian reviewers also suggested that utilitarianism had threatened musical culture. Measuring aspects of life according to their usefulness, utilitarian reformers had pronounced music a trivial "art of amusement" of no greater value than the game of push-pin (Bentham 253). Acceptable for foreigners, hired servants, and women with nothing better to do, music seemed useless for a gentleman.[3]

Under the heading "Gentlemanly Ignorance," *The Musical Herald* of 15 August 1846 reported that "a large portion of the old stock is still around us. . . . They will usually laugh and chuckle at the idea of your thinking it possible that they could know anything of music; as if to be intensely ignorant of a subject were one of the finest things imaginable." To illustrate this fashionable musical ignorance, editor George Hogarth (father-in-law of Charles Dickens) reprinted Charles Lamb's poem articulating English hostility toward classical music:

> Some cry up Haydn, some Mozart,
> Just as the whim bites; for my part,
> I do not care a farthing candle
> For either of them, or for Handel.

> The devil with his foot so cloven,
> For aught I care, may take Beethoven;
> And, if the bargain does not suit,
> I'll throw him Weber in, to boot . . . (Lamb 46)

John Bull apparently found music beyond his understanding and beneath his interest.

Instead of musical talent, Bull valued more pragmatic and profitable skills. *All the Year Round*, a weekly journal conducted by Charles Dickens, labeled England "this practical shop-keeping nation of ours" (22 October 1864) and observed on 5 November 1864:

> John Bull does not take to proficiency on any instrument kindly. Considering how adroit he can be with his hands and eyes, as a shot, as a whip, it seems, at first sight, strange that the neatness and readiness requisite for the management of strings or pipes, should, with him, "range at so low a figure."

Indeed, many Victorian writers accounted for England's amusicality by pointing to its preeminence as a "practical shop-keeping nation." In a society devoted to business transactions, commerce, financial gain, and industrial progress, how could music appear anything other than trivial and purposeless?

One senses in nineteenth-century periodicals that *some* critics had a dawning awareness of the double-edged nature of this commercial and industrial success. John Bull might be practical, worldy-wise, and wealthy, but was he not missing out on a poetic dimension of life? As the *John Bull Magazine* observed in November 1821 in a column entitled "English Manners," "All is business among the men of England — gain is their god, and his worship all their glory." *Douglas Jerrold's Shilling Magazine* expanded this argument in May 1847 in "A Word or Two on Music," noting that "In the earnestness of our commercial pursuits, and the absorbing nature of our business habits, we overlook the advantages which would follow the cultivation of a general taste for music." In an article entitled "Music a Useful Art," *The Musical Herald* of 26 September 1846 castigated Englishmen for their utilitarianism and their "lamentable want of sympathy with the arts":

> There seems to exist in this country a notion, that nothing, strictly speaking, ought to be encouraged, but what embraces practical utility. This feeling, no doubt, derives its origin from the fact that the English are what Bonaparte designated them — "a nation of shopkeepers," implying thereby, that the great object of an Englishman's existence is buying and selling; profit and loss, rates of exchange, premiums, and policies, being the staple commodities of the national brain, which considers all other matters beside the purpose of life that are not immediately connected with commercial advances.

John Bull, continues *The Musical Herald*, considers a piece of music "not . . . with reference to its intrinsic, but to its marketable value!''

Rather than the sweet sounds of music in England, bemoaned other columnists, one hears only the clink of coins and the din of factories. *The Musical World* of 24 November 1837 translated the remarks of a French commentator in *Le Monde Parisien* who had observed that "the only kind of harmony understood in England is the shrill scream of a Manchester steam-engine, or the heavy fall of the hammers that beat time in the forges of Birmingham.'' A year later in the same publication, another writer sniped that England's only true national music was the sound of money:

> This John Bullism in music is the more absurd because it is so *essentially* and *exquisitely* John Bullish, because it discovers, particularly, the most antimusical part of our national character — its unfortunate enthusiasm for money-getting. . . . [We] need to sharpen those ears hitherto deafened by the eternal din of trade, and the vile incessant clinking of penny against penny — that bad national music of ours!

The "heavy Saxon'' valued bank notes more than musical notes, added *The Musical World* of 6 February 1858.

The silencing of music by the discord of machinery and coins epitomized England's materialism. Arthur Wallbridge in *Douglas Jerrold's Shilling Magazine* blasted the typical Englishman in his May 1846 column entitled "A Man of Good Sound Sense'':

> The "man of good sound sense'' . . . exhibits his disdain for all who in his own day, make any objects but wealth and worldly advancement the business of their lives. . . . Artists he looks upon as silly, idle fellows. . . . Musicians he usually speaks of as "fiddlers'' [and wonders] what Beethoven was in the habit of 'making' a week. . . . Every stage of the earth's progress no doubt produces creatures proper to that stage; but as reptiles have been succeeded by men, let us hope that "men of good sound sense'' may be succeeded by men with a loving reverence for truth, goodness, and beauty.

Although it was more than a decade before Darwin's *The Origin of Species* would appear, Wallbridge used an evolutionary model to call for a higher type of Englishman than the stolid, sensible archetype. Similarly, a contributor to *All the Year Round* on 27 December 1862 argued that Englishmen should come up with "a better figure for future use'' than the "gross, overfed, vulgar, unintellectual, arrogant'' John Bull.

Other writers were less sanguine that any change could be effected, for they believed England's musical inferiority resulted from factors inherent to its location and climate. "The present inferiority of England is a geographical question,'' argued *The Musical World* in a 24 November 1837 column entitled

"English Music." As an island, England received few impulses from abroad and was thus slow to improve, the article continued. Egerton Webbe offered further geographical rationalizations in *The Musical World* of 4 August 1837:

> The general inferiority of English performers to those of some other European countries, may be traced to sources partly physical. . . . In a country like Italy, warm and joyous, everything *conspires* to music. It is like a grove in summer; the sun is shining, the leaves are rustling, the air is so pleasant, — the birds *must* sing. The climate of Italy is so genial and sustaining, that no national misfortunes can depress the temper of the people. They are as glad as children, and, like the birds, they *must* sing. No sharp east winds, pregnant with rheumatism and the spleen, come driving into their mouths the moment they have opened them, to nip the song in the bud. . . . An English singer always sings with an eye to a potential tooth-ache, and never opens his mouth.

Harsh weather, argues Webbe, leads to poor singing.

Although Webbe considered climate one explanation for English amusicality, he recognized that national character played a role, too: "Whether . . . we consider the national climate or the national character we shall equally find an explanation for the inferiority of our vocalists." Like others, Webbe pointed the finger of blame at English commercialism ("An Englishman sings on business"), but he also suggested that the problem went deeper. An Englishman's reluctance to engage in music reflected qualities of reserve and restraint endemic to English society. Thus not only the fear of sharp east winds kept the English singer's mouth shut; national characteristics also explained why he never opened his mouth unreservedly. John Bull was more inhibited and restrained than his continental brothers, argued a *Musical World* article the next month:

> The English have no lack of enthusiasm in the abstract, but they have a marked want of enthusiasm in action. They can be energetic enough on paper, and in private; they can make zealous scholars, and inspired poets; they can even drive enthusiasm to the verge of extravagance — so it be all in private, and out of sight. But they dare not *display* feeling, they shrink from the avowal of sensibility, they will not "compromise" themselves by the disclosure of such a weakness.

Webbe labels this phenomenon "the national characteristic of reserve and suppression of feeling."

And what accounted for this national characteristic? John Bull is reserved, columnists suggest, because (1) his religion discourages display; (2) his philosophy celebrates reason, restraint, and proper conduct; (3) his climate is cold and inhospitable; (4) his country's insular topography discourages an outgoing personality; and (5) his economy encourages self-interest and deceit rather than community feeling and openness. Webbe concludes his essay with this latter point, claiming that "The root of this [English reserve], as of nearly all our other failures and short-comings, is that cursed self-seeking and love of money, which emprisons nature, and locks up all the fountains of love and genius with the winter of insincerity."

Whatever the original causes might have been that led to England's musical decline, it became increasingly clear that the problem would continue as long as Englishmen received little or no musical education. Because music was not a required part of public education or part of a gentleman's private instruction, early Victorians often regarded music as an art foreign to their understanding, as mysterious and alien.

Indeed, music had literally become a foreign art — an art dominated by Italians, Germans, French, and other foreigners. One senses a vicious circle here: Because musical education and performances had been discouraged in England, the art declined among Englishmen; foreigners thus became preeminent in the art, filling a marked void in English culture; Englishmen, seeing the prevalence of foreign musicians, pronounced music a "foreign" and "unEnglish" art and regarded its practitioners with suspicion and prejudice. As Reverend Hugh Reginald Haweis observed in *Music and Morals* (1871), "Music in England has always been an exotic" (410).

Prejudice against foreigners surfaces throughout Victorian periodical writing on music. While the English enjoyed foreign virtuosi and found their performances exciting, they often regarded them as subhuman freaks. Victorians hailed Paganini as "the pale magician of the bow," a man who "forms a class by himself" and plays like "a devotee about to suffer martyrdom," a "supernatural figure [who seems] to belong to another race, and to discourse in the weird music of another world" (Hunt 2: 115–17; Haweis, *My Musical Life* 339). Yet this admiration was often mixed with hostility. Although admitting that Paganini was in a class by himself, *The Times* on 19 May 1831 vehemently protested the high prices he charged: "There can be nothing in his art, a mere instrumental performer, so great a prodigy, as to deserve such a price." It is clear that *The Times* reflected the view of its public: in the same issue, one indignant reader wrote the editor, "Why should John Bull suffer such imposition as is evidently intended to be practised upon his pockets by the announcement of the prices to be paid to hear that celebrated violin player?"

Paganini was in fact forced to lower his prices in England because of stubborn opposition. Newspapers attacked him for his avarice and depicted him as subhuman, as in this *Examiner* poem of 22 June 1831:

> Of monsters in the air or deep
> Four-footed, furr'd, or finny,
> There's none to be compared at all

to Signor Paganini.

A poster mounted in London echoed this sentiment and warned the public against Paganini and other "Foreign Music-Monsters":

> Do not suffer yourselves to be imposed upon by the Payment of Charges which are well worthy the name of extortion; rather suffer under the imputations of a want of Taste than support any of the tribe of Foreign Music-Monsters, who collect the Cash of this country and waft it to their own shores, laughing at the infatuation of John Bull. (Pulver 251)

Newspapers even criticized Jenny Lind, the popular "Swedish nightingale." According to *The Observer* of 27 June 1847, she was an *artiste* who charged too much money for something of too little worth. Although some Britons obviously were willing to pay high prices for good music, others resented foreigners for profiting from England's need to "import" music.

Foreign musicians thus became the targets of English xenophobia and racial prejudice. Some writers dismissed Italian and Jewish performers with the remark that their "race" was more child-like and primitive, giving them an innate predisposition for music. Italians were sensual, of passionate "blood"; the "barbaric" Jews took to the universal language of music because they were an amoral people without a country. These performers seemed sullied and decadent. *The Musical World* of 6 February 1858 labelled foreign virtuosi "exotic trumpery, which the British soil itself is far too healthy to generate."

Some of the English attacks on foreign musicians smack not so much of prejudice as of sour grapes. After all, John Bull found "Country without Music" hardly an appealing descriptor for his homeland. Some foreign columnists had been fatuous in their self-praise and merciless in their attacks on England. Scotland's *Blackwood's Magazine* boasted (in an article reprinted in the 29 August 1846 *Musical Herald*):

> Taken all in all, we are not convinced that there is any other body of national music in the world that surpasses that of Scotland in force, in character, in versatility, or in genius. We certainly feel not a little exultation at our superiority in this respect, over our neighbours of England, to whom we are willing to bow with a proud humility in many other subjects of competition, but whom, we rejoice to think, we can always outdo in the matter of mountains and music.

Foreigners delighted in hearing musical jokes with John Bull as butt, such as the story of the English manager of a concert-hall who yelled at a French horn player awaiting a symphonic entrance, "I'll have no resting in my theater. Play on, sir!" *The Musical Herald* of 29 August 1846 included the story of an English singer who felt immensely gratified by the cries of "Basta, basta!" she heard from the Italians in her audience: she assumed they had mistaken her for the great Italian singer, Pasta, but in reality, "basta" means "enough! nonsense! silence!"

This ridicule was hard to take. Some English writers responded with defensiveness, taking issue with the unflattering label, as in this *Morning Star* comment from 2 September 1859:

> Critics have been so much in the habit of averring that the English are not a
> musical people, that the assertion has taken its place among those accepted
> axioms which no one ever dreams of attempting to refute; and yet it would be
> difficult to condense into the same number of words a greater amount of error.

The Musical World of 20 December 1856 attacked "those highly enlightened foreign quidnuncs, who assert that England is not a musical nation." After all, remarked *The Times* on 26 June 1859, "Handel . . . passed the greater part of his life in England . . . so that we may almost consider him as one of our countrymen." Furthermore, offered *The Musical Herald* of 18 July 1846, "England is perfectly entitled to boast, without the smallest presumption, that she was the first to discover . . . the genius of Beethoven." *The Evening Herald* of 23 August 1859 boasted of English church music, pointing out that the oratorio is "essentially English — it is our pride, our glory, our nationality."

Unlike foreign virtuosi, the *Times* chauvinistically observed on 1 May 1857, native singers perform with "that quiet *English* demeanour." In an essay called "Neglect of English Musicians," *The Dramatic & Musical Review* of 25 June 1842 objected to "the remarkable preference shewn to foreigners in this country, *because they are foreigners*," and commended those concerts "in which the vocalists and music have been thoroughly English." *The Musical Herald* of 15 August 1846 maintained that "a pretty English girl may depend upon it she never looks so attractive as when singing a pretty English ballad," and *The Musical World* on 20 December 1856 boasted that "No voices are better than the English, and in no country more than this is the love and knowledge of music advancing more rapidly among amateurs."

Music *was* advancing in England, perhaps because of the tremendous efforts on the part of the English press to alter the attitudes of John Bull. For several decades, critics had sought ways to convince him that music was worth his while. *The Musical World* of 4 August 1837 had appealed to his national sentiment:

> We want nothing of Italy but her voice — nothing of Germany but her science.
> Let them keep their styles to themselves — we won't trouble them for them.
> Style is the image of character. I trust we have a character of our own; and
> certain I am that it is as well worth imagining as that of Germany or Ita-
> ly . . . Manufacture an item of your own — . . . Bull!

1. Thomas Rowlandson, "John Bull at the Italian Opera" (1811). Courtesy of the Newberry Library, Chicago.

Like American companies advising true patriots not to buy Japanese cars, Victorian music critics called on their neighbors to support British composers, performers, and instructors rather than squandering money on "bearded and mustachioed foreigners." This reference to wasted money bothered commercially-minded John Bull: "It is not the grimace of this German, or the voluptuousness of that Italian singer, that shocks our English sense of propriety, so much as that they have *got the money*," observed *The Musical World* on 22 November 1838.

Other writers appealed to John Bull's utilitarianism. If Bull was going to dismiss music as "not a useful art," perhaps he needed to be shown that it did indeed have its uses. "Give me the man who sings at his work. He will do more in the same time. — he will do it better. — he will persevere longer" (Nettel 20). So remarked Thomas Carlyle, offering to any discerning English entrepreneur the tantalizing suggestion that music could increase worker productivity. Songs, noted John Hullah, were "an important means of forming an industrious, loyal, and religious working class," a way of imparting ideas and values (Nettel 106). George Hogarth claimed that music was "pregnant with moral and social benefits" for those "who earn their daily bread by the sweat of their brow." Far from being an idle or frivolous amusement, Hogarth continues, music "may be rendered an auxiliary to the course of religion and virtue, and an instrument in the improvement of society" (Hogarth 274). Reverend Curwen suggested that an employer should teach his workers songs such as "Begone dull sloth" and "Try again" and that patriotism could be encouraged by teaching them songs of national sentiment. Furthermore, musical activity could reduce drunkenness and debauchery among the lower classes: congregational singing was "the indirect means of aiding worship, temperance, and culture, of holding young men and women among good influences, of reforming character, of spreading Christianity" (Curwen xiv–xv).

One detects in many of these remarks a mixture of sentimentalism and political manipulation. Reverend Haweis, quoted widely in Victorian periodicals, maintained that the influence of music on the poor was quite angelic because it made them "forget the hard, persistent images of pain and trouble, and the coarse realism that dampens joy." Music, he added (perhaps with an eye to reaching shrewd John Bull), would thus "save the country millions in poor-rates" (*My Musical Life* 118). Late-Victorian George Bernard Shaw would later ridicule this calculating attempt to spread music to the masses: "What we want is not music for the people, but bread for the people. . . . When we get that I imagine the people will make tolerable music for themselves" (*London Music* 139).

Victorian music critics claimed that music had benefits not only for the grumbling poor but for the general population as well. Music could help prevent consumption, headaches, and other ailments, for as William Gardiner noted with scientific seriousness, the Germans spit blood less often than the English because their lungs were engaged in the healthy exercise of vocal music (450). In an article entitled "Vocal Music Conducive to Health," 15 August 1846, *The Musical Herald* reported that "Singing tends to expand the chest, and thus increase the activity and powers of the vital organs."

Music now seemed not a useless amusement but an exciting panacea. Not only could it placate the poor, curb drunkenness, instill patriotism, increase productivity, and prevent blood-spitting, it also could reduce the crime rate (*Times*, 29 August 1859) and improve prison discipline (*The Musical Herald*, 29 August 1846). As Reverend Haweis foresaw, music's destiny in Victorian England was as a "vast civiliser, recreator, health-giver, work-inspirer, and purifier of man's life" (*My Musical Life* 118).

Such a "recreator" or "purifier" seemed increasingly necessary in an age of competition, urban complexity, and dehumanizing workdays. *The Musical World* of 12 March 1840 observed that singing in a chorus could "cheat the toiling man of his thoughts of ledgers, day-books, and all the troubles of bookkeeping, and ease his weary carcass of its remembrances of office desks, high-stools, and pen-cramped fingers." *The Gloucester Journal* of 17 September 1859 similarly viewed music as therapeutic: "Music is also frequently a refreshing restorative for the system, and a soother of the overwrought brain. It is impossible to over-estimate her good influence, especially in this age of keen commercial competition." Those engaged in "the stern materiality of trade" or working "in those struggling centres of industry" have an absolute need of recreation and "fly to music as a relief from the oppressiveness of those pursuits."

To provide a haven from the strife-ridden commercial life was a woman's role, agreed many Victorian men. Sermons encouraged women to strive to make their homes heavenly oases in an unheavenly world. Music was one means to this end: it provided a young woman with an innocent pastime (preventing her from reading "licentious novels, which are hourly sapping the foundations of every moral and religious principle") and simultaneously provided her husband with refreshment and tranquility at the end of a troubled day.[4] *Douglas Jerrold's Shilling Magazine* (May 1847) alluded to this feminine paradise in this query of efficiency-minded John Bull:

> Would you call that hour *wasted* in which your heart swelled with joyful affection for a daughter, a sister, or a wife, while her thrilling voice, "which Music loved and called her own," unsealed the fountain of deep feelings, and encircled with a sacred halo the dear delights of home? Would you consider that influence worthless, which, at the close of the day, should soften the icy crust which the world's cold breath had spread over your heart's surface, or extract with fairy touch the iron from your careworn soul?

Through a woman's music, a man could escape the sordidness of his work life.

What were the consequences of music's new "worth" or "usefulness"? The art became increasingly acceptable in nineteenth-century England and underwent an unprecedented expansion. As Bernarr Rainbow observes, music became part of the curriculum in English public schools by the middle of the century, and there was a new market for musical instruments, sheet music, music-sellers, performers, and instructors.[5] Employers sponsored bands, choral societies, and lectures on music appreciation. Many musical periodicals commenced publication, such as *The Musical Herald, The Musical Standard, Musical World, Dramatic and Musical Review, Musical Magazine, Musical Notes*, and *Musical Review: A Record of Musical Science, Literature, and Intelligence*. What nineteenth-century England lacked in music, it seemed to make up for in *words* about music.

At the urging of politicians, entrepreneurs, and philanthropists, music spread rapidly to the masses. Popular manuals such as Joseph Mainzer's *Singing for the Million* and F. J. Fetis's *Music on Everyone's Doorstep: Concise Explanation of Everything Needful to Judge this Art and Speak about it without Study* were translated and disseminated, spreading a smattering of music theory to the public. Between the years 1843 and 1860, 25,000 students attended John Hullah's singing classes and 39,000 copies of "The Messiah" arranged in a new, easily understood singing system were sold (Parratt 596). England prided itself on its mammoth musical events, such as the giant Handel Festival at the Crystal Palace in 1859. *All the Year Round* on 22 October 1864 exulted, "Though the Germans shake their heads and know better, there is no help for it! The English are now a great singing people." Determined not to remain the land without music, England became a nation teeming with musical dilettantes.

This rapid musical growth was not without unfortunate consequences. Encouraged to view music as useful, some Victorians regarded it more as an expedient tool than as an art having intrinsic merit.

For an aspiring middle-class family, music could be one means toward the end of social advancement. A young woman might use her musical "accomplishment" to ensnare a husband, displaying to him glimpses of the paradisiacal sanctuary she could create for him. Although Hannah More had written of an 18-year-old young woman who practiced 14,400 hours of piano but married a man who disliked music, such an outcome did not keep English families from trying to make their daughters into "accomplished" artists.[6]

Victorian music entrepreneurs exploited this situation by directing their advertisements to the covert motive behind the new middle-class interest in music. The phrase "brilliant but not difficult" could help sell sheet music, and piano teachers advertised that their instruction could make "pupils of *ordinary capacity* and *ordinary industry* . . . capable of emulating Corelli, Handel, Haydn, and Mozart!'' A review of a piece by Bayer noted, ''These variations will fulfill their purpose most surely in the hands of young pianists who would sometimes like to gleam in the tinsel of this art without having to wipe sweat from their brows'' (Loesser 296, 291). Music-making became such a serious part of an ambitious young woman's day, one London journalist complained in the January 1846 *Connoisseur*, that ''in families the piano has extinguished conversation and the love of books.'' But a critic in *The Musical Herald* of 9 May 1846 complained that, on the contrary, music's function as a mere social tool created situations where conversation extinguished music:

> One young lady, who has had what might be a decent patrimony spent on music-masters, sits down to the piano and boldly attacks the last *Fantasia* of Thalberg; while another favours the company with Grisi's new bravura at the Opera-house. Their discordant efforts are lost amid the clatter of tongues; for it generally happens that the commencement of a piece of music is a signal for conversation.

This critic attacks both the poor qualities of the music and the rudeness of the ''listeners.''

The increased quantity of music sold, taught, performed, and discussed led at times to a decline in quality. As Edward Hodges observed in *The Musical World* on 1 April 1836, ''Music, in this our day, is very much talked about, very much practised, apparently very much encouraged, but certainly very little understood.'' Another *Musical World* critic remarked in a column of 23 June 1837 on ''Popular Ignorance with Regard to Music'' that ''It is scarcely hazarding too much to confirm that a larger portion of nonsense is uttered in conversation respecting music than on any other topic.''

The Victorian music periodicals themselves — *The Musical World, The Musical Herald*, and others — reveal an enthusiasm for music not always accompanied by a sound understanding. The Table of Contents for the first volume of *The Musical Herald*, for instance, is an utter hodge-podge, demonstrating a shallowness of approach to music (see figure 2). Within a single volume, editor George Hogarth includes articles entitled ''A Musical Cow,'' ''Sacred Music,'' ''The Deaf not Insensible to Music,'' ''Moral Tendencies of Music,'' and ''Influence of Music on Deer.''

The popular taste in music also seemed shallow. In columns entitled ''Popularity'' and ''Public Amusements,'' *The Musical Standard* complained that the Victorian public liked only unnatural and flashy music, such as overtures with cannons fired and brilliant displays by eccentric virtuosi. Too often, musical performances were included in programs also featuring acrobats, dog exhibitions, and other curiosities. A commentator in *The Musical Standard* of 1 June 1863 observes:

CONTENTS OF THE FIRST VOLUME.

MUSICAL LITERATURE.

	PAGE
Address to the Reader	1
Musical Education in England	ib.
The Proper Performance of Church Music	3
Making Notes	ib.
Jeu d'Esprit, by the late Charles Lamb	4
The Music of the Ancients	5
Reasons for Learning to Sing	6
The Transposing Pianoforte	7
Musical Entertainments of the Metropolis	9
A Royal Amateur	ib.
The Present State of the Opera in England	10
The Song of Roland, in English and French	11
The Mission of Genius	13
Shield's "Loadstars"	16
Pianoforte Playing	ib.
The Influences of Music	19
Tartini's Dream	ib.
The Miserere of Allegri	ib.
The Origin of Oratorios	20
"Since first I saw your Face"	ib.
The Songs of Burns. By Allan Cunningham	21
Gluck's Principles of Dramatic Music. By Dr. Burney	23
French and Italian Taste in Music	ib.
Moral Tendencies of Music	24
Old English Masques	ib.
Pious Uses of Music	26
Musical Character of the Germans	27
Ignorant Contempt of Music	29
Sympathy. By Bishop Heber	ib.
Shakspeare's Use of Music	30
Current Nonsense	31
The Deaf not insensible to Music	ib.
Music in Spain	ib.
Old English Musical Plays	33
Sacred Music	34
Vocal Music in Society	35
Power of Music	ib.
Vocal Music conducive to Health	ib.
The Beggar's Opera	37
Scottish Music	38
Influence of Music in Prison Discipline	39
English and Foreign Ecclesiastical Music	43
The Birmingham Musical Festival	45
The Handel Society	47
Social Music of Germany	ib.
The Commemorations of Handel	50
The Hereford Festival	ib.
Gentlemanly Ignorance	51
On Poetical and Musical Ear	ib.
Pianoforte Playing	53
The Musical Chair in the University of Edinburgh	54
The One Thing Needful on the Musical Stage	ib.
A Substitute for the Metronome	55
Popularity of Musical Composers	ib.
John Cramer's Opinions of the Fashionable Style of Instrumental Music	ib.
Music as a Medicine	56

BIOGRAPHICAL NOTICES.

	PAGE
Allesandro Stradella	2
Madame Malibran	6
Dr. Jeremiah Clark	8
Henry Purcell	17, 22
Catalani	25
Rossini and Beethoven	29
Earl of Mornington	30
Shield's Reminiscences of Hadyn	35
Madame Camporese	39
Quinault	41
Auber	42
Haydn's Quartetts	43
Mademoiselle Sontag	46
Lulli	49
Thomas Britton, the Small Coal Man	53

POETRY.

The Power of Music, by Mrs. Norton	42

REVIEW.

Israel in Egypt. By G. F. Handel	43

VARIETIES.

	PAGE
Effects of Music on Animals	4
Losing the Key	ib.
Madame Malibran	ib.
The Swedish Nightingale	7
French Opera	ib.
A Complimentary Message	ib.
Mendelssohn, the Composer	ib.
Music in Spain	8
Corelli	ib.
The Enraged Musician	ib.
Handel and Buononcini	ib.
Dragonetti	ib.
Objects of Music	10
Norma Virium	ib.
Enthusiasm defined	ib.
Influence of Music on Deer	12
Part Singing in the Navy	ib.
Epigram on a bad Fiddler	16
The Privilege of Genius	ib.
Jarnovick	ib.
Anecdote of Rossini	18
Dragonetti	ib.
Greek Tragedies at Potsdam	ib.
Mathematical Music	19
Signora Parepa	20
Importance of a Comma	22
A Musical Hoax	23
Anecdote of Haydn	ib.
Palestrina	26
Mr. Wilson and Scottish Song	ib.
Metastasio's Operas	ib.
Effect of Civilization on the Voice	28
Anecdote of La Fontaine	ib.
Royal Amateurs	ib.
Musical Nationality	ib.
Star Gazing	30

	PAGE
Fashionable Music	31
The Double Bass	32
M. Benedict	ib.
Rossini	ib.
The Academie Royal de Musique	10,
Donizetti	ib.
Lower Rhine Musical Festival	ib.
Jenny Lind	ib.
The Musical Festivals	ib.
An Elegant Compliment	ib.
A Village Choir	34
Melodium Expressif	ib.
Important, if true	35
The Minor Key	ib.
An American Composer	36
The New Instrument, the Serpentcleide	ib.
Greediness of Praise	ib.
Russian Voices	ib.
Hummel	ib.
Singing Italian	ib.
An Aged Musician	38
Fischer	39
The Messrs. Strutt	40
A Man of Genius and a Pedant	ib.
A Slight Mistake	ib.
Mr. Wilson's Songs of Scotland	42
Catalani	ib.
Effects of Music on Madness	43
Bologna	44
Belgium—Malibran a Saint	ib.
Music in Society	ib.
Rubini	ib.
Coleridge's want of Ear	ib.
Rossini	ib.
Dragonetti	ib.
A Composer on Horseback	46
The Critical Press	ib.
National Music	48
Eylber, Kapellmeister of the Imperial Chapel, Vienna	ib.
Music a Useful Art	ib.
Power of the Human Voice	ib.
The Italian Opera	ib.
Music in Liverpool forty years ago	50
Berlin	ib.
Mendelssohn's Impromptu at the Birmingham Festival	ib.
Ancient Music	51
Vienna	ib.
Meyerbeer	52
Rincke	ib.
Balfe	ib.
German Appetite for Music	ib.
A Musical Cow	ib.
Trait of Malibran	ib.
Sebastian Bach	ib.
Economy of Wind	55
To Correspondents, 12, 20, 24, 28, 36, 40, 48, 52, 66	
A Dictionary of Musical Terms, 4, 8, 12, 16, 20, 24, 28, 32, 36, 40, 44, 48, 52, 56	

2. Tables of Contents, from *The Musical Herald: A Journal of Music and Musical Literature*, ed. George Hogarth, Vol 1, 1846. Courtesy of the Newberry Library, Chicago.

Alas! for the times . . . O, generous public! — respectable, educated public! . . . Lose no time in striving to abate the evil — help us to gain a hearing for true music. We do not wish to drone out classical dulness, but to set the beauties of our great and glorious masters before those who, we would fain hope, have only to hear them to enjoy them. Once implant the love of genuine music in the minds of those now led astray by debasing exhibitions, and they will shrink with loathing from "sensational Ethiopians," "comical *comiques*," "cures," "cantatrices," "clog dancers," and all the host of modern music-hall monstrosities.

A program at the Royal Aquarium Westminster in 1878 "began with the appearance of a mermaid and a live whale, followed up with performing fleas, passed into the realm of musical culture with an organ recital — a rendering of the 'Jewel Song' from *Faust* — and ended with Zazel being fired seventy feet from a cannon" (Briggs 33).

Rather than concerning himself with music's quality, John Bull seemed preoccupied with its decibel level and quantity. Victorian newspapers gleefully reported the number of people participating in and attending concerts and the number of instruments and music manuals sold in a given year. Some of the newer composers aimed more at the number of notes in a piece than at its overall beauty, more at the size of the orchestra than at the subtlety of the instrumentation. Manufacturers added new keys and devices to musical instruments and replaced wood with metal, aiming at efficient mass production rather than careful craftsmanship.

Some music critics sensed that these "improvements" harmed rather than aided the cause of music in England. Critics in *The Musical World* used phrases such as "the modern high velocity school," "the cold climate of mechanical dexterity," and "the 'fantastic tricks' of modern note-splitters" to capture their bitterness toward a new era of music more interested in technical display than artistic depth. For George Hogarth, writing on 15 April 1836, this musical phenomenon paralleled the widespread loss of poetry in modern life.

It is a pity that, highly cultivated as music now is, so much of its romance should be lost. . . . Many a beautiful address have the old lyric poets made to their harps, or their lutes; but what modern son or daughter of song has ever thought of apostrophising the violin or the piano-forte? Modern music, in short, is as unpoetical as modern war; and Paganini, with his fiddle under his chin, as unpoetical an object, when compared with an old minstrel, as his Grace of Wellington in the full splendour of his field-marshal's uniform, when compared with an Achilles armed with his shield and spear, or a steel-clad warrior of the middle ages. . . . Modern music and modern instruments . . . are complex and artificial. . . . We must submit to the loss of the spirit of romance, in music as in everything else, because romance is fast vanishing from the world. This is perhaps the necessary consequence of a highly advanced state of society, when reason assumes the empire over the mind, and considerations of utility become predominant.

Throughout nineteenth-century essays on music, one detects this strain of nostalgia.

The pianoforte in particular epitomized the negative side of modern music. Many Victorians regarded the piano as merely a piece of furniture or a status symbol, and contemporary piano music reflected the public's ostentation and shallowness.[7] In a 6 June 1846 column on "Pianoforte Playing," a *Musical Herald* critic editorializes, "I would have fewer notes, and more meaning: less address, and more sentiment; less impetuosity, and more elegance; less of noise, and more of tune: I would that they should not abuse the resources of so rich, so powerful, an instrument; and use them not as an end, but as a means." Another *Musical Herald* columnist laments on 24 October 1846, "What will pianoforte playing come to! . . . The more the powers of the piano have been enlarged by the manufacturer, the more they have been perverted by the performer." The piano has degenerated into "a machine for the exhibition of tricks of legerdemain" and a "social nuisance."

So John Bull apparently had failed. By approaching music with an eye to its utility and by focusing on statistics rather than aesthetics, he had only created new problems. The country seemed filled with dilettantes playing superficial music to philistines pretending to appreciate their efforts. As Don Juan would later remark in Shaw's *Man and Superman*, Act III, "Hell is filled with musical amateurs" (135).

Yet the new interest in music at least spread the art to more people and helped redeem it from its low place in public opinion. Many Victorian critics began to perceive that if music were to attain a higher quality in England, it needed to be promoted on a more idealistic, spiritual level. It had to be recognized as an art whose purpose was not to control workers or display social standing, but rather to add a sublime dimension to life.

This change in attitudes did not occur overnight. In fact, study of nineteenth-century remarks on music reveals not a linear progression but an ongoing debate. Music had its admirers and its detractors in each decade, with more and more voices and reasons being added on each side of the argument. Critics were often ambivalent themselves: a single commentator could reveal both a love of music and a suspicion of its frivolity.

Reverend Haweis, for instance, often indulged in silly remarks about music. Yet elsewhere he pleaded its case with unequalled eloquence:

> The people understand music to be a pleasant noise and a jingling rhythm; hence their passion for loudness, and for the most vulgar and pronounced melody. That music should be to language what language is to thought, a kind of subtle expression and counterpart of it; that it should range over the wordless

region of the emotions, and become in turn the lord and minister of feeling, sometimes calling up images of beauty and power, at others giving an inexpressible relief to the heart by clothing its aspirations with a certain harmonious form — of all this the English people know nothing. (*Music and Morals* 410)

Music must be, Haweis continues, "felt here, as it is in Germany, to be a kind of necessity — to be a thing without which the heart pines and the emotions wither — a need, as of light, and air, and fire" (*Music and Morals* 411).

Musicians were more than "noisemakers for the people"; they offered an art which stimulated a range of emotions and gave glimpses of another, better world. A commentator in *All the Year Round* of 25 April 1868 observed, "Music can express joy, hope, love, tenderness, sorrow, melancholy, martial ardour, and deep religious feeling; or, by a discordant note, it may possibly express fear or anger. . . . All music, in fact, is sacred." *Douglas Jerrold's Shilling Magazine* of May 1847 referred to music as a "divine and exquisite power." *The Musical Herald* on 20 June 1846 reprinted an essay on "The Influences of Music" that described a listener's passionate feelings while hearing hymns in a cathedral:

> At such time the things of earth, its cares, its passions, its very self is forgotten — we are young in spirit once more, young, and trusting, and hopeful; the work of years is gone, we are not the creatures we were a few moments before — "of the earth earthly;" — we feel that of a truth "there is another and better land," and feeling this, even though transitorily, we are better for it still.

Similarly, an article entitled "Music, Its High Ends and Purposes" in the 15 March 1838 *Musical World* extolled music as an elevating art which brings "the remembrance and images of joys yet unseen, and hopes as yet unrealized."

John Bull thus was exhorted to cultivate music not only to stem the flow of money to foreigners, to mold the lower classes, or to display a taste that never went beneath the surface; he needed music in order to develop refinement and sensibility; he needed it to develop soul. "How much longer are we English to assist foreign nations in misunderstanding us, by holding up that ridiculous lay-figure of our race known by the style and title of John Bull?" asked *All the Year Round* on 27 December 1862. No longer, continues the writer, should Englishmen accept as their national portrait the stock caricature of the obese, vulgar, unintellectual, pedestrian, amusical Bull with a massive knob-stick under his arm and a plodding bull-dog at his side.

> I protest against this detestable object as anything like a reasonable and correct expression of the great English race in its totality. A compound of a grazier,

a butcher, a licensed victualler, and a backer of prize-fighters . . . is no fit
representation of our Anglo-Saxon stock. Who invented this pictorial libel? . . .
Why are we to be any longer bound by it? Perhaps it was intended as a
compliment to our stolid king, George the Third, who . . . was certainly not
remarkable for either profundity or brilliancy of intellect. . . . I see no reason
why we should not select a better figure for future use. Graziers, butchers, and
licensed victuallers are very good and useful men; but I conceive they do not
stand quite high enough for the national ideal. . . . Let us get rid of John Bull,
who has given so much occasion to foreigners to denounce us as a coarse,
heavy, and soulless race.

John Bull, or British Character, needed an inner growth to match the expansion of his empire.

The debate over John Bull and his "Land ohne Musik" spawned eloquent
essays and probing criticism that went beneath the symptoms to the root cause.
What is perhaps most striking — moving, even — about these editorials is
their honesty: the willingness of Victorians to admit and attack their own
shortcomings. As Walter Houghton writes, "nearly every fault and failing
of the Victorian mind was exposed by the Victorians themselves. . . . The
worship of material progress, the anti-intellectualism, the dogmatism, the
commercial spirit, the exaltation of force, the marriage market, and the insin-
cerities of conformity, moral pretension, and evasion — all of these Victorian
weaknesses were recognized and attacked" (424). England's dearth of music
thus inspired an abundance of commentary analyzing and attacking British
character.

The results were encouraging. By the end of the century, England had
begun a musical renaissance of its own. Elgar, Vaughn-Williams, Britten,
and other twentieth-century English composers attained a reputation never
granted Sir Sterndale Bennett and his ilk, and English performers, conductors,
and orchestras no longer provoked foreign ridicule.

Although John Bull had narrowed the gap between himself and his European counterparts in respect to music, he retained an independent streak. Late
Victorians William S. Gilbert (1836–1911) and Arthur Sullivan (1842–1900)
rejected both the unrelenting high-seriousness of German opera (and by implication German national character as well) and the stilted and overwrought
qualities of Italian opera. Instead they developed an entirely new, English
type of opera. Operettas such as *HMS Pinafore* and *The Mikado* satisfied
music connoisseurs yet simultaneously appealed to the public. Just as Charles
Dickens had designed his novels not as stuffy classics for a literary elite but
as entertainment for the entire reading public, so Gilbert and Sullivan sought
to make their musically sophisticated compositions a matter of delight for the
populace.

Some began to suspect that John Bull had perhaps grown to dislike music
over the years because music had become too inaccessible and austere. As

The Morning Chronicle had observed of a typical performance (15 December 1858), "This concert belongs to the class which now-a-days is termed 'grand' — a phrase which means that the programme is long enough to tire everybody out." An *All the Year Round* columnist admitted in a 17 October 1868 article on "Tyranny of Art" that although beautiful melodies such as "Home Sweet Home" could bring tears to his eyes, compositions labelled "good music" by "musical tyrants" left him cold: "I own fairly that I loathe good music. I wish I liked it; I wished I liked everything. But I don't like it."

Instead of forcing John Bull to like, pretend to like, or imitate music that failed to reach him, late Victorian composers developed an indigenous English music that recognized the inherent value of English folk melodies and comic songs. John Bull might be evolving into a man of taste and musical discernment, but he steadfastly refused to lose his refreshing, down-to-earth vitality, integrity, and love of humor in the process.

University of Wisconsin—Madison

NOTES

1. The special Autumn 1986 issue of *Victorian Studies* in which Temperley's essay appears provides an excellent introduction to Victorian music and culture, but the issue does not adequately acknowledge the role played by the Victorian press in acquainting the public with England's alleged musical inferiority and seeking (through amusing, sprightly articles) to change its attitudes.
2. The quotations from *The John Bull Magazine and Literary Recorder, The Musical World*, and other Victorian periodicals are identified by date in the text. I gratefully acknowledge the Newberry Library for a fellowship to research this material. Most helpful in its Rare Book Collection was a series of *Scrapbooks* compiled by Charles Lewis Graneigen (1806–79). In this 16-volume set, Graneigen cut out articles on music from newspapers and magazines from 1843–79, identifying them by journal, title, and date but not page number.
3. Lord Chesterfield, for instance, informed his son, "I insist upon your neither piping nor fidding yourself. It puts a gentleman in a very frivolous, contemptible light" (276). For a discussion of the Methodist objections to secular music, see Bronson, Nettel, and Routley.
4. Burgh pronounces music a "harmless amusement" providing young women with "an antidote to the poison insidiously administered" by novels (vi–vii). Conversely, nineteenth-century novelists had plenty to say about musicians; for studies of musical scenes in Victorian novels, see Auerbach, Loesser, and Smith.
5. See Rainbow's *The Land Without Music* and his essay on "The Rise of Popular Music Education."
6. More's *Strictures* protest the general notion of trivial female "accomplishments." The image of an unmusical young woman displaying a smattering of musical skills for the sole purpose of attracting a husband recurs in innumerable novels of the period.

7. For discussions of the piano in Victorian society, see Burgan, Ehrlich, and Loesser.

WORKS CITED

Auerbach, Emily. "The Domesticated Maestro: George Eliot's Klesmer." *Papers on Language and Literature* 19.3 (Summer 1983): 280–92.

———. *Maestros, Dilettantes, and Philistines: The Musician in the Victorian Novel.* New York: Peter Lang, 1989.

———. "The Musicians of Charles Dickens." *The Sphynx* 15 (December 1984): 249–65.

Bentham, Jeremy. *Works of Jeremy Bentham.* Edinburgh: William Tait, 1842.

Briggs, Asa. *English Musical Culture, 1776–1876–1976.* Cincinnati: U Cincinnati Publications, 1977.

Bronson, Bertrand. "Some Aspects of Music and Literature in the 18th Century." *Music and Literature.* U.C.L.A.: Clark Memorial Library, 1963.

Burgan, Mary. "Heroines at the Piano: Women and Music in Nineteenth-Century Fiction." *Victorian Studies* 30.1 (1986): 51–76.

Burgh, A. *Anecdotes of Music, Historical and Biographical: in a series of letters from a Gentleman to his Daughter.* London: n.p., 1814.

Chesterfield, Lord. *The Letters of Phillip Dormer Stanhope, Earl of Chesterfield.* Ed. Lord Mahon. Philadelphia: Lippincott, 1892.

Chorley, Henry Fothergill. *The National Music of the World.* 1862. London: Spottiswoode, 1886.

Colman, George. *John Bull; or the Englishman's Fireside: A Comedy in Five Acts.* London: n.p., 1805; prologue by T. Dibdin.

Curwen, John. *Grammar of Vocal Music.* London: n.p., 1843.

Ehrlich, Cyril. *The Piano: A History.* London: Routledge, 1964.

Fetis, Francois-Joseph. *Music on Everyone's Doorstep: Concise Explanation of Everything Needful to Judge this Art and Speak About it Without Study.* Paris: A. Mesnier, 1830. Trans., London: Clarke, 1844.

Gardiner, William. *The Music of Nature.* 1832. Boston: Oliver Ditson, 1837.

Graneigen, Charles Lewis. *Scrapbooks, 1843–1879.* Newberry Library Rare Books Collection, Chicago.

Haweis, Reverend Hugh Reginald (H.R.). *Music and Morals.* New York: Harper, 1871.

———. *My Musical Life.* 1883. London: Longmans, 1902.

Hogarth, George. *Musical History, Biography, and Criticism.* 1835. London: John Parker, 1838.

Houghton, Walter E. *The Victorian Frame of Mind, 1830–70.* New Haven: Yale UP, 1957.

Hunt, Leigh. "Paganini." *The Poetical Works of Leigh Hunt.* Boston: Ticknor & Fields, 1857. 2: 115–17.

Lamb, Charles. "Free Thoughts on Several Eminent Composers." *Essays of Elia.* New York: A. L. Burt, 1885.

Loesser, Arthur. *Men, Women, and Pianos.* New York: Simon & Schuster, 1954.

Mainzer, Joseph. *Singing for the Million: A Practical Course of Music Instruction.* London: Simpkin, Marshall, 1841.

More, Hannah. *Strictures on the Modern System of Female Education.* 1799. Philadelphia: Budd & Bartram, 1800.

Nettel, Reginald. *The Englishman Makes Music*. London: Dolson, 1952.

Parratt, Walter. "Music." *The Reign of Queen Victoria*. Ed. Thomas Humphry Ward. London: Smith, Elder, 1887. 2: 596.

Pulver, Jeffrey. *Paganini, the Romantic Virtuoso*. London: Herbert Joseph, 1936.

Rainbow, Bernarr. *The Land Without Music: Musical Education in England 1800–1860 and its Continental Antecedents*. London: Novello, 1967.

———. "The Rise of Popular Music Education in Nineteenth-Century England." *Victorian Studies* 30.1 (1986): 25–49.

Routley, Eric. *The Musical Wesleys*. New York: Oxford UP, 1968.

Rubinstein, Anton. *Autobiography of Anton Rubinstein*. Trans. Aline Delano. Boston: Little, Brown, 1890.

Ruskin, John. "Traffic." *The Crown of Wild Olive*, Lecture II. Vol. 1 of *Complete Works of John Ruskin*. London: George Allen, 1905.

Shaw, George Bernard. *London Music in 1888–89 as Heard by Corno di Bassetto, Later Known as Bernard Shaw*. New York: Dodd, Mead, 1961.

———. *Man and Superman: A Comedy and a Philosophy*. Baltimore: Penguin, 1946.

Smith, D. J. "Music in the Victorian Novel." *Kenyon Review* 25 (Summer 1963): 517–32.

Temperley, Nicholas. "The Lost Chord." *Victorian Studies* 30.1 (1986): 7–23.

REFORM, RESCUE, AND THE SISTERHOODS OF *MIDDLEMARCH*

By Michael Cohen

EARLY IN MIDDLEMARCH, after we have been hearing about Dorothea's ambitious but unformed schemes, comes this sentence: "Women were expected to have weak opinions; but the great safeguard of society and of domestic life was, that opinions were not acted on" (ch. 1; 3). The comment bears on all the opinions — strong *and* weak, of women *and* of men — that are not acted upon in the book. Looking back in ironic condescension to a time when provincial England, both midlands and marches, was benighted, the sentence implies that we are now in a utopian present of 1872 when society and domestic life have been reformed. In reality after the Second Reform Bill in 1867 the political landscape seemed to some — *Middlemarch*'s narrator among them — strewn with wrecked reforms, or at least "checked" ones.

Middlemarch itself may well have helped bring about some specific reforms in The Married Women's Property Act. This act, really a series of parliamentary decisions begun in 1870 and amended in 1874, 1882, and 1893, had its most significant provisions written in 1882, ten years after the publication of *Middlemarch*. One of the main concerns of the act — as of Dorothea's and Ladislaw's dilemma — has to do with a married woman's separate property, distinct from her husband's, after marriage and in widowhood.[1] But the book itself is about false reform and failed reforms. George Eliot ends it with a contrast between then and now, "those times when reforms were begun with a young hopefulness of immediate good which has been much checked in our days" ("Finale"; 576), yet in fact the reforms are checked within the span of the novel. The genuinely-attempted reforms (as opposed to the more questionable mythological reforms of Casaubon and the still more dubious religious ones of Bulstrode) are medical and political; each of these reforms is also connected to reform in attitudes toward women. These different kinds of reform are linked at key points throughout the book. The "Prelude" asks where a modern woman is to find her epos when she cannot, like St. Theresa, find it "in the reform of a religious order" (xiii). The "Finale" juxtaposes the sentence about checked reforms quoted above with the unresolved question of exactly what it is Dorothea should have done: "Many who knew her, thought it a pity that so substantive and rare a creature should have been absorbed into the life of another, and be only known in a certain circle as a wife and mother. But no one stated exactly what else that was in her power she ought rather to have done" (576).

Middlemarch is a novel about a woman looking for a heroic role as reformer in the public arena, who finds herself instead attempting a series of private rescues.[2] Reform is the public or social manifestation of what at the private and personal level is the desire for rescue. Both reform and rescue are expressions of a liberal impulse toward freedom and equality, and so public reform connects thematically with the private rescue plots so often found in nineteenth-century British novels, especially those depicting sisters, from Austen and Scott through Collins and Gaskell to Eliot. Neither the public reforms undertaken around Dorothea nor the rescues she undertakes have unequivocally happy results. But all are connected by Dorothea and her sisterhoods.[3]

Dorothea's Sisters

DOROTHEA'S SISTER CELIA is near her throughout the novel. The images of two sisters, Casaubon's mother and Will Ladislaw's grandmother, watch over her in her blue-green boudoir. And figurative sisterhoods extend all around Dorothea. Sometimes these depend on a three-way dynamic. The sisterhood of Dorothea and Rosamond is constructed partly by their rivalries but also by resemblances between Rosamond and Dorothea's literal sister Celia, the fairer, vainer sister.[4] Rosamond and Celia, though profoundly different in their attitudes toward marriage and sexuality — Celia is not a coquette — are both cool women who despise impulse and emotional display; their similar voice qualities are made much of by the narrator. Rosamond and Dorothea are rivals for Lydgate and for Ladislaw, and they are linked briefly by the imagery of the book. Rosamond is compared frequently with a flower on a stem, while Dorothea is a haloed saint and a martyr. But in the last book Dorothea loses her halo, changes out of deep mourning, and acquires at least once — just before she and Ladislaw conquer the obstacles to their marriage — the flower-on-a-stem image that has distinguished Rosamond (ch. 88; 557). A more surprising linkage is that between Mrs. Bulstrode and Dorothea: Mrs. Bulstrode's loyalty to her husband when he is in disgrace, when his bubble of religious reform is exposed for hypocrisy, sisters her with Dorothea, passionately loyal to Casaubon as he sinks under the weight of his illness and the futility of his studies.

But one of Dorothea's "sisters" is not even a woman. The character of Will Ladislaw shows what U. C. Knoepflmacher has called "a transference to the male of the deprivation and suffering [Eliot] finds in the lot of women" (139). Ladislaw is constructed as a sister to Dorothea through his experience of dependence, through his susceptibility to being formed by her idealizing conception of him, and finally by being the object of one of Dorothea's rescues. Ladislaw is simultaneously an assertion that gender differences are largely artificial and an illustration of the novel's suspicion that there may be limits to reforming relations between men and women.

Dorothea is also "sistered" with other fictional heroines in overt allusions as well as inevitable echoings of other books. *Middlemarch* cannot help but allude to books that have treated the same society and classes it treats, as well as the same questions about marriage and money, sex and gender. Thus there are echoes of *Emma, Pride and Prejudice, Little Dorrit,* and *Wives and Daughters,* as well as an explicit reference to *The Woman in White.* Emma Woodhouse and Marian Halcombe, Elizabeth Bennet and Amy Dorrit, Molly Gibson and Cynthia Kirkpatrick are all sisters of Dorothea and mirrors held up to her at one time or another; the likenesses are brought to our attention so that we may more readily see the differences. Though none of these books asks *Middlemarch*'s question about how a woman is to satisfy her ambition for accomplishment outside "a certain circle as a wife and mother," they all ask other questions about women's relation to men and to other women. What is the correct proportion of money and romance in marriage? How much and what kind of dependence and independence should each marriage partner have? In Eliot as in Austen, the main character's most important society after marriage, as before it, consists of a sister, and so this last question is aptly discussed by the sisters, Celia and Dorothea (ch. 72; 507–8), as it had been earlier by Elizabeth and Jane Bennet. Then there is a woman's difficulty in correctly assessing how a prospective husband feels about her and about women in general. After marriage, what changes? How does one live with an incompatible mate? Eliot treats this last question with a depth and seriousness not previously seen in the novel, though her treatment is indebted to Gaskell's examination of the Gibson marriage and Austen's glimpses into the marriages of the Bennets and the Collinses. When *Middlemarch* echoes some of the situations in *Wives and Daughters,* it does so for the purpose, it seems to me, of tempering the optimism of Gaskell's book. The smart provincial medico in *Middlemarch,* unlike Mr. Gibson in *Wives and Daughters,* is neither the anchor of his little society nor proof against the managing efforts of his none-too-scrupulous wife. Moreover the heroine here wants — at least initially — something more than to bask in her husband's glory. Alluding to the answers other books have found, *Middlemarch* constructs its own original turn on each of the questions.

How, for example, does one choose one's mate? Does one pick in advance on the basis of money and family? Does one trust to impulse and intuition, after love at first sight? Does one vet the prospective bridegroom for a year or two? Dorothea thinks she knows Casaubon before she marries him. She decides after a few meetings (during which she spends much of her time dealing with the advances of Sir James Chettam) that he is the perfect spiritual match for her. The narrator asks us to put this leap to conclusions in a timeless context: "Dorothea's inferences may seem large; but really life could never have gone on at any period but for this liberal allowance of conclusions, which has facilitated marriage under the difficulties of civilisation. Has any one ever pinched into its pilulous smallness the cobweb of pre-matrimonial acquaintanceship?" (ch. 2; 13). This remark recalls Charlotte Lucas's conviction, in *Pride and Prejudice*, that knowledge of one's prospective husband is either not possible or not desirable. After Jane Bennet and Charles Bingley have spent four evenings in company with each other, Charlotte says, "if she were married to him to-morrow, I should think she had as good a chance of happiness, as if she were to be studying his character for a twelvemonth. Happiness in marriage is entirely a matter of chance. . . . it is better to know as little as possible of the defects of the person with whom you are to pass your life" (ch. 6; 23). Elizabeth Bennet condemns this opinion as "not sound," but it would hardly be accurate to say the book does. While Elizabeth and Darcy carefully maneuver to learn each other's faults and then either reform or explain them away, Jane and Bingley fall in love at first sight, are kept apart by others while they learn nothing further about each other, and then marry with every prospect of perfect happiness.

Where does *Middlemarch* come down on the question its narrator poses and Charlotte Lucas had answered in the earlier book? Certainly the Casaubons' marriage is no parallel of the Bingleys'. Dorothea jumps to conclusions about her first husband's real nature. She mistakes Casaubon in every respect important to her: she thinks him "a man who could understand the higher inward life, and with whom there could be some spiritual communion; nay, who could illuminate principle with the widest knowledge: a man whose learning almost amounted to a proof of whatever he believed!" (ch. 2; 13). She is dismally wrong. But her romance with Will Ladislaw is not a confirmation of Elizabeth Bennet's approach. Dorothea and Ladislaw have three years in which to study each other's character, but the happiness of their marriage is not guaranteed by the mutual knowledge they have gained, in the way we are invited to believe Elizabeth's and Darcy's is. Once again *Middlemarch* suggests a variation on the previous answers. Ladislaw's character has been not so much assessed as created by Dorothea. "That simplicity of hers, holding up an ideal for others in her believing conception of them, was one of the great powers of her womanhood" (ch. 77; 532), and Ladislaw's susceptibility to it is part of their fit. Ladislaw is Dorothea's will/Will; she constructs him to match her idealism, and he allows himself to be so constructed.

Dorothea and *Middlemarch* Courtship

THE YOUNGER SOCIETY OF *Middlemarch* is largely composed of men who have been either declared or potential suitors of Dorothea and the women they marry. The courtships are the narrator's initial method of showing us these people. We learn a great deal about the men — except Casaubon, about whose true nature the narrator is coy, letting us find it out as Dorothea does, after their marriage. We learn also about the women, and links to be formed among them. And Dorothea's character is presented for our scrutiny by a sometimes ironic and sometimes sincere voice.

Three of the four men, Chettam, Casaubon, and Ladislaw, are suitors of Dorothea; the fourth, Lydgate, is a potential suitor who takes himself out of the action early because he thinks he knows what it would be like to be married to her: "To his taste, guided by a single conversation, here was the point on which Miss Brooke would be found wanting, notwithstanding her undeniable beauty. She did not look at things from the proper feminine angle. The society of such women was about as relaxing as going from your work to teach the second form, instead of reclining in a paradise with sweet laughs for bird-notes, and blue eyes for a heaven" (ch. 11; 64). When Lydgate looks at Rosamond, on the other hand, he sees a woman "who was instructed to the true womanly limit and not a hair's-breadth beyond — docile, therefore, and ready to carry out behests which came from beyond that limit" (ch. 36; 243). Later, when he discovers how unanswerably Rosamond can turn blue eyes and the limits of her education into power, he tries to generalize his discomfort by the thought that "It is the way with all women." But he remembers Dorothea, and

> this power of generalising which gives men so much the superiority in mistake over the dumb animals, was immediately thwarted by Lydgate's memory of wondering impressions from . . . Dorothea's looks and tones of emotion about her husband when Lydgate began to attend him — from her passionate cry to be taught what would best comfort that man for whose sake it seemed as if she must quell every impulse in her except the yearnings of faithfulness and compassion. (ch 58; 409)

Lydgate wonders dreamily in his new state of awareness what it would really be like to be married to Dorothea. Later still, in the bleak part of the book's "Finale" that deals with Rosamond and Lydgate, the question why he did not marry Dorothea comes up again: Lydgate had called Rosamond "his basil plant; and when she asked for an explanation, said that basil was a plant which had flourished wonderfully on a murdered man's brains. Rosamond had a placid but strong answer to such speeches. Why then had he chosen her? It was a pity he had not had Mrs. Ladislaw, whom he was always praising and placing above her" (575).

Lydgate is put off by Dorothea and attracted to women who are husband-killers. His first love was the Parisian actress, Laure, who killed her husband onstage in what may have been merely an accident, but certainly agreed with her intent: "*I meant to do it*," she says unequivocally, "I do not like husbands. I will never have another" (ch. 15; 105). This declaration is offputting for Lydgate, who wants to be her husband. Laure's candid admissions link her with Rosamond. So frequently the flower in the early part of the book — in Lydgate's eyes "flowers and music, that sort of beauty which by its very nature was virtuous, being moulded only for pure and delicate joys" (ch. 16; 113) — Rosamond becomes the basil plant that flourishes on her dead husband's brains. Rosamond dislikes marriage. She does not herself locate the cause of her malaise, being deluded into imagining Will Ladislaw preferable to her own choice: "He would have made, she thought, a much more suitable husband for her than she had found in Lydgate." But the narrator continues, "No notion could have been falser than this, for Rosamond's discontent in her marriage was due to the conditions of marriage itself, to its demand for self-suppression and tolerance, and not to the nature of her husband" (ch. 75; 520).

Dorothea's husband-killing is a reader's fantasy. Dorothea's husband — like Laure's — actually dies, but she is innocent — unlike Laure and Rosamond — of killing either his physical body or the body of his ambitious intent. And yet within half an hour of the first time she speaks her mind to Casaubon, in chapter twenty-nine, he is clinging to the library steps in his study, gasping for breath (196). The idea of wishing Casaubon dead would no doubt horrify Dorothea, however fervently readers may wish it. Lydgate remembers Dorothea's passionate entreaty during Casaubon's illness "to be taught what would best comfort" her husband. And even at the worst of times with Casaubon, Dorothea does not dislike the institution of marriage, nor being married. In a revealing conversation with Celia after Casaubon's death and just before the novel's resolution, she makes it obvious that she wants a husband — one in particular — even as she protests that she does not. "As if I wanted a husband!" says Dorothea. "I only want not to have my feelings checked at every turn" (ch. 72; 508). She then immediately bursts into tears. Celia's reaction is to tell her how "shamefully" she submitted to Casaubon's unreasonable requests of her: "I think you would have given up ever coming to see me if he had asked you." Such attendance is a test for

Celia in which sisterhood must stand out against wifeliness. The bigoted Sir James attempts later to prevent Celia from seeing her sister because Dorothea has married a man beneath her class, without a fortune, and a foreigner into the bargain. But Celia quashes the prohibition with little effort. Now she tells Dorothea that "of course men know best about everything, except what women know better," and gets her sister to laugh. "Well, I mean about babies and those things," explained Celia. "I should not give up to James when I knew he was wrong, as you used to do to Mr. Casaubon" (508). As unlike as the two sisters may be, they are alike in being able to live within the conditions of marriage which chafe Rosamond. Laure and Rosamond do not like marriage. Celia and Dorothea do. And as trivial as Celia can sometimes be, she is honest with Dorothea and has things to teach her sister about self-knowledge early in the book and about sisters needing to avoid submerging themselves in wifehood later.

Each of the other three men is an active suitor for Dorothea. Sir James Chettam's unreconstructed male-supremacist attitudes are those most witheringly dealt with in the book; though the narrator keeps assuring us earnestly of his good nature, we are not convinced. Chettam is not a reformer. Thus he is distinguished from practically every other male character in the book, because practically every other male is a hopeful reformer, an incompetent one, a venal one, or a hypocritical one. Infatuated with Dorothea, convinced that she must like him, he muses complacently about how he could be helped out of his fog by asking advice of this decisive woman:

> In short, he felt himself to be in love in the right place, and was ready to endure a great deal of predominance, which, after all, a man could always put down when he liked. Sir James had no idea that he should ever like to put down the predominance of this handsome girl, in whose cleverness he delighted. Why not? A man's mind — what there is of it — has always the advantage of being masculine, — as the smallest birch-tree is of a higher kind than the most soaring palm, — and even his ignorance is of a sounder quality. Sir James might not have originated this estimate; but a kind Providence furnishes the limpest personality with a little gum or starch in the form of tradition. (ch. 2; 12)

Limp men do not interest Dorothea, although she is fooled about Casaubon, but *there* she imagines an intellectual and spiritual stiffness. She considers Chettam silly (ch. 4; 22) and the idea of his being a suitor of hers ridiculous (ch. 1; 4). But the episode is not complimentary to Dorothea. That Chettam is paying court ought to be apparent to her. The narrator says coyly, "It is difficult to say whether there was or was not a little wilfulness in her continuing blind to the possibility" of his courting her (ch. 3; 21).

In showing Dorothea's naivety about Sir James's intentions, *Middlemarch* invites a comparison between Dorothea and Austen's Emma Woodhouse.

Dorothea and Emma both mistake their ardent suitors, imagining that their all-too-obvious devotion is meant for other women. Emma is convinced that the attentions of Mr. Elton are meant for Harriet Smith, whom she has adopted as a sisterly protégée. The results are nearly disastrous, since Emma talks Harriet into rejecting a good offer of marriage from someone Harriet cares about. Dorothea's mistake resolves itself somewhat more gracefully, since she imagines Sir James Chettam to be pursuing her sister, and he takes that hint just as soon as he is convinced Dorothea does not care for him. Emma is chagrined by her experience, but she does not have to live with the results of her matchmaking. Dorothea, on the other hand, has Sir James for a brother-in-law, and when she is widowed she moves into his sphere of control, at least briefly, finding herself "only in another sort of pinfold than that from which she had been released" (ch. 50; 341). But another way to look at Celia's graceful acquiescence to Dorothea's matchmaking is that it has rescued her sister from embarrassment or worse.

Dorothea is like Emma in being willful and intelligent. Both engage us. Both are introduced as lacking a certain amount of self-knowledge. Celia knows more of her sister than Dorothea knows herself when we first see the Brooke sisters. In Book One, for example, Celia says of Dorothea: "She likes giving up." Dorothea answers, "If that were true, Celia, my giving-up would be self-indulgence, not self-mortification" (ch. 2; 10). But the narrator has already assured us of the truth of Celia's observation: "Riding was an indulgence which she allowed herself in spite of conscientious qualms; she felt that she enjoyed it in a pagan sensuous way, and always looked forward to renouncing it" (ch. 1; 3). Dorothea is the object of a good deal of ironic playfulness in this first part:

> She would perhaps be hardly characterised enough if it were omitted that she wore her brown hair flatly braided and coiled behind so as to expose the outline of her head in a daring manner at a time when public feeling required the meagreness of nature to be dissimulated by tall barricades of frizzed curls and bows, never surpassed by any great race except the Feejeean. This was a trait of Miss Brooke's asceticism. (ch. 3; 16)

At this point Dorothea's "asceticism" could be thought the vanity of nonconformity, and Dorothea an interesting comic heroine, but still one very much like Emma Woodhouse at the beginning of *Emma*. But having introduced Dorothea with all her limitations, the narrator does something no book of Austen's does in taking us right out of the ironic mode in an apology for the heroine:

> The intensity of her religious disposition, the coercion it exercised over her life, was but one aspect of a nature altogether ardent, theoretic, and intellectually

consequent: and with such a nature, struggling in the bands of a narrow teaching, hemmed in by a social life which seemed nothing but a labyrinth of petty courses, a walled-in maze of small paths that led no whither, the outcome was sure to strike others as at once exaggeration and inconsistency. (ch. 3; 17)

There is no irony in these careful distinctions and corrections nor in this instruction of our feelings toward Dorothea. If Eliot wants us to compare her heroine and Emma, she also wants us to see the differences. The greatest difference is in Dorothea's romantic heroism: instead of a heroine constructed by the male romantic lead in his image — an Emma made by Mr. Knightley — Eliot gives us a heroine who constructs the hero, in the person of Will Ladislaw, in her image.

Casaubon and "Checked" Reforms

CASAUBON IS NOT CREATED in Dorothea's image of him, not constructed as Ladislaw is by "that simplicity of hers, holding up an ideal for others in her believing conception of them, . . . one of the great powers of her womanhood" (ch. 77; 532). Casaubon's attitude toward women is not revealed by the same incidental glimpses into the mind of a possible suitor that we are given for both Chettam and Lydgate. We discover only slowly that Casaubon believes in a more profound subjection of women than the other men are capable of entertaining. He wants to be Dorothea's husband even after he is dead. She can resist him while he is alive: "While he lived, he could claim nothing that she would not still be free to remonstrate against, and even to refuse" (ch. 48; 332). But the claim he makes upon her, that she thinks relates only to his work and continuing what would have been, had he completed it, "the doubtful illustration of principles still more doubtful" (331), is that she agree to obey him, after his death, in any and every wish. The night before his death he tells her solemnly that he has a request, and when she asks what it is he replies: "It is that you will let me know, deliberately, whether, in case of my death, you will carry out my wishes: whether you will avoid doing what I should deprecate, and apply yourself to do what I should desire" (331). She does not agree to Casaubon's absurdly open-ended wish, but only because his death prevents her brow-beaten acquiescence. All that remains of his will to control her after his death is his literal last will.

Casaubon's provision that Dorothea will lose her inheritance from him if she marries Ladislaw is mean spirited, suspicious, and perfectly on the mark in its suspicion. But its significance goes beyond the personally insulting. Casaubon's death is one of those places in *Middlemarch* where improvement is promised but does not come about. Dorothea appears at her husband's death to have personal freedom and the means to accomplish some of her ambitious schemes for general betterment. In fact she is presented with a cruel dilemma that shows her she can have one only at the expense of the other. Finally she chooses the personal freedom, having realized that she has never exercised any wider freedom. When Celia pleads that if she does not marry she can go on doing what she likes, Dorothea replies: "On the contrary, dear . . . I never could do anything that I liked. I have never carried out any plan yet" (ch. 84; 566). Her theater of action has to narrow to the personal when she takes action; if she is to have any freedom of action at all she must give up some of her larger plans to better the world. And she does choose — Dorothea's Will rather than Casaubon's will. But the very next sentence after her embrace with Ladislaw is "It was just after the Lords had thrown out the Reform Bill . . ." (ch. 84; 560), linking her decision with at least the temporary arrest of reform.

Casaubon's action in cutting off Dorothea's inheritance would not have been legally binding at the time he supposedly made it, in 1831. *Middlemarch* fudges the historical evidence slightly in pursuit of a larger historical truth. English common law had always recognized a dower right of widows, and in Dorothea's case, because there were no children to inherit, this would have amounted to half Casaubon's real property. But the power of testation over the dower right had been steadily increasing before the nineteenth century, and in 1833 the Dower Act provided that a husband "could expressly bar his wife's right of dower, without her consent," by means of a will (Holcombe 22). In other words the reform-minded eighteen-thirties were moving backward in regard to reforming married women's property rights. The very circumstances that enable Casaubon's action in his will (or would within a year or two) show that there is no reform in the area — the rights, the place, and the freedom of women — that legal, political, and medical reforms metaphorically point toward throughout the book. Casaubon is enabled, in a slight rearrangement of legal chronology, to have a portion of his wish to be her husband after his death by controlling Dorothea's property after his death — not her separate property, but that to which English common law had historically considered a widow entitled by virtue of her having lived in sanctioned marriage with her husband.[5]

But what the episode says about the early seventies and "reform much checked in our days" is as significant as its slightly inaccurate historical reference to the thirties. *Middlemarch* has always that ironic double reference: it is about the thirties *and* about the early seventies. As Eliot was writing the book, in 1869, the House of Commons passed a Married Women's Property Bill by a vote of 131 to 33. It was not a new idea, having been first introduced as a bill in 1857. But when it went up to the House of Lords in 1869 it was dropped. Considered again by the Lords in 1870, the bill was gutted; according to Lee Holcombe, "the Lords tore the Commons' bill to shreds, striking out fourteen of its seventeen substantive clauses and replacing them with new provisions, and amending the other three" (177). The Commons passed the bill, but by the time Eliot published the last number of *Middlemarch* in 1872 the parliamentary efforts to amend the Married Women's Property Act of 1870 were already underway, and they did not cease until amending acts had been passed in 1874 and 1882. Though there have been further amendments in the twentieth century, English law has never restored anything like the original common law dower right that would impel some settlement on a surviving spouse by countermanding a will.

Although the Victorians were probably as talented as we are when it comes to reconciling contradictory principles, it must nevertheless have disturbed some that a wife divorced for adultery under the 1857 Matrimonial Causes Act was entitled to maintenance — alimony — while her sister, the chaste widow, could not see a penny of her dead husband's property, whether or not she had any of her own, if he had so willed. Given this anomaly in the effects of the divorce and property laws, it might seem likely that the 1857 Matrimonial Causes Act would have been the more hotly contested issue. But it was not. Parliamentary debate about women's property reform began at the same time, in the middle fifties; but it was not until the end of the next decade that even an unsatisfactory first step was taken toward securing separate property rights for women. The 1870 Act's provisions, immediately seen as inadequate, were contested and amended for another dozen years. The inference to be drawn from this struggle is that women's property represented a far more threatening issue for reactionaries than did the divorce question. The Married Women's Property Act, however flawed in practice, aimed at effecting a material equality between men and women that its more perceptive opponents in Parliament recognized as genuinely revolutionary (Holcombe 164). Eliot, too, recognized that pressure toward property reform was movement toward equality of rights and, more importantly, equality of ambition. But the 1870 Act itself was so feeble as to appear to Eliot, and probably many others, as reform that was being "checked" rather than carried through.

The identification of "reform" with Dorothea's novel ideas about what a woman might accomplish happens early in *Middlemarch*: Eliot writes that "all people, young or old (that is, all people in those ante-reform times), would have thought her an interesting object if they had referred the glow in her eyes and cheeks to . . . young love" (ch. 3; 16). Dorothea's glow is ambition for something more:

> But perhaps no persons then living — certainly none in the neighbourhood of
> Tipton — would have had a sympathetic understanding for the dreams of a

> girl whose notions about marriage took their colour entirely from an exalted
> enthusiasm about the ends of life, an enthusiasm which was lit chiefly by its
> own fire, and included neither the niceties of the *trousseau*, the pattern of plate,
> nor even the honours and sweet joys of the blooming matron. (ch. 3; 17)

That now, in 1872, there are persons with a "sympathetic understanding"
of Dorothea's notions does not mean that the sympathy has extended to
enthusiastic reform. Behind the narrator's comments is an acknowledgment
that though Dorothea's ambition might not be such an anomaly in the present,
an increase in the number of such women has not meant great changes —
there may be something self-limiting about women's emancipation.

The Sisterhood and Rescue
of Will Ladislaw

IF THERE IS A SINGLE CHARACTER who illustrates the novel's doubts about what
might be achieved in bringing men and women together, that character is
Will Ladislaw. Ladislaw, alone of the male characters who come within the
sphere of Dorothea's charm, does not assess her from a male supremacist
view. At their first meeting, when Dorothea professes to be ignorant about
art and unable to judge his sketch, Ladislaw's assessment is unfavorable,
mistaken (for reasons that already point to attraction), but not superior:

> Ladislaw had made up his mind that she must be an unpleasant girl, since
> she was going to marry Casaubon, and what she said of her stupidity about
> pictures would have confirmed that opinion even if he had believed her. As it
> was, he took her words for a covert judgment, and was certain that she thought
> his sketch detestable. There was too much cleverness in her apology: she was
> laughing both at her uncle and himself. But what a voice! It was like the voice
> of a soul that had once lived in an Æolian harp. This must be one of Nature's
> inconsistencies. There could be no sort of passion in a girl who would marry
> Casaubon. (ch. 9; 53)

He thinks her insincere and without passion — two mistakes, but both deriving
from an incipient jealousy about her approval, whether of art or of husbands.
There is no sign here that he knows himself to be superior, even as a judge
of art. And a moment later, as he thinks back about the comic aspects of the
scene, he laughs with "no mixture of sneering and self-exaltation" (54).
Later, in Rome, Will considers Dorothea's reverence for Casaubon a husband
worship that would be a weakness in any woman (ch. 21; 144). He retracts
his earlier doubts about her sincerity and lack of passion but conjectures that
"she must have made some original romance for herself" (145) in the marriage to Casaubon. He longs to rescue her, but since Casaubon is neither

dragon nor Minotaur (ch. 22; 153), but "a benefactor with collective society at his back" (ch. 21; 145), Will must forbear, and in the outcome it is Dorothea who rescues *him* rather than vice-versa.

Though Casaubon is no Minotaur and Dorothea's blue-green boudoir is not quite a labyrinth, nevertheless her room, Casaubon's living will and testamentary will, and Sir James's suppression of her projects are all restraints and enclosures. She lives in "the stifling oppression of that gentlewoman's world, where everything was done for her and none asked for her aid"; she endures "the gentlewoman's oppressive liberty," and the narrator calls it "moral imprisonment" (ch. 28; 189). True, also, in breaking for freedom from Casaubon's wealth and Casaubon's will, she falls first into another sort of "pinfold" — Sir James Chettam's — and afterwards is "absorbed into the life of another, and . . . only known in a certain circle as a wife and mother" ("Finale"; 576). But Ladislaw seems to represent Dorothea's own choice over the constraint of Casaubon, and among the men Ladislaw is preferable because his sensibility has been trained by a universal feminine experience of dependency. Henry James correctly observes that Ladislaw is "a woman's man" (654) — correctly and perhaps ironically — while he mistakenly imagines Lydgate to be "the real hero of the story" (655). Ladislaw *is* a woman's man, though not a womanly one. The attraction he immediately feels for Dorothea is frankly sexual, while his reaction does not spin itself out as Chettam's and Lydgate's do with faintly masked visions of a sultan and his harem. And he recognizes that his desire to effect a rescue of Dorothea is futile and must give way to acceptance of being rescued.

Ladislaw has been schooled in dependency. *Middlemarch* explores all kinds of dependencies, and Ladislaw, who is led through many varieties, comes out looking fairly self-sufficient. He begins with Casaubon's help, a benefaction that seems pure charity until it is examined more closely. At its first mention, during Dorothea's visit to Casaubon's manor-house at Lowick, talk of Casaubon's support of Ladislaw is juxtaposed with Mr. Brooke's comment about the French king's wish for a fowl in all his subjects' pots. Dorothea's indignant opinion is that it is "a very cheap wish. . . . Are kings such monsters that a wish like that must be reckoned a royal virtue?" (ch. 9; 51). A few moments later Casaubon explains, in his ponderous and circumlocutious way, his providing for Ladislaw: "putting his conduct in the light of mere rectitude" (54). After a few visits with Dorothea in Rome during which her formative influence — "that simplicity of hers, holding up an ideal for others in her believing conception of them" (ch. 77; 532) — starts to work on him, Ladislaw declines any further help from Casaubon. Will and Dorothea begin to realize that Casaubon's benefactions are not charity but simple justice; Casaubon sees that they realize it, and he reacts with an emotion that is as near as he comes to rage. Casaubon forbids Ladislaw his house and begins to contemplate his testamentary exclusion of him from Dorothea's life. He reenacts his family's disinheriting of Ladislaw's grandmother.

The images of the two sisters, Casaubon's mother and Ladislaw's grandmother, are Dorothea's constant companions in her blue-green boudoir. The sisters are types of the two men most important in her life. Dorothea's room was once Casaubon's mother's room, where miniatures of the two sisters hang opposite each other. Dorothea, when about to enter her own socially correct but unfortunate marriage, heard about the sister's "unfortunate marriage" and looked at the close-set grey eyes and the "nose with a sort of ripple in it" (ch. 9; 50) just a few minutes before she met Ladislaw with his grey eyes too near together and nose "with a little ripple in it" (52).

Ladislaw moves from dependence on Casaubon to dependence on Mr. Brooke, uneasily remains there for a while, and then finds himself more or less unwillingly a free agent. But during this time he rejects without hesitation a miserly offer of maintenance from Bulstrode, an offering Bulstrode construes as charity but which is no more than partial restitution to the heir whom he cheated out of an inheritance. These plot developments enable Ladislaw frequently to assert his independence even though he is almost continuously economically dependent. Then at the book's climax, he moves into Dorothea's money. But Dorothea must break through his resistance to the idea; he keeps insisting "We can never be married":

> At last he turned, still resting against the chair, and stretching his hand automatically towards his hat, said with a sort of exasperation, "Good-bye."
> "Oh, I cannot bear it — my heart will break," said Dorothea, starting from her seat, the flood of her young passion bearing down all the obstructions which had kept her silent — the great tears rising and falling in an instant: "I don't mind about poverty — I hate my wealth."
> In an instant Will was close to her and had his arms round her, but she drew her head back and held his away gently that she might go on speaking, her large tear-filled eyes looking at his very simply, while she said in a sobbing childlike way, "We could live quite well on my own fortune — it is too much — seven hundred a-year — I want so little — no new clothes — and I will learn what everything costs." (ch. 83; 560)

The scene recalls one in which Amy Dorrit tells Arthur Clennam that she has *no* money and therefore the obstacle to their marriage has been removed. Arthur is in the Marshalsea for debt, having lost all his money and that of his partner, but before his partner comes to tell him his debts are settled and his old life ready to be taken up, Amy Dorrit has been nursing him. He tells her that they "must learn to part again" (885). She has been urging him to accept her money (before she was informed that all had been lost in Merdle's fall), in terms like Dorothea's: "I have no use for money. I have no wish for it. It would be of no value at all to me but for your sake" (Bk. 2, ch. 29; 828).

Eliot, characteristically, alludes to the scene while reversing its import. In order to qualify for happiness by marrying Arthur Clennam, Little Dorrit has to lose not only this paternal inheritance but a later one she acquires through her uncle. Money for her would mean independence, so it must go. For Dorothea, *her own money* represents a measure of independence, but the use of Casaubon's money means subservience to Casaubon's continuing will, "The Dead Hand" of Book Five of the novel. But Dorothea's independence is Ladislaw's dependence; this rather fundamental compromise in the economics of marriage, when both parties are not equally rich, *can* go in the direction of male dependence. Ladislaw's resistance has to be broken through, and it is done here very simply through an emotive equation of Will and Dorothea: "Her lips trembled, and so did his" (ch. 83; 559). Her "young passion bear[s] down all the obstructions which had kept her silent" and they embrace. She holds him away for the wholly supererogatory, rational comments about how they can live well on her money. "I will learn what everything costs" (560), says Dorothea, when she has already learned this, and it is Will who has yet to learn.

The assertion of Will Ladislaw's "sisterhood" with the heroines of recent romantic fiction, with Amy Dorrit, with Dorothea herself, may be the boldest blow the book strikes for its causes. But it was risky. Henry James illustrates the risk when he reads Ladislaw as "a woman's man" (654) and implies that he is "womanish" or "feminine." In the middle-class construction of gender, which included economic independence for the male and dependence for the female, Ladislaw *was* feminine.

Ladislaw has been deliberately constructed to raise the kind of objection James makes, and also — perhaps to discredit that very objection by suggesting that it is encoded ethnic bigotry — Ladislaw is made a "foreigner." Actually, he merely has some Polish blood, and in Middlemarch he is surrounded by the "tribes of Toller, Hackbutt, and the rest, . . . who sneered at his Polish blood, and were themselves of a breed very much in need of crossing" (ch. 60; 417). Ladislaw's foreignness allows for another allusion, this time to Collins's *The Woman in White*. Shortly after Casaubon's death, Celia tells her sister about the will's provision against her marrying Ladislaw. Celia has no suspicion that Dorothea might be romantically interested in that direction: "Of course that is of no consequence in one way — you never *would* marry Mr Ladislaw; but that only makes it worse of Mr Casaubon." Then she repeats a judgment of the vicar's wife: "Mrs Cadwallader said you might as well marry an Italian with white mice!" (ch. 50; 339). Equating Ladislaw with Count Fosco and his pet mice expresses succinctly the Middlemarch tribe's xenophobic meanness, but it also brings to mind the differences between the two men rather than their similarities: nothing could be more unlike Fosco's imposition of his will on all those around him than Ladislaw's malleability. "An Italian with white mice! — on the contrary," Dorothea thinks, "he was a creature who entered into every one's feelings, and could take the pressure of their thought instead of urging his own with iron resistance" (ch. 50; 344). Ladislaw's yielding quality is less universal, more specifically aligned to Dorothea's will than she knows at this point, but it is literally a "saving" feature in that it allows Dorothea's rescue of him.

Ladislaw's rescue is accomplished only after Dorothea goes through a period of intense sexual jealousy when she imagines he loves Rosamond.[6] After this crisis Dorothea sees the rescue of Ladislaw *and* of Lydgate and Rosamond "an obligation on her as if they had been suppliants bearing the sacred branch. . . . The objects of her rescue were not to be sought out by her fancy: they were chosen for her" (ch. 80; 544). Dorothea temporarily rescues Lydgate by giving him money and her trust in his innocence. She rescues Rosamond from her infatuation with Ladislaw and thus saves Lydgate too, though this marriage's "hidden as well as evident troubles" (544) will not disappear because one catastrophe has been averted.

The rescues attempted and accomplished by women in nineteenth-century novels are impelled by a movement toward equality and the erasure of difference. Dorothea's power to save, to rescue, comes from her ability to get on a level with another person. Ironically, this power unnerves Casaubon and perhaps even hastens his death. Dorothea's encounters late in the book as she takes on the rescue of Lydgate, of Rosamond, and of Ladislaw depict her first as an imposing or awe-inspiring figure: Lydgate thinks she has "a heart large enough for the Virgin Mary" (ch. 76; 530), Rosamond feels "something like bashful timidity before a superior" (ch. 81; 548), and even Ladislaw is put off by what he perceives as her "queenly way of receiving him" — in her agitation she forgets to put out her hand to him or to sit down (ch. 83; 557). But these scenes move rapidly toward equality. Lydgate perceives that Dorothea is a woman with whom a man can be friends — something he "never saw in any woman before" (ch. 76; 530). Ladislaw and Dorothea are emotively equated in the reconciliation scene we have already looked at. Rosamond's meeting with Dorothea begins with Dorothea's apparent superiority and Rosamond's getting smaller and smaller (ch. 81; 547), but soon both women are reduced to helpless childishness (549) and are clinging to each other like very young sisters in a shipwreck.

Middlemarch is such a wonderful book that we expect it to teach us how men can get past their stupid notions of supremacy and how women can join each other as sisters to help and ensure that passage. But it does not. If anything it warns that the road to reform is longer than some had thought and that the solutions of previous books no more provide an answer than does this book. In *Middlemarch* every reform is costly. The Featherstone almshouses and the Bulstrode cholera hospital are built on the wrongs of women. What is gained in breaking gender stereotypes so that the heroine can marry is lost again because marriage itself is a narrowing of Dorothea's scope of influence to "a certain circle as a wife and mother." How that could have been avoided the narrator does not address: "no one stated exactly what else that was in her power she ought rather to have done" ("Finale"; 576). Dorothea is willing to submerge herself while her husband pursues reform; Rosamond is not willing to do the same. All this suggests an either/or, zero-sum view of reform — a forecast that women reformers will have to forfeit a great deal and that reform will not come about merely as a result of domestic compromise between pairs of reasonable people.

Murray State University

NOTES

1. We know of George Eliot's early interest in the cause of the Married Women's Property Act: she writes Sophia Hannell in January of 1856 that proposed changes to the laws concerning married women's property "would help to raise the position and character of women. It is one round of a long ladder stretching far beyond our lives" (*Letters* 2: 227).

2. My reading of *Middlemarch* is indebted to the work of many critics, especially those writing on political reform, on the idea of novels being in conversation with each other, on female heroism, rescue, and sisterhood, on the "feminization" of male characters, and on the complicated question of Eliot's feminism. Jerome Beaty (1957) sketched the political events of the years 1829–32 referred to by Eliot; Patrick Brantlinger (1977) related the disillusionment at failed reforms in *Middlemarch* to a widespread rejection of reform idealism in the decades after the middle of the century, evident in other novels such as *The Warden* and *Pendennis*. Bert G. Hornback (1988) argued that the political is always turned back toward the personal in the book. That novels might be in conversation with each other is a premise of Jerome Meckier's *Hidden Rivalries in Victorian Fiction* and is implicit in Susan Morgan's *Sisters in Time*. Morgan also writes about a nineteenth-century transformation of a masculine heroic tradition into a feminine one in the novel. I have been much influenced in my thinking about Will Ladislaw by U. C. Knoepflmacher's discussion of Eliot's androgynous narrators and the resolution of her own "internal gender divisions" through "a transference to the male of the deprivations and suffering she finds in the lot of women" (134, 139). Also relevant to what I call the "sistering" of Will Ladislaw is Carolyn Heilbrun's important book *Toward a Recognition of Androgyny* and Susan Morgan's discussion of the "feminization" of Chad and Strether in James's *The Ambassadors*. Disagreements about Eliot's "feminist credentials" (in Jeanie Thomas's words, 392) divide those who write about *Middlemarch* and its author. Feminists such as Lee Edwards, Patricia Beer, Marlene Springer, and Ellen Moers restate the question Virginia Woolf asked: Why is Dorothea Brooke not allowed the fulfillment of accomplishment that Eliot herself achieved? Feminist critics also attack Eliot's wariness of female suffrage and her conviction that men and women have

innate differences not culturally caused. But Eliot has strong feminist defenders: Kathleen Blake, Patricia Meyer Spacks, Zelda Austen, Jeanie Thomas, and Dorothea Barrett, among others, who argue that Dorothea shows women's social trammels in 1872 more realistically than Eliot's experience would indicate, and that the novel as a whole, as well as Dorothea's own life, shows that amelioration of social conditions is possible but gradual. Two excellent reviews of feminist criticism of *Middlemarch* are Ellin Ringler's (1983) and Jeanie Thomas's (1987). Anne E. Patrick (1987) also reviews the criticism while arguing that the book "contains a systematic critique of gender stereotyping, one that is integral to the action of the novel and central to its chief thematic concern" (223). Patrick's title, "Rosamond Rescued," points to her own rescue of Rosamond from full blame for the Lydgates' marriage problems, rather than to *Dorothea's* rescue of Rosamond. Finally, Barbara Hardy sees the book in a way that is almost a reversal of my own view — for her it is a psychologically flawed version of the male sexual rescue, rather than a psychologically astute depiction of Dorothea's rescue of Will (and others). Hardy argues that Ladislaw delivers Dorothea from the impotent Casaubon, even though Will himself self-disparagingly denies he is a rescuer at all (145, 153), Casaubon is dead before the rescue takes place, and Ladislaw seems intent on going away until Dorothea closes with him.

3. George Eliot's opinions about reform are complex, but they tend to be simplified into a uniform conservatism by scholars such as Gordon Haight. This comes about partly because of Eliot's reservations about extending the franchise — evident in *Felix Holt*, in her "Address to Working Men" in the January 1868 *Blackwood's*, and in her letters (for example 4: 403, 4: 496). But she also believed Mill's argument for extending the franchise to women a good one (*Letters* 4: 366), even though she saw clearly that working for women's suffrage was likely to be futile for a long time to come, and discouraged her friend Sara Sophia Hennell from doing so (4: 390).

Another ground of her conservatism, more troubling to feminists, is her belief in a "difference of function" between the sexes (letter to Emily Davies, August 8, 1868), a difference clearly going beyond the biological to what she sees as a difference of moral influence. But she is adamant on the necessity for giving men and women absolutely equal intellectual opportunities.

The letter which seems to me to bear most closely on the questions of reform in *Middlemarch* is an early one, written at the time of the revolutions of 1848. Eliot writes to John Sibree, Jr., to tell him she joins him in his happiness about the events in France. She makes clear that what she would like to see happen in her own country is not *political* reform, but a more profound *social* reform:

> I should have no hope of good from any imitative movement at home. Our working classes are eminently inferior to the mass of the French people. In France, the *mind* of the people is highly electrified — they are full of ideas on social subjects — they really desire social *reform*. . . . Here there is so much larger a proportion of selfish radicalism and unsatisfied, brute sensuality (in the agricultural and mining districts especially) than of perception or desire of justice, that a revolutionary movement would be simply destructive — not constructive. Besides, it would be put down. Our military have no notion of "fraternizing." . . . Our little humbug of a queen is more endurable than the rest of her race because she calls forth a chivalrous feeling, and there is nothing in our constitution to obstruct the slow progress of *political* reform. This is all we are

fit for at present. The social reform which may prepare us for great changes is more and more the object of effort both in Parliament and out of it. But we English are slow crawlers. (1: 254)

Eliot's conviction that revolution would be put down may have come from hearing accounts of the Peterloo massacre, which occurred three months before she was born, or perhaps from her own experience with the election riots caused by the 1832 Reform Bill. But the important distinction between social and political reform illuminates her later jaded attitudes about what can be accomplished through legislative processes, the limited value and the danger of the extended franchise, and the difference between Reform Bills and real reform.

4. Mary Garth, Rosamond Vincy, and Dorothea have other three-way sisterly links, though Mary is somewhat apart from the main actions in which Rosamond and Dorothea participate. The group of the Garths and Fred Vincy is in a kind of idyllic place off to the side of Middlemarch where reform actually *succeeds*. Caleb Garth is a practical reformer who does his bit to make things better for the people on the farms he tends. Fred is genuinely reformed by the efforts of Mary, who is a spiritual sister of Dorothea's and Rosamond's — she went to school with Rosamond — but differentiated from Rosamond in her contentment with her place and from Dorothea in her satisfaction with the way she can serve. The narrator identifies Dorothea with St. Theresa while observing of Mary that in relation to "the saints of the earth . . . Mary was not one of them" (ch. 33; 218), linking the two women with the image of sainthood while asserting their difference.

5. It could be argued that dower protection under the old common law system of marriage provision gave way to a *better* system of clearly defined settlements. But as Susan Staves points out, the loss of the dower right had "considerable ideological significance" (5). Staves presents the complexities of the issue in the second chapter of *Married Women's Separate Property in England, 1660–1833*. Her discussion makes clear that although by technical rule of law a man in 1831 could not have prevented a wife's dower right by will, yet the Dower Act of 1833 only made explicit what had already been taking place for many years: the replacement of dower rights by contractual settlements.

6. During Dorothea's period of jealousy, which is a kind of sexual dark night of the soul, the narrator uses the most bizarre image of the book, putting Dorothea and Rosamond together as true and false mothers, and thus "sistering" them in a fashion. Dorothea imagines Solomon's judgment carried through to its literal, bloody conclusion, with the divided child as her own heart and Ladislaw her true child/lover, and Ladislaw also divided into the true and false lover. Rosamond in this vision becomes false claimant to the child, "the lying woman who had never known the mother's pang." But she is also Dorothea's sister because Solomon's two suppliant women are sistered by their love of the child, as two women are made sisters by their rivalry for a child/man — and Ladislaw is described as being such a child/man, like Shelley and like Daphnis. *Wives and Daughters* also uses the image of Solomon and the two claimants, when Molly thinks about Roger and Cynthia. Paintings similarly assert the sisterhood of women who are rivals, from the Old Testament subject of *Moses Brought before Pharaoh's Daughter* by Hogarth, 1746, or Francis Hayman's version, *The Finding of the Infant Moses*, 1746 (both painted for the London Foundling Hospital); or "modern life" variations such as Frederick Barwell's *Adopting a Child*, 1857, which

also includes, as do the Moses pictures, both adoptive and birth mother. The sisterhood and near identity of *sexual* rivals is asserted comically by such pictures as James Tissot's *In The Conservatory* ("The Rivals" — 1878) and seriously by others such as Millais's *Retribution* (1854). Many of these pictures assert with a startling likeness of the faces the figurative truth of sisterhood through mutual love and pain: the adoptive mother and the blood mother, the true and false claimant to the child, the rivals for the adult male — all are sisters under the skin, and the pictures sometimes make them skin-deep twins as well.

WORKS CITED

Austen, Jane. *The Novels of Jane Austen.* Ed. R. W. Chapman. 3rd ed. Oxford: Oxford UP, 1965.

Austen, Zelda. "Why Feminist Critics Are Angry with George Eliot." *College English* 37 (1976): 549–61.

Barrett, Dorothea. *Vocation and Desire: George Eliot's Heroines.* London: Routledge, 1989.

Beaty, Jerome. "History by Indirection: The Era of Reform in *Middlemarch.*" *Victorian Studies* 1 (1957–58): 173–79.

Beer, Patricia. *Reader, I Married Him: A Study of the Women Characters of Jane Austen, Charlotte Brontë, Elizabeth Gaskell, and George Eliot.* New York: Barnes and Noble, 1974.

Blake, Kathleen. *Love and the Woman Question in Victorian Literature: The Art of Self-Postponement.* Sussex: Harvester P; Totowa, New Jersey: Barnes and Noble, 1983.

Brantlinger, Patrick. *The Spirit of Reform: British Literature and Politics, 1832–1867.* Cambridge, MA: Harvard UP, 1977.

Collins, Wilkie. *The Works of Wilkie Collins.* 30 vols. New York: Peter Fenelon Collier, 1895. Rpt. New York: AMS, 1970.

Dickens, Charles. *Little Dorrit.* Ed. Harvey Peter Sucksmith. Oxford: Clarendon Press, 1979.

Edwards, Lee R. "Women, Energy, and *Middlemarch.*" *Woman: An Issue.* Ed. Lee R. Edwards, Mary Heath, and Lisa Baskin. Boston: Little, Brown, 1972. 223–38.

Eliot, George. *The George Eliot Letters.* Ed. Gordon S. Haight. 7 vols. New Haven: Yale UP, 1954–55.

———. *Middlemarch.* Ed. Bert G. Hornback. Norton Critical Edition. New York: W. W. Norton, 1977.

Gaskell, Elizabeth Cleghorn. *Wives and Daughters.* Ed. Frank Glover Smith. Introduction by Laurence Lerner. Harmondsworth: Penguin, 1969.

Haight, Gordon S. *George Eliot: A Biography.* New York: Oxford UP, 1968.

Hardy, Barbara. *Particularities: Readings in George Eliot.* Athens: Ohio UP, 1982.

Heilbrun, Carolyn. *Toward a Recognition of Androgyny: Aspects of Male and Female in Literature.* London: Gollancz, 1973.

Holcombe, Lee. *Wives and Property: Reform of the Married Women's Property Law in Nineteenth-Century England.* Toronto: U of Toronto P, 1983.

Hornback, Bert G. Middlemarch: *A Novel of Reform.* Boston: Twayne, 1988.

James, Henry. "George Eliot's *Middlemarch.*" *Galaxy* (March 1873): 424–28. Rpt. in *Middlemarch,* ed. Hornback. 652–55.

Knoepflmacher, U. C. "Unveiling Men: Power and Masculinity in George Eliot's Fiction." *Men by Women.* Ed. Janet Todd. New York: Holmes and Meier, 1982. *Women & Literature* 2 (1982): 130–46.

Meckier, Jerome. *Hidden Rivalries in Victorian Fiction: Dickens, Realism, and Revaluation.* Lexington: UP of Kentucky, 1987.

Moers, Ellen. *Literary Women.* Garden City, N.Y.: Doubleday, 1976.

Morgan, Susan. *Sisters in Time: Imagining Gender in Nineteenth-Century British Fiction.* New York: Oxford UP, 1989.

Patrick, Anne E. "Rosamond Rescued: George Eliot's Critique of Sexism in *Middlemarch.*" *The Journal of Religion* 67 (1987): 220–38.

Ringler, Ellin. "*Middlemarch*: A Feminist Perspective." *Studies in the Novel* 15 (1983): 55–61.

Spacks, Patricia Meyer. *The Female Imagination.* New York: Knopf, 1975.

Springer, Marlene. "Angels and Other Women in Victorian Literature." *What Manner of Woman: Essays on English and American Life and Literature.* Ed. Marlene Springer. New York: New York UP, 1977. 124–59.

Staves, Susan. *Married Women's Separate Property in England, 1660–1833.* Cambridge: Harvard UP, 1990.

Thomas, Jeanie G. "An Inconvenient Indefiniteness: George Eliot, *Middlemarch*, and Feminism." *University of Toronto Quarterly* 56 (Spring, 1987): 392–415.

Woolf, Virginia. *A Room of One's Own.* New York: Harcourt, Brace, 1929.

IT THOUGHT IT WERE A MOUSE-TRAP: THE *SYLVIE AND BRUNO* BOOKS AS ARCHETYPAL MENIPPEAN SATIRE

By Edmund Miller

SATIRE HOLDS HUMAN FOLLY up to ridicule with a view to correcting the folly. Roman rhetoricians identified three modes of satire by the names of their chief exponents, Horace, Juvenal, and Menippus. Horatian satire mocks gently. Juvenalian satire castigates harshly. Both these modes are characterized by the author's announced intention to do something very like "anatomize" follies in a sense that Robert Burton, author of *The Anatomy of Melancholy*, would have appreciated: that is, to list, dissect, and criticize openly. Horatian satire and Juvenalian satire are called modes of formal satire because they make this criticism directly.

The third mode of satire recognized by Roman rhetoricians and practitioners, Menippean, is less familiar and somewhat more difficult to characterize. Abundant examples of complete works by Horace and Juvenal survive, but we have only fragmentary vestiges of the works of Menippus of Gadara. The *Satyricon* of Petronius Arbiter is perhaps the best known surviving illustration of a type of satire once regarded as representing an important third mode. But the *Satyricon* is itself only a fragment, and of course it cannot have the authority as a model that would be accorded a work by the author who gave his name to this type of satire. The marks of Menippean satire as they have come down to us from antiquity are fairly clear. But the genre can be defined only by examining the surviving works of less representative, later classical authors who claim Menippus as their master.

It is my contention that the *Sylvie and Bruno* books by Lewis Carroll are archetypal Menippean satire: that is, they are not simply outstanding examples of the mode, but, taken together as a single work, *Sylvie and Bruno* and *Sylvie and Bruno Concluded* illustrate the genre of Menippean satire as well as the *Satyricon*, the Dialogues of Lucian, or any other surviving classical text. Because our contemporary culture takes a special interest in issues of theory, the theoretical tradition which the work illustrates is something readers will wish to know about. Placing the *Sylvie and Bruno* books in the tradition of Menippean satire will also show the work to be more worth the effort of reading than has been the case and yet will make it, simultaneously, easier to read.

Mikhail Bakhtin has noted the general kinship between the carnival nature of Menippean satire and fantasy literature (94–95). And Carroll's specific affinity for Menippean satire has been noted persuasively by Northrop Frye, who so cited the *Alice* books in *Anatomy of Criticism*, the seminal work in which he reintroduced the term into the lexicon of modern criticism. But the *Sylvie and Bruno* books are far more Menippean than the *Alice* books. While Frye's theoretical formulations have been somewhat muted by later developments in genre theory (discussed in Hernadi 131–51) and qualifications of his sharp divisions between genres have been suggested by such writers as Scholes and Klaus, the modal characteristics of the genre of Menippean satire as he described them still provide the focus of all subsequent discussion. Indeed, I am proposing that Frye's theoretical formulations are in a sense sounder than his practical application of these principles since I shall argue that the *Sylvie and Bruno* books are also far more precisely Menippean satires by his definition than is his own suggested archetype, *The Anatomy of Melancholy*.

Carroll signals to us that he himself sees the *Sylvie and Bruno* books as satire of some sort by mentioning Horace in the preface to each part of the work. In the first of these prefaces, in the midst of a grim passage placing the unpleasant reality that "this night shall thy soul be required of thee" in an explicitly Christian context, Carroll quotes Horace to the effect that we may suddenly lose everything and be sent into exile. The passage is also interesting for its sly misdirection. The lines are quoted in Latin and followed by a footnote number. It is natural to suppose that the footnote will provide a translation of the lines. Even a classicist able to read the lines as easily as the English text in which they are embedded would naturally look down to see how the translation had succeeded in capturing the meaning. Members of the general public and the schoolgirls whom Carroll made his special concern would certainly need a translation and look to the note expecting to find one. But the footnote disappoints these expectations and instead elaborates the theme that we should expect death by announcing that as the lines were being written (by Carroll, not Horace) a message arrived announcing the "sudden death of a dear friend." In addition to symbolically bringing death to our expectations and providing a surprising testimony to the point under discussion, the passage also foreshadows the troubling seeming death of Arthur Forester in the work itself (*Sylvie and Bruno Concluded*, 772; ch. 18).

The reference to Horace in the preface to *Sylvie and Bruno Concluded* is more casual, being merely a passing observation that a particular section seems to have been written twenty years earlier than the complete book and thus "more than twice the period so cautiously recommended by Horace for 'repressing' one's literary efforts!" (660). Still, taken together, the references to Horace in the two prefaces certainly show that Carroll had at least one satirist in mind while he was compiling the work. And it is not surprising that it is the gently mocking Horace rather than the harsh Juvenal whom he has in mind. We cannot expect him to have had the no-longer-extant works of Menippus explicitly in mind.

Menippean satire, in distinction from formal Horatian and Juvenalian satire, is called informal satire because its method is to draw an exaggerated picture of the world from which implicit criticism of the way one conducts oneself can easily be understood. There is no announced authorial intention in the body of the work, and criticism is suggested by indirection. Menippean satire is inevitably narrative because it does not employ the commentary of the formal modes of satire and so must weave its moral from plot. But it is satire, and therefore the plot as it unfolds offers a criticism of the world as the author sees it. In a cavil in the preface to *Sylvie and Bruno Concluded*, Carroll objects that he cannot be held "responsible for *any* of the opinions expressed by the characters" (659). In this passage he firmly grasps the baton of Menippus. For what is at issue is more than the recognition that the work is fiction. The question is the applicability of the opinions of the characters to moral judgments concerning the real world. If Carroll had not been writing narrative, the question would not have arisen. But if he had not been writing satire, he would not have turned right around as he does in this preface and embraced the very opinions for which he has just disclaimed responsibility, for he goes on to say he is "much in sympathy with 'Arthur' " in his strictures on Sermons and Choristers (663). Carroll has presented Arthur as the touchstone of rational Christianity in such a way that his views ought to seem the right views to the reader. They are not just views such as "might probably be held by the persons into whose mouths" they are put (659), to quote Carroll's disclaimer again.

Some narrative is likely to occur from time to time in any sustained literary discourse, so narrative is not banned entirely from use in formal satire — witness Horace's famous story of the Country Mouse and the City Mouse. But in formal satire the author provides explicit moral commentary in his own voice to exemplify his thesis. And this is something that Carroll has carefully avoided, not so much with the disclaimer in the preface as with the creation of his passive third-person-observer narrator.

This principle of indirection at the basis of informal satire requires that the narrator's voice in Menippean satire be reduced to a minimum. The narrator must allow readers to draw their own conclusions about the quality and moral weight of the actions he describes. If he comments, it must be as a naïve observer of the passing scene. Whereas the narrator's voice is omniscient but characterized by very personalized attitudes in formal satire, in informal satire the narrator cannot be fully omniscient or he would know how to evaluate the actions he describes, and he cannot have much of a personality or he would express opinions about these actions.

In the surviving ancient works and fragments, we sometimes encounter what modern theorists of point of view would call journalistic or reportorial omniscience, in which the narrator describes the actions but not the thoughts of the characters and never comments on the implications of these actions. In classical works the narrator is never the sort of first-person omniscient narrator favored by many eighteenth- and nineteenth-century novelists, the narrator who tells the story in the third person but comments on the doings of the characters in a first-person authorial voice addressed to the "Dear Reader." The classical narrator of Menippean satire is also not a true first-person participant in the modern sense. Such a persona is usually present on the scene in the technical sense as a first-person narrator, but is only marginally involved in the physical action and moral valuation of the plot — is in the modern sense, a first-person observer narrator. Of course, theory and practice do not always work hand in hand, and in fact the narrator of the *Satyricon*, for example, participates to a very large extent in the on-going action of that work.

Carroll's narrator for the *Sylvie and Bruno* books is so self-effacing that the reader never learns his name, although Bruno called him "Mr. Sir" regularly after he determines that he is not "Duke of Anything" despite being big enough to be two dukes. This narrator does give expression to many feelings and beliefs throughout the course of the two volumes. For example, he comments favorably on the beauty and sensitivity of Lady Muriel Orme, on the sweet nature of Sylvie, on the engaging directness of Bruno, and on the astuteness and wit of Arthur, and he comments negatively on the moral depth of Eric Lindon. But all these points are obvious to the reader apart from the narrator's commentary. Indeed the reader notices many things the narrator seems to miss, for example the reason for Arthur's reticence in making his romantic feelings known to Lady Muriel and her reluctance to break off her formal betrothal to Eric. The feelings he expresses are, in fact, not really personal; he has the role of chorus in expressing the reader's feelings. And he does not advance the action himself, as he might have for example by telling the would-be lovers about one another's feelings. He wants these two to get together almost more than they do themselves, but like the reader he is powerless to take any action to bring about this desirable resolution.

There are, however, a few places where the narrator's voice is somewhat more insistent. For example, in chapter 14 of *Sylvie and Bruno* the narrator addresses the reader directly: "I want to know — dear Child who reads this! — why Fairies should always be teaching *us* to do our duty, and lecturing *us* when we go wrong, and we should never teach *them* anything?" (557).[1] But this chapter and the next one actually represent an independent story written for a children's magazine and incorporated without change in the finished book. There is a certain Menippean casualness in Carroll's neglect to change even such an obvious blunder as qualifying the narrator's first reference to Sylvie by name in this section with the parenthetical "I found out her name afterwards" (578; ch. 14). In these chapters the narrator also actively intervenes in the story. Mr. Sir helps Bruno discover that kindness is better than revenge by suggesting that Bruno show Sylvie that he is upset with her by weeding her garden rather than by tearing up the flowers as he had been doing. But although taking a more active part in the story than he does in the continuing plot in either England or Fairyland, the narrator is again here expressing sentiments Carroll expected his intended readers to share. Carroll is here helping his child readers to discover their inherent Christian charity. Although the work does not adhere to modern conventions of consistency in these matters, even with such variations in point of view as those in the two chapters under discussion, Carroll's narrator in the *Sylvie and Bruno* books is always reasonably compatible with the narrative requirements of traditional Menippean satire. The very inconsistencies are even perhaps traditional.

Another traditional characteristic of Menippean satire is the mixing of various levels and types of discourse — polite language with scurrilous, controlled Ciceronian periods with loose Senecan periods, Latin with Greek, prose with verse. In fact, Eugene Kirk calls unconventional diction the chief mark of classical Menippean satire, by which he means that it typically brought together sorts of language not usually found in the same place: "Neologisms, portmanteau words, macaronics, preciosity, course vulgarity, catalogues, bombast, mixed languages, and protracted sentences were typical of the genre, sometimes appearing all together in the same work. In outward structure," Kirk says, "Menippean satire was a medley" (xi). Included were "fantasitic voyages, dreams, visions, talking beasts," also "pardoxes" (xi). "The theme often called for ridicule or caricature of some sham–intellectual or theological fraud. Yet sometimes the theme demanded exhortation to learning, when books and studies had fallen into disuse and neglect" (xi). All of this should sound very familiar to readers of *Alice's Adventures in Wonderland* or *Sylvie and Bruno*, except of course the coarse vulgarity, and even on this point the *Alice* books are awash with all the rudeness anyone could possibly want, and the *Sylvie and Bruno* books specifically deal with a range of bad linguistic behavior from childish cruelty to drunken incoherence and even treasonous subterfuges. "LESS BREAD! MORE TAXES!" (*Sylvie and Bruno* 501; ch. 1). And at any rate the classical genre did not require that the whole possible range of language forms appear in any one work.

But the identification of the *Sylvie and Bruno* books with Menippean satire is much stronger. In addition to a local mixing of forms, Menippean satire tends to present an appearance of a body of material so overwhelming that it could not be contained within the work. Menippean satire, for example, shares with epic the characteristic of beginning in medias res. *Sylvie and Bruno* certainly does this. Not only are we dropped into the middle of a staged revolutionary uprising in Outland, but we are brought into this without knowing that this parallel universe is only one of several that play a part in the book. Menippean satire shares with classical romance the characteristic of episodic presentation. To this picaresque character of Menippean satire, the *Sylvie and Bruno* books conform with a vengeance. Menippean satire also shares with romance an ambiguity of closure that amounts to openendedness. One is not quite sure that it has ended. And Menippean satire shares with real life a peculiar affinity for digression that would be taken as a mark of careless, inept, or incomplete work in any other literary mode. I shall discuss these last two points — openendedness and digression — in some detail when I take up the question of the conclusion. The point of all these various aspects of Menippean overwhelming is undoubtedly to suggest that the world is out of joint. And it is in their inclusiveness that Carroll's *Sylvie and Bruno* books show their explicit conformity to the classical genre of Menippean satire. There is a whole spectrum of variety to the texture of the prose. There is even some macaroni in the form of a few Latin phrases and some Dogland dialogue transcribed in the native tongue — you should excuse the expression — of Dogee. There is the newspaper clipping that erroneously announces Arthur's death. There is the interpolated story from *Aunt Judy's Magazine*. There is the whole structure of a mixing of scenes from English country life with scenes in Fairyland. There are the time-travel stories concerning the Professor's Outlandish watch.

And of course no reader of Carroll needs to be told that he mixes prose and verse, the most obvious sort of Menippean medley of modes of discourse and the most commonly encountered in the classical models. Yet there are permutations to the mixing of modes in the *Sylvie and Bruno* books that are not seen in the *Alice* books. In the *Alice* books the verses are for the most part digressions only. Only the nursery rhyme about the Knave of Hearts is integrated into the plot, and this is, of course, not an original rhyme of Carroll's or parodied by him. In *Through the Looking-Glass* Carroll makes beautiful use of "Jabberwocky" and the White Knight's song "A-sitting On A Gate" to comment on the nature of Looking-Glass life, and "Jabberwocky" also memorably serves as a text for Humpty Dumpty's illuminating literary analysis, but it is not part of the action of the plot.

The verses in the *Sylvie and Bruno* books are as many and as various as those in the *Alice* books. "The Pig-Tale" has been found striking enough to be published separately as a children's book. In the work itself this is the lecture eventually presented by the character called the Other Professor. And his presentation is interrupted by dialogue scenes advancing the plot as well as by Bruno's naïve but astute literary commentary: "It's a miserable story! . . . It begins miserably, and it ends miserablier. I think I shall cry" (*Sylvie and Bruno Concluded* 809; ch. 23). But as much is done in the *Alice* books, which are of course Menippean satires too (see Chadwick-Joshua).

But in the *Sylvie and Bruno* books verse can sometimes do much more by helping to process the medley of forms and by providing symbolic commentary on the plot. A clear illustration of verses functioning this way is "The Gardener's Song," which occurs a stanza at a time throughout the work rather than as a single descent into verse — to use Mr. Boffin's term from *Our Mutual Friend*. And these scattered verses are not simply random interludes or digressions (although digression is itself of course a characteristic of Menippean satire). They are used rather as part of the narrative technique bridging the transition between worlds. For example, when the Gardener is first introduced, he sings,

> He thought he saw an Elephant,
>   That practised on a fife:
> He looked again, and found it was
>   A letter from his wife,
> "At length I realise," he said,
>   "The bitterness of Life."
>   (*Sylvie and Bruno* 526; ch. 5)

Sylvie and Bruno encounter the Gardener while running to catch up with a beggar who has been rudely chased away from the palace. Being good of heart they know that it was wrong of Uggug to dump water down on the beggar (*Sylvie and Bruno* 521; ch. 4), and so they want to share their cake with him. The Gardener unlocks a door in the garden wall for them, enabling them to continue their pursuit of the beggar on this errand of mercy, and when they catch up with him he leads them into a magic bejeweled cave where he is suddenly transformed into their father in all his regalia as King of Elfland. This transformation is exactly as probable as the nonsense transformation of the stanza of "The Gardener's Song" that we have just heard. The beggar is an elephant because he is as out of place on the palace grounds as an elephant is in Victorian England. He is also like an elephant because he is dangerous but useful. He is dangerous because he is, after all, a seeming stranger inviting these innocent children to follow him into a hidden cave with no more explanation or justification than "Follow me!" This is certainly a situation to make respectable Victorian parents uneasy. In fact, if anything, Carroll emphasizes the danger when he describes the beggar as "snatch[ing]" the cake from the children and "devour[ing] it greedily." In fact he is said to have "glowered 'More, more!' and glared at the half-frightened children" just before issuing his peremptory command "Follow me!" (*Sylvie and Bruno* 528; ch. 5). Yet this dark situation takes an improbably happy turn. The beggar turns out to be kindly disposed to the children; his dark cave turns out to be magically bejeweled and stocked with exotic fruit; he metamorphoses into the King of Elfland; and this King of Elfland turns out to be the children's own father, with whom they are happily reunited. The substantive difference here is no less than the reinterpretation of the elephant as a letter, and it is suggestive that it is a letter from a wife, introducing an unexpected familial relationship just such as the one discovered by the children.

The nature of the transformation described in the stanza of "The Gardener's Song" leads the anonymous hero to contemplate "the bitterness of life," as the song puts it. It is perhaps the job of Sylvie and Bruno throughout the work to grow up to an understanding of the bitterness of life, but at any rate this particular scene teaches them the nature of the reality of the world they inhabit. They are learning an important lesson about life. Life is a "phlizz," a strawberry-colored banana that is completely tasteless and probably not very nourishing. While the lesson about the physical world is not relevant to the very different physical world inhabited by the reader, it should be noticed that the lesson in the rewards of charity is applicable to the real world and that Carroll very specifically wanted the reader to see this. There is a reward to Christian charity, but it is spiritual, that is to say, something not to be expected in the coinage of this world. As the King of Elfland tells his son as he is about to eat the completely tasteless strawberry banana, "[T]hen you'll find out what *Pleasure* is like — the Pleasure we all seek so madly, and enjoy so mournfully!" (*Sylvie and Bruno* 529; ch. 6).

In addition, almost any stanza of "The Gardener's Song" could stand as a description of both the book's theme and its technique.

> He thought he saw an Argument
> That proved he was the Pope:
> He looked again, and found it was
> A Bar of Mottled Soap.
> "A fact so dread," he faintly said,
> "Extinguishes all hope!"
>
> (*Sylvie and Bruno Concluded* 785; ch. 20)

Here we have both the theme of false belief supplanted by true and the salutary effect of coming to a right understanding. The reference to the Pope makes the religious implication explicit. The reference to soap suggests that right thinking is cleansing. Yet the despair of the anonymous hero of the song at his chastening discovery that he is not quite so grand a personage as he thought is a warning to the reader to distrust all hasty generalizations especially in a world where it is so easy to make such a vast mistake. And the spiritual world is just such a world.

The shifts of point of view in the *Sylvie and Bruno* books — shifts of substantive reality, shifts back and forth between Fairyland and the English town of Elveston, and shifts between the included tales and the main narrative — are specific indicators of the work's nature as Menippean satire because they call attention both to the overall structure and to the casual and digressive texture of the narrative.

These shifts of presentational mode and point of view are often uneasy and remind us that the work is indeed satire in its intent to reform society and not merely Menippean satire in the structural sense of presenting mixed modes. An example of the uneasiness of a transitional passage occurs in the narrator's initial meeting with the heroine of the English strand of the story, Lady Muriel Orme. Because of her sweet disposition, her physical beauty and elegance, and the logical clarity of her advanced but not radical ideas, the narrator immediately associates her in his conscious mind with the magical Sylvie he knows from his secret fugue states. But when he actually first awakes from Fairyland in the English railway carriage, Lady Muriel appears before him replacing the fairy presence not of Sylvie but of My Lady Tabikat, Uggug's Mother (*Sylvia and Bruno* 522–23; chs. 4–5). The message seems to be that even an embodiment of all Christian perfection like Lady Muriel is always on the brink of falling away from that perfection. One small lapse and she becomes Tabikat. We have to work at Christian perfection just as the Red Queen had to run as fast as possible to stay where she was and keep from falling behind (see Plackis on the Christian themes of the *Alice* books).

The presentational shifts give a special character to the way the *Sylvie and Bruno* books begin in the middle of things. In chapter 2 of *Sylvie and Bruno* the narrator recognizes Lady Muriel's position in the narrative (although he does not yet know her name), saying to himself, "And this is, of course, the opening scene of Vol. I. *She* is the Heroine" (507). Of course, in the surface narrative at this time he is merely commenting on her as a type, but a transparent metatextual observation is being made at the same time. And the observation turns out to be true, not misleading, about the place of Lady Muriel at least in the English strand of the narrative. But this is not, in fact, the opening scene of volume I. It is chapter 2 and very much the middle of

things, for we have already in chapter 1 witnessed the makings of a complicated plot involving events in a parallel Fairyland universe supplied with the
constituent kingdoms of Outland, Elfland, and Dogland. In fact, the shifts
between the parallel universes of England and Fairyland mean that to some
extent we are always in the middle of things. For the *Sylvie and Bruno* books
begin in medias res not only like a classical epic — in the middle of a
temporal sequence of which earlier events are subsequently narrated at
length — classical Menippean satire also begins in the middle of things in
the sense that it begins abruptly. *Sylvie and Bruno* certainly does this. And
classical Menippean satire keeps us in the middle of things by resisting closure
and undermining narrative expectations.

Another characteristic which Kirk has noted in historical Menippean satires
is the special relationship of author to audience. The author usually seems to
be writing down to the audience in some sense, as a teacher sharing knowledge, perhaps cabalistic secrets, with catechumens who have theretofore been
excluded from this knowledge by initiates. Poking fun at the privileged class
wins readers over, and the narrative method of presentation makes it possible
for these readers to understand and assimilate the truths expounded (xii). This
attitude toward audience closely corresponds to Carroll's situation. Although
Carroll here still claims to be addressing schoolgirls, the vocabulary of the
work is quite advanced (Miller 143n.4). In addition, the point of view is
obviously highly sophisticated. But the clearest indication of the educative
purpose of the book is its central theclogical theme that to love is to be
loved, for by love Carroll explicitly means Christian charity, as the included
Christian parables and Arthur's philosophical remarks make clear.

WHEREAS THE SYLVIE AND BRUNO books are representative Menippean satire,
The Anatomy of Melancholy is not. In *Anatomy of Criticism*, borrowing the
term from Burton, Northrop Frye proposes "anatomy" as an alternative
name for Menippean satire, preferable, he says, as less cumbersome and less
antiquarian (309–12).[3] The suggested change of terminology is one indication
of the archetypal status Frye accords *The Anatomy of Melancholy* as Menippean satire. But *The Anatomy of Melancholy* (while being very like the
Scholes and Klaus genre "essay") is unlike classical Menippean satire in
some important senses.

The Anatomy of Melancholy has no announced satiric form at all. That is
to say, while satire is certainly a fundamental element of the texture of the
work, it makes no claim to satire as genre. The satiric texture of the work
supports the thesis that everybody is mad, a thesis advanced quite soberly
without irony or hyperbole. We inevitably find human folly used as evidence
to support this thesis. The ridicule that Burton makes of everyone's follies is
not his end but his means. Since the satiric mode ostensibly limits itself to

ridiculing corrigible faults, there is perhaps even some question whether madness could qualify as a legitimate object of satiric attack.

But of course Frye suggests not merely that Burton's work uses satire as its primary mode but that the work is a Menippean satire in the generic sense. *The Anatomy of Melancholy* shares with formal satire an important element of structure, one not characteristic of Menippean satire. Formal satire is characterized by the author's announced intention to "anatomize" follies: to list them, dissect them, and criticize them directly. *The Anatomy of Melancholy* is, of course, not narrative. The implicit narrative method of Menippean satire is completely alien to Burton's method. Even more interesting, the other modern works presented by Frye as in the tradition of Menippean satire are in fact narratives: *Gulliver's Travels, The Beggar's Opera, Candide, Gryll Grange, Gargantua and Pantagruel, Patience, Don Juan, The Complete Angler, The Sot-Weed Factor,* even *Tristram Shandy,* and of course both *Alice's Adventures in Wonderland* and *Through the Looking-Glass.*

And not only is *The Anatomy of Melancholy* without narrative continuity, it is also very markedly characterized by the insistent voice of Democritus Junior. The persona is the major defining characteristic of formal satire; differences in personae define the division between Horatian satire and Juvenalian. An amused persona makes for Horatian satire; a bitter one, for Juvenalian satire. Burton, perhaps unfortunately for our ideas of neatness, somehow seeks to be both at the same time: he sees madness as an inherent and unchangeable affliction of humankind, and yet still he is unrelenting in his coruscating exposition of this fact.

Even if Democritus Junior were a persona of a sort more closely identifiable within the tradition of formal satire, *The Anatomy of Melancholy* would still be unusual formal satire because — as already suggested — Burton sees madness as incorrigible. Carroll sees madness as a dream. There is no problem without a solution because it is always possible to escape problems by moving to another world, a real thesis in Christian theology for him, not simply a narrative technique. Indeed he uses the mixed medley of forms characteristic of Menippean satire precisely to illustrate this theme.

Burton does flirt with Menippus, but he does not seem to recognize Menippean satire as generically distinct from other sorts of satire. "Barking Menippus" is only one among Burton's myriad authorities; he can say, "I did sometime laugh and scoff with Lucian, and satirically tax with Menippus, lament with Heraclitus, sometimes again I was *petulant; splene cachinno,* and then again, *urere bilis jecur,*" bitterly mirthful, and then again burning with rage (886.19). And Burton certainly does not acknowledge any special generic precedent for his work in the satires of Menippus. If fact, there is no such precedent.

Generically *The Anatomy of Melancholy* is a "systematic psychology," and as such its generic antecedents are to be found in other "systematic" works, in the *Summa Theologica* and ultimately in Aristotle. This genre might usefully be identified as "anatomy" if we could keep it carefully distinguished from the varieties of satire, with which it has no necessary connection. Of the various other modern works cited as Menippean satires, a few — for example, *The Praise of Folly*, the Martin Marprelate tracts, many of Milton's controversial works — share these characteristics of anatomy. But an anatomy, or systematic work, does not necessarily have a satiric texture and intent. It is only in this non-satiric sense that Frye's own book can be seen as the anatomy it announces itself to be in its title, *Anatomy of Criticism*. This work is certainly not a satire in intention or effect.

Burton is at pains to make clear the provenance of his work, if not necessarily the genre, by including as a sort of table of contents a Ramist schema outlining the scope of the work. Peter Ramus was the fashionable new rhetorician of the Renaissance. He and his followers often outlined their material as if to show that the new logic was just as "systematic" as the old Aristotelian logic. Burton might have felt a special need to provide evidence that his work is highly structured and complete just because the thesis and mode of the work naturally suggest to readers that it cannot possibly be systematic. Even Burton's famous digressions are carefully labeled and thus bound by the systematization of the whole.[4] And these digressions are real digressions, digressions from which there is a return to the main point. In classical Menippean satire the satiric point of a digression is made in part by the author's getting lost and failing to return to the episode from which he digressed. A Menippean digression is a shaggy dog story. In Carroll's work just this sort of traditional Menippean digression is described in the following passage as the Other Professor prepares to recite "Peter and Paul":

> The Professor put his hands over his ears, with a look of dismay. "If you once let him begin a *Poem*," he said to Sylvie, "he'll never leave off again! He never does!"
> "Did he ever begin a Poem and not leave off again?" Sylvie enquired.
> "Three times," said the Professor.
> Bruno raised himself on tiptoe, till his lips were on a level with Sylvie's ear. "What became of them three Poems?" he whispered. "Is he saying them all now?"
> "Hush!" said Sylvie. (*Sylvie and Bruno* 556; ch. 10)

In this light only *Tristram Shandy* of the various modern works that have been called Menippean satires actually enters into the spirit of the classical genre.

Though comprehensive and complete, the *Sylvie and Bruno* books are by contrast with Burton's book very unsystematic. They are not an anatomy in a sense Burton could have recognized. Inevitably, the *Sylvie and Bruno* books suggest more of the quality of Menippean digression than does *The Anatomy of Melancholy*. Although Carroll does not get lost in digressions which break down the structure of the work itself, both in quality and extent there is more than enough peripheral to the plot — to the major plot in each of the parallel universes — to please Laurence Sterne, Petronius, or Varo, the earliest of the Menippean satirists whose works survive.

The ending to *Sylvie and Bruno*, which was revealed with the publication of *Sylvie and Bruno Concluded* to be only a provisional ending, is the key to seeing the work as the archetype of Menippean satire. Among other things, this "*sort* of conclusion" (as Carroll calls it, *Sylvie and Bruno Concluded* 660; Preface) to *Sylvie and Bruno* strikingly illustrates the qualitative difference between digression in the *Sylvie and Bruno* books and digression in *The Anatomy of Melancholy*. *Sylvie and Bruno* by itself is on analysis not complete because the fairy scenes leave off with the Warden still fraudulently in place as Emperor of Outland and the English scenes leave off with the relationship of Arthur Forester and Lady Muriel Orme unresolved. It is true that Arthur has decided to give her up and to seek personal fulfillment by working to better the lot of the underprivileged in India, but it is obvious to us and to the narrator that Lady Muriel loves him and not Eric and that Eric is, at any rate — despite his charm and heroism — not worthy of her because of his agnosticism. Yet only one reader wrote to Carroll to note these loose ends after the first volume was published. Of course others may have felt the incompleteness and either confidently expected a sequel or simply remained dissatisfied. But even the original reviewers did not make the point. And I think most modern readers feel sufficiently overwhelmed by the bulk and variety of material in the volume that they do not feel there had to be a sequel. On the other hand, the volumes are not typically published separately nowadays, so it is hard to recover our naïve impressions.

The texture of *The Anatomy of Melancholy* is of course satiric, with Juvenalian leanings to the fore, and thus the mode of the work plays against the genre, which could be called "anatomy," and makes *The Anatomy of Melancholy* finally almost sui generis. By contrast, the *Sylvie and Bruno* books are very much part of a traditional genre. In fact, they illustrate a larger number of traits classically associated with Menippean satire than any other modern work and, especially in light of the ambiguity of closure, do so with greater clarity. This understanding is important for Carroll studies because it validates the more subtle use of the Menippean tradition in Carroll's greater works.

The *Sylvie and Bruno* books are often dismissed as a failed experiment. One frequent criticism is the archness of Bruno's babytalk. But Sleary's lisp is surely more arch in *Hard Times*, and yet in the not-too-distant past the

Leavises had convinced most of the profession that *Hard Times* is the model of a perfectly constructed novel. The *Sylvie and Bruno* books are also criticized, perhaps more cogently, for the dullness of the English scenes. But these scenes are considerably more lively than anything in Trollope, and while their subtlety is of a different kind, they are as alive with implication as anything in Jane Austen. Indeed, Barbara Pym has become a modern master by recapturing this texture with subtle allusiveness. In addition, the fairy scenes are said to be confusing; the English scenes are said to be moralistic. The whole is called sentimental.

But there is a purpose to all the cited defects of the work. Even Bruno's babytalk calls attention to the educative function of the work. The English scenes tell moral tales in a real-world context just as the fairyland scenes tell moral tales in a metaphoric context. Even the uneasiness of the shifting from one world to another has a Christian moral purpose in calling our attention to the need for eternal vigilance. And I think this is the real problem that modern readers have with the work. It is hard to read. We normally allow our minds to wander from time to time as we read even the most engaging material because we are confident that when we refocus attention we will be but a little way beyond where we were the last time we gave full attention. However, it is part of the moral of the book to teach us that we must never let our attention wander. As noted at the outset of this discussion, as Menippean satire the *Sylvie and Bruno* books make a special claim on the attention of both scholars and general readers. For scholars, the work provides a touchstone of this lost classical genre. General readers can more easily understand the work when they are aware of its traditional, formal structure and implicit expectations. In addition, by seeing the work as Menippean satire, all readers may more readily understand the relationship of the difficulties encountered in reading to the Christian moral. And although the Christian doctrine may not persuade contemporary readers, the sophisticated generic presentation richly rewards thoughtful scrutiny.

C. W. Post Campus,
Long Island University

NOTES

1. Note too an inconsistency between the chapters that advance the plot in the Fairyland sections on the one hand and on the other hand this chapter and the next few following chapters in which Mr. Sir speaks to the Fairies and is seen by them. That the human characters can later speak to the fairies when they materialize as children is an entirely different matter.
2. It is not without reason that the preface to *Sylvie and Bruno* calls for the publication of more fully expurgated versions of Shakespeare and the Bible so that these works may be available for the edification of children.

3. Frye's description of *The Anatomy of Melancholy* as Menippean satire is repeated and documented by Bud Korkowski. Korkowski, however, curiously supposes that Frye's suggestion of "anatomy" as an alternative term for Menippean satire implies somehow that Frye thinks *The Anatomy of Melancholy* is not Menippean satire. Korkowski does show that between 1575 and 1650 the term "anatomy" was used to describe works of widely varying type (75). The use of the term by authors exclusively during the Renaissance is for Korkowski another mark against its modern reintroduction as a genre term. Korkowski does not call attention to the real differences between *The Anatomy of Melancholy* and Menippean works. And as Kirk he inaccurately summarizes his own early article (256–57).

4. The reader interested in Burton's manipulation of digression is directed to Fox's fine study.

WORKS CITED

Bakhtin, Mikhail. *Problems of Dostoevsky's Poetics*. Trans. R. W. Rotsel. n.p.: Ardis, 1973.

Carroll, Lewis. *The Complete Illustrated Works of. . . .* Ed. Edward Guiliano. New York: Avenel, 1982.

Burton, Robert. *The Anatomy of Melancholy*. 3 vols. Everyman's Library, nos. 886–88. 1621 (1651); London: Dent, Dutton, 1932.

Chadwick–Joshua, Jocelyn. "*Alice's Adventures in Wonderland* and *Through the Looking-Glass*: A Menippean Assessment and Rhetorical Analysis of Carroll's Alice Books." *Dissertation Abstracts International* 49 (1988): 1461A.

Fox, Ruth. *The Tangled Chain: The Structure of Disorder in the Anatomy of Melancholy*. Berkeley: U of California P, 1976.

Frye, Northrop. *Anatomy of Criticism: Four Essays*. Princeton: Princeton UP, 1957.

Hernadi, Paul. *Beyond Genre: New Directions in Literary Classification*. Ithaca: Cornell UP, 1972.

Kirk, Eugene P. *Menippean Satire: An Annotated Catalogue of Texts and Criticism*. New York and London: Garland, 1980.

Korkowski, Bud [later known as Eugene P. Kirk]. "Genre and Satiric Strategy in Burton's *Anatomy of Melancholy*." *Genre* 8.1 (1975): 74–87.

Miller, Edmund. "The *Sylvie and Bruno* Books as Victorian Novel." *Lewis Carroll Observed: A Collection of Unpublished Photographs, Drawings, Poetry, and New Essays*. Ed. Edward Guiliano. New York: Clarkson N. Potter, 1976. 132–44.

Plackis, Anashia Poulos. "Alice: Carroll's Subversive Message of Christian Hope and Love." *Dissertation Abstracts International* 47 (1987): 3049A.

Scholes, Robert, and Carl H. Klaus. *Elements of the Essay*. New York: Oxford UP, 1969.

FAMILY SECRETS AND THE MYSTERIES OF *THE MOONSTONE*

By Elisabeth Rose Gruner

> What brought good Wilkie's genius nigh perdition?
> Some demon whispered — "Wilkie! have a mission."
> Swinburne, "Wilkie Collins"

SWINBURNE'S FAMOUS JUDGMENT on Wilkie Collins is not generally applied to *The Moonstone*, the work which T. S. Eliot called "the first and greatest of English detective novels" (377). While few readers today would go so far as to concur with William Marshall's opinion that the novel reveals a "general absence of social criticism, overt or implied," still it is rarely considered one of Collins's "message" novels — and probably for this reason it has received far more critical attention than those later works (77–78).[1] But *The Moonstone*, like those later novels with purpose which Swinburne found so unaesthetic, is a novel dominated by a social message — a message probably both riskier and more central to Collins's own life and those of his readers than some of those which pervade his later works, such as his diatribes against vivisection, prison life, the cult of athleticism, and Jesuits. Not easily reducible to "beware opium," "don't bring back sacred diamonds from India," or "don't steal your cousin's jewels," the message of *The Moonstone* yet involves all three of these strictures. The novel calls into question what writers like Sarah Ellis had celebrated as "one of [England's] noblest features . . . the home comforts, and fireside virtues" of the Victorian family, and it asks us not to trust in its appearance (Ellis 2). Drugs, imperialism, and theft are subsumed into the larger question of family relations (cousinly or closer) which is at the heart of *The Moonstone*. What is the Victorian family, and whose purposes does it serve? Collins asks, and the answer does not come back in the family's favor.[2]

Theorists of detective fiction usually discuss the genre's interest in the discovery and expulsion of a crime, perceived as a foreign element which has invaded a secure community or family.[3] While this tendency is apparent in *The Moonstone*, one of the genre's founding texts, a contradictory impulse runs equally strongly through the novel, one with profound implications for the security of the Victorian family. For *The Moonstone* is, to a great extent, motivated by an impulse to secrecy, not to tell, to cover up the family's complicity in crime. Franklin Blake's editorial strategy seems designed to this end: he has chosen witnesses loyal to the family, unreliable as observers (Gabriel Betteredge remarks, "It is one of my rules in life, never to notice what I don't understand"), and often monomaniacal to the point of selective blindness (Collins 75). They are, singly or together, almost incapable of telling "the truth." But the impulse to conceal is built as well into the very material of the novel, Collins's most important source for *The Moonstone*, the Road murder case of 1860, which remains unsolved today.

If we read *The Moonstone* in the context of the famous murder case on which it was in part based, we find a scathing commentary on the Victorian family in Collins's selective recapitulation of the details of the case. Far from remaining within the protected private space which Victorian ideology reserved for family, the Kent family in the Road case and the Verinder-Herncastle-Ablewhite clan of *The Moonstone* cross boundaries and break traditions, rules, and commandments. Yet, Collins implies, these transgressions are not anomalous; the reasons for them are deeply imbedded in the Victorican ideology of the domestic sphere, especially in the concept of domestic privacy. For Collins the Victorian family, far from protecting one from the increasingly complex and dangerous public world, is itself the source of many of its own complexities and dangers.

I

EARLY IN THE MORNING of 30 June 1860, the murdered body of four-year-old Francis Savile Kent was found in an outhouse close by his father's house.[4] (The house, known as Road House or the Road-Hill House, furnishes the popular name for the case.) The circumstances of the case soon made it clear that a member of the Kent household must be the murderer, and the case became a cause célèbre in both the local and the national press.

The case received national attention, as Richard Altick notes, primarily "because it occurred in a substantial middle-class family" (130). The murder and the arrests of two young female members of the household (first Savile's sixteen-year-old half-sister, Constance, then his twenty-one-year-old nursery governess Elizabeth Gough) raised the disturbing possibility that the security of the Victorian home was an illusion. Anthea Trodd writes:

> The whole Road case affronted the popular conception of the domestic sanctuary in the most violent manner imaginable. . . . A young lady had been dragged

from under her father's roof into a police-court, and her reputation and prospects irretrievably blighted. . . . (442–43)

She adds, "All the features of the case recommended themselves to intense publicity," and Collins was certainly aware both of the case and of its publicity value (Trodd 441). As Collins and the rest of the newspaper-reading public must certainly have known, Francis Savile Kent (known as Savile) had been stabbed several times and his throat was cut, although he did not appear to have bled profusely. (This detail, as hardened readers of detective fiction now know, raises the possibility that the child was stabbed after death.) The child was the son of Samuel Kent and his second wife Mary (née Pratt) — who had been a nursemaid and governess in the Kent household before the death of the first Mrs. Kent.

The appearance of the house and the testimony of the servants made it clear that the house had not been broken into, so the local police suspected those in the house: the family and the servants. It was suggested that Elizabeth Gough had admitted a lover into her room and that they had murdered the child when he awoke inopportunely. This was the most comforting suggestion possible, in an entirely uncomfortable affair, since it exonerated the immediate family and cast blame on a servant and — to some eyes — an outsider. When Jonathan Whicher, the celebrated Scotland Yard detective (and the model for Collins's Sergeant Cuff), entered the picture almost two weeks after the murder, he seized on one (missing) piece of evidence and arrested sixteen-year-old Constance Kent, Mr. Kent's third daughter by his first marriage. The missing evidence was one of Constance's nightgowns, entered into the washing book but never received by the washerwoman. Since no bloodstained clothes were found in the house, Whicher surmised that Constance's missing nightgown was the bloodied evidence which could have incriminated her, and that she had destroyed it. Other examinations of the evidence, however, have turned up reports of no less than three nightgowns, one belonging to Constance's elder sister Mary Ann, stained by what witnesses euphemistically called "'natural causes"'; Constance's, which some witnesses claimed to have seen — unstained — the morning after the murder; and a mysteriously bloodied "night shift" which was discovered hidden in the boiler-stove and then lost by the bumbling police. By the time Whicher entered the case several days later, there was only the one — now missing — nightgown of Constance's to be reckoned with, and he arrested her. Her putative motive was jealousy of her stepmother and her father's second family.[5]

Local opinion was against Whicher, and soon after Constance was released on the grounds of insufficient evidence, Whicher resigned from the force in disgrace. Elizabeth Gough was arrested some months later after a second investigation and released when she was proved to know no one in town, thus disproving the "outside lover" theory. Five years later, in 1865, Constance Kent confessed to the crime, and a weeping judge condemned her to death in a melodramatic courtroom scene. Constance's lawyer called no witnesses for her defence in the initial hearing and spoke in the second trial only to record her plea of guilty; Constance herself maintained a stony silence throughout the proceedings.

Like Rachel and Lady Verinder in Collins's transformation of the case, Constance, her stepmother, and Elizabeth Gough appear to have been hostile to or at least uncooperative with the police investigating the case. As Bridges remarks, this seems particularly strange on Mrs. Kent's part, as she was by all accounts a fiercely devoted mother who could be expected to be zealous in her prosecution of her son's murderer. Like Rachel's belligerent silence after the theft of her diamond, Mrs. Kent's refusal to cooperate seems to imply some special knowledge of the case which her personal concerns required her to hide; as the injured parties, both would seem to have had the most to gain by cooperating with the investigation. Constance's confession itself, which failed to account for many circumstances of the murder (including motive, and, especially, the lack of blood), appeared to many contemporary commentators to have been dictated, perhaps by her confessor in the Anglican convent where she had spent the last two years. In a letter written after her confession, Constance pointedly disavowed revenge or jealousy as a motive for the murder, although no other motives were ever suggested. Her confession and subsequent silence failed to convince many of her guilt, including, it seems, the judge who reluctantly sentenced her.[6]

Perhaps the most disturbing aspect of the whole disturbing Road case was the reluctance of the family to assist in the investigation of the crime. The suggestion that the family was not all it seemed, especially because its members would lie or at least remain silent even in the investigation of such a brutal murder, is inescapable. The Kent family's silence seems to imply that no one is innocent, least of all the young women whose innocence, in other circumstances, the family could have been expected most zealously to protect. Family secrets, the Kent case seems to say, are both disturbing and dangerous, and murder may not even be the worst of them.

II

THE MOONSTONE, DESPITE ITS narrative technique based on eyewitness testimony and a stated devotion to "the interests of truth," is a novel characterized and perhaps even motivated by secrets (39).[7] The prologue's narrator has kept a secret which protects John Herncastle's theft of the moonstone, Mr.

Candy's secret trick keeps Franklin Blake's motivations mysterious, Godfrey Ablewhite's secret life must be uncovered to solve the crime, and Franklin Blake's secret from himself complicates both the mystery and his relationship with Rachel. Most obviously, perhaps, both Rachel Verinder and Rosanna Spearman keep secrets to hide Franklin's, and in some sense their own, guilt. Like the mystery of the Road case which inspired it, the plot of *The Moonstone* is complicated by the silence of women. Rachel, Rosanna, and even Miss Clack conceal their own motivations and what they know of others' in order to protect secrets of their own, thus complicating and ultimately doubling the plot: Franklin Blake's "strange family story" becomes both a mystery and a courtship novel, a story of both theft and passion (39). And the secrecy which creates this mystery is deeply implicated with the family's privacy.

The Victorian family depended on the privacy which earlier generations had carefully cultivated with innovations like corridors and locks and had increased by rejecting earlier practices like fostering out children and boarding in apprentices.[8] In *Sesame and Lilies*, John Ruskin eulogized the family home in terms of its security and privacy:

> within [a man's] house . . . need enter no danger, no temptation, no cause of error or offence. This is the true nature of home — it is the place of Peace; the shelter, not only from all injury, but from all terror, doubt, and division. In so far as it is not this, it is not home; so far as the anxieties of the outer life penetrate into it, and the inconsistently-minded, unknown, unloved, or hostile society of the outer world is allowed by either husband or wife to cross the threshold, it ceases to be home; it is then only a part of that outer world which you have roofed over, and lighted fire in. (59)

As Sissela Bok notes, domestic privacy and secrecy are closely related:

> The private constitutes, along with the sacred, that portion of human experience for which secrecy is regarded as most indispensable. In secularized Western societies, privacy has come to seem for some the only legitimate form of secrecy; consequently, the two are sometimes mistakenly seen as identical. (7)

In this context, the notion of "family secrets" becomes almost redundant: the family's privacy necessarily involves a certain amount of secrecy, even if the two are not, as Bok notes, identical.

As Patrick Brantlinger has noted, sensation novels like *The Moonstone* rely on secrecy for their appeal: "the plot unwinds through the gradual discovery — or, better, recovery — of knowledge, until at the end what detective and reader know coincides with what the secretive or somehow remiss narrator-author has presumably known all along" (19). Even the supposed "eyewitness" character of *The Moonstone*'s narration requires, because of its retrospectivity, a certain suppression of evidence in the retelling. Betteredge, for example, confesses that he is concealig his present knowledge of the case in his reconstruction, leaving his readers "in the dark" (233); and Miss Clack ("condemned to narrate," 241) similarly includes in her narrative an exchange of letters which indicates her inability to "avail . . . herself of the light which later discoveries have thrown on the mystery" (241; 285).

The absence of testimony from several key witnesses, among them Penelope Betteredge (whose diaries, we are told, provide many of the important facts in Gabriel's narrative), Godfrey Ablewhite, and Rachel Verinder, is even more disturbing than possible omissions in the testimony we do have. Obviously their silence is a necessary element in the novel's mystery plot, but these characters are silenced for another reason as well: they are witnesses to the development of a counterplot involving a young woman's sexual passion and desire.[9] The counterplot of Rachel's passion for Blake is witnessed by Penelope and doubled in Godfrey's secret suburban life, but because this second story is told only or at least primarily through the voice of the demented Miss Clack it remains buried through most of the novel. Clack — like Franklin, keeping a secret from herself — provides a grotesque parody of Rachel in her determined suppression of her own and, by implication, of Rachel's desire.[10]

Rosanna Spearman provides another parallel to Rachel: her passion for Blake is an open secret, known at least to Penelope and Limping Lucy, and the narrative gives her, unlike Rachel, a voice — albeit a voice from beyond the grave. Her "testimony" — the letter to Blake — is both a clue to the eventual solution of the theft mystery and a hint at the other, buried mystery; it is Rosanna who tells us, far more explicitly than Clack or Betteredge, of Rachel's desire for Franklin. It is Rosanna who unites the mystery and the marriage plots by her recognition that the paint on Franklin's nightgown is evidence against him, evidence of at least an illicit visit to Rachel's room, if not of his theft of the moonstone.

Female secrecy is, of course, not unique to *The Moonstone*. Elaine Showalter believes that "secrecy was basic to the lives of *all* respectable women" of the mid-nineteenth century. She quotes Jane Vaughan Pinkney's *Tacita Tacit*, a novel of 1860: "Women are greater dissemblers than men . . . by habit, moral training, and modern education, they are obliged to . . . repress their feelings, control their very thoughts" (2). Margaret Oliphant went further than to note the tendency toward concealment; she endorsed it and regretted that young women in modern novels (particularly sensation novels, with which *The Moonstone* shares many generic characteristics) could not keep their feelings secret. She wrote in 1867, just one year before *The Moonstone* was published:

> That men and women should marry we had all of us acknowledged as one of the laws of humanity; but up to the present generation most young women had

been brought up in the belief that their own feelings on this subject should be religiously kept to themselves. (259)

But the secrecy which Oliphant calls for in modern heroines becomes dangerous in *The Moonstone* when it becomes epidemic, as the women who in concealing their passions also conceal a crime and set off a chain of circumstances which includes theft, suicide, and murder. The family's reliance on secrecy for its normal maintenance quickly translates, in *The Moonstone*, into an almost pathological — and certainly criminal — secrecy. The secrecy of Collins's own family life seems benign by comparison to the secrecy which permeates both the Road case and *The Moonstone*.[11]

Collins makes it clear that the family is not, as Ruskin would have it, a place of peace; and the mysteries of *The Moonstone* do not arise from a foreign invasion which can be expelled, leaving the family complacently untouched — they are inherent in the very nature and structure of the family. The secrecy which, as Bok and Showalter agree, is part of family life, is primarily women's part. But the women of *The Moonstone*'s extended family, like the women of the Road case, keep their secrets too well, covering up crime rather than expose their passionate secrets to a prying public (primarily the police, but also — especially in the Road case — the press). Like the mystery of the Road Murder of 1860, in which Collins found the original of Sergeant Cuff and the evidence of the missing nightgown, *The Moonstone*'s mystery operates on at least two levels, only one of which — the fictional theft of the diamond or the actual murder of the child — can be publicly acknowledged. And, as the Road Murder seems to hinge on a familial conspiracy of silence, so *The Moonstone*'s mysteries hinge on the silence and the secrecy of the Verinder-Herncastle clan, especially its women.

III

IN ITS BARE OUTLINES, there seems to be little to connect the Road murder with *The Moonstone* beyond the ineptitude of the local police and the evidence of the missing nightgown. But Collins's focus on the social pathology of female silence seems also to derive from his understanding of the Road case. It is the silence which Constance and Rachel share which unites the cases and sets these women apart from many of their fictional counterparts, at least in the sensation novels Mrs. Oliphant deplores; it is a silence which brings them under suspicion of one crime but may in fact have been designed to conceal another. In Rachel's case, and Collins probably believed in the Road case as well, the second "crime" is illicit passion. In a letter to Collins on 24 October 1860 Dickens outlined his theory of the Road murder. As Dickens puts it:

Mr. Kent intriguing with the nursemaid, poor little child awakes in crib and sits up contemplating blissful proceedings. Nursemaid strangles him then and there. Mr. Kent gashes body to mystify discoverers and disposes of same. (qtd. in Bridges 187).[12]

Dickens's theory neatly domesticates the widespread — and more popular — theory of Elizabeth Gough's guilt, which involved a lover coming in from outside the house. Trodd cites other contemporary reports which did, however, in more guarded terms, express variations on the same theme (443).[13] Bridges proposes Constance's 1865 confession, then, as a form of self-sacrifice intended to protect her family, keep the secret, and lay the matter to rest. While Rachel keeps silent to protect her cousin-lover and to hide her own feelings for him, Bridges theorizes that Constance's silence (and her stepmother's), and the odd way in which she broke it, were designed to protect her father and to hide his — and Elizabeth's — illicit passion.

Collins's two passionate and silent women — Rachel and Rosanna — recall aspects of Constance and Elizabeth without providing an easy parallel. Rosanna, a servant in love with her master, recalls Elizabeth Gough — but hides a criminal past rather than an (allegedly) adulterous present. And Collins conflates the two roles of Constance and Elizabeth (knower and lover) into the single character of Rachel, thus increasing the pressure on the family to solve or hide its own crimes and its own deviations from familial norms. Of course Rachel is neither murderer or fornicator, nor even an accomplice to any serious crime; yet her silence in the face of a police investigation suggests that Collins could expect her passion to be widely read as almost as guilty as the adulterous Elizabeth's. Any woman who would allow herself to be suspected of theft (or, in Elizabeth and Constance's case, murder) must, the reasoning goes, be hiding something far worse.

As Richard Altick notes, behind the shocking violence of the murder lay other shocking circumstances in the Kent family. The first Mrs. Kent was widely believed to have gone mad after bearing her third child "but her loss of mind did not deter her husband from begetting six more [children] on her body" (Altick 131). Bridges hypothesizes that the first Mrs. Kent was not indeed mad but jealous of her husband's relationship with Mary Pratt the governess (and her successor), and she notes the striking similarities between the situations of the first Mrs. Kent with Mary Pratt, and the second Mrs. Kent (née Mary Pratt) with Elizabeth Gough. Whatever the particular circumstances, the Kent home clearly concealed a most unfamilial (or un-Ruskinian) reality.

So, of course, does the Herncastle-Verinder clan. Mr. Ablewhite, Senior, acknowledges a seamy family history when he attributes Rachel's stubbornness to her Herncastle blood, implying that she is, unlike himself, "descended from a set of cut-throat scoundrels who lived by robbery and murder'' (305). The moonstone, then, is not the only legacy Rachel has received from the wicked colonel; in some ways, however, it seems to be emblematic of them all. Perhaps we need to examine the moonstone itself more closely to determine just what these characters are protecting with their secrets.

IV

IT IS A COMMONPLACE OF Collins criticism to see the moonstone as symbolic of Rachel's virginity — this bright jewel that ''seemed unfathomable as the heavens themselves,'' which Rachel displays proudly in the bosom of her dress (97).[14] Hutter, building on this connection, notes the more important detail that the diamond is flawed, perhaps ''suggest[ing] some of the sexual prejudice so strongly attached to women in the nineteenth century'' (200–1). More threateningly, because the diamond would be more valuable cut into smaller stones, the flaw may suggest that a woman's value is not in her wholeness and self-sufficiency but in her multiplicity and her reproductive ability. In fact, as a symbol of woman's status as ''exchange value,'' one could hardly do better than the flawed diamond. For, as Luce Irigaray notes, only virgins are exchange value for men. Once violated (divided, cut up, married) they become use value, recognized only for their ability to reproduce themselves. Rachel and her (uncut) diamond are both more valued in a capitalist economy for their potential than for themselves.[15] Lady Verinder, recognizing this, puts Rachel's inheritance in trust to protect her from a too-rapacious consumer such as Godrey Ablewhite. Only the Hindu priests, who are outside of English life and the capitalist economy, are able to value the diamond for itself; no one (with the possible exception of Franklin Blake) seems able to value Rachel for herself.

John Reed, in his interesting examination of *The Moonstone*'s anti-imperialist implications, makes a similar claim for the symbolic value of the diamond but focuses on its status as sacred gem and stolen object:

> In itself ambiguous, its significance lies in its *misappropriation*. Because it is so desired by *men*, it signifies *man's greed*. . . . More particularly, however, the Moonstone becomes the sign of England's imperial depredations — the symbol of a national rather than a personal crime. (286; my emphasis)

While I agree with Hutter that Reed ''oversimplifies the novel'' in this symbolic reading, his insights are helpful (196). For, as he points out, Rachel Verinder has no more right to the diamond than Godfrey Ablewhite — it belongs, in fact, to the Indians from whom Franklin and Betteredge try so hard to protect it and to whom it is finally returned. Like a woman's virginity, its greatest value is a symbolic one: it is less valuable to the possessor (Rachel) than the desirer (whether Ablewhite or the Indians), it is most valuable in exchange, and the desirer is only and always male. The diamond thus points in (at least) two directions: outward, towards England's treatment of its colonies, and inward, to its treatment of women at home.[16] And Rachel's insistence on maintaining control of it challenges both of these (analogous) power structures: she refuses to treat the diamond as a prize, preferring to maintain it in its native setting (the Indian cabinet), and she refuses to give up her own independent judgment. Jenny Bourne Taylor claims that "Rachel thus tacitly upsets the conventions of feminine propriety . . . she is dark, positive, purposeful, independent — yet silent" (200). Constance Kent, who once ran away from home to escape her stepmother's tyranny, was similarly accused (by her father) of a wish "to be independent" (Bridges 39). Her habitual reserve and self-dependence are among the characteristics John Rhode — who believes in her guilt — notes when he claims that "in a sense, the crime saved her character. Before it . . . she was a wayward, passionate girl . . . and she would probably have developed into a selfish, headstrong woman" (83).[17] The Verinder family lawyer, Bruff — more sympathetic to Rachel than Rhode is to Constance Kent — comments that Rachel's "absolute self-dependence is a great virtue in a man . . . [but] has the serious drawback of morally separating her from the mass of her sex" who are, presumably, more compliant (319).

Bruff's comment points out a characteristic which all of Rachel's observers note. Rather than claiming that she has been changed by the theft of the diamond into a secretive person, Gabriel, Clack, Lady Verinder, and Bruff agree that she has always been "secret and self-willed" (262; see also 87; 205). Bruff's correlation of secrecy with self-will corresponds with Bok's observation that "secrecy guards against unwanted access by others — against their coming too near, learning too much, observing too closely. Secrecy guards, then, the central aspects of identity" (13). Rachel's secrecy, both after the theft of the diamond and after her broken engagement with Ablewhite, signifies her insistence on maintaining herself as a separate identity and her refusal to be known and thereby possessed.

Why does Rachel's secrecy so annoy her family, when she seems simply to be complying with the Oliphantian code of self-suppression? I believe it is because she, and Constance Kent, and Elizabeth Gough, are forced into the ironic position of defending their identities through the very means Oliphant would use to urge their suppression. Silence for Oliphant signifies a lack of desire — for these women, it signifies an excess.[18]

When Franklin steals the diamond and Rachel refuses to condemn him, we can see that she is tacitly accepting his right to her sexuality, even to her virginity — but not her identity (Hutter 202–3; Lawson 67).[19] Her silence, however, cuts two ways: while protecting Franklin, it puts Rachel herself under suspicion, as well as endangering Rosanna Spearman. While Rachel keeps silent, the truth will remain hidden. Thus the plot of the mystery — the discovery of the diamond — is inextricable from woman's passion, and her identity.

If the mystery plot is inextricably linked with passion, perhaps marriage, the courtship plot is similarly mysterious. Not only must Rachel conceal her passion for Franklin until he becomes a "suitable" suitor, but the moonstone itself becomes a pawn in the marriage negotiations. Money and marriage are often related, both in novels and in life; in *The Moonstone* Gabriel Betteredge first hints at the connection which will later loom large by giving us his own history.

> Selina, being a single woman, made me pay so much a week for her board and services. Selina, being my wife, couldn't charge for her board, and would have to give me her services for nothing. That was the point of view I looked at it from. Economy — with a dash of love. I put it to my mistress, as in duty bound, just as I had put it to myself.
> "I have been turning Selina Goby over in my mind," I said, "and I think, my lady, it will be cheaper to marry her than to keep her." (43)

Betteredge's euphemistic "services" implies an illicit relationship with Selina not unlike the one Rachel and Franklin metaphorically begin when he enters her boudoir. And, as Betteredge's account implies, money enters into both relationships. Rachel seizes on Franklin's implied debts to explain his "theft" of the diamond: "I had reason to know you were in debt, and . . . that you were not very discreet, or very scrupulous about how you got money when you wanted it" (400). When Franklin comes to Rachel for an explanation of her actions, she immediately assumes that as he has inherited his father's wealth, perhaps he has come to "compensate [her] for the loss of [her] Diamond" (392). The compensation for the symbolic loss (of virginity) will of course be marriage, but here Rachel's concern is with literal, monetary compensation.

Jean E. Kennard argues that the conventional marriage plot of the Victorian novel most often involves a choice between suitable and unsuitable suitors and that each of the suitors "represents one pole of value in the novel in which he appears" (13). Rachel's suitors take on roles which mask their suitability, however: Godfrey appears as "the Christian Hero" and Franklin as a philandering debtor and suspected thief (Collins 239). According to Kennard, when these roles are sorted out — a sorting out which here requires the solution to the mystery — the marriage plot can be satisfactorily, conventionally, concluded. In *The Moonstone*, however, the sorting out muddles the "poles of value": we establish that Godfrey is both a philandering debtor and a thief, but we never really establish that Franklin is neither. In fact he is certainly, according to Betteredge's testimony, at least a philanderer and a debtor. Twice constrained from returning to England by "some unmentionable woman," on his return he borrows money from Lady Verinder to repay an earlier debt (Collins 48). The conclusion of the courtship plot does, however, literalize the "poles of value": Franklin, who has inherited his father's wealth, is simply worth more than Godfrey.

But Franklin is Rachel's choice even before his father's death makes him wealthy; so while convention demands a fortune for the novel's heroine, Collins also provides her with passion. Rachel's love for Franklin survives her conviction that he is a philanderer, a debtor, and even a thief — it is only his seeming hypocrisy in calling the police which threatens to destroy her love. For the reader, her passion is an ill-kept secret, but among the characters of the novel only the voiceless Penelope seems to be privy to Rachel's passionate secret — as to so many other secrets of the novel.

Penelope, one of *The Moonstone*'s silent women, only comes to us filtered through her father Gabriel. Her narrative silence helps conceal Rachel's love, since her correct observations are always followed by her father's contradictory opinions. Her silence does more than conceal Rachel from us, however; it also conceals herself. Since her diaries supply dates and times for Gabriel, he suggests that "she should tell the story instead of me, out of her own diary, [but] Penelope observes, with a fierce look and a red face, that her journal is for her own private eye, and that no living creature shall ever know what is in it but herself" (46). Her insistence on her own privacy, which mystifies her father, is a more benign version of another important silence in the novel: Rosanna Spearman's. Both women are, of course, servants, and as such are barely even named by the other narrators of the novel — Miss Clack remembers Penelope only as "the person with the cap-ribbons" (259). But servants are part of the extended family, at least in Gabriel's view, and as such privy to and part of family secrets. Resented for "her silent tongue and her solitary ways," Rosanna, as Gabriel informs us, is hiding a criminal past; and, as we later discover, she is also hiding an unsuitable and uncontrollable passion (55). In this, she not only doubles Rachel but provides another connection to the Road case: like Elizabeth Gough, she is a servant in love with a master, although her passion is not, like Gough's, adulterous. By comparison, Penelope's "Sweethearts" seem insignificant — and they are, except as evidence of the need for concealment in even the most complacent and commonplace of families (46).

The women of *The Moonstone*, from Penelope to her mistress and including Rosanna and Clack, are forced to conceal their passions, forced to conform to Oliphant's rules. But this conventional concealment has fatal consequences;

Collins seems to suggest that these rules are not, in fact, designed so much to protect female modesty or propriety as to conceal the criminal underpinnings of the Victorian family. While the secret of Penelope's sweethearts seems to have no effect on her household, the ''necessary'' concealments practiced by the other three women create the mystery, complicate relationships, and prevent simple solutions. Again, the line between benign and fatal secrets is not easy to draw.

Because she is complying with Oliphantian strictures against self-revelation, Rachel must not speak until Franklin proposes. But Franklin is not in a position to propose through most of the novel — he is poor, and his chosen lover suspects him of a crime. The situation is a stalemate: only Rachel can solve the crime, but because Franklin is the suspect, she cannot solve it without revealing her passion (and her acceptance of his presence in her bedroom at night). Despite its mysterious underpinnings, however, Rachel's dilemma is not unlike that of any other courtship heroine; any such heroine, of course, must not speak of love until she is spoken to. According to Kennard, she must also learn to read her suitor correctly and must ''adjust . . . to society's values'' (18). Ruth Bernard Yeazell similarly argues that marriage in the Victorian novel is usually a metaphor recognizing the heroine's internal growth and an enactment of the ''union of Self and Other . . . [resolving] the tensions between the individual and the larger human community'' (34–35; 37). Although she already finds him desirable, Rachel must learn to see Franklin as acceptable. Her ''growth,'' then, may look to us like regression, as it involves both a rejection of her former status as self-dependent and a recognition of society's commercially-derived values; she must relinquish her ''unnatural,'' unwomanly, anti-social silence and allow herself to be mastered by the now-wealthy Blake. After Franklin has inherited his father's money, he confronts Rachel about her silence; only then can he claim that ''while her hand lay in mine I was her master still!'' (393).

Of course, Godfrey Ablewhite's mercenary machinations also make him an unsuitable suitor. Again, it is Betteredge who first makes Ablewhite's character clear: ''Female benevolence and female destitution could do nothing without him'' — for he uses female benevolence to create female destitution (89). Ablewhite's aborted engagement to Rachel and his secondary theft of the diamond are both evidence of his deviance from acceptable behavior. As Barickman, and others, point out:

Godfrey Ablewhite's secret . . . involves Victorian sexual roles at their worst; he hypocritically becomes a champion of charitable ladies while he is keeping a mistress, embezzling another man's money, and preying upon Rachel in order to gain control of her money. (143)

It is not so much Ablewhite's preoccupation with wealth as his hypocrisy which condemns him; ironically, he is really guilty of just the kind of hypocrisy of which Rachel suspects Blake.

So Franklin becomes the right suitor when Rachel learns to read him "correctly," when Ezra's hypothesis about his behavior proves a more satisfying one than her own; she must believe that he came to protect, not steal, her virginity. And Collins, having upset convention by valorizing his passionate, secret, self-willed heroine and exposing the hypocrisy and criminality of the Victorian family, quietly reinscribes her into the system with her marriage to Franklin.

V

THE MOONSTONE IS, THEN, a detective story, but it is also a family story. Indeed, it is perhaps not even the "*strange* family story" Franklin believes it to be, but simply a story about the necessary concealments families practice (39; my emphasis). Gabriel even comments on the text's reliance on secrets, insisting in the "Eighth Narrative" that his "purpose, in this place, is to state a fact in the history of the family, which has been passed over by everybody, and which [he] won't allow to be disrespectfully smothered up in that way" (518). Godfrey Ablewhite — himself a member of the family — *has* been rather disrespectfully smothered up, but not so Gabriel's news.

Yet even in this triumphant conclusion, Gabriel himself contributes to the pervasive silence of the novel by cutting Franklin off with "You needn't say a word more, sir," and leaving the news of Rachel's pregnancy — which may stand both as visible evidence of female passion and as final proof of her capitulation to her status as "use value" — unspoken (519). The family, even in its triumphant return, is still relying on secrecy, is still, perhaps, not entirely innocent. The "scattered and disunited household," disrupted by the theft and Rachel's cover-up, is never wholly restored (225). Although Rachel and Franklin are married, Rosanna, Lady Verinder, and Godfrey are dead, Gabriel is retired, and Clack is exiled.

Cuff's failure to solve the crime on his own, like Whicher's failure in the Road Murder, clearly implies that there are family secrets which the police cannot penetrate — secrets not, perhaps, worse than murder or theft, but more difficult to reveal. Cuff's low interpretation of Rachel's behavior considers the possibility of "family scandal," but this version of the family scandal, involving as it does debts and pawnbrokers, is entirely *outside* what Ruskin and even Gabriel Betteredge would recognize as the sphere of family, in the more common and public realm of the police. And, in fact, when this realm becomes central to the case in Ablewhite's unmasking, Cuff acquits himself brilliantly. As D. A. Miller shows in his discussion of *The Eustace Diamonds*, fictional police are notoriously inept when forced to act within the sphere of family; thus "the plot of the novel 'passes on,' as it were, the initial offense until it reaches a place within the law's jurisdiction" (13; see also 33–57). But it is not really the family's inviolability which the police cannot penetrate; it is precisely its inseparability from the public sphere which confounds them. For the police, like the family, still believed in the family's privacy in the mid-1860s; remember that the police in the Road case waited to be invited in, preserving a boundary which had presumably already been broken. While we may want to read Godfrey's crime as a crime outside the sphere of family, involving as it does pawnbrokers and Indians and London and its suburbs, we cannot separate the spheres so easily. Like Rachel's implied crime, Godfrey's is both a family scandal and a police matter; the two spheres are inextricably linked, and no amount of artistic pleasure in neat solutions can separate the two. "The complexity and even incomprehensibility of the truth" are not, as Kalikoff would have it, "related to the invasion of the respectable," so much as they are related to the instability of the respectable (125). No family is secure, Collins's novel implies, from the dangers of its necessary concealments.

The lesson of *The Moonstone*, like the lesson of the Road Murder, is that the family is complicit in the failings of the larger society; murder and robbery are not invasions from without but manifestations of societal tensions — involving especially the dangerous desires of greed and sexuality — within. The fabled privacy of the domestic sphere protects it not from the public world but from discovery. If we are to understand the Victorian family at all, we must examine its pathological need for secrecy and understand, as does Collins, the kinds of secrets it protected.

University of Richmond

NOTES

1. John R. Reed and D. A. Miller are two notable exceptions to this trend, although they find different (and, in Miller's case, deeply buried) messages in the novel. Even Philip O'Neill, however, in his recent attempt to unify the Collins oeuvre in terms of social criticism, finds little to say about *The Moonstone*, reading it primarily as an allegory of literary criticism. But see Sue Lonoff, who writes of *The Moonstone* that "none of [Collins's] novels is as profoundly critical of Victorian values . . . and none is more subtle in linking its political, social, and religious censure to its central images and symbols" (211). Lonoff finally sees Collins's social criticism as less conflicted than I do, but her reading is nonetheless perceptive and interesting.

2. I take the term "family" in its broadest possible sense here, meaning both "blood kin" and "members of a household." As we will see in my discussion of the Road case and Collins's novel, the "traditional" nuclear family is something of a chimera. The Kent household comprised parents, children of two mothers, and

servants; the Verinder household consists of only one parent, a daughter, and servants — as well as frequent visitors, most of them cousins. Most of the primary characters in *The Moonstone* — Rachel, her mother, Godfrey Ablewhite, Franklin Blake, Drusilla Clack, Rosanna Spearman, and Gabriel Betteredge — are members of the same "family," either by blood or service. See Steven Mintz for a review of recent work in family history (esp. 11–20).

3. See, for example, W. H. Auden. George Grella also claims that "the fabric of society will be repaired after the temporary disruption" of crime (38). Many readings of *The Moonstone* depend on seeing the criminal Godfrey Ablewhite as an outsider; Beth Kalikoff, for example, claims that the crime in *The Moonstone* represents an "invasion of the respectable" (125; see also Miller 41–46). Yet Ablewhite and Blake stand in exactly the same relation to Rachel; both are her cousins, and both are clearly established and accepted as family members — thus Ablewhite's father, Rachel's nearest male relative, becomes her guardian on her mother's death.

4. The case is detailed by Yseult Bridges, John Rhode, Richard Altick, and Mary S. Hartman. As Bridges's is the most detailed account, my summary of the case relies most heavily on her reconstruction of it (as verified by Hartman).

5. Bridges here relies on the testimony of the police and an account of the crime written by Mr. Kent's doctor and friend, J. W. Stapleton (72–73; 77–84).

6. Contemporary accounts of the trial reveal that Constance was asked three times to enter a plea before she would say the word, "guilty," and that the judge was forced to pause twice while pronouncing the sentence to choke back sobs (Bridges 237–39).

7. In my use of the concept of secrecy, I am relying on Sissela Bok's discussion of the topic. Her definition makes it clear that while not all secrets involve deception or are necessarily wrong, our conceptions of secrecy almost always involve "prohibition, furtiveness, and deception" as well as "sacredness, intimacy, privacy, [and] silence" (6). "The defining trait of secrecy," she says, is "intentional concealment" (9) — although she later discusses the possibility of keeping a secret from oneself — also an issue for Franklin Blake (see, 59–72).

8. Ian Watt discusses the rise of domestic privacy in relation to the novel in chapter six of his *The Rise of the Novel* (see esp. 188). See also Michelle Perrot's claim that "the nineteenth-century family tended to subsume all the functions of private life" (97). Lawrence Stone's evidence concurs with Watt's and Perrot's; he characterizes the intense privacy of the mid-Victorian family as an "explosive intimacy" (423; see also 169). Hartman, writing specifically of the Kent case, claims that "new middle-class privacy provided relative isolation from outside pressures," especially with regard to the treatment of children and Mr. Kent's alleged adultery (117).

9. Jenny Bourne Taylor writes, "Rachel's silence is the essential secret that generates the Story; but in its very structural indispensability this suppression turns the conventions of moral management into hysterical repression on the one hand, and on the other suggests that the ascription of hysteria is the uncomprehending response to female autonomy" (201).

10. Beth Kalikoff argues that "Clack is a comic distortion of the other passionate women in the novel. Cloaking all her prejudices and greed beneath excessive religiosity, she seeks attention, love, and money" (122).

11. The irregularities of Collins's family life are now well known, although they were perforce "secrets," at least from the novel-reading public, during his lifetime and

have been obscured rather than clarified by his biographers. He lived for most of his adult life with a mistress, Caroline Graves, and her daughter Harriet; and he kept for some years a "second family" consisting of Martha Rudd and her three children by Collins. Martha Rudd and Caroline Graves were equally provided for in Collins's will. Nuel Pharr Davis's highly imaginative biography makes the most of these irregularities, to the extent of using Collins's fiction to "comment" on the still sketchy picture of his domestic life (see, for example, 164, 166). Robert Ashley's biography refers to Caroline Graves as an "alleged 'intimacy' " and, while reporting speculation that she was his mistress, suggests as well that Collins's bequest to her may simply have been a reward to "an affectionately respected housekeeper" — a hypothesis which is by now largely rejected (72, 77). The two relationships are also discussed by Kenneth Robinson.

12. It seems more likely that the child was — like Godfrey Ablewhite — smothered, not strangled. In the outline of means and motive, however, both Bridges and Hartman substantially agree with Dickens.

13. Lonoff puts forth the more traditional view that "the [Road] murder itself has nothing in common with the crime or the plot of *The Moonstone*" (179).

14. Psychoanalytic critics such as Charles Rycroft and Lewis Lawson have made the most of this symbolism. Rycroft's perceptive and often amusing reading also notes the Franklin Blake gives up cigar smoking during his courtship: Collins provides both hero and heroine with symbolic representations of their sexuality (Rycroft 235; see also Lawson 66).

15. Irigaray writes:

> *The virginal woman . . . is pure exchange value.* She is nothing but the possibility, the place, the sign of relations among men. In and of herself, she does not exist: she is a simple envelope veiling what is really at stake in social exchange. . . . The ritualized passage from woman to mother is accomplished by the *violation of an envelope*: the hymen, which has taken on the value of *taboo*, the taboo of virginity. Once deflowered, woman is relegated to the status of use value, to her entrapment in private property; she is removed from exchange among men. (186; emphasis in original)

While these comments seem problematic as a rendering of contemporary women's experience, they do clearly point up Rachel's (and her flawed diamond's) status. They may also recall to us the situation in the Kent household, in which Mr. Kent seems to have moved from one virgin to another (his first wife to Mary Pratt to Elizabeth Gough) as if they were interchangeable. The "madness" of the first Mrs. Kent and the silence of the second in the face of his virgin–consumption seems to signal the powerlessness of the woman who has been relegated by motherhood to the private sphere.

16. See Mark M. Hennelly, Jr., for a discussion of Collins's research into gemology. Hennelly sees the diamond itself as uniting the major themes of the novel, which he characterizes as both detective and domestic.

17. Apparently Constance's most unforgivable behavior was cutting off her hair and running away from home — at age thirteen — with her younger brother William (see Hartman 110).

18. Hartmann writes of Constance's confession, "Ironically, this act of confession was finely 'female,' just the sort of submissive, sacrificial, and self-destructive

act which, in lesser forms, was explicitly demanded of all respectable creatures of her sex'' (127). Anita Levy discusses the way in which what in one context is good and "feminine" becomes in other contexts destructive and "masculine," especially in her discussion of the "Venus Hottentot" and the "Bushwoman" dissection (69–72). She writes:

When anthropological writing contrasted the "bad" female, disruptive of familial and sexual order, with the "good" female, the upholder of that order, it pinpointed female choice as the decisive factor in the transition from nature to culture. . . . Most important, anthropological writing helped middle-class women to understand their gender as a contradictory phenomenon precisely because it was both crucial to woman's identity and the gravest threat to it. Being female meant (as it does today) constant self-regulation; neither too little nor too much femininity would do. (74)

19. I seem to be arriving, by some what different methods, at John Kucich's thesis that "Victorian repression produced a self that was actually more responsive libidinally, more self-sufficient, and — oddly enough — more antisocial than we have yet understood" (3). While I would not claim that Rachel's secrecy is typical of Victorian repression — certainly Bruff and Betteredge find it unusual enough to remark on it — it seems to be operating as Kucich defines the term here.

WORKS CITED

Altick, Richard D. *Victorian Studies in Scarlet*. New York: Norton, 1970.

Ashley, Robert. *Wilkie Collins*. New York: Roy, 1952.

Auden, W. H. "The Guilty Vicarage." *The Dyer's Hand and Other Essays*. New York: Random House, 1948. 146–58.

Barickman, Richard, Susan MacDonald, and Myra Stark. *Corrupt Relations: Dickens, Thackeray, Trollope, Collins, and the Victorian Sexual System*. New York: Columbia UP, 1982.

Bok, Sissela. *Secrets: On the Ethics of Concealment and Revelation*. New York: Vintage, 1984.

Brantlinger, Patrick. "What Is 'Sensational' about the 'Sensation Novel'?" *Nineteenth-Century Fiction* 37 (June 1982): 1–28.

Bridges, Yseult. *The Tragedy at Road–Hill House*. New York: Rinehart, 1955.

Collins, Wilkie. *The Moonstone*. 1868. Ed. J. I. M. Stewart. Harmondsworth: Penguin, 1969.

Davis, Nuel Pharr. *The Life of Wilkie Collins*. Urbana: U of Illinois P, 1956.

Eliot, T. S. "Wilkie Collins and Dickens." *Selected Essays, 1917–1932*. New York: Harcourt, 1932. 373–82.

Ellis, Sarah Stickney. *The Women of England, Their Social Duties, and Domestic Habits*. New York: Appleton, 1839.

Grella, George. "Murder and Manners: The Formal Detective Novel." *Novel* 4 (Nov. 1970): 30–48.

Hartman, Mary S. *Victorian Murderesses: A True History of Thirteen Respectable French and English Women Accused of Unspeakable Crimes*. New York: Schocken, 1977

Hennelly, Mark M., Jr. "Detecting Collins' Diamond: From Serpentstone to Moonstone." *Nineteenth-Century Fiction* 39 (June 1984): 25–47.

Hutter, Albert D. "Dreams, Transformations, and Literature: The Implications of Detective Fiction." *Victorian Studies* 19 (Dec. 1975): 181–209.

Irigaray, Luce. *This Sex Which Is Not One.* 1977. Trans. Catherine Porter with Carolyn Burke. Ithaca, NY: Cornell UP, 1985.

Kalikoff, Beth. *Murder and Moral Decay in Victorian Popular Literature.* Ann Arbor: UMI Research P, 1986.

Kennard, Jean E. *Victims of Convention.* Hamden, CT: Archon, 1978.

Kucich, John. *Repression in Victorian Fiction: Charlotte Brontë, George Eliot, and Charles Dickens.* Berkeley: U of California P, 1987.

Lawson, Lewis A. "Wilkie Collins and *The Moonstone.*" *The American Imago* 20 (Spring 1963): 61–79.

Levy, Anita. *Other Women: The Writing of Class, Race, and Gender, 1832–1898.* Princeton: Princeton UP, 1991.

Lonoff, Sue. *Wilkie Collins and His Victorian Readers: A Study in the Rhetoric of Authorship.* New York: AMS, 1982.

Marshall, William H. *Wilkie Collins.* New York: Twayne, 1970.

Miller, D. A. *The Novel and the Police.* Berkeley: U of California P, 1988.

Mintz, Steven. *A Prison of Expectations: The Family in Victorian Culture.* New York: New York UP, 1983.

O'Neill, Philip. *Wilkie Collins: Women, Property and Propriety.* Totowa, NJ: Barnes & Noble.

Oliphant, Margaret. "Novels." *Blackwood's Edinburgh Magazine* 102 (Sept. 1867): 257–80.

Perrot, Michelle, ed. *From the Fires of Revolution to the Great War. A History of Private Life.* Vol. 4. Trans. Arthur Goldhammer. Cambridge, MA: Harvard UP, 1990.

Reed, John R. "English Imperialism and the Unacknowledged Crime of *The Moonstone.*" *Clio* 2 (June 1973): 281–90.

Rhode, John. "Constance Kent." *The Anatomy of Murder.* Ed. Simpson, Helen, John Rhode, Margaret Cole, E. R. Punshon, Dorothy L. Sayers, Francis Iles, and Freeman Wills Crofts. New York: Macmillan, 1937, 43–86.

Robinson, Kenneth. *Wilkie Collins: A Biography.* New York: Macmillan, 1952.

Ruskin, John. "Of Queen's Gardens." 1871. *Sesame and Lilies; The Two Paths; The King of the Golden River.* London: Dent, 1970. 48–79.

Rycroft, Charles. "A Detective Story: Psychoanalytic Observations." *Psychoanalytic Quarterly* 26 (1957): 229–45.

Showalter, Elaine. "Desperate Remedies: Sensation Novels of the 1860s." *Victorian Newsletter* 49 (Spring 1976): 1–5.

Stone, Lawrence. *The Family, Sex and Marriage in England 1500–1800.* Abridged ed. New York: Harper, 1979.

Swinburne, Algernon Charles. "Wilkie Collins." *The Complete Works of Algernon Charles Swinburne.* Vol. 15. Ed. Sir Edmund Gosse and Thomas James Wise. London: Heinemann, 1926. 289–306.

Taylor, Jenny Bourne. *In the Secret Theatre of Home: Wilkie Collins, Sensation Narrative, and Nineteenth-Century Psychology.* London: Routledge, 1988.

Trodd, Anthea. "The Policeman and the Lady: Significant Encounters in Mid-Victorian Fiction." *Victorian Studies* 27 (Summer 1984): 435–60.

Watt, Ian. *The Rise of the Novel: Studies in Defoe, Richardson and Fielding.* Berkeley: U of California P, 1957.

Yeazell, Ruth. "Fictional Heroines and Feminist Critics." *Novel* 8 (Fall 1974): 29–38.

THE SORROWS OF CARLYLE: BYRONISM AND THE PHILOSOPHIC CRITIC

By Andrew Elfenbein

THOMAS CARLYLE NEVER FORGOT that Byron's rank had opened doors that were closed to him as the son of a Scottish peasant. In *Sartor Resartus*, Carlyle embodied in Diogenes Teufelsdröckh the voice of a new class that could replace Byron's, the class of the professional intellectual. Where Byron had depended on rank, the intellectual would depend on innate merit; where Byron had been a casual dilettante, the intellectual would be a serious philosopher. *Sartor Resartus* set out to represent Byron as all that the professional intellectual must learn to overcome.

Carlyle's challenge in *Sartor Resartus* involved how best to represent this ideal to a public whose taste was dominated by the literature of Byronism. His solution was not to reject this literature wholly, but to transform it into a vehicle for bourgeois spirituality. Unlike the writers who spurned Byron simply because he was popular, Carlyle had no distaste for a mass audience per se. Even as he attacked Byron's flaws, he envied Byron his popularity because Byron had reached the audience that he wished to reach. Yet Carlyle despised the kind of writing that his audience seemed to want, such as novels with Byronic characters or biographies of Byron. *Sartor* represents his parodic rewriting of this popular literature, a strenuous attempt to redirect public taste toward the voice of the professional intellectual.

Both Charles Richard Sanders and Michael Timko have written usefully about Carlyle's relation to Byron by analyzing his comments about Byron in his early periodical essays. Sanders counters *Sartor*'s impression of a flat rejection of Byron by pointing out Carlyle's heavily qualified admiration for certain aspects of Byron: ''Byron, 'the noblest spirit in Europe,' was one of the 'inheritors of unfulfilled renown.' He was immature but full of promise; if he had lived, he would have probably done mighty things'' (92). Timko supplements Sanders with his discussion of Byron as an apotropaic figure for

147

dangers in authorship for Carlyle. For Timko, Carlyle "sees Byron at various times as either a potential rival [to himself] or as a rival to his one great hero-artist, Goethe" (119). I am interested in developing a different kind of argument from that of Sanders or Timko by paying close attention less to Carlyle's explicit pronouncements about Byron than to his more subtle engagement with contemporary forms of Byronism in *Sartor Resartus*.

A revised understanding of how Byron was accessible to Carlyle changes the way the relationship between the writers has to be interpreted. Both Sanders and Timko make little distinction between a nineteenth-century Byron and a twentieth-century one, as if Byron were a stable, ahistorical entity. But in the early 1830s, when Carlyle wrote *Sartor*, "Byron" was a figure who existed chiefly as the product of the numerous texts of Byronism, which were only partly related to Byron's poetry: biographies, reviews, annotated editions, illustrations, dramatic adaptations, and much else. *Sartor* represents a response to three levels of Byronism: the broad stereotypes of Carlyle's periodical reviews, the Byronism of fashionable novels, and the portrait of Byron in contemporary biographies, particularly that of Thomas Moore. Trying to get behind the image of a monolithic Byron to understand the varying levels of mediation at which *Sartor* addresses the discourses of Byronism can transform our understanding not only of the Carlyle-Byron relationship but of *Sartor* itself.

FRASER'S, THE JOURNAL IN which *Sartor* first appeared in 1833–34, has long been recognized as a vital influence on its style (Tennyson 133–41). It also played a central role in shaping *Sartor*'s treatment of Byron. Its writers, particularly William Maginn, were obsessed with Byron and included more material about him than any comparable journal; their attitudes toward Byron were uniformly hostile. I will first look at *Sartor*'s most mediated relationship to Byronism in terms of the way it responds to William Maginn's 1830 review in *Fraser's* of Bulwer-Lytton's fashionable novels.[1] These novels, as contemporary reviewers recognized, were directly influenced by Byron's life and work (Adburgham 131–33). Bulwer-Lytton's smash success *Pelham*, for example, concerns the intense friendship between Henry Pelham, a dandy with a sarcastic wit like that of Byron in *Don Juan*, and Reginald de Glanville, a dark and brooding aristocrat who conforms to the stereotypes of the Byronic hero in poems like *Childe Harold's Pilgrimage*. Bulwer-Lytton himself confessed that he created Glanville as a member of the "would-be Byron School" (452). Maginn's review of Bulwer-Lytton's novels, especially of *Pelham*, has often been discussed as an important influence on Carlyle's "The Dandiacal Body" in *Sartor Resartus*, in which Teufelsdröckh mentions having read in "some English Periodical . . . something like a Dissertation on this very subject of *Fashionable Novels*!" (278). Teufelsdröckh also paraphrases a section from Bulwer-Lytton's *Pelham* about rules for fashionable dress, which Maginn had printed and ridiculed. Yet the article's significance has not been looked at in the larger context of Byronism and Carlyle's reaction to it.

Maginn's "Mr. Edward Lytton Bulwer's Novels; and Remarks on Novel Writing" savagely attacks Bulwer-Lytton, particularly *Pelham*, which it treats as unregenerate dandyism. The essay excerpts enough of Bulwer-Lytton's work to make its Byronic tendencies clear; Maginn quotes a remark from *Pelham* on the excellence of *Childe Harold*, and, in reference to *Paul Clifford*, refers to "the Lara or the Corsair of Byron" as a model for Bulwer's portrayal of passion (530). Although Carlyle had never associated Byron with the dandies before reading this article, he repeatedly did so afterward. For example, in his brief "Schiller, Goethe, and Madame de Staël," written in the spring of 1831, he wrote that Byron's letters were written "not with philosophic permanent-colours, but with mere dandyic ochre and japan" (*Works* 26: 503), and in his notebook that December he wrote, "Byron we call 'a Dandy of Sorrows, and acquainted with grief.' That is a brief definition of him" (*Note Books* 230).

Yet the relevance of Maginn's article to *Sartor* goes beyond the connection of Byron with dandyism; it also involves the role of philosophy in literature. In his earlier essays, such as "Jean Paul Friedrich Richter Again," Carlyle had attacked Byron for his aristocratic dilettantism, to which he opposed his own philosophical seriousness (Elfenbein 91–95). *Pelham* includes many conversations on philosophical topics, which give the novel an air of intellectual seriousness lacking in other fashionable novels. Maginn was not impressed by the philosophy and took Bulwer-Lytton to task for his dilettantism: "With this pretension to metaphysical science, and this real ignorance as to its elementary principles, it is not extraordinary that Mr. Bulwer's novels should be so deficient in arrangement and unity" (514); in particular, he blamed Bulwer-Lytton for being ignorant of German idealist philosophy and relying on Reid, who merely "had an indistinct perception of a system of philosophy which has since been perfected by Kant and Schelling in Germany, and by Stewart and Coleridge in England" (513). Maginn suggests that Bulwer-Lytton did not know the very philosophical systems that Carlyle had been studying and whose ideas had influenced his approach to literary criticism. He unmasked the philosophizing of Bulwer-Lytton's Byronic novels as another facet of the dilettantism that Carlyle despised in Byron himself.

According to Maginn, Bulwer-Lytton's ignorance of philosophy arose because "it is a favourite notion with our fashionable novelists, to sacrifice the middle classes equally to the lowest and highest," although "it is from the middle classes that men of genius have in general risen" (514–15); Bulwer-Lytton had "failed to prove his capacity to paint the lower and truly philosophical orders of mankind" (532). In discussing philosophical issues, Bulwer-Lytton chose to compete with philosophic critics like Carlyle; according to

Maginn, he failed because of his class bias. The aristocracy represented by Bulwer-Lytton was incapable of philosophy; only the middle class was "truly philosophical." Although the novel itself was not an aristocratic form, Bulwer-Lytton's tremendously popular novel about fashionable aristocrats represented another facet of the domination of literature by the aristocracy that Carlyle deplored in the success of Byron. Fashionable novels, particularly those produced by Byronism, provided Carlyle with a target that mediated for him many of his complaints about Byron. In *Sartor Resartus*, he presented, in contrast, a philosopher who properly belonged to no class except that of the professional intellectual.

At the end of September 1830, Carlyle hit on the idea of writing an essay on clothes, the first incarnation of *Sartor*, which would serve as an indirect critique of these Byronic dandy novels, with their obsession with clothes (*Note Books* 176).[2] He had contemplated the metaphor of clothes in his notebooks and essays before this time. But the importance of clothes in the Byronic fashionable novel seems to have inspired him to appropriate the clothes metaphor as a path to transcendent truth, thereby winning over the fashionable novel to the side of philosophic criticism.[3] He took the fascination with clothes, a motif from the pseudo-philosophic, fashionable novel *Pelham*, and used it as the basis for his more "genuine" philosophy; *Sartor Resartus* is an unfashionable novel of fashion. Rather than presenting his philosophy straight, Carlyle demonstrates that he can manipulate the tropes of fashionable Byronic literature for "higher" ends.

For example, in the "Adamitism" chapter, clothes for Teufelsdröckh represent the arbitrary hierarchies of society that disguise the true equality of humanity:

> Often in my atrabiliar moods, when I read of pompous ceremonials, Frankfort Coronations, Royal Drawing-rooms, Levees, Couchees; and how the ushers and macers and pursuivants are all in waiting; how Duke this is presented by Archduke that, and Colonel A by General B . . . on a sudden, as by some enchanter's wand, the — shall I speak it? — the Clothes fly-off the whole dramatic corps; and Dukes, Grandees, Bishops, Generals, Anointed Presence itself, every mother's son of them, stand straddling there, not a shirt on them; and I know not whether to laugh or weep. (60–61)

Novels like *Pelham* offered the middle-class reader a privileged view of high life, as Byron's poetry had offered a privileged view of an aristocrat's mind. Teufelsdröckh presents his own version of penetrating to the secret interiors of the aristocracy, which undoes any fascination that aristrocratic privacy might possess. There is no secret erotic charge to this imagined display of nakedness, only a leveling emphasis on the fact that we are "bound by invisible bonds to *All Men*" (60).

Having dismissed social class as a mere effect of clothes, Teufelsdröckh in the "Pure Reason" chapter reveals that clothes, metaphorically conceived, are the garment of the spirit: "The thing Visible, nay the thing Imagined, the thing in any way conceived as Visible, what is it but a Garment, a Clothing of the higher, celestial Invisible. . . ?" (67). He replaces dilettantish philosophy with his version of the German idealism of which Bulwer-Lytton was ignorant, so that the Byronic fashionable novel comes to appear philosophically impoverished beside the greater wisdom of Carlyle's text about clothes. The Clothes Philosophy undercuts the dilettantism represented for Carlyle by Byron and Bulwer-Lytton by providing a different perspective on clothes: rather than being emblems of high society, they are emblems of high spiritual truth.

The fashionable novel was only one form in which Byronism affected *Sartor*. Another mode of fashionable literature, the Byron biography, played an even larger role. Three major biographies of Byron appeared in 1830: James Kennedy's *Conversations on Religion with Lord Byron and Others*, John Galt's *Life of Lord Byron*, and, the most important, Thomas Moore's *Letters and Journals of Lord Byron, with Notices of his Life*, which became the year's best seller. In "Signs of the Times," (1829), Carlyle had announced that Byron "already begins to be disregarded and forgotten" (*Works* 27: 78); even *Sartor* maintained that "the very Byron, in some seven years, has become obsolete" (47). The small outpouring of material about Byron in 1830 proved Carlyle wrong. All three biographies, particularly Moore's, were widely reviewed; in many cases, the comments of reviewers marked the beginning of the Victorian rejection of Byron.[4]

In *Fraser's*, William Maginn, with the possible participation of J. A. Heraud, reviewed the first volume of Moore's biography in March, Kennedy's in August, and Galt's in October. The review of Galt is particularly interesting with regard to the genesis of *Sartor* because it seems to have been written with Carlyle in mind. Galt's biography received generally poor reviews, but Maginn defended it against its critics, particularly those at the *Athenaeum*. Nevertheless, he attacked Galt, like Bulwer-Lytton, for his incompetent philosophy: when Galt "ventures into the stream of philosophy," he "soon gets out of his depth and flounders woefully" (366). What Galt failed to give, according to Maginn, and what was really needed, was "a full development of [Byron's] character — a metaphysical analysis of his mental qualities, his idiosyncratic complexion" (348); Maginn described precisely the kind of biographical analysis that Carlyle had perfected in his earlier essays. Maginn also seems to have had Carlyle in mind when he objected to Byron's selfish complaining, dilettantism, and incoherence in terms that paraphrased Carlyle's estimate in "Goethe." He acknowledged Carlyle's influence explicitly when he said that "Göthe [*sic*] would have taught him [Byron] differently"

(370) and quoted lines by Goethe as "they are translated by his friend, Mr. Thomas Carlyle" (370). He even echoed the phrase "snarl and snap like dog distract" (356), which Carlyle had used in "Goethe." Maginn had already tried to interest Carlyle in *Fraser's* by sending him the first six issues; Maginn's review of Galt's *Life of Byron* was an implicit invitation to Carlyle to write a "metaphysical analysis" of Byron for the journal.[5]

The invitation worked, but not for *Fraser's*. In November, Carlyle wrote to the editor of the *Edinburgh Review* asking to write about Byron:

> Occasionally of late I have been meditating an Essay on *Byron*; which, on appearance of Mr Moore's Second Volume, now soon expected, I should have no objection to attempt for you . . . [M]y chief aim would be to *see* him and show him, not, as is too often the way, (if I could help it) to write merely "about him and about him." . . . Dilettantism, and mere toying with Truth, is, on the whole, a thing which I cannot practice: nevertheless real Love, real Belief, is not inconsistent with Tolerance of its opposite . . . For *Byron*, no Books were wanted except Mr Moore's two vo[lumes] to which Galt's might be added: except the *Plays* and *Don Juan*, which also would be needed, all his Poems are already here.[6] (*Letters* 5: 196–97)

Macvey Napier, the editor, turned Carlyle down, because the review of Moore had already been given to Macaulay; instead, he sent him William Taylor's *Survey of German Literature* to review. Nevertheless, Carlyle read the first volume of Moore's biography by late 1830 or early 1831.[7] In January, he asked his brother to retrieve his essay on clothes from *Fraser's* because he wanted to give Teufelsdröckh more biography: "I can devise some more Biography for Teufelsdreck, give a second deeper part, in the same vein, leading thro' Religion and the nature of Society, and Lord knows what" (*Letters* 5: 215). It is no coincidence that Carlyle decided to revise *Sartor* to give Teufelsdröckh more biography at about the same time that he was reading the first volume of Moore's biography of Byron. Byron's life as told by Moore became a decisive negative model for the biography of Teufelsdröckh in the second volume of *Sartor*.[8]

MOORE'S BIOGRAPHY, WRITTEN as a refutation of Leigh Hunt's, in some ways supported the view it was supposed to refute. Moore reproduced Hunt's negative images of Byron's mobility but removed much of their openly hostile edge. Whereas Hunt made Byron seem frivolous, Moore made him seem like a lively child: "In all the excursions, whether of his reason or his fancy, he gave way to this versatile humour without scruple or check, — taking every shape in which genius could manifest its power, and transferring himself to every region of thought where new conquests were to be achieved" (2: 788). The combination of the "authentic" voice of Byron's letters with a consistent characterization of him in terms of mobility allowed Moore to develop an interpretation that explained the paradoxes in Byron's career without damning him, exalting him, or shuttling between the two. The result gave a coherent picture of "Byron the man" at the expense of "Byron the myth," which was unmasked as Byron's "pride of personating." It was an instant best seller and was more frequently reprinted than any other version of Byron's life. For Carlyle, who had always discussed Byron in terms of the man, not the poet, Moore's best-selling biography gave him a more detailed and concrete image than he had ever had before of Byron as a powerful but unphilosophical aristocrat, ruled by the impulses of a moment, against which he could pose his ideal of the classless philosopher, Diogenes Teufelsdröckh.

The name Diogenes Teufelsdröckh recalls Byron's character in its emphasis on divided nature. The periodical reviewers of Moore's *Life* saw in Byron an archetypal embodiment of duality, perhaps applying to Byron his own description of Napoleon as "antithetically mixt." Even his physical presence, with his clubfoot and handsome face, seemed an emblem of division; as Macaulay noted, "He had a head which statuaries loved to copy, and a foot the deformity of which the beggars in the street mimicked" (2: 614). Maginn maintained that Moore portrayed Byron as "half monster — half god" (1831, 242). Lockhart noted that Byron's comment on Burns, "What a strange compound of dirt and deity!" might better have been applied to himself (219). Carlyle's own essays had been divided between their presentation of Byron as a divine prophet, as in "Burns," and as a howling animal, as in "Goethe." Byron provided Carlyle's age with a particularly striking example of the ancient topos of duality, and Teufelsdröckh's divided nature is as much Byronic as Calvinist.

The Byronism of Teufelsdröckh's name also involves his Satanic attributes: Byron was repeatedly associated with Satan, as in Southey's tag for Byron's school of poetry, the Satanic school. Carlyle associates Teufelsdröckh's Satanism with his humor; the editor says that his perverse and satirical qualities makes one "look on him almost with a shudder, as on some incarnate Mephistopheles" (32). He finally gives up his biography because of the "painful suspicion" that Teufelsdröckh, with his "humouristico-satirical tendency," has written autobiographical documents that "are partly a mystification!" (202). Byron's satirical mystifications were often commented on in writings about him, especially Moore's *Life*, which noted that he succumbed to the temptation "of displaying his wit at the expense of his character" because he liked "to astonish and *mystify*." Moreover, it was "difficult, in unravelling the texture of his feelings, to distinguish at all times between the fanciful and the real" (1: 135, 201).[9]

The Byronic influence is present not only in Teufelsdröckh's name; the events of his life in book 2 of *Sartor Resartus* are a continuous revision of the events of Byron's life as told by Moore. The editor justifies the need for Teufelsdröckh's biography in terms of the Byronic equation between man and author. Like Byron, Teufelsdröckh cannot be understood "till a Biography of him has been philosophico-poetically written, and philosophico-poetically read" (75). This language recalls Maginn's desire in his review of Galt's biography for a "metaphysical analysis of [Byron's] mental qualities, his idiosyncratic complexion." Carlyle hints at his debt to Moore's biography near the end of the "Sorrows of Teufelsdröckh" chapter, when the editor explains the need for Teufelsdröckh to pass through a stage of passionate suffering akin to Byron's: "For what is it properly but an Altercation with the Devil, before you begin honestly Fighting him? Your Byron publishes his *Sorrows of Lord George*, in verse and in prose, and copiously otherwise" (156–57). Previous critics have not commented on the reference to Byron's prose, which is puzzling if applied to the prose published during Byron's life. Byron's contributions to the *Liberal* or his prefaces and notes to poems hardly qualify as the *Sorrows of Lord George*. Carlyle must refer to the prose letters published in Moore's *Life*, which, as Macaulay's review suggested, reveal the "sad and dark" story of Byron's early unhappiness (2: 614). This small reference points to a larger debt to Moore throughout this section of *Sartor*.

Like the novels of Bulwer-Lytton, Moore's biography was a piece of fashionable literature; the popularity of both represented to Carlyle the dangerous fascination in the early 1830s with novelistic images of high society. Teufelsdröckh's unfashionable life begins as a point-by-point reversal of the young Byron's; all that happens to him is written against Byron's early experiences. The overall effect of this revision is to emphasize the effects of class, which becomes the symbolic ground for Carlyle's attack on Byron. Both Byron and Teufelsdröckh are only children, but they come from radically different backgrounds. Moore devotes several pages to Byron's illustrious ancestry; Teufelsdröckh is an orphan given to the Futterals by a mysterious stranger. Carlyle makes a particular point that Teufelsdröckh's origins are not noble; Teufelsdröckh has looked "through all the Herald's Books, in and without the German Empire" and found no record of his name (86). Teufelsdröckh uses the humbleness of his origins to bolster his strength of character: "Wouldst thou rather be a peasant's son that knew, were it never so rudely, there was a God in Heaven and in Man; or a duke's son that only knew there were two-and-thirty quarters on the family-coach?" (99). Moore noted the bad effect that Byron's early elevation to nobility had on him: "Had he been left to struggle on for ten years longer, as plain George Byron, there can be little doubt that his character would have been, in many respects, the better for it" (1: 20).

The highly moral peasant family that adopts Teufelsdröckh serves as a direct criticism of the family structure that turned Byron into a selfish aristocrat. Though Tuefelsdröckh's lack of a father during childhood parallels Byron's, he at least has a strong substitute in his foster-father, Andreas Futteral. Like Byron's father, Andreas is a military man, but he has retired and become "Cincinnatus-like" (82), in contrast to the wild and irresponsible Captain Byron. Their mothers present a similar contrast. Both are religious: Mrs. Byron "was of a very religious disposition" and taught Byron "while yet an infant, to repeat a great number of the Psalms" (Moore 1: 9); Gretchen taught Teufelsdröckh "less indeed by word than by act and daily reverent look and habitude, her own simple version of the Christian Faith" (99). Carlyle's emphasis on Gretchen's deeds reflects back unfavorably on Mrs. Byron, who, despite her piety, was a woman "full of the most passionate extremes" (Moore 1: 11). Moore describes her as a violent, often uncaring mother whose passions, arising from her aristocratic haughtiness, were responsible for flaws in Byron's character. The differences of the children reflect those of the parents. Teufelsdröckh as an infant "seldom or never cried" and felt that "he had other work cut-out for him than whimpering" (89); Byron "even when in petticoats . . . showed the same uncontrollable spirit with his nurse, which he afterwards exhibited when an author, with his critics" (Moore 1: 8).

Carlyle's project is not simply to reverse Moore's version of Byron's life, but to suggest how Teufelsdröckh is a redeemed Byron, who fulfills the potential that was ruined in the real Byron. Despite social disparity, similarities indicating unusual poetic sensitivity can easily be seen between the two. Both are almost obsessive readers. Teufelsdröckh recalls that "what printed thing soever I could meet with I read" (101), and Moore quotes a letter by Byron in which he writes, "I read eating, read in bed, read when no one else read, and had read all sorts of reading since I was five years old" (1: 40). Byron spent much of his childhood in Scotland, as had Carlyle, and developed a love for the mountains at sunset that is like Teufelsdröckh's: "After I returned to Cheltenham, I used to watch them every afternoon at sunset, with a sensation which I cannot describe" (Moore 1: 17). Though Teufelsdröckh is supposed to grow up in Germany, the landscape he describes looks suspiciously like the Scotland of Carlyle and Byron: "[T]here, many a sunset, have I, looking at the distant western Mountains, consumed, not without relish, my evening meal" (93).

Both experience a crisis of identity in their early adolescence, which reinforces Carlyle's use of class as a means of moral distinction. Without warning, they are suddenly alienated from all that has been familiar to them. Gretchen and Andreas have pretended that Teufelsdröckh is their grandnephew, but after Andreas's death, Gretchen tells him "that he was not at all of this kindred'' (107). Suddenly, Teufelsdröckh feels set apart from humanity: ''A certain poetic elevation, yet also a corresponding civic depression, it naturally imparted: *I was like no other*'' (107). When Byron is ten, the fifth Lord Byron dies; Byron, his grandnephew, becomes the sixth Lord Byron. Though he asks his mother ''whether she perceived any difference in him since he had been made a lord, as he perceived none himself,'' Moore notes that ''the child little knew what a total and talismanic change had been wrought in all his future relations with society, by the simple addition of that word before his name'' (1: 20). Byron is unable to answer to his name in school when *dominus* is prefixed to it for the first time; like Teufelsdröckh, he suddenly feels that he is ''like no other.'' Characteristically, however, Byron's alienation comes from a move up the social ladder, a move that had catastrophic results for his moral development, as Moore suggests. Teufelsdröckh's ''civic depression'' emphasizes that he has none of Byron's worldly advantages; his achievements will be solely the result of his intrinsic merits.

Their sensitivity leads both young men to erotic catastrophe; they love with an all-absorbing intensity of passion that is destined to fail. Byron's lost love is Mary Chaworth; his attachment to her ''sunk so deep into his mind as to give a colour to all his future life'' (Moore 1: 53). Carlyle revises this episode when Teufelsdröckh falls in love with a woman nicknamed Blumine, whom he meets at an ''*Aesthetic Tea*'' (134) run by the aristocratic Zähdarms. Blumine's real name is never given, and this absence characterizes her general shadowiness. She loves Teufelsdröckh but is forced by her ''Duenna Cousin'' (144) to break off the relation because of his lack of prospects. He plunges into despair: ''through the ruins as of a shivered Universe was he falling, falling, towards the Abyss'' (146). The pathetic force of circumstance that forces Blumine to leave him makes Byron's unreturned love for Mary, as presented by Moore, seem self-absorbed and egotistical. Carlyle's presentation ensures that Teufelsdröckh knows a depth of sorrow of which Moore's Byron is incapable; he experiences the tragic loss of a man, while Byron undergoes merely the infatuation of a boy.

Teufelsdröckh's disappointment in love brings him to his most explicitly Byronic phase. According to the editor, he can only do one of three things: ''Establish himself in Bedlam; begin writing Satanic Poetry; or blow-out his brains'' (146). To the editor's surprise, he does not choose any of these: ''He quietly lifts his *Pilgerstab* (Pilgrim-staff), 'old business being soon wound-up'; and begins a perambulation and circumambulation of the terraqueous Globe'' (147). Carlyle is here at his trickiest. We are supposed to understand that Teufelsdröckh has rejected the Byronic alternative of writing Satanic poetry, but Carlyle could not have chosen a more explicit reference to Byron than to have Teufelsdröckh go on a pilgrimage. As Teufelsdröckh becomes Childe Harold, Carlyle tries to preserve a few marks of difference from

Byron by praising his combination of "intensity of feeling" with "stoicism in external procedure" (147). The editor marvels that Teufelsdröckh "was meek, silent, or spoke of the weather," while underneath "a whole Satanic School [was] spouting, though inaudibly, there" (148); he is living up to the Satanism of his name.[10] Moore's Byron also masks his pain, and his "bursts of vivacity on the surface [were] by no means incompatible with a wounded spirit underneath" (1: 188). Yet Teufelsdröckh does not resort, like Byron, to vivacity, but to "meek, silent" stoicism. Still resembling the baby who would not whimper, the adult Teufelsdröckh keeps his pain to himself.

His pilgrimage is not fully underway until he sees the shocking vision of Blumine and his English friend Herr Towgood in a "gay Barouche-and-four" attended by servants and postillions wearing wedding-favors (151). The Satanic School in him at last wins out: "Life has become wholly a dark labyrinth; wherein, through long years, our Friend, flying from spectres, has to stumble about at random, and naturally with more haste than progress" (152). In case we miss the connection here between Teufelsdröckh and Byron, the editor notes, "From which is it not clear that the internal Satanic School was still active enough?" (155). These events are paralleled closely in Moore. Like Teufelsdröckh, Byron sees Mary Chaworth and her husband immediately before he sets off on his pilgrimage, and the sight plunges him into despair: "His passions had, at the very onset of their career, forestalled the future; and the blank void that followed was by himself considered as one of the causes of that melancholy, which now settled so deeply into his character" (1: 182). Carlyle closes the chapter on the "Sorrows of Teufelsdröckh" with the reference to the *Sorrows of Lord George* discussed above. Teufelsdröckh is undergoing the same "Altercation with the Devil," from which Byron never emerged completely victorious.

The shock of rejection leads Teufelsdröckh and Byron to the nadir of their spiritual journey. Carlyle again is careful to present Teufelsdröckh's "Everlasting No" as having far purer depth and moral intensity than Byron's. Moore describes Byron's bitterness as arising out of revenge and impatience: "Baffled, as he had been, in his own ardent pursuit of affection and friendship, his sole revenge and consolation lay in doubting that any such feelings really existed. . . . What others would have bowed to, as misfortunes, his proud spirit rose against, as wrongs" (1: 186). Though Moore maintains a distanced tone, he views Byron's despair as petty and self-indulgent. Byron is exceptional only in his inability to bear his misfortunes with patience. Teufelsdröckh, in contrast, does not feel revenge or scorn so much as cosmic emptiness: "It is all a grim Desert, this once-fair world of his; wherein is heard only the howling of wild-beasts, or the shrieks of despairing, hate-filled men" (161). Far from being upset by worldly disappointments, as Byron is, Teufelsdröckh feels the vast hollowness of a world without faith, in which a mechanistic philosophy has turned all into "one huge, dead, immeasurable Steam-engine, rolling on, in its dead indifference" (164). The editor emphasizes that Teufelsdröckh's despair is only a stage "wherefrom, the fiercer it is, the clearer product will one day evolve itself" (158). Unlike Byron's aimless bitterness, Teufelsdröckh even at his most forlorn is developing moral strength.

At the end of "The Everlasting No," Teufelsdröckh realizes that he has been crippled by a needless fear of death, because he has the ability to suffer "all that the Devil and Man may, will or can do" against him (167). This realization allows him to reject the Everlasting No and emerge from his despair. Yet he has not fully overcome Byron, because no new faith yet replaces his emptiness. During this interim — the "Centre of Indifference" — Teufelsdröckh undergoes many adventures that the editor claims to be unable to describe in detail:

> — But at this point the Editor recalls his principle of caution, some time ago laid down, and must suppress much. . . . Of Lord Byron, therefore, of Pope Pius, Emperor Tarakwang, and the "White Water-roses" (Chinese Carbonari) with their mysteries, no notice here! (178)

The editor's elaborate disclaimer pokes fun at the ones made by Moore, who had been sharply criticized by some reviewers for divulging the more unsavory sides of Byron's life.[11] Byron's appearance functions as an "in-joke" through which Carlyle signals the beginning of the end of Teufelsdröckh's Byronic phase. Byron is now only an exotic worthy whom Teufelsdröckh meets in his pilgrimage, just as Harold described exotic worthies in *Childe Harold*. The humor lies in the fact that the editor does not need to dwell upon Teufelsdröckh's adventures because readers will already know their general shape from having read *Childe Harold* and Moore's *Life*. The reference to Chinese Carbonari in particular may derive from Byron's involvement with the Italian Carbonari; Lockhart had noted in his review that Byron's connection with the Gambas had "led to his becoming mixed up, to a much greater extent than we were till now aware of, in the Carbonaro politics" (214).

Almost the only episode in Teufelsdröckh's pilgrimage that the editor does describe involves a complex revision of episodes in Moore. Teufelsdröckh, alone "in the solitude of the North Cape," muses on a promontory over the ocean, while viewing "nothing but the granite cliffs ruddy-tinged, the peaceable gurgle of that slow-heaving Polar Ocean" (179). Although Carlyle moves Teufelsdröckh geographically northward, his position recalls that of Byron in Greece, who "when bathing in some retired spot, [used] to seat himself on a high rock above the sea . . . lost in that sort of vague reverie, which, however formless and indistinct at the moment, settled afterwards on his pages, into those clear, bright pictures which will endure for ever''(Moore 1: 254). Teufelsdröckh is visited not by poetic visions, but by ''a man, or monster, scrambling from among the rock-hollows; and, shaggy, huge as the Hyberborean Bear'' who assails him ''with his importunate train-oil breath'' (179–180). When the man will not go away despite Teufelsdröckh's courteous request for privacy, he draws a gun and says, ''Be so obliging as retire, Friend (*Er ziehe sich zurück, Freund*), and with promptitude!'' The Hyperborean, whom Teufelsdröckh fears is a Russian smuggler, leaves ''with apologetic, petitionary growl'' (180).

Just as Carlyle translates Teufelsdröckh from Byron's Greece to the North Cape, so the Hyperborean represents a northward movement from Byron's exotic Greek corsairs to a Russian smuggler. With this geographic dislocation comes a coarsening of character, as if the Hyperborean were a Byronic Corsair grotesquely stripped of surface refinements. His savagery recalls Carlyle's association of Byron with savage wildness in his early essays, as when in ''Goethe'' he wonders what good it does Byron ''to snarl and snap in malignant wise, 'like dog distract, or monkey sick' '' (*Works* 26: 218). Moore's biography emphasizes Byron's violent, potentially murderous nature, as when he is ''heard to say, in an under voice, 'I should like to know how a person feels, after committing a murder!' '' (1: 235). Moreover, as Joseph Sigman has pointed out, Teufelsdröckh's rejection of the Hyperborean recalls Jesus's ''Get thee behind me, Satan'' (221); for Teufelsdröckh, rejecting the Hyperborean becomes an emblem of rejecting the Satanic school. The Hyperborean is a burlesque of the savage, Satanic characteristics that Carlyle typically associated with Byron, as well as a parodic projection of the Byronic wildness in Teufelsdröckh himself. Teufelsdröckh is a purified version of Byron, the Hyperborean a parodically debased one.

While Byron drew poetic inspiration from his elevated outlook over the sea, Teufelsdröckh draws the moral that gunpowder ''makes all men alike tall''; because of it, ''savage Animalism is nothing, inventive Spiritualism is all'' (180). Byron too had a high regard for guns, according to Moore, and he always had arms about him because ''the mortification which he had . . . to endure at school, from insults . . . hazarded on the presumption of his physical inferiority, found consolation in the thought that . . . the law of the pistol would place him on a level with the strongest'' (1: 27). Like Teufelsdröckh, Byron believes that guns make all men alike tall. Yet Teufelsdröckh despises violence and only approves of guns because they eliminate the tyranny of the physically strong. His attitude toward duels is contemptuous, while Moore's Byron is always about to fight one.

Although Carlyle seems to wish to transfer Byron's violent qualities away from Teufelsdröckh onto the Hyperborean, the transfer is not as simple as it seems. Teufelsdröckh's behavior in the episode retains a residual violence. We might have expected that Teufelsdröckh's "inventive spiritualism" would have been demonstrated by some quick-witted maneuver to avoid the Hyperborean; instead, he links spirituality with gunpowder. He seems not to have overcome Byron's violence so much as found a more euphemistic rhetoric in which to describe it. The spiritualization of gunpowder is in itself a violent fiction, a dark underside to Carlyle's desire to make unspiritual objects, such as clothes, fashionable novels, or the biography of Byron, into spiritual ones.

The almost violent dismissal of the Hyperborean is tantamount to a dismissal of the Byronic aspects of Teufelsdröckh: immediately after the episode, the editor notes that "the Satanic School, was now pretty well extirpated and cast out" (181). It is replaced by the "Everlasting Yea," Teufelsdröckh's general sense of affirmation brought about by a realization of the power of his will:

> I asked myself: What is this that, ever since earliest years, thou hast been fretting and fuming, and lamenting and self-tormenting, on account of? Say it in a word: is it not because thou art not HAPPY? Because the THOU (sweet gentleman) is not sufficiently honoured, nourished, soft-bedded, and lovingly cared-for? Foolish soul! What Act of Legislature was there that *thou* shouldst be Happy? A little while ago thou hadst no right to *be* at all. What if thou wert born and predestined not to be Happy, but to be Unhappy! Art thou nothing other than a Vulture, then, that fliest through the Universe seeking after somewhat to *eat*; and shrieking dolefully because carrion enough is not given thee? Close thy *Byron*; open thy *Goethe*. (191–92)

The Byronic Teufelsdröckh is a "sweet gentleman" who expects to be "honoured, nourished, soft-bedded, and lovingly cared-for." The progress of the passage suggests that underneath the sweet gentleman is the shrieking vulture; gluttony for happiness reduces him to another version of the Hyperborean's savage animalism. Yet the savagery does not seem to be solely Byron's; Teufelsdröckh is vulture-like himself in the way he pounces on his own Byronic tendencies. This moment revises the scene in which his pistol forces the retreat of the monstrous Hyperborean. As there, we sense that Byron has been closed out with a ferocity that is not as far from savage animalism as it would like to pretend.

Teufelsdröckh channels his ferocity into an intense sense of mission: "Be no longer a Chaos, but a World, or even Worldkin. Produce! Produce! Were it but the pitifullest infinitesimal fraction of a Product, produce it, in God's name!" (197). We expect that Teufelsdröckh, having closed his Byron, will become Goethe. Yet there is an odd falling off between his ringing affirmation of potential and the actuality of his fate. Instead of becoming Goethe, he becomes Professor of Things-in-General at the university in Weissnichtwo, where he gives occasional orations in the coffee-house, though no formal lectures; he is the first absent-minded professor in English literature. The appropriateness of this most unByronic profession lies in its close connection to that of the philosophic critic. The academic professor was the next step up the cultural ladder from the philosophic critic. In Carlyle's day, writers for the reviews often had academic connections. For example, John Wilson, the guiding force behind *Blackwood's*, was professor of Moral Philosophy at the University of Edinburgh; Carlyle had inquired about applying for the same position at the University of London in 1827 and actually applied unsuccessfully for a similar job at St. Andrews a few months later. Although not a journalist himself, Teufelsdröckh is a dedicated reader of the periodical reviews. He sits at the Weissnichtwo tavern "reading Journals" (19), his room is littered with "Periodical Literature" (24), and he announces that "the Journalists are now the true Kings and Clergy" (45). The editor imagines that he might publish articles on Teufelsdröckh's clothes philosophy in "widely-circulating Critical Journals" (10).[12] The new form of selfhood that Carlyle imagines in response to Byron's problems arises in the new class of professional intellectuals, like academics and philosophic critics. As David Riede notes, "Carlyle is a kind of literary sansculottist, evolving a romantic formulation of the *true* man of letters as revolutionary prophet arising from the lower orders to restore true order" (107).

The political importance of this class becomes apparent in "The Dandiacal Body," which explicitly relates Teufelsdröckh's philosophy to fashionable literature. The editor notes, "The all-importance of Clothes, which a German Professor, of unequalled learning and acumen, writes his enormous Volume to demonstrate, has sprung up in the intellect of the Dandy without effort, like an instinct of genius" (272). By putting the chapter late in the book, Carlyle allows the dandies to appear as one more incarnation of the aristocratic Byron who was rejected in "The Everlasting Yea." Like him, they are "sweet gentlemen." Yet the dandies are not merely an unusual social group; they represent a politial development with disastrous implications. The light-hearted tone of the chapter, in which Teufelsdröckh describes the dandies and fashionable novels as a religious sect of whose tenets he disapproves, darkens tremendously when the dandies are contrasted with the wretchedness of "Poor-Slaves" (285), the Irish peasantry whose condition is spreading beyond Ireland. He concludes by predicting that the sects are "two bottomless boiling Whirlpools" that will overwhelm England, until "we have the true Hell of Waters, and Noah's Deluge is outdeluged" (286). This outcome seemed threateningly possible in the troubled years immediately preceding the 1832 Reform Bill. As Carlyle wrote in his notebook, "Haystacks and corn-stacks burning over all the South and Middle of England! Where will it end? Revolution on the back of Revolution for a century yet?" (178–79).

The division of England into the Dandies and the Poor-Slaves excludes the class of the bourgeois intellectual represented by Teufelsdröckh. The chapter implicitly poses this class as the only possibility for staving off the apocalyptic consequences of the increasing division between rich and poor. Carlyle wrote in his notebook, "Not that we want *no* Aristocracy, but that we want a *true* one" (179). The true Aristocracy consists of intellectual men of intrinsic merit, rather than those like Byron whose merit is judged by birth. In their hand lies not only the future of literature but the political salvation of England itself.

OUR ESTIMATE OF TEUFELSDRÖCKH'S success in rejecting Byron and creating "philosophic permanent-colours" is filtered through the book's omnipresent editor. The editor's relation to Teufelsdröckh can be thought of as Carlyle's revision of Moore's relation to Byron. By foregrounding the editor's role, Carlyle criticizes Moore's seemingly objective stance, which produced a superficial version of Byron by overlooking all that made him significant. The contrast between the editor's blandness and Teufelsdröckh's wild prose reworks the contrast between Moore's tepid Johnsonian style and the witty verve of Byron's letters. When the editor notes that his style has become contaminated by Teufelsdröckh's — "Thus has not the Editor himself, working over Teufelsdröckh's German, lost much of his own English purity?" (293) — his loss suggests that he has sympathized with the importance of his subject in a way unavailable to Moore. His modest description of digging for the truth beneath Teufelsdröckh's "printed and written Chaos" (80) masks Carlyle's more profound "editing" of Moore's text. It is as if he were trying to delve beneath the superficial surface of Moore's biography to get at a core of vital potential latent in the subject that was never allowed to develop. Teufelsdröckh's life is the life that should have been written about Byron.

Yet Carlyle's editor is not merely Teufelsdröckh's greatest admirer; he is also his harshest critic. While Teufelsdröckh is the apotheosis of what Riede calls "the *true* man of letters," the editor, with his fussy concern for the reactions of the British reader, is a parodic version of Carlyle's potential to degenerate into a magazine hack. While Carlyle was writing *Sartor*, Francis Jeffrey insisted that he would never find an audience: "No man who despises and contemns educated and intelligent men, at the rate you do, will ever have any success among them. . . . I wish I could persuade you that you are not an inspired being, and never will be the founder of a new religion" (qtd. in David Wilson 201). The editor is Carlyle's version of what Jeffrey would have liked him to become. Like Jeffrey, the editor frequently points out Teufelsdröckh's failings: "Thus does the good Homer not only nod, but snore" (46); "Beware, O Teufelsdröckh, of spiritual pride" (100); "Does your Professor take us for simpletons?" (287). The editor's carping, like the wildness of Teufelsdröckh's language, permits Carlyle to avoid the crudeness of seeming to preach in his own person. Without subverting Teufelsdröckh, the editor lets Carlyle suggest that he himself subscribes to more temperate versions of Teufelsdröckh's doctrines. At the same time, the editor's comments foreground the importance of the act of interpretation itself, although we are not always asked to agree with his interpretations. The ability to understand, judge, and respond to Teufelsdröckh properly is as important as Teufelsdröckh himself.

The editor's relation to Teufelsdröckh is a diminished version of Teufelsdröckh's relation to Goethe. In the command "Close thy *Byron*; open thy *Goethe*," Goethe represents the perfection of the heroic ideal. The editor's negative comments are a reminder that Teufelsdröckh himself has not attained this perfection; he is not a hero but a man striving to attain heroism. As long as he has not reached Goethe, Teufelsdröckh retains residual traces of Byron, which are particularly evident in the editor's reminiscences of him. His initial appearance suggests he has not sustained the brotherhood with his fellow men that he proclaimed in "The Everlasting Yea." If he has moved beyond Byronic despair, he has not quite conquered Byronic solipsism. When he looks out from his window onto the town, he says, "All these heaped and huddled together, with nothing but a little carpentry and masonry between them. . . . But I, *mein Werther*, sit above it all; I am alone with the Stars" (23). The editor calls this room Teufelsdröckh's "speculum or watch-tower" (20); Carlyle mistakenly uses "speculum," mirror, for "specula," watch-tower. The mistake is overdetermined in its suggestive confusion of internal and external. When Teufelsdröckh looks out on the world, he does not quite see himself as in a mirror, but he sees a vision of the world that bolsters his sense of his own specialness. A similar confusion of internal and external occurs when Teufelsdröckh calls the editor "*mein Werther*." He seems to see the editor as a younger, sentimental version of himself, although the editor never gives hints of having undergone any experiences like the "Sorrows of Teufelsdröckh."

Only at the end of *Sartor Resartus* does Teufelsdröckh move away from this solipsism toward a more active, Goethian ideal of heroism. This active heroism turns out to be his most direct imitation of Byron. He mysteriously disappears from Weissnichtwo, and the editor tries to reconstruct his last days. He discovers that when Teufelsdröckh learned of the Paris Revolution of 1830 shortly before his disappearance, he commented "*Es geht an*" (It is beginning); as Harrold notes, the words are a translation of the French "Ça ira," the song of the French Revolution (296). The Post-Director reports that he has corresponded with the Saint-Simonians, a radical French sect (296). He is blamed by certain "Evil-wishers, or perhaps mere desperate Alarmists" for having caused an uprising of tailors in Berlin. The editor's private theory is that he has come to London, which in 1831 was rocked by tensions over reform. Although the editor never says that Teufelsdröckh is actually preparing to fight a revolution, these events strongly hint that he has become involved in revolutionary activities (see Vanden Bossche, "Desire" 75). Given the consistency with which Teufelsdröckh's life mirrors Byron's, his final activities suggest a revision of Byron's departure from Italy to fight for Greek independence. In "Goethe" and "Burns," Carlyle spoke of the last stage of Byron's life as his best, the one in which he was beginning to achieve spiritual victory. The most fitting fate he can imagine for his hero is to return to the Byronic model at its best, having rejected it as its worst. Goethe never went off to fight for freedom. The final pages of *Sartor Resartus* suggest that Teufelsdröckh has closed his Goethe and reopened his Byron. Presumably, he will be able to accomplish the victory that Byron was able only to glimpse.

The function of "Byron" in *Sartor Resartus* has little to do with Carlyle's reading of Byron's poetry or with what Byron means to an academic audience in the late twentieth century. Rather, I want to stress the importance of cultural mediation in shaping the ways that "Byron" and Byronism become for Carlyle the emblems of a literary system hostile to all that he wished to represent. Influence, in this case, involves far more than an intersubjective relation between two authors; it involves Byronism as a literary and cultural movement that seemed to prevent a man with Carlyle's background from achieving success as a writer. In this context, *Sartor Resartus* looks less like an odd translation of German philosophical ideals than a polemical appropriation and redirection of the forms of writing dominating the British literary marketplace in the early 1830s.

University of Minnesota

NOTES

1. I follow the *Wellesley Index to Victorian Periodicals* in attributing many of the reviews most important to Carlyle to William Maginn, the guiding spirit behind *Fraser's* (2: 320–26); J. A. Heraud may also have contributed, but I will use Maginn's name throughout. All the articles were anonymous; Carlyle would not have known that they were by Maginn.
2. S. B. Liljegren argued that the *Fraser's* article was the inspiration for the entire book, and that "The Dandiacal Body" was the first version of *Sartor*. Tennyson rightly dismisses this view (132–33); however, I would still argue that the *Fraser's* article had a vital influence in shaping the first third of *Sartor*.
3. For a good discussion of the political resonances that the clothes metaphor would have had for Carlyle at this time, see Vanden Bossche, *Carlyle* (41–44).
4. John Wilson, the *Blackwood's* reviewer, had one of the most positive reactions to Moore: "And blind and base must they be who feel not — that with all his faults and frailties — Byron was, throughout childhood — boyhood — youth —

and up to manhood's spring-prime, — a noble being'' (417). John Gibson Lockhart's review in the *Quarterly* was less favorable; he emphasized Byron's lack of solidity: ''[A]ccording to Mr. Moore, the distinguishing characteristic of Lord Byron is neither more nor less than that he had no fixed principles or motives of action of any kind''; this ''moral side of the picture is fatal to anything like a high impression of dignity'' (223). Macaulay's essay in the *Edinburgh Review* became a standard nineteenth-century estimate; it centered on the terrible darkness of Byron's life. Like Carlyle, Macaulay found that Byron's time had passed, and ''a few more years will destroy whatever yet remains of that magical potency which once belonged to the name of Byron'' (2: 642). Maginn's review of Moore's first volume in *Fraser's* opened the March 1830 issue, and the review of the second appeared a year later. Despite grudging admiration for Byron's originality, he despised Byron's aristocratic privileges, his ''green sickness for notoriety'' (131) and his affectations: ''His sequestration was ostentatious; he affected solitude; but his solitariness was that of a statue on a column in a marketplace'' (133).

5. Although Carlyle does not mention reading this review specifically, his letters indicate that he was reading *Fraser's* regularly during this time. On October 19, he asked his brother John about the October issue, in which the second part of John's article on St. John Long appeared (*Letters* 5: 175, 202); it seems highly probable that Carlyle saw the issue soon afterwards.

6. Rodger L. Tarr notes that the Carlyle edition of Byron still surviving is Jane's copy of the five volume 1821 edition (''Thomas'' 252). This may be the edition to which Carlyle refers; it would have lacked the plays and *Don Juan*.

7. The earliest evidence for his having read Moore's book appears in a passing reference to Byron's letters, cited above, in ''Schiller, Goethe and Mme. de Staël.'' The letters in which Byron mentions Madame de Staël occur near the end of Moore's first volume and were published there for the first time. Carlyle's essay was not published in *Fraser's* until 1832, but on 6 June 1831, he wrote to his brother, ''By the way, Fraser, I think, has still a little Paper of mine, 'Goethe, Schiller and Madame de Staël': request him to return it if it does not suit'' (*Letters* 5: 284). If in June *Fraser's* had had the piece for some time, Carlyle must have written it earlier in 1831, which in turn suggests that he read the first volume of Moore during the winter or early spring of 1830–31. Further evidence for his having read Moore appears in the letter he wrote to Napier in 1832, after Napier suggested that he write an encyclopedia entry on Byron. Carlyle indicated his unwillingness but added: ''If . . . you still persist, then be so good as transmit me your copy of *Moore's Life of Byron* (the second volume of which I have never seen)'' (*Letters* 6: 149). He implies that he had at least seen the first volume, which ends with Byron about to leave England after his marriage's failure.

8. With regard to the composition history of *Sartor*, I follow Tennyson in assuming that the original essay on clothes roughly corresponded to what is now book 1 and parts of book 3 (141–45), and that Carlyle wrote book 2 when he retrieved the essay from *Fraser's* to supplement and alter the biography given in the ''Reminiscences'' and ''Characteristics'' chapters of what is now book 1. For a different argument, see Tarr, ''Manuscript.''

9. Lockhart in his review of Leigh Hunt's recollections claimed that ''Lord Byron, we have no sort of doubt, indulged his passion for mystifying, at the expense of this gentleman [Hunt], to an improper and unjustifiable extent'' (415).

10. Carlyle associated Byron explicitly with the Satanic school in a letter to his brother in November 1831: he noted that employment was often difficult to find and "thus Byron writes Satanic Poetry" (*Letters* 6: 46).
11. In its review of the first volume, *Fraser's* noted "the disregard of personal feeling with which living individuals are treated by name" (143), and Lockhart objected to the way in which Moore had displayed Byron's love affairs so as to become "the instrument of placing before the public . . . full length pictures of this particular species of profligacy" (205).
12. Tennyson has noted how the structure of *Sartor* itself represents an expansion of the structure of Carlyle's earlier periodical reviews (114–25).

WORKS CITED

Adburgham, Alison. *Silver Fork Society: Fashionable Life and Literature from 1814 to 1840*. London: Constale, 1983.

Carlyle, Thomas. *Sartor Resartus: The Life and Opinions of Herr Teufelsdröckh*. Ed. Charles Frederick Harrold. New York: Doubleday, 1937.

———. *Two Note Books of Thomas Carlyle*. Ed. Charles Eliot Norton. New York: Grolier Club, 1898.

———. *Works of Thomas Carlyle*. Ed. H. D. Traill. 30 vols. London: Chapman and Hall, 1896–99.

Carlyle, Thomas, and Jane Welsh Carlyle. *The Collected Letters of Thomas and Jane Welsh Carlyle*. 18 vols. to present. Ed. Charles Richard Sanders, et al. Durham, N.C.: Duke UP, 1969–.

Elfenbein, Andrew. "Carlyle, Lockhart, and Byron: A Note." *Carlyle Annual* 12 (1991): 91–95.

Galt, John. *The Life of Lord Byron*. London: Colburn and Bentley, 1830.

Houghton, Walter E., ed. *The Wellesley Index to Victorian Periodicals*. 5 vols. Toronto: U of Toronto P, 1966–89.

Kennedy, James. *Conversations on Religion with Lord Byron and Others*. London: John Murray, 1830.

[Lockhart, John Gibson.] Review of Leigh Hunt's *Lord Byron and Some of His Contemporaries*. *Quarterly Review* 37 (1828): 402–26.

———. Review of Thomas Moore's *Life of Lord Byron*. *Quarterly Review* 44 (1831): 168–226.

Lytton, Edward Bulwer-Lytton, Lord. *Pelham, or The Adventures of a Gentleman*. 1828. Ed. Jerome J. McGann. Lincoln: U of Nebraska P, 1972.

Macaulay, Thomas Babington. "Byron." *Critical and Historical Essays*. 2 vols. London: Dent, 1967. 2:613–42.

[Maginn, Williams.] Review of Thomas Moore's Life of Byron. *Fraser's* 1 (1830): 129–43.

———. Mr. Edward Lytton Bulwer's Novels; and Remarks on Novel Writing. *Fraser's* 1 (1830): 509–32.

———. Review of John Galt's *Life of Lord Byron*. *Fraser's* 2 (1830): 347–70.

———. On Moore's Life of Byron. *Fraser's* 3 (1831): 238–52.

Moore, Thomas. *Letters and Journals of Lord Byron; with Notices of His Life*. 2 vols. London: John Murray, 1830.

Riede, David. "Transgression, Authority, and the Church of Literature in Carlyle." *Victorian Connections*. Ed. Jerome J. McGann. Charlottesville: UP of Virginia, 1989. 88–120.

Sanders, Charles Richard. "The Byron Closed in *Sartor Resartus.*" *Studies in Romanticism* 3 (1964): 77–108.

Sigman, Joseph. " 'Diabolico-angelical Indifference': The Imagery of Polarity in *Sartor Resartus.*" *Southern Review* (Adelaide) 5 (1972): 207–24.

Tarr, Rodger L. "The Manuscript Chronology of *Sartor Resartus*: Some Speculations." *Carlyle Annual* 11 (1990): 97–104.

———. "Thomas Carlyle's Libraries at Chelsea and Ecclefechan." *Studies in Bibliography* 27 (1974): 249–64.

Tennyson, G. B. *Sartor Called Resartus: The Genesis, Structure, and Style of Thomas Carlyle's First Major Work.* Princeton: Princeton UP, 1965.

Timko, Michael. *Carlyle and Tennyson.* Iowa City: U of Iowa P, 1987.

Vanden Bossche, Chris R. *Carlyle and the Search for Authority.* Columbus: Ohio State UP, 1991.

———. "Desire and Deferral of Closure in Carlyle's *Sartor Resartus* and *The French Revolution.*" *Journal of Narrative Technique* 16 (1986): 72–78.

Wilson, David Alec. *Carlyle to* The French Revolution *(1826–1837).* London: Kegan Paul, 1924.

[Wilson, John]. "Moore's *Byron.*" *Blackwood's* 27 (1830): 389–420.

THE EMPIRE AS METAPHOR: ENGLAND AND THE EAST IN *THE MYSTERY OF EDWIN DROOD*

By John S. DeWind

MANY HAVE NOTED THAT Charles Dickens's *The Mystery of Edwin Drood*, like Wilkie Collins's *The Moonstone*, possesses a pervasive Eastern background.[1] Most notably John Jasper induces typical images of oriental violence and pageantry by using opium, and the twins Helena and Neville Landless appear in England having travelled from Ceylon where they have suffered considerable abuse. Much other Eastern imagery exists in the novel, and its widespread presence has tempted various commentators to assert that a pattern of meaning may be shown to exist in it. Edgar Johnson wrote in his biography that toward the end of his life, Dickens, the great social commentator, was beginning to develop an anti-imperialist critique (1124–26).

Against Johnson's notion of Dickens becoming aware of imperialist oppressions might be placed that of Ina Rae Hark who sees all things Eastern as exercising a malignant effect on the West through characters who are superior and selfish and "ignore the needs of others" (Hark 160). Both writers were correct to assert a consistent meaning to the Eastern references, but I believe they interpret them incorrectly.[2] Dickens was an ardent imperialist and believer in Western civilization, as his attitude toward the Indian Mutiny of 1857–58 shows. In his correspondence he fantasized about exterminating a hateful Indian race, and he translated his feelings into literature in "The Perils of Certain English Prisoners . . ." composed with the help of Collins, which appeared in *Household Words* as the special Christmas number of 1857.[3] On the other hand, Hark is mistaken in believing that the East is always associated with unhealthy influences. Particularly she goes wrong in asserting that Rosa Bud's attraction for Lt. Tartar is regressive (Hark 162). Dickens certainly shows the East as a source of evil impulses, but this image of the East is one descended from the Mutiny, that is, it is an image of the East broken loose and independent from England. Against this image are set alternate ones in

169

which England and the East meet in a harmonious whole in which the former balances, controls, and channels the latter, and together they symbolize a full and happy life. The prospective marriages of Rosa Bud and Lt. Tartar and Mr. Crisparkle and Helena Landless, with which Dickens's friend and fellow editor John Forster wrote the novel was to end, would have presented twin pictures of this full life.[4] In short, imperialism provided an image of opposite impulses coming together in a fruitful whole. This image of balance contrasts with that of John Jasper in which "Eastern" impulses displace and subsume "English" ones. The prevalent Eastern imagery interconnects with the other dominant images in the novel, those of suffocation, water and land, wetness and dryness, light and dark, and with such matters as character and differing kinds of time. Giving a consistent account of the Eastern imagery clarifies much about these other matters which have figured so prominently in criticism of the novel.

Like Collins, Dickens introduces the Eastern element into the novel from the very beginning, but by avoiding Collins's apparatus of a prologue in which important action is set in India, he maintains the East as a vague, misty, more securely symbolic place. Rather, Dickens begins in the middle of things, allowing an initial view of Jasper's own mind as the choirmaster attempts to make sense of his opium visions while waking:

> An ancient English Cathedral town? How can the ancient English Cathedral town be here! The well-known massive grey square tower of its old Cathedral? How can that be here! There is no spike of rusty iron in the air between the eye and it, from any point of the real prospect. What is the spike that intervenes, and who has set it up? Maybe it is set up by the Sultan's orders for the impaling of a horde of Turkish robbers, one by one. It is so, for cymbals clash and the Sultan goes by to his palace in long procession. Ten thousand scimitars flash in the sunlight, and thrice ten thousand dancing-girls strew flowers. Then, follow white elephants caparisoned in countless gorgeous colors, and infinite in number and attendants. Still, the Cathedral Tower rises in the background, where it cannot be, and still no writhing figure is on the grim spike. Stay! Is the spike so low a thing as a rusty spike on the top of a post of an old bedstead that has tumbled all awry. (Dickens ch. 1, 37)

The Eastern content of Jasper's visions is all quite the usual stuff — the cruelty and violence of the despot, the sensuality of the dancing girls, and the exotic coloring of the whole scene. Jasper attaches this scene to the actual spike on the bedpost which makes an incongruous contrast with the cathedral tower in the background, characterized by its weight and its colorless gray and square form. The vision provides almost a picture of Jasper's life with its two discordant elements. The cathedral tower represents his dull, oppressive respectability — his conscious life, crushing in its boredom and lack of satisfaction; the eastern visions stand for the fantasies drawing on unconscious impulses and achieved by taking opium, by means of which he escapes. The relationship between the two realms is signalled by the spike mistaken for part of the fantasy and intruding into a place where it does not belong, mixing unconscious desire into the conscious world. Right from the start a disturbed psychology expresses itself by means of disturbed relations between East and West, in which an Eastern impulse from below invades the Western surface. If the vision provides an initial picture of Jasper's mental disease, it implicitly suggests that mental health is characterized by a quiescent relationship in which the East lies still in quiet support of a busy Western life.

Some critics have suggested a further Eastern connection for Jasper — that he is a Thug committing a ritual murder in the service of Kali. This outlandish notion, first suggested by Howard Duffield in an article published in 1930 and given prominence by Edmund Wilson, should not be excluded either historically or thematically, but neither is there any good reason to accept it.[5]

Dickens further draws on the Eastern metaphor in introducing the Landless twins, Helena and Neville. The two appear almost preternaturally from Ceylon, coming from that domain in an oddly unfinished form which can only be completed by experience in the West. In Ceylon they exist almost as primitives submerged in a wild life of emotion. Dickens's initial description, given from Crisparkle's point of view, seems to refer to animals as much as people:

> An unusually handsome lithe young fellow, and an unusually lithe girl; much alike; both very dark, and very rich in colour; she of almost the gypsy type; something untamed about them both; a certain air upon them of hunter and huntress; yet withal a certain air of being objects of the chase rather than followers. Slender, supple, quick of eye and limb; half shy, half defiant; fierce of look; an indefinable kind of pause coming and going on their whole expression, both of face and form, which might be equally likened to the pause before a crouch or bound. (ch. 6; 84–85)

And in the next paragraph Crisparkle thinks of the two as "beautiful barbaric captives brought from some wild tropical dominion" (85). Underlying their appearance as nervous animals and primitives has been a life of raw emotion caused by neglect and cruelty from their stepfather. Neville reveals much of the character of the twins when he tells Crisparkle, on an acquaintance of a few minutes, in reference to his stepfather that, "It is well he died when he did, or I might have killed him" (ch. 7; 88). The two young people have almost no existence in the world of the everyday. What for Jasper is stifling is for them non-existent; subject to open and continual brutishness and meanness, they live by immediate emotion equally open to love and hatred, both exercised by them with an innocent and direct power. Helena loves Rosa immediately and deeply and also tends to "ferocity" (94), and she maintains a "slumbering gleam of fire in [her] . . . intense dark eyes" (96) directed toward those whom she feels to be a threat to her newly-acquired friend. Neville relates how she once bit and tore her hair off when the two needed to be in disguise during an attempted escape from their stepfather. Also, within a very short while, Neville falls passionately in love with Rosa and has a quarrel with Edwin in which he could well have taken his life if others did not intervene. Neville's extreme, uncontrolled, and dangerous emotions directed in different ways at Edwin and Rosa are just the ones that Jasper cultivates in his opium reveries toward the two. Neville and Helena have been forced into an oriental world in Ceylon, a place similar to the one that Jasper has sought out in his visions — cruelty, violence, sensuality, and color characterize both worlds, and by keeping Ceylon far in the background, with life there only related distantly by Helena and Neville, Dickens keeps it more a psychological state than a geographical one.

If in Jasper and the Landless twins Dickens portrays characters with little surface life and much in the psychological depths connected to the East, he creates another class of characters who are almost all surface with no depth. For them he provides appropriate Oriental connections indicative of their superficiality. Rosa Bud, as her very name indicates, is more a girl than a woman; she is still largely untouched by life, and she may be said to demonstrate this when she asks Edwin to take her to the Lumps of Delight Shop for a "Turkish sweetmeat" (ch. 3; 58). Such a trip amounts to her current contact with the Orient, though she has heard more about it. Miss Twinkleton has taught her girls about the pyramids which in Rosa's account become, "Tiresome old burying grounds! Isises and Ibises, and Cheopses, and Pharaohses; who cares about them? And there was Belzoni or somebody, dragged out by the legs, half choked with bats and dirt. All the girls say serve him right, and hope it hurt him, and wish he had been quite choked" (59). The East, appearing now as Egypt, constitutes a matter of indifference for Rosa, and Belzoni, the explorer, seems a fool for taking an interest. However, that his doing so should lead to his near suffocation is quite appropriate. Rosa herself is often short of breath when near Jasper or when he is the subject of conversation, and during the scene at the sundial, when he most fully reveals his Eastern fantasies, telling her of "Paradises and Hells of visions into which I rushed, carrying your image in my arms" (ch. 19; 228) — she also feels suffocated. Dickens writes, "Her panting breathing comes and goes as if it would choke her" (229); as soon as she escapes his presence, she faints. Jasper's intense life of "Oriental" sensuality can only be a threat to the Rosa whose desires are fulfilled by a candy.

A different Oriental future looms for Rosa during the early part of the novel, for she and Edwin are to go to Egypt after their marriage, where he will be an engineer. The Orient would be a natural destination after their marriage though neither has much idea of what it contains; matching Rosa's lack of interest in the place are Edwin's callow and superficial views, for he has never been there either, and though he criticizes her indifference, he seems to know quite as little. He remarks with offhanded contempt to Neville that he is "going to wake up Egypt a little" (ch. 8; 96). If the two were happy there it would be completely a matter of luck. Rosa tells Edwin to read her palm, a trick she attributes to "you Egyptian boys"; however, when she asks, "Can't you see a happy Future," there is no reply, and Dickens adds in the following narrative that neither of the two can even see a "happy Present" (ch. 3; 62).

Rosa and Edwin's superficiality belongs to their youth and each possesses some understanding of his or her own condition and each feels the lack in the other. When they have brought their own prospective marriage to an end, each feels attracted to a sympathetic character with more "Eastern" experience. Indeed, at his final departure from Rosa, Edwin wonders "whether it might come to pass that he would know more of Miss Landless" (ch. 13; 169), and much later Rosa feels attracted to Lt. Tartar, whose very name refers to a resident of the Orient and who in his "twelve or fifteen years of knocking about" (ch. 17; 215) in the Royal Navy has no doubt come to see a good deal of the East.

However, Thomas Sapsea cannot be excused from the charge of superficiality on the grounds of youth. He is an old fool, and all the greater one because he is convinced he is not. His great claim for himself, inscribed even on his wife's tombstone, is that he knows the world. Unlike Lt. Tartar however, he has never seen that world, only laid his hands on its products as an auctioneer. This far and no further has he delved into the Orient. He explains to Jasper, "I see some cup and saucers of Chinese make, equally strangers to me personally. I put my finger on them, then and there and I say 'Pekin, Nankin, and Canton.' It is the same with Japan and Egypt, and with bamboo and sandalwood from the East Indies; I put my finger on them all" (ch. 4; 64). In fact Sapsea's attitude to the foreign consists of equal portions of fear and ignorance blending together into a rich chauvinism concerning all "verminous peoples" (ch. 12; 148), a category which includes all nationalities besides the English. Jasper easily manipulates him in building a case against the dark-hued Neville, who suggests to Sapsea an "un-English complexion" (ch. 15; 188) to the mystery.

Other characters are more carefully balanced between their conscious lives of a proper social existence and their unconscious lives of private emotions based on desire and fear. For example, with Lt. Tartar, Dickens defines him as someone with an extensive experience of the world and through his name places him as someone linked specifically to Eastern experience. His name may have another meaning in the reiteration of the word "tar." As a sailor, even a sort of double sailor, Tartar has moved expertly through the medium of water in coming to know the world, and in the opposed imagery of land and water, Dickens creates another metaphorical image of the structure of the mind, just as Collins did with the Shivering Sand in relation to Roseanna Spearman.[6] Tartar's ability in water was achieved even before he became a sailor, for as Chrisparkle's old student, when he was "the smallest of juniors" (ch. 20; 243), he managed to save the full-sized senior Crisparkle from drowning. The incident suggests the danger of water — in submerging oneself in the element one may lose the power to reach the surface again with the result of suffocation. Rosa's mother, a woman so much like her daughter that Grewgious mistakes the one for the other, suffered this fate during a "party of pleasure" (ch. 9; 105). Rosa herself feels threatened with suffocation from Jasper's desire, and thus Tartar impresses her especially. After hearing of his early feat, she thinks, "If Heaven . . . had but sent such courage and skill to her poor mother's aid" (ch. 20; 244), and soon after Rosa transfers the lesson to herself when she contemplates Tartar's figure as that of someone who "could have caught her up and carried her out of any danger . . ." (246).

However, Tartar is not a completely formed figure — secure as he is within water, his existence above has been cramped and restricted by the necessity of living in a ship. When he enters the novel he is attempting to adjust to a wider, more relaxed life on land. He explains to Neville his current mode of living by saying, "I chose this place, because, having served last in a little corvette, I knew I should feel more at home where I had a constant opportunity of knocking my head against the ceiling" (ch. 17; 215). Constriction in this case provides comfort, and a moment later he explains tending his window boxes by saying "having been accustomed to a very short allowance of land all my life, I thought I'd feel my way to the command of a landed estate, by beginning with boxes" (215). In Tartar's case his deceased uncle provided the land, and he adapts himself slowly to be able to use it productively. He is somewhat like Neville and Helena in that so much of his life is elsewhere and below the surface, and so he may justly tell Neville he is a "corresponding set" (214), but with the essential difference that he possesses a secure place in both worlds. Tartar prepares himself for his future on his estate, but Neville and Helena, though deep in an education to adjust themselves to England, are fundamentally, even by their name, Landless and therefore in a sense always adrift and open to being swept away by odd currents. In opposition, pure Englishman Mr. Sapsea, forever at his ease on dry land, has no moisture in him; he even possesss the frightening ability to dry up others — indeed to "sap" the "sea" from them.

Crisparkle like Tartar participates in the two worlds, but also remains an unfinished character. He dives regularly into the water — a practice he took up after Tartar saved him, and he has advanced further towards becoming a complete person. He more securely rests on "land" as is shown by his suitability as an instructor for those who have no such footing. Both Neville and Helena benefit from his tutelage and his faith in them. He presents a healthful combination of freedom and restriction to the two, constantly providing an opportunity for confidences, and then using his influence to mold the resulting expressions into socially acceptable forms. He moves skillfully between the private and public spheres of life and in doing so presents the most integrated character in the book. However, at the end of the list of adjectives describing him, Dickens includes "boylike," and there is something unrealized about the Minor Canon so apt at bringing others into their majority. He still lives with his mother and in that relationship gladly embraces pretended infirmity. For example, he persists in the falsehood that he cannot read clearly, wearing spectacles despite having the "eyes of a microscope and telescope combined" (ch. 6; 80), so that his mother may display her own good eyes. This practice typifies a kind of beneficent holding back in Crisparkle — it makes for a charming relationship with his mother but one in which his deference to her keeps his whole personality in the position of boyish son. Dickens writes that at thirty-five Crisparkle listens to his mother recite the Lord's Prayer in much the way he did at the age of three (79). The persistence of this unchanged ritual indicates a sameness through time that Dickens elsewhere shows to be objectionable as a denial of the very processes of life. However, one must note that the novel is incomplete as well as the character. According to Forster, Dickens intended to marry Crisparkle to Helena at the end. Such an ending would presuppose a vast further development in Crisparkle — he too was to evolve into something fuller than at the early stages of the book.

Nevertheless, lacking the end of the book, what strikes one about the first half is that none of the characters is fully mature and whole; none has had a full and balanced experience of life.[7] As the Princess Puffer says, "Well, there's land customers, and there's water customers" (ch. 19; 266). The result is that a strange instability pervades the novel; identity tends not only to the lopsided but to a blurry indistinction, to mercurial shifts, to odd resemblances and ambiguities, to sudden aggressions and flights, to peculiar weaknesses and powers. In no one are the uncertainties of character greater than in John Jasper, and he acts as a central disturbing force with the other characters around him, manipulating and distorting them, recreating his own oddnesses in them, forcing himself on them, and hampering them in their pursuits. He possesses all the aggressive qualities of Luke Honeythunder and Thomas Sapsea, made all the more dangerous because he also possesses depth and subtlety. Yet for all the force the private monster shares with those two public ones, a certain insubstantiality also adheres to all these men; their very aggressiveness is linked to a fundamental emptiness or lack of character.

Jasper's thinness of character derives from the extent to which he allows his conscious life in Cloisterham to be restricted. In his case, limitation provides no comfort, only frustration, pain, and despair. The very name of the city suggests its being shut up from the business of the world, and such is the air it exudes. Dickens writes: "An ancient city, Cloisterham, and no meet dwelling-place for anyone with hankerings after the noisy world" (ch. 3; 51). Later he adds, "All things in it are of the past" (52). The two sentences almost suggest that time in the city has ceased to function. The "noisy world" in which change takes place lies elsewhere — and in the city all things have already become what they are through past time and now remain in an unchanging, presumably finished state. However, elsewhere Dickens makes clear that such an appearance is a false one, when he writes; "A drowsy city, Cloisterham, whose inhabitants seem to suppose, with an inconsistency more strange than rare, that all its changes lie behind it, and that there are no more to come. A queer moral to derive from antiquity, and yet older than any traceable antiquity" (51). The residents of the city mistakenly imagine themselves without any future but rather think they face a continual recreation of what is already past. They imagine themselves complete prisoners of what has gone before, and in holding this illusion, Jasper shows himself a fit resident.

The music master sees only an awful sameness in his life; he tells Edwin, "The cramped monotony of my existence grinds me away by the grain" (ch. 2; 48). A moment later he compares himself to a cloistered monk in the cathedral saying, "The echoes of my own voice among the arches seem to mock me with my daily drudging round. No wretched monk who droned his life away in that gloomy place before me can have been more tired of it than I am" (48). Dickens fills the passage with a repetition suggestive of sameness.[8] Jasper's voice is repeated in the echo, he enacts a repeated daily round, and his activity repeats the repeated activities of monks long ago, only including a change in that he is more tired of it than his forebears were. Mr. Grewgious, in looking in the door of the cathedral where Jasper works, says "it's like looking down the throat of Old Time" (ch. 9; 117). Jasper does seem consumed by the past, and he is more explicit in another passage: following his round precludes any future when he tells Neville (goading him by doing so) that, "You and I have no prospect of stirring work and interest, or change and excitement, or of domestic ease and love. You and I have no prospect (unless you are more fortunate than I am, which may easily be), but the tedious, unchanging round of this dull place" (ch. 8; 101).

Jasper's sense of being constricted and consumed by the past creates a theme on which Dickens plays several variations. Rosa and Edwin feel something similar in that their marriage has been planned by their fathers, long deceased by the time the novel opens. Thus do the dead and buried reach through the past to lay a grip upon the present. Edwin complains about being cut off from a choice in his marriage, of the difficulty of telling if there exists a real basis for the union, and of his fears that he has been forced on Rosa and she on him. Rosa too cannot act naturally under the paternal wishes, set years before, which attempt to predict growth and affection in the young people. Less articulately she tells Helena that it makes Edwin and her a "ridiculous couple" (ch. 7; 94). They cannot tell if they are repeating parts written for them or actually have genuine feelings appropriate to their appointed roles. In fact an actual, specific play seems more lively and true than the performance Edwin and Rosa put on. On the night of her birthday Rosa has a mock ball and one of her classmates plays Edwin. She refuses to dance with him because she is tired of him, and the young actress imitates Edwin's ennui in a way that greatly amuses Rosa. She says of the girl, "Oh, she did it so well!" (ch. 3; 56). The feeling of being stuck in assigned roles haunts the young people through the beginning of the book.

Helena and Neville are held in thrall to the past in a different way — specifically their brutalized past in Ceylon among what Neville calls "abject and servile dependents, of an inferior race," with whom he fears he has "contracted some affinity" (ch. 7; 90). Both fear that their experiences in Ceylon form an insuperable barrier to conducting a normal life in England. Furthermore the darkness of the twins suggests that the legacy of Ceylon is broader than just that of experience. Dickens surely means to suggest that the Landlesses are somehow the product of a mixture of blood. In quarreling with Neville, Edwin manages to hit an especially sensitive point by referring to the young man's dark complexion. In fact, this allusion drives Neville from verbal insults to open force. Oddly by referring to Neville's most unbreakable ties to Ceylon, Edwin evokes the response most associated with that country in the novel — that of violence. This impulse to violence surfaces elsewhere with Neville repeatedly, most characteristically in the gesture of clenching his fists — an action which he does unconsciously and to which Crisparkle always takes exception. Under the further provoking influence of opium, which is surely what Jasper mixes in the drinks he prepares for the young men on the night of their quarrel, Neville loses control in a way that is at least partially a reversion to the past — to his racial makeup and parentage, and to experiences of his childhood. Both Neville and Helena understand the whole purpose of their efforts in England to be that of trying "to make up for lost time" (ch. 8; 98) or to overcome the force of their "antecedents" (ch. 10; 127), which are associated with the netherworld of the East.

Another character suffering from the haunting gloom of time gone is Mr. Grewgious, and in his case also the effect of the past is to remove him from the present. As he explains humorously to Rosa, "I was the only offspring of parents far advanced in life, and I half believe I was born advanced in life myself" (ch. 9; 114). He further tells her that he came into the world as a very dry "chip." His dryness does not indicate that he has no depth but rather that he has never found a way of expressing it. His lack of experience makes him angular, and angularity makes it difficult for him to have experience. What he does at least in the early stages of the book always has the air of a mechanical repetition of something already done in the past. Thus, when he first meets Rosa, all his actions with her are performed from a memorandum prepared before, and each action is laboriously ticked off after it is performed. Yet Mr. Grewgious has more complexity than he presents to Rosa. The emotions of the man came into play when he was young. He loved Rosa's mother, but never acted on that love, instead watching Rosa's father move before him and win the woman. Mr. Grewgious was not born entirely old but became thoroughly so in presiding over these unsatisfied past emotions. All that is most alive in him looks backward, and his most profound duties are those of a guardian of the past wishes of others concerning the living. And yet, in serving the cause of the dead, he can display quite wonderful expressiveness, as when he gives the ring to Edwin. Introduced as a minor character given a few peculiar "Dickensian" traits, Grewgious quickly increases in stature and in many ways is a parallel figure, perhaps intended as an equal, to Jasper. Grewgious too is a guardian, with a stifling past and no future, and yet he acts with an entirely different effect on his wards. The past limits him, reduces him, dries him out, but he also expands in accepting those limitations, becoming a heroic figure in defending Rosa.

The past also dominates the rather dry person of Thomas Sapsea, but he is as unaware of the full extent of this condition as he is of most things, for Sapsea, despite all his force of character, has virtually no independent identity; all his power acts rather only as a means of duplicating some other action or person.[9] Thus, he can only repeat what has been established in the past. This trait of his finds illustration in his toast to Jasper at their first meeting; he says "When the French come over / May we meet them at Dover." Dickens adds, "This was the patriotic toast in Mr. Sapsea's infancy and he is therefore fully convinced of its being appropriate to any subsequent era" (ch. 4; 64). The toast has no meaning in the present, and it is typical of Sapsea that its past meaning is one of hostility to the foreign. Just as Sapsea shapes his whole person by imitating the Dean, so does he speak mechanically, reproducing the dead language of cliché over and over, always as if it were fresh, and he the ingenious originator of it. One can make a small collection of his utterly conventional wisdom. In conversation with Jasper he says, on looking for a marriage partner, ". . . as I say, it is not good for a man to be alone" (65). On his wife's death, "As I say, Man proposes, Heaven disposes" (66). Later with Datchery, Sapsea similarly prefaces his words, "As I say, . . . the arm of the law is a strong arm, and a long arm." And the auctioneer refers to ". . . what I call the secrets of the prison house" (ch. 18; 222). He is a man so imprisoned in the past and what has been done and said, that he does not know he is in jail, having no consciousness of any other existence except a hated foreign one. Rather he simply reproduces the past in his person with little understanding and much unintended bizarre effect.

If Dickens creates a large number of characters trapped in the past, he makes Jasper distinct in his response to the problem. The other young people struggle to free themselves, attempting to create independent and free lives in the present so they may influence their futures, and the older ones persist — in sufferance or self-satisfaction at their positions. Jasper feels desperate to liberate himself. He cannot persist, but he makes no attempt to alter the daily monotony that he finds so suffocating; instead he escapes by using opium to attain to a luxurious visionary state. At the opium den he tells the old woman, "When I could not bear my life, I came to get the relief, and I got it" (ch. 22; 270). With regard to time Jasper's use of opium both gives relief and intensifies his problem. Taking the drug does allow him to lose consciousness of a present that feels thoroughly circumscribed, and it gives him freedom to experience whatever he can imagine. Thus, he can indulge all the emotions that otherwise go unexercised, enjoy all the color that is lacking in the gray walls of the Cathedral. If his present feels constricted, in his opium dreams Jasper operates through what he calls "vast expanses of time" (ch. 22; 269). Dickens like Collins in *The Moonstone* equates the "Oriental" unconscious not only with untamed emotion but also with enormous reaches of time, time that stretches back and forth from the essentially timeless primitive.

Yet if Jasper finds freedom in the unconscious, his experience of it oddly mirrors his conscious life, for at least in part his unconscious life is one of endless and exact repetition. He explains to the opium woman that his visions always begin with "a journey" (presumably the killing of Edwin), that indeed his whole purpose in taking opium and the ensuing relief he gains comes from taking that journey. After it come more varied visions, probably including ones of Rosa, but these seem secondary. He tells the woman at her opium den, referring to the journey, "Well; I have told you. I did it, here, hundreds of thousands of times. What do I say? I did it, millions and billions of times" (269). Not only does he repeat the act endlessly, but to the surprise of the old woman, who otherwise understands the pleasures of such fantasy, he always does it in just the same way. The following dialogue takes place between them:

"I'll warrant you made the journey in many ways, when you made it so
often."
"No, always in one way."
"Always in the same way?"
"Aye."
"In the way in which it was really made at last?"
"Aye."
"And always took the same pleasure in harping on it?"
"Aye." (269–70)

Opium provides visions of great interest for Jasper, but it also creates these
in a very narrow, obsessive world.

One can see that Jasper's flight from the present intensifies his ailment in
another way. If Cloisterham is figuratively suffocating, under the influence
of opium it becomes literally so. One feature of the prolonged smoking of
the drug that Dickens stresses is the loss of breath. The old opium woman
suffers from "a grievous cough" (ch. 14; 178); Edwin sees her suffering
from it when she makes her first trip to Cloisterham, and under its influence
she undergoes a kind of seizure in which a "film" comes over her eyes and
she shakes. Edwin has seen Jasper undergo the same process, and Tope saw
it before him. The Verger relates of Jasper at a performance at the Cathedral
that "Mr. Jasper's breathing was so remarkably short . . . when he came in
that it distressed him mightily to get his notes out: which was perhaps the
cause of his having a kind of fit on him after a little" (ch. 2; 41). To employ
Dickens's other metaphor of water and land, Jasper has only a tenuous,
suffocating existence on the land, which becomes all the slighter when he
continuously and protractedly takes to plunging into the water for relief. The
balance of water and land in the man is all askew, and his remedy only makes
it worse, threatening him with complete loss of present time for an amorphous
and shadowy experience of a realm where the great enormous past dominates.

The key moment for Jasper is of course his murder of his nephew; by this
action he brings to a culmination the ill effects of his illusions about time,
decisively severing himself from the present and any chance of the beneficial
change that always is possible in the continuous passage of time. By murder-
ing the boy, he attempts to bring his unconscious life into reality. This is no
longer diving into water but rather an effort to flood the small portion of land
remaining to him. Jasper succeeds in his aim, and the effect is that in a sense
he ceases to exist in time, the present no longer works on him, and he is
exiled into a fantastic and frightening dream world cut off from the reality
of everyday events. In short, he is mad. Dickens symbolizes Jasper's break
with the present time by having the hands of the cathedral clock come off
during the night of the murder — they have been "torn off" by the dark and
violent storm (ch. 14; 183). From this moment on, Jasper's mind is a "horrible wonder apart" (ch. 18; 223). He is fixed only on further bringing his

oriental fantasy world to life and, except for this obsession, is hardly alive at all. Dickens writes that Crisparkle remains open to discussion with Jasper of the mystery, but adds, "The determined reticence of Jasper . . . was not to be so approached. Impassive, moody, solitary, resolute, concentrated on one idea, and on its attendant fixed purpose, that he would share it with no fellow-creature, he lived apart from human life" (ch. 22; 264). If before the murder he wondered whether to enact his obsession and even offered Edwin a veiled warning of the impending danger, afterwards Jasper only thinks of how to accomplish his ends — everything else has ceased to matter.

Three characters are most prominent in Jasper's fantasy life — Edwin, Rosa, and Neville. All the others are only significant as witnesses to be manipulated into confirming the truth of what Jasper would show about the central three. These three all feel the pull of Jasper's effort to drag them into the dark world he has created in his mind, and each one experiences that effort as an attempt to obliterate time.[10] For Edwin the eclipse of the present is most pronounced; he is the busiest character of the three, most in the present of all of them, and just before his murder, he has broken off the restrictive engagement with Rosa — the most prominent way in which he is bound by time past. Thus, the murder directly and physically stops a fast-flowing, changeable, and full current of time. The young man who was just gaining a larger present suddenly has only a past. Just before going to the fateful meeting at Jasper's he has his watch wound and set at the jeweller's — the reader discovers the time is exactly two-twenty. At this encounter Edwin finds out that Jasper has a complete inventory of all his jewelry — his watch and stick-pin. Edwin says he has everything he needs, but the jeweller hopes he might make a future sale: "Still (the jeweller considers) that might not apply to all times, though applying to the present time" (ch. 14; 177). The onward flow of time might change one's needs. Of course, Jasper's knowledge does not apply even to the present; Edwin has already stepped out of the past course set for him and, as a result, carries a new piece of jewelry at that particular present — the ring to be returned to Mr. Grewgious. When Edwin heads toward Jasper's, it is after having heard from the old woman that Ned is a threatened name. He goes to his uncle's amid portentous references to time. After the encounter with the old woman, Edwin finds himself near the cathedral and quite unsettled. Dickens writes, "Alone, in a sequestered place, surrounded by vestiges of old time and decay, it rather has a tendency to call a shudder into being" (179). And when Edwin finally goes to Jasper's door it is with the old woman's words recurring in his mind, the day darkening, and a storm coming on. Dickens writes of those words, "There is some solemn echo of them in the Cathedral chime, which strikes a sudden surprise to his heart . . ." (179). Jasper's attack on the innocent Edwin is no doubt another such surprise, and when the reader next encounters Edwin's watch —

recovered by Crisparkle from under the water at the Cloisterham Weir — it is found that "it had run down" (ch. 16; 199). Time has literally ceased for Edwin.

For Rosa there is a similar contrast, though not so dramatic, between time before the murder and time after. The book begins with her birthday, an event that the usually intent Jasper forgets, and before the murder Rosa moves further forward in time by breaking the engagement. She describes her agreement with Edwin to end their engagement in terms of time, of not being too late. Dickens gives the following dialogue between them, just after they have ended all prospect of marriage:

> "If we knew yesterday," said Rosa, as she dried her eyes, "and we did know yesterday, and on many, many yesterdays, that we were far from right together in these relations which were not of our own choosing, what better could we do today than change them? It is natural that we should be sorry, and you see how sorry we both are; but how much better to be sorry now than then?"
> "When, Rosa?"
> "When it would be too late. And then we should be angry besides." (ch. 13; 165)

Rosa's last thought in separating from Edwin is that she will no longer take music lessons from Jasper. After the murder Jasper's first approach to her is that the music lessons should be resumed — past time should be reinstituted. However, what he proposes is really more radical than that, for what he wants is to detach Rosa from the present altogether by having her enter the world of his unconscious. He reveals to her the essential content of his opium visions — his violent contempt for Edwin, his insane and threatening love for Rosa herself, and finally his determination to make Neville appear the murderer. Though Jasper's words are not completely direct, he fully displays the chaotic emotions that rule his unconscious, all the while attempting to make Rosa submit to his will. During the entire conversation he leans against a sundial, which, no matter what his posture, he covers completely — "setting as it were, his black mark upon the very face of day" (ch. 19; 228) by blotting out a natural expression of the continuing passage of time.

Just as his body blocks present time so the whole effect of his declarations to Rosa is to induce something like an opium fit in her that would remove her from the present into his obsessively restricted realm. I have already mentioned that before him she has difficulty breathing. In addition, soon after her breath becomes short, she experiences another symptom of an opium fit. Dickens writes that "A film comes over the eyes she raises for an instant, as though he had turned her faint" (229). Finally however she breaks away from the man when further frightened by his most violent climactic statements which include a list of "sacrifices" which Jasper offers, including what he calls "my past and my present wasted life" (231). Later, she actually does faint; the faint is very like the condition that Jasper was attempting to induce in that it involves the complete obliteration of everyday consciousness of the present, and Dickens writes that "Rosa no sooner came to herself than the whole of the latter interview was before her. It even seemed as if it had pursued her into her insensibility, and she had not had a moment's unconsciousness of it" (ch. 20; 232). The force of what Jasper has said is not addressed to Rosa's present, awake self, and thus she continues to feel its influence even when that self has entered a state of suspension in a faint.

Rosa flees from Cloisterham and Jasper's vicinity, but for the remaining portion of the novel she exists in a kind of limbo of suspended time, neither retreating nor advancing, neither giving in to Jasper's will nor able to quite shake off his influence in blotting out the present. In exile in London, Rosa experiences two different kinds of time. First, in her encounter with Tartar at Mr. Grewgious's house, she feels a wonderful and confusing pleasure with him which is just the opposite of what Jasper evokes in her. If Jasper poses a danger, Tartar seems a trustworthy person capable of saving her. Both address themselves to her undeveloped emotions based in the unconscious. The encounter with Tartar is like a fairy tale, just as the one with Jasper might be likened to a horror story; both kinds of literature are removed from the actual passage of time in the everyday world, but rather refer only to different internal psychological states.[11] Rosa's title in Tartar's room is "First Lady of the Admiralty, or First Fairy of the Sea" (ch. 21; 248). When Helena across the way in the window of Neville's rooms asks how Rosa came to be at Tartar's window, the young girl replies, "I . . . I don't quite know . . . unless I am dreaming" (249). Rosa feels that her waking consciousness of the present is not operating in this encounter, and her experience in Tartar's room is a sleeping interlude which ends when time intrudes again. She has a similar experience during the outing on the river which climaxes in an Edenic "everlasting green garden" (referring to another kind of timeless literature, that of the early chapters of Genesis before history began with the Fall). When the party leaves the garden, the place seems "unregainable and far away" (258). Dickens writes at the end of Rosa's interview with Helena, "But Mr. Tartar could not make time stand still; and time, with his hardhearted fleetness, strode on so fast that Rosa was obliged to come down from the bean-stalk country to earth and her guardian's chambers" (252).

The above passage suggests that Rosa is pulled back into an everyday experience of time, but this is not the case, for her more prosaic existence is ruled by the principle of "gritty stages" in London when no pleasant gardens are about.[12] Placed between the feuding Mrs. Twinkleton and the Billickin, Rosa finds that in London "everything has a strange and an uncomfortable appearance on it of seeming to wait for something that wouldn't come'' (ch. 21; 258). Rosa is not so much in time as waiting for time to begin operating again — for things to happen. In this restricted state, she lives in literature again — now of a romantic sort. Miss Twinkleton hampers the girl's fantasy by verbally editing the love-stories she reads aloud to her, but finally Rosa discovers books ''of voyages and sea-adventure'' (263), books which address experience in the water, and these Miss Twinkleton will permit her to hear unabridged. Present time is curiously suspended in London for Rosa — Jasper's influence holds back the hopeful developments that began with the dissolution of the engagement to Edwin.

For Neville the rising above his ''antecedents'' follows much the same pattern of Rosa's attempt to win control of present time, but for him the battle is much more closely fought, as he exists so little in the present to begin with, and Jasper constantly subverts him even before the murder. His initial attack on Edwin — very much a regression to his Ceylonese life — occurs under doubly unfavorable circumstances: he unconsciously experiences the effects of the opium that Jasper mixes into the mulled wine,[13] so that he is removed to his former ''Oriental'' state of existence, and he is goaded by Edwin about his oriental origins. During the same scene Jasper insists that, like himself, Neville has ''no prospect'' — no present or future — and soon Neville has lost control of his passions being completely engulfed in the primitive world of the unconscious. Against this unpropitious beginning Neville struggles with the help of Mr. Crisparkle; soon he has the additional burden of not only hating Edwin but also of having fallen in love with Rosa, and thus being further like Jasper. In this condition the best Neville can tell Mr. Crisparkle concerning a softening of his strong feelings is that ''the time may come when your powerful influence will do even that with the difficult pupil whose antecedents you know, but it has not come yet'' (ch. 10; 129). The statement is ambiguous — it both shows that Neville is not essentially changed but that there does exist hope for a future time — something that Jasper would never allow. By the time of the murder the best that can be said of Neville is that he has placed complete confidence in Mr. Crisparkle, and, as he says to Helena, ''I do want to conquer myself'' (ch. 3; 51), that is, to develop a ''Western'' self that can control his Eastern impulses. However, when he goes to Jasper's reconciliation dinner he is in a raw and vulnerable condition — the best remedy for his state that he can devise is to go off on a long hiking trip alone.

When the next day he is detained in connection with Edwin's disappearance, the regression is immediate. Once arrested he walks as a man ''in a dream'' (though one far worse than Rosa's), his waking life seemingly suspended, and under questioning he complains variously that ''I feel as if I had lost my senses'' and ''I seem to be mad'' (ch. 15; 186, 187). Returning to

Cloisterham, three men walk together presenting a kind of emblem of Neville's state of mind. On one side of Neville is Jasper, silent, concentrating, and implacable, and on the other is Mr. Crisparkle asking questions, weighing answers, searching for explanations — continuing in his role as Neville's mentor and instructor attempting to construct a framework of reason around the case by which Neville may support himself. Neville perseveres with Crisparkle's help, but forever afterwards he is a solitary and isolated character cut off from much ordinary human contact. The most important symbol of his condition is that he never goes into the sunlight — the whole time of day associated with ordinary wakefulness simply does not exist in Neville's life. Neville shows high spirits when Mr. Crisparkle visits him in London until the Minor Canon says, "I want more sun to shine upon you" (ch. 17; 209). Suddenly Neville has no spirit left — sunlight seems to him only a medium by which he stands accused and vulnerable; daylight does not provide a time of ordinary intercourse with the world for him. He only ventures out under cover of darkness.

Like Rosa at the sundial, Neville experiences Jasper's doings as a "black mark upon the very face of day" — one which he is so unable to lift that he embraces it and goes on submerged, out of balance, with no hold on the present. Time passes in an alteration of day and night, but Neville always remains in the same monotonous darkness. Neville as a good student tells Crisparkle that "The ordinary fulness of time and circumstances is all I have to trust to" (209). Crisparkle endorses the comment, but Neville's next remark puts it in an odd perspective; he says, "So I believe, and I hope I may live to know it" (209). He speaks as someone not in the flow of time and then wonders if he can experience its "ordinary fulness." That he fears death may intervene is sensible; someone completely removed from experience, outside the passage of time, is very near death already — perhaps in something like the coma preceding it. Furthermore Jasper's haunting of Neville's rooms — as Mr. Grewgious sees — can only have the effect of reminding the young student of the world's accusation, the claim that Neville acted on oriental character traits, which the young man fully knows he possesses, to a sufficient degree to have committed murder.

From the above discussion of Eastern and other connected imagery two directly opposed conclusions may be drawn. On the one hand, we have some material to show how mistaken George Orwell was when he pronounced, "The outstanding, unmistakeable mark of Dickens' writing is the *unnecessary detail*" (Orwell 59). Quite the contrary, the more closely one studies the detail of this novel, one finds the smallest points are significant. That Rosa takes a Turkish sweetmeat, that John Jasper forgets her most recent birthday, that Sapsea puts his finger on merchandise to be auctioned, that Lt. Tartar is an expert swimmer, that Mr. Grewgious mistakes Rosa for her mother, that

Edwin gets his watch wound and set are small points along with hundreds of others, yet as one reads and rereads, all these points leap into prominence and establish patterns of meaning throughout the book until the text, unfinished as it is, seems quivering and pulsing with life. The Eastern imagery has been woven into a consistent fabric, in which each point informs the rest, and it is also connected to other webs of interlinked imagery, giving the novel an intense, almost feverish, quality.[14] The book is in fact the work of an extraordinary artist of the specific, necessary detail.

On the other hand, the study of the Eastern imagery reveals another side of Dickens: that the great artist was also a conventional man of his times, accepting many of its stereotypes and received opinions with little critical sense. In short, he dealt in the broadest, most foolish sort of generalizations. The imagery that Dickens employs with such subtlety is drawn from a few popular clichés as persistent as they are inane; for him the Orient is a realm that is timeless and unchanging, that is filled with opium fumes, exotic color, and pageantry; it is a place where the emotions have free play. First of all one finds that sensuality, but also cruelty and torture, are practiced there, for life in the Orient, that of ''inferior'' races, is both abundant and cheap. Dickens's use of such imagery was supported by his conventional political views concerning non-European peoples, formed from such experiences as having followed the Indian Mutiny of 1857–58 and the suppression of disorders by blacks in Jamaica by Governor Eyre in 1865 in the English press, and having seen the condition of American blacks first-hand during a tour of the United States in 1867–68. In all three instances he showed contempt and fear of the foreign people of a different race, emotions not so different from those of Thomas Sapsea.[15] We are presented with the paradox of a great artist who could display the faults of one of his grossest characters.

Dickens the ordinary man picked up the received ideas of his time about the Orient, and he assumed that the progressive, civilized, and hard-working West should rule the unchanging and luxurious East for the benefit of both. He thought the results dangerous when this tie was broken or altered towards one of an impossible equality; indeed, outside his novels he tended to become a bit hysterical when he thought this was happening. He also found in this political relationship (which in fact was a temporary one determined by changing relations of power) a metaphor for divided human consciousness (a permanent potential condition of the species). His ideas on human consciousness were not weak or ill-thought out at all, and in developing them in a novel, he used to the fullest the enormous powers of Dickens the artist. In the book, the imperialist metaphor works primarily in one way — rebellion from below leads to the overthrow of normal consciousness and the performance of monstrous actions by John Jasper. However, Jasper is an aberration, and the process that goes so wrong in his psychology contrasts with a healthful pattern

that Dickens surely meant to explore more thoroughly in the latter half of the
novel — one based metaphorically on a vision of just, beneficial rule of the
East by the West.

City College of New York

NOTES

1. One of the best discussions of the links between the two novels is to be found
   in the introductory chapters to Charles Forsyte (42–50). He notes the competition
   between the two men and the origin of their common interest in divided consciousness and the East.
2. Angus Wilson shows how faulty the notion that Dickens was an anti–imperialist
   is (25).
3. For a full account of Dickens's attitude toward the Indian Mutiny, see William
   Oddie.
4. There is a vast literature challenging Forster's account and offering alternate
   ingenious solutions. Indeed, most of the work that deals with the novel has been
   concerned with the question of how the book ends, from 1873, when Thomas
   P. James published a complete edition of the novel with his "Medium's Preface"
   recounting how the spirit of Dickens dictated the latter half of the book to him,
   to the present when the recent Broadway show based on the book offered its
   audience three endings among which to choose by vote. This literature has thrived
   by asking and giving various answers to a series of questions: Has Edwin been
   killed? If not, where is he? If so, by whom? Who is the apparently disguised
   character Dick Datchery? Who is the old woman who sells opium? For an account
   of the many solutions published up to the 1960s see Philip Collins (290–95).
   Interest in the "case" has in no way waned since then. All such solutions must
   ignore or explain away what Dickens told John Forster. I see no convincing
   reason to suspect that Dickens misled Forster or that the latter misrepresented
   Dickens. Forster wrote:

   The story . . . was to be that of a murder of a nephew by his uncle; the originality
   of which was to consist in the review of the murderer's career by himself at the
   close, when its temptations were to be dwelt upon as if, not the culprit but some
   other man, were the tempted. The last chapters were to be written in the condemned cell, to which his wickedness, all elaborately elicited from him as if told
   of another, had brought him. Discovery by the murderer of the needlessness of
   the murder for its object, was to follow hard upon commission of the deed; but
   all discovery of the murder was to be baffled till towards the close, when by
   means of a gold ring which had resisted the corrosive effect of the lime into
   which he had thrown the body, not only the person murdered was to be identified
   but the locality of the crime and the man who committed it. So much was told
   to me before any of the book was written; and it will be recollected that the ring,
   taken by Drood to be given to his betrothed only if their engagement went on,
   was brought away with him from their last interview. Rosa was to marry Tartar,
   and Crisparkle the sister of Landless, who was himself, I think, to have perished
   in assisting Tartar finally to unmask and seize the murderer. (Forster 3: 425–26)

As good an argument as any that Forster is unreliable may be found in Forsyte (27–36).

5. See Wilson's use of this argument in the chapter on Dickens in *The Wound and the Bow*. A good account of the pros and cons is in Wendy S. Jacobson. She concludes there is no compelling reason to accept the notion that Jasper is a Thug. William M. Burgan suggests that Jasper is not literally a Thug but is characterized with imagery that links him to Thuggee just as Grewgious is similarly linked to Masonry.

6. For good discussions of water imagery see Ina Rae Hark and Charles Mitchell.

7. Roussel points out the unfinished nature of the various characters and argues, incorrectly I believe, that they will remain so. The imperial combination of West and East provides an image of a union Roussel takes to be impossible, one that would realize Grewgious's notion of a "globular lover" who would unite dreams of fantasy with acceptance of reality. As I argue above this union was to be accomplished in the marriages with which, as Forster wrote, the novel was to end. Rosa's fantasy life is quite distinct from Jasper's and has a distinct goal. Roussel fails to make this distiction.

8. See Roussel (384) on how Edwin and Rosa are held in the past.

9. See Roussel (391) and Mitchell (232) on the various ways that Sapsea acts as a repetition of what has gone before. In what follows I've pointed out some additional ways.

10. For partial discussions of ways Jasper kills time, see Paul Gottschalk and Stephen Franklin.

11. See Roussel (392–94), who points out the timeless nature of fairy tales and the fantasies they contain.

12. I think Roussel goes wrong on this; see his article (392).

13. Jasper's drugging of the wine would explain its excessive effect on both Edwin and Neville.

14. Some other connected imagery is that of doubles, that of vegetation and its cycles, and that related to the artist.

15. Here is a sampling from Dickens's letters. On the Indian Mutiny and particularly the Kanpur Massacre, he wrote in October 1857:

> And I wish I were Commander in Chief in India. The first thing I would do . . . would be to proclaim . . . that I considered my holding that appointment by leave of God, to mean that I should do my utmost to exterminate the Race upon whom the stain of the late cruelties rested . . . and that I was there for that purpose . . . to blot it out of mankind and raze it off the face of the Earth. . . . (*Letters* 2: 889)

On the Jamaican disturbances, he wrote in November 1865:

> That platform-sympathy with the black — or the Native, or the Devil — afar off, and that platform indifference to our own countrymen at enormous odds in the midst of bloodshed and savagery, makes me stark wild. . . .

And he goes on, "the whites might have been exterminated, without a previous hint or suspicion that there was anything amiss" (qtd. in Kaplan 481).

On American blacks he wrote in January 1868:

The melancholy absurdity of giving these people votes . . . would glare at one out of every roll of their eyes, chuckle of their mouths, and bump in their heads, if one did not see . . . that their enfranchisement is a mere party trick to get votes. (*Letters* 3:618)

WORKS CITED

Burgan, William M. "Masonic Symbolism in *The Moonstone* and *The Mystery of Edwin Drood.*" *Dickens Studies Annual* 16 (1987): 257–303.

Collins, Philip. *Dickens and Crime*. 2nd ed. London: Macmillan, 1965.

Dickens, Charles. *The Letters of Charles Dickens*. 3 vols. Ed. Walter Dexter. London: Nonesuch P, 1938.

———. *The Mystery of Edwin Drood*. Harmondsworth: Penguin, 1974.

Duffield, Howard. "John Jasper — Strangler." *American Bookman* 70 (Feb. 1970): 581–88.

Forster, John. *The Life of Charles Dickens*. 3 vols. Boston: Estes and Lauriat, 1872–73.

Forsyte, Charles. *The Decoding of "Edwin Drood"*. London: Gollancz, 1980.

Franklin, Stephen. "Dickens and Time: The Clock without Hands." *Dickens Studies Annual* (1975): 1–35.

Gottschalk, Paul. "Time in *Edwin Drood.*" *Dickens Studies Annual* (1970): 265–72.

Hark, Ina Rae. "Marriage in the Symbolic Framework of *The Mystery of Edwin Drood.*" *Studies in the Novel* 9.2 (Summer 1977): 154–68.

James, Thomas P. "Medium's Preface." *The Mystery of Edwin Drood*. Brattleboro: T. P. James, 1873.

Jacobson, Wendy S. "John Jasper and Thuggee." *Modern Language Review* 72.3 (July 1977): 526–37.

Johnson, Edgar. *Charles Dickens: His Tragedy and Triumph*. 2 vols. Boston: Little Brown, 1965.

Kaplan, Fred. *Dickens, A Biography*. New York: Morrow, 1988.

Mitchell, Charles. "*The Mystery of Edwin Drood*: The Interior and Exterior of Self." *ELH* 33.2 (June 1966): 228–46.

Oddie, William. "Dickens and the Indian Mutiny." *Dickensian* 68.1 (January 1972): 3–15.

Orwell, George. *Dickens, Dali and Others*. New York: Harcourt, Brace and World, 1946.

Roussel, Roy. "The Completed Story in *The Mystery of Edwin Drood.*" *Criticism* 20.4 (Fall 1978): 383–402.

Wilson, Angus. "Introduction." *The Mystery of Edwin Drood by Charles Dickens*. Harmondsworth: Penguin, 1974.

Wilson, Edmund. *The Wound and the Bow*. New York: Oxford UP, 1947.

OBSERVATION AND DOMINATION IN HARDY'S *THE WOODLANDERS*

By Cates Baldridge

CONTRARY TO A LONG-STANDING consensus, *The Woodlanders* does not lack either the specificity or the contemporary relevance of *The Mayor of Casterbridge* or *Tess of the d'Urbervilles* in its depiction of those aspects of modernity which threaten the traditional rural community. True, at first glance Fitzpiers and Charmond seem to bear a stronger resemblance to the rakes and adventurers of previous literary genres than to bourgeois entrepreneurs and industrialists such as Farfrae and Alec Stoke-d'Urberville — that is, they appear to be, like Sergeant Troy, antagonists from an earlier, less politically engaged phase of Hardy's career. Furthermore, the fact that the novel was begun and abandoned just after *Far From the Madding Crowd* in the mid eighteen–seventies and then taken up again over a decade later in an unknown state of completion has encouraged the tendency of critics to label it an anomaly among Hardy's later productions. It is my contention, however, that by looking at *The Woodlanders'* oft-noted concern with observation (Miller 109–11; Boumelha 111; Gregor, "Introduction" 12–14; Thesing 44–52) from a Foucauldian perspective, we shall discover that the interlopers bring to the woodlands various attitudes toward the act of seeing which are intimately bound up with the advent of modernity. I do not refer merely to the new physical means of observation facilitated by Fitzpiers's scientific apparatus, but rather to a pervasive orientation toward the fundamental purposes and effects of viewing in all its forms — an orientation which insures the destruction of the traditional community.

Michel Foucault discusses this distinctly modern complex of attitudes concerning what can be extracted from an act of observation when, in tracing Europe's transition from an early-modern to what he terms a "carceral" society, he notes that

> side by side with the major technology of the telescope, the lens and the light beam, which were an integral part of the new physics and cosmology, there

191

were the minor techniques of multiple and intersecting observations, of eyes
that must see without being seen; using techniques of subjection and methods
of exploitation, an obscure art of light and the visible was secretly preparing a
new knowledge of man. (171)

As we shall discover, it is precisely such a new and "obscure art of light
and the visible" which woodland natives like Giles and Marty are unfamiliar
with, for they bring to the act of observation much different preconceptions —
preconceptions which Hardy explicitly links with their endangered traditionalism. Conversely, Fitzpiers and Charmond come upon the scene already fully
inhabiting a conception of seeing which takes for granted that observation
always and everywhere produces a "knowledge of man" indispensable to
the acquisition and maintenance of power. By invoking Foucault I do not
mean to suggest that Hardy represents Fitzpiers as attempting to impose
anything very close to a regime of carceral discipline upon Little Hintock. I
do, however, argue that some of the "technologies of the visible" which
Foucault identifies as indispensable to modern bureaucracies of surveillance
are also perceived by Hardy to be the hallmarks of modernity's attack upon
Little Hintock, and that Foucault's enterprise can thus be helpful in defining
more precisely what, in the 1880s, was topical and relevant about the disruptive forces which Fitzpiers embodies.

If we first turn to Marty and Giles's many *un*observed acts of surveillance — acts in which their concealed position would seem to offer these
woodlanders some sort of advantage — and focus especially upon the immediate effects of those acts, we discover a curious pattern: such seeing almost
always serves to confirm disabling beliefs the pair already hold concerning
their prospects, casting water upon any incipient sparks of ameliorative action
and insuring their continued economically subordinate and erotically powerless position among the text's various protagonists. Early on, for instance,
Marty — concealed by chance behind a hedge — observes Melbury and his
wife conversing about the timber merchant's plan to steer Giles and Grace
into marriage as reparation for his own amorous chicanery in years past. His
wife, soothing her husband's fears about the match, assures him that though
Giles is poor, "love will make up for his want of money" for "he adores
the very ground she walks on" (Hardy 56). Marty "start[s]" at the news yet
cannot help but listen until all is out, whereupon she exclaims that she "had
half thought" such was the state of affairs all along and departs while uttering
a despairing self–confirmation of her worst fears: "And Giles Winterborne
is not for me!" (58). The palpable effect of this conclusion drawn from her
surveillance is precipitous, for she returns home and immediately acquiesces
to Barber Percomb's demand that she cut off her hair in order that Mrs.
Charmond might have a wig. This defacement will go far toward insuring

that she never escapes the very spinsterhood she laments, as indicated by the narrator's assessment that Marty boasts "but little pretension to beauty, save in one prominent particular — her hair" (48). Indeed, Marty herself has already admitted as much, telling Percomb that she "value[s her] looks too much to spoil 'em" (51). As Pamela Jekel points out, Marty's role in the remainder of the novel remains that of a passive and resigned spectator (151–52) who gains nothing from her stoic watching beyond successive confirmations of her melancholy presuppositions.

In like manner, Giles's acts of surveillance serve only to render stillborn any chance of his romantic fulfillment or upward mobility. Upon bringing Grace home to her father's house from Sherton Abbas, he finds himself gazing through the parlour window at the family reunion:

> The fire was as before the only light, and it irradiated Grace's face and hands so as to make them look wondrously smooth and fair beside those of the two elders; shining also through the loose hair about her temples as sunlight through a brake. Her father was surveying her in a dazed conjecture, so much had she developed and progressed in manner and in stature since he last had set eyes on her. (86)

What is also typical about this episode, however, is the freezing effect Giles's peering has upon him, for "observing these things Winterborne remained dubious by the door, mechanically tracing with his fingers certain timeworn letters carved in the jambs." This hesitation quickly turns to a negative resolve: "No, he declared to himself, he would not enter and join the family; they had forgotten him." As he walks away, we are told that he is "a little surprised" that his efforts have met with "such indifference as this," and while the narrator confirms that the Melburys are in fact talking upon subjects "in which he ha[s] no share," the point is that Giles has, on the basis of his brief observation, preemptively precluded the most obvious method of remedying the situation — that of entering the house and joining in the conversation. Instead, Winterborne wanders off, uttering an unheard lament quite similar to Marty's: "He hazarded guesses as to what Grace was saying just at that moment, and murmured, with some self-derision, 'nothing about me!' " (86–87).

Variations on the above occur throughout the novel's first half. On a winter morning Giles unobtrusively follows Grace and Melbury to a woodland timber auction, whereupon he takes up position behind the pair in order to survey "how one [snow]flake would sail downward and settle on a curl of [Grace's] hair, and how another would choose her shoulder, and another the edge of her bonnet." This operation unfortunately takes up "so much of his attention that his biddings [proceed] incoherently" — to the extent that he possesses "no idea whether he [has] bought faggots, poles, or logwood." Only after the auction is over does Giles realize that he has all the while "been unwittingly bidding against [Grace's] father, and picking up his favourite lots in spite of him" (95–96). Winterborne's brand of surveillance, then, is here, as elsewhere, anything but an efficient tool for gaining insight or advantage. Indeed, the process seems to distract rather than inform him, to be a passive rather than an active undertaking, and one which leaves him worse off than before.

That evening — the one preceding Grace's visit to Mrs. Charmond at Hintock House — Giles approaches Melbury's dwelling and observes "Grace lighting several candles, her right hand elevating the taper, her left hand on her bosom, her face thoughtfully fixed on each wick as it kindled, as if she saw in every flame's growth the rise of a life to maturity" (97). Upon talking to her father and discovering what has "led Grace Melbury to indulge in a six-candle illumination" (99), he suddenly balks at the prospect of speaking with her, even as Melbury gives the most promising of declarations:

> As Giles remained in thought without responding, Melbury continued: "But I'll call her downstairs."
> "No, no; don't do that, since she's busy," said Winterborne.
> Melbury, feeling from the young man's manner that his own talk had been too much at Giles and too little to him, repented at once. His face changed and he said, in lower tones, with an effort: "She's yours, Giles, as far as I am concerned."
> "Thanks — my best thanks, sir. But I think since it is all right between us about the biddings, that I'll not interrupt her now. I'll step homeward, and call another time." (98)

Once again, an act of observation convinces Giles that there is no use in talking, with the result that his suit remains cold.

When Winterborne makes observations in the company of Fitzpiers, his fecklessness — and its probable deleterious consequences — become doubly evident. This first occurs when Giles, perceiving Grace coming down the road fresh from her visit to the manor, also descries the doctor "quizzing her through an eyeglass" (107–8). Winterborne, coming up beside her, wonders whether he should alert her to the fact that she has been the object of this more than casual examination but "decide[s] in the negative" (109) and holds his tongue. Later, when a similar conjunction of Giles's and the doctor's observations occur, the narrator goes out of his way to paint Winterborne as helpless before Fitzpiers's more efficacious peering. The latter has picked up Giles for company on a midnight medical call, and as they return to Little Hintock Winterborne's inability to thwart his companion's gaze is cast in Biblical terms:

> They had reached the top of Hintock Lane or Street, if it could be called such where three-quarters of the roadside consisted of copse and orchard. One

of the first houses to be passed was Melbury's. A light was shining from a bedroom window facing lengthwise of the lane. Winterborne glanced at it, and saw what was coming. He had withheld an answer to the doctor's inquiry, to hinder his knowledge of Grace. But "who hath gathered the wind in his fists? who hath bound the waters in a garment?" — he could not hinder what was doomed to arrive and might just as well have been outspoken. (166–67)

Much, of course, has been written about Winterborne's almost perverse passivity (see Giordano 143–50; Thurley 106–10; Williams 167), but what I have here attempted to emphasize is how closely this seeming helplessness is bound up with acts of observation that one might commonsensically expect to be helpful rather than otherwise. Furthermore, as the above examples show, it is simply not the case that Giles is chronically presented with inherently disheartening *objects* of scrutiny. Rather, there seems to be — for him — something intrinsic to the *act* of observation itself which renders the process inimical to the accumulation of power. He peers closely, but is never the gainer; he observes minutely, but learns only the lessons of passive resignation. As we shall later discover, this complex of attitudes and expectations is intimately connected to Winterborne's knowledge of, and intercourse with, his anachronistic woodland demesne.

In direct contrast to Winterborne's clandestine observations, those of Fitzpiers tend to empower the doctor and lay the groundwork for future action. This difference can be seen most clearly in his surveillance of Suke Damson, Marty, and Grace as they all attempt to pass through the newly-painted gate visible from Fitzpiers's parlour window. Suke, her "skirts tucked up and her hair wild . . . grasp[s] the gate without looking," a misstep which draws from her "an exclamation in language not too refined" and prompts a roll in the grass to remove the stain. " 'Ha, ha, ha!' laugh[s] the doctor" (161) as if already anticipating his own amorous encounter with this "hoyden" on Midsummer's Night. The next subject to pass through is Marty, she too staining her clothes — in this case mourning garb — by brushing against the planks. Her fatalism bred of unrequited love is plainly displayed to the watching Fitzpiers as he observes her to be "little surprised" and to wipe off the "disfigurement with an unmoved face and as if without abandoning her original thoughts" (161). Grace is the final passer-by, and even before she reaches the gate the doctor perceives that she walks "as delicately as if she had been bred in town and as firmly as if she had been bred in the country," and that her bearing generally is that of one who knows "her appearance to be attractive" but who charmingly forgets this fact "in a general pensiveness" (162). Although his best guess is that the woman in question is Mrs. Charmond rather than Grace, the quickness with which Edred surmises the key personality traits of two future lovers stands in stark contrast to Winterborne's visual exercises in futility. Indeed, the most striking thing about the above observations is their blatantly *instrumental* nature, as if the doctor were constructing a zoology of the local females — and ranking them according to their probable usefulness to himself.

Fitzpiers's employment of the parlour window as a *camera obscura* is merely one instance within a larger enterprise, for it is suggested from the first that Fitzpiers is bringing to Little Hintock a different species of observation altogether — one which the natives are unfamiliar with, and which in important aspects far surpasses their own. The doctor surveys Grace "through an eyeglass," but this is hardly the only artificial aid to scrutiny he has at his disposal. Grace, on her first night home, notices the light which burns into the wee hours from Edred's laboratory. At first it is remarkable only because of its persistence, but her curiosity is soon "widely awakened" when the light "gradually changed colour, and at length shone blue as sapphire. Thus it remained several minutes, and then it passed through violet to red." Such a phenomenon, we are told, is "no less than a marvel in Hintock," and the narrator goes on to underscore how utterly alien this new form of illumination is to the isolated village: "Almost every diurnal and nocturnal effect in that woodland place had hitherto been the direct result of the regular terrestrial roll which produced the season's changes; but here was something dissociated from these normal sequences, and foreign to local knowledge" (88–89). Fitzpiers's light, because it stands against nature rather than arising from it, because its function is to investigate the natural rather than to stand as a marker of man's acquiescence before its supposedly immutable rhythms, appears instantly formidable: it constitutes indeed a new "art of light and the visible." And it is not long, of course, before Little Hintock learns that the doctor in fact means to practice surveillance in a decidedly "unnatural" manner, by peering beneath nature's curtain of flesh and exposing to view the minutiae of Grammer Oliver's and John South's brains. Grammer herself declares that Fitzpiers's eyes "seem to see as far as the north star" (90), though eventually she comes to be frightened at the prospect of such an unprecedentedly searching gaze being turned upon her own body and begs Grace to "save a poor old woman's skellington from a heathen's chopper" (170). Later, when Grammer comes to forecast Giles and Grace's marriage, she phrases it in words which emphasize the doctor's aggressive inquisitiveness, his "X-ray vision" if you will: "Instead of my skellinton he'll carry home her living carcase before long" (195). Put succinctly, Fitzpiers makes good on his promise to "inaugurate a new era forthwith" (149) amidst the woodlands.

The above passages pertain to the fact that Edred Fitzpiers is an amateur scientist, but merely labelling the new complex of attitudes he brings to the act of seeing as "Baconian" or "the scientific method" is at best incomplete and perhaps misleading. Rather, it is better understood as what Foucault, referring to the hallmark technique of modern disciplinary institutions, labels "the uninterrupted play of calculated gazes" (177). To live under such a regimen is to recognize that the gaze of the observer is inseparable from the exercise of power — to understand that it is in fact a *projection* of power in the same instant that it remains a method for amassing the information which makes possible the continued exercise of power. Thus the unadorned, unaccompanied gaze itself attains an unprecedented power to chasten, to terrify, and to control:

> He who is subjected to a field of visibility, and who knows it, assumes responsibility for the constraints of power; he makes them play spontaneously upon himself; he inscribes in himself the power relation in which he simultaneously plays both roles; he becomes the principle of his own subjection. By this very fact, the external power may throw off its physical weight; it tends to the non–corporal; and, the more it approaches this limit, the more constant, profound and permanent are its effects: it is a perpetual victory that avoids any physical confrontation and which is always decided in advance. (202–3)

Foucault's assertion will prove helpful as we turn to those episodes in which the characters are knowingly beneath one another's gaze, for in a significant number of these the objects of scrutiny fall into what can only be described as "weird seizures" wherein their will and even their rationality seem to mysteriously desert them. The first, and doubtless the most striking, of these encounters occurs between Fitzpiers and Grace when the latter comes to petition Edred to revoke his bargain with Grammer Oliver and is unwittingly admitted to the room in which the doctor is sleeping upon the couch. Grace, unwilling to awaken him herself, turns around to reach for the bell-pull, catching as she does the doctor's reflection in a mirror:

> An indescribable thrill passed through her as she perceived that the eyes of the reflected image were open, gazine wonderingly at her. Under the curious unexpectedness of the sight she became as if spell–bound, almost powerless to turn her head and regard the original. However, by an effort she did turn, when there he lay asleep the same as before.
> Her startled perplexity as to what he could be meaning was sufficient to lead her to abandon her errand precipitately. (176)

Even though Fitzpiers is not (as one might initially suppose) shamming sleep, the important point is that Grace seems to believe she is — given the unusual circumstances — being actively spied upon, for she reacts in a way which, as we shall find, is typical of those who feel themselves under the kind of "calculated gaze" discussed above. Thus the heroine experiences an "indescribable thrill" and a "startled perplexity," and she is "almost powerless to turn her head and regard the original." This "spell-bound" state of disorientation and weakness is, as Foucault suggests, the reaction to be expected of any individual who suddenly feels herself under the weight of a stare which she somehow understands to be first and foremost an instrument of power, a device for classifying, analyzing, and thereby subduing the person being scrutinized. Such a gaze cannot help but weaken those it plays upon, for by its very nature it objectifies them — turning them into (or rather defining them as) a phenomenon to be studied rather than a person to be encountered. During such acts of seeing, the direction of sight is always and inevitably "downward" from observer to observed.

That Grace, even as the recipient of affection, should be a mere "object" in the sense discussed above, is implied in Fitzpiers's own philosophy of love. As the doctor explains to Winterborne, "love" is simply "a joy accompanied by an idea which we project against any suitable object in the line of our vision, just as the rainbow iris is projected against an oak, ash, or elm tree indifferently." He goes on to admit that "if any other young lady had appeared instead of the one who did appear, [he] should have felt just the same interest in her, and have quoted precisely the same lines from Shelley about her, as about this one [he] saw" (165). Under such a conception, the objects of even the fondest glances are by definition interchangeable, and the being surveyed is robbed of her selfhood by being defined as a mere "conductor" for the "emotive fluid" of the brain. Indeed, at times the objects seem to be in danger of vanishing altogether, as when Fitzpiers declares himself to be in love only with "something in [his] own head, and no thing-in-itself outside it at all" (165). This leads Ian Gregor to label Fitzpiers a kind of solipsist, since he is "incapable of feeling the reality of any world outside himself, whether it is the woods or the people who live there. In common with Mrs. Charmond he sees that world as composed of discrete objects, existing for his own purposes, and where he puts down money for Grammer Oliver's brain, she puts it down for Marty's hair" (*Great Web* 151). I would supplement this remark only by pointing out that what Gregor sees as a moral failing specific to Fitzpiers, Foucault describes as an endemically modern method of approaching *all* acts of observation, and that this way of looking at the doctor seems truer to Hardy's ironic point about the individual's relationship to historical forces: the doctor is only a paltry Mephistopheles, yet the way of life he represents will lay waste the benign traditionalism of Little Hintock in short order.

Grace, for her part, certainly responds to Edred's gaze as if she were under the sway of "a power that seems all the less 'corporal' in that [,being visual,] it is more subtly 'physical' " (Foucault 177), for in his presence she exhibits a puzzling stupor, as if the mere touch of his vision were enough to rob her of the ability to resist and indeed of much of her higher faculties. Even before the doctor's courting has begun in earnest, she experiences "a premonition that she could not resist him'' and, in the weeks that follow their initial encounter, finds that her suitor exercises "almost a psychic influence" over her, which renders her strangely passive: "Fitzpiers acted upon her like a dram, exciting her, throwing her into a novel atmosphere which biassed her doings until the influence was over, when she felt something of the nature of regret for the mood she had experienced'' (210). This influence is later described as an "intoxication" which "cause[s] her to float with the current" before the "coercive, irresistible Fitzpiers" (216). Significantly, this state of stupefaction is not one which causes Grace to feel particularly intimate with her fiancé — rather, it seems only to emphasize the inequities of power which already exist within their relationship due to the difference in class:

> He left her at the door of her father's house. As he receded and was clasped out of sight by the filmy shades he impressed Grace as a man who hardly appertained to her existence at all. Cleverer, greater than herself, one outside her mental orbit, as she considered him, he seemed to be her ruler rather than her equal, protector, and dear familiar friend. (219)

In *The Woodlanders*, then, power often seems inversely tied to visibility, and to be watched is frequently to be weakened. As Foucault has demonstrated, this state of affairs is an important signature of the advent of modernity:

> In traditional forms of power, like that of the sovereign, power itself is made visible, brought out in the open, put constantly on display. The multitudes are kept in the shadows, appearing only at the edges of power's brilliant glow. Disciplinary power reverses these relations. Now, it is power itself which seeks invisibility and the objects of power — those on whom it operates — [who] are made the most visible. It is this fact of surveillance, constant visibility, which is the key to disciplinary technology. (Dreyfus and Rabinow 159)

Thus to say that the text depicts Fitzpiers as employing something like "the evil eye" is to succinctly characterize Hardy's reaction to the disciplinary gaze of the encroaching national culture.

There is another obvious interloper in the world of Little Hintock — Felice Charmond — and if the present argument is to convince, it must explain how she too subscribes to the modern attitudes toward seeing associated with Fitzpiers. At first glance, any useful connection between the doctor and the Lady of Hintock House may seem unlikely, since Mrs. Charmond is not at all the committed observer of her environment that Edred is. Again, though, what is important is not so much *what* one sees as what kind of expectations and assumptions one has about what observations imply for the perceiver and the perceived.

We can begin by recalling that both Charmond and Fitzpiers attempt to buy pieces of the woodlanders' bodies, for it is the nature of Felice's purchase which shows her pertinent affinities with the doctor. Whereas the open doors, unshaded windows, and bright hearth fires of Little Hintock allow its inhabitants to be viewed off guard with some frequency, Mrs. Charmond is almost never observed without her knowledge — all her "viewings" are staged, and Marty's hair is for her merely a prop designed to heighten the effect she will have upon those who behold her. Felice was, before her marriage, an actress, and this detail is all to the point, for "acting" entails a *purely* instrumental attitude toward observation, albeit on the part of the perceived rather than the perceiver. In a theatrical production every pose is struck in order to produce a specific effect upon one's audience. What makes this rather obvious point germane to the novel is that Charmond lives all her life as if she were still upon the boards. When Grace comes to Hintock House, for instance, Felice's entrance has a decided air of calculation about it and is furthermore accompanied by an act of observation reminiscent of Fitzpiers's: "Mrs. Charmond was at the end of a gallery opening from the hall when Miss Melbury was announced, and saw her through the glass doors between them" (100). The Lady's manner, the narrator implies, is carefully studied (101), and we are further told that she is "far too well-practiced a woman" to let an incautious word foil her "idea of making use of this gentle acquaintance" (104). Finally, upon departing, Charmond is keenly aware of the picture thrown back when both she and Grace are before the mirror, wherein "Grace's countenance had the effect of making Mrs. Charmond appear more than her full age" (104), a circumstance which immediately causes Felice to drop her new acquaintance. Later, when Fitzpiers is summoned to Hintock House on the pretext of Charmond's carriage-spill, the curtain rises upon an even more elaborate stage-set:

> Fitzpiers duly arrived at Hintock House, whose doors he now saw open for the first time. Contrary to his expectation there was visible no sign of that confusion or alarm which a grave accident to the mistress of the abode would have occasioned. He was shown into a room at the top of the staircase, cosily and femininely draped, where by the light of the shaded lamp he saw a woman of elegant figure reclining upon a couch in such a position as not to disturb a pile of magnificent hair on the crown of her head. A deep purple dressing-gown formed an admirable foil to the peculiarly rich brown of her hair-plaits; her left arm, which was naked nearly up to the shoulder, was thrown upwards, and between the fingers of her right hand she held a cigarette, while she idly breathed from her delicately curled lips a thin stream of smoke towards the ceiling. (241)

Added to all this is the curious physical situation of Hintock House and Felice's strong antipathy toward the place. In one sense it is almost hidden, for "to describe it as standing in a hollow would not express the situation of the manor-house; it stood in a hole." But this location in fact renders its inhabitants a likely focus of surveillance, for every window in the house can be pierced directly by the eye of approaching visitors. "From the spot which Grace had reached a stone could easily have been thrown over or into the birds'-nested chimneys of the mansion. Its walls were surmounted by a battle-mented parapet; but the grey lead roofs were quite visible behind it, with their gutters, laps, rolls, and skylights, together with letterings and shoe-patterns cut by idlers thereon." Indeed, the edifice sits in a kind of natural auditorium, where "the roots of the trees were above the level of the chim-neys" and grazing sheep look "quietly into the bedroom windows" (99). Hintock House is in fact a kind of reversible Panopticon, in which those without can practice surveillance on the inhabitants and vice-versa, a fact underscored by Timothy Tangs's comic tumble down the slope, precipitated by his suddenly "observing Mrs. Charmond gazing at him" as he takes a shortcut across the lawn "in opposition to express orders" (255). It is little wonder, then, that Felice Charmond dislikes her country house, is depressed by it, and frequently seeks to escape from it. As the narrator informs us, it is no place for those who suffer the "ache of modernism":

> The situation of the house, prejudicial to humanity, was a stimulus to vegeta-tion, on which account an endless shearing of the heavy-armed ivy went on, and a continual lopping of trees and shrubs. It was an edifice built in times when human constitutions were damp-proof, when shelter from the boisterous was all that men thought of in choosing a dwelling-place, the insidious being beneath their notice; and its hollow site was an ocular reminder by its unfitness for modern lives of the fragility to which these have declined. (100)

Felice is thus just as implicated in the instrumental attitudes toward seeing as Fitzpiers, even though she is far more often the observed than the observer. The former actress, like the doctor, understands the act of seeing as one inextricably linked to power, as an operation from which new knowledge and advantage are nearly always to be gained if the transaction is properly engineered.

Perhaps the best indication that this modern "art of light and the visible" which the interlopers practice is not to be narrowly equated with "the scien-tific method" is that the disconcerting power associated with acts of observa-tion is fully present in the relationship between the Melburys and Giles Win-terborne. Grace and her father, of course, are anything but philosophers or scientists, but both of them — especially the former — possess a knowledge of the world outside of Little Hintock, which is unavailable to Giles. Indeed, the heroine is best described as a figure with one foot in the traditional community and the other in the alien sphere of the Victorian middle class, and while it has been pointed out that her education there has been social rather than intellectual (Williams 164–65), it is apparently enough, in Hardy's mind, to have endowed her with a gaze every bit as debilitating to the object of scrutiny as Fitzpiers's, provided only that it is aimed at a native woodlander. Mr. Melbury, as that native enjoying the highest place in the Hintock social scale and the most familiarity with the realm that begins at Sherton Abbas, can boast a similar ability to discombobulate Giles with a penetrating look.

To take a somewhat comic example of this, Winterborne's loss of rationality during his ill-fated Christmas dinner begins as soon as the eye of Grace's father "passe[s] with pitiless directness of criticism into yet remoter recesses of Winterborne's awkwardly built premises" (115) to discover how ill prepared is the host to serve his guests. More embarrassing moments ensue; his despair of impressing — and anxiety over offending — Grace increases, and soon Giles is "presiding in a half-unconscious state. He could not get over the initial failures in his scheme for advancing his suit; and hence he did not know that he was eating mouthfuls of bread and nothing else, and continually snuffing the two candles next him till he had reduced them to mere glimmers drowned in their own grease" (118). By the end of the evening Winterborne has suffered a diminution of his humanity equal to that which befalls Grace beneath the eyes of Fitzpiers, for Melbury "critically regard[s] Giles's person, rather as a superficies than as a solid with ideas and feelings inside it" (120). Mr. Melbury then flouts his family's comparative acquaintance with instrumental observation by declaring that his daughter's "fortune has been told by men of science — what do you call 'em? Phrenologists." He goes on, in a phrase reminiscent of the narrator's concerning Fitzpiers's activities, to assert that Giles "can't teach her anything new. She's been too far among the wise ones to be astonished at anything she can hear among us folks in Hintock" (121).

Giles appears to intuit the debilitating power of Grace's gaze in the famous "Niflheim" passage, where he seems intent upon escaping from her view precisely at the time when her associations with the outside world are being thrown up as the best arguments against his hopes of marriage. As Grace prepares to deliver the discouraging news, Winterborne climbs "higher into the sky, . . . cutting himself off more and more from all intercourse with the sublunary world" until he has "worked himself so high up the elm, and the mist [has] so thickened, that he [can] only just be discerned as a dark grey spot on the light grey zenith" (140). It is at this point that Grace tells him that the "engagement, or understanding" between them is off. Winterborne, answering in "an enfeebled voice which barely reached down the tree" that he has "nothing to say," attempts to render himself completely invisible by sitting "back upon a bough, plac[ing] his elbow in a fork, and rest[ing] his head upon his hand. Thus he remained till the fog and the night had completely inclosed him from her view." The narrator, citing a belief that women are peculiarly open to advances from lovers they have just rejected, speculates that "something might have been done by the appearance of Winterborne on the ground beside Grace. But he continued motionless and silent in that gloomy Niflheim or fogland which involved him, and she proceeded on her way" (141). The passage is striking, for it appears as if Giles were neurotically afraid of the very weight of Grace's eyes upon him, as if he thought that her viewing of him would make her rejection twice as cruel, twice as final. Many critics have pointed to this as one of the most glaring examples of Giles's irksome passivity (see, for instance, Alexander 23; Giordano 146), but on the novel's terms his almost childlike refusal to come out into the open may be justified, for as we have seen, the assessing observation of a woodlander by an interloper seems to induce its own kind of psychic Niflheim, and thus Giles's fear of losing more dignity by descending than remaining hidden above may partake of a touch of wisdom as well as mere cowardice and timidity.

By now turning to the equally famous "Autumn's Brother" passage we can compare in close conjunction the differing results of the woodlanders' and the interlopers' acts of surveillance. The scene opens at an exceptional moment in Grace and Edred's marriage which nevertheless neatly underscores the text's insistence that observation and power relations are inextricably mixed, for as Grace watches Fitzpiers ride away to another assignation with Mrs. Charmond, the peculiarities of time and place combine to turn the tables on the doctor and to make *him* the unconscious target of his wife's scrutiny: "His way was east, the evening sun which stood behind her back beaming full upon him as soon as he got out from the shade of the hill." The fact that he has chosen to ride Darling also facilitates Grace's observations, for "the conspicuous coat of the active though blanching mare made horse and rider easy objects for the vision." Indeed, some moments later we are informed that Edred's "plodding steed render[ed] him distinctly visible yet," and later still we get the following: "the sky behind [Fitzpiers] being deep violet she could still see white Darling in relief upon it — a mere speck now — a Wouvermans eccentricity reduced to microscopic dimensions" (259–61). The phrasing of this last strongly suggests that Edred has momentarily assumed the position he has up till now maneuvered the woodlanders into. The effect of this sight upon Grace is immediate: as soon as Giles has ascended the hill from which she has so long been watching her husband's departure, she addresses her former lover "under a sudden impulse to be familiar with him." This liberation from the hitherto dreamy bondage continues apace:

Her heart rose from its late sadness like a released bough; her senses revelled in the sudden lapse back to Nature unadorned. The consciousness of having to be genteel because of her husband's profession, the veneer of artificiality which she had acquired at the fashionable schools, were thrown off, and she became the crude country girl of her latent early instincts. (261)

The fact that this escape is couched in terms of a return to her spontaneous woodland ways does not diminish her momentary resemblance to Fitzpiers-as-observer, for he too employs his arts of surveillance not to uphold the official moral code of the larger culture from whence he has emerged, but to follow the dictates of his instincts. Thrust by chance into a similar point of vantage (in both senses of the word), we are informed that Grace experiences an "abandonment to the seductive hour," a "revolt for the nonce against social law," and a "passionate desire for primitive life" (262). She, like her husband after his survey of the village women, feels empowered to transgress the dictates of bourgeois respectability.

The same scene, however, finds Winterborne again discombobulated, and again because of an act of seemingly useful surveillance which does him harm rather than good. Walking beside Grace, "looking at her, his eye lingering on a flower she wore in her bosom," he suddenly falls into a reverie:

> Almost with the abstraction of a somnambulist he stretched out his hand and gently caressed the flower.
> She drew back. "What are you doing, Giles Winterborne?" she exclaimed with severe surprise.
> The evident absence of all premeditation from the act, however, speedily led her to think that it was not necessary to stand upon her dignity here and now. (262)

Giles himself is taken aback by his own dissociated state, for "his action of forgetfulness had made him so angry with himself that he flushed through his tan." With "tears of vexation" in his eyes, Winterborne laments what he takes to be his recent mental decline: " 'I don't know what I am coming to!' he exclaimed savagely. 'Ah — I was not once like this!' " What is significant about this scene is that Giles's sleepwalking blunder is the direct result of a previous act of covert observation he committed some days previously — the very kind which garners advantages for Fitzpiers and occasionally for Grace — as he himself explains: "It would not have occurred to me if I had not seen something like it done elsewhere — at Middleton lately." Grace is quick to realize that he is talking about an interlude he observed between her husband and Charmond, and she concludes that "association of ideas" (262–63) has forced him to unconsciously repeat the act. Thus once again, the very practice which so signally aids the doctor's designs — and, what is more, a specific instance of it whose content should by rights significantly further Giles's own prospects — only serves to fill Winterborne's mind with information and images detrimental to his dignity and self-possession. In *The Woodlanders* a little observation can be a dangerous thing, depending upon who one is.

But why exactly *should* the observations of the native woodlanders be so systematically associated with fecklessness and even paralysis? After all, both Giles and Marty are, in a physical sense, highly competent surveyors of the world around them.

> The casual glimpses which the ordinary population bestowed upon that wondrous world of sap and leaves called the Hintock woods had been with these two, Giles and Marty, a clear gaze. They had been possessed of its finer mysteries as of commonplace knowledge; had been able to read its hieroglyphs as ordinary writing; to them the sights and sounds of night, winter, wind, storm, amid those dense boughs, which had to Grace a touch of the uncanny, and even of the supernatural, were simple occurrences whose origin, continuance, and laws they foreknew. They had planted together, and together they had felled; together they had, with the run of the years, mentally collected those remoter signs and symbols which seen in few were of runic obscurity, but all together made an alphabet. (399)

In a perverse way, though, this is precisely their downfall, because the woodlanders consistently associate keen observation with reiterated lessons in fatalism and the stoic acceptance of an adverse fate. In the midst of the forest the Darwinian struggle — utterly devoid of a teleology — is, for those who have eyes for it, everywhere to be seen. There, "the Unfulfilled Intention, which makes life what it is, was as obvious as it could be among the depraved crowds of a city slum. The leaf was deformed, the curve was crippled, the taper was interrupted; the lichen ate the vigour of the stalk, and the ivy slowly strangled to death the promising sapling" (93). Thus described, the natural processes of the forest, which both Marty and Giles know so intimately, appear as a futile struggle of each against all in which it is impossible for any individual to prevail. Habituation to such scenes has bred not horror but an attitude of acceptance toward the iron law of nature, and so the Hintock people watch with mild amusement the "mistakes" of the "more sanguine trees" whose premature buddings are "incontinently glued up by frozen thawings," and they behold the "similar sanguine errors of impulsive birds" whose nests are "swamped by snow-water" in a way which "prevent[s] any sense of wearisomeness in the minds of the natives" (174). Marty, for instance, finds a wry allegory for the futility of human relationships in the misfortunes of the forest birds, for when a roosting couple fall into "a desperate quarrel" and thereby tumble "one over the other into the hot ashes" of the workmen's fire, flying up again "with a singed smell," she is moved to proclaim: "That's the end of what is called love" (192). In like manner the first moanings of new-planted saplings lead her to muse that "they sigh because they are very sorry to begin life in earnest — just as we be" (106). Although Giles objects to this sentiment at the time, we are later told that his own "abeyant mood" upon hearing of Grace's possible divorce springs "from a taciturn hesitancy taught by life as he knew it" (334). This kind of instruction, Hardy makes clear, is lost upon the interlopers, for "these were features of a world not familiar to Fitzpiers" (174). Grace too can traverse copses in which "every object . . . [wears] that aspect of mesmeric passivity which the quietude of daybreak lends to such scenes" — in which a "helpless immobility" and a "meditative inertness . . . [possess] all things"; she can only find such shadings "oppressively contrasting with her own active emotions" (219). The outsiders may observe the forest but never in such a way as might interfere with their exercise of power.

Of course Winterborne is quite skilled at manipulating his environment, and his genuine talent as a woodsman might seem to cast his seasoned observations in just as "instrumental" a mode as Fitzpiers's, though directed at different objects. Interestingly, though, Giles's facility is mainly tactile rather than visual. The profusion of trunks in the Hintock forest radically limits the usefulness of sight, and thus Winterborne, attempting to keep pace with Grace and her father on the way to the auction, is "obliged to follow by ear" (94). Indeed, it is in the nature of branches to be a danger to the opened and directed eye, as Giles must remind Mrs. Charmond's impatient American suitor on Midsummer's Night (202). When Winterborne actually begins to plant, he "seem[s] to shovel in the earth quite carelessly," yet there is "a sort of sympathy between himself and the fir, oak, or beech that he [is] operating on." This sympathy is centered in his hands, for "Winterborne's fingers were endowed with a gentle conjuror's touch in spreading the roots of each little tree, resulting in a sort of caress under which the delicate fibres all laid themselves out in their proper directions for growth." This operation, shaped by long experience, is performed under the shadow of the chronically diminished expectations discussed above: "He put most of these roots towards the south-west; for, he said, in forty years' time, when some great gale is blowing from that quarter, the trees will require the strongest holdfast on that side to stand against it and not fall" (105–6).

Perhaps the most telling indication of the contrast Hardy means to draw between the observations of the woodlanders and interlopers, however, is to be found in the extended metaphor he employs when discussing Giles's and Marty's familiarity with the forest. The pair, remember, has learned "to read its hieroglyphs as ordinary writing," to decipher "those remoter signs and symbols which seen in few were of runic obscurity, but all together made an alphabet." Whereas this text strikes Grace Melbury as possessing "a touch of the uncanny, and even of the supernatural," Giles and Marty observe it "from the conjuror's own point of view, and not from that of the spectator" (399). The diction throughout this passage depicts the forest as a text both ancient and hierophantic, whose secrets are open only to those who have invested long years of arduous study. This choice is telling, for it places the woodlanders and the outsiders in the positions, respectively, of scholastics and empiricists. We have already seen how the observations of the doctor — and to a lesser extent those of the Melburys — suggest, among other things, the operations of empirical science; here then are Giles and Marty appealing with like consistency to the sacred texts of established authority. The forest is, for them, not a mere tissue under an optic but a venerable compendium of wisdom and lore, whose well-thumbed pages endlessly reiterate the vanity of human wishes and the futility of all aspiration. It is little wonder, then, that Giles's observations seems to forestall action and close off possibilities, for Winterborne is merely extending the deeply imbued *habits* of reading he has acquired amidst the bark and leaves of his pervasive surroundings. If he thus exhibits a general fecklessness and "a mordant unwillingness to preen himself to attract and flatter his mate" (Giordano 143) — as witnessed by his balkings after the sightings of Grace through lighted windows — it is because his expectations about the act of observation are closely intertwined with a pessimistic fatalism. In his case, the forest is a kind of parchment even though it is still rooted in the ground, and the message he glosses there must render him passive in comparison to the more empirical and empowering scrutiny Fitzpiers casts upon the Hintock community. For Giles, to observe one's environment is to re-consult an authoritative text which necessarily humbles and discourages the reader; for Fitzpiers, observation is coextensive with the projection of one's desires upon the world. To put it another way, when Winterborne sees, he reads; when the doctor scrutinizes, he is already writing, inscribing his surroundings with his mark.

There is a stark irony in all this, of course, since Hardy's own perceptions of the prospects for effective action are much closer to Giles's than to Fitzpiers's. The situation is nearly identical to that found in the later novels more generally admired, for here, as in *The Mayor of Casterbridge* and *Tess of the d'Urbervilles*, the side which is successfully manipulating and exploiting nature for its own short-term advantage — and thereby destroying the traditional community championed by Hardy — knows precious little about the long-term lessons to be learned from that nature. As Perry Meisel remarks, the interloping culture is composed of "inherently impotent, while circumstantially powerful, forces" (111): Giles and Marty read the text aright, but it harms rather than helps them, for Fitzpiers's breezy *mis*readings imbue him with a reckless and optimistic opportunism which brushes them aside.

We can now say with some assurance, I think, that *The Woodlanders*, whatever its faults, cannot be roundly accused of neglecting to define the nature of the enemy or of presenting the reader with villains who spring wholly from antiquated literary traditions rather than contemporary social realities. Hardy's representation of the "clear and present danger" bearing down on Little Hintock is ambitiously broad, but not therefore vague or diffuse. What Fitzpiers and Charmond (and to a lesser extent the Melburys) are bringing to the rural community is a new and fiercely instrumental conception of seeing — a conception in which sight and power are virtually equated and which posits a malleable world which can be simultaneously interrogated and altered, rather than an immutable one whose glowering face forever commands a passive acceptance of the status quo. To say that the new "art of light and the visible" they bring to the woodlands is nearly synonymous with the Enlightenment is to pun in a serious key, for what renders Giles and Marty helpless before the doctor and his ilk are their antiquated expectations about the relationship between acts of observation and human will. For the former, observing the world functions as a check to hubris, while for the latter it is the indispensable vehicle for making human aspiration manifest. We can say that *The Woodlanders* depicts that moment in the history of encroaching modernity at which, according to Foucault, "the individuality of the memorable man" was displaced by that of "the calculable man" (193). Foucault, of course, is here speaking only of those individuals who are the objects of scrutiny, but Fitzpiers belongs to that peculiarly modern species of men who assume that *all* gazes "calculate" *by definition*, that every individual subjected to observation is always being calculated, and that every observer is unavoidably a calculating entity. Our last word of Giles, on the other hand, paints him precisely as the last "memorable" man, Marty having transposed his life into a chapter within the larger text of the forest, where his ignominious end reiterates the fatalistic message writ large upon the face of the woodlands:

> "Now, my own, own love," she whispered, "you are mine, and only mine; for she has forgot 'ee at last, although for her you died! But I — whenever I get up I'll think of 'ee, and whenever I lie down I'll think of 'ee again. Whenever I plant the young larches I'll think that none can plant as you planted; and whenever I split a gad, and whenever I turn the cider wring, I'll say none could do it like you. If ever I forget your name let me forget home and heaven! . . . But no, no, my love, I never can forget 'ee; for you was a good man, and did good things!" (439)

In the world of *The Woodlanders*, then, an alien and (temporarily) triumphant modernity arrives not amidst coal smoke or dragging a steam thresher, but rather emerges from optics — both mortal and manufactured — whose very composition relentlessly transforms acts of seeing into projections of power.

Middlebury College

WORKS CITED

Alexander, Anne. *Thomas Hardy: The Dream Country of his Fiction.* Totowa: Barnes & Noble, 1987.

Boumelha, Penny. *Thomas Hardy and Women: Sexual Ideology and Narrative Form.* Totowa: Barnes & Noble, 1982.

Dreyfus, Hubert L., and Paul Rabinow. *Michel Foucault: Beyond Structuralism and Hermeneutics.* Chicago: U of Chicago P, 1983.

Foucault, Michel. *Discipline and Punish: The Birth of the Prison.* Trans. Alan Sheridan. New York: Pantheon, 1977.

Giordano, Frank, Jr. *I'd Have My Life Unbe: Thomas Hardy's Self-Destructive Characters.* Tuscaloosa: U of Alabama, 1984.

Gregor, Ian. "Introduction." *The Woodlanders.* New York: Penguin, 1986.

———. *The Great Web: The Form of Hardy's Major Fiction.* Totowa, NJ: Rowman and Littlefield, 1974.

Hardy, Thomas. *The Woodlanders.* Ed. James Gibson. New York: Penguin, 1986.

Jekel, Pamela. *Thomas Hardy's Heroines: A Chorus of Priorities.* Troy: Whitston, 1986.

Meisel, Perry. *Thomas Hardy: The Return of the Repressed.* New Haven: Yale UP, 1972.

Miller, J. Hillis. *Thomas Hardy: Distance and Desire.* Cambridge, MA: Harvard UP, 1970.

Thesing, William B. " 'The Question of Matrimonial Divergence': Distorting Mirrors and Windows in Hardy's *The Woodlanders.*" *Thomas Hardy Yearbook* 14 (1987): 44–52.

Thurley, Georffrey. *The Psychology of Hardy's Novels: The Nervous and the Statuesque.* St. Lucia: U of Queensland P, 1975.

Williams, Merryn. *Thomas Hardy and Rural England.* New York: Columbia UP, 1972.

SIR WALTER BESANT AND THE "SHRIEKING SISTERHOOD"

By Earl A. Knies

THOUGH HIS NAME IS hardly recognized now — perhaps less so than that of his estranged sister-in-law Annie Besant — in his own day when Walter Besant talked, a great many people listened. And he talked incessantly — in fiction, critical essays, interviews, letters to the editor, his eight-year weekly column in the women's magazine *The Queen*, and in the official journal of the Society of Authors, *The Author*, which he founded in 1890, edited, and, for the most part, wrote until his death in 1901. His was a powerful voice for the dignity of authorship and the need for greater parity between author and publisher — a voice so insistent in its accusations of government failure to honor literary figures that Besant was knighted in 1895, ostensibly for his contributions to the dignity of literature. His voice was also constantly raised in support of social causes. His novel *All Sorts and Conditions of Men* (1882) was a major impetus for the founding of the People's Palace in East London, a place where the working men and women of that previously neglected area might add a cultural dimension to their drab lives. A later novel, *The Children of Gibeon* (1886), spoke out powerfully against the "sweating" of seamstresses and raised the consciousness of the English public about the gross exploitation of these women. In *Katherine Regina* (1887) he dramatized the need for proper affordable housing for gentlewomen who had to work, and he was instrumental in founding the Women's Labour Bureau.

He was, in fact, a constant champion of women — at least those women who were forced to work. But he had no sympathy for the "Shrieking sisterhood" (a label he borrowed from Eliza Lynn Linton),[1] those women he thought were advocating a blurring of sexual lines and in the process threatening to destroy the family, which he regarded as the very foundation of society. Sarah A. Tooley, interviewing Besant in 1897, recognized, with some ambivalence of her own, that his attitudes toward women were not easy to pigeonhole: "One may at the outset say that Sir Walter Besant is partial to the feminine type known as the 'womanly woman,' and that he especially admires

211

a woman at home" who finds the joy of love in letting a man work for her and pour into her ample lap "the harvest of his labours." Besant also voted against opening Cambridge degrees to women, yet "he is quick to recognise the absolute futility of telling all women to confine themselves to domestic duties, and wishful to safeguard those who enter professional life against injustice" (109). Besant's ambivalence seems to result from an honest, but far from successful, attempt to come to terms with the changes taking place in women's lives during the last decades of the nineteenth century.

Besant's first notable confrontation with the issue of women's rights came in the 1882 novel (first published anonymously) *The Revolt of Man*. It is set around the year 2100, after the "Great Transition" when "Transfer of Power" from men to women, "the last and greatest step of civilisation," has been brought about by

> the gradual substitution of women for men in the great offices; the spread of the new religion; the abolition of the monarchy; the introduction of pure theocracy, in which the ideal Perfect Woman took the place of a personal sovereign; the wise measures by which man's rough and rude strength was disciplined into obedience. . . . (3)

Parliament now consists of the House of Peeresses, the House of Commons having been abolished because "in a perfect State, the best rulers must be those who are well-born, well-educated, and well-bred" (25). However, Constance, Countess of Carlyon, Lady Home Secretary, is uncomfortable with the rule of women. In her speech summing up the general condition of men in society, she shows that the whole of the educational endowments of the country have been seized for women, that married men with property "have no protection from the prodigality of their wives," that single men's wages are hardly adequate to buy basic clothing; she complains of "the long hours during which men have to toil in solitude or in silence, of the many cases in which they have to do housework and attend to the babies, as well as do their long day's work . . ." (16).

The social structure is matriarchal, even geriarchal, as Katherine Stern (101) has noted. Now men take their wives' names, and titles descend through the female line. Women old enough to be their grandmothers choose young men for husbands, leaving young women to look and long in frustration. In matters of marriage it is "man's chiefest honour to be chosen: his highest duty to give, wherever bidden, his love, his devotion, and his loyalty" (40). Not surprisingly, religion teaches that men are required to obey, that all women are set in authority over them. The perfect man is marked by meekness, modesty, submission, and docility (43).

One might at this point wonder whether this is a satire against demands for women's rights or one in support of them. Constance sighs when she thinks of the men "working at their looms from morning until night, cooking the dinners and looking after the children, while the women sit about the village pump or in their clubs, to talk unmeaning politics . . ." (23). She insists that she does not ask for unconstitutional and revolutionary measures — only "such an education of [men's] reasoning faculties as will make them reasoning creatures. . . . there is more in life for a man to do than to work, to dig, to carry out orders, to be a good athlete, an obedient husband, and a conscientious father" (29).[2]

It is not hard to see why the *Women's Suffrage Journal* called the book "a chameleon-like production, the true intent of which seems as difficult to determine as the colour of the classic reptile in Bewick's fable" (1 Sept. 1882: 137). The *Saturday Review* claimed that the book can be read by everybody who has "the wit to appreciate it with a great deal of pleasure and amusement," while at the same time recognizing it is unlikely to please Miss Lydia Becker or "the unfortunate male creatures whom Miss Becker sweeps along in her sceptered pall." Nevertheless, the reviewer recognizes that the book's attack on women's rights is by no means one-sided: "The author has contrived . . . to insinuate a good deal of criticism by way of back stroke on the less justifiable peculiarities of the existing position of women. An undercurrent of 'How would you like this yourself?' runs all through the book" (53 [1882]: 535).

But despite flashes of sympathy, the weight seems finally to be on the side of disapproval. The women have really made a mess of their power. Parliamentary debate becomes "exchange of unrestrained insults, rude personalities, humiliating recrimination." (The reviewer for the *Women's Suffrage Journal* thought that sounded just like the current Houses of Parliament.) Wise Professor Dorothy Ingleby later admits that "we, who have usurped the power, have created nothing, improved nothing, carried on nothing" (137). "There was a time," she says, "when everything was advanced — by men. . . . We took from men their education, and science has been forgotten. We cannot now read the old books; we do not understand the old discoveries; we cannot use the tools which they invented, the men of old . . ." (142–43).

Besant's real sympathies seem to lie with the young women who long for the good old times, when women ruled at home while men did all the work.

> Oh, to end these weary struggles, — these studies, which led to examinations; these examinations, which led to diplomas; these diplomas, which led to nothing; these agonising endeavours to trample upon each other, to push themselves into notoriety. . . . Oh, to rest, to lie still, to watch the men work! Oh . . . to be worshipped by a lover young and loyal!" (220–21)

The highest function of a woman, the wise professor tells Lord Chester the night before the decisive battle, is to cheer and comfort (305–6). Grace

Ingleby, her daughter, tells Constance that after the revolt women will take their own place — as housewives — and be loving and faithful servants to men. But men will be women's servants in return because love knows no mastery. Nevertheless, man must be the ruler outside the house; the true place of woman is as the mother and wife, the giver of happiness and love (316).

At the end we see Besant's mixed attitudes once more. The men of the middle class are forced out of their homes to become part of the army, and they are a puny, sickly race for reasons that many middle-class women of Besant's own day could recognize:

> they were not allowed to work at any occupation which brought in money, because it was foolishly considered ungentlemanly to work for money, or to invade, as it was called, woman's Province of Thought. Yet . . . they had very little hope of marrying; and mostly they lounged at home, peevish, unhappy, ignorantly craving for the life of occupation. (344)

But women (young women) revert to stereotype. They are pleased that they do not have to go into the professions, that they have no responsibilities and consequently have "unlimited time to look after dress and matters of real importance." The old method of courtship returns, with young men wooing young women instead of elderly women buying young men. The "sweet feminine gift of coquetry" is revived along with dancing, laughter, good books and art, and the old religion which worships the "Divine Man" (352–54). And the earl of Chester is crowned king at Westminster Abbey after his marriage, which *he* proposes to Constance. Everything is just the way it used to be; woman's reign has shown only that woman is not fit to reign and that true happiness and orderly, progressive government result when men and women keep to their proper spheres.

The work was generally well received. The writer for the *Nation* saw it as satire directed against the woman's rights agitation which, "like most satires of the kind, endeavours to turn the cause into ridicule by a picture of some of its probably remote consequences" (34 [1882]: 505). The *Spectator* noted that the reversal of the sexes is as old as Aristophanes, but "the present-day movement in the direction of feminine independence is sufficiently prominent among the social phenomena of the period, to give a raison d'etre to a modern treatment of so ancient a fancy" (55 [1882]: 1383). The *Athenaeum* praised the novel as "a happy idea well worked out," one which must rank "amongst the best literary confections of its kind," and added, "if the implications now and again seem to press too hardly upon certain theories and aims of the present day, few will be so thin-skinned as to take offence at the details of this entertaining and skilful burlesque" (29 Apr. 1882: 537).

The writer for the 1893 series in the *Echo* on "Novels and Novelists" did take offense, however:

> Mr. Besant starts with a prejudice as to woman's position in the world. He is of the old school who believes in her due subordination, and sees in her a pretty ornament for the house, that should wait with smiles and caresses her lord and master, man; not a separate being with a personality of her own to develop. She must not vote. She should not speak. Her proper sphere is the home. And Mr. Besant has maintained his thesis in a clever satire, forecasting a future society where woman rules, but occasions by her tyranny and folly "The Revolt of Man." (N.O.B. 1)[3]

But if Besant was able to achieve an easy victory through fantasy in his novel, he found formidable foes in the real world. He declared on more than one occasion that he was no Ibsenite, and *A Doll's House* was particularly troubling to him — so much so that he joined those who provided alternate endings or sequels to the play. His version[4] begins twenty years after the play ends. Torvald Helmer is now a drunkard who has lost his job in the bank; his eldest son is also an alcoholic, and his youngest son — like his mother before him — a forger. Only the daughter, Emmy, seems to have escaped corruption, and she is beloved by Nils Krogstad the younger. His father is now married to Christine Linde and is a most respectable man: mayor of the town, manager of the bank, the leader in every religious and philanthropic effort. His sons are a professor, a lawyer, an officer of engineers; and he wants Nils to follow him in the bank.

Nora has returned to town for no apparent reason; Christine, learning she is there, visits her and in the process manages to revive in her a spark of feeling for her children. Nora's subsequent visit to Emmy, however, receives such a cold welcome that she does not reveal her name. And as she leaves, Emmy prophetically trembles at the thought of "the ruined home cursed by the sins of her parents" (323). The curse soon becomes clear. Nils's father firmly rejects his son's plan to marry Emmy and take her off to America as a farmer's wife, and when he learns of Emmy's brother's forgery, he offers to let him off if she will give up Nils. Of course she does, then drowns herself, and her body is being brought back as Nora is on her way to the railway station to leave forever. When she learns who the dead girl is, she is moved momentarily but suppresses her emotion: "In a word, Norah Helmer, the apostle of the new and better creed, was threatened with some of the weakness of the ordinary woman; . . . but she was mistress of herself; she rose to the occasion; she became perfectly cold and indifferent." The driver has the last word: "It seems that it is a poor girl who has drowned herself for shame. She had a bad mother and a bad father. It is sad. Madame will be in time to catch her train" (325).

The final lines seem to share the blame, but the whole force of Besant's sequel is clearly against Nora. Torvald's memory of twenty years ago (318) suggests that the deterioration of the family is caused by her leaving. But the scene with Christine makes the point most strongly. Before she enters, the disapproving narrator castigates Nora for abandoning husband, home, and children "to find — Herself." Now convinced that religion is imposture, that the ordinary laws of life are designed to keep women in slavery, and that "the first duty of every woman [is] owed to that something — Herself," she begins to live "the life of perfect freedom" and to write novels that horrify the old-fashioned — novels which advocate abolition of the family and make "love the sole rule of conduct" (320). Nora has become a "New Woman" novelist, joining those writers — male and female — who were trying to invert and subvert the old morality of sexual and marital relationships. But Christine will have none of it: "Norah, no woman ever did a more cruel, a more wicked, or a more selfish thing than you, when you deserted your husband and your children" (321).

The *Spectator* found Besant's continuation "a rather dreary and unattractive embodiment of the author's well-known views on one branch of the great 'woman question' " (69 [1892]: 297). Ibsenites said it was beneath notice, but George Bernard Shaw saw it as having "enormous importance as a representative middle class evangelical verdict on the play" and wrote a sequel to Besant's sequel, "Still after the Doll's House."

In his "Author's apology" at the beginning, Shaw says he assumes people are "familiar with Ibsen's epoch-making play . . . which struck London in 1889 and gave Victorian domestic morality its death blow." He could not, however, claim equal renown for Besant's sequel, written "in the sincere belief that he was vindicating that morality triumphantly against a most misguided Norwegian heretic" (126). But of course there would be no reason to write a sequel/rebuttal to something that hardly anyone had read; in a letter to Charles Charrington, Shaw explained his real motive:

> the ball must be kept rolling on every possible pretext, so that . . . everybody who has not seen the Doll's House will feel quite out of it, especially in the provinces. . . . There will be discussion, and repetition of Doll's House Doll's House Doll's House here, there, & everywhere, which is the desideratum. (*Letters* 1: 239–40)

And what better way than to use the popularity of Besant and his reputation as a spokesman for traditional values regarding the relations of the sexes.

The *Nation's* reviewer of Besant's sequel admits that many worthy people felt consternation lest Nora's impetuous desertion of her husband

> should be widely held justifiable, and establish a righteous precedent. To this is added the author's profound personal alarm. If wives and mothers once begin

to take an interest in themselves, as creatures possessing mind and spirit, who can measure the imminent calamity for society? What is to become of Mr. Besant's social pleasure-house if the heresy of individualism is to insinuate itself into the foundation? Without presuming to belittle the possibility of the gloomy Norseman's vicious effects on British morals, there doesn't seem any reason for being scared out of one's wits about it. (55 [1892]: 436)[5]

But Besant continued his attacks on Ibsen. In his column in the *Queen* for 28 January 1893, he responded to a woman indignant about his conclusion to *A Doll's House* that nothing Ibsen has suggested or advised "has advanced the world a single step. That a woman is no longer to be brought up as a doll, a foolish, pretty, half-educated toy, I have been taught ever since I could read, and that is fifty years ago. To trot out this stale old truism as a new and hitherto unheard of doctrine is absurd." However, it is not Nora the doll but Nora the independent woman who really upsets Besant. "Then we are called upon to admire a woman who, because she has suddenly learned this new doctrine, goes away, abandons the most sacred duties, and leaves her children — her children, mind — to hirelings! . . . I loathe and abhor such a woman." He ends, however, by claiming that he is "always on the side of those who would give every woman as well as every man all the facilities possible for the widest and the fullest education; and I should be a proud man indeed if one of my own daughters would take a better place in the first class than her father could manage" (122).

A few months later (29 April), Besant is attacking the "New Woman" (and Ibsen) in doggerel. "A Woman's advice to Women" a hundred years ago found blessedness in constancy and a sense of duty to him "whom Heav'n has made your choice." Today, however, women are advised to guard their rights by legal deed before marriage, since "no church-made vow / Is thought to bind a woman now." Neither husband nor children should distract the modern woman's mind from high pursuits:

> Forbid it! To yourself be true.
> Let all else slide — excepting — you.
> The noblest, newest, grandest thing
> (Thus the Norwegian sage doth sing)
> Is Freedom. . . . (*Queen* 650)

In the *Queen* for 20 May 1893, Besant cites as a model of womanhood the middle class mother in whom there

still lingers a feeling that it is better — say less selfish — for a mother to give up her maiden efforts at becoming a bad painter or a tenth-rate musician in order to direct the minds of her boys and girls so that they may have a chance of the big prizes of life. . . . The women of the highest development that I have had the honour of knowing have not been the women of Arts, Literature, or Science, but the women who lived for their children. From such work there may spring such a development of the spiritual nature as the Norwegian Sage has never imagined. (798–99)

To find an alternative to Ibsenism in the real world, Besant turned to Judaism for a model. In *The Rebel Queen* (1893), Isabel Albu inherits her father's fortune at the age of twenty and becomes the wealthiest heiress in France. Though she might have married anyone she wanted, she chooses the promising young scientist Emanuel Elveda, a fit mate, she thinks, a man of broad views and generous instincts. Before marriage she had read all the books about the rights of women and expected that a man of science, for whom reason should be stronger than religion, would readily fall in with her emancipated opinions. But their religion, Judaism, rules Elveda's thinking about the relations between the sexes, and when, a month after their marriage, he demands wifely submission, she refuses. A year's trial separation makes both of them more obstinate than ever. To all of Isabel's arguments he has but one reply: "It is the law of the Lord, . . . the woman is subject to the man" (22). And so they separate for good.

Elveda leaves without being told that he is the father of a daughter, Francesca, born during the separation. The girl is brought up believing she is a Spanish Moor, since Isabel wants to cut herself off entirely from Judaism and its belief in women's inferiority. Isabel becomes a leading feminist on the strength of her book *Women in Western Europe*, a bulky treatise tracing the position of woman in Europe from the fourth century to the present time — "a terrible book to those who had time to read it through . . ." (23). Francesca is brought up as a disciple.

The complex plot, full of coincidence, brings Elveda to London, where Isabel and Francesca have settled after wandering the world "observing and working." Elveda does not come in search of his wife, however, but to bring a scientific formula for his friend Harold Alleyne, a young chemist (who, it turns out, is in love with Francesca). Ultimately Francesca learns that Elveda is her father, and at the end of the novel she has rejected her mother's feminism and is leaving to tour "the Land of our Fathers" with Elveda, ultimately to return to marriage with Harold Alleyne.

The book gets its title from a play by Francesca reflecting her mother's teachings. The "Rebel Queen" is Vashti, who refuses to obey when the king bids her come forth to be examined by his friends and all the people, to "learn what manner of woman is she in whom the king delighteth." She strips off her jewels and fine things and flees to the desert. At this point, Francesca's play departs radically from the Biblical account. Vashti's successor, Esther, comes in search of the secret of love because she fears her beauty, and consequently her power, are in decline. She pleads: "If it is only my face that the king loves, make him love that face a little longer." When she leaves, Vashti scornfully declares: "She is but a slave. . . . Only those women are strong who are free. . . . I am the first woman in the world who has dared to disobey her lord. . . . Vashti, who refused to be the slave of man" (39–40).

The play ends with muted hope for the future: "Ye are women," said Vashti, "therefore ye are in chains. . . . the last emancipation of all shall be the emancipation of woman from man. . . . Have patience: the time of freedom shall surely some day come" (41).

Early in the novel Isabel complains about the unequal treatment of Jewish males and females brought about by the belief in the Divine Order, a belief "that the man shall learn everything, do everything, and be responsible"; for the woman there is obedience, which is "the whole of the Law for Woman." With these ideas she was brought up, says Isabel, in spite of her intellect, her gifts, her great fortune; and at first she acquiesced, even though she found it horrible to be the slave "of such men as one sees." Once she went into the outer world where there was a freer air, however, she discovered that "given the pick of women, they can meet on equal terms the pick of men; yes, in science, in scholarship, in anything not requiring your strength of muscle, the woman is as good as the man" (8).

But Elveda prefers his conception of the Divine Order, or "if you please, Nature," to Isabel's evidence, and she sees how pointless it is to go on: "You wrap yourself in the cloak of the Truth Absolute" (9).

The issues are acted out by the second generation as well. When Harold Alleyne proposes to Francesca early in the novel, offering equality in marriage, she replies that a household where husband and wife are equal does not exist and cannot yet exist. "We must educate the world in order to make it possible." In fact, she thinks Harold really wants "an old-fashioned marriage with an old-fashioned wife — a professional wife; a woman who makes her married life her profession . . . and thinks of nothing but her house, her husband, and her family." Harold recognizes "the influence of the Norwegian Sage" in all this, and Francesca continues to express her fears that she might not do justice to herself if she is always thinking about others, that she might be false to herself out of devotion to love. "These ideas are in the air," replies Harold. "Girls catch them as they catch the bacillus of some new disease" (66–67).

Though Francesca rejects Harold's proposal, she is upset by the emotions it has aroused and the sense that her mother's position is falsely based: "You say that I have sat inattentive at your meetings. It is because the subject seems altogether altered. . . . There is a voice within me that keeps on asking the same question, 'If women are the equals of men, why don't they prove it?' '' Isabel suggests that Francesca should read her book again, but she replies that she knows it by heart.

> When we discussed the position and condition of women at Newnham I used to employ your facts and your arguments. . . . They convinced everybody; but, somehow, they moved nobody. . . . We all agreed that we were the equals of man; we would never, never, never show submission to any man. And now I hear that they are all marrying in the usual way without any more heroics about submission. (173–74)

So Francesca moves out of her mother's house to get a complete change of scene and companions, unwittingly moving into the house where her father, under a different name, is a boarder. Even more important, she is exposed to Jewish family values, and while listening to an aged patriarch talk about the happiness brought to him by women who knew their place, she experiences an epiphany:

> before her eyes there arose a vision of four generations — a dozen families, all glorified and made happy by the women who took their place in the household lower than the men yet without rebellion — all made happy by the women. These four generations might stand for all the generations since the world began, this being the Divine Order according to these simple people. (230–31)

Her fear of committing injustice to herself through thinking of others finds no support here. Happiness for women comes through obedience to husband or father, through working for each other rather than themselves. Jewish families are the happiest in the world because everything is ordered according to the Law of the Lord: "The father rules, and the wife and children obey. Christians are miserable because they will not acknowledge the Law" (230–31).

By the end of the novel she has discovered that she is Jewish and gladly accepts a redefined relationship between the sexes: "I have never understood until now how [women's] obedience brings order and happiness into life. Now I have seen it and I know what it means. Oh, women are not the equals of men! Let us cease to fight against the Laws of Nature." She sees Isabel's house as a "Temple of a False God," "a Temple of Religion which shuts out humanity. The preachers are not real women; they must destroy their nature before they can preach and teach these things" (370–71).

In their final interview, Emanuel and Isabel vigorously maintain their original positions. Isabel has lost her fortune and her daughter, but there is a certain poignancy and even heroism in her rejection of his charge that she is still a rebel against the Laws of Nature and the Laws of God: "[C]all it what you like," she replies,

For twenty years I have striven to uphold the equality of woman. . . . I have against me the united forces of religion, tradition, prejudice, and brutality. . . . I have succeeded, however, so far that the world has learned the actual condition of women in Europe, at least. I have shown what the enforced submission of women has led to, over this civilised continent. And I have gathered round me a band of women devoted to the cause of their own enfranchisement. (360)

Nevertheless, Emanuel (and Besant) firmly reject this viewpoint. Instead of a wife and mother contented with the "Eternal Laws of Nature," Isabel has become a rebel waging a feeble war against the "Order of Heaven," a Lilith, a lonely, friendless and loveless woman who has trampled on the Law (362–63).

At the end, leaving for the Holy Land with her father, Francesca believes she has found in nature and God's law a happiness she had never imagined before. The world has grown real for her, "the Passing Show has become part of the Eternal Drama" in which she too plays her humble part. She has her father and cousins, kith and kin, and even patient Harold Alleyne, who will suffer her to be with her father a little longer before she returns, her education completed, to become his submissive wife (388–89).

The reviewers seemed more upset with the didacticism of the novel than with the doctrine. Said the *Spectator*:

A good many of Mr. Besant's books have been pretty well loaded with explicit or implicit preaching, and though we fully sympathise with his views . . . that nature and revelation are entirely wrong in emphasising the difference between men and women, we do not think that any exposition of these views ought to usurp the place of a story. (71 [1893]: 583)

The *Saturday Review* felt that even those who disagree with Mr. Besant will acknowledge "that he has put into the mouth of Mme. Elveda as good sense — if also as good nonsense — as has ever been put forth in favour of the 'great cause' of equality for the sexes — equality in the sense, not of *justice*, but *sameness*" (76 [1893]: 415–16). The topic seemed almost old hat to George Saintsbury. He found Isabel's defeat in resisting her husband and campaigning for the revolt of women "a subject of which Mr. Besant is thoroughly master," but here subordinate in interest to his surprisingly successful handling of the Chosen People (*Academy* 44 [1893]: 388). The woman question was indeed a familiar topic to readers of Besant's novels and essays, but in the works above it received particularly intense examination.

PERHAPS BESANT WAS happiest dealing with women's issues in his weekly column for the *Queen*, "The Voice of the Flying Day," where he had the opportunity to speak as the spirit — and letters from feminists and other more supportive correspondents — moved him. "I believe that a great many gentlewomen read this 'Voice' of mine,'' he announced in his column for 3 August 1895. ''I am told so by correspondents, and I have every reason to believe, with pride and gratitude, that this is the case'' (199). In an obituary essay, W. Morris Colles speaks of ''the flood of letters which [readers wrote Besant] from all parts of the world and upon every imaginable topic of the time . . .'' (960).

Established with Victoria's permission to use the name, the *Queen* was a ''Ladies Newspaper and Court Chronicle'' aimed at those who ''naturally attended Court functions, and those who would have loved to have been invited.'' The two subjects it felt most strongly about were women's suffrage and education, but it was never ''even faintly militant in its feminism. It was a magazine of fashion and etiquette, a social magazine, therefore one that subscribed, by its very nature, to the superiority of men'' (Crewe 7, 53). Until she died in 1898, Eliza Lynn Linton's column followed Besant's each week — obviously no attempt to provide a feminist balance for his voice.

Here he could expect a sympathetic audience for his satiric attack on the woman lecturer in New York who has been claiming, ''among the Sacred Rights of Women, nothing less than the right with a capital R — to be ugly — with a capital U if they please'' (5 March 1898: 398). Besant classes himself with the old-fashioned folk who are delighted by loveliness of face and form, graciousness of manners, and ready sympathy of mind in women. He admits a possibility of a third camp, ''creatures neither men nor women; but the desertions will be frequent, and the camp will speedily fall to pieces. Go on, therefore, Prophetess of Ugliness. Complacently survey thy absence of charms in the largest procurable looking glass.''

His column for 26 November 1892 rendered poetically a report that ''At the Birmingham Conference of Women's Emancipation one lady . . . said that men might be stronger than women, but that women had the use of dynamite as well as men. Men had been women's mortal enemies, and would be for all time to come.'' The speaker, pince–nez clinging to her nose, her voice ''like many files a–rasping,'' calls on women of all ages and marital status to reject the promises of man, who with his strength has knocked women down for ages. But now weapons will bring about equality:

> For his strong arm and iron will, his cunning and resource,
> We can meet with strength of Science, and the might of Nature's force.
> Hear me, Sisters! We will smite him; we will blast and dynamite him;
> We will rend him and affright him and dismember him and slight him;
> We will. . . .

(Here the meeting broke up in confusion, as the speaker produced from a hidden pocket a handful of soft white stuff resembling putty.) (867)

When Sarah Grand published her paper on the "New Woman" in the *Lady's Realm*, Besant replied more seriously. Particularly offended by her portrait of the "Old Woman," he grants that she had no household duties and no learning, but she was "a steady force making quietly for temperance, purity, delicacy, and refinement." The "New Woman" is the "Woman of the Honour Lists," who "claims all knowledge as her right as much as it is the right of men. . . . When she arrives it will be a wonderful world indeed." But she is not likely to satisfy the practical demands of life. If the "New Woman" succeeds in shaping a "New Man," there will still remain the need for the kind of man for the rougher work of the world — and with him will remain his companion the "Old Woman" (*Queen* 20 Aug. 1898: 292).

In fact, "It is not the 'shrieking sisterhood' which has contributed to the elevation of girls — though we must acknowledge the fruits of their persistence — so much as Charlotte Yonge" (*Queen* 29 July 1899: 174). Yonge, he said in his 12 March 1898 column, may not be responsible for the "New Woman," "but she is largely responsible for the possibility of the New Woman; and for the intellectual side, the self-respecting side, the side of study and thought, she is mainly responsible; also, I think, for the aesthetic side. . . . It is an atmosphere of feminine grace and culture." Before Yonge (forty years ago), average girls were ignorant of everything solid and important, considered incapable of serious study or serious conversation: "Meekness, submission, obedience, ignorance of things social, political, historical, literary, artistic — these were the qualities that were expected in women" (444–45).

Yonge might have found parts of this catalogue surprising. In her collection of essays, *Womankind*, she admits that she has "no hesitation in declaring [her] full belief in the inferiority of woman, nor that she brought it upon herself" by being the first to fall and then drawing "her husband into the same transgression" (1). She later encourages women to be strong-minded but not in "a bad sense in discarding all the graces of humility, meekness, and submission, which are the true strength and beauty of womanhood" (240). This "New Woman" sounds very much like Besant's "Old Woman."

During 1893, Besant was preoccupied with the question of women and work. In his column for 16 September he reported pleasure that the *Spectator* was as "delightfully Philistine as myself" on the subject; one effect, it said, is to throw women out of their natural position, "which is to depend on men and make them happier in return" (470).[6] Besant admitted in his column on 30 September that there is "a great quantity of work which can only be done by women — writing work, teaching work, all kinds of work." Such work is beneficial to society if the women do it voluntarily and not out of necessity. But it is "disastrous" when women "invade" the work of men (546). "For," he explains on 7 October, "it halves the wages, and lowers the position of the workers, and it drives men out of the country, or forces them to compete with women at lower pay; it deprives men of their wives, and women of their husbands" (586).

One of his strongest and most comprehensive statements on women's work and the relations of the sexes is occasioned by a woman's complaint that he treats the subject in a "half-jesting manner which is offensive to those who take the subject seriously." Besant turns the tables, charging that many earnest people

> appear to be pursuing the most mischievous course possible. . . . (1) They are . . . stirring up that most unnatural of all hatreds — Sex hatred. This they do by constantly representing men as oppressors; . . . marriage . . . as a condition in which the wife is nothing but a drudge or a puppet; and the interests of women . . . separate from those of men. (2) They rejoice whenever a woman succeeds in turning out a man and taking his place at a lower wage. . . . (3) They perpetually stimulate girls to compete with the man who ought to be working for them; they make them unhappy and discontented with . . . the old works of love and charity and kindness which make so many women's lives one long continual blessing to all around them; and they drive into intellectual or artistic professions too many who are intellectually unfitted for the work.

Besant finds inexpressibly sad the letters which have reached him from all quarters on the subject of women's work, each proclaiming "a mad rush of women into the labour market; and they all proclaim . . . the fact that, unless something be contrived to check the evil, the labour market, which is only kept in order by the nice balance of capital and labour, . . . will speedily become the slave market." This leads Besant to an apocalyptic vision of the future: "a world of women workers, underpaid, sweated, doing work hitherto done by men, condemned to celibacy and to life-long sweated labour. . . . I cannot bear to think of tender women . . . being driven under the lash of the pitiless sweater. . . . Indeed, madam, I am very earnest" (*Queen* 4 Nov. 1893: 748).

Even as he writes the words above, Besant receives by post, he says, a copy of the *Woman's Herald* for 26 October addressed to him. He knows what is coming — "more castigations," and indeed he finds an article marked in blue pencil containing one and a half columns of "the funniest abuse possible."

The humor is difficult to find, but the castigation is pointed enough. "Mr. Walter Besant is once more pressing women to remember — with a view to furthering them — men's interests, comforts, and pleasures, and to forget their own with true womanly forgetfulness.'' The writer is not moved by Besant's pity for "bright young fellows" driven west to that "enormous territory with its boundless resources.'' She prefers that to seeing "bright young girls driven downwards, sunk in slums, or pushed to the wall, either to wear their lives away in want and despair, or in hopeless drudgery and moral misery. . . .'' Answering Besant's assertion that the average woman loathes the thought of entering the labor market, the writer replies that "it stands to common sense that she would not enter it unless compelled to do so; probably she loathes it less than she loathes the marriage laws, written or unwritten, that convert her into a child, a puppet, or a drudge.'' If, as Besant says, England needs to encourage marriage by every means in its power, then let it establish "legislative and moral equality between men and women in every pathway of life; and let the 'Voice of the Flying Day' lend its eloquence to teach men to walk side by side with the other sex, and not to ride rough-shod over it'' (563).

But Besant's comments were not without effect. By 18 November he is happily reporting the receipt of letters from various parts of the country assuring him that "Prophetesses of Sex Hatred'' have made little progress in Great Britain and Ireland. He calls his readers' attention to a letter in another column from Isabel Somerset, co-editor of the *Woman's Herald*, which, he says, puts the case for woman and the part played by men in the "Woman Question'' far more eloquently than he can; he hopes the letter will be read and taken to heart by those "mischievous and malignant'' people who would "bring about division of women into hostile camps and classes'' (830).

Lady Somerset's letter, dated 7 November, begins with an apology for the attack on Besant in her paper while she was abroad. "Knowing Mr. Besant to be not only by profession a novelist, but by performance a philanthropist, I feel sure that he does not wish to deprive any woman of the right to do whatever she can do well as a means of earning an honourable self-support. . . .'' The *Woman's Herald*, she continues, has as its predominant purpose "to seek the things that make for peace, and not for war, between the sexes'' (831).

But noting that women continued to take jobs from men, Besant in his 9 December column calculated the costs: the loss of 10,000 jobs for men and a savings of £500,000 per year in salaries. Men will have to emigrate, and 10,000 families will not be called into existence. Since 10,000 families may account for an average of four children each, the country will lose

the work, brains, productive power, fighting power, colonising power of 40,000 men and women. Putting the productive power of one person at £100, we have a loss in the next generation of £4,000,000 a year. Which is better — to save £500,000 a year; or to secure the services and strength of 40,000 English men and women, reckoned at £4,000,000 a year? (966)

Besant does not, however, explain what services these potential new workers would perform if there is a shortage of work now; they (especially the women), it seems, would just contribute to the problem.

Why do women work? In his column for 14 October 1893, Besant lists the six principal reasons:

> 1. Because their intellectual activity will not allow them to rest at home. [These women (George Eliot for example) may study medicine, science, history, teach, write, lecture, become a journalist or an editor.] Any of these lives are better to such a brain than the old fashioned social round and domestic duties. . . . These are the happy workers; but these are not the average.
> 2. Because they must earn money somehow. Among these are the unhappy workers, the unwilling women who . . . miss the life they would prefer.
> 3. Because they want to make a little more money for dress or for spending. A very considerable class.
> 4. Because they have taken up a Cause, and feel called upon to speak, act, write, and work for it.
> 5. Because they have become "advanced" women, and they want, above all things, to show that they are as good as men.
> 6. Because their home lives are so deadly dull and unsocial, and lonely and vacuous, that they want a change. (626)

Although he appears to have presented these reasons at random, sorting them out seems easy enough. Here as elsewhere he cites the intellectual woman as an exception, but because there are so few of them they do not significantly affect his perception of the relations between the sexes. Moreover, his example, George Eliot, seems not precisely to his taste. He admires "her great intellectual power and wonderful gifts," but he finds Mrs. Gaskell "a more charming and delightful novelist, so beautiful and womanly in all her instincts, as well as being a most accomplished writer" (Tooley 114). As for the other motives for women's work, Besant is strongly sympathetic to the woman who must work (#2) and quite *un*sympathetic to the "advanced" woman trying to demonstrate her equality (#5). The capital letter in #4's "Cause" suggests Besant's limited approval of that motive, and #6's dreadful home life would no doubt be a better excuse than #3's petty avarice. And yet, having drawn those seemingly obvious conclusions about Besant's position, one finds him a week later (21 October 1893) rejecting the bitter complaints of several ladies against women who work but do not have to, thereby taking work away from those who need it. It is a serious question, he admits, but he does not see how women can be convinced to sit in lofty idleness against their inclination so that others may not be injured (667). He seems to agree with the *Spectator* critic that although the woman who works "is injuring herself, and may even be injuring civilisation, the right . . . is absolute, — a right which cannot be suppressed or taken from them without violent oppression" (9 Sept. 1893: 331).

Besant's *Fifty Years Ago* (1888) contrasts England in Victoria's coronation year with Besant's own day. Chapter 7 details changes in the social and intellectual position of women, quoting a book by Mrs. John Sandford ("nowadays she would have been Mrs. Ethel Sandford, or Mrs. Christian-and-maiden-name Sandford"), to represent the older point of view: independence is unfeminine, contrary to nature, and offensive. A really sensible woman "*is conscious of inferiority, and therefore grateful for support*" (Besant's italics). Besant acknowledges that such a book would now be received with a storm, but his "Conclusion" suggests some sympathy for Sandford's position. Besant feels "the example of the women who speak, who write, who belong to professions, and are, generally, aggressive, threatens to change the manners of all women." Already more assured and self-reliant, less deferential to men's opinion, they "boldly deny any inferiority of intellect, though no woman has ever produced any work which puts her anywhere near the highest intellectual level" (264–65).

Commemorating Victoria's sixtieth anniversary in *The Queen's Reign* (1897), Besant again traces progress for women, much of it with apparent approval. But in chapter 7, "The Day of New Ideas," he sees women getting out of hand: "At the present moment there is a wild and insensate game of 'grab' going on. Women admit of no restrictions, they claim everything. They are not satisfied with the whole intellectual field, they would overrun the field of physical labour." But he feels this folly will soon be replaced by more sensible counsels, an acceptance of biological destiny (or at least responsibility): "It will be recognised that Nature assigns limitations and prescribes certain kinds of work for men, and certain other kinds for women. Above all, it should be remembered that if a man owes himself to his country as a soldier or a workman, so a woman owes to her country the duties of maternity" (82).

In his last column for the *Queen*, on 29 December 1900, Besant notes that the air is heavy with summaries of the dying century, and the summary of woman's progress should be most interesting because of the "amazing revolution of the last thirty years":

> I remember when universal conquest, the reign of woman, the domination of the feminine — *i.e.*, the pure and unclouded — intellect, was a dream said to be common in certain haunts of the new woman. I wrote at that time a little story [*The Revolt of Man*], in which I pictured the realisation of that dream in the reign of woman; not, I hope, ill–naturedly. . . . To this day whenever I meet one of those extinct volcanoes, the emancipated woman of the seventies, she reminds me with an acrid smile of that work. Women are still as much emancipated as ever, but they are so very, very much more sensible. (1046)

Nevertheless, though emancipated and sensible, women are still not equal. "May we, without offence," Besant asks — knowing full well he may not —

"lay down the general principle that to man belongs the present and to woman the future?" He does not mean that women's achievements will eventually supersede men's, but that men discover and women apply. As he puts it elsewhere: "Woman does not create but she receives, moulds, and develops" ("Collaboration" 209). Women have made no significant contributions to science and technology — there have been no female Darwins, Tyndalls, Edisons, Listers, Kelvins. Perhaps these are not real, natural limitations, he says, but perhaps they are, and "if after another thirty years of the highest and widest education no scientific leader arises among women, we shall, perhaps, be justified in considering that in woman's work there are these limitations" (*Queen* 29 Dec. 1900: 1046–47).[7]

Though by 1900 Besant does not want to deny flatly that women may be the equal of men in more ways than current achievements have proven, he seems much more comfortable with the old idea of separate spheres and its assertion of simultaneous inferiority and superiority, a role which "at one and the same time empowered and confined" women (Levine 12). Besant's poetic tribute upon the death of Eliza Lynn Linton gives his (and her) sense of improper and proper behavior in women:

> She fought for Woman: yet with women fought,
> The sexless tribe, the shrieking sisterhood;
> Who made them masks of men, and fondly thought
> Like men to do: to stand where men have stood.
>   . . . .
> She fought for Woman, and for all the gifts
> Which consecrate her Priestess of Mankind:
> Eternal Priestess, she who leads and lifts
> The Man who, but for her, crept dark and blind. (*Queen* 23 July 1899: 134)

He ends with the prediction that Linton's work will last "Wherever women live in God's own way."

Still, much as Besant would have liked the latter to be true, he was too practical a man to believe that it any longer was. He had watched the changes taking place with an attentive eye, and he knew others would surely come. The priestesses had cast off their cumbersome robes in favor of rational dress which allowed them to ride bicycles and play tennis. So the best he could hope was to slow the process with his resistance, try to prevent the worst excesses with his ridicule, and devote his primary attention to those women's problems that he considered important and needing immediate attention. When a woman accused him of sneering at the movement for women's franchise (*Queen* 25 June 1898: 1088), he rejected the charge, but predicted the vote would be a long time coming; and in the meantime, what he found most pressing was the problem of factory girls suffering from "phossy jaw" (a condition caused by phosphorus used to manufacture matches). Besant was willing to watch New Zealand's experience with the women's franchise for ten years rather than leap to an unwise conclusion about giving the vote to women in England,[8] but he felt the need to address practical evils immediately. So he wrote against sweating of women factory workers by capitalists, and women authors by the Society for the Promotion of Christian Knowledge; he repeatedly urged that parents create an endowment to protect against their daughters' uncertain future; he concerned himself with decent accommodations for working gentlewomen and helped establish the Woman's Labour Bureau to enable them to find suitable employment; he disliked women working but argued that if men's wages are raised, so should theirs. Besant clearly would have preferred that women remain at home, but no one argued more strongly for fairness when they could not or would not stay there.

Somewhat playfully, George Saintsbury, reviewing *Armorel of Lyonesse*, labeled Besant "stout champion . . . of the right supremacy of man and decrier of modern theories of gynaecocracy" (35). The *Saturday Review*, speaking with equally partial accuracy, said "no one has inquired with less prejudice into the wrongs of women or been a more zealous champion for their good" (76 [1893]: 415–16). Sarah Tooley diplomatically brought the extremes together: "Indeed, Sir Walter Besant's attitude to women, though not so much in keeping with the spirit of the time as one could wish, has a tendency to disarm criticism" (109). In his own day many people, male and female, applauded him for his strong views on women's proper sphere; many others — largely, but not exclusively, female — attacked him for the same reason; and Besant seems to have appreciated the one and enjoyed the other. He loved a fight, and the "shrieking sisterhood" provided him with worthy antagonists for much of his professional life. But the mixed feelings of less radical women about the Besantine paternalism may have defined him more accurately. A woman writing to the *Author* for 1 February 1892 spoke for many when she identified his "kindly condescending" to the feminine reading public: "We note the kindness," she said, "but the condescension also" (282).

In his "Voice of the Flying Day" for 3 February 1900, Besant "rejoiced" in the success of one of his practical causes: Bryant and May's match factory will no longer use the dangerous phosphorus which causes "'phossy jaw'" (168). When he died in 1901, women's suffrage was still well in the future, where Besant thought it belonged. "Forward! But not too fast" — the motto for the journal *Woman / For all Sorts and Conditions of Women* — might well have been his own. Because so many people of his own day agreed and disagreed with him, his insistent, influential voice still needs to be heard to give us a proper sense of the late nineteenth-century debate over women's rights and wrongs.

Ohio University

NOTES

1. In an obituary for Linton in the *Author* (9 [1898]: 76–77), Besant wrote that "She had no sympathy with what is commonly called the 'new' woman — what Mrs. Linton herself called, in a series of essays upon them [in the *Saturday Review* during 1870], the 'shrieking sisterhood.' "

2. The reversal has kinship with an earlier satirical piece punningly titled "Latest Intelligence from the Planet Venus," published in *Fraser's Magazine* in 1874 under the initials B.T. On Venus only women can vote and sit in the House of Commons, and eldest daughters of deceased Peers inhabit the Upper House. But recently there has been a movement advocating enfranchisement of males, an idea vigorously opposed in a speech by the leader of the Opposition. It ends:

   That any wrong is done to men by the existing arrangement, I entirely deny. Most of them are married, and it is so seldom that a wife's political opinions differ materially from her husband's, that the vote of the former may fairly be said to represent both. . . . It is a fatal mistake to try to turn men into women, to shut them up indoors, and set them to study blue-books and reports in their intervals of business, to enforce on them an amount of thought, seclusion, and inaction so manifestly uncongenial to their physical constitution. . . . (763–66)

   This speech causes male suffrage to be overwhelmingly rejected, as we might expect in a satire uncompromised and uncomplicated by the ambivalence that Besant shows in *The Revolt of Man*.

3. Elaine Showalter is also offended by the novel but sees no clever satire, only a "mean-spirited" book (41–43).

4. It was published first in the *English Illustrated Magazine* in 1889 and reprinted in the collection entitled *Verbena Camilla Stephanotis* in 1892. Archibald Henderson says Besant's sequel "attracted no little attention" in Norway and Germany and was translated in a daily newspaper and in book form (405).

5. Fred W. Boege offers an explanation for Besant's fear: "As Mr. Average Opinion, he was too deeply shocked to see the difference between a symbolic drama and a manual of conduct for unhappy wives. If it was good for Nora to leave her family, why not for Mrs. Doe, Mrs. Smith, or Mrs. Besant?" (44).

6. The *Spectator* allowed only two reasons why women should be free to work: necessity, and their natural right to choose to work. But there was little sympathy for the latter. The *Spectator* agreed with Frederic Harrison, Besant, and the majority of the trades-unions that it would be better if women did not do hard work for gain or work outside the house at all. Women's labor drives down men's wages and, because of its cheapness, stands in the way of developing better machines. Moreover, "In working, they diminish the possibility of their being good daughters, sisters, wives, and mothers, and these are their true functions, not earning money" (9 Sept. 1893: 330–31).

7. The idea appears frequently in his novels, most notably *The Revolt of Man, Children of Gibeon*, and *The Changeling*.

8. Besant sees little likelihood that the New Zealand experience will prove successful: "[U]ntil the contrary is proved, I mean to go on thinking that everything which tends to . . . make men and women regard their interests as separate,

instead of identical . . . is self-condemned at the outset. . . . '' (*Queen* 24 Feb. 1894: 280).

WORKS CITED

B., N. O. "Novels and Novelists. / VI. — MR. WALTER BESANT." *Echo* 2 Oct. 1893: 1.

Besant, Walter. "The Doll's House — and After." *English Illustrated Magazine* 7 (1889): 315–25.

———. *Fifty Years Ago*. London: Chatto & Windus, 1888.

———. "On Literary Collaboration." *New Review* 6 (1892): 200–9.

———. *The Queen's Reign . . . The Story of the Victorian Transformation*. London: Werner, 1897.

———. *The Rebel Queen*. New York: Harper, 1893.

———. *The Revolt of Man*. Edinburgh: Blackwood, 1882.

———. "The Voice of the Flying Day." *The Queen, the Lady's Newspaper*. 26 Nov. 1892: 866–67; 28 Jan. 1893: 122; 29 Apr. 1893: 650; 20 May 1893: 798–99; 9 Sept. 1893: 331; 16 Sept. 1893: 470; 30 Sept. 1893: 546; 7 Oct. 1893: 586–87; 14 Oct. 1893: 626; 21 Oct. 1893: 667; 4 Nov. 1893: 748; 18 Nov. 1893: 830–31; 9 Dec. 1893: 966; 24 Feb. 1894: 280; 3 Aug. 1895: 199; 5 Mar. 1898: 398; 12 Mar. 1898: 444–45; 25 June 1898: 1088; 20 Aug. 1898: 292; 29 July 1899: 174; 3 Feb. 1900: 168; 29 Dec. 1900: 1046–47.

Boege, Fred W. "Sir Walter Besant: Novelist (Part Two)." *Nineteenth-Century Fiction* 11 (1956): 32–60.

"Books [*Revolt of Man*]." *Spectator* 55 (1882): 1383–85.

Colles, W. Morris. "The Late Sir Walter Besant." *The Queen, the Lady's Newspaper*. 15 June 1901: 960.

Crewe, Quentin. *The Frontiers of Privilege: A Century of Social Conflict as Reflected in "The Queen."* London: Stevens, 1961.

"E. Lynn Linton." *The Queen, the Lady's Newspaper*. 23 July 1898: 134.

Henderson, Archibald. *George Bernard Shaw: Man of the Century*. New York: Appleton, 1956.

Levine, Philippa. *Victorian Feminism: 1850–1900*. Tallahassee: Florida State UP, 1987.

"Novels of the Week [*Revolt of Man*]." *Athenaeum* 29 Apr. 1882: 537.

"Obituary." *Author* 9 (1898): 76–77.

P., S. "A Plea for the Mild Domestic Novel." *Author* 2 (1892): 282.

"The Rebel Queen." *Saturday Review* 76 (1893): 415–16.

"Recent Novels [*Revolt of Man*]." *Nation* 34 (1882): 505.

"Recent Novels ["Doll's House — and After"]." *Spectator* 69 (1892): 297.

"Recent Novels [*The Rebel Queen*]." *Spectator* 71 (1893): 583–94.

"Review [*Revolt of Man*]." *Women's Suffrage Journal* 1 Sept. 1882: 137.

"The Revolt of Man." *Saturday Review* 53 (1882): 534–35.

"The Right of Women to Work." *Spectator* 71 (1893): 330–31.

Saintsbury, George. "New Novels [*Armorel of Lyonesse*]." *Academy* 39 (1891): 35.

———. "New Novels [*The Rebel Queen*]." *Academy* 44 (1893): 388.

Shaw, George Bernard. *Bernard Shaw: Collected Letters, 1874–1897*. 2 vols. Ed. Dan H. Laurence. London: Reinhardt, 1965.

——— "Still after the Doll's House." *Short Stories, Scraps and Shavings*. London: Constable, 1934. 127–39.

Showalter, Elaine. *Sexual Anarchy: Gender and Culture at the Fin de Siècle*. New York: Viking, 1990.

"Some Novels ["'Doll's House — and After"]." *Nation* 55 (1892): 436–37.

Somerset, Lady Isabel. "Women's Work." *Queen* 18 Nov. 1893: 831.

Stern, Katherine. "The War of the Sexes in British Fantasy Literature of the Suffragette Era." *Critical Matrix* 3 (1987): 78–109.

T., B. "Latest Intelligence from the Planet Venus." *Fraser's Magazine* n.s. 10 (1874): 763–66.

Tooley, Sarah A. "The Women's Labour Bureau: Sir Walter Besant's New Scheme." Bookman. (New York) 6 (1897–98): 108–15.

"The Voice of the Flying Day." *Woman's Herald* 26 Oct. 1893: 563.

Yonge, Charlotte. *Womankind*. New York: Macmillan, 1882.

A CINDERELLA AMONG THE MUSES: BARRETT BROWNING AND THE BALLAD TRADITION

by Marjorie Stone

In their 1867 edition of *Bishop Percy's Folio Manuscript*, John H. Hales and Frederick J. Furnivall picture the ballad before the Romantic revival as a "Cinderella" among the Muses:

> She had never dared to think herself beautiful. No admiring eyes ever came near her in which she might mirror herself. She had never dared to think her voice sweet. . . . She met with many enemies, who clamoured that the kitchen was her proper place, and vehemently opposed her admission into any higher room. The Prince was long in finding her out. The sisters put many an obstacle between him and her. . . . But at last the Prince found her, and took her in all her simple sweetness to himself. (xviii–xix)

Some readers might pause over the class and gender-inflected assumptions in this ingenuous fairy story of a gallantly patronizing "Prince" taking a low-born maiden "to himself," not to speak of the cultural hegemony implied, given that the "Prince" was English and so many of the ballads were Scottish. But few would dispute the importance of the union Hales and Furnivall so fancifully describe. Every student of Romantic poetry is aware of the profound significance of the ballad revival, reflected in Bishop Percy's *Reliques of Ancient English Poetry* (1765), in Sir Walter Scott's "minstrelsy," and above all in the *Lyrical Ballads* published by Wordsworth and Coleridge in 1798.

Yet the ballad is seldom recognized as an important Victorian genre, even though it attracted major and minor poets throughout the nineteenth century. G. Malcolm Laws, Jr.'s catalogue of Victorian literary ballads is longer than his catalogue of Romantic ballads (151–58). As Laws suggests, the ballad was held in particular esteem by Pre-Raphaelite poets like D. G. Rossetti and Swinburne (89–93). Tennyson, like Hardy after him, also employed innovative variants on the form throughout his long career, in works such as the

"The Sisters," with its refrain "O the Earl was fair to see!", "The Lady of Shalott," the immensely popular "Lady Clara Vere De Vere," "Edward Gray," "Lady Clare," "Locksley Hall," "The Revenge: A Ballad of the Fleet," and "Rizpah." Ballads are particularly numerous in his 1842 *Poems*, reflecting their prominence in a period marked by the success of Macaulay's *Lays of Ancient Rome* (1842) and the continuing sway of Sir Walter Scott's ballads and narrative poems. The ballad has an even higher profile in Elizabeth Barrett's 1844 *Poems*, commended by the *English Review* for containing "some of the best ballad-writing" encountered "for many a day" (272). Indeed, Barrett's "peculiar skill" in "this species of poetry," a form she had made "peculiarly" her own, was frequently praised in the reviews of the two volumes that established her as Tennyson's rival in 1844 (Kelley and Hudson 9: 365, 341). Although Barrett was no "Prince," she too took that "Cinderella" among the Muses, the ballad, to herself — not so much because of its "simple sweetness" but because its energy, its frank physicality, its elemental passions, its strong heroines, and its sinewy narrative conflicts allowed her to circumvent the passionless purity conventionally ascribed to the middle-class Victorian woman. In her own appropriations, the lowly maiden is used to interrogate the inscriptions of sexual difference it appears to encode.

For a number of reasons, some having to do with the ballad genre itself, others with the general approach to Barrett Browning's works, her achievement in the ballad form is insufficiently appreciated today. Even recent feminist critics tend to disparage her ballads, ironically by placing them in the context of a separate "feminine genre" of ballad-writing which is, in Dorothy Mermin's words, "sentimental" and "retrogressive" (91). This essay will argue for a different perspective on the Victorian ballad and Barrett Browning's ballads in particular. Her revisionary innovations in the genre can be more fully appreciated when we re-situate her ballads in the matrix of the Romantic ballad revival and the tradition it produced, ranging from Bishop Percy to the Pre-Raphaelite poets and Thomas Hardy. By considering the intertextuality of a number of her ballads, and by reconstructing the horizon of expectation against which they were written and read, I hope to show how poems like "A Romance of the Ganges," "The Romaunt of Margret," "The Poet's Vow," "The Romaunt of the Page," and "Rhyme of the Duchess May" echo and adapt the motifs and conventions of traditional ballads and Romantic narrative verse in ways that point forward to the ballads of the Pre-Raphaelite poets.

I use "intertextuality" here in the broad sense it has come to have as the prescriptive definitions of structuralism and semiotics have yielded before the recognition that repertoires of anonymous social and literary codes cannot be easily extricated from traditional questions of particular sources and influences. Some of the conventions and motifs Barrett deploys in 1838 and 1844 ballads were so widely disseminated and frequently imitated that they undoubtedly are intertextual in the stipulative sense emphasized by Roland Barthes and others (39). Yet the border between this form of intertextuality and identifiable influence is often difficult to determine. Like the works analysed by Antony Harrison, many of Barrett Browning's ballads also involve "self-consciously intertextual uses of precursors" to expose ideological values and presuppositions (1).

Barrett Browning's more self-conscious intertextuality is particularly apparent in her modification of what Nancy K. Miller terms "female plots" — that is, the plots that "culture has always already inscribed" for women, plots reinscribed in "the linear time of fiction" (208). Like Charlotte Brontë, Barrett Browning has often been faulted for her handling of plot. Mermin observes that it was fortunate Barrett Browning did not write novels because she "had no gift for inventing plots" (186) and the stories in her ballads are "invariably silly," if "entertaining" (90). But in many instances, the "silly" stories that Mermin objects to in Barrett's 1838 and 1844 ballads are no more absurd than the plots they play against in the traditional ballads collected by Percy, and in Romantic ballads and narratives written by Gottfried Bürger, by Scott, and by Wordsworth and Coleridge.

The revisions in several of Barrett Browning's ballads cast additional light on her complex adaptation of plots and motifs in precursor texts. These revisions also indicate that, contrary to prevailing assumptions, Barrett Browning engaged in careful and often extensive rewriting of some of her ballads, both at the manuscript stage and after they had appeared in periodicals and annuals. Her alterations in the ballads, like the significant textual changes she introduces in successive editions of her other works, point to the need for a modern scholarly edition of her poems.[1] This essay considers some of the changes she made in "The Poet's Vow" between its first publication in 1836 and its appearance in subsequent editions of her works, and in "The Romaunt of the Page," between the manuscript draft, its initial publication in the 1839 *Findens' Tableaux*, and its republication in the 1844 *Poems*.[2] In the case of "The Poet's Vow," her revisions serve to extend the critique of Wordsworth readily apparent in the initial version of the poem — a critique she effects in part by drawing on the plots and motifs of the old anonymous ballads in the Percy collection. In "The Romaunt of the Page," however, it is certain of the Percy ballads themselves that she most directly writes against.

As in the case of "Rhyme of the Duchess May," the most substantial revisions in "The Romaunt of the Page" expand the role and motivation of the poem's male protagonist, revealing how Barrett Browning progressively complicated her "female plots" by portraying their intersections with the

social systems that create and encompass them. The changes in "The Romaunt of the Page" and "Rhyme of the Duchess May" thus look forward
to the last of the 1844 ballads to be written, "Lady Geraldine's Courtship,"
with its male protagonist Bertram, and to *Aurora Leigh*, where the conflicts
between Romney's reformist socialist ideals and his conservative assumptions
about gender are portrayed at some length. In short, Barrett Browning shows
how the "female plots" constructing Aurora as a subject are inseparable from
the gender plots of Romney and his society, thereby establishing an ideological nexus she first began to explore in her ballads.

i

THE 1844 POEMS BROUGHT before a wide public, both in England and America,
two of Barrett's ballads previously published only in the 1839 and 1840
editions of *Findens' Tableaux*: "The Romaunt of the Page" and "The Lay
of the Brown Rosary." Several new poems identified as "ballads" by contemporary reviewers also appeared in 1844, most notably "Rhyme of the
Duchess May," "Bertha in the Lane," "Catarina to Camoens," "The Romance of the Swan's Nest," and "Lady Geraldine's Courtship." These
poems were acclaimed by general readers as well as critics. Barrett was highly
amused by "an account in one of the fugitive reviews of a lady falling into
hysterics" after reading "Rhyme of the Duchess May," and a similar story
of a "gush of tears" down "the Plutonian cheeks of a lawyer" as he read
"Bertha in the Lane" (Kenyon 1: 247). As Mermin notes, "Barrett's ballads
were her most consistently popular poems in the nineteenth century" (71).
They were often reprinted in selected editions of her poems, while particular
favourites, such as "Rhyme of the Duchess May" and "Lady Geraldine's
Courtship" were republished separately in illustrated editions until well past
the turn of the century.[3]

The vogue for ballads in the mid-Victorian period inevitably led to parodies
like those in the frequently reprinted "Bon Gaultier" *Ballads*, published in
1845 by Sir Theodore Martin and W. E. Aytoun. One of its later editions
included a parody of "Rhyme of the Duchess May" entitled "The Rhyme
of Lancelot Bogle" (Bratton 227). Such parodies no doubt contributed to the
relatively low profile of the ballad in modern constructions of the Victorian
poetical canon — and, in Barrett Browning's case, to the disappearance of
her ballads from literary history altogether. The assumption that a popular
literary work is necessarily of little artistic value has lingered longer in the
case of Victorian poets than in the case of novelists such as Dickens or Wilkie
Collins.

Paradoxically, in the case of popular literary ballads, the effects of this assumption have been exacerbated by narrow definitions of the genre that privilege the anonymous or "authentically" popular folk ballad over literary "imitations." J. S. Bratton shrewdly notes the limitations of such constraining definitions in the case of Francis J. Child's enormously influential collection, *The English and Scottish Ballads*, and detects the "same assumption of the innate superiority of the traditional ballad" in studies of the literary ballad by Albert B. Friedman and Anne Ehrenpreis (4–7). But Bratton's study risks perpetuating some of the very assumptions it criticizes in focusing on the Victorian popular ballad and reclassifying some literary ballads as popular. Thus it attempts a "redrawing of the line which separates 'art' and 'popular' poetry" (8), rather than a questioning of the line itself. In shifting this line, Bratton gives no attention to Barrett Browning's very popular literary ballads. Such omission is typical of literary histories published between 1900 and 1980. Her ballads have particularly suffered from definitions of the genre privileging the "authentic" folk form because they move farther away from this model than literary ballads like Keats's "La Belle Dame Sans Merci" and D. G. Rossetti's "Sister Helen."

These general assumptions about the popular literary ballad seem to underlie Alethea Hayter's 1962 dismissal of Barrett Browning's ballads as "synthetic" confections with a "certain narrative sweep and excitement" appealing to "people who did not normally read poetry at all." Hayter adds in extenuation that Barrett Browning "never really took them seriously" (81–82), supporting this conclusion with the well-known lines in *Aurora Leigh*:

> My ballads prospered; but the ballad's race
> Is rapid for a poet who bears weights
> Of thought and golden image. (*Aurora Leigh* 5.84–86)

Traces of Hayter's disparaging tone persist in recent feminist reinterpretations. Thus Angela Leighton approaches one of Barrett's earlier poems, "A Romance of the Ganges" (first published in the 1838 *Findens'*), and "The Lay of the Brown Rosary" as "ballads which Elizabeth Barrett wrote in response to a demand . . . for morally educative poems" directed towards "a primarily female readership" (32). Leighton finds these "confused and precipitate" ballads to be of psychological interest only (37), like "The Romaunt of Margret," first published in 1836 in the *New Monthly Magazine*. Kathleen Hickok similarly dismisses "The Lay of the Brown Rosary" as "an uninspired jumble," "The Romaunt of Margret" as completely conventional, and "Rhyme of the Duchess May" as a spasmodic poem (173–75).

In a series of articles subsequently incorporated into *Elizabeth Barrett Browning: The Origins of a New Poetry*, Mermin was the first to reinterpret

Barrett Browning's ballads as poems providing "a covert but thorough-going reassessment, often a total repudiation, of the Victorian ideas about womanliness to which they ostensibly appeal" (71). "Beneath their apparent conventionality," Mermin persuasively argues, the ballads sceptically examine "the myths and fantasies of nineteenth-century womanhood," including "the virtues of self-repression and self-sacrifice" they seem to affirm (90–91). At the same time, however, Mermin doubts that Barrett Browning herself was entirely aware of the subversive elements in her own poems. "Almost all her ballads cry out to be read as feminist revisions of old tales," but they were not interpreted as such by Victorian readers, Mermin emphasizes. "Elizabeth Barrett told the old stories in a style and tone that gave no hint of revisionary intention, and she discarded the ballad form without discovering how to use it effectively against itself" (95).

Helen Cooper and Glennis Stephenson assume a more thorough-going revisionary intent on Barrett's part: Cooper in reading Barrett's medieval ballads as an examination of "the sexual economy of courtship and marriage" (70), and Stephenson in analysing their subversion of "chivalric conventions" and gender roles (29). Nevertheless, like Mermin, they emphasize the limits of Barrett's revisionism and approach it within the context of a feminine genre of ballad writing which is "squarely in the tradition" of Letitia Landon (Mermin 107). Cooper suggests that Barrett followed Landon and Felicia Hemans in using her ballads to explore "issues of domesticity" (31), and that their publication in annuals "apparently located" them in "a female genre" (70). Similarly, while Stephenson explores the "complexity" of "The Lay of the Brown Rosary," she argues that Barrett tended to "devalue" all of her *Findens'* ballads (24).

There is good reason to question some of these assumptions and their critical implications. In the first place, they depend upon categorizations that are not clearly evident in many early and mid-Victorian references to the ballad. Early Victorian concepts of the ballad seem to have been remarkably broad and inclusive, both in terms of genre and in terms of gender. Neither Barrett Browning nor the majority of her readers seem to have approached her ballads in the context of a separate, feminine tradition. Barrett Browning also took her ballads more seriously than some of her playfully disparaging remarks about the *Findens'* contribution and herself as a "writer of ballads" indicate (Kelley and Hudson 7: 218). More importantly, she clearly did sometimes consciously use the ballad form "against itself" in complicating or subverting traditional ballads, and some Victorian readers, at least, recognized how much she was writing in the wake of Bishop Percy and his imitators.

Recent discussions of Barrett Browning's works by Mermin and Cooper separate her "romantic ballads" with their female protagonists from works such as "The Poet's Vow," even though this poem has stronger formal affinities with the ballad genre, as narrowly defined, than works like "The Lay of the Brown Rosary." Resituating her ballads within the matrix created by the Romantic ballad revival requires an approach less marked by such artificial distinctions. A relatively broad operative definition of the ballad also seems called for, since conceptions of the ballad were more amorphous and comprehensive in the early Victorian period than they became after Child's collection of "authentic" ballads appeared. Many of the works described by Barrett's reviewers as ballads might more probably be classified as romances or romantic tales today, in particular "Lady Geraldine's Courtship," with its subtitle "A Romance of the Age." In *Romantic Narrative Verse*, Hermann Fischer acknowledges the difficulty of distinguishing between these forms, and he traces some of the historical and literary developments that contributed to their amorphousness by the 1830s and '40s. Among much else, Fischer points out that when Scott attempted to describe the new genre of "romantic poetry" or romantic verse narrative in 1813, he did "not distinguish between [sic] ballads, lays and romances" (53); morever, Scott's own poetical works reflect an "eclectic mixture" of conventions from "the ballad and romance tradition" (90). Scott's eclecticism led to "rich variations of subject and form" in romantic narrative verse, with the result that "the 'genre' was constantly being extended and becoming vaguer in definition" (120–21), until its "ramification" led to what Fischer terms its "dissolution" (146). Although Fischer acknowledges that variants on such verse were "repeatedly resurrected by poets such as Macaulay, Matthew Arnold, Tennyson and Browning," he describes it as an exhausted and merely popular form after 1830. Barrett Browning is not included among the few women writers he dismisses as Scott's prolific imitators (111).

Barrett Browning's titles for her "ballads" ("romaunt," "lay," "rhyme," "romance") and her references to these works in her letters suggest that for her, as for many of her contemporaries, these terms were loosely synonymous. Harriet Martineau, for instance, similarly refers to these works in a letter to Barrett as "your Rhyme, Romaunt, lay-style of poems" (Kelley and Hudson 9: 141). Thus I use the term "ballad" here as Barrett Browning and other Victorians used it, to refer to all of her narrative poems with clear affinities either with the characteristic features of the ballad form (the ballad stanza, the refrain, dialogue, tragic and/or topical subject matter) or with the larger tradition of "minstrelsy" and Romantic narrative verse. I have made an exception, however, in the case of the group of narrative poems with dramatized speakers, including "Catarina to Camoens," "Bertha in the Lane," "Lady Geraldine's Courtship," "The Runaway Slave at Pilgrim's Point," "Void in Law," and "Mother and Poet." These works were sometimes described as "ballads," and they share many characteristics with both folk ballads and the ballads of the Romantic revival: there are clear echoes of the old Scottish ballad, "Lady Bothwell's Lament," in "Void in Law," for example. But since this group of poems displays even stronger affinities with the developing form of the dramatic monologue, I have chosen to approach them elsewhere, and made only incidental comments on their ballad traits below.

Barrett Browning often expressed her love for "the old burning ballads, with a wild heart beating in each!" (Kelley and Hudson 6: 268). The old Scottish ballads were praised by the historian Henry Hallam for their "Homeric power of rapid narration" (qtd. in Willmott lxxiii), and it should not be forgotten that, as James Borg notes, "the ballad was viewed as the prototype of the epic" in the early nineteenth century (74). As Barrett herself puts it in her survey of English poets from Chaucer to Wordsworth, "The Book of the Poets," the ballad is "a form epitomical of the epic and dramatic" (*Works* 6: 296). Given this assumption, it is unlikely that Barrett saw her ballads — even her ballads for *Findens'* — as mere diversionary exercises in a "feminine" genre. On the contrary, she may well have approached her ballad writing as a natural preparation for the writing of epic, a view that her own career subsequently bore out as she moved from writing simpler to more elaborate ballads and narratives between 1836 and 1844, culminating in "Lady Geraldine's Courtship," which she clearly saw as the prototype of *Aurora Leigh* (Raymond and Sullivan 3: 42). The significance of her ballads in her own eyes is further reflected in the prominence she gives them in planning the contents of the 1844 *Poems* (Kelley and Hudson 6: 260).

Unfortunately space did not permit Barrett to include a survey of the "anonymous & onymous ballads" in "The Book of the Poets," as she explained to Mitford (Kelley and Hudson 6: 17). "We must not be thrown back upon the 'Ballads,' lest we wish to live with them for ever," she fondly observes as she passes them by (*Works* 6: 296). Barrett does find room, however, to speak of "the *réveillé* of Dr. Percy's 'Reliques of English Poetry,' " which sowed "great hearts" like Wordsworth's with "impulses of greatness" (299–300, 298). Barrett acquired her own copy of Percy's *Reliques* in 1826 (Kelley and Coley 156). Her love of the Percy ballads was shared by Mitford and some of her literary acquaintances, as Mitford's own comments (see below) and Robert Willmott's 1857 edition of the *Reliques* indicate. "The Book of the Poets" also alludes to the "Scottish Minstrelsy" inspired by the *Reliques* (299–300). Scott's epic narrative *Marmion* (1808) is one product of Scottish minstrelsy that enters into the intertextuality of Barrett's 1844 ballads, contributing to the resonance of her depiction of a woman disguised as a page and a nun buried alive in "The Romaunt of the Page" and "The Lay of the Brown Rosary" respectively. The pronounced Gothic strain in the "The Lay of the Brown Rosary" also owes something to Scott, although it reflects more closely the lingering influence of "Lenora," the immensely popular German ballad by Gottfried Bürger that was so important a prototype for Wordsworth, Coleridge, Scott, and Southey in the 1790s, as Mary Jacobus (209–32) and Stephen Parrish (86–90) have shown. Fischer notes that the influence of German works like Bürger's ballads contributed to the public taste between 1798 and 1830 for "the outwardly sensational and exaggeratedly thrilling" and for "rebellious amoral 'heroes,' " a taste fully exploited by Byron in his romantic tales (46).

It is important to note that Barrett's contemporary reviewers were quick to link her ballads to such precursors in the larger ballad tradition. After reading "The Poet's Vow" in October 1836 in the *New Monthly Magazine*, Mitford wrote to Barrett, "I have just read your delightful ballad. My earliest book was 'Percy's Reliques,' the delight of my childhood; and after them came Scott's 'Minstrelsy of the Borders,' the favourite of my youth; so that I am prepared to love ballads. . . . Do read Tennyson's 'Ladye of Shalot' " (Kelley and Hudson 3: 195). *The Spectator* noted the resemblance of "The Romaunt of the Page" and "The Lay of the Brown Rosary" to the "old ballads," while *The Critic* described them as "revivals of the old English ballad, to which Miss BARRETT appears to be extremely partial" (Kelley and Hudson 9: 326, 370). Similarly, John Forster compared "Rhyme of the Duchess May" to the Scottish border ballad "Edom o' Gordon" included in Percy's *Reliques*; while Sarah Flower Adams in the *Westminster Review* observed of the same poem, "it has all the rapidity of action of 'Leonore,' [and] the descriptive power of Scott and Campbell, united with the deep pathos of the earlier Scottish ballads" (Kelley and Hudson 9: 347, 376).

It was not Scott and company, however, who were the most important precursors for Barrett the balladist, but Wordsworth and Coleridge. As Charlotte Porter and Helen A. Clarke noted in 1900, ballads such as "The Poet's Vow" belong to "the totally modern class of symbolic ballads" of which "The Ancient Mariner" is such a notable example (*Works* 1: xliii). Mary Howitt, whose ballads Barrett often praised (Kelley and Hudson 7: 164; Horne 1: 230), was similarly influenced by "The Ancient Mariner" in works such as "The Voyage of the Nautilus" and "The Old Man's Story," although these poems are less "symbolic" than Coleridge's or Barrett's. Like Elizabeth Gaskell, who echoed Coleridge in depicting the fallen woman Esther in *Mary Barton*, Barrett was particularly drawn to "Christabel," with its sinister symbolic mother-daughter relationship and its highly innovative irregular metre. Jacobus observes that many of the *Lyrical Ballads* are like "Christabel" in releasing "subconscious impulses" in "dramatic confrontations" (225). Much the same can be said of two of Barrett's ballads that echo "Christabel," "The Lay of the Brown Rosary" and "Isobel's Child." The latter, published in 1838, resembles Coleridge's poem in its loose ballad form, in its Gothic imagery and setting, and in its symbolically indirect treatment of the dark undercurrents in a mother's possessive love for her dying infant. Sara Coleridge was one Victorian reader who noticed that "Isobel's Child" was "like 'Christabel' in manner" (Kelley and Hudson 8: 333).

Barrett Browning's focus on abandoned or betrayed women in early ballads such as "The Romance of the Ganges' has reinforced the assumption that she was writing primarily in a sentimental female tradition. But such figures were a staple in traditional ballads such as "Lady Bothwell's Lament," in German ballads by Bürger like "The Lass of Fair Wone," and in lyrical ballads by Wordsworth such as "The Mad Mother" and "The Thorn." "The Runaway Slave at Pilgrim's Point," which Barrett Browning referred to as a "long ballad" (Raymond and Sullivan 3: 310), adapts motifs from "The Lass of Fair Wone" and the "The Thorn" (the mother's act of infanticide and burial of her child beneath the roots of a tree), as well as from "The Mad Mother": one manuscript version of "the Runaway Slave" was entitled "Black and Mad at Pilgrim's Point" (Kelley and Coley 324).

It is ballad traits, "The Runaway Slave" reveals how much Barrett Browning's interest in the form was, like Wordsworth's as Tilottama Rajan describes it, "social not antiquarian" (140). Indeed, the conflation of the traditional ballad and the topical, polemical broadside ballad that Rajan discerns in her Bakhtinian reading of Wordsworth's lyrical ballads may have been one reason why Barrett Browning saw Wordsworth as a greater poet than Scott. Scott was not a "great poet" in her view, though she conceded that he was highly accomplished in "poetical-antiquarianism" (Kelley and Hudson 7: 80). Like Wordsworth (see Rajan 139), Barrett Browning was interested in using the ballad form to create a community of readers cutting across class-lines and, in the case of "The Runaway Slave," sexual and racial divisions.

Particularly in her later career, however, Barrett Browning was inclined to be more radically polemical than Wordsworth in her appropriation of the ballad for political purposes. "The Runaway Slave," with its abolitionist agenda, and the 1854 political ballad, "A Song for the Ragged Schools of London," follow Shelley's more than Wordsworth's example. In the latter Barrett Browning is clearly writing in the tradition of the topical broadside ballad, using the form as Shelley had used it in "Song to the Men of England" and "The Mask of Anarchy," and as it was widely used by the Chartists in England during the 1840s. As I have argued elsewhere, "A Song for the Ragged Schools" adapts and strategically revises Shelley's rhetorial tactics in "A Mask of Anarchy" to reach an audience more female than male (Stone 161–62). Its inspiration was also woman-centered. According to Robert Browning, the ballad was originally written to help raise money not for the ragged schools in general, but for "the 'Refuge for young destitute girls' " which Elizabeth's sister Arabella helped to "set going" — "the first of its kind" (209).

Like "A Song for the Ragged Schools," Barrett's earlier, less polemical ballads of the 1830s and 1840s seem designed to appeal to a community of women readers. Although "Lady Geraldine's Courtship" with its male protagonist skilfully combines an appeal to both male and female readers, Barrett Browning seems to have written many of her ballads as a woman speaking to women, not like Wordsworth, as a "man speaking to men." William Herridge observed in 1887 that her ballads "appeal with especial force to the author's own sex, and strike almost every note in the scale of woman's thought and emotion" (612–13). As Herridge's terms suggest, it was not to the feelings alone that Barrett Browning's ballads appealed, even though she praised the ballad form to Horne because "all the passion of the heart will go into a ballad, & feel at home" (qtd. in Mermin 90). "Her narrative ballads have a swift directness and an impressive pictorialism which hold the imagination and stir the blood," James Ashcroft Noble observed (163). The "swift directness," most apparent in "Rhyme of the Duchess May," may have been acquired in part from her early immersion in ballads by Byron such as "The Destruction of Sennacherib." The pictorial quality reflects the influence of both Byron and Scott. But the vivid scene-painting, most apparent in the "Rhyme of the Duchess May," never impedes the narrative movement, as it so often does in Scott's narrative verse. Unlike Scott's narratives and unlike Wordsworth's "lyrical" ballads, Barrett Browning's ballads typically exhibit a strong narrative propulsion, despite the fact that she herself did not value narrative as the highest element in poetry (Kelley and Hudson 4: 109). "It is the *story* that has power with people," she acknowledged (Kenyon 1: 247).

Nevertheless, within this strong narrative propulsion, the convolutions and excesses that disrupt or exaggerate "plausible" sequentiality register Barrett Browning's critique of the plots encoding women's lives in the texts of precursor balladists, both "anonymous & onymous." As Nancy Miller points out, often plots seem "plausible" because they embody the assumptions of the dominant ideologies that determine the conditions for their constant reiteration (208). Barrett Browning's transformations, like Hardy's in "The Ruined Maid," undermine such plausibility and the ideologies that sustain it. Rajan observes that, because the ballad is a "cultural palimpsest inhabited by traces of more than one ideology," it "functions as a psychic screen on which desires having to do with ideological authority and hermeneutic community are projected and analysed" (141–42). Barrett Browning's ballads function in precisely this way in their strategic revisions of conventions, motifs, and in some cases, precursor texts familiar to early Victorian readers. Most notably, in her ballads of the 1830s and '40s, Barrett employs the starker power structures of medieval society to foreground the status of women as objects in a male economy of social exchange and to unmask the subtler preservation of gender inequities in contemporary Victorian ideology. Thus, like some of the modern women writers discussed by Patricia Yaeger, she engages in "a form of textual violation that . . . overgoes social norms by doubling them, by making them visible" (117).

In many cases, her transformations were simply ignored by Victorian reviewers, who imposed the old "plausible" plots of praisable female behavior on her revisionary narratives. But such responses to the ballads cannot be taken to prove a lack of revisionary intention on Barrett's part. Nor do such reviewers necessarily speak for the large body of female readers who may have read Barrett's ballads otherwise. For instance, in Eliza Fitzgerald's copy of Barrett Browning's poems now in the Armstrong Browning library, one of the passages marked most heavily in "The Romaunt of the Page" stresses the courage of the woman-page in meeting the Saracens.[4]

Often the narrative convolutions in Barrett Browning's ballads draw the reader's attention to ironies intensified by her transformative allusions to earlier works. In this respect, her ballads are again very different from Wordsworth's. Despite Wordsworth's democratizing project in the *Lyrical Ballads*, Rajan detects an "elision" of political and social concerns in his reduction of "narrative to a lyric tableau that constructs the world in terms of feeling rather than events or situations" (145). The result is an apolitical "hermeneutics of sentimenalism" that privileges archetypal and universal feeling over political, social, and gender differences. Barrett Browning's focus, on the contrary, is on configurations of plot and character that foreground ideologically grounded gender differences in their intricate intersections with other hierarchies of power: humanity over nature, God over humanity, knight over page, parent over child, priest over nun, and, in "The Runaway Slave," master over slave.

ii

"THE POET'S VOW," THE 1836 ballad in which Barrett Browning most noticeably echoes the *Lyrical Ballads*, illustrates this striking difference between her handling of the ballad form and Wordsworth's. As Cooper suggests, "The Poet's Vow" is a critique of the Romantic ideology positing nature as female, "the silent other" (37). Possessed by the conviction that mankind has afflicted Earth with the curse of the fall, the nameless and representative poet referred to in the poem's title vows to forswear contact with humanity, consecrating himself to communion with nature instead. Publicly declaring his vow, he bestows his "plighted bride" Rosalind upon his "oldest friend" Sir Roland, offering his own lands as Rosalind's dower (lines 136–40). Declining to be the object in this male exchange, the betrayed Rosalind, still "half a child," rejects the "cruel homily" the poet has found in "the teachings of the heaven and earth" (165–72). Years later, after the poet alone in his hall has withered within from "rejection of his humanness" (266), Rosalind dies and instructs that her bier be placed before his "bolted door": "For I have vowed, though I am proud, / To go there as a guest in shroud, / And not be turned away" (371–75). On her breast, like a Lady of Shalott who refuses to be judged merely by her "lovely face," she bears a scroll:

> I left thee last, a child at heart,
>   A woman scarce in years.
> I come to thee, a solemn corpse
>   Which neither feels nor fears.
> . . . .
> Look on me with thine own calm look:
>   I meet it calm as thou.
> No look of thine can change *this* smile,
>   Or break thy sinful vow:
> I tell thee that my poor scorned heart
> Is of thine earth — thine earth, a part:
>   It cannot vex thee now. (416–19, 423–29)

As Mermin suggests, the echoes of Wordsworth's "A Slumber Did My Spirit Seal" are "unmistakable," reflecting Barrett Browning's recognition of the "unprivileged position of woman" in the Romantic myth of a female nature (65–66). To speak with the voice of nature is to speak with the voice of the dead — or, as in Wordsworth's poem, with the voice of the male poet who chooses to commingle with nature and the dead. In either case, the individual woman is buried.

The crucial difference, of course, in Barrett Browning's rewriting of the Romantic man-nature love relationship is that in "The Poet's Vow" we *do* hear the voice of the still unburied Rosalind speaking from her scroll as an individual woman, not as a mythic female presence articulated by a male poet. Rosalind speaks, moreover, with the passion and bitterness of the betrayed women who so often appear in the ballads collected by Percy. She bears a particularly striking resemblance to the dead Margaret in "Margaret's Ghost" who appears at her lover's bedside to indict him for betraying his plighted troth (Percy 3: 210–313).[5] By superimposing a traditional ballad plot of human love and betrayal on Wordsworth's representation of the poet's love for nature, Barrett Browning foregrounds the narrative conflicts he deliberately elides in his identification of Lucy with the earth and in his deliberate focus on apparently universal feelings rather than on the drama of conflicting human desires.

In substantially revising "The Poet's Vow" first for her 1838 volume, *The Seraphim, and Other Poems*, and then for her 1850 *Poems*, Barrett Browning intensified both the narrative conflicts between the poet and Rosalind, and the forcefulness and passion of her ballad heroine. In the process, she also extended her subtle critique of Wordsworth. For example, in both the *New Monthly Magazine* version and the 1838 version of the poem, the section entitled "The Words of Rosalind's Scroll" begins with, "I left thee last, a feeble child / In those remembered years." In revising, Barrett Browning removed the emphasis on Rosalind's feebleness and made it clear that, though she was "a woman scarce in years" (417) like Wordsworth's Lucy when her lover consigned her to her fate, she now speaks as a woman with a woman's desires and a woman's strength. The revisions also intensify Rosalind's bitter scorn for the poet's "sinful vow" (426). In both the *New Monthly Magazine* version of "The Poet's Vow" and in the 1838 version, the second stanza of Rosalind's scroll ends with the lines, "My silent heart, of thine earth, is part / It cannot love thee now," not with the forceful declaration, "I tell thee that my poor scorned heart / Is of thine earth — thine earth, a part: / It cannot vex thee now" (427–29). The syntactic doubling in the revised version, "of thine earth — thine earth," undoes Wordsworthian ideology by simultaneously exaggerating and contradicting the identity of woman with nature that he assumes in the Lucy poems.

"The Poet's Vow" provides a further critique of Wordsworth in demonstrating the limited redemptive influence of recollections of early childhood. Barrett Browning's deletion of "those remembered years" is logical, given that the past is not remembered in any living way by her poet. Other revisions serve to emphasize the memories that the poet *should* have shared with Rosalind. For instance, in the *New Monthly Magazine* and the 1838 versions, Rosalind instructs her nurse to gather "little white flowers . . . Which I plucked for thee" and place them on her bier, whereas in the revised version she refers to the flowers "*he* and I" plucked "in childhood's games" (341). The flowers thus bear a message for the poet, as the scroll more overtly does. But, as the passionate scorn of the scroll's words indicates, Rosalind has little faith in the efficacy of the flowers or memory alone. Nor is she herself moved chiefly by the tender recollection of childhood in addressing the poet as she does. Barrett Browning's revisions to "The Poet's Vow" make it clear that it is passion, not memory, that motivates Rosalind. Thus the lines "I have prayed for thee with the wailing voice / Thy memory drew from me" in the two earliest versions of the poem are replaced with, "I have prayed for thee with bursting sob / When passion's course was free" (437–38).

Yet another dimension to Barrett Browning's intertextual debate with Wordsworth is apparent in the epigraph from "Lines Left upon a Seat in a Yew-tree" which she added to the poem in 1838 — "O be wiser thou, / Instructed that true knowledge leads to love." In Wordsworth's poem, this advice is prompted by the example of a hermit who withdrew from the world and died in the pride of his solitude. Moralizing upon this example, the poet instructs the reader to "be wiser." In "The Poet's Vow," however, it is the Wordsworthian poet himself who withdraws into the pride of solitude and who therefore needs instruction. In effect, then, Barrett Browning turns Wordsworth's advice back on the poet's own example.

Other revisions in "The Poet's Vow" serve to emphasize the ironic contradiction between the poet's "vow" to mate himself with the "touching, patient Earth" (68) and his broken vow to Rosalind. Significantly, the poet's description of Rosalind as his "plighted bride" (138) does not appear in the *New Monthly Magazine* version of the poem. Rosalind's declaration of *her* vow to appear as a corpse before the poet's bolted door ("For I have vowed . . .") is an even more notable addition to the poem. In both the *New Monthly Magazine* version and the 1838 version, no vow on her part is mentioned as she less forcibly states, "For there, alone with the lifeless one, / The living God must stay." The emphasis on Rosalind's vow in the revised version foregrounds both the ambiguities of the title and the narrative doublings that the poem's convoluted plot enacts. Not only is the poet's vow itself doubled, given that the poet breaks his vow to Rosalind in making his vow to the Earth. The figure of the poet is also doubled, as Rosalind employs her scroll to carry out her own vow. In implying that the representative poet of the title may be female, Barrett Browning subverts the traditional assumption that the poet is male — an assumption that the poem initially seems to perpetuate. More telling, perhaps, we may note that of the two poets in "The Poet's Vow," it is the woman whose words are more powerful in their effect. She becomes "Triumphant Rosalind!" (458) when the words of her text and the text of her body combine to "wring" (452) a cry from the "long-subjected humanness" (466) of the poet who has "vowed his blood of brotherhood / To a stagnant place apart" (53–54).

Such passages in "The Poet's Vow" point to its parallels with Tennyson's "The Palace of Art," where the proud and sinful soul of the speaker becomes "a spot of dull stagnation" (line 245). In fact, this is one of several passages in the revised version of "The Poet's Vow" that points to the influence of Tennyson's 1842 *Poems*.[6] But the influence also seems to have run in the other direction. For instance, Barrett Browning's description of the solitary poet looking down from his lattice to see "Three Christians" (285) going by to prayer may have influenced the ending of "The Two Voices."[7] Whatever the pattern of mutual influence may have been, it seems clear that, independently of each other, Tennyson and Barrett were engaged in writing strong critiques of Romantic solipsism in the 1830s. Indeed, Peter Bayne aptly describes "The Poet's Vow" as "the ethical complement" of "The Palace of Art" in its treatment of "the cardinal sin of isolation from human interests" (38). But of the two, "The Poet's Vow" is the more pertinent and telling critique of the major Romantics because Barrett Browning's representative poet is a lover of nature, whereas Tennyson's protagonist in "The Palace of Art" is a sterile aesthete and a lover of art, a type that less often appears in Romantic poetry.

Barrett Browning's focus on the poet's love of nature in "The Poet's Vow" reflects her critique of Coleridge as well as Wordsworth. This critique is accomplished principally through an echo of "The Rime of the Ancient Mariner" that calls in question Coleridge's vision of the mariner's redemption. After the poet looks down from his lattice on the "Three Christians" going by to prayer in "The Poet's Vow," he observes a bridal party and then a little child watching the "lizards green and rare" (300) playing near the wall. All of these sights leave him unmoved — even the child who remains "Unblessed the while for his childish smile / Which cometh unaware" (301–2). The spontaneous release that comes to the Ancient Mariner when he blesses "unaware" the watersnakes does not come to Barrett Browning's poet. The child's spontaneous response to Nature's beauty cannot undo the effects of a crime against the poet's own humanity originally motivated by a misplaced love of Nature. This passage points to the revisionary intent of Barrett Browning's poem and to her reasons for making her alienated figure a poet who sins against his "humanness" rather than a mariner who sins against nature, as in Coleridge's poem. Despite its use of supernatural incidents, "The Rime of the Ancient Mariner" powerfully reinforces the idea expressed elsewhere in the *Lyrical Ballads* by Wordsworth: that nature and natural feeling, defamiliarized by the poet, offer redemption from sin. The poem is therefore in keeping with Coleridge's well-known description in chapter fourteen of the *Biographia Literaria* of the complementary aims that he and Wordsworth had in focusing on the supernatural and the natural respectively. But the poet's feeling of fusion with nature that brings redemption in "The Rime of the Ancient Mariner" becomes the very source of alienation in "The Poet's Vow."

This alienation is only overcome in the poem's conclusion when the "wail" of the poet's "living mind" fuses with Rosalind's "senseless corpse" (462–63). While "earth and sky" look on "indifferently," God smites the poet with his own "rejected nature" (478–83), and he joins Rosalind, his fellow poet, in death, as William joins Margaret in her grave in the Percy ballad after her ghost has haunted him. "They dug beneath the kirkyard grass, / For both one dwelling deep" (491–92). Despite the tone of reconciliation here, one is more struck by the note of revenge in the conclusion to "The Poet's Vow," again typical of many Percy ballads like "Margaret's Ghost" or "Thomas and Annet," which concludes with a double murder and a suicide.[8] In Barrett Browning's rewriting of the Romantic poet's communion with nature, the supernatural joins "Triumphant Rosalind" in recalling the arrogant male poet to a recognition of her humanness as well as his.

The focus on female subjectivity in the second half of "The Poet's Vow" is intensified in Elizabeth Barrett's other ballads of the 1830s, among them, "A Romance of the Ganges," "The Romaunt of Margret," and "The Romaunt of the Page." As Hickok implies, the first of these has much in common with the exotic poems of "pseudo-Oriental sentimentalism" popular in the early nineteenth century: poems such as Letitia Landon's "The Hindoo Girl's Song" (172). "A Romance of the Ganges" has even closer affinities with the traditional ballad, however. Although the poem was written to accompany an illustration in the 1838 *Findens' Tableaux: A Series of Picturesque Scenes of National Character, Beauty, and Costume*, Barrett downplays the exotic elements of "costume," setting, and nationality. Instead, as in "The Poet's Vow," she focuses on the burning passions of love and revenge so pervasive in the old ballads. But in "A Romance of the Ganges," these passions are exclusively female, as the male lover becomes no more than an absent catalyst for the narrative conflict between the betrayed Luti and her unwitting rival Nuleeni. With a further twist, Barrett transforms the two women of "A Romance of the Ganges" from rivals in love into accomplices in revenge, much as Tennyson does in "The Sisters," a ballad which she later praised (Kelley and Hudson 6: 212). Thus Luti leads the child-like Nuleeni to vow to "whisper" to her bridegroom on her wedding day, "*There is one betrays, / While Luti suffers woe*" (lines 161–62). And to her "little bright-faced son" (165) when he asks, "What deeds his sire hath done," (167) Nuleeni vows to whisper, "*There is none denies, / While Luti speaks of wrong*" (171–72).

When Nuleeni, in wondering innocence, softly asks why Luti would wish to define a "bride-day" with a "word of *woe*" and a sinless child's ear with a "word of *wrong*" (174–81), her fellow maiden cries out:

> "Why?" Luti said, and her laugh was dread,
> And her eyes dilated wild —
> "That the fair new love may her bridegroom prove,
> And the father shame the child!" (182–85)

As Mermin notes, we begin to see in "A Romance of the Ganges" the "strong, angry heroine who dominates" most of Barrett Browning's ballads (72). Indeed, Luti's cry for revenge registers an unrepentant excess that is formal as well as emotional, for her fierce declaration appears in four extra lines that spill over the limits of the eight-line ballad stanza that Barrett employs elsewhere in "A Romance of the Ganges." It is as if the river flowing in insistent monotone through the poem's constant refrain, "The river floweth on" — resisting as well as marking each stanza's containment — has suddenly risen in angry overflow. As the refrain implies, and the narrative makes clear, Luti's bitterness and grief flow from herself to Nuleeni. Thus, the curious use of the female pronoun without a clear referent in the first stanza proves justified: "The wave-voice seems the voice of dreams / That wander through her sleep: / The river floweth on" (7–9). The pronoun in the final line — "She weepeth dark with sorrow" — is similarly ambiguous, in its possible reference to both Luti and Nuleeni. Luti could be any woman, the poem implies, and her sorrow every woman's.

In the earlier ballad "The Romaunt of Margret," the "running river" in which the protagonist encounters the shadow of her own darkest fears murmurs a parallel story of betrayal and "failing human love" (lines 39, 240). The shade that rises from the river to confront Margret torments her with the thoughts that the love of her brother, her father, her sister, and her lover — all, all will prove inconstant. The poem derives some of its power from the haunting effect of its relentlessly darkening images: the sound of "silent forests" growing between the pauses of the shade's voice (68); the recurrent trembling of its movement on the grass "with a low, shadowy laughter" (201); the shadows falling "from the stars above, / In flakes of darkness" on Margret's face (204–6) — until finally she drowns herself in despair, fusing with her dark double and, ironically, with the inconstancy of the river, in death. But even more of the power of "The Romaunt of Margret" derives from the ambiguities which Barrett subtly develops. Were Margret's dark doubts justified or not? Does she suffer from the inconstancy of others' love or the inconstancy of her own faith in love? Is the love of the knight who has given her no sign but an apparently heartfelt "look" a "transient" love because he is unfaithful or because he is dead (197, 210)? "The wild hawk's bill doth dabble still / I' the mouth that vowed thee true" (211–12) "the shade whispers with grisly relish. As Hayter suggests, lines such as these give "The Romaunt of Margret" "the true sadness of the old ballads" and their "genuine cold grue" (32).

The narrative frame of the poem, presenting an anonymous minstrel singing the "wild romaunt" of Margret to the accompaniment of a harp, suggests how closely and consciously Barrett was writing within the tradition revived by Percy's *Reliques*. Indeed, she may have felt particularly drawn to the minstrel tradition because, although Bishop Percy declared in the first edition of the *Reliques* that no "real Minstrels were of the female sex" (xviii), the fourth edition adopted by Willmott acknowledged that there "seem to have been women of this profession" for "no accomplishment is so constantly attributed to females, by our ancient Bards, as their singing to, and playing on, the Harp" (lxvi).[9] In "The Romaunt of Margret," the minstrel's sex is not revealed. But the intensity of the narrator's response to Margret's fate in the poem's concluding stanza — "Hang up my harp again! / I have no voice for song." (236–37) — may imply that the minstrel too is a woman.

Cooper observes that the minstrel's apparent identification with Margret manifests the "confused relationship of the narrator to her tale" (34) and her inadequacy to conclude her story. The minstrel's declaration, "Hang up my harp again!" is a conventional framing device, however. More importantly, it marks Barrett's movement into a deliberately ambiguous coda in which she develops the *Doppelgänger* motif at a metanarrative level as the minstrel concludes — but does not resolve — the tale of Margret's dark inner conflicts:

> O failing human love!
> O light, by darkness known!
> O false the while thou treadest earth!
> O deaf beneath the stone!
> Margret, Margret. (240–44)

The minstrel's final series of laments can be read either as a reflection of her keen identification with Margret's anguish in the face of "failing human love," or as her condemnation of Margret's own failing love. In effect, then, the minstrel mirrors the division within Margret herself embodied throughout the poem in the refrain, "Margret, Margret."

In its subtle double depiction of the dialogue of the mind with itself, "The Romaunt of Margret" justifies Cornelius Mathews's observation that Barrett's handling of the ballad form is "subjective" (Kelley and Hudson 9: 342). Yet, at the same time, like Wordsworth's complex narrative frames in the *Lyrical Ballads* (Rajan 145, 153), the narrative frame in "The Romaunt of Margret" undermines the inscription of the writer as transcendental subject. What we encounter instead is the divided post-Romantic subject that Loy D. Martin has related to the production of the dramatic monologue. The dramatic elements in "the Romaunt of Margret" are highlighted by one reviewer's comment, "We know not anything much newer or more striking, than the *prima intenzione* of 'Margret'; save, . . . in 'the Notion' (as the Americans might call it) of Mr. Browning's 'Pippa' " (Kelley and Hudson 8: 417).

iii

"THE ROMAUNT OF PAGE" IS a less "subjective" ballad than "The Romaunt of Margret," yet ultimately it is a more complex one that achieves its effects by subtly revisioning the conventional figure of the woman-page so prevalent in the drama, in ballads and in Romantic narrative verse. As Dianne Dugaw suggests in *Warrior Women and Popular Balladry, 1650–1850*, the female page has many features in common with the transvestite heroine who appears in the "Female Warrior" ballads popular throughout the seventeenth and eighteenth centuries, ballads in which a woman disguised as a man follows her lover to war or to sea (146, 172). Barrett Browning was undoubtedly familiar with one of the most famous of the female warrior ballads, the variant on "Mary Ambree" included in Percy's *Reliques*. In illuminating the social and historical conditions that explain the immense popularity of the "Female Warrior" ballads among all social classes, Dugaw's study indirectly suggests why a literary ballad like "The Romaunt of the Page" had such a widespread appeal at a time when popular ballads like "Mary Ambree" were dying out because of an increasingly inflexible "semiotics of gender" (164).

Mitford revealed her critical acumen in making "The Romaunt of the Page" the lead poem in the 1839 *Findens' Tableaux of the Affections: A Series of Picturesque Illustrations of the Womanly Virtues*. She also singled it out in the "Preface" and praised it privately to Barrett: "Let me say, my sweetest, that the 'Romaunt of the Page' (which is a tragedy of the very deepest and highest order) always seems to me by far the finest thing that you have ever written; and I do entreat and conjure you to write more ballads or tragedies — call them what you will — like that; that is to say, poems of human feelings and human actions" (Kelley and Hudson 5: 135). Reviews of the 1839 *Findens'*, with the exception of *The Literary Gazette*, were equally laudatory, describing "The Romaunt of the Page" as "full of fancy and originality," "shewing true and original genius," "a poem with the spirit of the elder and better day of poetry in every line of it," "full of the early spirit of English poetry" (Kelley and Hudson 4: 405–6). As the last two descriptions indicate, like Mitford, reviewers linked "The Romaunt of the Page" to the early ballads recovered in the Romantic revival. Henry Chorley was atypical in relating the poem to the exclusively female tradition of Hemans's "Records of Woman" in his *Athenaeum* reviews of *Findens'* and of the 1844 *Poems* (Kelley and Hudson 4: 409; 9: 320). Chorley's association seems somewhat justified: the conclusion of "The Romaunt of the Page" may have been influenced by Hemans's ballad "Woman on the Field of Battle" (which appeared in *Songs of the Affections*, however, not *Records of Woman*). But there is much more reason to interpret "The Romaunt of the Page" as an ironically allusive adaptation of narrative and character configurations in both Scott's *Marmion* and some of the Percy ballads, "Child Waters" definitely, and perhaps "The Not-Browne Mayd" as well.

In "Woman on the Field of Battle" Hemans pictures a "gentle and lovely form" with "golden hair" (lines 1, 11) slain on the battlefield, much as Barrett's woman/page is slain by the Saracens. A passage in the manuscript of "The Romaunt of the Page," not included in either the *Findens'* or the 1844 version of the ballad, may echo Hemans's poem, as Barrett describes the slain page with the wind lifting "aside her golden hair" to "show the smile beneath it fair."[10] Only one motive could have led a woman to such a death, Hemans declares in her ballad: not glory, but love, which "Woman's deep soul too long / Pours on the dust'' (235). Love is also a motive contributing to the fate of Barrett's heroine, but in this case it is only one element in a subtle mix of circumstances, motives, and passions. Whereas Hemans presents a static, sentimental tableau of womanly sacrifice, showing no interest in the narrative that leads up to it, Barrett develops an ironic series of narrative conflicts in which a knight and a lady are alike victimized by a system of gender relations in which women function as objects of exchange.

These conflicts and the passions that accompany them were intensified by the substantial revisions Barrett made in ''The Romaunt of the Page'' for its reissue in the 1844 *Poems*, revisions unnoted in existing interpretations of the poem. Chorley observes in his review of the 1844 *Poems* that she ''much simplified'' ''The Romaunt of the Page'' in revising the *Findens'* version (Kelley and Hudson 9: 320). But the observation is inaccurate. While Barrett did eliminate some of the archaic diction, along with the interesting epigraph from Beaumont and Fletcher (''The trustiest, loving'st, and the gentlest boy / That ever master had''), she made the narrative itself fuller, more complex, more ironic, and more conflicted by developing the psychology of the knight and the page. Nevertheless the knight, because he is so ideologically blinded by the very system that victimizes him, emerges as more culpable than the page in both the *Findens'* and the 1844 version. He is as unchivalric and ungrateful as Child Waters, and although unwittingly, he betrays his lady as much as Marmion betrays his woman-page Constance. Significantly, a reference to the knight speaking ''kindly'' to the page in the manuscript (in the original version of line 63) is deleted in the published versions of the poem.

Using an *in medias res* construction, Barrett begins with a knight and a page returning from ''the holy war in Palestine'' (1. 3), where the page has saved the knight's life ''once in the tent, and twice in the fight'' (11). In the manuscript the knight is nameless, while in the *Findens'* version he becomes Sir Hubert — but the poet refers to him by name only once, as if to stress his role as a representative knight. As thoughts of home fill the minds of both, the nameless page recalls the dying prayer of his mother, while the knight points out to the page that, although he has proven himself in battle, he is too silent to serve well in the bower of the knight's lady. The page leads the knight to speak more of his lady: is she ''little loved or loved aright'' (100), asking a question that takes a more pointed form than it does in the manuscript, where this line appears simply as ''And tell me if that loved aright''? Gloomily, the knight explains that he does not even know what his lady looks like — that he married her in haste and darkness before leaving for Palestine, out of a sense of obligation to his friend Earl Walter, who lost his life in avenging the honor of the knight's own dead father. When the Earl's wife died, she sent for the knight and asked him to marry her daughter, the ''sweet child'' made ''an orphan for thy father's sake''

(162–63). Bitterly the knight recalls how his bride rose from the ceremony "[a]nd kissed the smile of her mother dead, / Or ever she kissed me" (180–81).

In revising "The Romaunt of the Page" for her 1844 *Poems*, Barrett greatly expanded the knight's inset narrative of the marriage forced on him by circumstance and the chivalric code — a narrative reversing the conventional plot in which a knight or a "stranger (to all save the reader)," as Robert Browning facetiously remarked, wins a bride because the father owes his life or some other debt to him (Kintner 2: 881). In the *Findens'* version and in the manuscript, Earl Walter is a nameless "Baron," and stanza 16, the first half of stanza 17, and stanza 19 do not appear; while very different versions of stanzas 15 and 18 present a brief narrative of the actions and circumstances leading up to the marriage. The additions in stanzas 17 and 19 create sympathy for the knight and develop his motives and passions with some psychological depth as he declares that it would have been better if he had avenged his own father and died rather than have "murdered friend and marriage-ring / Forced on my life together" (146–47).

Responding with tears of grief to the knight's tale, the page explains that his own sister was married as the knight's lady was but that she "laid down the silks she wore" and followed her new husband to the "battle-place" "[d]isguised as his true servitor" (186, 189, 188). The knight reacts with a "careless laugh":

> "Well done it were for thy sister,
> But not for my ladye!
> My love, so please you, shall requite
> No woman, whether dark or bright,
> Unwomaned if she be." (191–96)

Here again, Barrett's revisions intensify the conflict between her two characters and, in this case, emphasize the ideological system of "true womanhood" she is critiquing. In the manuscript, the knight simply laughs "loudly." In *Findens'*, his laugh is "gay," not "careless," and the last three lines of his declaration are briefer and less unequivocal: "No woman bright, my love requite / Unwomaned if she be." In the manuscript, the last line is still less extreme — "If she loved not womanly." The revisions indicate that, in the knight's eyes, any wife who follows her husband to battle disguised as a page destroys the very core of her womanhood.

This is a dogma that the page strongly questions in another passage that Barrett revised to intensify the conflict between the knight and the page:

> "Your wisdom may declare
> That womanhood is proved the best

> By golden brooch and glossy vest
>   The mincing ladies wear;
> Yet it is proved, and was of old,
> Anear as well, I dare to hold,
>   By truth, or by despair." (198–204)

In the manuscript, the first line of this passage simply reads as "It seems that everywhere." In *Findens'* it is "Some wisdoms may declare." But in the 1844 version, Barrett makes it plain that it is the knight's limited "wisdom" that the page is questioning. The last three lines of this passage are also more emphatic in the 1844 version. In the manuscript and *Findens'* there are only two lines: "And yet 'tis almost proved as well / by truth . . . or by despair" in the manuscript, and the equally tentative "Yet almost is it proved as well" in *Findens'*. In the 1844 version, however, the page emphasizes how true love is "proved" both in the present and "of old."

As the page passionately defends his hypothetical sister's actions to the scornful knight, Barrett presents her ironically paradoxical vision of the "womanly virtues" the 1839 *Findens'* was meant to celebrate:

> "Oh, womanly she prayed in tent,
>   When none beside did wake!
> Oh, womanly she paled in fight,
>   For one beloved's sake! —
> And her little hand, defiled with blood,
> Her tender tears of womanhood
>   Most woman-pure did make!" (207–13)

Such a combination of heroic valor "in fight" and womanly devotion is also quite typical of the "Female Warrior" ballads that Dugaw explores, but in early nineteenth-century variants on these, as in "The Romaunt of the Page," insistent "gender markers" like Barrett's phrase 'little hand" became much more common (149).

Little hand or not, such a woman-servitor is wholly unacceptable in the eyes of Barrett's knight, who reiterates his belief in a more conventional type of womanly virtue that hides behind a veil. "No casque shall hide her woman's tear" (220), he declares, in an ironically prophetic, punning line that does not appear in the manuscript. According to the knight, womanly virtue is "[s]o high, so pure, and so apart" from the world that it shines like "a small bright cloud / Alone amid the skies!" (230–33). When the page asks, what if his lady "mistook thy mind / And followed thee to strife" (223–24), he asserts that he "would forgive" her and "evermore / Would love her as my servitor / But little as my wife" (227–29). The revision of "mistook thy will" (in the manuscript) to "mistook thy mind" in the first published version indicates what the page is up against here: not a mere matter of will, but of mindset or ideology. In such a context, the "strife" the page refers to is as much marital as martial.

When the little cloud that provokes the knight's comparison disappears behind a blacker one, the page sees the Saracens approaching. But while "the page seeth all," "the knight seeth none" (241), presumably because his eyes are still dazzled by what Barrett scornfully referred to as the "cloud-minding theory" of true womanhood. As Stephenson has shown (29–32), the poet emphasized in her letters to Mitford that the chivalric theory of idealized womanhood was as confining for women as the "pudding-making and stocking-darning" theory. " 'Twas a stroke of policy in those ranty-pole barons of old to make their lady-loves idols, and curb their wives with silken idleness," another Victorian woman astutely remarked (qtd. in Poovey, *Uneven* 147). The sterility of the chivalric ideal of passive womanhood is dramatically revealed in "The Romance of the Swan's Nest," in many ways the counterpart of "The Romaunt of the Page." In this depiction of a young girl's fantasies, the female who opts for the conventional lady's role of inspiring rather than following her knight — of being his idol rather than his disguised page and "servitor" — is as bitterly betrayed as her more active opposite. As Cooper suggests (97), Little Ellie's fate in "The Romance of the Swan's Nest" shows how "dreaming courtly fantasies . . . gnaws at women's energy, sexuality, and identity" as insidiously as the rat gnaws at the reeds surrounding the empty swan's nest in the poem's ending.

"The Romaunt of the Page" concludes with the page sending the blind knight on ahead to safety, while the loyal "servitor" drops her disguise, and the embittered wife exclaims,

> "Have I renounced my womanhood
>   For wifehood unto *thee*,
> And is this the last, last look of thine
>   That ever I shall see?
>
> Yet God thee save, and mayst thou have
>   A lady to thy mind,
> More woman-proud and half as true
>   As one thou leav'st behind!" (276–83)

Disillusioned by earthly love, Earl Walter's daughter turns to God's love and faces the "Paynims," a "Christian page" who taunts the enemy as boldly as any knight might do (295, 301). "False page, but truthful woman" (297), she dauntlessly dies beneath the scimitar, meeting its downward sweep "[w]ith smile more bright in victory / Than any sword from sheath" (325–26).

Mermin observes of this conclusion that the protagonist of "The Romaunt of the Page" "succumbs to an ideal of 'womanly virtues' that the poet both scorns and shares" in that she chooses "a woman's fate — unrecognizing, self-sacrificing death" (91–92). Hickok similarly views the poem as "a sentimental tale of extreme wifely devotion and self-sacrifice," although one used to "arraign the maleficence of current nineteenth-century notions about women" (173). Certainly, some Victorian readers interpreted "The Romaunt of the Page" in sentimental and conventional terms: for example, Thomas Bradfield cited the "cloud" metaphor for woman's honor out of context as proof of Mrs. Browning's "profound admiration of the devotion so characteristic" of medieval women (178).

What such readings do not address, however, is the fact that Barrett's heroic page never acts more like a man, in conventional terms, than when she is "truthful woman." Even her smile flashes like a sword. Moreover, her motives are mixed rather than "pure" in that, like so many ballad-women, she is driven as much by revenge as devotion. In revising "The Romaunt of the Page," Barrett progressively intensified the woman-page's more vindictive motives. Thus, in the manuscript version, the page wishes her knight may find another lady "More woman-proud, yet all as true / As one thou leavest behind." In *Findens'*, she wishes him a lady "More woman-proud, not faithfuller / Than one thou leav'st behind!" The change from "not faithfuller" to "half as true" is startling, bringing out the anger implicit in line 250, where "ride on thy way" is substituted for the more tender address "my master dear" appearing in the *Findens'* version. The page's possessive pledge to be near to her master as "parted spirits cleave / To mortals too beloved to leave" (259–60) has a rather ominous note to it as well, intensified in the revision from the *Findens'* version, "as parted spirits are near / The thrice beloved they loved here." Does the outraged wife plan to bless her husband from above, like Catarina, or to haunt him? Perhaps the thought of her will indeed haunt him when he arrives home and realizes that the page who sacrificed himself for him was also the wife he so fiercely resented — a quite probable narrative extrapolation that is not considered in interpreting the page's sacrifice as "unrecognized." He may be "a knight of gallant deeds," as he is introduced in the revised 1844 version. (In *Findens'* he is simply "a knight upon a steed.") But he may discover, as the reader already has, that in this particular "romaunt," the page and not the knight performs the "gallant deeds."

The ironies permeating "The Romaunt of the Page" are intensified when Barrett's revisioning of the lady-page figure is read against its prototypes in ballads like "Child Waters" and "The Not-Browne Mayd" and in Scott's *Marmion*. The immediate inspiration of "The Romaunt of the Page" was the illustration Mitford sent to the poet, picturing a woman disguised as a page, wearing a very short skirt and hiding behind a tree in the foreground, while a knight rides away from her in the background.[11] But it is clear that the conventions of the old ballads and "Child Waters" in particular were in Barrett's mind when she composed the poem. Apologizing to Mitford for the length of her "long barbarous ballad," she quips, "I ought to blush — as ladyes always do in ballads — 'scarlet-red.' " Then she adds, "By the way, the pictured one pretty as she is, has a good deal exaggerated the ballad-receipt for making a ladye page — Do you remember? — 'And you must cut your gowne of green / An *INCH* above the knee'! — She comes within the fi fa fum of the prudes, in consequence" (Kelley and Hudson 4: 33, 38).

The "receipt for making a ladye page" cited here is Child Waters's own, in the ballad of the same title (Percy 3: 58–65). Hardly the conventional model of chivalry, he instructs his female companion Ellen, swollen with child by him, to cut off her skirt and her hair and run barefoot as his "foot-page" by his side. He is not even "so curteous a knighte, / To say, Put on your shoone." Nor is this the end of Ellen's ordeals. At Child Waters's bidding, she must run by his side into the "north countrie," swim a swollen river, stable and feed his horse, find him a paramour to spend the night with (while she lies at the foot of the bed!), and then feed his horse again. Finally, as she is moaning with labor pains in the stable, Child Waters's mother hears her, the gallant knight in his "shirte of silke" arrives to see the babe born, and, like Griselda, Ellen is rewarded. Child Waters tells her to be of "good cheere": he will marry her. But the poem ends before the marriage takes place.

The frankly physical treatment of Ellen's ordeals supplies an interesting subtext to the declaration of Barrett's knight that, if his lady followed him as his page, he would love her as his "servitor" but not as his wife. In other respects, however, "The Romaunt of the Page" works against, not with, the text of "Child Waters" by reversing its plot and making marriage the beginning and cause of the page's ordeals, not the end. Moreover, the "Romaunt" shifts the focus in its title and its narrative perspective to the woman-page rather than the knight. In Barrett's ballad, it is the knight who is tested and found wanting, not the woman who is tested and rewarded.

A testing of woman's devotion similar to that appearing in "Child Waters" appears in "The Not-Browne Mayd," in which the minstrel depicts a "SHE–HE" debate between a Baron's daughter and a "squyer of lowe de-gre" in order to defend women against the men who malign their constancy (Percy 2:26–42). As the squire repeatedly tells his lady that he is a "banyshed man" who must go the "grene wode" alone, she vows that she will give up and endure all to be with him: she will sacrifice her good name; she will fight by his side, though "women be / But feble for to fyght"; and she will cut her hair and her "kyrtel by the kne" as he requests. He then denounces her as a light woman who would vow such for any man, much as the knight denounces any woman who would follow him into battle in "The Romaunt of the Page." But after further protestations on the "not-browne mayd's" part, and further testing, the squire declares her to be a constant woman — and reveals that the entire dialogue has been based upon a ruse. He is not a banished man; indeed, he is an Earl's son who vows to marry her. The gender conflicts in the poem are not really resolved, however, since the lady is left questioning the "wyle" her lover has used with her as well as the constancy of men. "[O]ne of the most beautiful & true of our Ballad-poems, is the antique original of the 'Notte browne Mayde,' " Barrett observed in 1843, objecting to Matthew Prior's version of it in "Henry and Emma" — a modernization that "desecrated" the original (Kelley and Hudson 7: 266).

Marmion more directly suggests the perils that attend the woman who proves her love by following her knight as his page, although Scott's text depicts the old story of women suffering from male falsehood, whereas Barrett's shows both sexes suffering from a false ideology. When Constance breaks her religious vows to follow Marmion disguised as "a horse-boy in his train," he treats her as such, making her not only his servitor but also his whore (Scott 54). *Marmion* suggests why, in the more prudish 1830s, Barrett was careful to have her heroine marry her knight before following him as his page. Betraying his promise to marry Constance, Marmion pursues the wealthy young Clara instead. Clara is forced to flee to St. Hilda's convent and a novitiate's veil in order to elude him, so that Marmion's wickedness almost leads to the symbolic burial of one woman and the literal burial of another, when Constance is immured alive in the dungeon walls of Lindisfarne Monastery for breaking her vows. Like Barrett's page, the forsaken Constance is constant in love, and in revenge. Before she goes to her doom, she gives up the information that will prevent Marmion's marriage to Clara and bring about his downfall. The passages describing Constance's vow to take revenge are among the most powerful in Scott's entire poem, and it is highly likely that, given the immense popularity of *Marmion*, they influenced Barrett's depiction of her lady-page. Certainly the subtle counterpoint she creates in "The Romaunt of the Page" between the narrative action and the memorial chant for the dead Lady Abbess — "*Beati, beati, mortui!* / From the convent on the sea" (line 71) — seems to have been suggested by *Marmion*. Scott's epic is similarly structured by a counterpoint between Marmion's military exploits and the quieter scenes depicting the Lady Abbess of St. Hilda's travelling to Lindisfarne Monastery, with the sounds of her nuns' voices carrying across the wave much as the dirge of St. Mary's nuns is carried from the convent "on the sea" in "The Romaunt of the Page." Significantly, this prophetic dirge first interrupts the narrative at the point where the lady disguised as a page blushes "sudden red" as ladies in ballads conventionally do and confesses to the knight that his lady's bower is "suited well" to her (68, 70). As in the case of Scott's Constance, however, female desire is checked by death. In *Marmion*, the Abbess of St. Hilda is one of three church authorities who condemn Constance to her living burial in the walls of the monastery. In "The Romaunt of the Page," the link between the Abbess and the page is forged in two lines Barrett appears to have added to her conclusion: "Dirge for abbess laid in shroud / Sweepeth o'er the shroudless dead" (341–42).[12]

iv

BARRETT'S ADAPTATION OF elements in *Marmion* is even more apparent in "The Lay of the Brown Rosary," the ballad in the 1840 *Findens'* that, next to "The Romaunt of the Page," was one of her most popular works before the 1844 *Poems* appeared. "The Lay of the Brown Rosary" is a ballad that anticipates Charlotte Brontë's *Villette* in its adaptation of Gothic conventions to represent intense psychic conflicts. Like Brontë, Barrett symbolically develops the figure of the buried nun popularized by Scott's *Marmion* and other works. But whereas Scott's central focus in *Marmion* is male and military, Barrett's, like Brontë's after her, is on the conflicts of female desire with institutionalized repression that speak so powerfully in the interstices of his narrative through the narrative flashbacks and the monastic interludes that link Constance with Clare. The *Doppelgänger* motif linking Onora, the heroine of "The Lay of the Brown Rosary," with the defiant cursing nun, buried alive for her sins, makes this poem a "subjective" ballad like "The Romaunt of Margret," but it is a more daring work, too complex in its play of intertextual allusions to consider fully here. Along with *Marmion*, "The Lay of the Brown Rosary" also seems to draw on *Faust*, "Christabel," Bürger's "Lenora," and possibly some of the Percy ballads, fusing elements from these texts in a highly original way with Barrett's own innovations, among them the heroine's dream, which she herself thought of as "rather original in its manner" (Kelley and Hudson 6: 276). Any analysis of "The Lay of Brown Rosary" is further complicated by the extensive revisions made in the poem between its first appearance in the 1840 *Findens' Tableaux* and its publication in 1844: among others, the change of the heroine's name from Lenora (a direct link with Bürger's ballad) to Onora.

"Rhyme of the Duchess May" also reflects Barrett's adaptation of motifs from Bürger's "Lenora," in this case, as we have seen, creating a connection readily detected by the *Westminster* reviewer Sarah Flower Adams. By echoing Lenora's swift, dark gallop to the bridal bed of the grave with the ghost of her slain lover, Barrett subtly foreshadows the fate of the orphan Duchess

May and her newly-wed husband Sir Guy of Linteged as they flee to his castle, evading her guardian, the Earl of Leigh, and the cousin whose hand in marriage she spurns: "Fast and fain the bridal train along the night-storm rod [*sic*] amain" (line 89). Reminiscent of "Lenora" too, "The Duchess May" depicts what one Victorian critic aptly described as a "dark bridal" concluding with a "double death-ride" (Massey 527). Facing certain defeat after a fourteen-day siege by the Leighs in which his castle has "seethed in blood" (43), the anguished Sir Guy seeks to save the lives of his loyal men by riding from his castle tower to a sacrificial death — accompanied, against his will, by his young bride, who leaps into the saddle with him at the last minute. Contemporary readers were especially taken by this spectacular and novel climax, which Mermin astutely interprets as "in effect a bold, bizarre sexual consummation" (93) — even if it does occur three months after the Duchess's actual marriage to Sir Guy.

"Rhyme of the Duchess May" adapts situations and scenes from the old Scottish ballad "Edom o' Gordon" as well as from Bürger's "Lenora," although its "double death" leap was probably suggested by Benjamin Haydon's painting, "Curtius Leaping into the Gulf."[13] The hero of "Edom o' Gordon" is not the brutal border raider referred to in the title but the fiercely loyal Scottish lord's wife who takes a stand on her castle walls and valiantly resists Gordon and his men in her husband's absence (Percy 1: 99–106). Like the "Female Warrior" in the Percy variant of "Mary Ambree," who also mounts the walls of a besieged castle and "all undaunted" faces the enemy (Percy 2: 212–216), the Scottish wife in "Edom o' Gordon" may have provided Barrett with an image of heroic womanhood like that "miracle of noble womanhood" later introduced by Tennyson into the "Prologue" to *The Princess* (Ricks 223–24). But she rejects the futile and passive sacrifice of the Scottish lord's daughter in the old ballad, who is lowered over the castle walls in a "pair o' sheits" — only to be spitted on "the point of Gordon's spear" until "the red bluid dreips" over her yellow hair (68–69). Instead, she depicts a more active and heroic sacrificial leap on the part of the Duchess, whom she made more forceful and willful in revising her poem. As in the case of "The Romaunt of the Page," Barrett's revisions to "Rhyme of the Duchess May" also intensify and complicate the psychological and narrative conflict between the newly-wed wife and husband. The most substantial addition to the Berg draft greatly expands upon the complex mix of nobility and blind condescension in Sir Guy's treatment of the Duchess as a representative woman, who "will weep her woman's tears" and "pray her woman's prayers." This addition makes Sir Guy less a stock character and more a prototype of Romney in *Aurora Leigh* and, like Barrett's most significant addition to "The Romaunt of the Page," it reveals her growing interest in representing female lives in the context of ideologies of gender. Other revisions in "Rhyme of the Duchess May" refine the artistry of the verse form itself, as Barrett employs the poem's unusual stanza and the refrain, "Toll slowly," to create both the pulsing, headlong rush of passion and action and the stillness of deathful peace pervading the ballad's frame story of a reader in a churchyard, beside the grave of a three-year-old child.

This reader is like yet different from the minstrel who narrates the tale in "The Romaunt of Margret." In revising "Rhyme of the Duchess May," Barrett more fully developed the narrator's ambivalence towards the "burn-ing" intensity of the passions the poem presents. She also altered the date on the child's grave from 1453 to 1843, the year in which she was writing. The divided framing subject here is thus not an anonymous traditional minstrel but the modern narrator/reader herself or himself — the connection between the two effectively implied by Barrett's depiction of the narrator *as* a reader in "Rhyme of the Duchess May." We might consider too that the medieval scenes and gender relations Barrett depicts in her "ancient rhyme" (line 21) may have seemed paradoxically quite modern in the early 1840s, when the medieval revival was in full swing and the earl of Eglinton had recently staged a mammoth tournament, attended by tens of thousands, on the grounds of his castle, and featuring "knights on horseback in full armour, a Queen of Beauty, jesters, heralds, pavilions and a banquet" — all turned into a "fiasco by two days of torrential rain" (Culler 159).

Deborah Byrd suggests that Victorian women poets like Barrett Browning turned to the Middle Ages because it was envisioned "as a time in which at least some women had control over their property and destiny and the courage to venture into the 'male' arenas of politics and war" (33). There is much truth in this. The women Barrett Browning encountered in the Percy ballads and even in Scott's romances were not yet confined by what Mary Poovey has analysed as the cult of the "proper lady." In fact, in its frankly physical depiction of strong, heroic, or long-suffering women like Ellen in "Child Waters," the traditional ballad, that "Cinderella" among the Muses, very often was not the bashful maiden Hales and Furnivall quaintly imagined. At the same time, however, Barrett Browning was no celebrator of the often brutal and violent gender and human relations that prevailed in the Middle Ages when a "black chief" was "half knight, half sheep-lifter" — like Edom o' Gordon and his kind — and a "beauteous dame" was "half chattel and half queen" (*Aurora Leigh* 5. 195–96). Thus she both echoes and strategi-cally revises traditional ballads in order to dramatize the crudely overt power structures of the society that also produced the chivalric idealization of women. These power structures are blatantly apparent, for instance, when the younger Lord Leigh threatens to take the Duchess May in marriage over the "altar" of her husband's corpse: "I will wring thy fingers pale in the gauntlet of my mail . . . 'Little hand and muckle gold' close shall lie within my hold, / As the sword did, to prevail'' (149–52). If, as Michel Foucault suggests, a changing ''technology of power'' transformed brutal and external social constraints into more internalized and carefully concealed ''humane'' forms by the nineteenth century (qtd. in Lootens 122–23), ballads like Barrett Browning's reverse that strategic transformation in their depiction of gender relations.

Barrett Browning's later ballads typically use contemporary rather than medieval settings. The often noted progression in her ballads from medieval to modern contexts is manifested not only in ''Lady Geraldine's Courtship'' but also in the very interesting unpublished ''The Princess Marie,'' in the ''Sonnets'' notebook now in the Armstrong Browning Library, dating from the 1842–44 period. This unfinished poem in ballad stanzas focuses on Princess Marie, daughter of King Louis Philippe of France. Phillip Sharp, who supplies a helpful account of its historical context, along with a somewhat unreliable transcription of the manuscript, describes ''The Princess Marie'' as a ''domestic poem about a head of state'' (169). But what really seems to have interested Barrett in the Princess Marie was not her relation to Louis Philippe, but her skill in sculpture and the human cost of her devotion to her art. Thus, ''The Princess Marie'' is not only a ballad in which Barrett Browning turns to contemporary subjects but also one anticipating her focus on the woman-artist in *Aurora Leigh* and in the powerful late ballad-monologue, ''Mother and Poet.''

Although they move farther away from their prototypes in the old English and Scottish ballads and the narrative verse of the Romantic Revival, most of Barrett Browning's ballads after 1844 continue to exhibit some of the features considered in this essay: in particular, the ironic manipulation of traditional ballad plots and motifs (often through narrative reversals or doublings), the focus on female subjectivity and the conflicts of female desire, and the exploration of ideological links between the ''female plots'' shaping women's lives and the gender plots of encompassing ideologies. The female perspective, complicated by lingering ironies, is apparent in the deceptively simple ''Amy's Cruelty,'' for instance, where Barrett Browning explores female as well as male possessiveness in love. The manipulation of traditional ballad conventions is perhaps most evident in the often praised ''Lord Walter's Wife.'' Like ''The Not-Browne Mayd'' in the Percy collection, ''Lord Walter's Wife'' contains elements of the debate or flyting match concerning female constancy. Yet typically, Barrett Browning subverts conventional expectations by dramatizing the contradictions and sexual double standard in male perceptions of women and by again showing a man tested and found wanting, not the woman he flirts with and condemns.

The ironies in ''Lord Walter's Wife'' are more direct than those in ''Amy's Cruelty'' and in many of Barrett Browning's earlier ballads. Indeed, they were too direct for William Thackeray who, in his well-known exchange with Barrett Browning, considered the poem too frank in its "account of unlawful passion" to be published in the *Cornhill Magazine*, "written not only for men and women but for boys, girls, infants, sucklings almost," as he emphasized with histrionic hyperbole (Kenyon 2: 444–45). Perhaps Thackeray was in part responding to the omniscient narrative perspective in "Lord Walter's Wife" that clearly identified the poem's voice with Barrett Browning herself — that is, with "Browning's wife and Penini's mother," to use his own words. Barrett Browning had published ballads before "Lord Walter's Wife" that treated "unlawful" passions even more frankly — most notably, "The Runaway Slave at Pilgrim's Point." But she had used dramatic speakers in these poems. The license these speakers gave her was no doubt one reason why, like Robert Browning, she was attracted to dramatic poetical forms, and to the dramatic monologue in particular.

Barrett Browning's ballads, with their paradoxical combination of the medieval and the modern and their strong, transgressive women, had an influence on subsequent writers that remains to be explored. Their impact on the Pre-Raphaelite poets, in particular, is often acknowledged in passing, yet still largely uninvestigated. Over a century ago, Arthur Benson commented on Mrs. Browning's "fancy for pure romantic writing, since developed to such perfection by Rossetti," singling out for praise "The Romaunt of the Page" and "Rhyme of the Duchess May" (224). In 1900, Porter and Clarke, editors of her complete works, similarly observed that "Rossetti and others of the pre-Raphaelite brotherhood" had followed Barrett Browning in writing "modern ballads," "archaic in diction and suggestion" but striking "new themes." "But her ballads were first," Porter and Clarke remind us. "They are miracles of sympathetic reproduction of an old *genre* in new substance" (*Works* 2: xiii). Hayter suggests one reason why the influence of Barrett Browning on the Pre-Raphaelites was "forgotten," despite Porter and Clarke's reminder, in noting how critics after 1900 characteristically apologized for and dismissed the many traces of "Mrs. Browning" in the works of D. G. Rossetti and William Morris (231–32). As long as this subtle work of cultural "forgetting" lies unanalyzed and unopposed, and as long as Barrett Browning's ballads continue to be excluded from standard surveys of Victorian poetry, while the Victorian ballad itself remains a form denigrated for its very popularity, there will be a missing link in the history of the ballad revival that continues to influence a wide range of writers today. Bob Dylan, whose "Desolation Row" is now studied alongside T. S. Eliot's "The Waste Land," might describe himself too as a "writer of ballads."

Dalhousie University

NOTES

1. Barrett Browning substantially altered the opening of *A Drama of Exile*, for instance, in the 1853 edition of her *Poems*. Although Margaret Reynolds and Julia Markus have produced excellent editions of *Aurora Leigh* and *Casa Guidi Windows* respectively, a scholarly edition of Barrett Browning's remaining works has not, so far as I am aware, been undertaken to date. In contrast, at least four scholarly editions of Robert Browning's works have been produced or undertaken in the last twenty years.

2. "The Romaunt of Margret" and "The Lay of the Brown Rosary" were other ballads revised by Barrett Browning between successive publications. The latter is the ballad she most substantially revised after its initial publication.

3. The following editions are typical: *Lady Geraldine's Courtship*, illustrated by W. J. Hennessy and engraved by W. J. Liften (New York: Charles Scribner & Co., 1870); *Rhyme of the Duchess May*, illustrated by Charlotte M. B. Morrell [London: Sampson Low & Co., 1873]; *Lady Geraldine's Courtship* in the Vest-Pocket Series of Standard Authors, also illustrated (Boston: J. R. Osgood & Co., 1876); *Lady Geraldine's Courtship*, illustrated by G. C. Wilmshurt and decorated by Franklin Booth (New York: D. Appleton & Co., 1907); *Rhyme of the Duchess May* one of the Envelope Books (#2.) illustrated by Katherine Cameron (Edinburgh: T. N. Foulis [1907]); *Lady Geraldine's Courtship* (London: Siegle, Hill & Co., 1911. Langham Booklets). See Warner Barnes's bibliography for additional reprints.

4. Lines 299–300 in Fitzgerald's copy, vol. 2 of *Poems* by Elizabeth Barrett Browning, 3rd edition (London: Chapman & Hall, 1853) 14. I am grateful for permission to refer to Eliza Fitzgerald's copy of Barrett Browning's 1853 *Poems* and to manuscripts of Barrett Browning's in the Armstrong Browning Library, directed by Roger L. Brooks. I particularly wish to thank Betty A. Coley for the generous sharing of her expertise.

5. Barrett Browning owned the 5th edition of the *Reliques*, acquired in 1826 (Kelley and Coley 156). Since I did not have access to this edition, I have used the first, supplementing it with Willmott's, which is based on the fourth edition.

6. The numerous echoes of Tennyson's 1842 *Poems* in the revised version of "The Poet's Vow" reflect the influence of "Locksley Hall" as well as 'The Palace of Art." John Kenyon loaned the 1842 *Poems* to Barrett in May when they first appeared. Thanking him, she said that she had only seen "one" of Tennyson's "two preceding volumes" before, "having enquired for the other vainly" (Kelley and Hudson 5: 348). *The Browning Collections* indicates that Barrett had a copy of Tennyson's 1830 volume *Poems, Chiefly Lyrical*, inscribed "Nov. 1st, 1836" (Kelley and Coley 193).

7. Before Barrett's 1844 *Poems* appeared, Tennyson was reported to have said to Moxon, "There is only one female poet whom I wish to see . . . & that is Miss Barrett" (Kelley and Hudson 7: 4). The conclusion to "the Two Voices" was not completed until 1837 or early 1838 (Ricks 101), after "The Poet's Vow" had appeared in the *New Monthly Magazine* of October 1836. Barrett highly praised "The Two Voices" when it appeared (Kelley and Hudson 6: 220) and marked several passages in her copy of the 1842 *Poems* (Kelley and Coley 192).

8. The latter does not appear in the first edition of the *Reliques*; see the Willmott edition, 518–21.

9. Because I have not had access to all editions of the *Reliques*, I have not been able to determine when or why this significant revision was made.

10. Berg Collection. The ms appears in the notebook identified as Berg Notebook Three in *The Browning Collections* (D1399), which Kelley and Coley describe as containing "drafts for *Poems* 1844" (373). But almost all of the poems in this notebook appeared in the 1838 volume *The Seraphim, and Other Poems*. It appears to be the earliest of the four Berg notebooks. For permission to consult and quote from the Berg notebooks, I am grateful to the Henry W. and Albert A. Berg Collection, The New York Public Library, Astor, Lenox and Tilden Foundations.

11. All of the *Findens'* pictures for which Barrett Browning wrote poems are reproduced in Kelley and Hudson 4: 192–93.

12. I could find nothing corresponding to these lines in the Berg manuscript, but at points the writing on the last page is too faded to be legible.

13. My brief comments here on the intertextuality and the manuscript revisions of "Rhyme of the Duchess May" summarize work-in-progress on an article extending the argument of this one. "A Cinderella Among the Muses" is partially based on a chapter in the book I am currently completing on Elizabeth Barrett Browning for Macmillan's Women Writers Series. This book will also include a chapter on the group of Barrett Browning's ballads I have chosen to treat as dramatic monologues.

WORKS CITED

Barnes, Warner. *A Bibliography of Elizabeth Barrett Browning*. Austin: U of Texas P, 1967.

Barthes, Roland. "Theory of the Text." *Untying the Text: a Post-Structuralist Reader*. Ed. Robert Young. London: Routledge and Kegan Paul, 1981. 31–47.

Bayne, Peter. *Two Great Englishwomen: Mrs. Browning & Charlotte Brontë, with an Essay on Poetry, Illustrated from Wordsworth, Burns, and Byron*. London: James Clarke, 1881.

Benson, Arthur. *Essays*. London: Heinemann, 1896.

Borg, James M. "The Fashioning of Elizabeth Barrett Browning's *Aurora Leigh*." Diss. Northwestern U, 1979.

Bradfield, Thomas. "The Ethical Impulse of Mrs. Browning's Poetry." *Westminster Review* 146 (1896): 174–84.

Bratton, J. S. *The Victorian Popular Ballad*. London: Macmillan, 1975.

Browning, Elizabeth Barrett. *Aurora Leigh*. Ed. Margaret Reynolds. Athens: Ohio UP, 1992.

———. *Casa Guidi Windows*. Ed. Julia Markus. New York: The Browning Institute, 1977.

———. *The Complete Works of Elizabeth Barrett Browning*. Ed. Charlotte Porter and Helen A. Clarke. 6 vols. New York: Thomas Y. Crowell, 1900; rpt. AMS P, 1973.

———. "The Poet's Vow." *New Monthly Magazine*. 48 (October, 1836): 209–18.

———. "The Romaunt of the Page." *Findens' Tableaux of the Affections: A Series of Picturesque Illustrations of the Womanly Virtues*. From paintings by W. Perring. Ed. Mary Russell Mitford. London: Charles Tilt, 1839. 1–5.

———. *The Seraphim, and Other Poems*. London: Saunders and Otley, 1838.

Browning, Robert. *Letters of Robert Browning Collected by Thomas J. Wise*. Ed. Thurman L. Hood. New Haven: 1933.

Byrd, Deborah. "Combating an Alien Tyranny: Elizabeth Barrett Browning's Evolution as a Feminist Poet." *Browning Institute Studies* 15 (1987): 23–41.

Cooper, Helen. *Elizabeth Barrett Browning, Woman and Artist*. Chapel Hill: U of North Carolina P, 1988.

Culler, A. Dwight. *The Victorian Mirror of History*. New Haven: Yale UP, 1985.

Dugaw, Dianne. *Warrior Women and Popular Balladry, 1650–1850*. Cambridge Studies in Eighteenth-Century English Literature and Thought 4. Cambridge: Cambridge UP, 1989.

English Review. [?Eliot Warburton.] 4 (December 1845): 263–73.

Fischer, Hermann. *Romantic Verse Narrative: The History of A Genre*. Trans. Sue Bollans. Cambridge: Cambridge UP, 1991.

Hales, John H., and Frederick J. Furnivall, eds. *Bishop Percy's Folio Manuscript: Ballads and Romances*. Vol. II. Part I. London: N. Trubner & Co., 1867.

Harrison, Antony H. *Victorian Poets and Romantic Poems: Intertextuality and Ideology*. Charlottesville: UP of Virginia, 1990.

Hayter, Alethea. *Mrs. Browning: A Poet's Work and its Setting*. London: Faber and Faber, 1962.

Hemans, Felicia. *The Poetical Works of Mrs. Hemans*. Ed. W. M. Rossetti. New York: Hurst & Co., n.d.

Herridge, William T. "Elizabeth Barrett Browning." *Andover Review* 7 (June 1887): 607–23.

Hickok, Kathleen. *Representations of Women: Nineteenth-Century British Women's Poetry*. Westport, CT: Greenwood P, 1984.

Horne, Richard Hengist. *Letters of Elizabeth Barrett Browning to Richard Hengist Horne. With Comments on Contemporaries*. Ed. S. R. Townshend Mayer. 2 vols. London: Richard Bentley & Son, 1877.

Jacobus, Mary. *Tradition and Experiment in Wordsworth's "Lyrical Ballads" (1798)*. Oxford: Clarendon P, 1976.

Kelley, Philip, and Betty A. Coley. *The Browning Collections: A Reconstruction With Other Memorabilia*. Winfield, KS: Wedgestone P, 1984.

Kelley, Philip, and Ronald Hudson, eds. *The Brownings' Correspondence*. 9 vols. to date. Winfield, KS: Wedgestone P, 1984–.

Kenyon, Frederic G., ed. *The Letters of Elizabeth Barrett Browning*. 2 vols. New York: Macmillan, 1897.

Kintner, Elvan, ed. *The Letters of Robert Browning and Elizabeth Barrett Browning 1845–1846*. 2 vols. Cambridge, MA: Harvard UP, Belknap P, 1969.

Laws, G. Malcolm, Jr. *The British Literary Ballad: A Study in Poetic Imitation*. Carbondale and Edwardsville: Southern Illinois UP, 1972.

Leighton, Angela. *Elizabeth Barrett Browning*. Key Women Writers Series. Ed. Sue Roe. Brighton: Harvester P, 1986.

Lootens, Tricia. "Elizabeth Barrett Browning: The Poet as Heroine of Literary History." Diss. Indiana U, 1988.

Martin, Loy D. *Browning's Dramatic Monologues and the Post-Romantic Subject*. Baltimore: Johns Hopkins UP, 1985.

[Massey, Gerald.] "Last Poems and Other Works of Mrs. Browning." *North British Review* 36 (1862): 514–34.

Mermin, Dorothy. *Elizabeth Barrett Browning: The Origins of a New Poetry*. Chicago: U of Chicago P, 1989.

Miller, Nancy K. *Subject to Change: Reading Feminist Writing*. New York: Columbia UP, 1988.

Noble, James Ashcroft. "Elizabeth Barrett Browning." 1892. *Joanna Baillie to Jean Ingelow*. Vol. 8 of *The Poets and the Poetry of the Nineteenth Century*. Ed. Alfred H. Miles. 12 vols. London: Routledge; New York: E. P. Dutton, 1905. 155–64.

Parrish, Stephen Maxfield. *The Art of the Lyrical Ballads*. Cambridge, MA: Harvard UP, 1973.

Percy, Thomas. *Reliques of Ancient English Poetry, Consisting of Old Heroic Ballads, Songs, and other Pieces of our Earlier Poets, Together with some few of later Date*. 3 vols. London: J. Dodsley, 1765.

Poovey, Mary. *The Proper Lady and the Woman Writer: Ideology as Style in the Works of Mary Wollstonecraft, Mary Shelley, and Jane Austen*. Chicago: U of Chicago P, 1984.

———. *Uneven Developments: The Ideological Work of Gender in Mid-Victorian England*. Chicago: U of Chicago P, 1988.

Rajan, Tilottama. *The Supplement of Reading: Figures of Understanding in Romantic Theory and Practice*. Ithaca: Cornell UP, 1990.

Raymond, Meredith B., and Mary Rose Sullivan, eds. *The Letters of Elizabeth Barrett Browning to Mary Russell Mitford 1836–1854*. 3 vols. Winfield, KS: Wedgestone P, 1983.

Ricks, Christopher, ed. *Tennyson: A Selected Edition*. London: Longman, 1989.

Scott, Sir Walter. *Marmion*. Ed. Thomas Bayne. Oxford: Clarendon P, 1889.

Sharp, Phillip. "Poetry in Process: Elizabeth Barrett Browning and the Sonnets Notebook." Diss. Louisiana State U, 1985.

Stephenson, Glennis. *Elizabeth Barrett Browning and the Poetry of Love*. Ann Arbor: U.M.I. Research P, 1989.

Stone, Marjorie. "Cursing as One of the Fine Arts: Elizabeth Barrett Browning's Political Poems." *Dalhousie Review* 66 (1986): 155–73.

Walker, Hugh. *The Literature of the Victorian Era*. Cambridge: Cambridge UP, 1910.

Willmott, Robert Aris, ed. *Reliques of Ancient English Poetry, By Thomas Percy*. London: Routledge & Sons, 1857.

Yaeger, Patricia. *Honey-Mad Women: Emancipatory Strategies in Women's Writing*. Gender and Culture Series. Ed. Carolyn Heilbrun and Nancy K. Miller. New York: Columbia UP, 1988.

WORKS IN PROGRESS

Richard Dellamora's "E. M. Forster at the End" is based on a chapter in his forthcoming book *Apocalyptic Overtures: Sexual Politics and the Sense of an Ending*.

Barbara T. Gates's essay, "Retelling the Story of Science," is from a forthcoming book, *In Nature's Name: Women and Nature in Nineteenth-Century Britain*.

Margaret F. King's " 'Certain Learned Ladies': Trollope's *Can You Forgive Her?* and the Langham Place Circle" is part of a project on the impact of the Langhamites' discourse on Trollope's fiction of the 1860s and on mainstream journalism.

Donald E. Hall's essay, "Muscular Anxiety: Degradation and Appropriation in *Tom Brown's Schooldays*," is drawn from a book-length project, "The Literature of Threat: Feminism and English Male Novelists, 1840–1870."

Jill L. Matus's essay, "Looking at Cleopatra: The Expression and Exhibition of Desire in *Villette*," is part of a project exploring representations of female sexuality in Victorian bio-medical, social scientific, and literary texts.

E. M. FORSTER AT THE END

By Richard Dellamora

IN THE 1890s IN ENGLAND there occurred both a renaissance of cultural production by male homosexuals and a major onslaught against them that took as its focus Oscar Wilde, the cynosure of upper-class masculine difference. The successful prosecution of Wilde on charges of "gross indecency" in 1895 brought this renewal to an end with a crash that has continued to be heard across several generations of middle-class men sexually and emotionally attracted to other men. The effect on the generation born around 1880 was particularly severe as instances the case of E. M. Forster, who was 16 years of age at the time of Wilde's debacle. Young men like John Gray, Aubrey Beardsley, and Alfred Douglas, who were in their late teens or early to mid-twenties between 1890 and 1894, experienced moral and practical support when they questioned hegemonic values. Forster too found friendship and encouragement among homosexuals such as Oscar Browning, G. Lowes Dickinson, and others; and he became romantically entangled with H. O. Meredith while an undergraduate at King's College, Cambridge. But Meredith was at least nominally straight, and sexual fulfillment eluded Forster for many years. Not until he fell in love with a young man named Mohammed el Adl while in Alexandria during World War I did he become sexually experienced.

In the meantime, Forster enjoyed friendships with homosexual men and supportive women while also undergoing a series of intense, sexually frustrated relationships with heterosexual or bisexual men. While no definitive answer is available as to why Forster's homosexuality was for so long blocked at the site of the genitals, the end of relatively open homosexual self-expression posed major difficulties in his personal life and in the career that unfolded for him during the first decade of the new century as an ironic observer of the tragicomedy of English upper-middle-class life and manners.

"Albergo Empedocle" (1903), Forster's first published short story, was suitable for publication in one of the homosexual magazines that had appeared at Oxford and London early in the preceding decade. After 1895 these were gone or else under changed editorial policies. Wilde had made writing for a double audience the height of chic, but the glamor disappeared after male homosexuality had been negated in the most public fashion. Male heterosexual writers too lost the opportunity critically to assess gender norms.[1] And the relatively public opportunities for socializing and collaborative work that male homosexuals had briefly enjoyed no longer existed. As a young homosexual writer with a keen eye for the details of bourgeois domestic life, Forster found himself without a suitable social or publishing context. That he overcame these limits in a string of successful novels, climaxing in the publication of *Howards End* in 1910, was a triumph that could not be sustained indefinitely. Forster expresses the situation as early as a diary entry of June 16, 1911. Shortly after the success of *Howards End* and at a time when he was in his early thirties, he writes: "Weariness of the only subject that I both can and may treat — the love of men for women & vice versa."[2]

Even when Forster in his fiction resolutely focuses on male-female relations, they have as a limiting term the dangers posed by excessive investments between men. The threat of what Victorian sexologists defined as sexual inversion actively shapes the representation of conventional sexuality in Forster's writing, and this fact is already true in "Albergo Empedocle." In referring to this novel situation, which pertains not only to Forster's difficulties but to his social milieu, I use the term *the heterosexual contract*, by which I mean the prescribed investment of young men in relations with women whose main significance is their relation to social (re)production. This contract, which defines both male-female relations and the male relations that frame them, marks a significant change from the male homosocial construction of sexuality prevalent in the mid-Victorian period.[3] The contract demands a "forgetting" of desire between men that Forster figures at the literal level through the use of amnesia. As for young women, in their roles as fiancées or wives, they must sacrifice the slightest suggestion of a female difference that might exist outside the limits of the phallogocentric order.[4]

The new context has implications for the structure of Forster's fiction, in particular for the function of irony with respect to the reader as an excluded third term who is, nonetheless, implicated in the text by the way in which desire is structured between a narrator and narratee.[5] In a recent study, Ross Chambers has argued that oppositional writing depends primarily upon irony, a trope that can be put into operation only in the presence of a reader, who provides a necessary third term in addition to the first two. Chambers distinguishes two such operations: an irony of negation, which negates values of the dominant culture to whose members the text is in the first instance addressed; and an irony of appropriation, whereby the text suggests different desires to a reader or group of readers in opposition, wittingly or unwittingly, to the values of the dominant group (Chambers 237–241). Remaining for the most part within the limits of reader-response theory, Chambers does not exploit the possibility that structural irony affords for calling into existence as yet indeterminate social groupings. "Albergo Empedocle," while addressed to conventional readers of *Temple Bar*, the journal in which it first appeared, appeals to a second set of readers who share Forster's need both to express and to dissemble a special interest in male intimacy.

This latter group are in an oppositional relation to the heterosexual contract along with its affiliations of class, rank, and nationality — even if, like Harold, the protagonist of the story, they aren't quite aware of the fact. In "Albergo Empedocle," male-male desire places one at the margin of the heterosexual contract but not altogether outside it.[6] This positioning at the margin is necessary if the processes of group-formation are to occur but also opens possibilities of self-deception and of failure in personal relations that neither Harold nor Tommy, the framing narrator of the story, escapes.[7]

The significance of the setting of Forster's story amid Greek ruins on Sicily brings to mind the end during the 1890s of the discussion, dating from the late Enlightenment, of the significance of intimacy between males in the institution of pederasty as it had existed in different forms at ancient Athens and Sparta. While Forster as a boy was recoiling from the philistine atmosphere of Tonbridge School, Victorian philology entered a final phase as Walter Pater and Wilde, between 1890 and 1892, continued ironically to undercut the uses to which Greek models were conventionally put in elite education. Even when Greek studies were used to serve the political, social, and economic purposes of male elites, philology performed a useful function in foregrounding the connection between male intimacy and cultural and social production. As part of conventional education, such ties were subjected to critique by writers like Pater and Wilde; on the other hand, the debates compelled homosexual polemicists to theorize connections between masculine desire and positive outcomes in cultural and social relations. In slightly different terms, male homosexual discourses were necessarily preoccupied with the utilities of male intimacy. The forced abandonment of this project for young people of Forster's generation was to have negative consequences for the process of transforming Great Britain into a fully democratic state.[8]

In "Albergo Empedocle" Forster responds to both of these endings by drawing on tropes of metempsychosis and amensia. On a visit with his bride-to-be and her parents to Sicily, Harold dreams that he has lived before as a Greek at Girgenti, the site of the former city of Acragas, a major commercial and cultural center during the Age of Pericles. The experience seems to suggest that while it may no longer be possible to think Greek, it is possible to *become Greek*. This rapture, however, can be achieved only at the cost of disconnection from normal existence; in other words, only at a moment when it has become impossible any longer to envisage a hermeneutics of Greek love does the protagonist overleap the work of intellection by assuming for himself a metaphoric identification with a Greek Other. This projection is precipitated by the refusal of Mildred, Harold's fiancée, and her family to comprehend the possibility of being-different. Harold is pushed into a break-down and has to be repatriated by force to that other island, Great Britain, the counter to Sicily in the story. There he becomes the permanent ward of a mental hospital: "Long before Harold reached the asylum his speech had become absolutely unintelligible; indeed, by the time he arrived at it, he hardly ever uttered a sound of any kind" (62).

Under the pressure of rejection by others, metempsychosis becomes an identification that captures the subject within a virtually complete solipsism. The recovery of a prior existence is incompatible with modern life because "we" (that is, the late Victorians) are amnesiacs. "We" have forgotten what it means to think Greek — even though as few years ago as the early 1890s writers were showing us how to do so.[9] Accordingly, while philology retains the grammar and syntax of ancient Greek, in Forster's rhetoric it has lost — as have modern subjects generally — the capacity of enunciation. Only Tommy, whose avowals of "love" for Harold equivocally frame the story, shares his friend's belief: "I firmly believe that he has been a Greek — nay, that he is a Greek, drawn by recollection back into his previous life. He cannot under-stand our speech because we have lost his pronunciation" (62). Tommy, however, does not speak Harold's language either or, rather, he can only speak it with the language of the body, the most equivocal of utterances, in the kiss he receives from Harold at the end of the story. The role that Tommy plays needs to be regarded warily since his witness leaves Harold fixed in place as the subject of an existence almost totally estranged from "ours" and onto which, in view of Harold's muteness, Tommy is free to project what he will. Yet his fidelity to a love that cannot be voiced in return is the one space that Forster finds for expressing desire between men.

The extremity of Harold's situation suggests yet one more ending, this time generic, implied in Forster's short story; and that is the end of realist narrative, particularly in the novel, as a story in which two male rivals struggle for possession of a woman.[10] When Forster uses male-homosocial triangulation, he uses it differently so as to show that, at least in his fiction, the mediation of desire between men in a female object has ceased to consti-tute the terms of normal sexuality. Writing from a tacit homosexual subject-position, Forster frames relations between men and women with an eye to desire between men. This framing poses the possibility of another narrative trajectory to some readers while presenting male-female relations not so much as normal but as representative of the institution of heterosexuality. In this context, Forster describes the implications for female subjectivity of the posi-tion of women as "wife" or "woman" within this order. This representation, particularly in Mildred, contributes to the critique of marriage but operates as well so as to limit Forster's awareness of the ways in which female subjectivities can exist in resistance to the formation of gender. Forster demonstrates the cost to women of their positioning within heterosexuality but at the expense of failing to respond to their capacity to differ from their prescribed roles.

In "Albergo Empedocle," the triangle of Harold, Mildred, and Tommy focuses on Harold. Despite the fact that Tommy and Harold's mutual if asymmetrical desires for each other set the interpretive horizons of the story, after Harold's experience Mildred reveals another, more forceful triangle at work: that of herself, her future husband, and her father, Sir Edwin. Mildred takes the following view of Harold's experience: "Worn out," Harold "had fallen asleep, and, . . . had indulged in a fit of imagination on awaking. She had fallen in with it, and they had encouraged each other to fresh deeds of folly. All was clear. And how was she to hide it from her father? (55) As the family expedition indicates, Harold is marrying not just Mildred but also her family. In return, the contract guarantees Mildred a fixed place in the scheme of things.

As Eve Kosofsky Sedgwick has shown in her discussion of Charles Dickens's *Our Mutual Friend* (1864–65), woman's work in the triangle, as it functions in mid-Victorian fiction, is to save the male from his own indecisive and unrecognized desires (1985, 177). Harold conforms to this script when he insists that Mildred validate his dream by kissing him with passion, something previously absent in their relations (57). His demand for her knowing acceptance belongs yet more properly to a moment late in male homosocial existence when, as Sedgwick shows, this time by way of her reading of "The Beast in the Jungle," a short story that Henry James also published in 1903, woman as "friend" serves the function of cherishing the secret of John Marcher, a man so deeply closeted that he forgets that he has told her his "secret" (Sedgwick 1990, 210).

Like a number of late Victorian wives who married men attracted to other men,[11] Mildred's ambivalent relation to her status as woman makes her initially prepared to undertake this exacting role but only on condition that she too can become Greek — that is, that within her role as wife she can occupy the place of an imaginary Other to Harold and thereby become more nearly his equal. When she decides that supporting Harold will, to the contrary, require self-sacrifice on her part while reinforcing her subordination as woman and her exclusion from "Greek" culture, she turns on him with vehemence. As for Harold, he is innocent of what his secret might be or why it needs to be a secret at all (50–51). His incomprehension signals that the male-homosocial role of woman as the friend or wife who keeps a man's secret does not in this story provide an effective bound to errant desires. Harold's Greek experience has begun to move him outside the terms of the contract. What he needs are interlocutors who can share his memories.

I. A Roman Ending

"ALBERGO EMPEDOCLE" begins with a letter that seems to set in place the sort of male homosocial triangulation that is a familiar aspect of realist narrative in Victorian fiction. As described by Harold, however, the situation sounds not quite right:

> We've just come from Pompeii. On the whole it's decidedly no go and very tiring. What with the smells and the beggars and the mosquitoes we're rather off Naples altogether, and we've changed our plans and are going to Sicily. The guidebooks say you can run through it in no time; only four places you have to go to, and very little in them. That suits us to a T. Pompeii and the awful Museum here have fairly killed us — except of course Mildred, and perhaps Sir Edwin.
> Now why don't you come too? I know you're keen on Sicily, and we all would like it. You would be able to spread yourself no end with your archaeology. For once in my life I should have to listen while you jaw. You'd enjoy discussing temples, gods, etc., with Mildred. She's taught me a lot, but of course it's no fun for her, talking to us. Send a wire; I'll stand the cost. Start at once and we'll wait for you. The Peaslakes say the same, especially Mildred.
> My not sleeping at night, and my headaches are all right now, thanks very much. As for the blues, I haven't had any since I've been engaged, and don't intend to. So don't worry any more.
> Yours,
> Harold (36)

In fairly evident transcoding, Harold's dissatisfaction with traveling expresses an underlying awareness that the engagement mentioned at the end of the letter is a mistake. The pre-nuptial tour is, in reality, a series of detours that "go" nowhere and whose predetermined stops on the way have "very little" in them, except, that is, for threatening Harold with annihilation. Pompeii and its "awful museum" are associated in his mind with marriage, the family, philistine culture, and the burdens of imperium: in other words, with the responsibilities upon which he is about to enter. For his part, Harold would rather be on another trip, one that would "suit" him "to a T" — that is, to a T/Tommy.

In this light, it is not surprising to find Harold resisting his fiancée in her role of *cicerone*. As Tommy writes, submaliciously, a bit later: "Mildred . . . was the fount of information. It was she who generally held the Baedeker and explained it. She had been expecting her continental scramble for several years, and had read a fair amount of books for it, which a good memory often enabled her to reproduce'' (37). The key word here is memory, figured in the Baedeker, which connotes repetition. Memory in this sense only appears to ''scramble'' since it knows where it's headed, having learned its object by rote before meeting it. In contrast to this work of memory is recollection or metempsychosis or the belief, held by Empedocles who once lived at Acragas, in ''the transmigration of souls'' (41). This latter condition, implicitly recalling efforts within nineteenth-century philology to recover Greek consciousness, enables one to be constituted as wholly other.

Early on in the story, Mildred defends Harold's capacity for imagination against her father, who doubts that Harold has any. As well, it is Mildred who sets matters in motion by telling Harold en route to Girgenti that ''[t]oday you must imagine you are a Greek'' (42). Yet Mildred's capacity for sympathy is put cruelly to the test when Harold experiences his prior existence at Acragas. His continuing psychic stability depends on her sharing this belief with him; with no sense of exaggeration, he says to her: ''I might have died if you hadn't believed me'' (50). And Mildred does try. ''Oh, Harold,'' she says, ''I too may remember. . . . Oh, Harold! I am remembering! . . . [I]n the wonderful youth of Greece did I speak to you and know you and love you. We walked through the marble streets, we led solemn sacrifices, I armed you for the battle, I welcomed you from the victory. The centuries have parted us, but not for ever. Harold, I too have lived at Acragas!'' (53) Without a guidebook to con, however, Mildred fails. Her difference, which accommodates no difference, is fake, as she says later: ''pure imagination, the result of sentimental excitement'' (54). Harold's sleep, however, has converted him into a truth-sayer. In response to her claim to have lived at Acragas, he quietly responds: '' 'No, Mildred darling, you have not' '' (53).

The reader shortly learns that, contrary to his report to Tommy, headaches and insomnia do continue to trouble Harold. Mildred shows no awareness of these symptoms of bodily and spiritual dis-ease. To her as to her father, Harold might just as well be a piece of classical statuary. His external deportment conforms to the observation of an educator like Jowett that:

> You may look at a Greek statue and be struck with the flexure of the limbs, the majestic folds of the drapery, the simplicity, the strength; And yet scarely any topics arise in the mind of the uncritical [viewer]. . . . The highest art is colourless like water, it has been said; it is a surface without prominences or irregularities over which the eye wanders impressed by the beauty of the whole with nothing to detain it at a particular point. . . . It is a smooth surface over which the hand may pass without interruption, but the curious work lies beneath the surface: the effect only is seen from without. The finer the workmanship the more completely is the art concealed.[12]

This remark is, if not colored, then shadowed by the preterition that draws attention to while denying the fact that Greek ''limbs'' may draw ''the eye'' (and "the hand") to a "particular point," a point which redirects attention from a surface without openings to "the curious work" accessible only from the inside. Precisely Harold's presentation of "a surface without prominences or irregularities" makes him a suitable candidate as son-in-law, almost too suitable. Sir Edwin Peaslake remarks: "Of course I'm very fond of him, he's a thoroughly nice fellow, honest as the day, and he's good-looking and well-made — I value all that extremely — but after all brains are something. He is so slow — so lamentably slow — at catching one's meaning" (44).

In Sicily, however, Harold betrays a disturbing propensity to imagine that he is "someone else," a "dodge" (39) he confesses that he occasionally resorts to when he has trouble falling asleep — or when he has "the blues" (40). When Sir Edwin discovers this capacity, he is shocked: "It is never safe to play tricks with the brain," he admonishes. "I must say I'm astonished: you of all people!" (40) It's even worse after Harold's dream when Sir Edwin demands that unless the young man acknowledge that he has been deluded, the marriage will not take place. What is troubling ("queer" in Sir Edwin's usage) is Harold's ability to change when he encounters something or someone different.

As the mention of Sir Edwin in Harold's letter indicates, Harold's contract is only incidentally with Mildred even as it is only incidental that she has something to say about the Greek temples at Girgenti: she can repeat what she has read. Similarly, in the role of wife and mother, she will repeat the genealogy of the Peaslakes. The corporate character of the engagement is implicitly extended in the brief reference at opening to another ending, the destruction of Herculaneum and Pompeii as a result of an eruption of Vesuvius in 79 A.D. Pompeii signifies English as an analogue of Roman culture both in the static density of existence as recovered from the ashes in archaeological digs and in the characteristic twinning of Roman with British imperium in nineteenth-century English thought.[13] The sense of closure impressed on Harold during his visit to "the awful Museum" helps set the stage for the crisis at Girgenti.

On the train from Palermo, Harold's view of Sicily comments ironically on England's economic and political position at the end of the century: "They had hardly crossed the watershed of the island. It was the country of the mines, barren and immense, absolutely destitute of grass or trees, producing nothing but cakes of sallow sulphur, which were stacked on the platform of every wayside station. Human beings were scanty, and they were stunted and dry, mere withered vestiges of men. And far below at the bottom of the yellow waste was the moving living sea, which embraced Sicily when she was green and delicate and young, and embraces her now, when she is brown and withered and dying" (42). This contrasting vision suggests both the industrial devastation occurring in England and the actual as opposed to the putative effects of Empire since Sicily's denudation is a leading result of centuries of foreign invasion and domination. Tommy/Forster's outburst contrasts, however, to the commentary of the 10th edition of *The Encyclopaedia Britannica* (1902), which blandly remarks on the systematic transfer of capital from Sicily to the north after the unification of Italy:

> Like all southern Italy, Sicily in 1860 was poor, notwithstanding the possession of notable reserves of monetary capital. On the completion of Italian unity part of this pecuniary capital was absorbed by the sudden increase of taxation, and a much greater part was employed by private individuals in the purchase of lands formerly belonging to the suppressed religious corporations. . . . Both the revenue acquired by taxation and the proceeds of the land sales were almost entirely spent by the State in northern Italy, where the new Government, for administrative and military reasons, had been obliged to establish its principal organizations, and consequently its great centres of economic consumption. (9: 618)

The Peaslakes identify with Sicily's conquerors. After the small upset that occurs when Sir Edwin learns about Harold's "dodge," Mildred restores quiet by returning to the guidebook: she "passed on to the terrible sack of Acragas by the Romans. Whereat their faces relaxed, and they regained their accustomed spirits" (41).[14]

Tommy's "keen" interest in Sicilian archaeology, however, associates him with the world, both pastoral and civic, of Greek Sicily, which offers in Acragas a far different model of colonization from Italian, Roman, or English. Harold's letter betokens the wish to recover this existence in company with Tommy (even if the wish can only be uttered in negation and displaced onto Mildred). In the absence of Tommy, the possibility of recovery is open to Harold only in something like the form of his experience at Girgenti, where he falls asleep in the afternoon sun between the legs of a toppled colossal statue of Atlas and wakes convinced that, in an earlier life, he has lived as a citizen of Acragas.

> [There] were two fallen columns, lying close together, and the space that separated them had been silted up and was covered with flowers. On it, as on a bed, lay Harold, fast asleep, his cheek pressed against the hot stone of one of the columns, and his breath swaying a little blue iris that had rooted in one of its cracks. . . .
> Sleep has little in common with death, to which men have compared it. Harold's limbs lay in utter relaxation, but he was tingling with life, glorying in the bounty of the earth and the warmth of the sun, and the little blue flower bent and fluttered like a tree in a gale. The light beat upon his eyelids and the grass leaves tickled his hair, but he slept on, and the lines faded out of his face as he grasped the greatest gift that the animal life can offer. (47–48)

Mildred frames the scene as a tourist should: "He looked so picturesque, and she herself, sitting on the stone watching him, must look picturesque too. She knew that there was no one to look at her, but from her mind the idea of a spectator was never absent for a moment. It was the price she had paid for becoming cultivated" (47).

By 1903, high culture, including Greek culture, had been thoroughly commodified for the consumption and adornment of members of Mildred's class. Exotic locales provided the props for situating members of this group in preformulated ways. Mildred responds to such a scene as a masculist observer would. Her gaze is from the position of one who is always already an object within such a scene. This framing excludes the possibility that instead of responding in a "cultivated" way Mildred might be changed by contact with "animal life" or by a pastoral existence that combines both spontaneous and cultivated responses. Hence the metonymic function of the travel-book, whose mapping determines before one leaves home what knowledge will or will not be ascertained while abroad.

For a middle- or upper-class male homosexual, Greek culture could be commodified in another way in the form of sexual tourism — whether the object of desire remained fantasmatic as it did for Forster on his Italian and Greek tours of 1902 and 1903 or whether it was acquired in more practicable ways. When Baron von Gloeden, for instance, photographs young Sicilian peasants in the ungarb of ancient youth, the discrepancy between sign and signifier indicates the inability of representation to suture the difference between material and imaginary reality. Nonetheless, these images, with the blessing of local Sicilians, drew homosexuals to the villa at Taormina from which von Gloeden sold his postcards.[15] Forster pitches the attraction in another register. In "Albergo Empedocle," Greek culture provides the opportunity of imagining a "better love," as presumably it does for Tommy, whose interest in Sicily is described as that not of a tourist but of an archaeologist. Yet even when resolutely scientific or highminded, trips like Forster's visit to Girgenti in 1902 exist within a structure of erotic fantasy that is marked by class and ethnic snobbery. Forster/Harold/Tommy's aspiration to a better love is distinguishable but not dissociable from the other meanings of fin-de-siècle tourism. For these men, absorption in Greek culture, though oppositional in Chambers's use of the word, signifies economic and national distinction.

Against these significations, Forster buttresses the oppositional meaning of Harold's experience through intertextual reference to polemical texts of the homosexual renaissance of a few years before. Mildred's gaze at Harold recalls that of the Prior at the sleeping figure of Apollo/Apollyon in Pater's "Apollo in Picardy," an imaginary portrait of 1893 (Dellamora 1990, ch. 9). In the story, Pater uses the setting of a monastic community in order to analyze the psychological effects of homophobia on a male homosocial subject. The blue iris recalls the hyacinths that blossom after the murder, probably at the hands of the Prior, of his young companion, Hyacinth (*MS* 169). Harold's habit of looking out the window of the asylum recalls the Prior's similar practice after he is judged to be insane and placed under house arrest. "Gazing . . . daily for many hours, he would mistake mere blue distance, when that was visible, for blue flowers, for hyacinths, and wept at the sight" (*MS* 170). In Forster's less ironic text, we simply don't know what Harold sees. The references to Pater, however, provide textual means of overcoming the limiting terms of the spectator envisaged by Mildred.[16]

II. Sweet Nothings

AT THE END OF "ALBERGO EMPEDOCLE" the narrator observes:

> Most certainly he is not unhappy. His own thoughts are sweet to him, and he looks out of the window hour after hour and sees things in the sky and sea that we have forgotten. But of his fellow men he seems utterly unconscious. He never speaks to us, nor hears us when we speak. He does not know that we exist.
> So at least I thought till my last visit. I am the only one who still goes to see him; the others have given it up. Last time, when I entered the room, he got up and kissed me on the cheek. I think he knows that I understand him and love him: at all events it comforts me to think so. (63)

Just as the story begins with a missive from Harold to Tommy, it ends with another, with Harold's chaste kiss. In a story in which the reader has learned something of the semiotics of kissing, this kiss is a bodily sign of Greek love in contrast both to the proffered kiss of conscious desire that Mildred rejects at Girgenti and to the "decorous peck" (50) that had earlier sealed her engagement. In a world that has become amnesiac by resolutely turning away from thinking Greek — and Tommy includes himself among the "we" who have forgotten — Tommy can at best be only nearly sure what the language of the body means when, in the final words of the story, he says: "I think he knows that I understand him and love him: at all events it comforts me to think so" (63). Tommy needs comfort because, though his absence from Sicily was necessary, it meant that he was not at hand at Harold's moment of truth. Accordingly, Tommy has missed, perhaps for good, his own chance to re-enter Greek subjectivity.

In adhering to the Christian counsel to visit the sick, Tommy does on the other hand give witness to his love for Harold. Indeed, in Tommy's telling, his love frames the story even though at the start that love appears to have been baffled and remains so throughout. Harold, Tommy confides, is "the man I love most in the world" (37). Yet the role of witness and the confidence with which Tommy uses the verb are odd in view of the ignorances that usually attend love within the story. In addition, by proffering this knowledge to the reader as though it were fairly straightforward, Tommy posits a line of shared cognition between Harold, himself, and the reader despite the fact that the story is structured in such a way as to leave such a possibility in suspension. At no time do Harold and Tommy clearly understand love in the same way. Instead, the assumption of intelligibility on Tommy's part depends on a reading-effect. In the experience of readers of the story, there may exist relations that will complete Tommy and Harold's untold, unconsummated "love."

Tommy makes a utopian appeal to a reader who has recovered the ability to *think Greek*, who understands touch, and who has enough imagination to project a world in which it would make sense to say as Harold does: "I was better, I saw better, heard better, thought better . . . I loved very differently. . . . Yes, I loved better too" (51, 52). By this appeal, Tommy calls into being a reader of the future who may be described as the subject of a gay erotics. Moving beyond the frame of the heterosexual contract, the text implies the potential existence of cultural and social spaces in which men will be able to voice and to enact their mutual sexual and emotional bonds.

At this point, the endings that accompany Forster's hesitant beginnings as a writer help explain discrepancy between hope and contingencies. Forster, who was born on New Years Day, 1879, was sixteen years old during the Wilde trials of 1895. As "a little cissy" (King 17) aware of the distances, including distances of desire, between himself and others his age, Forster was both appalled and instructed by the punishment meted out to Wilde, the only homosexual of his class who seemed able simultaneously to appeal to newly emergent groups, including male homosexual and lesbian ones; sharply to satirize the powers that be; yet to continue to enjoy entry and success in the worlds both of middlebrow and highbrow culture.[17] Two years later, when Forster left Tonbridge School to enter King's College, he found a place at which the conditions for a life of Greek harmony still seemed to exist:

> Body and spirit, reason and emotion, work and play, architecture and scenery, laughter and seriousness, life and art — these pairs which are elsewhere contrasted were there fused into one. People and books reinforced one another, intelligence joined hands with affection, speculation became a passion, and discussion was made profound by love.[18]

Forster achieved this sense of wholeness especially as a result of being selected for membership in the Apostles, the Cambridge undergraduate society of which Alfred Tennyson and Arthur Henry Hallam had been early members and which achieved new distinction at the turn of the century through the membership of men like Bertrand Russell, Alfred North Whitehead, Lytton Strachey, Leonard Woolf, and John Maynard Keynes. Moreover, the line into this group was affective: Forster was sponsored for membership by H. O. ("Hom") Meredith, a handsome, bright, athletic, sexually confused young man, with whom Forster fell in love. While arguments in defense of male homosexuality were put forward at the weekly meetings, members kept quiet about their sexual involvements; and Forster and Meredith's intimacies were confined to "kisses and embraces" (Furbank 1: 98).

In a biography of Forster that is marked by homophobia, Francis King comments that "Meredith, a basically heterosexual man, probably took the physical lead, either out of kindness or out of curiosity, but Forster was the one who was in love" (34). Yet there is evidence that Meredith signed the heterosexual contract with difficulty. Shortly after he and Forster became friends, Meredith became engaged to Caroline Graveson, then "had a nervous breakdown" (Furbank 1: 140). In 1906, Meredith wrote to Keynes from Manchester: "I think I am dead really now. . . . Or perhaps I should say I realise now what was plain to others two years ago. I come to life temporarily when I meet Forster." Furbank remarks: "Forster, as was his habit in friendship, made vigorous efforts to rouse Meredith out of his apathy. They would go for long walks, endlessly discussing Meredith's problems, or sometimes walking in total silence while he brooded" (1: 141). In this relationship, Forster appears to have played the role of "Tommy."

Homosexual members of the Apostles or, later, Bloomsbury lived in a country in which their exchanges could subject them to ignominy, to blackmail, and to legal prosecution. Under the relatively new terms of the Labouchère amendment, the prohibition of "gross indecency" brought a far wider range of acts between men — including kissing — within the net of the Law. Indeed, even those Saturday night deliberations about the nobility of male love were potentially liable to prosecution. Within these circumstances, Forster, referring to himself as a homosexual, uses the term "minority." Returning from a trip to Greece in 1904, he describes himself as though he were part of a barren Mediterranean landscape:

> I'd better eat my soul for I certainly shan't have it. I'm going to be a minority if not a solitary, and I'd best make copy out of my position. There is nothing contemptible or cynical in this. I too have sweet waters though I shall never drink them. So I can understand the drought of others, though they will not understand my abstinence. (Furbank 1: 111)

For Forster in 1904, being a minority meant living privately and celibately. In face of this sort of isolation, it is not surprising that the insulation of groups like the Apostles increased or that homosexual involvements came to appear to be a "cult" to outsiders (Annan ch. 7, 8).

Forster's decision not to reprint "Albergo Empedocle" during his lifetime is in keeping with the extreme sense of apartness expressed in the preceding quotation. Yet it is a part of the continuing interest of this story that it calls into existence the members of a minority *group*. This structure depends in turn upon contingencies: on the existence of a homosexual radical culture before 1895, on its subsequent suppression, and on the continuing effects of the work of gender in Victorian Greek studies. Even when it was no longer possible to contest the meaning of masculinity within philological inquiry, the efforts of writers like Pater, Wilde, and others continued to lend fortitude to men like Forster.

Forster is often thought of as a man with a double career: the first climaxed with the publication of *A Passage to India* in 1924, after which he ceased to publish new fiction. The second career is a posthumous one as the writer of gay short stories and the novel, *Maurice*, which were published after his death in 1970. The two parts of Forster's career, however, and the frustration of his work as a novelist after 1924 are conditioned by the institution of heterosexuality, which both impels the novels that deal with conventional sexuality and ensures that, in various ways, as in "Albergo Empedocle," they work out a complex relationship to a specifically homosexual desire. In this sense, there are not two careers but one marked by continual compromise and resistance.

III. Another Difference

AND, FINALLY, MILDRED, archetype of what Noel Annan refers to as "the self-satisfied, uneducated, conventional Edwardian girl, whom Forster knew so well, corseted by the conventions of her class and determined, come what may, to impose her will" (111). Her representation in "Albergo Empedocle" demonstrates the production of "woman" — in marriage or a picturesque setting — as a heterosexual institution. Viewed in this light, the sympathetic woman of the James short story is a logical impossibility. In a story that refers in many ways to the love that dare not speak its name, Mildred vindictively insists on naming Harold a "charlatan and cad" (56). She does so, moreover, in defense of herself as a woman, convinced that in turning back her wish to participate in his other life, Harold means to subordinate her:

> How patiently he had heard her rapturous speech, in order that he might prove her silly to the core! How diabolically worded was his retort — "No, Mildred darling, you have not lived at Acragas." It implied: "I will be kind to you and

treat you well when you are my wife, but recollect that you are silly, emotional, hypocritical; that your pretensions to superiority are gone for ever; that I have proved you inferior to me, even as all women are inferior to all men. Dear Mildred, you are a fool!'' (55–56)

Mildred's reaction shows that, in her scrutiny of Baedeker, she has been in search of cultural capital for herself, something she needs to offset the assured superiority of her better educated male coevals. This capital prominently includes the Greek studies that put a premium on male relations — so that the translation of Harold into Greek experience must either be recoded by Mildred or else be felt by her to be utterly demeaning.

Mildred responds in terms of her position as a future wife: what is implicitly in contest is her rivalry over Harold with Tommy, a rivalry she translates into cognitive terms. Mildred perceives her failure to be one of ''archaeology'' (55), the field of Tommy's expertise. The knowledge possessed by male subjects of elite education excludes her. She won't bear it. She lashes out. In a barely concealed metaphor, she kills Harold. Or, at least, Tommy thinks so: ''I . . . believe that if things had happened otherwise he might be living that greater life among us, instead of among friends of two thousand years ago, whose names we never heard. That is why I shall never forgive Mildred Peaslake as long as I live'' (63).

As enforcer of the contract and an outmoded novelistic realism, Mildred merits Tommy's anger. Yet the word ''cad'' suggests some of the ambiguities in gender and sexual relations in these years. Forster himself would use the term at Alexandria a number of years later at a moment when anxieties of class, gender, and race combined to prompt him to lose confidence in his first lover, Mohammed el Adl. In a letter of April 4, 1918, to Florence Barger, the wife of a former Cambridge classmate and a lifelong friend and confidante, Forster writes: ''I thought he had meant to insult me, and left in a fury. He was puzzled and distressed, but very dignified. All through it is *I* who have endangered the thing. . . . I have found it so hard to believe he was neither a traitor or [sic] cad.''[19] Poised on the fine line that separated friend from traitor, lover from cad, Forster was in position to understand the volatile insecurity that a young upper-class woman might feel shortly before her marriage.

The writer of ''Albergo Empedocle'' was younger, less experienced, and less reflective than the Forster of 1918. He represents Mildred through the medium of Tommy's animosity, an effect reinforced by the way in which other characters likewise see her. Mildred's father, unconsciously observing the Coleridgean distinction between fancy and imagination, thinks ''that, although she might sometimes indulge in fancies, yet when it came to action she could be trusted to behave in a thoroughly conventional manner'' (45).

This comment in indirect discourse, written by Tommy/Forster, is as reliable but only as reliable as is the narrator. Tommy assures the reader: "I am well acquainted with all who went then, and have had circumstantial information of all that happened, I think that my account of the affair will be as intelligible as anyone's" (36).

The containment of Mildred's subjectivity within her function as woman prompts questions about the capacities of the narrator to envisage feminine difference. As for Forster, in contrast to his ability to register masculine differences, he gives no clue that Mildred might have a capacity to be different from the roles that she has been called upon to play. Yet the non-negotiability of Mildred in the role of a May Bartram or a Florence Barger does indicate the high price that women who invested in such a compromise had to be willing to pay. Her refusal to pay this price is a noteworthy revolt and could be admirable though unfortunately, in Forster's ironic presentation, she revolts not in the direction of dis-identification with "woman" but in the direction of an accentuated identification with her place in the heterosexual contract. The expression of feminine differences would have to wait for writers such as Radclyffe Hall who, in "Miss Ogilvy Finds Herself" (1926), writes her own story of a subject of same-sex desire who is rapt into another world. But in Hall's story, the protagonist is *Miss* Ogilvy.

Trent University

NOTES

1. The scandal attending publication of *Jude the Obscure* later in 1895 registers the negative impact for male heterosexual writers of the Wilde scandal. See Dellamora 212–17.
2. Quoted in Oliver Stallybrass, "Introduction," in Forster 1975, 16. Biographical information in the opening paragraphs is from Summers, ch. 1.
3. See the discussions in Sedgwick 1985, esp. ch. 9, and 1990, ch. 4.
   I adapt the phrase, "heterosexual contract," from Teresa de Lauretis 1987, esp. pp. 260, 277 n. 1; and from Monique Wittig 24–25. See also de Lauretis 1990, 128–29. Where I supplement her work is in suggesting that the contract is implemented with special aggressivity in the years immediately following Wilde's imprisonment.
4. My suggested dates for the installation of this shift in the construction of conventional sexuality parallel the development, in Continental psychoanalysis, of Freud's model of female sexual difference, a model that Mary Jacobus argues instates "the phallus" as "an arbitrary and divisive mark around which sexuality is constructed" (122). For a discussion of the problematic of "woman" in male modernity, see Jardine, ch. 4.
5. See Chambers 24, 32.
6. Chambers 217.
7. I say "framing" because the opening text, Harold's letter to Tommy, oversteps the role of narrator that Tommy otherwise plays.

8. I follow Sinfield's argument. See esp. ch. 5.
9. I mean showing us how in the sense described by David Halperin in a discussion of heroic male friendship in the *Iliad* and other early texts. Halperin argues that interpretations of "homosexuality" in these works tell us more about the understanding of sexuality in the culture of the interpreter than in the cultures in which the works themselves were first performed or written (87).
10. See Sedgwick 1985, esp. ch. 9.
11. See Amor, Thwaite, and King (22–23).
12. Quoted in Higgins 90.
13. Dowling. Similarly, in "Ansell," another early story, the narrator's upper-class father is distressed when his son loses interest in the history of Rome after he makes friends with a garden boy: "[M]y father did not like my entire separation from rational companions and pursuits. I had suddenly stopped reading and no longer cared to discuss with him the fortunes of the Punic War or the course of Aeneas from Troy" (Forster 28).
14. Acragas is the Greek name for Girgenti, known to the Romans as Agrigentum and, since 1927, as Agrigento, a change of name consonant with the Fascist program of invoking an earlier empire. Forster visited the town in April 1902.
15. Waugh 30. Information provided by Tom Waugh in a phone conversation on August 11, 1992.
16. For more on the connections between Pater and Forster, see Martin 1982.
17. One of the features of the last fifteen years of the century, as discussed in George Gissing's *New Grub Street* (1891) and in such recent studies as Jonathan Freedman's *Professions of Taste* (1990), is the emergence of what is now referred to as "middlebrow" taste. Middlebrow taste, which might be described as the revenge of Philistinism on Matthew Arnold, was — and is — averse to *thinking Greek*.
18. Quoted in King 19.
19. Quoted in Gardner 218. The letter is not included in the *Selected Letters*.

WORKS CITED

Amor, Anne Clark. *Mrs. Oscar Wilde: A Woman of Some Importance*. London: Sidgwick and Jackson, 1983.

Annan, Noel Gilroy Annan, Baron. *Our Age: English Intellectuals Between the World Wars — A Group Portrait*. New York: Random House, 1990.

Chambers, Ross. *Room for Maneuver: Reading (the) Oppositional (in) Narrative*. Chicago: U of Chicago P, 1991.

Dellamora, Richard. *Masculine Desire: The Sexual Politics of Victorian Aestheticism*. Chapel Hill: U of North Carolina P, 1990.

de Lauretis, Teresa. "Eccentric Subjects: Feminist Theory and Historical Consciousness." *Feminist Studies*, 16 (Spring 1990): 115–50.

——— "The Female Body and Heterosexual Presumption." *Semiotica*, 67, no. 3/4 (1987): 259–79.

Dover, K. J. *Greek Homosexuality*. New York: Vintage, 1980.

Dowling, Linda. "Roman Decadence and Victorian Historiography." *Victorian Studies*, 28 (Summer 1985): 579–607.

Forster, E. M. *The Life to Come and Other Stories*. Ed. Oliver Stallybrass. Harmondsworth: Penguin, 1975.

————. *Selected Letters: Volume 1, 1879–1920*. Ed. Mary Lago and P. N. Furbank. Cambridge, MA: Harvard UP, 1983.

Foucault, Michel. *The Use of Pleasure: Volume 2 of the History of Sexuality*. Trans. Robert Hurley. New York: Vintage, 1986.

Freedman, Jonathan. *Professions of Taste: Henry James, British Aestheticism, and Commodity Culture*. Stanford: Stanford UP, 1990.

Furbank, P. N. *E. M. Forster: A Life*. 2 vols. London: Secker & Warburg, 1977.

Gardner, Philip. "The Evolution of E. M. Forster's *Maurice*." In Judith Scherer Herz and Robert K. Martin, jt. ed., *E. M. Forster: Centenary Revaluations*. Toronto: U of Toronto P, 1982. 204–23.

Halperin, David. *One Hundred Years of Homosexuality and Other Essays on Greek Love*. New York: Routledge, 1990.

Higgins, Lesley. "Essaying 'W. H. Pater Esq.': New Perspectives on the Tutor/Student Relationship between Pater and Hopkins." In Laurel Brake and Ian Small, jt. ed., *Pater in the 1990s*. Greensboro, NC: ELT Press, 1991. 77–94.

King, Francis. *E. M. Forster*. London: Thames and Hudson, 1988.

Jacobus, Mary. *Reading Woman: Essays in Feminist Criticism*. New York: Columbia UP, 1986.

Jardine, Alice. *Gynesis: Configurations of Woman and Modernity*. Ithaca: Cornell UP, 1985.

Malek, James S. "Forster's 'Albergo Empedocle': A Precursor of *Maurice*." *Studies in Short Fiction*, 11 (1974): 427–30.

Martin, Robert K. "Forster's Greek: From Optative to Present Indicative." *Kansas Quarterly*, 9 (1977): 69–73.

————. "The Paterian Mode in Forster's Fiction: *The Longest Journey* to *Pharos and Pharillon*." In Judith Scherer Herz and Robert K. Martin, jt. ed., *E. M. Forster: Centenary Revaluations*. Toronto: U of Toronto P, 1982. 99–112.

Nadel, Ira. "Moments in the Greenwood: *Maurice* in Context." In Judith Scherer Herz and Robert K. Martin, jt. ed., *E. M. Forster: Centenary Revaluations*. Toronto: U of Toronto P, 1982. 177–190.

Pater, Walter. *Miscellaneous Studies*. London, 1910; rpt. New York: Johnson Reprint Co., 1967.

Sedgwick, Eve Kosofsky. *Between Men: English Literature and Male Homosocial Desire*. New York: Columbia UP, 1985.

————. *Epistemology of the Closet*. Berkeley: U of California P, 1990.

Sinfield, Alan. *Literature, Politics, and Culture in Postwar Britain*. Berkeley: U of California P, 1989.

Summers, Claude J. *E. M. Forster*. New York: Ungar, 1983.

Thwaite, Ann. *Edmund Gosse: A Literary Landscape: 1849–1928*. Chicago: U of Chicago P, 1984.

Waugh, Tom. "Photography, Passion and Power." *The Body Politic* (March, 1984): 29–33.

Wittig, Monique. *The Straight Mind and Other Essays*. Foreword by Louise Turcotte. Boston: Beacon P, 1992.

RETELLING THE STORY OF SCIENCE

By Barbara T. Gates

BECAUSE THE BRITISH CULTURAL and educational bias favored men in the nineteenth century, none of the great discoveries of natural and physical science belonged to women. Yet many women took an intense interest in those discoveries and throughout the century sought knowledge of the workings of the universe. Botany, the fern craze; geology, the rock-collecting craze; entomology, the bug-hunting craze — all of these were more female than male pursuits. Charles Kingsley's *Glaucus* (1855), a book written to inform a hypothetical London merchant about the wonders of the seashore, asks the merchant to look at what pleasures his daughters have gained from their ''pteridomania'' over ferns and to imagine what equivalent joys he himself might find in a study of the seashore (4–5). In the nineteenth century, women formed large portions of the audience at public lectures on science and read whatever was available to them by way of written explanation.

But more than this, from the late eighteenth century onward women themselves frequently retold the story of science. They functioned mainly as educators and popularizers, carefully explaining new views of the physical and natural world to women, children, and the working classes. Typically, the scientific theories they conveyed were those which had become accepted; they eschewed the controversial partly in order to enhance their authority. Their originality lay not in the substance of what these women were trying to convey but in the distinctive counter-discourse that they evolved as they narrated the story of science.

I do not wish to suggest that there was a gender war in terms of the scientific texts of the nineteenth century — to search out and stress binary oppositions between male and female scientific narratives. I do not think that the women popularizers believed they were hampered by their gender. Their writing gave them voices and in many cases livelihoods as well. These women found their audience, and they seemed to like the job of informing it. And they were appreciated: up until the end of the century, their volumes sold as well as men's. When George Eliot and George Henry Lewes arrived in

Ilfracombe in 1856 — awkward and ill-equipped novices in seashore life but ready to learn enough for Lewes to be able to write *Seaside Studies* in 1858 — they would have been as likely to have been carrying Annie Pratt's *Things of the Sea Coast* (1850) as they would Phillip Gosse's *Aquarium* (1854) or Kingsley's *Glaucus*. Men and women both popularized science, but women established a set of narrative paradigms that they made their own and that are revealing in terms of women's writing and women's authority in nineteenth-century culture.

On my first review of the earlier part of the century, I was struck by the sheer numbers of popularizations by women; on my second, by the numbers of volumes that heavily favored dialogue as the means of telling their story. Women popularizers imagined their audience to be receptive but previously-uninformed women and children who would function as virtual *tabulae rasae*, querying and then waiting to receive the scientific word. They wrote in the name of nature but in large part for the sake of women. And dialogue was found to be the perfect vehicle for conveying to women those "[m]any things which were thought to be above their comprehension, or unsuited to their sex," to quote Maria Edgeworth in her *Letters for Literary Ladies* (1795) (1).

Most turn-of-the-century writers of dialogue were motivated by a commitment to natural theology. In describing the wonders of nature, they believed they were also describing the wonders of creation and, ultimately, of a creator. Most were equally motivated by a belief in the accessibility of proof. For Priscilla Wakefield in *Domestic Recreations; or Dialogues Illustrative of Natural and Scientific Subjects* (1805), "the curious phenomena that nature presents, is [sic] one of the most rational entertainments we can enjoy: it is easy to be procured; always at hand; and, to a certain degree, lies within the reach of every creature who has the perfect use of his senses, and is capable of attention" (77–78). For women like Wakefield, moral education and scientific observation were not at odds. On the contrary, observing and teaching about the natural world amounted to a calling. Since women saw themselves as the moral educators of each other and of the young, it only made sense that they should be the ones to offer a proof-laden version of natural theology to women and children. They became important purveyors of what I shall call the narrative of natural theology.

In *Writing Biology*, Greg Myers establishes two categories in order to describe twentieth-century science writing: the "narrative of natural history," which refers to a popular account of nature which is diverting, full of anecdotes, and non-theoretical — the sort of thing one finds in natural history magazines — and the "narrative of science," which describes a work that must meet the standards of a discipline and is heavily committed to model-building (142–43, 194–96). The purpose of the latter is primarily to establish the credibility of a scientist within the scientific community. Students of the nineteenth century will notice that Myers's distinctions can easily apply to the Victorian era; Thomas Henry Huxley and many mid- to late-century women popularizers, for example, utilized the "narrative of natural history"; Charles Darwin the "narrative of science." But this is to anticipate my own story.

At the turn of the century, William Paley, not Darwin, was the naturalist to be reckoned with. His *Natural Theology* (1802) claimed that each discovery of natural science was new proof of the wisdom and power of a divine creator. But Paley's deity had personality and was separate from nature. For Paley, nature was primarily valuable as a means of deducing deity. For half a century, women took the substance of Paley's work as the stuff of their popularizations of natural history, producing narratives of natural theology. Margaret Bryan, for example, who taught science to women both in her home and by way of her pen, prefaced her *Lectures on Natural Philosophy, the Result of Many Years' Practical Experience of the Facts Elucidated* (1806) with the statement, "I have followed the very excellent divine Dr. Paley, in his Natural Theology: — a work comprehensive in its nature, important in its application, and extensive in its elucidations of the divine wisdom and omnipotence of our great Creator."

If for the substance of their narratives women took Paley, for their model of narrative discourse they took an animal lover and mother of twelve, Sara Trimmer (1741–1810). Trimmer's *Easy Introduction to the Knowledge of Nature and Reading the Holy Scriptures, Adapted to the Capacities of Children* (1780) offered a sequence of conversations between a mother and her two children. Together the three take outdoor walks and talk about morality and the wonders of nature. Often they sound as though they are proceeding through a catechism of questions and answers. In 1796, Trimmer followed the *Easy Introduction* with her immensely popular *Fabulous Histories, Designed for the Instruction of Children, Respecting Their Treatment of Animals*. This later book tells the natural history of animals via a family of fictional children, the Bensons, who become recipients of their mother's knowledge of and sensitivity toward animals. Trimmer, like many of the women popularizers who would follow her, made up stories to convey facts and created female figures as repositories of the natural wisdom essential for sensitizing growing children to non-human nature. No aspects of children's querying, no questions that they might need to raise go unanswered by the mothers in Trimmer's dialogues.

Trimmer's work was influential for decades and became a model for writers like Charlotte Smith, who also produced a set of *Rural Walks in Dialogues Intended for the Use of Young Persons* (1795), in her case, to support her own children. The task proved difficult for Smith, as she reveals in her preface: "I wished to unite the interest of the novel with the instruction of the schoolbook, by throwing the latter into the form of dialogue, mingled with narrative, and by giving some degree of character to the group. I have found it less easy than I imagined" (iv). Smith's preface also reveals her worry that her work might be judged harshly and appear "insipid" to those for whom it was not intended. Readers must realize that she is not to be blamed by "persons who seem not sufficiently to consider that such books were not meant for their entertainment, but for the instruction of the rising generation" (v). Disclaimers like Smith's became a tradition in women's popularizations of science. They point up the self-consciousness of women who felt themselves excluded by the scientific community and who wrote for audiences which they perceived to be equally excluded.

Even Jane Marcet (1769–1858), unquestionably the most popular of the women writing scientific dialogue in the nineteenth century, believed disclaimers were in order. Marcet attended lectures by Humphrey Davy, and her own work was in turn read by Michael Faraday, a young bookbinder's apprentice who went on to scientific fame and who considered his own entry into science due to her. Nevertheless, in her *Conversations on Chemistry, Intended More Especially for the Female Sex* (1805), a book that sold 160,000 copies in its day and went through sixteen editions in less than forty years, Marcet felt it "necessary to apologize for the present undertaking, as her knowledge of the subject is but recent, and as she can have no real claims to the title of chemist" (v).

Marcet evolved the "conversation," a type of dialogue she devised as a result of her own needs in learning science. When she first attended lectures in experimental chemistry, she found herself overwhelmed by the rapidity of the demonstrations. But as she began to have conversations with friends about what she had heard and seen, she realized that the subject of chemistry came clearer. She therefore decided that "familiar conversation was, in studies of this kind, a most successful source of information; and more especially to the female sex, whose education is seldom calculated to prepare their minds for abstract ideas, or scientific language" (v). For her books, she chose a set of characters who became familiar to generations of readers. They were Mrs. Bryan, a teacher, and Emily and Caroline, her pupils. In Marcet's conversations, as in many dialogues by women popularizers, one of the two students already had some knowledge of the subject to be discussed. This allowed Marcet to speak to readers with a degree of sophistication as well as to those with little or none. Mrs. Bryan, of course, reflected a real-life person, Margaret Bryan, already familiar to us, and indicates the beginnings of a female tradition in women's popularizations. In Marcet's book on chemistry, the three women converse their way through the discoveries of Henry Cavendish, Antoine Lavoisier, Davy, and others. In the book on natural history,

Conversations on Natural Philosophy (1819), the work of earth scientists and physicists becomes the topic. The fictional Mrs. Bryan carefully controls dialogue to make her points. "I do not," she remarks, "wish to confine you to the systematic order of a scientific treatise: but if we were merely to examine every vague question that may chance to occur, our progress would be but very slow" (2). Marcet's characters never wasted time with dialogue, only took time to get things right by conversing productively.

After Mrs. Marcet's successes, the dialogue was even more widely adopted by women and was considered, too, by men. In 1827, Charles Lyell began writing a "Conversations in Geology," to be a companion volume to Marcet's work on chemistry, but the eminent geologist reconsidered and set to work on one of the century's most famous narratives of science instead — his *Elements of Geology* (1838). Earlier, in 1822, Delvalle Lowry had offered a two-volume *Conversations in Mineralogy*, noting that "the mode of conversation has not yet been adopted in this branch of natural history" (v). In her preface, Lowry praised Marcet. In her own dialogues, she created a character called Mrs. L. who carefully instructs young women in her own home and sounds very like Bryan and like Lowry herself.

Despite her admiration of Marcet, Lowry found that her own work presented her with a contradiction that also began to face other discerning writers of scientific dialogue: as a teacher, Lowry was dedicated to direct observation and hands-on experimentation, but as a writer, she was offering something less. As she carefully warned in her preface, "very little knowledge of Mineralogy can be obtained from books, without an acquaintance with Minerals themselves" (ix). Lowry got around her dilemma in part through ample use of illustrations in her text. But she also felt hampered by the form of the conversation, which forced her to use textual devices she might rather have omitted. In her words:

> As it did not appear consistent with the nature of conversations, to particularize all the different synonymes of Minerals, I have inserted the principal in the Index; placing them after the English names. I have avoided as much as possible the use of technical terms in my descriptions; as a great many . . . have been generally adopted by English Mineralogists, I have endeavoured to define them in the first part of the work; and near the end is an Alphabetical List of one hundred and eighty-seven names of Minerals, with their derivations from the Greek, Latin, and German. (vii)

Lowry also sent her readers to museums of mineralogy to see collections at first hand.

Lowry's sense of being cramped by the dialogic form represents the perspective of popularizers who were moving toward observation and experiment. Many women in the 1820s thought like Lowry, although many others still continued to deliver Paleyan narratives of natural theology. Maria Hack's *Harry Beaufoy; or the Pupil of Nature* (1821), a popular fiction about a ten-year-old boy, is prefaced with the words: "Though I have purposely avoided placing the formidable words '*Natural Theology*,' in the title-page, yet parents will perceive, at a glance, that the admirable work of Dr. Paley has been used as the basis of this little volume" (ix). Hack goes on to tell the story of Harry and the mother who instructs him in everything from the ligaments in chicken legs — by snatching a bird from her maid's platter — to gardens and microscopes, mainly through dialogue placed in the context of story. Consistently, Harry is made to see the wisdom and ingenuity of a divine artificer.

But increasingly, both the narrative of natural theology and widespread use of dialogue were fading from view. Evolution was in the air, Paley was being displaced by new scientists, and the dialogue, which came of age along with natural theology, was outliving its own credibility. People were, in general, better informed scientifically, partly because of the dialogues themselves. And learning by question and answer was becoming more frequently satirized — by Charles Dickens, for example. In *Our Mutual Friend*, his Miss Peecher and Mary Anne fall into a mock dialogue of "learning." Wherever she goes, whatever she is asked, young Mary Anne reels off the expected rote answer, so inured is she to interrogation.

Nevertheless, for half a century the scientific dialogue had suited both its women practitioners and their audiences. Certainly it established women as scientific authorities. Questions imply answers, and authorities of one sort or another are needed to supply them. The female instructors in the dialogues, whether they were mothers — almost Mother Natures — teachers, aunts, or older cousins, knew what they were talking about, so much so that when in 1869 Charles Kingsley decided to write a popular book of lessons in geology for children, he titled it *Madame How and Lady Why*. Kingsley's book, addressed to young boys, made these two female figures aspects of Nature herself, the ultimate authority on how and why. But the real-life instructors were experts, too. Like all good educators, they seem to have studied their subject well enough to translate it from professional jargon into the vernacular and to cull just the right examples from their store of knowledge to impress their pupils with self as well as science.

They also knew how to reach consensus. At the outset, dialogue both opens discourse and starts to interrupt narrative. It also challenges the authority of scientific language, for the inquirers on both sides need again and again to make sure that they and their listeners are speaking the same language. This process of interruption and realigning of communication continues to the narrative's end, when the knowledge involved becomes the property of all members of the dialogue. Since their audience was not comprised of scientists — as it would have been had they been unfolding the narrative of science — fictional authorities in the dialogues could be patient enough to get to the heart of the matter while providing others with time in which to learn. They did not have to foretell, but carefully to retell. The experiments they purportedly ran and the observations they made were all controlled to the end of others' learning. They, like their authors, did not project the picture of a lone scientist on the eve of a new discovery but of an alert woman sharing an interest in the world around her. While altering the shape of science writing, they added a social dimension to the story of science. And, in the case of the women telling the story of natural theology, they also added the dimension of the values, something women would continue to do in their popularized versions of science, as in their other writing about nature, throughout the nineteenth century.

By the 1840s, new forms began to enhance the dialogue. In her *Young Naturalist's Journey* (1840), for example, Jane Loudon offered a type of narrative that would widen its scope. In Loudon's "journey," a fictional young girl and her mother travel throughout the British Isles and meet, query, and parley with people who own or have extensive knowledge of exotic animals. Anecdotal in the extreme, Loudon's book is a narrative of natural history, not natural theology, and is informed by other vehicles for popularizing science. It was when she was turning over the pages of the *Magazine of Natural History* looking for information about animals that Loudon was stimulated to write her own book. "Stripped of their technicalities," she believed the magazine articles could "be rendered both interesting and amusing to children" (ix). She went on to carefully authenticate her own originality, adding that "the adaptation of them has cost me quite as much time and labour as the writing of an entirely new work. . . . Anecdotes here related of the animals are strictly true; though the incidents of the journey, and the persons introduced are partly imaginary" (x).

Loudon patterned her main characters after her own daughter and herself, producing this book and dozens of others in order to support the two of them after the death of her husband John Claudius Loudon, the landscape gardener. In the *Journey* the subject that most interests Loudon is animal adaptation — like that of the mole to its underground hideaways. If there is some Paleyan reference to the beauty of adaptation in Loudon, the main emphasis is on the creatures themselves, not on a conjectured creator. Moreover, the journey is a railroad journey, not a turn-of-the-century ramble in nearby rural surroundings. With Loudon we enter wider worlds in terms of both natural history and geography, worlds that many women were eager to explore and depict.

Loudon's book, no doubt coupled with her many authoritative studies of botany for women, was seminal and led to imitations like Margaret Plues's

Rambles in Search of Ferns (1861), a first-person, fictional handbook describing a long holiday with friends in various parts of England. Plues's narrator makes visits in order to see the ferns indigenous to each part of the country, then authoritatively explains them to her native but less well-informed hosts and, of course, to her readers as well. But Plues and Loudon had only described British botany. Loudon's botanicals, like *The Ladies' Flower Garden of Ornamental Annuals* (1840) and *British Wild Flowers* (1846), were part of a movement toward botany that had attracted British women as illustrators and enthusiasts throughout the second quarter of the nineteenth century. These books were designed to familiarize women with the plants they could see with their own eyes and grow with their own hands.

In the 1860s, a wider world of botany was opened to reading and traveling women, and they in turn tried to interest other women in that world. In 1868 Elizabeth Twining's beautifully worked *Illustrations of the Natural Orders of Plants with Groups and Descriptions* was prefaced to promote this new catholicity of vision. Twining, whose family owned tea plantations in many corners of the English empire, wanted to show British plants in relation to others. "By thus placing our native plants in groups with foreigners, we acquire a more correct idea of the nature of our Flora, and the character it has when compared with that of other countries" (ii), she explained. Proud of her pioneering efforts at popularizing comparative botany, she helped her readers to see their favorites in a new light. Loudon and earlier popularizers had sympathized with women's difficulties with the Linnean system of classification. Twining chose an even more difficult system to follow — De Candolle's — because his ordering allowed her readers "a ready perception of the geographical distribution of any particular tribe. Also what proportion our British Flora bears, both in quantity and quality, to the whole range of the Natural Orders" (ii).

By mid-century, other women popularizers had already favored this outward expansion in search of a wider world. Possibly, it was because, as women, they felt the constrictions of both British society and the British scientific community. Becoming pioneers and going beyond British borders offered women horizons against which to stand as authorities and granted them a stature more equivalent to that of men. Rosina M. Zornlin, author of over half a dozen books popularizing science in the 1850s — among them *Outlines of Geology* (1852), *Recreations in Geology* (1852), and *The World of Waters* (1855) — certainly opted to commend the new vantage points. In her *Recreations in Physical Geography, or the Earth As It Is* (1855), she praised the work of travel writers and showed how it applied to her own work: "descriptions of small and detached portions of the earth's surface kindle in us a desire to become acquainted with all that is remarkable on the face of the globe: in short, with all that descriptive geography . . . can impart to us'' (4). This desire then led to a need to understand physical geography, and hence to her book.

By mid-century, too, audiences for scientific writing had become more demanding and more sophisticated. Speaking on behalf of the reader or student of science, in *The Scientific Lady,* Patricia Phillips explains that ''women were no longer content to be supplied with their science in a haphazard manner'' (191). Writers responded by expanding the world of popularizations and bringing new sciences before new audiences. Nevertheless, female devotion to the moralizing of scientific discovery also remained. Zornlin, so aware of the far-ranging, so devoted to getting an accurate picture of geology and geography to the working classes — ''to the cotter no less than the large landed proprietor, to the artisan as well as the master manufacturer, to the miner as well as the owner of mines'' (preface to *Physical Geography* vii) — and so convinced of the ''truth'' of science, nevertheless, clearly stated that truth was ''God's'' truth (*Recreations in Geology* 365). And Margaret Gatty, writer of the authoritative *British Seaweeds*, completed in 1862 after fourteen years of painstaking research, continued for decades to reissue editions of her *Parables of Nature* (1855), one of the most popular books of the last half of the nineteenth century. The *Seaweeds*, in two volumes, were — like Anna Atkins's comprehensive and beautiful volume of photographic cyanotypes, *British Algae* (1843) — intended to supplement William Harvey's *Manual of British Algae*. Unlike the *Seaweeds*, the parables, although based in scientific knowledge, were meant to illustrate morals of one sort or another. In the parable, ''A Lesson of Faith,'' for example, the stages of metamorphosis became demonstrations of patience. In the course of this narrative, an impatient caterpillar eventually learns that it will become a butterfly but learns this in nature's time, not its own. One cannot will beauty or the ability to fly. If one is a caterpillar, nature bestows the gift; if a child, God does. Another parable, ''Knowledge not the Limit of Belief,'' displayed Gatty's more specific scientific knowledge. In this parable, a zoophyte, a seaweed, a bookworm, and a naturalist parley about a controversy that had earlier interested Gatty: whether a zoophyte was or was not a plant, and a seaweed an animal. The naturalist solves the problem, showing that despite popular opinion and the bookworm's protests, the zoophyte is animal, the seaweed a plant. Even the two creatures themselves are humbled by this discovery and become ''disciples'' of a higher power — the naturalist — as children must in turn become disciples of God.

Women like Gatty and Zornlin continued to carry a responsibility as moral teachers along with their challenge to popularize science in more sophisticated and less amateurish ways. Injunctions for the role of moralist were deeply entrenched and had been in place at least since Trimmer's day. They had been laid down by Trimmer herself and by such influential figures as Erasmus

Darwin, who in his *Plan for the Conduct of Female Education in Boarding Schools* (1797) recommended that women inculcate in other younger women "sympathy, when any thing cruel presents itself; as in the destruction of an insect" (47). Darwin went on to illustrate his point:

> I once observed a lady with apparent expressions of sympathy say to her little daughter, who was pulling off the legs of a fly, "how should you like to have your arms and legs pull'd off? would it not give you great pain? pray let it fly away out of the window": which I doubt not would make an indelible impression on the child, and lay the foundation of an amiable character. (47)

Darwin's recommendations were often reinforced in conduct books like Maria Grey and Emily Shirreff's *Thoughts on Self-Culture, Addressed to Women* (1851), where women again were charged with the duty of inculcating in the young sympathy and benevolence for all "inferior beings." Still later in the nineteenth century, Darwin's grandson, Charles, would influence Patrick Geddes and J. Arthur Thomson in their widely read study of *The Evolution of Sex* (1889), which characterized women as having evolved "a larger and habitual share of the altruistic emotions" and as excelling "in constancy of affection and sympathy" (270–71).

SMALL WONDER, THEN, that a need to sympathize remained with women even when a new generation of post-Darwinian women appeared as popularizers toward the end of the century. Most remarkable among these was Arabella Buckley, Sir Charles Lyell's secretary, whose writing career I would like to document in some detail. With Buckley we enter a new era in popularization by women. Personally familiar with the leading scientists and scientific theories of her day, she had little of the diffidence we have seen in earlier women popularizers. In her first book, *A Short History of Natural Science* (1876), she recalls how she "often felt very forcibly how many important facts and generalizations of science, which are of great value in the formation of character and in giving a true estimate of life and its conditions, are totally unknown to the majority of otherwise well-educated persons" (vii–viii). This is to say nothing of children, who are fed only a few elementary and scattered facts about science and therefore are unprepared "to follow intelligently the great movement of thought" (viii). Her own book was intended "to supply that modest amount of scientific information which everyone ought to possess, while, at the same time, it will form a useful groundwork for those who wish afterwards to study any special branch of science" (viii). She would write narratives of natural history in hopes of stimulating future narratives of science.

With Buckley's *History* the dialogic form had virtually died. There are no fictional questioners, so that when Buckley raises questions in her history, she makes it clear that it is she who has both the discernment to pose and the knowledge to answer them. She is clearly the authority here. This is also true in her second book, *The Fairy-land of Science* (1879), where she expatiates on the dangers of questions and answers as she instructs children in wonders of a science that should seem to them as magical as the wonders of fairyland, and far more accessible. In the *Fairy-land* Buckley advises her young readers not to be constantly asking questions of other people, "for often a question quickly answered is quickly forgotten, but a difficulty really hunted down is a triumph forever" (13).

History obviously fascinated Buckley, as did analogies between scientific forces and imaginary fairies, but neither of these gave full scope to her distinctive penchant for narrative. Only retellings of the story of evolution did that. Thoroughly grounded in evolutionary theory and in all aspects of the new geology, Buckley set out this knowledge in a series of books whose narratives are brilliantly original. It is difficult to imagine a popularizer of Darwin who could out-narrate Darwin's own remarkable story, with its high drama of struggle and its presiding Nature who both is and is not the principle of natural selection. But, as Darwin himself knew, the story of evolution was many stories. His revisions and his own later comments on what he meant by natural selection show is own openness to reinterpretation. Buckley, then, was one of many later interpreters of Darwin who took advantage of the capaciousness of the story of evolution. Like Huxley, she could help to write a narrative of natural history based upon Darwin's narrative of science.

This she did in two highly imaginative volumes, *Life and Her Children* (1881) and *Winners in Life's Race* (1883). In these books, Buckley presents seven divisions of life: *Life and Her Children* covers the first six, from the amoebas to the insects, and *Winners in Life's Race*, the seventh, the "great backboned family." Life, or the life force, is only a partial heroine in this story. It drives all creatures to seek further life for themselves but does not exhibit the sympathy that Buckley would most admire in a heroine. That role would be reserved for the vertebrates of the animal kingdom. In this way, as in many ways, Buckley's story does not recapitulate Darwin's, with its confusion between a benevolent seeming natural force, Nature, and a more indifferent one, natural selection.

In *Life*, the first of the two volumes on evolution, Buckley reviews the struggle for existence and adaptations of the simpler animals, concluding with an interesting appraisal of ants that prepares for her second volume. Her entire chapter on ants is highly authoritative: Buckley supports every observation and anecdote with scientific accounts by eminent authorities and leads us to ant colonies throughout the globe. But ants leave her with a final troubling question: whether these creatures, with all their socialized behavior, are also marked by sympathy. Her conclusion is that the ant's place in Life's scheme need allow for no such thing — ants are devoted to community, not to each other. It remained for the backboned creatures to illustrate kindness.

Winners shows these backboned creatures in far greater detail than its predecessor had depicted the invertebrates and reveals the original ways in which Buckley handled narrative problems that had also faced Darwin. Having written a history in her first work, Buckley knew well how to depict events imagined through time. But the story of evolution called for a different kind of history, a different kind of time. The need to get beyond life spans, not just of individuals but of entire species, forced Buckley to reach past the strategies she had previously relied upon. The need to describe a history that was pre-verbal and antecedent to human consciousness sent her deep into images.

In an early chapter Buckley recalls how "with a history so strange" she wishes to "open the great book of Nature still further, and by ransacking the crust of the earth in all countries . . . try and find the explanation, which will no doubt come some day to patient explorers" (210) — the explanation of the "missing links." But neither science nor history could take Buckley and her readers into such uncharted waters. Having learned, as did Darwin, that "[o]rganicism is more space than time oriented" (Beer 108), Buckley therefore altered her focus in her final chapter. She asks her readers to begin "forgetting the enormous lapse of time required" and to "allow the shifting scene to pass like a panorama before us" (334). She could then move with kaleidoscopic swiftness to a review of the progress of backboned animals.

Buckley loved sight and the instruments that allowed people better to see the universe. The magic lantern, the telescope, photographic equipment, and the spectroscope would all be the focus of her next book, *Through Magic Glasses* (1890). But seven years earlier, in *Winners*, words were the focalizers for a narrative that puts Buckley's readers on something like a conveyor belt at a world's fair: we glide into and past dramatic dioramas of vertebrate beasts. First we find ourselves in a sea full of stone-lilies and huge crustaceans, looking at tiny fish with gristly skeletons; then we move on to watch those fish evolve into giants with enormous jaws; next we enter a dual world, where creatures can shift from water to the now-forested land, and the age of amphibians has dawned. Before we can move on again, Buckley stops to tell us that though we witness exterior changes in the animals, even greater changes are taking place inside the animals. A look at a contemporary tadpole might show us some semblance of those changes.

But back to the dioramas. Dense forests of the coal period pass away, and the huge reptiles enter the scene. "Meanwhile' (337), and Buckley pauses our journey again, the tree of life begins to branch: marsupials and birds both enter, the birds showing us their reptilian ancestry, the marsupials more mysteriously — because of missing links — concealing theirs, though amphibians probably spawned them somewhere back in time. With scenery of the chalk period, we resume our vision of the age of reptiles. "We find them everywhere — in the water, with paddles for swimming; in the air, with membranes for flying; on the land hopping or running on their hind feet" (339). "This is," Buckley tells us, "no fancy picture, for in our museums, and especially in Professor Marsh's wonderful collection in Yale Museum in America, you may see the skeletons of these large reptiles, and build them up again in imagination as they stood in those ancient days when they looked down upon the primitive birds and tiny marsupials" (339). Of course, this building up again is exactly what Buckley's imaginary dioramas have been accomplishing.

What stops Buckley's journey in pictures is a "strange blank" — the mysterious end of the age of reptiles. But Buckley seems to realize that her panorama has served its narrative purpose. She returns to a "history" (342) of the mammals and humankind's appearance on the scene, and this allows her a place for her favorite improvement upon Darwin: her belief in the evolution of sympathy. Before she launches into her explanation of this phenomenon, Buckley looks for awhile at adaptation, then instinct. These usher her into the realm of feeling, exactly where she wishes to be. The loyalty of pet snakes, the sacrificial miming of injuries by parent birds trying to distract enemies away from their young, the instinct of herding for protection — all these lead her to speculate that "one of the laws of life which is as strong, if not stronger, than the law of force and selfishness, *is that of mutual help and dependence*' (351). This law was not a special gift to human beings, as Christians might like to believe, but a gradual development through the animal world. In considerable contrast to the social Darwinians of her day, Buckley concludes her book with "the great moral lesson taught at every step in the history of the development of the animal world, that amidst toil and suffering, struggle and death, the supreme law of life is the law of SELF-DEVOTION AND LOVE" (353). For Buckley the *raison d'etre* for evolution was not just the preservation of life but the development of mutuality as well.

Buckley's last book, *Moral Teachings of Science* (1891), is devoted to this idea, and is written to unite science and philosophy — to study morality from "within outward" and "without inward" (4). For Buckley, "these are not really two, but only different methods of arriving at one result, namely, the knowledge of the laws by which we and all the rest of nature are governed" (5). Life for her has become universal; she sets out to examine a natural and human world where struggle predominates but mutuality works to benefit individuals of all groups, including human beings. Although Buckley plants us firmly in the world of sympathy, as a post-Darwinian she takes us entirely out of the world of Paley. "[W]e must remember," she reminds us, that this [evolution, development] has not taken place by special guidance along certain beneficent lines, since degradation and partial deformities result as by products of the struggle for life; but that the overwhelming preponderance of healthy, happy, and varied existence has been brought about by the steady working of natural laws among which the struggle to survive and the constant action of natural selection are the most important. (54)

Buckley's moral ecology was not embraced by her contemporary, Alice Bodington, whose essays, in her *Studies in Evolution and Biology* (1890), attempted to bring the story of evolution scientifically up to date for turn-of-the-century readers. Bodington's whole tone is an even greater departure from those of earlier women popularizers than is Buckley's. Buckley found no need for disclaimers: Bodington find them wholly absurd. Her preface, entitled "to the Reader," makes this fully clear.

A stigma is supposed to rest, for some mysterious reason, upon the person who ventures to write upon any branch of science without being an original discoverer. I am at a loss to imagine why it is considered almost wrong to write about physical science without having made original experiments. A historian is not required to have fought in the battles he describes, nor a geographer to have personally traversed the wilds of Africa. Why cannot a wide view be taken by some competent person of the results of the labours of hundreds of scientists, so that we may more clearly see what manner of fabric is being reared? (ix–x)

This is a direct plea on behalf of the expansiveness of the narrative of natural history — a preserve that women shared with men — versus the narrative of science — the more narrow, exclusively male preserve. Bodington wanted to be able freely to enter into the shared preserve without the condemnation of scientists. She especially wanted to be unobstructed in her attempt to supplement Darwin's narrative where Darwin seemed passé.

She made this clearest in her essay "The Mammalia: Extinct Species and Surviving Forms," where, like Buckley, she took exception to Darwin's idea of natural selection. The "great master," as she calls him, "had only grasped one form of the law governing evolution . . . whereas we now see that the infinite, delicate variations in the world of organic beings are owing to the intense irritability and susceptibility to molecular changes of protoplasm, and the consequent action of the environment upon it" (22). What she objected to in Darwin is what Buckley objected to in Paley: his determinism. To her, "natural selection evoked some unknown force vaguely of the nature of will. The action of the environment upon protoplasm requires nothing but ordinary and well-known phenomena of organic chemistry" (23). Bodington preferred this explanation because it gave natural selection a lesser role in "the great drama of development" (23).

Bodington went on to discuss post-Darwinian theories of extinction. To her mind, catastrophism was utterly dead, killed by frequent, new discoveries of missing links. She therefore proposes a natural law of her own, one *"governing the duration of species"* (27). Species and even orders of animals "may be *prematurely* destroyed by glacial epochs, or drying up of marshes, or inundations of the sea, but if they are exposed to no possibility of perishing by external accidents, *the species dies out of old age"* (27). Ever the popularizer, Bodington used her ready wit to name these "Liberal-Conservative animals," those who have the best chance of long term survival because they "do not change too quickly or slowly" (27). When she concluded her essay on mammals, Bodington identified her intended audience — non-professionals who do not realize that, despite the many discoveries since Darwin's time, obscurities still veil the story of "the appearance, duration, and disappearance of species" (60). This permitted her to urge her readers, especially the travelers and anthropologists among them, to continue hunting for missing links.

In its choice of audience, Bodington's post-Darwinian work makes an interesting contrast with Buckley's. Bodington was clearly not writing for children but for intelligent adults, giving her room to poke fun at the fanciful, Buckley's stock and trade. Whereas Buckley illustrated the romance of science and of geological history, Bodington employed wit and humor to drive home the peculiarities of species' evolutionary adaptations. Spoofing science fiction, she complained of its tired exploration of people from other planets who "always turn out to be distressingly like ourselves." She would have preferred "a planet inhabited permanently by a set of old maids, where gentlemen were grudged even a few days of life, and one matron presided over the whole community, where there were no paupers and no starvation, and children were brought up as in the Republic of Plato" — her unique demonstration of female sympathy and compassion. But more interesting still would be a world "where everyone had their mouths in the middle of their bodies . . . and their eyes at the ends of their fingers and toes," like some of the animals she had just been describing. These adaptations would play havoc with the accustomed style of dinner party but would probably also be too much for the human imagination. "We might," suggests Bodington, "find our reason tottering, as that of the clergyman did, who wished that all his congregation had tails they could wag when they were specially pleased with his sermons" (20). With this kind of playful wit, Bodington's essays capture humor along with their subjects. Bodington's main thrust was to educate; she wanted to make "clear and plain" to persons of "ordinary intelligence" those many new observations of scientists who "buried" their work "in the pages of scientific journals, to be read only by specialists" (143). All the same, she could see no reason not to make the narrative of natural history as amusing and pleasurable as possible.

Nor, at the end of the century, could many others. Bodington worked the same vein as did men like J. G. Wood, who both wrote and lectured. Although women like Arabella Buckley and Mary Kingsley lectured on the subjects in which they had expertise, science lecturing was predominantly the domain of men, whose lectures helped them to build reputations and to sell books. Wood himself developed a unique art which he called "sketch-lecturing." He would speak, then illustrate his subject before his audience's eyes, dramatically conjuring up huge images of hydrozoa, fish, or other animals in colored pastilles, which he applied directly to a large black canvas. When he died, the year before Bodington's *Studies* appeared, Wood was heralded as the great popularizer of his day; when he wrote his *Boy's Own Book of Natural History* in 1883, the year of Buckley's *Winners*, he himself claimed that there was "no work of a really popular character in which accuracy of information and systematic arrangement are united with brevity and simplicity of treatment" (iii).

Yet we have just seen two to rival him — Buckley and Bodington — both supporters of the theory of evolution that he, with his conservative religious bias, had trouble condoning. By the end of the century, women, long purveyors and champions of the popularization of science, were now more well-informed, original, and creative popularizers than they had been in the past. But they were also perceived as competitors in a literary struggle for survival and were more frequently discounted by men like Wood. Edmund Gosse, for example, in a supposed tribute to the popular natural history writer Eliza Brightwen that introduces her posthumous *Life and Thoughts of a Naturalist* (1909), all but kills his subject with condescension. "This little book," he says of Brightwen's autobiography as he compares it with her natural history, "in its simplicity, in its *naïveté*, will not be comprehended by any but those who are already in sympathy with its author and in measure conversant with her methods" (x). By implication, then, those methods were simple and naïve, rather like Kingsley's description of the young women's "pteridomania" with which I began this chapter. Kingsley had minimized the young women's pursuit in order to make his intended audience, the London merchant, feel superior to his daughters. They had only taken up ferns in preference to "the abomination of 'Fancy work,' that standing cloak for dreamy idleness" (*Glaucus* 4), whereas the merchant should take up the study of seashores as an amateur naturalist. As the century wore on, botany, along with the seashores, was becoming the province of men, although it had certainly been the science most attractive to women. In 1887, J. F. A. Adams's essay in *Science*, "Is botany a suitable study for young men?," offered botany as an area to be studied by "able-bodied and vigourous brained young men" (116) as well as by women. Adams's attitude, like Kingsley's and Gosse's, reveals how scientific endeavor, like the narrative of science, had become linked to masculine intellectual qualities that were certainly not simplicity nor naïveté, and how women had begun to lose their status as interpreters of the narrative of natural history.

In part this loss of status also occurred because their special audience of children and women had diminished. Natural history education had reached the schools — first girls' schools, then boys' — and had reduced the need for science books in the home. In the first half of the century, mothers and grandmothers had bought books by women popularizers and had virtually educated themselves along with their children. My own copy of Annie Pratt's *Things of the Sea Coast* was a gift from a grandmother to her grandson in 1852. But as time went on, mothers and grandmothers were progressively less responsible for children's knowledge of science. Concomitantly, formal education in natural history for girls, an important ingredient in their curricula for decades, was lessened, while at the same time it was increased for boys. Young men became more knowledgeable in science, more likely to learn their science from men, and more and more likely to be the future narrators of the narrative of natural history as well as the narrative of science. This overall "demise" of science as a female interest — as Patricia Phillips describes it in chapter eight of *The Scientific Lady* — was especially noticeable after the Taunton Commission's report in 1868–69. It was then that the focus of women's education shifted from natural science to the classics, ostensibly to bring women's study more on a par with men's. By the time of the Bryce Commission report in 1894–95, many of the bright young women in secondary schools who showed a special desire to study science were discouraged from taking classes in scientific subjects, and encouraged instead to perfect a knowledge of classics. Thus in the name of equalizing formal education for women, fewer young women were given access to narratives of science in secondary schools, while at almost the same time, fewer were reading narratives of natural history in their homes. Ironically, then, the economics of the book trade and the masculinization of science — through appropriation by and education of men — joined along with educational reforms on behalf of women to prevent women from speaking so freely in nature's name.

University of Delaware

WORKS CITED

Adams, J. F. A. "Is botany a suitable study for young men?" *Science* 9 (1887): 116–17.

Beer, Gillian. *Darwin's Plots*. London: Routledge and Kegan Paul, 1983.

Bodington, Alice. *Studies in Evolution and Biology*. London: Elliot Stock, 1890.

Brightwen, Eliza. *Life and Thoughts of a Naturalist*. London: T. Fisher Unwin, 1909.

Bryan, Margaret. *Lectures on Natural Philosophy, the Result of Many Years' Practical Experience of the Facts Elucidated*. London: Thomas Davison, 1806.

Buckley, Arabella. *The Fairy-land of Science*. London: Edward Stanford, 1879.

————. *Moral Teachings of Science*. London: Edward Stanford, 1891.

————. *A Short History of Natural Science*. London: John Murray, 1876.

————. *Winners in Life's Race*. London: Edward Stanford, 1883.

Darwin, Erasmus. *Plan for the Conduct of Female Education in Boarding Schools*. 1787. New York: S. R. Publishers, Ltd., 1968.

Edgeworth, Maria. *Letters for Literary Ladies*. London, 1795.

Geddes, Patrick, and J. Arthur Thomson. *The Evolution of Sex*. London: Contemporary Science Series, 1889.

Hack, Maria. *Harry Beaufoy; or the Pupil of Nature*. 1821. London: Darton and Harvey, 1845.

Kingsley, Charles. *Glaucus; or, the Wonders of the Shore*. Cambridge: Macmillan, 1855.

Loudon, Jane. *The Young Naturalist's Journey, or Travels of Agnes Merton and Her Mother*. London: William Smith, 1840.

Lowry, Delvalle. *Conversations in Minerology*. London: Longman, Hurst, Rees, Orme, and Brown, 1822.

Marcet, Jane. *Conversations on Chemistry, Intended More Especially for the Female Sex*. London: Longman, Hurst, Rees, and Orme, 1805.

————. *Conversations on Natural Philosophy*. London: Hurst, Rees, Orme and Brown, 1819.

Myers, Greg. *Writing Biology*. Madison: U of Wisconsin P, 1990.

Paley, William. *Natural Theology, or, Evidences of the Existence and Attributes of the Deity, Collected from the Appearances of Nature*. London: R. Faulder, 1802.

Phillips, Patricia. *The Scientific Lady: A Social History of Woman's Scientific Interests, 1520–1918*. London: Weidenfeld and Nicholson, 1990.

Plues, Margaret. *Rambles in Search of Ferns*. London: Houlston and Wright, 1861.

Smith, Charlotte. *Rural Walks in Dialogues Intended for the Use of Young Persons*. London: T. Cadell and W. Davies, 1795.

Trimmer, Sara. *An Easy Introduction to the Knowledge of Nature, and Reading the Holy Scriptures, Adapted to the Capacities of Children*. London: Longman, Robinson, and Johnson, 1789.

————. *Fabulous Histories, Designed for the Instruction of Children, Respecting Their Treatment of Animals*. London: Longman, Robinson and Johnson, 1796.

Twining, Elizabeth. *Illustrations of the Natural Orders of Plants with Groups and Descriptions*. London: Sampson Low, Son, and Marston, 1868.

Wakefield, Priscilla. *Domestic Recreations; or Dialogues Illustrative of Natural and Scientific Subjects*. Philadelphia: Robert Carr, 1805.

Zornlin, Rosina M. *Recreations in Physical Geography, or the Earth As It Is*. London: John W. Parker and Son, 1855.

"CERTAIN LEARNED LADIES": TROLLOPE'S *CAN YOU FORGIVE HER?* AND THE LANGHAM PLACE CIRCLE

By Margaret F. King

IN HIS 1856 REVIEW of *Can You Forgive Her?*, Henry James complains of the incongruity between Alice Vavasor's "temporary ill-treatment" of John Grey and the severity with which it is censured. "There are few of Mr. Trollope's readers," writes James, "who will not resent being summoned to pass judgment on such a sin . . . , to establish by precedent the criminality of the conscientious flutterings of an excellent young lady" (409). By calling into question the judgment implicit in the title's plea for mercy, James anticipates recent critics' preoccupation with the gaps and fissures in *Can You Forgive Her?*: disjunctions between sympathetic female characterization and anti-feminist narrative commentary, between the initially transgressive trajectories of female desire and their ultimate re-direction toward marriage and motherhood, between the competing ideals of self-fulfillment and (female) self-denial.[1] But the question raised by the disparity James himself identifies remains an important one: Why *does* Trollope violate the conventions of realism to sensationalize an offense that even to a contemporary seemed venial? The answer, I believe, lies in the relationship between *Can You Forgive Her?* and the discourse of mid-century British feminists, particularly those nicknamed the "ladies of Langham Place" — discourse that was for Trollope both a narrative resource to be utilized and a cause for anxiety, to be suppressed.

The key to this relationship, which may supply the answer to James's question, appears in Chapter 11 of *Can You Forgive Her?*, where the narrator alludes to and answers another question:

What should a woman do with her life? There had arisen round [Alice Vavasor] a flock of learned ladies asking that question, to whom it seems the proper

307

answer has never yet occurred. Fall in love, marry the man, have two children, and live happy ever afterwards. I maintain that answer has as much wisdom in it as any other that can be given; — or perhaps more. The advice contained in it cannot, perhaps, always be followed to the letter; but neither can the advice of the other kind, which is given by the flock of learned ladies who ask the question. (140)

This passage suggests to me that Alice's story is partly a narrative response to a specific "flock of learned ladies," headquartered by late 1859 in London's Langham Place, who led the assault in mid-century Britain on the patriarchally defined "proper answer" to what Victorians termed the Woman Question. By looking first at the discourse produced by the Langham Place circle and then at the shift from feminist to confessional discourse in Alice Vavasor's narrative, I hope to show that the hyperbole of the latter discourse, foreshadowed by the title question, is part of a strategy for silencing the threat posed by the former, which is introduced to make Alice's story narratable. I shall argue, finally, that while the same strategy is repeated, with variations, in the novel's other narratives of Glencora Palliser and Arabella Greenow, in the latter narrative it is disrupted by the subversive conventions of comedy. As these conventions liberate the play of desire within women's language, that desire emerges in the low comic subplot more or less triumphant.

I

IN MID-CENTURY LONDON, whose geography Trollope borrows for the London chapters of *Can You Forgive Her?*, the "learned ladies" of Langham Place would have literally "arisen round" Queen Anne Street, where Trollope locates the house of Alice Vavasor and her father. Blandford Square, where in 1855 Barbara Leigh Smith (later Bodichon) first convened the original members of the group as the Married Women's Property Committee, is only six or seven blocks away. Even closer are Cavendish Square and Langham Place, the initial and subsequent headquarters of the English Woman's Journal Company, where the original circle expanded to encompass not only Bodichon, Anna Jameson, Anna Mary Howitt, Maria Rye, and Bessie Rayner Parkes but also Matilda Hayes, Isa Craig, Adelaide Procter, Emily Faithfull, Emily Davies, and Jessie Boucherett.

By 1863, the Langham Place feminists had attracted notice through a variety of initiatives to improve the lives of British women: a Society to Promote the Employment of Women, with a network of regional branches; a Female Middle-Class Emigration Society; training and employment sites for women that included a law stationer's office, a business school, and the Victoria Press; a Ladies' Institute to house women in these training programs;

and at the Langham Place headquarters a women's employment registry, library, and dining room. Individually, the women associated with Langham Place had also published monographs and delivered speeches, particularly before the National Association for the Promotion of Social Science, on the need to reform the laws and customs controlling women's property and voting rights, employment, and education. But their collective identity dates most clearly from the establishment in 1858 of a shareholders' company to finance and publish the *English Woman's Journal*. Never a commercial success, the *Journal* ceased separate publication after six years, to be succeeded by other Langham Place periodicals: the short-lived *Alexandra Magazine*, with which it merged, and the more enduring *Victoria Magazine* and *Englishwoman's Review*. Between 1858 and 1864, as it provided a monthly forum for the discussion of women's issues, the *Journal* served as the discursive and organizational matrix for the first major wave of nineteenth-century British feminism. Not only by its content but also by the nature of its production and the discursive practices of its editors, the *Journal* challenged the subtext of legal and economic dependence for women contained within the mid-Victorian narrative of marriage, motherhood, and happy-ever-aftering.

Admittedly, by its almost exclusive appeal to women's issues, the *English Woman's Journal* unavoidably supported what Mary Poovey has called "the characteristic feature of the mid-Victorian symbolic economy: the articulation of difference upon sex and in the form of a binary opposition rather than a hierarchically ordered range of similarities" (6). But by entering the public arena of political and economic debate, its editors and contributors also breached the barriers between the so-called "male" and "female" spheres upon which the Victorian ideology of gender depended. As publishers, editors, and (after the establishment of the Victoria Press in 1859) printers of the *Journal*, the ladies of Langham Place exercised a control enjoyed by few British women before them over the production, reproduction, and dissemination of female discourse.[2] Besides publishing their own essays, they reviewed, excerpted, and thus increased the circulation of the work of other feminists like Caroline Dall and Harriet Martineau.[3] Equally important, they invited their readers to participate in the construction of the *Journal* not only by reading it but also by submitting letters of suggestion and inquiry, which were printed each month in "Open Council." As a vehicle for discursive interaction, the *Journal* gave both ordinary and extraordinary women a public voice and offered them a means, however limited, of transcending the isolation that Mill would cite as a major cause of women's subjection. In addition, they utilized the periodical format to engage in an ongoing dialogue with anti-feminist discourse.[4] Trollope found himself and his brother engaged in such dialogues: the *Journal* published a scathing review of Thomas Adolphus Trollope's "sneering" book, *A Decade of Italian Women*, and in a more

charitable critique of Anthony Trollope's *North America* countered at length
his arguments against middle-class women's wholesale entry into the paid
labor force. By their skillful control of the discursive resources of the *Journal*,
the editorial staff made it the "pressure-group periodical" that, according to
Brian Harrison, "virtually brought the British feminist movement into existence in the 1860s" (282). In doing so, the women of Langham Place themselves enacted an alternative or at least supplemental female narrative to the
one legitimized in *Can You Forgive Her?*

The Langham Place circle also challenged the culturally defined "natural"
narrative of a Victorian woman's life by the kinds of articles they included
in the *English Woman's Journal*. Underscoring the gap between the ideal of
the husband-supported wife-mother and mid-century reality, *Journal* contributors repeatedly noted the findings of the 1851 census, including the high
number of "surplus" women of marriageable age and the even higher number
of women who were either single and self-supporting or married and employed.[5] And whereas they sought in several articles to "address the plight
of the governess," whose specter made any marriage seem preferable to no
marriage, the ladies of Langham Place also pointed out in the *Journal* article
"What Are Women Doing?" that by 1861, middle-class women were employed as "authors and able editors, actresses, professional singers, painters,
sculptors; milliners, dressmakers, hairdressers and artists in hair; law-copy-
ists, telegraph-clerks, post-mistresses; lodging-house keepers, innkeepers,
shopkeepers of various kinds, and saleswomen; last, but not least, the great
army of teachers" (52). As examples of what could be achieved outside the
domestic sphere, they included profiles of such women as Florence Nightingale, the physician Elizabeth Blackwell, female professors at the University
of Bologna, poets Isa Craig and Elizabeth Barrett Browning, mathematician
Sophie Germaine, and novelist-critic Mme. de Stael. Coupled with the census
figures, articles like these exploded the Victorian myths that the housebound
wife-mother was a universal (middle-class) norm and that the only alternative
for middle-class women was the governess's literal and figurative impover-
ishment.

The ladies of Langham Place also called into question the "happy ever
after" promised as the pay-off for marriage and motherhood. Besides publi-
cizing the hearings of the newly established divorce courts, they pointed out
that whereas a "woman is regarded as making in marriage an absolute and
unconditional gift and surrender of her person and property into the hands of
her husband," "[f]rom the most important and injurious of female disabilities
single women are, in this country, exempt" (Tabor 124–25).[6] Out of this
gendered imbalance of marital power, they argued, "has grown that servility
of mind and body . . . at the root of all the relations between the sexes, and

which aims the deadliest blow at domestic peace and happiness, at human worth and dignity'' (''Female Education'' 223).

Rather than idealize middle-class wives as Angels in the House, the *Journal* likened them to heathen idols of the hearth, forced to sit at home ''silent, motionless, with Berlin wool or novel in hand, until their blood stagnates in their veins, their limbs refuse to move, and they become as *useful* or as *useless* as the little figures were of old, perched on pagan altars'' (A. R. L. 76). But because the domestic norm had been so thoroughly internalized, most women, ''though created neither children, slaves, nor invalids, shun all serious reflection upon the great end of existence, terrified by the threat that the phantom will modify, or injure, their existing domestic interests'' (''The Disputed Question'' 365). In the face of this inertia and women's legal, educational, and economic disabilities, the Langham Place circle sought ''to throw down the barriers, so that women may be free to choose their own way of life — to earn their living independently, and to marry or not to marry, as they may deem it well or prudent'' (''The 'Saturday Review' '' 204). It is particularly to this advocacy of women's power of ''self-defini-tion''[7] — and the discourse in which it was articulated by Langham Place circle — that I believe Trollope responds in *Can You Forgive Her?*

Trollope was well acquainted with the concerns of the ladies of Langham Place through his friendship with Emily Faithfull, the director of the Victoria Press, whom he dubbed ''that female Caxton of the Age'' (Letter to W. H. Russell, *Letters* 1: 220). At her request he contributed stories to two Victoria Press publications — to *Victoria Regia* in 1861 and to *A Welcome* in 1863. Out of this professional relationship grew a personal friendship. Miss Faithfull was a guest at the Trollopes' Waltham Cross home at least once, in 1863. Earlier, when Trollope visited the United States in 1861–1862, he gave ''one of Miss Faithfull's cards,'' along with a description of the Victoria Press, to an American woman who complained that the English were not doing enough for women's rights (*North America* 224).[8]

Despite Trollope's friendship with Emily Faithfull, the ''Rights of Women'' chapter of *North America*, published fourteen months before he began *Can You Forgive Her?*, makes clear what was at least his ''official'' opposition to the mid-century Anglo-American feminist movement.[9] Behind his arguments that women are destined by God, nature, and their reproductive organs for domestic dependency lies his fear that if enabled to support them-selves and persuaded that the single state can be both respectable and happy, most women will choose not to marry. ''If women can do without marriage,'' he asks, ''can men do so? And if not, how are the men to get wives if the women elect to remain single?'' (259). Clearly, Trollope recognized that by seeking to re-configure women's position within the economic system, ''cer-tain learned ladies'' threatened to undermine the basis of the patriarchal class/ kinship system: the exchange of women in marriage.

II

IN NORTH AMERICA, Trollope responds to this threat with a patriarchal definition of women's rights: "The best right a woman has is the right to a husband" (265). In *Can You Forgive Her?*, he responds with a thrice-told tale of domesticated female desire. Although the conventions of comic improbability allow Arabella Greenow to combine self-direction with domesticity, no such integration is possible in the more serious and realistic plots of Alice Vavasor and Glencora Palliser. There, marginalizing women's desire for self-direction as deviant, Trollope reappropriates it through a narrative of transgression, penitence, and forgiveness, at the end of which female desire is reinscribed within the boundaries of monogamous domestic dependence.

Paralleling and reinforcing the ideological implications of this narrative structure is a discursive strategy by which Trollope first voices and then attempts to silence the discourse of mid-century feminists. In order to produce the "narratable," which D. A. Miller defines as "the instances of disequilibrium, suspense, and general insufficiency from which a given narrative appears to arise" (*Narrative* ix), Trollope interjects into *Can You Forgive Her?* language that echoes concerns articulated by the Langham Place circle. But as Alice's and Glencora's plots move beyond the moment of transgression, this discourse of transgressive desire is supplanted by confessional discourse, which signals the internalization of patriarchal norms and authorizes the disempowerment and domestication of both protagonists.

The role that female transgression and confessional discourse will play in the novel is foreshadowed by its title. Not only does the pronoun *her* assign the female to the object position in the title question, but also, lacking an antecedent, it invites a virtually endless series of synonymous female substitutions. And the auxiliary verb *Can* (as opposed to *Will* or *Won't* [*You Forgive Her?*]) implies that this unspecified female's trespass is so heinous that she may be beyond forgiveness altogether.[10] *You*, the other pronoun in the title, situates the reader in the powerful, traditionally male positions of subject and confessor. Although the role of confessor within the nineteenth-century middle-class home often fell to women, as part of what Nancy Armstrong calls "the power of domestic surveillance" (19), to the extent that these female confessors reinforced patriarchal values, they served as male surrogates. Given the central role that Western culture has assigned confession in "the production of truth" (Foucault 1: 58), the confessor, who not only grants or withholds absolution but also in a sense elicits the confession, occupies a privileged position within that culture. Thus the novel's title forecasts a system of gendered relationships within the narrative in which an asymmetrical distribution of power is embedded within a series of binary oppositions: [male]/reader/subject/confessor versus [female]/text/object/

penitent. Foreshadowed here is the primary strategy within the novel by which female desire is represented and regulated. To the extent that it strays outside the (erotic, economic, and linguistic) boundaries of domestic dependence, it is characterized as deviant, subjected to the omniscient, collusive gaze of narrator and reader, and reinscribed within the boundaries of domestic dependence through a ritual of confession and forgiveness — a ritual of speaking/ writing and hearing/reading in which not only the characters but also the reader and narrator participate.[11]

The transgression of the primary protagonist, Alice Vavasor, occurs in two stages: her disengagement from a "worthy" man whom she loves and her engagement to a "wild" man whom she does not love. In the first phase, although her income is inherited rather than earned, Alice's "full command of her own fortune" (43) allows her to ignore the wishes of family and friends without fear of economic reprisals and, as the *English Woman's Journal* had advocated, to "choose . . . to marry or not to marry" as she deems it "well or prudent." Even though she loves John Grey, she refuses to marry him and contemplates a life of spinsterhood with her cousin Kate. Alice's decision to take both herself and her inheritance out of circulation threatens the very foundation of middle-class male power and the ideology of domesticity by which that power was authorized. It is in Trollope's effort to motivate her refusal to marry Grey that the feminist discourse of the 1850s and early 1860s is most clearly echoed.

Immediately after inveighing against the pernicious influence of certain "learned ladies," Trollope's narrator most fully articulates Alice's desire for some "scope for action" beyond the domestic sphere, at least as demarcated by John Grey's Cambridgeshire estate:

> Alice Vavasor was ever asking herself that question ["What should a woman do with her life?"], and had by degrees filled herself with a vague idea that there was a something to be done; a something over and beyond, or perhaps altogether beside that marrying and having two children; — if she only knew what it was. . . .
>
> When she did contrive to find any answer to that question as to what she should do with her life, — or rather what she would wish to do with it if she were a free agent, it was generally of a political nature. She was not so far advanced as to think that women should be lawyers and doctors, or to wish that she might have the privilege of the franchise for herself; but she had undoubtedly a hankering after some second-hand political manoeuvering. She would have liked, I think, to have been the wife of the leader of a Radical opposition, in the time when such men were put into prison, and to have kept up for him his seditious correspondence while he lay in the Tower. She would have carried the answers to him inside her stays, — and have made long journeys down into northern parts without any money, if the cause required it. She would have liked to have around her ardent spirits, male or female, who

would have talked of "the cause," and have kept alive in her some flame of political fire. As it was, she had no cause. (141–42)

Though denying to Alice the most radical feminist aspirations of the day, the narrator characterizes her desire for some extradomestic mission as politically destabilizing, linking it to Radicalism, to political "opposition," even to sedition. At the same time, he attempts to nullify the threat it poses by trivializing it as "a hankering after some second-hand political manoeuvering," by humorously eroticizing it as the desire to carry seditious messages "inside her stays," and by reinscribing it within the marital paradigm where Alice's influence would be exercised only through her husband, with her role that of passively "bearing the word" from one male to (presumably) another.[12] The last two sentences, however, convey with some poignancy Alice's "serious reflection upon the great end of existence," which includes the devotion to some cause supported by other women — the kind of alliance that the Langhamites themselves represented. By thus motivating Alice's decision to break her engagement to John Grey, Trollope creates a character who initially resists what DuPlessis calls "the specific narrative and cultural orders of nineteenth-century fiction . . . the subordination of quest to love, the death of the questing female, the insertion into family life" (34–35).

Although he begins by motivating Alice's disengagement by her desire for a cause, Trollope introduces a second desire — for self-determination or at least an equal voice within marriage. Like the discourse of the Langhamites, Alice's articulation of this desire challenges the legal and social disempowerment of women in which mid-Victorian marriage was grounded. The narrator notes, with some regret, that Alice has given up her earlier concept of love as "total abnegation of self," seeing it now in more mundane, egalitarian terms. In such a relationship, Alice reasons, "why should not each yield something, and each claim something?" (68). She realizes, however, that the unequal distribution of power between the sexes, exacerbated within marriage by the wife's loss of her separate legal identity, precludes anything approaching the evenhanded give-and-take that she wants. As she explains to Lady Macleod, "People always do seem to think it so terrible that a girl should have her own way in anything. . . . I haven't much of my own way at present; but you see, when I'm married, I shan't have it at all" (64).

Both James Kincaid (181–82, 184–85) and Juliet McMaster (26) have noted the importance accorded the characters' speech acts, both written and oral, in *Can You Forgive Her?* Given this thematic centrality of discourse, it is especially significant that once Alice's desires for a cause and for autonomy have served to motivate her initial transgression, the articulation of those desires becomes progressively muted. In the presence of her fiancé, Alice is virtually struck dumb, "having things to say but not knowing in what words to put them'' (68). To a large extent, her silence results from Grey's domination of the discourse between them. Under the guise of masculine courtesy, he either obliges her to speak when she would rather not or silences her altogether. The embodiment of phallogocentrism, with (appropriately) ''a mouth like a god'' (144), Grey ''always *spoke* and acted as though there could be *no question* that his manner of life was to be adopted, *without a word* or thought of doubting, by his wife'' (68, italics mine). When, in his absence, Alice is able to write of her resistance to a marriage where all the concessions must be on one side and where Cambridgeshire domesticity may drive her mad, Grey responds by turning her own words against her. Appropriating her topos of madness, he reads her resistance to marriage as a sign of pathological melancholy and thus denies her authority as a writing and desiring subject. This discursive de-legitimation of her desires, especially the desire for self-determination, becomes more pronounced after her engagement to George Vavasor, when what was ''melancholy'' to John Grey becomes ''sin'' to the narrator — and to Alice herself.

Once Alice enters the second phase of her transgression by engaging herself to her cousin George, the basis of narratability changes. By introducing what Jean Kennard identifies as the ''convention of the two suitors'' (10–11), Trollope transforms what began as a female quest plot into a traditional love plot, shifting the central question from ''What will Alice do with her life?'' to the much less radical ''Whom will Alice marry?'' And by casting Alice's new fiancé as a Fury-possessed melodramatic villain, replete with a theatrically gaping scar and a bombastic repertoire of curses, Trollope shifts attention away from the political issues of gender and power that were raised by her initial transgression. Not only does George's violence, both contemplated and actual, destroy Alice's credibility as a judicious independent agent; it also enables Trollope to transform the central conflict into a struggle between absolute good and evil as embodied, according to the conventions of melodrama, by Alice's two suitors.[13] These conventions — especially the almost ontological evil that George embodies — prepare the reader for the ritual and discourse of confession, penance, and absolution by which Alice internalizes the patriarchal norms of her culture and acquiesces to a position of feminine dependency within the class/kinship system.

Central to the confessional rhetoric that describes and seeks to contain Alice's subversive desires are features of both the melodramatic discourse of the ''moral occult,'' with its ''desacralized remnants of sacred myth'' (Brooks 5), and the Evangelical discourse of Original Sin, which supplied the Victorians with a coded language for female sexual misconduct. From both discursive traditions, as well as from their Biblical and Miltonic progenitors, come not only explicit tropes of the Fall, as when Alice refers to her disengagement from Grey as both a ''fall from heaven'' and a ''lost . . . Eden,'' but also allusions to sexual defilement, most often characterized as sins against her own sex. In Chapter 37, close to the midpoint of the novel, as Alice reflects on her jilting of Grey and her engagement to George, such figures are interwoven into eight paragraphs of highly patterned and fervidly penitential rhetoric. They reach an almost parodic crescendo as the narrator, after a halfhearted plea for clemency, joins Alice and the "delicate reader" in deploring her "offence against womanhood":

> But let us own that she had sinned, — almost damnably, almost past forgiveness. . . . What; — doubt, of two men for whose arms she longed; of which the kisses would be sweet to bear; on which side lay the modesty of her maiden love! Faugh! She had submitted to pollution of heart and feeling before she had brought herself to such a pass as this. Come, — let us see if it be possible that she may be cleansed by the fire of her sorrow. (398)

Though divorced from an appropriate "signified," the signifying force of this rhetoric creates guilt by association — between mortal sin and sexual impropriety on the one hand and Alice's more venial transgressions on the other.

On close examination, the intensity of this denunciation seems less a response to Alice's engagement to George *per se* than it is to her desire for autonomy. Recalling Eve's decision in *Paradise Lost* to work apart from Adam, this desire is explicitly linked to Alice's fall into the clutches of the Satanic George: "She had gloried in her independence, and this had come of it!" (397). Later, embedded between clauses that sum up Alice's double transgression, this desire is condemned in terms recalling both Grey's early pathological reading of it and the prideful desire behind the fall of Milton's Eve: "[Alice] had said that she would become the wife of a man to whom she could not cleave with a wife's love; and, *mad with a vile ambition*, she had given up the man for whose modest love her heart was longing" (398, italics mine). Alice's desire to choose a course for her life beyond the confines of wifehood and motherhood poses a much more serious threat to male middle-class hegemony than does her wandering between two suitors. The rhetorical excess of these paragraphs — the extreme censure of Alice's behavior to which James took exception — is one effort to contain that threat.

At the end of the novel, as Alice accepts Grey's forgiveness and his offer of marriage, the punishment and extinction of her desire for autonomy are completed. Here a second escalation of penitential discourse concludes with her confession to Grey that she has "done that which no woman can do and honour herself afterwards" (771). Such self-abasing language prepares for the martial rhetoric of the subsequent love scene, where tropes of conquest and surrender foreshadow the economic and sexual realities of mid-Victorian wedlock. At this point, Alice's crimes of the heart seem forgotten — but not her desire for independence, which, in a final act of contrition, she repudiates:

> And there must now, she acknowledged, be an end to her pride, — to that pride which had hitherto taught her to think that she could more wisely follow her own guidance than that of any other who might claim to guide her. She knew now that she must follow his guidance. She had found her master, as we sometimes say, . . . She was from henceforth altogether in his hands. . . . She had taken her fling at having her own will, and she and all her friends had seen what had come of it. She had assumed the command of the ship, and had thrown it upon the rocks, and she felt that she never ought to take the captain's place again. (774)

Clearly, just as Alice herself will soon be contained by Victorian marriage, so her desires have already been contained by Victorian domestic ideology, which her renunciation of autonomy shows she has internalized.

III

PENITENTIAL DISCOURSE, especially the rhetoric of the fallen woman, is ironically much less prevalent in the complementary narrative of Glencora Palliser's contemplated adultery, but then so is the rhetoric of mid-century feminism. To be sure, like the Divorce and Matrimonial Causes Act of 1857 and the publicity that the *English Woman's Journal* gave to divorce trials, Glencora's unhappiness with Plantagenet Palliser and her comments on the "tyranny" and "cruelty" of husbands undermine the Victorian idealization of marriage as a harmonious union where the wife flourished under her husband's benign guardianship. Even more destabilizing, her contemplated adultery with Burgo Fitzgerald suggests that rather than providing an inviolable enclosure for female desire, marriage is bounded by only a permeable membrane, through which that desire may freely circulate.

On the other hand, Glencora's desire never strays, as Alice's does, beyond the boundaries of the traditional love plot and the choice between two men, even when, "not . . . expecting joy or the comfort of love from either of them," she is convinced "that on either side there must be misery for her" (607). The only autonomy she had wanted, which her relatives had denied her, was the freedom to marry the man she loved. Whereas by contemplating adultery she threatens the ideal of marital fidelity, Glencora does so in the name of another, equally powerful mid-Victorian ideal: companionate marriage.[14] In actuality, although forced marriages were legally proscribed, property, class, and parental wishes continued to exert a powerful influence on actual Victorians' choice of marriage partners. Marriage for love, however, was clearly the dominant ideal in Victorian fiction. Because Glencora's union with Palliser is a throwback to the supposedly discredited aristocratic model of arranged marriages, her rebellion against that paradigm is actually less radical than the rebellion of her cousin, who resists the inequitable distribution of power in marriage that the companionate ideal obscured. Even more conventional is the second trajectory of Glencora's desire: to "give [Palliser] a son," which displaces her desire for Burgo as the narratable element in her story and which, when fulfilled, creates for her desire a terminus within marriage.[15] Most important, despite her protestations of undying passion for Burgo, Glencora — unlike Alice — never acts on her transgressive desire. From a patriarchal perspective, as George Levine points out, "Part of what is so attractive about Glencora is that her fits of independence and defiance — in relation at least to the man's world — are necessarily fruitless" (17). Nevertheless, confessional rhetoric plays an important role in validating the norms of domesticity by which Glencora's desire is ultimately regulated.

Ironically, Glencora's confessor for most of the subplot is her cousin Alice, who listens reluctantly to her repeated articulation of marital unhappiness and adulterous yearning. Like John Grey in her own story, albeit less successfully, Alice initially tries to stifle these subversive confessions, admonishing her cousin to "be silent," "not [to] say such words," and "not to speak of [Burgo]" (701, 305, and 461). More successfully, at least for ideological purposes, Alice offers in counterpoint to Glencora's transgressive discourse a normative discourse of female submission and respectability. Having urged Glencora to "be true to her marriage-vow, whether that vow when made were true or false" (306), Alice later censures Glencora's waltzing with Burgo as "misbehaving . . . in public" and her contemplated elopement as "misery and destruction," "ruin and disgrace" (648–49).

On the mimetic level, the ease with which the usually taciturn Alice delivers "wise lectures" on the very norms that she herself has violated reflects the pervasive power in her culture of the discourse of feminine respectability. On the ideological level, these lectures undercut Glencora's gestures toward autonomy by bracketing them as deviant. And although her stance toward Glencora's relationship with Burgo in many ways mirrors that of the odious Mrs. Marsham and Mr. Bott, the disinterested discretion with which Alice judges Glencora's transgressive desire makes her judgments much more palatable than theirs. Even those judgments delivered after Glencora has decided not to elope with Burgo are ideologically useful, because they underwrite the self-regulation of Glencora's desire and articulate the social consequences of the adultery she has rejected.

Signalling the domestication of Glencora's desire to choose her own sexual partner is a shift in her (infrequent) use of the rhetoric of the fallen woman. Initially, because her passion is in no sense aligned with the sexual union sanctioned by her marriage, Glencora inverts the conventional view of the fallen woman, arguing that her marriage is merely legalized prostitution:

> "I am not honest. By law I am his wife; but the laws are liars! I am not his wife. I will not say the thing that I am. When I went to him at the altar, I knew that I did not love the man that was to be my husband. But him, — Burgo, — I love him with all my heart and soul." (305)

As she makes this confession to Alice in the Abbey ruins, Glencora's discourse is not so much penitential as despairing. Faced with a choice that is no choice — between a loveless marriage and a disgraceful affair — she tells Alice, "I loathe myself, and I loathe the thing that I am thinking of" (306). But by the time she rejects the opportunity to elope with Burgo, the feminine ideal of marital fidelity has superseded the companionate ideal of a mutually gratifying union. When Glencora explains her decision to Alice, her deployment of the rhetoric of the fallen woman has become strictly conventional. Like Alice, she describes the sin she contemplates as a sin against her sex:

> "Do you suppose I have never thought of it; — what it would be to be a man's mistress instead of his wife? . . . When once I had done it I should hate and despise myself. I should feel myself to be loathsome [*sic*], and, as it were, a beast among women." (649)

However tragic in terms of romantic ideology, Glencora's acquiescence to this conventional condemnation of the fallen woman represents a victory for nineteenth-century domestic ideology, which was based on the self-regulation of female desire within the domestic sphere (Armstrong 81).

Coming as it does after Glencora has already tentatively decided against adultery and thus against sexual autonomy, her confession to Palliser is in one sense superfluous. Ideologically speaking, however, it is crucial, because it implies that what had been for Glencora competing ideals of marital fidelity and romantic love can be integrated into one harmonious whole. Unlike Alice's self-abasing confession to Grey, which elicits forgiveness in a context of self-righteous mastery, Glencora's almost defiant confession to Palliser elicits forgiveness in the context of a reciprocal confession — of love rather than sin, but still of vulnerability: "I would rather have you for my wife, childless, — if you will try to love me, — than any other woman, though another might give me an heir" (616). Suggesting the advent of genuine affection between Glencora and Palliser, this confession scene has led Levine to declare that of "the three plots, . . . only the story of Glencora is worked out fully and satisfactorily" (17).

Despite the seductive tenderness of this scene, the impression it gives of an equitable distribution of power with concessions on both sides is reversed in the next chapter. There, signalled by her destruction of Burgo's assignation letter, the domestication of Glencora's desire is reiterated by the tropes of male conquest in which she recasts the confession scene: "She knew that he had conquered her. . . . She had gone out into the tilt-yard and had tilted with him, and he had been the victor" (618). Though mild compared to the language describing Alice's capitulation to Grey, these figures underscore the dominance of the male confessor. The imbalance of power within the Pallisers' marriage is thus exacerbated, as the description of their trip abroad makes clear. Palliser, we are told, "behaved very well. But, then, he had his own way in everything." Glencora, on the other hand, behaves badly, continually challenging Palliser's authority. "But, then," the narrator concedes, "she had her own way in nothing" (707–08).

Once Glencora's resignation to marital fidelity guarantees that the child she produces will be Palliser's, Trollope rewards her with pregnancy. When this second trajectory of her desire is completed, her son displaces Burgo, the terminus of the first trajectory, and Glencora's desire is permanently sealed within the domestic sphere. Her transformation from potential (autonomous) magdalen to mother of "embryo dukes" (757) both mirrors and underwrites the centrality of women's reproductive capacity in defining not only their essential nature but also their value to men. Although Glencora gains from her incipient maternity both a sense of worth and a role in which she hopes to exercise authority, her pregnancy is described as Palliser's triumph, not hers — provided, of course, that the child she produces is male. And whatever authority she may claim as a mother, during her three days of labor, Glencora is "completely in . . . [the] power" of her husband, her male doctors, and that avatar of patriarchal omnipotence, the Duke of Omnium (829). Coupled with Glencora's acquiescence to monogamy, childbirth completes and valorizes the circumscription of her desire within patriarchally approved limits.

IV

AFTER THESE CLAUSTROPHOBIC NARRATIVES of suffocated desire, Arabella Greenow's speech and subplot are for me a discourse and narrative of comic — and specifically female — liberation. It can, of course, be argued that Arabella's story merely reinforces the patriarchal norms shaping the stories of Alice and Glencora. After all, the desires Arabella gratifies are from the outset circumscribed within the domestic sphere, and the comic ease with which she gratifies them distracts the reader from the extradomestic frustrations of the other protagonists. Moreover, as a middle-aged, vulgar widow who owes her fortune to a mercenary May-December marriage, Arabella is hardly a figure with whom Trollope's young female readers would identify. She is further distanced from readers by being situated within the satiric tradition of marriage-hungry widows like Lady Wishfort, stock characters in neoclassical drama.[16] Therefore, this argument might conclude, Arabella's high degree of self-determination — erotic, financial, and linguistic — is ideologically disempowered by the very conventions that enable it.

While acknowledging the strength of this argument, I contend that Arabella's narrative disrupts at least as much as it reinforces the ideology of domestic dependency that closes down transgressive desire in the two "realistic" narratives. Despite Arabella's satiric introduction, she also belongs, like the Ephesian widow, to a more ancient and purely comic tradition celebrating the movement from "the gravelike gloom of death into new life and love."[17] Her determination "not to waste the good things which fortune had given [her]" (101) aligns her with the most central value of Trollopian comedy.[18] As her narrative progresses, Arabella becomes increasingly a figure of comic delight, even admiration — a shift signalled by Kate's changing discourse about her. Initially labeling her aunt "of a bad sort" (89), Kate later describes her as "too wide-awake to put herself in any man's power," "very generous," and, "with all her faults," ready to "go through fire and water to serve me" (340–41). Arabella's generosity — her resolve to give pleasure to others as well as herself — diminishes her distance from Trollope's readers, increasing the ideological power of her narrative. In large measure, the comic, subversive power of Arabella and her subplot is directed against the patriarchal conventions, institutions, and power relations that exercise a virtual stranglehold on the other two plots and their heroines. To Deborah Morse's insight that Arabella inverts the "Two-Suitor Convention" by choosing the Wild Man over the Worthy Man (11), I would add that her entire subplot actually parodies that convention. Farmer Cheeseacre is a comic send-up of both the other two "worthy" suitors. As a rural landowner, he seems a low comic version of John Grey, with Oileymead as the parodic counterpart of Nethercoats, Grey's Cambridgeshire estate. Like Palliser, on the other hand, Cheeseacre is undeterred by a prior claim on his beloved's affections — in this case, the claim of the late Mr. Greenow. "If I find early mangels don't do on a bit of land," he responds philosophically to Arabella, "then I sow late turnips; and never cry after spilt milk. Greenow was the early mangels; I'll be the late turnips" (128). Cheeseacre's nemesis, Captain Bellfield, parodies only one of his serious counterparts. Like Burgo Fitzgerald if stripped of aristocratic connections and the romantic aura with which Glencora invests him, Bellfield is "simply an idle scamp, who had hung about the world for . . . years, doing nothing, without principle, shameless . . . (681). Given the comic imperfections of both suitors, Arabella subverts the Two-Suitor Convention not so much by choosing the "wild" man but by choosing at all. Because her worthiness can in no sense be defined by her choice of a husband, her narrative unsettles the normalizing power of this convention in the other two plots.

But primarily what Arabella's narrative destabilizes are the rhetorical conventions that constrain or mute Glencora's and Alice's expressions of transgressive desire. Arabella has internalized none of those norms of female propriety that lead the cousins to self-loathing and self-abasement. As the narrator remarks, "The charm of the woman was in this, — that she was not in the least ashamed of anything that she did" (102). Her freedom from any sense of transgression can be seen in the absence of confessional rhetoric from her discourse, direct or indirect. Rather, it is Arabella who extracts two confessions from her fiancé, both about his finances. In the first of these, which the narrator refers to as a "cross-examination," she "got much information out of him," but "not exactly all the truth" (674). In the second, she tells him, "As long as there's anything kept back, I won't have you," and this time, the narrator says, "I think he did tell her all, — or nearly all" (681). Like Palliser and Grey, she not only extracts confessions but also pronounces absolution: "she forgave [Bellfield] all his offences" (674). As the gendered reversal of confessional roles suggests, it is Bellfield's desire, more than Arabella's, which is contained and domesticated in marriage.

By using the confession to gratify rather than renounce her own desires, Arabella subverts its patriarchal function. She similarly destabilizes the sign systems of Victorian widowhood, parodying the codes of dress and discourse, text and textiles, that regulated the Victorian widow's conduct. Both codes were designed to reify the patriarchal myth that a woman's desire was so totally encompassed by marriage that at her husband's death, it ceased to exist.[19] But "there was that of genius," we are told, "about Mrs. Greenow, that she had turned every seeming disadvantage to some special profit, . . . so . . . that though she had obeyed the law to the letter, she had thrown the spirit of it to the winds" (426). "Gorgeous" in her widow's weeds, she enjoys the attentions of her two suitors while declaring that her desire is entombed with her late husband. Exploiting the play of the signifier — its refusal to be bound to a single signified — she creates within the language of suffocated female desire a space where that desire can flourish.[20]

Certainly, the "power," "authority," and "mastery" with which Arabella is repeatedly associated depends largely on her financial independence, the kind that the Langham Place circle advocated for all women, married or single. In contrast to Alice and Glencora, Arabella retains control of her fortune even after her (second) marriage. But it is her discourse, specifically her exploitation of the contextual determination of the relationship between "words" and "things," that most significantly undermines the strategies by which female desire is contained in *Can You Forgive Her?* As McMaster has demonstrated, closure in the narratives of Alice and Glencora occurs when "words" and "things" regain what the narrator sees as their "proper" relation to each other (20–37). The premise here is that this relation is fixed and monolithic. The moment of "truth" in their narratives, when the proper relation of words and things is fully restored, is represented as the moment of confession, which displaces and shuts down the errant discourse of transgressive desire. In Arabella's narrative, there is no such moment. Rather, her language continues to be shaped by and directed toward the gratification of desire rather than the production of "truth." Unlike Alice and Glencora, who obsessively reiterate the "facts" of a guilt-ridden past, Arabella simply makes up the past as she goes along. She invents, for example, progressively earlier dates for Greenow's demise in order to justify her premature re-marriage, just as she invents a story of Cheeseacre's friendship with Bellfield and the former's "violent attachment" to Charley Fairstairs. Though well aware that her fictions are recognized as such, Arabella has "a pleasure in telling her own story," recounting it "as though she believed every word that she spoke" (805). Like her creator, she delights in a narrative dictated not by the "truth" of confession but by imagination and desire.

This is not to say that Arabella is the perfect avatar of female autonomy. Her contentment with two seriously flawed husbands, as well as her determination to marry off everyone around her, reinforces an ideology that in other ways she challenges. Even her comic inversions of patriarchal paradigms leave intact the gendered oppositions and power relations on which those paradigms depend. Nevertheless, as "a woman of great resources," both financially and linguistically, she is able to exercise something approaching the self-direction advocated by the ladies of Langham Place but ultimately denied the other protagonists of *Can You Forgive Her?* Like the discourse of the Langham Place circle in the world outside the novel, to the extent that Arabella's articulation of desire eludes the twin nemeses of masculine control and feminine guilt, her subplot keeps patriarchal ideology in *Can You Forgive Her?* from having the last — or at least the only — word.

North Carolina State University

NOTES

1. See, for example, the studies cited at the end of this essay by Barickman, MacDonald, and Stark; Garrett; Kincaid; Levine; Morse; Nardin; and Overton.
2. Earlier Victorian women's forays into publishing are summed up by Nestor, who points out that the *English Woman's Journal* was significant as "the corporate venture" which started the women's movement's connection with print (95).
3. Actually, the most influential feminist whose ideas were publicized in the *Journal* was John Stuart Mill. The Langhamites supported his bid for a seat in Parliament. See "The Opinions of John Stuart Mill," *EWJ* 6 (1860): 1–11 and 193–202.

4. For an excellent discussion of the power of citation, see Yaeger 149–76.
5. See "How to Utilize the Powers of Women" 34, Boucherett 361, and "Statistics" 2–3.
6. On efforts leading ultimately to the passage of the Married Women's Property Acts of 1870 and 1882, see Holcombe.
7. The term is Newton's (5), whose "Introduction" (1–22) provides a thoughtful classification of types of female power.
8. These "cards" may have been those printed by the Victoria Press illustrating varieties of women's employment.
9. Qualifying Overton's argument that Trollope's "unofficial" creative self subverts such pronouncements in the novels, I contend they are at once subverted *and* supported in *Can You Forgive Her?*
10. See also the discussion of the title in Warhol 135–37.
11. On the disciplinary role of tolerance in Trollope's novels, see D. A. Miller, *The Novel* 11–16, 107–45.
12. On this archetypal female role in Romantic and Victorian literature, see Homans 29–33.
13. On these conventions, see Brooks 5–80.
14. I am indebted to Stone for the term "companionate marriage," but I believe it describes not so much an eighteenth-century ideal as the ideal of married love (albeit qualified) whose rise Peter Gay locates in the mid-nineteenth century, concurrently with the rise of feminism (97–100).
15. On the problematic nature of Glencora's fulfillment through motherhood, see Morse 21–24.
16. For a discussion of the misogyny behind the frequent appearances of this stock character, see Todd.
17. On the comic significance of the Ephesian Widow's narrative, see Bakhtin 221–23.
18. On Trollope's use of comic conventions, see Herbert.
19. On the gender-based distinctions in Victorian mourning etiquette, see Morley, esp. 64–76.
20. My approach to Arabella's playful use of language is indebted to the discussion of women's liberating language games in Yaeger, esp. chs. 3, 7, and 8.

WORKS CITED

Armstrong, Nancy. *Desire and Domestic Fiction: A Political History of the Novel.* New York: Oxford UP, 1987.

Bakhtin, M. M. "Forms of Time and the Chronotope in the Novel: Notes Toward a Historical Poetics." *The Dialogic Imagination: Four Essays.* Ed. and trans. Michael Holquist. U of Texas P Slavic Ser. 1. Austin: U of Texas P, 1981. 84–258.

Barickman, Richard, Susan MacDonald, and Myra Stark. *Corrupt Relations: Dickens, Thackeray, Trollope, Collins, and the Victorian Sexual System.* New York: Columbia UP, 1982.

[Boucherett, Jessie.] "On the Obstacles to the Employment of Women." *English Woman's Journal* 4 (1860): 361–75.

Brooks, Peter. *The Melodramatic Imagination: Balzac, Henry James, Melodrama, and the Mode of Excess.* New Haven and London: Yale UP, 1976.

"The Disputed Question." *English Woman's Journal* 1 (1858): 361–67.

DuPlessis, Rachel Blau. *Writing Beyond the Ending. Narrative Strategies of Twentieth-Century Women Writers*. Bloomington: Indiana UP, 1985.

"Female Education in the Middle Classes." *English Woman's Journal* 1 (1858): 217–27.

Foucault, Michel. *The History of Sexuality*, Vol. I: *An Introduction*. Trans. Robert Hurley. 1978. New York: Vintage, 1980.

Garrett, Peter K. *The Victorian Multiplot Novel: Studies in Dialogical Form*. New Haven: Yale UP, 1980.

Gay, Peter. *The Tender Passion*. New York: Oxford UP, 1986. Vol. 2 of *The Bourgeois Experience: Victoria to Freud*. 2 vols. 1984–86.

Harrison, Brian. "Press and Pressure Group in Modern Britain." Shattock and Wolff 261–95.

Herbert, Christopher. *Trollope and Comic Pleasure*. Chicago: U of Chicago P, 1987.

Holcombe, Lee. *Wives and Property: Reform of the Married Women's Property Law in Nineteenth-Century England*. Toronto: U of Toronto P, 1983.

Homans, Margaret. *Bearing the Word: Language and Female Experience in Nineteenth-Century Women's Writing*. Women in Culture and Society Ser. Ed. Catharine R. Stimpson. Chicago: U of Chicago P, 1986.

"How to Utilize the Powers of Women." *English Woman's Journal* 3 (1859): 34–47.

James, Henry. Rev. of *Can You Forgive Her?*, by Anthony Trollope. *Nation* 28 September 1865: 409–10.

Kennard, Jean E. *Victims of Convention*. Hamden, CN: Archon, 1978.

Kincaid, James R. *The Novels of Anthony Trollope*. Oxford: Clarendon, 1977.

L., A. R. "Facts *Versus* Ideas." *English Woman's Journal* 7 (1861): 73–84.

Levine, George. "Can You Forgive Him? Trollope's *Can You Forgive Her?* and the Myth of Realism." *Victorian Studies* 18 (1974–75): 5–30.

McMaster, Juliet. *Trollope's Palliser Novels: Theme and Pattern*. London: Macmillan; New York: Oxford UP, 1978.

Miller, D. A. *Narrative and Its Discontents: Problems of Closure in the Traditional Novel*. Princeton: Princeton UP, 1981.

———. *The Novel and the Police*. Berkeley: U of California P, 1988.

Morley, John Harwood. *Death, Heaven and the Victorians*. Pittsburgh: U of Pittsburgh P, 1971.

Morse, Deborah Denenholz. *Women in Trollope's Palliser Novels*. Nineteenth-Century Studies. Ed. Judith McMaster. Ann Arbor: UMI Research P, 1987.

Nardin, Jane. *He Knew She Was Right: The Independent Woman in the Novels of Anthony Trollope*. Carbondale: Southern Illinois UP, 1989.

Nestor, Pauline A. "A New Departure in Women's Publishing: *The English Woman's Journal* and *The Victoria Magazine*." *Victorian Periodicals Review* 15.3 (Fall 1982): 93–106.

Newton, Judith Lowder. *Women, Power, and Subversion: Social Strategies in British Fiction, 1778–1860*. 1981. New York and London: Methuen, 1985.

"The Opinions of John Stuart Mill." *English Woman's Journal* 6 (1860): 1–11 and 193–202.

Overton, Bill. *The Unofficial Trollope*. Brighton, Sussex, Eng.: Harvester; Totowa, NJ: Barnes & Noble, 1982.

Poovey, Mary. *Uneven Developments: The Ideological Work of Gender in Mid-Victorian England*. Women in Culture and Society Ser. Ed. Catharine R. Stimpson. Chicago: U of Chicago P, 1988.

Rev. of *A Decade of Italian Women*, by T. Adolphus Trollope. *English Woman's Journal* 3 (1859): 273–75.

Rev. of *North America*, by Anthony Trollope. *English Woman's Journal* 10 (1862): 61–66.

"The 'Saturday Review' and the 'English Woman's Journal': The Reviewer Reviewed." *English Woman's Journal* 1 (1858): 201–204.

Shattock, Joanne, and Michael Wolff, eds. *The Victorian Periodical Press: Samplings and Soundings*. Toronto: Leicester UP, 1982.

"Statistics as to the Employment of the Female Population of Great Britain." *English Woman's Journal* 5 (1860): 1–6.

Stone, Lawrence. *The Family, Sex, and Marriage in England 1500–1800*. New York: Harper, 1977.

Tabor, Mary C. "On the Condition of Women As Affected by the Law." *English Woman's Journal* 10 (1862): 124–27.

Todd, Barbara J. "The Remarrying Widow: A Stereotype Reconsidered." *Women in English Society 1500–1800*. Ed. Mary Prior. London; New York: Methuen, 1985. 54–92.

Trollope, Anthony. *Can You Forgive Her?* Ed. Stephen Wall. Harmondsworth, Eng.: Penguin, 1972.

———. *The Letters of Anthony Trollope*. Ed. N. John Hall. Vol. 1, 1835–1870. Stanford, CA: Stanford UP, 1983. 2 vols.

———. *North America*. 1862. Ed. Donald Smalley and Bradford A. Booth. New York: Knopf, 1951.

Warhol, Robyn R. *Gendered Interventions: Narrative Discourse in the Victorian Novel*. New Brunswick, NJ: Rutgers UP, 1989.

"What Are Women Doing?" *English Woman's Journal* 7 (1861): 51–53.

Yaeger, Patricia. *Honey-Mad Women: Emancipatory Strategies in Women's Writing*. Gender and Culture Ser. Ed. Carolyn G. Heilbrun and Nancy K. Miller. New York: Columbia UP, 1988.

MUSCULAR ANXIETY: DEGRADATION AND APPROPRIATION IN *TOM BROWN'S SCHOOLDAYS*

By Donald E. Hall

IN THE MANLINESS OF CHRIST (1879) Thomas Hughes condemns what he believes has been the gross misappropriation of some of the concepts underlying his fictional work. In particular, he decries those who misuse the terms "manliness" and "manfulness": these words "embrace more than we ordinarily mean by the word 'courage'; for instance, tenderness, and thoughtfulness for others."[1] Indeed, tenderness, of a sort, is central to the "manliness" dramatized in Hughes's most popular work, *Tom Brown's Schooldays* (1857), a novel that actively promotes carefully controlled expressions of nonsexual love between men. Nevertheless, Hughes's claim that he has been wholly misunderstood by those who equate his "manly" ideals with stubbornness and pugilism seems strained, for while certain forms of tenderness and thoughtfulness play key roles in *Tom Brown's Schooldays*, so also do expressions of violence and sexism. Brutal misogyny and a continuing fear of vulnerability attend Hughes's construction of a seemingly carefree and compassionate form of manliness. Therefore Hughes is perhaps justified in claiming that "courage" has no ordinary meaning in his works, for in *Tom Brown's Schooldays* courage often means a tenacious defiance of women and marginalized men. It is a novel that insists upon the value of "endurance . . . of standing out against something, and not giving in," one that claims that "every one who is worth his salt has his enemies, who must be beaten."[2] Who are these "enemies" in *Tom Brown's Schooldays*, the some*things* that men must stand out against? We soon discover that they are all *things* that challenge heterosexual male primacy.

Of course *Tom Brown's Schooldays* is not unique in this sense, for it fits into a pattern of anxious and often violent expressions of desire for control, a pattern that virtually defines the mid-nineteenth century phenomenon known as "muscular Christianity," but one that also extends beyond the traditionally recognized limits of the movement. From the 1840s through the '50s and '60s, the muscular trio of Hughes, Charles Kingsley and F. D. Maurice produced numerous popular novels, poems, essays, and sermons that affected both religious and political discourse. So widespread was the muscular phenomenon, that Wilkie Collins felt obliged to write an entire novel, *Man and Wife* (1870), in order to express fully his outrage over its effects. But despite the clear social significance of muscular Christianity, the movement has yet to receive adequate attention from literary and social historians. As the critic George Worth has argued repeatedly, muscular Christianity is often ignored because its extremism both embarrasses and mystifies the twentieth-century reader.[3] When it is mentioned, the movement is generally ridiculed, trivialized or over-simplified. Over-simplification is perhaps the most common reaction, for many recent examinations of nineteenth-century constructions of masculinity, such as Mangan and Walvin's 1987 edition *Manliness and Morality*, tend to dismiss the oppressive ideologies underlying muscular Christian texts in an attempt to recover their more "positive" aspects, such as their dramatization of heterosexual male bonding patterns.[4] I, on the other hand, believe that certain gynophobic and homophobic undercurrents in muscular Christian texts are well worth highlighting, for the ideologies informing *Tom Brown's Schooldays* and similar works are simply extreme versions of those underlying much of the literature of the mid-Victorian period. Hughes's novel foregrounds the fears of an era and thereby allows us a unique opportunity to explore anxiety-driven constructions of gender roles as well as examine a complex economy of arrogation and degradation. As we shall see, it is a text that amply bears out Tania Modleski's assertion in *Feminism Without Women* that "a man may hold femininity in contempt at the same time that he appropriates it."[5]

But in order to recognize how thoroughly anxiety pervades muscular Christian works, we must first establish a working definition of that slippery psychological signifier. Freud, in *Inhibitions, Symptoms and Anxiety*, states simply that "Anxiety is the reaction to danger," even as he carefully distinguishes between "real" and "instinctual" dangers.[6] For Freud, the latter consists primarily of manifestations of his infamous "castration anxiety," but later theorists have expanded the designation to include a variety of nonphysical, often ill-defined or imperfectly perceived threats to psychological security and well-being. Rollo May, in *The Meaning of Anxiety*, builds upon Freud when he asserts that "*Anxiety is the apprehension cued off by a threat to some value which the individual holds essential to his existence as a personality.*"[7] For May, anxiety is a diffuse response to a potential disruption in an individual's "security pattern," that is, his or her perception of the self's relationship to a social matrix. Threats may include aggressive actions by others, changing economic or political situations, or information that clashes with beliefs integral to one's self-perception.[8] May argues that anxiety is in fact overt and pervasive during periods of dynamic change, when common cultural values and components of identity are disrupted or challenged. But while he agrees with W. H. Auden's designation of the twentieth century as "The Age of Anxiety" in the poem of that name,[9] I would argue that nineteenth-century literature too evinces diverse and intense currents of anxiety, ones that may be "covert," to use May's terminology, but that indicate ongoing processes of social contestation and paradigmatic metamorphosis.

It is here that muscular Christianity becomes particularly useful, for in the hyperbolic discourse of the muscular Christians, we find many of these covert currents of anxiety rendered overtly; the movement was in fact born of reaction. Muscular Christianity originated as a response to John Henry Newman and the Tractarians, whose mysticism and attraction to asceticism was loudly and summarily branded "weak" and "effeminate" by the muscular Christians.[10] But as Norman Vance explores in his respected study of mid-Victorian religious tensions, *Sinews of the Spirit*, these terms were inextricably linked to numerous and diverse threats to the Victorian male's sense of stability and self-possession.[11] Historian Walter Houghton relates the fears of the muscular Christians to the profound insecurity of an age that was "deeply troubled with religious doubts, acutely aware of weakness and frustration."[12] He argues that the muscular Christians's glorification of brawniness and brutality was a reaction to the threats to psychological equilibrium posed by a world growing ever more confusing and fragmented. Houghton ties the anxieties of the age to scientific discoveries that called into question Biblical accounts of creation, to technological advances that rendered the world increasingly complex and hostile, and to industrial processes that isolated individuals from each other and the past. Muscular Christianity was an attempt to assert control over a world that had seemingly gone mad: "In such a mood, not of cynicism but of bitter exasperation, the objective correlative is the destructive force of a conquering hero."[13]

But it is equally important to remember that during the mid-nineteenth century threats to male hegemony were also pervasive and anxiety-producing. While Victorian binarism cast "male" and "female" and "masculine" and "feminine" as dichotomous terms in a rigid construct that relied on exclusion to determine gender roles, the resulting definitions were inherently unstable: life was and is too complex to be accounted for in terms of "angels in the house" and "queens in their gardens." Threat was therefore structural; in a binary construct, the other becomes an inevitable source of anxiety, and in the nineteenth century, a reductive gender paradigm produced contradictory perceptions of both power and powerlessness in women. The socially prescribed maternal role, for example, evinces such inherent instability and confusion; while almost all young Victorian boys were raised and governed by women, they were then asked to define their lives and abilities in strict opposition to those of their mothers, sisters, and nannies. Thus the image of the terrible mother who threatens the development and independence of her son appears often in Victorian literature; we see Alton Locke painfully but successfully battling the smothering influences of his powerful mother in Kingsley's novel of 1850 and a similar offensive mounted by little Georgy Osborne in Thackeray's *Vanity Fair*. As Karen Horney explores in "The Dread of Woman" and Nancy Chodorow affirms in *The Reproduction of Mothering*, such implicitly violent processes of binary differentiation contribute to a socially pervasive and culturally reinforced misogyny and gynophobia in men.[14]

Even so, threats to male equanimity during this era were not only implicit and structurally produced; the roots of Victorian male gender anxiety were, in fact, diverse and complex. Mary Poovey argues convincingly in *Uneven Developments* that because of its fundamental unworkability the Victorian opposition-based gender paradigm was always socially contested, and in a particularly widespread and explicit fashion around and after mid-century.[15] The publication of Margaret Fuller's *Woman in the Nineteenth Century* in 1845 marked the beginning of an era of stormy debate on the subject of men's and women's roles and rights, four decades that included campaigns for women's suffrage and property rights and the repeal of the Contagious Diseases Acts. In 1848, the Seneca Falls convention in New York garnered wide publicity for its "Declaration of Sentiments" which detailed men's oppression of women and for its "Resolutions" which called for a woman's revolution against patriarchal dictates. Elizabeth Helsinger, Robin Sheets and William Veeder draw on both fiction and nonfiction in *The Woman Question* to chart the diverse "voices of protest and prescription" that participated in the "complex" and "fluid" social dialogue that ensued.[16]

Certainly it is fair to say that most male poets, novelists, and essayists of the period responded anxiously to the many implicit and explicit threats to patriarchal privilege and power. The same decades during which the multifaceted British women's movement saw some of its most intense activity of the nineteenth century, readers find some of the most monstrous representations of powerful, transgressive women by male writers in all of literary history: Sairey Gamp in *Martin Chuzzlewit*, Becky Sharp in *Vanity Fair*, Lydia Gwilt in Collins's *Armadale*, and Miss Havisham in *Great Expectations* are among the many female characters of the era who violently threaten their male counterparts. Rollo May lends implicit support to Horney and Chodorow when he asserts that "anxiety gives rise to hostility."[17] In his novel *Yeast*,

Kingsley praises Tennyson's *The Princess* for showing us "the woman, when she takes her stand on the false masculine ground of intellect, working out her own moral punishment, by destroying in herself the tender heart of flesh, which is either woman's highest blessing or her bitterest curse."[18]

Tom Brown's Schooldays foregrounds the thinly veiled male hostility pervading this age of male gender anxiety. At age four, Tom initiates a veritable war between the sexes; he is "given to fighting with and escaping from" women, in particular, from nurse "Charity Lamb" (28), whose cariacaturish name captures the novel's heavy-handed insistence on her inappropriateness as a guide and role model for the manly young Tom. We are told that Charity Lamb's physical power barely approximates that of her four-year-old charge, and she "hadn't a chance with him wherever head-work was wanted" (29). In Hughes's exaggerated version of common Victorian gender conceptions, adult women are the mental equivalents of male toddlers. Thus by the time Tom reaches age ten, "the war of independence had been over for some time: none of the women now, not even his mother's maid, dared to offer to help him in dressing or washing" (53). But as is obvious in this quotation, even though Tom has supposedly vanquished women and the novel has reiterated their incapacity, they continue to remain sources of anxious concern. In fact, while women are often on the margins of muscular Christian novels, their repeated degradation seems central to the fragile masculinity and sense of male self-possession these books dramatize.

This becomes immediately apparent when Tom takes as a new companion the old, "rheumatiz"-ridden, ex-wrestler Benjy, who actually becomes "Tom's dry nurse" (31). But in spite of this seemingly transgressive appellation, Benjy is not an androgynous character, for he clearly weans Tom from charity figuratively as well as literally. Benjy, in fact, personifies misogyny and violence. His cottage, where Tom spends his days, is armed against imminent attack; he has decorated it with pistols and swords, making it not only a fortress but also a shrine to a particularly martial form of masculinity. The identity of the potential attackers becomes clear when Benjy and the narrator express vague fears about what will happen if "Master Tom should fall back again into the hands of Charity and the women" (45). Although the narrative never focuses directly on the basis for these fears, Hughes portrays women as fatal to men's equilibrium and strength. The narrator tells us of Willum Smith, whom he commends for attempting to break another man's head in a backswording match at the village fair. But tragedy strikes when Willum is momentarily distracted by his concerned sweetheart and falls with his own head bloodily broken (39).

The novel represents women as both ominously powerful *and* incarnations of mental and physical weakness; predictably, such representational and ideological dissonance feeds an intense fear of "womanishness" and vulnerability in men. At his first school, someone forgets to post a letter to Tom's "beloved" mother; Tom cries bitterly, but "his wrath was proportionally violent when he was aware of two boys, who stopped close by him, and one of whom, a fat gaby of a fellow, pointed at him and called him 'Young Mammysick!' Whereupon Tom arose, and giving vent thus to his grief and shame and rage, smote his derider on the nose and made it bleed" (59). The dynamics of this scene of violence are noteworthy, for the boy's feelings of vulnerability cause him to lash out at sources of threat, much as the muscular Christians did through the medium of their novels. Not surprisingly, Tom always has the tacit approval of the narrator in such assertions of "manliness." In the chapter entitled "The Fight," we are told that "fighting, rightly understood, is the business, the real highest, honestest business of every son of man" (218). "Boys will quarrel, and when they quarrel will sometimes fight. Fighting with fists is the natural and English way for English boys to settle their quarrels. What substitute for it is there, amongst any nation under the sun? What would you like to see take its place?" (231) Even Hughes's questions here seem muscular as he challenges the reader to find fault with his declarations. And it is no coincidence that a passage that reveals the text's implicit colonialism also reveals its gender politics, for in *Tom Brown's Schooldays* we find a strategy to counter the threats posed by women which, when scrutinized carefully, reveals intertwined processes of both domination and appropriation.

For as many recent critics have pointed out, the psychology of Victorian oppression is more complex than any simple model tracing linear vectors of action and reaction would allow. John Kucich notes in *Repression in Victorian Fiction* that constrictive belief systems and practices during the nineteenth century were always "self-conflictual, self-divided" and "shaped toward many different ends."[19] Thus it is intriguing, but perhaps not surprising, to find that the grotesque sexism of many Victorian male writers' characterizations coexisted uneasily with the same writers' tendency to appropriate certain aspects of the feminine for their male characters. Carol Christ argues in "Victorian Masculinity and the Angel in the House" that violence toward women almost always attends such a colonization of the feminine, a process that she clearly reveals as a male strategy for threat-reduction and self-aggrandizement.[20] And Christ's arguments concerning Tennyson and Patmore seem equally pertinent for a discussion of *Tom Brown's Schooldays*. Of course, a movement toward androgyny, if it led to an equitable redistribution of gender power for both men and women, would hardly be condemnable. In fact, Claudia Nelson, in her recent work *Boys Will Be Girls*, celebrates *Tom Brown's Schooldays* as a wholly laudable exploration of a revolutionary "manly androgyny."[21] But to do so, she must ignore the novel's gynophobic discourse and characterizations. In *Tom Brown's Schooldays* we find no radical process of depolarization, for Hughes's boy characters expand their own roles and abilities while continuing to scorn and abuse women. Rugby, Tom's second school, is portrayed as a womanless, male "paradise" where boys can revel in seeming autonomy and completeness.

The Victorian binary conception of domain is literally portrayed in *Tom Brown's Schooldays*, for Rugby is a male community whose identity explicitly depends upon the exclusion of women. Tom's journey to the school is one in which he gradually forgets his own mother and home and establishes a new identity around "the first place which he could call his own" (81). The school yard is in fact bounded by places of violence, as if all "womanishness" has to be left behind in order to enter there. Harry East, another schoolboy who soon becomes Tom's best friend, points out the limits of the school property: one of the farthest corners of the yard "is the place for fights," another corner is the "island" for "island fagging" (where young boys do strenuous labor for older students) and the space in between is "the big-side ground, where the great matches are played" (82–83). Once inside the boundaries, women are never to be spoken of; Tom cautions one new boy, "don't you ever talk about home, or your mother and sisters" (174).

But even as this enforced silence indicates that women remain vague sources of continuing threat, the novel attempts to demonstrate that mothers and sisters are practically dispensable in the Rugby world, for boys take on many of the roles usually assigned by the Victorians to women. This is evident in Tom's relationship with George Arthur, a shy boy whose protection and instruction the schoolmasters assign to him. Certainly Tom works to masculinize Arthur by taking him on swimming and fishing expeditions that build his constitution and drive from his mind all "morbid" longings for his home and mother. But while doing so, Tom in effect becomes a surrogate mother himself, taking on all of the nurturing ability and even the "little" worries that were (and often are) attributed to women alone, and thus cannot be called "paternal." Like Benjy, Tom becomes a "dry nurse," as he starts calling Arthur "young 'un" and hovering nervously around his charge:

"Why, young'un," said he, "what have you been after? You don't mean to say you've been wading?"

The tone of reproach made poor little Arthur shrink up in a moment and look piteous . . . .

". . . a fellow can't turn his back for a moment but all his work's undone. He'll be laid up for a week for this precious lark, I'll be bound."

"Indeed, Tom, now," pleaded Arthur, "my feet ain't wet, for Martin made me take off my shoes and stockings and trousers."

"But they are wet and dirty too — can't I see?" answered Tom. (206)

Tom is clearly jealous of his "young 'un" in this scene, but when he sees Arthur so intent on winning back his favor, he, in good motherly fashion, "swallowed the last mouthful of his bile, and is repaid by seeing his little sensitive plant expand again, and sun itself in his smiles" (206–07). The narrator tells us that

> Arthur at last, to his intense delight, was allowed to climb a small hedgerow oak for a magpie's nest with Tom, who kept all round him like a mother, and showed him where to hold and how to throw his weight; and though he was in a great fright didn't show it, and was applauded by all for his lissomness. (210)

The text calls even more direct attention to the explicitly maternal nature of Tom's relationship with Arthur when East says, "He'll never be worth a button, if you go on keeping him under your skirts" (181). But Tom is the most effective and active "mother" in the entire novel; his is a solicitude that fosters a boy's development toward manhood instead of threatening it as "Charity and the women" did in earlier chapters. The form of Tom's mothering is no different from that of the women, but his sex means that he is no threat to male primacy and equanimity.

The novel asserts that all men carry this potential completeness and autonomy within them, for it is not only Tom who plays a feminine role: Arthur is both an object of masculinization and a reformer of brutish boys. The Rugby schoolmasters actually give Tom the responsibility of looking after Arthur in order to assure Tom's moral growth and temper his "animal" instincts. Arthur quickly becomes a source of religious inspiration for Tom and his dormitory mates and even convinces them to pray every evening. He later serves as a voice of conscience that regulates Tom's proclivity for unethical shortcuts in his studies. Through such actions Arthur actually assumes the role of spiritual guide and moral purifier ordinarily assigned to Victorian women. The association is clear if one remembers the common stereotype of the "angel in the house": "Arthur was lying on the sofa by the open window, through which the rays of the western sun stole gently, lighting up his white face and golden hair. Tom remembered a German picture of an angel which he knew" (236). But while the angel role was particularly oppressive for Victorian women, it actually empowers Arthur, for his is decidedly an active rather than a passive role of purification. One might say that the theory of gender relations Ruskin expresses as an ideal in "Of Queens' Gardens" is projected onto a purely male terrain and therefore empowered with all of the dynamism attributed to masculinity.

For in order to realize fully this process of androgynous empowerment, all passivity and frailty must be purged from Arthur. As critic Samuel Pickering notes, "When fever broke out at Rugby, Arthur was 'still frail and delicate, with more spirit than body.' He now had body enough, however, to overcome the fever, something he would not have been able to do had he not met Tom.''[22] And as Arthur recovers from his illness, he comes to embody a muscular manliness that is the mirror image of Tom's. Later in the narrative, we find him shouting and clapping "furiously" for his school's cricket team (269). When he goes into the game to score an important run, he "feels prouder than when he got the three best prizes, at hearing Tom's shout of joy, 'Well played, well played, young 'un!' '' (274). Although Pickering refers to the two youths' transformation as a "union of body and spirit which Hughes thought good education should effect,''[23] we actually have a particularly misogynistic situation in which men are shown to make better women than women themselves because they can be strong and active as well as nurturing and inspirational. Many of Elaine Showalter's objections to the Dustin Hoffman role in the movie *Tootsie* can also be raised about Tom and Arthur's dynamic, "de-passivized" androgyny: it makes women practically superfluous in a world where men can do everything short of actually giving birth.[24] And Hughes's boys even infringe upon the ability to bear children through the character of Martin or Madman:

> One morning an old basket made its appearance, suspended by a short cord outside Martin's window, in which was deposited an amateur nest containing four young hungry jackdaws, the pride and glory of Martin's life for the time being, and which he was currently asserted to have hatched upon his own person. (195)

He not only tends "his nurselings" but also raises numerous other young animals in his room. Madman even exhibits unhatched eggs on sheets of pasteboard in a seeming attempt to reaffirm visually a reproductive capacity that elsewhere in the text is scorned in women.

In commentary above I call such appropriation "colonial" and this is true in several senses, for at the same time the novel details the boys' gradual aggrandizement of power, it also reveals an inner mechanism of exploitation and degradation. Even as the boys assert their autonomy, female servants continue to perform the drudge work of feeding and cleaning them. And even though women are relatively powerless in this section of the novel, the text reiterates their humiliation. The boys tease and torment Mary, the school's matron, whose name accurately signifies her symbolic value as a representative of all women. The youths' disdain for her becomes explicit when East opens several new boys' trunks in her presence: " 'Hullo, look here, Tommy,' shouted he, 'here's fun!' and he brandished above his head some pretty little night-caps, beautifully made and marked, the work of loving fingers in some distant country home" (170). The feminine night-caps are brandished as a trophy, their capture indicating both the boys' acquisition of the feminine and their actual power over women. The "little matron," as she is repeatedly called, finally promises the boys food if they will simply leave her in peace; the boys depart with a final mocking reference to her as "vicious" (170). The scene is particularly offensive because it is so clearly celebratory, as the boys prance about and revel in their male homosocial invincibility.

Thus women are not wholly absent from the Rugby world, even as men there are not truly autonomous. In all binary pairings, the existence of the privileged half of the binary constellation depends upon the existence of the degraded other. While male autonomy may be desired in *Tom Brown's Schooldays*, the novel actually celebrates male primacy, which women themselves are called upon to reinforce. Such is the case when George Arthur's mother enters Rugby briefly to visit her ill son. She contributes little to his recovery, which is managed by men, rather her sole purpose in the scene seems to be to praise Tom Brown's abilities and nearly divine capacity for love; she leaves him with, "Good night — you are one who knows that our Father has promised to the friend of the widow and the fatherless. May He deal with you as you have dealt with me and mine!" (246) That there is a higher power than the still earthly Tom is clear, but since patriarchal power in *Tom Brown's Schooldays* is revealed as potentially inclusive of every positive gender-associated quality, the heavenly Father is precisely the masculinized androgynous being that his singular generation of the novel's male-dominated world would indicate.

This emphasis on an androgynous omnipotence is explicit in the final sentence of the novel. Hughes writes,

> For it is only through our mysterious human relationships, through the love and tenderness and purity of mothers, and sisters, and wives, through the strength and courage and wisdom of fathers, and brothers, and teachers, that we can come to the knowledge of Him, in whom alone the love, and the tenderness, and the purity, and the strength, and the courage, and the wisdom of all these dwell for ever and ever in perfect fulness. (288)

The binary psychology underlying Hughes's conception of gender is clear; all of the active attributes in this passage are associated with men and the relatively passive qualities of "love and tenderness and purity" attributed to women. But equally important is the fact that the "Him" mentioned in the passage, God, is the incarnation of all of these things — a veritable repository of all possible gender roles and therefore truly an androgynous patriarch. And while the passage tells us that God "alone" possesses this completeness, the novel repeatedly indicates that his steward, Tom, is similarly empowered. Thus Tom's growth toward moral responsibility, which in this novel is explicitly a development toward Godliness, is in fact a movement toward a gender omnipotence.

This convergence of desires, in which religious security is inextricably tied to a desired male autonomy and an insisted-upon primacy, is just as evident in the works of Charles Kingsley. The heroes of *Yeast* and *Alton Locke* seek comfort from and find safe haven with men, from whom they also receive religious instruction. Gender and religious power structures both reflect and reinforce each other as the muscular Christians see themselves in God and God in themselves. The weakness and doubt that each hero occasionally evinces is purged and projected onto women or womanish men, whom the muscular Christians then repudiate. In *Alton Locke*, the shallow and change-able Lillian becomes the embodiment of the religious dilettantism and moral vacillation that at one point characterized Alton. She serves as a scapegoat who is finally punished for her sins as she dies of a fever that symbolically represents divine judgement upon weakness, doubt and irresponsibility. Simi-larly, Kingsley's novel *Two Years Ago* uses the weak and effeminate poet Elsley Vavasour as the novel's embodiment of the selfishness and moral corruption that is seen as poisoning contemporary society. In Vavasour's death, Kingsley dramatizes a turning point in social history, so that two years later, one of the characters announces the birth of a new "spirit" in which "men and women [are] asking to be taught their duty, that they may go and do it."[25] Their teacher will be the novel's hero Tom Thurnall, who by the end of the novel (and like the other Tom in this article) has assumed a prophet-like stature and gender-bending range of qualities that elicits something like worship from the other characters, including the stereotypically-drawn Grace Harvey, his future wife: "Grace lay silent on his arms: but her eyes were fixed upon him; her hands were folded on her bosom; her lips moved as if in prayer."[26]

As these passages clearly demonstrate, men and women are not segregated physically in all muscular Christian novels, for even though the muscular Christians portrayed women in degrading ways, they certainly did not re-nounce romantic and sexual contact with them. Even Tom Brown marries in the sequel to *Tom Brown's Schooldays, Tom Brown at Oxford*. Instead of being a call for male separatism, the muscular Christian agenda is specifically designed for use in heterosexual society. Their ideal is perhaps best summed up in a brilliant essay that appeared in *Fraser's Magazine* just a few years after the publication of *Tom Brown's Schooldays*. Its author, the novelist Francis Power Cobbe, exposes the greed and egotism of a male culture that consistently repulsed women's demands for property rights and suffrage. " 'Criminals, Idiots, Women, and Minors' " show how each of these four categories is treated in virtually the same manner by British law. The only difference is that women are an object of what Cobbe calls "consumption" by a male society. In speaking of the complete appropriation of wives' prop-erty allowed to men by the marriage laws of her day, Cobbe writes, we must seek an example in the Tarantula Spider. As most persons are aware, when one of these delightful creatures is placed under a glass with a companion of his own species a little smaller than himself, he forthwith gobbles him up; making him thus, in a very literal manner, 'bone of his bone' (supposing tarantulas to have bones) 'and flesh of his flesh.' The operation being completed, the victorious spider visibly acquires double bulk, and thenceforth may be understood to 'represent the family' in the most perfect manner conceivable.[27]

Even though Cobbe's use of all masculine pronouns in this passage obscures her point slightly, she deploys the metaphor to foreground dramatically the greed and violence of patriarchal consumption of the property, indeed attributes ("bone of his bone"), of weaker parties, specifically wives. Cobbe recognized well that for some Victorian men, social privilege was not enough; they desperately desired the imagined security that might be provided by complete "assimilation" of their partners/social inferiors/opponents. Her description serves well to highlight both the degradation and appropriation implicit in muscular Christian novels, where we find a seemingly easy and unproblematic acquisition by men of all that they might desire from women, a process that we would recognize as "subsumption" rather than consumption. Of course Cobbe's description of these dynamics is particularly powerful because of its simplicity; the psychological realities of even fictional portrayals of such appropriative moves are much more complex. Pernicious anxiety is the inevitable result of a strategy whereby one takes for oneself certain aspects of those individuals whom one otherwise degrades and fears.

Thus *Tom Brown's Schooldays'* use of a woman-less "world elsewhere" at Rugby carries with it some inevitable psychological baggage. In *A World Elsewhere* Richard Poirier demonstrates how the outside world invariably intrudes on a paradise constructed apart from "time, biology, economics."[28] In terms of our discussion, the gender-related anxieties manifested in the early chapters of *Tom Brown's Schooldays* are always already there in the new world of Rugby. But in a world without women, gender anxieties take a particular cast. The passivity and objecthood so integral to the Victorian construction of femininity are continuing sources of unease from which men can not easily escape when they covet and colonize other, more positive, aspects of the feminine. The purgation of George Arthur receives so much attention because Hughes draws clear lines marking which feminine characteristics may be appropriated by men and which are to be feared. Early in the novel, on the same page where Benjy is described as Tom's "dry nurse," we also find reference to a certain ghost story that "had frightened the old women, male and female, of the parish out of their senses" (31). Such a reference to male "old women" is obviously meant to demonstrate what Benjy was not: vulnerable and afraid. These male old women are also quite different from the male "mothers" whom we meet later. When the narrative

focuses directly on the schoolboys' appropriation of positive feminine characteristics, it also turns anxiously to certain "feminized" men for whom Tom
and the narrator have only opprobrium; of one "pretty little" boy, Tom says
uneasily, " 'Worst sort of breed . . . thank goodness, no big fellow ever
took to petting me" (183).

Tom's fear of "petting" is telling, for the term captures a potential vulnerability and physicality that remain sources of a profound and continuing anxiety
in the Rugby section of *Tom Brown's Schooldays*, where we find that men
may be used by other men just as women are used by men. As Joseph Allen
Boone notes in *Tradition Counter Tradition*, "the underside of the all-male
world, ironically, is often a microcosm of exactly those tensions from which
the quester seeks to flee with his band of comrades.[29] Such tensions in fact
abound at Rugby. On the most obvious level, the novel views the fagging
system with considerable alarm and roundly applauds educational reforms to
reduce exploitation of younger students. But it cannot so easily resolve less
systemic, more personal possibilities for male vulnerability. The most notori-
ous and explicit of the various scenes demonstrating the potential for degradation and abuse between men is that detailing the "roasting" of Tom. When
Tom refuses Flashman's demand for a lottery ticket, the unrepentant bully
retaliates.

> 'Very well then, let's roast him,' cried Flashman, and catches hold of Tom by
> the collar: one or two boys hesitate, but the rest join in. East seizes Tom's arm
> and tries to pull him away, but is knocked back by one of the boys, and Tom
> is dragged along struggling. His shoulders are pushed against the mantelpiece,
> and he is held by main force before the fire, Flashman drawing his trousers
> tight by way of extra torture. (145)

Tom "groans and struggles" but is "roasted" into unconsciousness. The
dynamics of this scene and the emotions generated in it seems to be those of
a rape. The narrative tense changes from the past to the present as the scene
builds to its "climax," one that critic Henry Harrington identifies as a literal
"initiation into the mysteries of sex."[30] But it is obvious that the novel
represents this initiation as horrific. We are told that afterwards "Flashman
and one or two others slink away; the rest, ashamed and sorry, bend over
Tom" (146). The "roasting" scene is thoroughly homophobic; not only is
it a cautionary tale designed to heighten men's fears about such attacks, but
it also highlights the significant opprobrium directed at other sexually taboo
behavior throughout the school. As Eve Sedgwick explores in *Epistemology
of the Closet*.

> [T]he continuum of male homosocial bonds has been brutally structured by a
> secularized and psychologized homophobia. . . . Because the paths of male
> entitlement, especially in the nineteenth century, required certain intense male

bonds that were not readily distiguishable from the most reprobated bonds, an endemic and ineradicable state of what I am calling male homosexual panic became the normal condition of male heterosexual entitlement.[31]

In life and in literature, homophobia is always most pronounced in those arenas where contact between men is most likely, and clearly, homophobic discourse is rabid within homosexually active, but ostensibly heterosexual communities, such as all-male schools. John Addington Symonds makes explicit what was only hinted at in Victorian literature; he writes in his memoirs that in school dormitories in the 1850s "one could not avoid seeing acts of onanism, mutual masturbation, [and] the sports of naked boys in bed together."[32] The narrator of *Tom Brown's Schooldays* alludes meaningfully to "miserable little pretty white-haired curly-headed boys, petted and pampered by some of the big fellows, who wrote their verses for them, taught them to drink and use bad language, and did all they could to spoil them for everything in this world and the next" (182). In a footnote, Hughes says he refused a friend's advice to delete the passage, saying "many boys will know why it is left in" (182). The "spoiled boys" whom he mentions are identified by historian John Chandos as those who engaged in homosexual activity with older students for affection or profit.[33] Interestingly, if we look at the construction of Hughes's sentence above, it is the younger, passive boys who are the object of interest; they are the miserable ones, and even though the "big fellows" are implicated in their abuse, Hughes's anxiety seems to hover around the figure of the feminized male. Thus the passive boys are the only ones who are fictionally punished for their activity; Tom and East have great fun shaking up, kicking and tripping one effeminate "little blackguard," who snivels and whines "like a whipped puppy" (182–83). While this scene was written before the "construction" of homosexuality in the late nineteenth century, one finds clear intimations in *Tom Brown's Schooldays* that such an act of definition was imminent. Already a binary psychology equates male/male sexual contact with a highly threatening form of vulnerability; all activity that places men in the traditional position of women carries with it the threat of a loss of the powers, rights, and privileges that cultural constructions of masculinity entail.

THUS TOM BROWN'S SCHOOLDAYS vividly captures many of the diverse gender-related tensions of its era. But while it has no real Victorian equal in its assertion of heterosexual male gender primacy and in its pervasive anxiety, it is so remarkably useful and intriguing because it is finally so unremarkable; it effectively highlights the fear of women and vulnerable men that pervades all muscular Christian novels and, indeed, many other works by male writers of the mid-nineteenth century. And this observation engenders yet another, for given such pronounced anxiety and painful insecurity, we must ask, "who exactly is vulnerable here?" Women and homosexual men were not the only individuals oppressed by Victorian constructions of masculinity; the anxiety that we find in so many male texts of the period afflicts precisely those individuals who seem to benefit most directly from Victorian gender constructions. Of course I am not attempting to claim victimhood for heterosexual Victorian men, but violence and oppression return often to plague their perpetrators. Certainly we find no credible or lasting equilibrium (outside of death) in muscular Christian novels, for there will always be another foe to conquer, another source of anxiety to contain, or another threatening woman or effeminate man who will cross the path of the brawny but psychologically beleaguered hero; bluster and bravado provide little defense against insidious self-doubt and a world growing ever more complex. Thus the concluding paragraphs of muscular Christian novels are as telling as they are contrived. *Two Years Ago* ends with the hero's breakdown and regeneration as a "little child," a seemingly arbitrary stopping point in an endless cycle of recurring anxiety that began eight hundred pages earlier with this hero's childhood. *Yeast* and *Alton Locke* conclude with frantic pilgrimages by their heroes, who desperately seek a utopia abroad — England remains ever-threatening and complicated. And most revealing of all is the conclusion of *Tom Brown's Schooldays*, for there we leave Tom praying at an altar, weeping and humbly asking for divine help in sustaining "a burden which had proved itself too heavy for him to bear" (287–88). While literally this denotes his feelings of loss concerning the death of a schoolmaster, figuratively it speaks to the heavy burden of masculinity that he and his fellow muscular Christians carried. And in the space beyond the final period of the novel, the reader can well imagine that tears will turn to rage once again and that the cycle of fear and degradation will continue.

California State University, Northridge

NOTES

1. Thomas Hughes, *The Manliness of Christ* (London, 1894) 21.
2. Thomas Hughes, *Tom Brown's Schooldays* (Harmondsworth: Puffin, 1973) 67, 210. All subsequent references to this text will be followed by the page citation in parentheses.
3. See George J. Worth, "Of Muscles and Manliness: Some Reflections on Thomas Hughes," *Victorian Literature and Society: Essays Presented to Richard D. Altick*, ed. James R. Kincaid and Albert J. Kuhn (Columbus: Ohio State UP, 1984) 300–14, and George Worth, *Thomas Hughes*, Twayne's English Authors Ser. 387 (Boston: Twayne, 1984).
4. J. A. Mangan and James Walvin, eds., *Manliness and Morality: Middle-class masculinity in Britain and America 1800–1940* (Manchester, UK: Manchester

UP, 1987); see especially Jeffrey Richards, " 'Passing the love of women': manly love and Victorian society," 92–122.

5. Tania Modleski, *Feminism Without Women: Culture and Criticism in a "Postfeminist" Age* (New York: Routledge, 1991) 90.

6. Sigmund Freud, *Inhibitions, Symptoms and Anxiety* (New York: Norton, 1959) 88.

7. Rollo May, *The Meaning of Anxiety* (New York: Ronald, 1950) 191.

8. May 191.

9. May 4–16.

10. This is not to say that there was no ambiguity on Kingsley's part concerning Roman Catholicism and mysticism. See Susan Chitty's biography *The Beast and the Monk* (London: Hodder and Stoughton, 1974) esp. 58–59, for her outline of the combination of attraction and revulsion that no doubt contributed to the harshness of Kingsley's condemnation of Newman and others.

11. See Norman Vance, *The Sinews of the Spirit: The Ideal of Christian Manliness in Victorian Literature and Religious Thought* (Cambridge: Cambridge UP, 1985) esp. 8–41.

12. Walter E. Houghton, *The Victorian Frame of Mind: 1830–1870* (New Haven: Yale UP, 1957) 216.

13. Houghton 216.

14. Karen Horney, "The Dread of Woman," in *Feminine Psychology* (New York: Norton, 1967) 133–46, and Nancy Chodorow, *The Reproduction of Mothering: Psychoanalysis and the Sociology of Gender* (Berkeley: U of California P, 1978) esp. 180–90.

15. Mary Poovey, *Uneven Developments: The Ideological Work of Gender in Mid-Victorian England* (Chicago: U of Chicago P, 1988).

16. Elizabeth Helsinger, Robin Sheets and William Veeder, *The Woman Question: Society and Literature in Britain and America 1837–1883*, 3 vols. (Chicago: U of Chicago P, 1983).

17. May 222.

18. Charles Kingsley, *Yeast, Charles Kingsley: The Works*, Vol. II (Hildesheim, Germany: Georg Olms, 1968) 26.

19. John Kucich, *Repression in Victorian Fiction: Charlotte Brontë, George Eliot, and Charles Dickens* (Berkeley: U of California P, 1987) 2–4.

20. Carol Christ, "Victorian Masculinity and the Angel in the House." *A Widening Sphere: Changing Roles of Victorian Women*, ed. Martha Vicinus (Bloomington: Indiana UP, 1977) 146–62.

21. Claudia Nelson, *Boys Will Be Girls: The Feminine Ethic and British Children's Fiction, 1857–1917* (New Brunswick: Rutgers UP, 1991) 38 ff.

22. Samuel Pickering, "The 'Race of Real Children' and Beyond In *Tom Brown's School Days*," *Arnoldian* 11.2 (1984): 44.

23. Pickering 45.

24. See Elaine Showalter, "Critical Cross-Dressing: Male Feminists and the Woman of the Year," *Men in Feminism*, ed. Alice Jardine and Paul Smith (New York: Methuen, 1987) 116–32.

25. Charles Kingsley, *Two Years Ago*, 2 vols. (New York: J. F. Taylor, 1899) I, 7–8.

26. Kingsley, *Two Years Ago*, II, 405.

27. Frances Power Cobbe, " 'Criminals, Idiots, Women, and Minors,' " *Fraser's Magazine* Dec. 1868: 789.

28. Richard Poirier, *A World Elsewhere: The Place of Style in American Literature* (Madison, WI: U of Wisconsin P, 1985) 49.

29. Joseph Allen Boone, *Tradition Counter Tradition: Love and the Form of Fiction* (Chicago: U of Chicago P, 1987) 259.

30. Henry R. Harrington, "Childhood and the Victorian Ideal of Manliness in *Tom Brown's Schooldays*," *Victorian Newsletter* 44 (1973): 16.

31. Eve Kosofsky Sedgwick, *Epistemology of the Closet* (Berkeley: U of California P, 1990) 185.

32. John Addington Symonds, *The Memoirs of John Addington Symonds*, ed. Phyllis Grosskurth (Chicago: U of Chicago P, 1984) 94.

33. John Chandos, *Boys Together: English Public Schools 1800–1864* (New Haven: Yale UP, 1984) 290.

LOOKING AT CLEOPATRA: THE EXPRESSION AND EXHIBITION OF DESIRE IN *VILLETTE*

By Jill L. Matus

THROUGHOUT HER NARRATIVE Lucy Snowe carefully scrutinizes those around her, drawing attention not just to what she sees but also to the act of looking. References to gaze, glance, the exchange of looks, shafts of the eye, observations, and sight abound in her narrative, which dwells on moments of private, secret, or surreptitious scrutiny and their consequences. The narrative foregrounding of moments of looking encourages one to think about Lucy, spectator, in terms of recent critical discussions of the gaze.[1] At first sight, Lucy appears to disturb and perhaps invert the traditional positions of female "to be looked-at-ness" and male looker (Gamman and Marshment 5). When she stares at Dr. John, recognising him as Graham Bretton, he immediately assumes that she has seen "some defect" in him that attracts her usually averted eyes (Brontë, *Villette* 163). Later in the novel, Lucy curbs Paulina's admiration for Graham's beauty by sarcastically casting him as the Medusa — a traditionally female role. She declares that she avoids looking at him because the sight of him may strike her "stone blind" (520). Also, Lucy does not look at men so much as at women, which seems further to unsettle traditional notions about the construction of the heterosexual subject. Although she watches Graham and M. Paul closely, her observance of women — Madame Beck, Ginevra, the women in the audience at the concert, the subjects of paintings in the gallery, the actress playing Vashti — is particularly intense. Yet when we consider Lucy's position as one who looks, it is difficult to characterize her as simply subversive; she is not really the woman who refuses the position of object of the gaze thereby threatening the dominance of the male viewer. Since no one looks much at Lucy or pays much attention to Lucy's looking, she can hardly be said to offer a disruptive, returning look "from the place of the other" (Heath 88; see also Newman's discussion of Heath 1029–41). Her gaze does not usually unsettle those around her or allow

345

her to appropriate control and power. Privately though, she does sometimes find bitter solace in priding herself on her acute powers of observation. Further, when she refers to herself as a spectator, it is not to assert dominance but to draw a contrast between herself as passive and the active players; she emphasizes that she is merely someone who looks on as opposed to joining in. Hers is the gaze of the outsider.

It is precisely because Lucy's situation in the novel challenges without merely inverting the traditional binary formulation — female as the object of the gaze, male as dominating subject — that her spectatorship is important and interesting. Theoretical attention to the gaze is after all a way of articulating concerns with the formation of gendered subjectivity. In order to think about the process of gendering, we focus on the subject's pleasure in looking, the path of desire, the fantasies and conceptions of the self in relation to others, the perceptions of sexual difference. We are interested in the question of the gaze ("Who's zoomin' who?" as Aretha Franklin puts it) also because it directs attention to the power and politics of looking. Since *Villette* is so clearly a novel about desire, yearning, and invisibility, to consider Lucy in terms of the outsider's gaze may be a useful way of engaging the novel's exploration of self-perception, desire, and gendered subjectivity.[2]

Lucy is a keen observer of the dynamics of sexual attraction; she looks to see what men see in other women and how women negotiate the problems of desire and its expression. She is also interested in what ways they attract attention and what the approbation from men affords as well as costs them. The fact that Lucy is often unseen, overlooked, and unrecognized provokes both resentment and hurt. For, while she does not want to be appropriated as an object of visual pleasure, which is, in the terms of current feminist discourse, the effect of the male gaze, she also does not want to be invisible.[3] The effect, however, of her "invisibility" is that she is excluded from the transactions of desire that patriarchy sanctions and she is hence extremely unsure of her desirability and sexuality. We can think of the novel, then, as a chart of her difficulties in addressing the wish to be reflected as an admired and desirable self. The narrative explores the place of the desiring feminine subject and asks, "What is the state between invisibility and making a 'spectacle' of oneself?"

This essay discusses that question by focusing on a particular moment in the novel that foregrounds male viewers and visual representations of women — Lucy's scrutiny of an ostentatious painting entitled *Cleopatra*, which depicts a voluptuous, semi-recumbent female figure. Brontë supposedly based the painting she describes in *Villette* on a "real" picture which she saw at the Brussels Salon in 1842, but this picture was not named *Cleopatra* at all and differs in significant ways from Brontë's fictional painting. Her "recognition" of a rather ordinary Orientalist painting as a version of Cleopatra illuminates how discourses of sexuality and race converge and overlap through long-standing Western stereotypes of the Egyptian queen and the burgeoning nineteenth-century fascination with the East and interest in Oriental exoticism. An entire chapter is devoted to Lucy's description and assessment of it, its placement in the gallery, how the men around her respond to it and to her looking at it. Since she is the only woman in a group of male viewers, who respond very differently from her, Lucy is chastised for her "temerity to gaze with sang-froid at pictures of Cleopatra" (280). She transgresses the boundaries of decorum by looking at this frankly sexualized female object and her position as viewer is unorthodox, even illegitimate. Loosening the knot of associations that the painting provides enables us to locate *Villette* in the context of mid-Victorian constructions of female sexuality and to explore how such constructions are grounded in the discourse of prostitution, which itself depends on assumptions about physical characteristics (weight, shape, bodily functions, colour) and class.

While there has been some critical focus on the nature of buried or repressed desire and yearning in *Villette*, there has been relatively little attention paid to the ways in which Brontë works out her version of female desire in opposition to traditional mid-Victorian notions about the sexualized woman.[4] Before turning to consider the painting and Lucy's scrutiny of it, I want first therefore to suggest the context in which Victorian constructions of female desire take place. Recently, Mary Poovey has argued that nineteenth-century discussions and public debates about the nature of desire in women, particularly in relation to prostitutes, provide a context for *Jane Eyre*. Poovey examines the underpinnings of "dominant" representations of the prostitute (the explicitly sexualized woman) and outlines the debate about female sexual desire (or its absence) in the case of the prostitute: do the ungovernable desires of some women lead to their fall, or does desire not exist at all in a woman until she has fallen? Framing the question of desire in this way produces two opposing images of the prostitute, the first, a "different" woman, lascivious and wanton; the second, a woman who falls into the clutches of sin and lust, not because of her passions, which are dormant or non-existent, but because she has been betrayed by her weak and generous heart.[5] The latter model suggests that women are all the same; the former that lust and desire are aberrant — aspects of the prostitute's pathological sexuality. One of the effects of public debates about prostitution was to acquaint women with formulations such as these, and to offer them the opportunity (in fiction, for example) to explore and revise ideas about female desire. As Poovey points out, "these discussions paradoxically provided the discursive conditions of possibility for women's conceptualizing their own sexuality, and therefore the opening that would eventually enable women to help change the way in which female sexual desire was represented and understood'' (Poovey 30).[6]

* * *

A PAINTING CALLED CLEOPATRA creates expectations that the subject is a representation of the historical queen, but the painting Lucy Snowe sees when she visits the art gallery in *Villette* depicts no particular anecdote associated with Cleopatra, nor includes any distinctive Cleopatra paraphernalia — asp, pearl dissolving in vinegar or wine, sumptuous barge, Antony or Caesar — though it does portray Cleopatra in a classic posture: lying on a couch in the midst of signs of excessive indulgence and feasting. Here is Lucy's deflating description:

> She lay half-reclined on a couch: why, it would be difficult to say; broad daylight blazed around her; she appeared in hearty health, strong enough to do the work of two plain cooks; she could not plead a weak spine; she ought to have been standing, or at least sitting bolt upright. She had no business to lounge away the noon on a sofa. She ought likewise to have worn decent garments; a gown covering her properly, which was not the case out of abundance of material — seven-and-twenty yards, I should say, of drapery — she managed to make inefficient raiment. Then, for the wretched untidiness surrounding her, there could be no excuse. Pots and pans — perhaps I ought to say vases and goblets — were rolled here and there on the foreground; a perfect rubbish of flowers was mixed amongst them, and an absurd and disorderly mass of curtain upholstery smothered the couch and cumbered the floor. (275–76)

As far as Cleopatra's well-documented orgiastic feasts are concerned, the description Lucy gives seems wonderfully to correspond in essential details to standard, "classic" accounts of the feasts, such as that by Socrates of Rhodes: both refer to the gold vessels (denigrated by Lucy as "pots and pans"), the expensive roses ("a rubbish of flowers"), and the couch spreads (a disorderly, smothering "mass of curtain upholstery") (*Athenaeus: The Deipnosophists* bk. 4; 147–48).[7] The rubbish of flowers — Lucy later refers specifically to the roses, which she is prepared to concede are nicely painted — brings to mind Cleopatra's extravagant floral budget. Historical record has it that she caused a talent of silver to be spent on roses and had them strewn all over the floors like a carpet.

As a subject in Western pictorial art, Cleopatra has a long and varied history in which her representation takes as many different forms as the idea of woman she is used to represent — Guido Reni's Cleopatra looks very like his penitent Magadalena. She contrasts with Tiepolo's regal Venetian princess or Artemesia Gentileschi's intense and passionate suicide.[8] With the rise of Orientalism in the nineteenth century, the figure of Cleopatra lends itself to

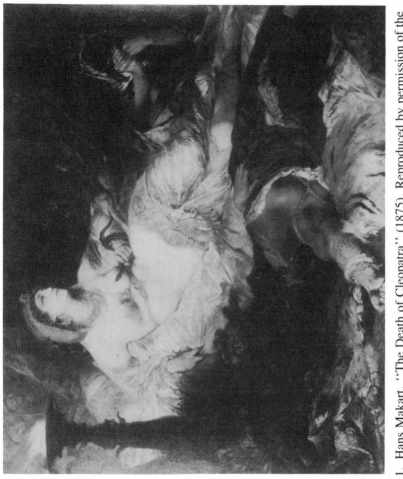

1. Hans Makart, "The Death of Cleopatra" (1875). Reproduced by permission of the Staatliche Kunstsammlungen Kassel, Kassel, Federal Republic of Germany.

representation as the acme of exotic Oriental sexuality. A good example of such representation is Hans Makart's *Death of Cleopatra* (1875) (fig. 1).[9] Part of the developing nineteenth-century discourse of the Orient was the construction of the sexualized Eastern woman. As travellers and scholars began to map their knowledges of the East, they wrote in great numbers about the libidinous and lascivious character of the Egyptian woman. Texts such as Edward Lane's *An Account of the Manners and Customs of the Modern Egyptians*, which had a very wide readership, attribute the libidinous nature of the women to the climate, the "want of proper instruction," and the encouragement by husbands of licentiousness in their wives:

> The women are permitted to listen, screened behind the windows of wooden-lattice work, to immoral songs and tales sung or related in the streets by men whom they pay for this entertainment; and to view the voluptuous dances of the ghawazee, and of the effeminate khawals. The ghawazee, who are professed prostitutes, are not unfrequently introduced into the hareems of the wealthy, not merely to entertain the ladies with their dances, but to teach them their voluptuous arts. (Lane 305)

Lane assures the reader that some of the stories of the "intrigues of women in 'The Thousand and One Nights' present faithful pictures of occurrences not unfrequent in the modern metropolis of Egypt" (304). While there was a steady proliferation during the nineteenth-century of scholarly texts, travel-ogues, and stories about the East, pictorial Orientalism also flourished in Europe, culminating in the establishment in Paris of the Salon des Peintres Orientalistes Français in 1893. From *The Great Odalisque* of Ingres (1814) to the famous *Women of Algiers in Their Room* (1834) by Delacroix (fig. 2), to Renoir's sultry *Odalisque* (1870) (fig. 3), representations of Oriental women acquired a tradition and iconography in which a great many painters expressed their fantasies of harem life and Eastern sexuality.[10]

If we place Lucy's description of the lavish disorder surrounding her Cleo-patra in the context of nineteenth-century versions of Oriental women, we see that it parodies not only Cleopatra's historic feasts, but also the way the harem and its inmates are represented in countless Orientalist paintings. Then again, both Cleopatra's sumptuous surroundings and the characteristically lush harem decor gesture toward an encompassing tradition in which the sensuality of a semi-recumbent female figure — she may be Venus, Cleopatra, or an anonymous odalisque — is suggested through contingent signs of lux-ury, excess, and abandon. What Lucy challenges, therefore, in her withering account of the painting are the artistic traditions and contemporary fashions of representing the eroticized female subject.

The historic Cleopatra was, however, not the subject of the painting by Edouard De Biefve (1802–82) that Brontë saw at the Brussels Salon in 1842.[11]

2. Eugène Delacroix, "Women of Algiers in Their Room" (1834). Reproduced by permission of the Musée de Louvre, Paris.

3. Auguste Renoir, "Odalisque" (1870). Reprinted by permission of the National Gallery of Art, Washington, D.C.

4. Edouard De Biefve, "Une Alme" (1842), from *La Renaissance: Chronique des Arts et de la Litterature 4* (1842–43).

De Biefve's canvas depicted an Egyptian dancing girl lying semi-recumbent on a couch (fig. 4) much as Lucy describes the subject of the Cleopatra painting in *Villette*. De Biefve's painting was entitled *Une Almé*.[12] Strictly speaking, *almeh* is the name for a singer; dancing girls should be called *ghawazee*, as Edward Lane refers to them. Edward Said notes that in Arabic *alemah* means a learned woman. "It was the name given to women in conservative eighteenth-century Egyptian society who were accomplished reciters of poetry. By the mid-nineteenth century the title was used as a sort of guild name for dancers who were also prostitutes . . ." (186; see also the section on "dancing girls" in Klunzinger 30–32).

If we compare the lithograph of De Biefve's painting with *Villette's Cleopatra*, it appears that Brontë magnifies and intensifies the figure's posture, dress, and surroundings. In comparison to Lucy's depiction of the massive queen of the Nile, De Biefve's subject looks rather contained — understated rather than underclothed. Yet in 1842 the painting caused quite a stir at its showing and in press reviews. One could go so far as to say that it scandalized the Brussels viewers because its subject was considered flagrantly and ostentatiously sexual. A contemporary review suggested that the painting was misnamed. Rather than a dancing girl, the reviewer reflected, this woman looked more like a voluptuous odalisque; a better title would have been *A Slave of the Harem* (Charlier 389). The remark is interesting because it suggests that the reviewer is drawing a distinction between the dancing girl and the odalisque, unaware that it was even then already blurred. Although some viewers of De Biefve's painting at the Brussels Salon in 1842 may have been puzzled that a dancing girl should be represented lying on a couch rather than dancing, others would have recognized that *almeh*, by the nineteenth century, is practically a synonym for prostitute. In the iconography of the sexual woman, therefore, the almeh and odalisque are both Cleopatras. Another reviewer remarks on the head of the figure, which "has a somewhat vulgar character, the face of a woman of low degree" ("Salon National de 1842" 92). Such a remark suggests the subject's profession as a prostitute/dancer, since the iconography of the prostitute in nineteenth century representations invoked the shape of head and bone structure, clues to a pathological and atavistic sexuality. Or perhaps the unlowered eyes and unaverted gaze (like the look of the recumbent prostitute in Manet's *Olympia*) make the subject seem provocative and therefore vulgar and low. Just as it is difficult today to see what outraged viewers of *Olympia* in 1865 and how that painting transgressed and subverted traditional representational codes, so the reaction of the scandalized Brussels viewers is puzzling. As Gustave Charlier points out, *Une Almé* seems a rather mundane and restrained Orientalist representation, but in the Brussels of 1842 it struck some commentators as hypersexualized and sensational, drawing both salacious appreciation — one reviewer is enthusiastic about "the devilishly" seductive almé — and censorious opprobrium. Male viewers in *Villette* respond in similar ways to the *Cleopatra*.

Brontë explains and intensifies De Biefve by casting *her* odalisque as a Cleopatra, returning to earlier associations of exotic sexuality with the East — following the serpent of the Nile, as it were, to its source. And after all, one does not need to make a great leap in association to get from De Biefve's dancing girl, who is not dancing but rather lying invitingly on a couch, to well-known representations of Cleopatra, supine on a sumptuous couch, contriving to ensnare Antony and lose him half the world. To substitute the anonymous, recumbent odalisque for the very queen of recliners is a perfectly logical exchange in the realm of stereotypic female sexuality. Furthermore, by emphasizing the iconographic markers of the Eastern *femme fatale*, Brontë makes very clear that her subject epitomizes a tradition of representation that embraces Cleopatra, the posed semi-nude, the lush harem interior, and the odalisque.

One can see from the ways in which Brontë cites Cleopatra elsewhere that her particular references to Cleopatra here are deliberate and considered. She refers to Cleopatra on a number of occasions in the Juvenilia, citing the Egyptian queen in company with other famous women, such as Helen of Troy and Madame de Staël, and referring to "the majesty of Cleopatra" (Wise and Symington 2: 390; see also Alexander). For example, the temptress Zenobia is compared to Cleopatra in the following way:

> What eyes! what raven hair! . . . She is perfectly grand in her velvet robes [,] dark plume, and crown-like turban . . . the prima donna of the Angrian court, the most learned woman of her age, the modern Cleopatria [*sic*] (qtd. in Gérin 51)

The fact that Brontë can conceive of Cleopatra as a majestic and learned *femme fatale* emphasises, I think, that Cleopatra was not automatically associated for her with large, coarse women. When Brontë labels the subject of her painting she is not thinking of Cleopatra as the intelligent, powerful, and ruthless Queen of Egypt, but Cleopatra as a dark, indolent, gipsy-queen, and in so doing she makes Cleopatra (Queen of Egypt) synonymous with nineteenth-century stereotypes of Egyptian women — latter day Cleopatras. What she chooses to blow up, as it were, in her painting is the notion of Cleopatra "i' the posture of a whore" (*Antony and Cleopatra* V.ii.219).

A recognition of the textual and visual sources of Lucy's description in accounts of Cleopatra and their relationship to the iconography of Orientalist art releases the full extent of the humor and parodic play by which Lucy deflates the diction and rhetoric of awe and splendour with her domestic, down-to-earth observations. Her pleasure in tartly puncturing high-flown descriptions is a manifestation of her desire to diminish the overblown Cleopatra type, for whom the catalogue of abundance, luxury, and laziness is a metonymy. Glut is here inevitably associated with slut. Possibly, the undisciplined Cleopatra inspires envy and hence resentment in the hard-working Lucy for whom life is no holiday. In an early chapter, Lucy teases the reader with a vision of the life she has *not* been living: "Picture me then idle, basking, plump, and happy, stretched on a cushioned deck, warmed with constant sunshine, rocked by breezes indolently soft" (94). The vocabulary of desirable ease and pampering — "idle," "plump,' "basking," and "indolent" — applies similarly to Cleopatra but in such a grossly exaggerated way as to make indolence and relaxation a sin. Lucy's response is, however, more than Protestant disapproval of any form of laxity. It is true that in order to register the chagrin of Lucy (who works very hard for her living) Brontë draws attention to the laziness of the Cleopatra (who should have been doing the work of "two plain cooks"), but Cleopatra's sloth is also an indirect way of signifying that she is a prostitute. Rather than commenting directly on the sexualized quality of the painting, Lucy emphasizes the sluggishness of her Cleopatra and the slovenliness of her surroundings. She is hardly pulling her weight (some fourteen to sixteen stone, Lucy estimates) as she lounges around in broad daylight, unsuitably clad amid clutter and disorder. Nineteenth-century studies of prostitution point repeatedly to grossness, stoutness, and excessive weight as characteristic of profligate women. Parent-Duchatelet, also referred to as the "Newton of Harlotry," published *De la prostitution dans la ville de Paris* in 1836. This work, which was for a time the most widely read and influential study of prostitution, informs that "prostitutes have a 'peculiar plumpness' owing to 'the great number of hot baths these women take.' Or perhaps to their lassitude, rising at ten or eleven in the morning, 'leading an animal life' " (qtd. in Gilman 94).[13] Beliefs about the inclination of prostitutes to plumpness and lassitude are barely distinguishable from accounts and common conceptions of women living life in the harem. Harriet Martineau, for example, regarded the harems she visited as little better than brothels, implying also that the life such women lead with excessive emphasis on "that which, with all our interests and engagements, we consider too prominent with us" makes them

> dull, soulless, brutish or peevish. . . . There cannot be a woman of them all who is not dwarfed and withered in mind and soul by being kept wholly engrossed with that one interest, — detained at that stage in existence which, though most important in its place, is so as a means to ulterior ends. The ignorance is fearful enough, but the grossness revolting. (Martineau 239)

Whether they produced scorn or titillation, such common assumptions were persistent, provoking refutation from those travellers and scholars concerned to dispel stereotypes:

They do not, as the common descriptions of harem life lead us to believe, recline the live-long day on a soft divan enjoying *dolce far niente*, adorned with gold and jewels, smoking, and supporting upon the yielding pillow those arms that indolence makes so plump. (Klunzinger 162)

Although Brontë had "visited" the Orient only in her readings of *The Arabian Nights*, she associates the harem with "tons of female flesh" and registers a similar abhorrence of indolence and sexual availability to that recorded by such visitors to the East as Harriet Martineau and Florence Nightingale. Indeed, Nightingale's passionate denunciation of polygamy and the role of woman as "the servant of man" recalls the terms of debates between Jane Eyre and Rochester. Shortly before they are to be married, Rochester exclaims that he would not exchange "this one little English girl for the Grand Turk's whole seraglio — gazelle eyes, houri forms and all!" Brontë writes: "The Eastern allusion bit me again." What is it that has bitten Jane Eyre except the relegation of herself to the condition of a sexual slave? She has already described Rochester as having smiled on her as a sultan smiles on a favored slave when she urges him to go and buy whatever he fancies in that line. He asks her what she will do while he bargains for "so many tons of flesh." Jane replies that she is going to liberate the enslaved, his harem inmates included (*Jane Eyre* 297–98). Her way of counteracting the power Rochester has as sultan is to seek independence; it is after all her fear of being a "kept" woman that urges her to write to her uncle in Madeira. In having another wife locked away, Rochester attempts to practise polygamy and become a kind of "bashaw" or pasha, though a pasha would from all accounts have been able to rid himself of a troublesome wife more easily than Rochester can. The insurrection in the harem threatened by Jane points also to the rebellion Bertha stages on the night before Rochester's abortive wedding to Jane. In their sparring, Rochester and Jane evoke a context in which male fantasies of the harem focus on the titillating availability of passive female flesh, while female assumptions about harem life emphasize passivity and availability as well as sloth and lassitude. Reflecting common cultural assumptions, Brontë's fiction represents exaggerated female sexuality either as a passive, degenerate slump or, if active, as evil and overpowering, a preying and devouring of the other. Bertha (dark, exotic, intemperate, with "giant propensities") is the extreme to which *Villette*'s Cleopatra points (*Jane Eyre* 334).

In *Villette* the image of the pasha is evoked, significantly, in relation to Graham at the point of his "abandonment" of Lucy for Paulina Home. Having waited seven weeks with no word from him, she finally receives a letter from his mother. The body of the letter details an occasion in which Graham falls asleep and his mother "invests his brows" with the "grand adornment'' (a sky-blue turban) that he won at the concert: "[H]e looked quite Eastern, except that he is so fair. . . . [T]here was as fine a young bey, dey, or pacha improvised as you would wish to see" (355). The characterization of Graham as pasha recalls the Eastern images used of Paulina and Graham as early as the third chapter, where the child Paulina is described as a "little Odalisque, on a couch" (87) and Graham, once he has won her affection, as "the Grand Turk" who cannot be "sufficiently well waited on" (82). Paulina could not be more unlike the sexualized women that Lucy would associate with the Cleopatra figure, but we remember that Paulina's mother was a Ginevra, given to self-indulgent excess and pleasure like her name-sake — Paulina's cousin Ginevra. Home (Paulina's last name) may be where the harem is, if one is in willing service to the pasha's self-absorption. This alternative scenario — being a slave to someone else's appetites — does not strike Lucy as much better than being a slave to one's own.

If we return to nineteenth-century assumptions about the sexualized woman as deviant and pathological, we see that such assumptions are underscored by the way in which the prostitute became synonymous with disease (Gilman 99–101).[14] The sense of the prostitute as physically and morally different from "normal" women was confirmed therefore by the association of the prostitute with disease and contagion, a view that was to express itself later in the legislation of the Contagious Diseases Acts. In Lucy's response to the painting, the discourse of prostitution is also evoked by the connotations of particular terms that Lucy uses to evaluate the picture. It is described at one point as an "enormous piece of claptrap" (276). While claptrap is insincere or empty language, it is also an artifice or ploy for winning audience approval. This piece of claptrap ensnares applause; it is an empty artifice seducing its viewers as Cleopatra is supposed to have ensnared and seduced hers. But if *clapier* is a brothel, what is trapped there is the clap, the connotations of which play into the stereotypic associations of the sexualized female with the prostitute, disease, and deviance. Gilman also suggests that the nineteenth-century perception of the prostitute "merged with that of the black," linking the perception of female sexuality to stereotypes of the primitive — the dark, savage "lower" order of things (99). Assumptions that blacks, seen as lacking in control, represented a primitive stage of civilization merged with assumptions about dark women as threatening unbridled sexuality and chaos.[15] Brontë describes her Cleopatra figure not only as fat and coarse, but also "dark," "dusky," "mulatto," "gypsy." If not exactly bestial, she is at one point referred to as "the Lioness." In the context of Gilman's findings on nineteenth-century sexual stereotypes, these are qualities associated with degeneration and the leading of a brutish, animal life.

There are important ways in which Lucy interacts with the painting, projecting her own anxieties about laxity and displacing her own struggle with a sexual identity onto it. By virtue of her association with the brutish and degenerate, the subject of the painting represents the claim of the primitive and the lack of control that Lucy fears in herself. License to recognize or own desire, especially libidinal desire, she immediately associates with licentiousness; relaxation becomes laxity. As Lucy indulges herself slightly at the gallery, her small shifts in the direction of permission are writ large in the distortion and magnification of the painting's subject. Just before she describes the Cleopatra canvas, Lucy discusses the familiar struggle within herself as she walks through the gallery looking at the paintings. The division she experiences as she forms a judgment is fatiguing. Part of herself demands that she admire what is appropriate to admire, but part struggles against received canons of taste and withholds approbation. After struggling for some time in this way, Lucy decides to let herself off the hook and simply to enjoy walking around the gallery. The result is that she "[sinks] supine into a luxury of calm before ninety nine out of a hundred of the exhibited frames." Her supine sinking anticipates the posture of the Cleopatra — "She could not plead a weak spine; she ought to have been . . . sitting bolt upright" (275). Does the portrait suddenly upbraid her for her own ease, however slight? Her lapse of vigilance must be punished, but since it is subconscious, it is projected onto the painting, which is then mocked and repudiated. The moment Lucy relaxes, a backlash of punitive retribution follows. Should Lucy continue the luxury of indulging herself she would surely see herself exaggerated and distended in a gross and overblown way.

The subject of the painting is later described as a "slug," a pulpy mass. Among other things this is an image of massive regression. Lucy does more than straighten up in asserting herself against the sight of the supine spineless slug; she mounts a scathing attack on the part of herself that is expressed in the canvas. From this transaction, we may begin to summarise the characteristic displacement of Lucy's emotions in the narrative. Her fierce sense of secrecy and privacy about her feelings is born from the knowledge that her own desires and yearning are unlikely to be reciprocated. Hence Lucy counsels stoicism, anticipates neglect, and keeps her desires well under control. She likens herself to Jael, driving nails into the temples of her Sisera — desire. She also concludes that if her soft, tender feelings were to command attention they would have to be exhibited, paraded brazenly, which she refuses to do. The desiring self must therefore be hidden and stifled for two reasons: one is that there is no one to recognize, summon, and cherish it. (Graham confirms this by repeatedly failing to recognize her as a woman, and M. Paul refutes it by endorsing and responding to that desiring, sexual self.[16]) The other reason is that if desire asserts itself, it will suffer disappointment; her proleptic identification with Madame Beck whom she sees as fighting desire and greeting the grisly hag of disappointment confirms her expectation of disappointment. And if not disappointment, then the desiring self will suffer spoiling, grow greedy and monstrous like Cleopatra, or conflagrate in demonic self-assertion like Vashti.

It is not only the subject of the painting that is gross and overbearing, but as far as Lucy is concerned the very painting itself — the whole "preposterous" production which "queens it" over all the others in the gallery. By what authority, Lucy asks, does such a representation command respect and attention? Not only is this canvas exhibited; it is itself exhibitionistic. By means of figurative transformation, the whole painting — that "notable production" — is its subject. It is a production of "pretentious size, set up in the best light, having a cordon of protection stretched before it, and a cushioned bench duly set in front for the accommodation of worshipping connoisseurs, who, having gazed themselves off their feet, might be fain to complete the business sitting" (275). Indeed, Lucy sounds here much like John Berger in recognizing how the evaluation of a "work of art" is highly dependent on the logistics of its exhibition. The way the subject has been executed and framed solicits a certain viewing of her; it is Lucy's perverse pleasure therefore to take a dim view of such solicitation. But there is perhaps more to it than simply Lucy's objection to the painting's shameful call for male attention. If the definition of prostitution as a "setting forth or placing in a public place" can be applied to the painting, it is clear from the response of those around Lucy that there are many clients available for seduction (see Bernheimer 1). The idea of a public setting forth applies, of course, to Lucy's narrative, which is characterized by lies, evasions, and secrets never shared with the reader. Whereas Brontë could be accused of resorting to images of shipwreck when Lucy does not want to be specific about disappointment and pain, and whereas Lucy is infuriatingly withholding, reticent, and inscrutable at times, the narrative seems to ask the reader to work at knowing Lucy and meeting her, as it were, half way. Lucy is going to make sure that her narrative is no brazen publication. As readers we are hardly exempt from the consequences of the following point of view: "There is a perverse mood of the mind which is rather soothed than irritated by misconstruction; and in quarters where we can never be rightly known, we take pleasure, I think, in being consummately ignored" (164). Just as Lucy prefers to be ignored than to advertise or exhibit herself, so she maintains a private purity in the face of imagined misperception.

* * *

CLEOPATRA SURFACES AGAIN later in the novel, in the context of another spectacle — the dramatic portrayal of Vashti. On this occasion Lucy compares her responses to the representations of Cleopatra and Vashti and delivers an impassioned diatribe against Rubens, whom she holds responsible for privileging women like the subject of the Cleopatra painting — large, buxom

women who (even these days) are identified by the epithet "Rubensesque."
Peter Paul Rubens is not known for any depictions of Cleopatra, but at this
point in the text "Cleopatra" is functioning as a generic label for all fleshy,
painterly subjects.

> Place now the Cleopatra, or any other slug, before her as an obstacle and see
> her cut through the pulpy mass as the scimitar of Saladin clove the down
> cushion. Let Peter Paul Rubens wake from the dead, let him rise from his
> cerements, and bring into this presence all the army of his fat women; the
> magian power or prophet-virtue gifting that slight rod of Moses, could, at one
> waft, release and re-mingle a sea spell-parted, whelming the heavy host with
> the down-rush of overthrown sea-ramparts. (340)

The paragraph is extraordinary in the way it conflates many aspects of the
novel's concern with female sexuality and its artistic representation. I begin
with the associations that Vashti, Saladin, Cleopatra, Moses, and Rubens
raise here. Vashti offers a challenge to Rubens who becomes a sign for the
kind of painter who produced the *Cleopatra*. Although he is no Orientalist,
he paints female subjects who remind Lucy of the women she labels as
Cleopatras. Her quarrel with such painters is that they have the power to
represent women and to influence perceptions of beauty and desirability. The
apostrophe to Rubens, whose women subjects are generally ample and fleshy,
brings to mind paintings such as "The Judgement of Paris," in which the
naked women parade and compete for the prize. Beauty is rewarded; those
not judged beautiful, as Berger points out in *Ways of Seeing*, are not beautiful
(52). As an object of beauty the woman may be encouraged to enjoy her
power over men and indeed to enjoy herself as a sight, though she may
also be condemned vain or narcissistic. The ramifications in Lucy's case are
particularly interesting. Since she is judged not beautiful, Lucy is not encouraged to look upon herself as a sight that produces pleasure; in fact she is not
encouraged to see herself at all. It is significant that her way of asking M.
Paul to declare that he loves and desires her is, "Do I displease your eyes
much?" (583). Her stab at Rubens's fat ladies comes from one who has been
so thinned as to vanish. In contrast to Cleopatra, half-reclined on a couch in
the posture of the whore, Lucy is secret, often self-effacing, denying her
materiality and doubting at times her own substantiality.

In an amazing transference of association, the "heavy host" refers not so
much to the Egyptian enemies of Moses but to the stout gang of Cleopatras
who have been the subjects (hosts) of many a painter like Rubens. Further,
the contraction that converts "heavenly" to "heavy" is instructive. These
are the divine creatures, graceful angels that men like Graham worship and
adore, transformed by Lucy's critical eye into overweight slugs. Since she is
slight, small, and thin, and since she associates large fleshy women with

gross sexual parade, she certainly relishes the slicing, paring, and cutting down to size that the passage fantasizes. In a face-off between Rubens's flabby Cleopatras and Vashti (armed with Saladin's scimitar or the rod of Moses) Lucy envisions a triumphant trouncing. Her reference to Scott's *The Talisman* and the scimitar of Saladin that clove the down cushion underpins one fantasy of demolition; the rod of Moses another. The analogy of Moses and the Egyptians sustains the Eastern flavor of all the allusions and analogies Lucy makes here and elsewhere, but it has another significant function. Since Lucy is fantasizing the dismissal of the artistic interpretations she despises and contrasting them with those she admires, Brontë quotes an Orientalist she respects — John Martin, whose *Destruction of Pharaoh's Host* she may very well have in mind here. Martin is an Orientalist painter in that many of his themes are Eastern and Biblical, but instead of Cleopatra, his composition focuses on the rod of Moses and the power it derives from the dynamic sea and sky, which direct attention toward it. If we imagine Lucy thinking of this painting, we see that it is of course Lucy herself who occupies the powerful position of Moses here and would like to liquidate this imaginary army of fat women with the wave of her wand. Something needs to slice through all this blubber and cut both subjects and inflated painters down to size. The power that Lucy envisions in relation to this painting is a phallic power — Saladin's sword, Moses' wand. This perception raises interesting problems in the coding of power and fantasies of action as male (see Mulvey 37). Yet Lucy does not want to play the man, as her insistence on retaining female garb in the school dramatic production reveals. She articulates here the difficulty of envisioning a representation of female desire and sexuality that is not tantamount of looseness and "giant propensities." Further, the representation of Vashti's passionate self-expression suggests that the assumption of power by a woman is overwhelming, uncontainable. That is, a female Moses would not be able to control the flood she summoned, just as the performance of the actress playing Vashti on this occasion sets the theater alight.

It is significant that the impassioned gauntlet thrown down to Rubens and his army of fat women is made in the context of the Biblical Vashti — one woman of the East who refused to be exhibited as the object of the male gaze. She contrasts interestingly with Cleopatra whose exhibitionism and feasting and seductive manipulation of men define her. Lavish feasts like Cleopatra's are described in the Book of Esther, which begins with Vashti's story: "the beds were of gold and silver upon a pavement of red, and blue, and white, and black, marble. And they gave them drink in vessels of gold . . . and royal wine in abundance, according to the state of the king" (*Esther* I.6–7). Vashti, one may say, could have found herself in the supine position of Cleopatra had she not shown some backbone. Having been commanded to appear so that all the people and princes could look upon her beauty — "for she was fair to look on" — she refused to obey. She dies fighting, breathing mutiny and resisting the "rape of every faculty" because she "*would* see, *would* hear . . ." (342). If Cleopatra represents the regressive slump of dark, unbridled sexuality, and Vashti the crimson flame of uncontainable and self-destructive passion, Lucy Snowe attempts to negotiate her own path by comparing these extremes. The alternatives seem unclear, however, for the woman who does not want to exhibit herself as a spectacle for male consumption, but who also realizes the destructiveness of demonic and self-consuming anger.

At what price visibility? I return to the question with which I began. Lucy Snowe's answer takes the form of a questioning of dominant discourses of desire in relation to the sexual woman and an assertion that passion and desire may exist in the woman who is not marked like the prostitute, just as passion and desire may be kindled for the woman who is not conventionally the object of the male gaze. Anticipating the criticism of some twentieth-century feminist readers, Harriet Martineau wrote an anonymous critical review of *Villette* in which she castigated the novel for its abiding concern with "love" and its representation of a woman who could only see life in those terms. She wrote: "There are substantial, heartfelt interests for women of all ages, and under ordinary circumstances, quite apart from love: there is an absence of introspection, an unconsciousness, a repose in women's lives . . . of which we find no admission in this book" (qtd. in Fraser 433).[17] Just as Martineau wrote in *Eastern Life: Present and Past* that it was dreadful to see the inmates of a harem in the grip of "that one interest," so she objected to what she saw as Brontë's inordinate concern with female desire. To Brontë, though, there was a world of difference between the sexual surfeit of the stereotypical harem slave and the passionate desire of Lucy Snowe to be seen and to be loved. And indeed, the ambiguous and troubling closure of the novel bears testimony to the difficult social negotiation of this difference. Lucy loves M. Paul and is seen, recognized, and rewarded by him, however problematic his despotic, Napoleonic demeanour may be for modern readers. Lucy survives, has economic independence, and is no man's slave. But Brontë does not allow Lucy to keep in sight that which reflects her desiring, sexual self, and she becomes understandably associated with frost and cold. From what Brontë shows us in this novel, it is difficult to disturb entrenched patterns of gendered looking and what they imply about the expression of desire. Her closure will not preserve or seal, therefore, that dissenting scenario in which the outsider becomes a player in the exchange of mutually desiring gazes.

University of Toronto—Scarborough

NOTES

1. Feminist and psychoanalytic discussions particularly have examined critically Freud's emphasis on the gaze as a crucial aspect on the construction of male sexual identity. In terms of the Freudian scenario, the sight of the "castrated" female is initially responsible for the production of male anxiety about sexuality and then, as the gazer asserts his difference, the anxiety is subsequently allayed. The domination of the "looking" position is supposed to be a means of empowering the looker, a scenario that writes the power relations between the subject of the controlling gaze and its subordinated object. This opposition is further mapped onto the binaries of male/female, active/passive, and so on.

2. My perspective on the gaze as a way of entering the novel's discourse of female desire and sexuality is indebted to Newman.

3. Hence the narrative attention paid to Graham's failure to recognize her when he meets her ten years later, and the emphasis on looks and eyes in the scene where Lucy finds out that Monsieur Paul loves her.

4. The most thorough and useful treatment of Brontë's sexuality is Maynard. See also Jacobus; Fraser 173; and Gilbert and Gubar 399–440.

5. Poovey is quoting from W. R. Greg's treatment of "the great social vice of Prostitution" published in the *Westminster Review* 1850; for further discussion of Greg's views see Walkowitz (42–45). On prostitution in the nineteenth century see also Gay, Kendrick, Nead, and Mahood.

6. Reading *Jane Eyre* in the context of the public debates about female desire allows Poovey to argue that Jane's return to Rochester is a deliberate and aggressive choice in favour of her desire for him, even though that desire is sanctioned and mythologized by its representation as the voice of nature. The problem of expressing desire and reconciling a passionate spiritual and sexual self is more extensively explored, if not resolved, in the case of Lucy Snowe.

7. Brontë's knowledge of Cleopatra's feasts may have come from her readings in ancient history. Monsieur Rollin's *Ancient History* was apparently recommended for study by Miss Wooler at Roe Head, and indeed Rollin offers an expansive treatment of the most famous classical accounts of Cleopatra's conspicuous consumption and sexual politics.

8. Renaissance depictions often show her with the asp, a familiar metonymic signifier of her identity. While death scenes continued to be popular, the Restoration favored scenes showing the famous episode in Pliny where Cleopatra dissolves a fabulously valuable pearl in a glass of wine in order to win a wager with Antony about who was the bigger spender. The seventeenth century was disposed to admire and indulge, even idealize, extravagant sensual love, but the nineteenth century was not.

9. Having been "seduced by Egypt" Makart altered his conception of Cleopatra, which he had previously treated in a "generalized Baroque manner." Influenced by Egyptologist Georg Ebers, he also invented genre scenes with an Egyptian flavor. His *Ancient Egyptian Dancing Girl* is clothed (or unclothed) in a costume identical to that of his Cleopatra.

10. Although the realistic style of painters who actually lived and worked in the east (John Frederick Lewis and Gerome, for example) was at one time held to reflect Oriental reality with scientific exactitude and objectivity and to advance the West's "knowledge" of Eastern women, such claims are today rigorously deconstructed. See Nochlin, "The Imaginary Orient" (33–60); and de Groot.

11. The identification of this painting and the one described in *Villette* was originally put forward by Gustave Charlier, who points out that Brontë both misnames and misdescribes the painting by De Biefve. Charlier was also able to show that another painting at the Salon is recognizable in Lucy's description of "La vie d'une femme." For information on De Biefve see Berko, who lists his name among Belgian Orientalists but offers no commentary on his work; see also P. Berko and V. Berko's dictionary of Belgian painters, which has a short entry on De Biefve but does not mention Orientalist themes at all. He was known for his portraits and his historic, mythological, and religious scenes. Also remarked on is his penchant for the large canvas, depicting pomp and circumstance; *Une Almé* is not mentioned.

12. Beneath the lithograph printed in *La Renaissance*, the following explanatory lines accompanied the title of the painting:

Les almés de l'Egypte, agiles bayadères,
Aux longs cheveux flottants, aux tuniques légères . . .

[Egyptian almees, light-footed dancing-girls
With filmy draperies and long floating curls . . .]

13. See also Walkowitz's discussion of Parent-Duchatelet's influence on British social scientists (36–44).

14. See also Poovey's discussion of the ideological work done by different versions of desire that developed in response to public concern about contagious diseases (30–37).

15. Among the "civilized orders," then, a loss of control was likely to be marked by a regression into this dark past, a degeneration into primitive expression of emotions in the form of either madness or unbridled sexuality. Indeed, *Villette* holds these two states — madness and sexual licentiousness — in a dangerous Scylla and Charybdis position, and it is interesting to note that not long before Lucy confronts the lascivious Cleopatra, she has recently suffered a "breakdown" — a madness caused by being left at the school for the summer with only "the crétin" to take care of (225–36). She is recovering at the home of the Brettons and enjoying the luxury of Dr. Graham's company when he suggests that she visit the gallery exhibition. The two versions of extreme derangement — madness and primitive sexuality — are thus counterpointed and associated in the novel.

16. Maynard observes that M. Paul is the only male viewer who responds to "the sexual reality behind the poor and foolish painting" (170); see his discussion of M. Paul's sexual and passionate nature (200).

17. See also Martineau's tribute to Charlotte after her death, in which she again refers to the vehement and morbid passion of Brontë's heroines (Fraser 486).

WORKS CITED

Alexander, Christine. *The Early Writings of Charlotte Brontë*. Oxford: Blackwell, 1983.

Athenaeus: The Deipnosophists. Trans. Charles Burton Gulick. Cambridge, MA: Harvard UP, 1961.

Berger, John. *Ways of Seeing*. London: BBC and Penguin, 1972.

Berko, P. *Orientalist Painters*. Brussels: Laconti, 1982.

Berko, P., and V. Berko. *Belgian Painters: A Dictionary of Belgian Painters born between 1750 and 1875*. Brussels: Laconti, 1981.

Bernheimer, Charles. *Figures of Ill–Repute: Representing Prostitution in Nineteenth–Century France*. Boston: Harvard UP, 1989.

Brontë, Charlotte. *Villette*. Harmondsworth: Penguin, 1979.

———. *Jane Eyre*. Harmondsworth: Penguin, 1966.

Charlier, Gustave. "Brussels Life in *Villette*." *The Brontë Society Transactions* 5 (1955): 386–90.

de Groot, Joanna. " 'Sex' and 'Race': The Construction of Language and Image in the Nineteenth Century." *Sexuality and Subordination*. Ed. Susan Mendus and Jane Rendall. London: Routledge, 1989. 89–128.

Fraser, Rebecca. *Charlotte Brontë*. London: Methuen, 1988.

Gamman, Lorraine, and Margaret Marshment, eds. *The Female Gaze: Women as Viewers of Popular Culture*. Seattle: The Real Comet P, 1989.

Gay, Peter. *The Bourgeois Experience: Victoria to Freud*. Vol. 2 *The Tender Passion*. New York: Oxford UP, 1984–86.

Gérin, Winifred. *Charlotte Brontë: The Evolution of Genius*. Oxford: Clarendon, 1967.

Gilbert, Sandra, and Susan Gubar. *The Madwoman in the Attic: The Woman Writer and the Nineteenth-Century Literary Imagination*. New Haven: Yale UP, 1979.

Gilman, Sander L. *Difference and Pathology: Stereotypes of Sexuality, Race and Madness*. Ithaca: Cornell UP, 1985.

Heath, Stephen. "Difference." *Screen* 19.3 (1978): 51–112.

Jacobus, Mary. "The Buried Letter." *Reading Woman: Essays in Feminist Criticism*. New York: Columbia UP, 1986. 41–61.

Kendrick, Walter. *The Secret Museum: Pornography in Modern Culture*. New York: Viking, 1987.

Klunzinger, C. B. *Upper Egypt, its People and its Products*. New York: Scribner, 1878.

Lane, Edward. *The Manners and Customs of The Modern Egyptians*. 1836. London: Dent, 1908.

Mahood, Linda. *The Magdalenes: Prostitution in the Nineteenth Century*. London: Routledge, 1990.

Martineau, Harriet. *Eastern Life: Present and Past*. 1848. London: Moxon, 1875.

Maynard, John. *Charlotte Brontë and Sexuality*. Cambridge: Cambridge UP, 1984.

Mulvey, Laura. "Afterthoughts on 'Visual Pleasure and Narrative Cinema' inspired by *Duel in the Sun*." *Visual and Other Pleasures*. Bloomington: Indiana UP, 1989. 29–38.

Nead, Linda. *Myths of Sexuality: Representations of Women in Victorian Britain*. New York: Basil Blackwell, 1988.

Newman, Beth. " 'The Situation of the Looker-On': Gender, Narration, and Gaze in *Wuthering Heights*." *PMLA* 105.5 (1990) 1029–41.

Nochlin, Linda. *The Politics of Vision: Essays on Nineteenth-Century Art and Society*. New York: Harper and Row, 1989.

Poovey, Mary. "Speaking of the Body: Mid-Victorian Constructions of Female Desire." *Body/Politics: Women and the Discourses of Science*. Ed. Mary Jacobus, Evelyn Fox Keller, and Sally Shuttleworth. London: Routledge, 1990. 29–46.

Rollin, Charles. *The Ancient History of the Egyptians, Carthaginians, Assyrians, Babylonians*. London: Printed for Cowie, 1827.

Said, Edward W. *Orientalism*. New York: Pantheon, 1978.

"Salon National de 1842." *La Renaissance: chronique des arts et de la littérature* 4 (1842–43): 92.

Steegmuller, Francis. *Flaubert in Egypt: A Sensibility on Tour*. Boston: Little, Brown, 1972.

Walkowitz, Judith R. *Prostitution and Victorian Society*. Cambridge: Cambridge UP, 1980.

Wise, Thomas James, and John Alexander Symington, eds. *The Miscellaneous and Unpublished Writings of Charlotte and Patrick Branwell Brontë*. The Shakespeare Head Brontë. 2 vols. 1936 and 1938.

REVIEW ESSAYS

FEMINISM, HISTORY, AND THE NINETEENTH-CENTURY NOVEL

By Deborah Epstein Nord

HERBERT SPENCER, whose intellectual relationship to George Eliot forms the subject of Nancy Paxton's *George Eliot and Herbert Spencer: Feminism, Evolutionism, and the Reconstruction of Gender* (Princeton: Princeton UP, 1991), also makes a brief appearance in Paula Marantz Cohen's *The Daughter's Dilemma: Family Process and the Nineteenth-Century Domestic Novel* (Ann Arbor: U of Michigan P, 1991). In Cohen's book, a reading of five novels through the lens of "family systems" analysis, Spencer figures as one of the two men Eliot loved who was *not* the partner of another woman: other objects of her affection — Robert Brabant, John Chapman, George Henry Lewes — enabled Eliot to reproduce aspects of her subordinate but complementary and companionate relationship to her father, while Spencer's solitariness threatened to engulf Eliot and stifle her independence. For Cohen, then, George Eliot and indeed the heroines of her novels, are to be understood above all as victimized but heroic daughters, those pivotal figures in the Victorian family who, in Cohen's reading of nineteenth-century fiction and culture, maintain family equilibrium through their relationship to the father and who are "destined to be the shaping force behind social organization as the nuclear family breaks down" (23). For Nancy Paxton, on the other hand, Eliot emerges as an intellectual historical figure struggling not with Strauss, Feuerbach, and Comte but with the evolutionism of Spencer, most importantly in its complicated and ultimately antagonistic relationship to feminism. As these two visions of Spencer and Eliot suggest, these works of criticism present us with radically divergent approaches to nineteenth-century fiction, and it is above all on their contrasting uses of feminism and of history that I want to focus here.

In her introduction to *The Daughter's Dilemma*, Paula Cohen distinguishes her own approach to issues of gender and literature from that of feminist critics who "read female authors as covertly struggling against a prevailing ideology that seeks to crush them": the authors, literary heroines, and real daughters of the past (Cohen does not always separate these categories in her writing) were not necessarily rebelling in their lives and art but "passing through" an ideology of the family on their way to the subjectivity necessary to feminist politics and criticism (7). The experience of the "nuclear family" — a term I believe Cohen uses in an anachronistic or at least an ahistorical way — resulted not in the madwoman's suffering and anger but in the "progressive realization of the daughter's power" (23). Cohen's understanding of the evolution of the family from the eighteenth century, shaped by the family systems theory of Gregory Bateson and others, gives the daughter the crucial role of mediation and accommodation, the part of family lynchpin, who keeps its structure intact by acting as scapegoat, safety valve, and regulator. In this vision the daughter can be seen as a powerful figure, and even her victimization and somaticization of family stress (as in the illness of anorexia) can be understood as means to unmask a crippled or obsolete family structure. Cohen's differences with the feminist criticism from which she distances herself in the Introduction can, in fact, be explained around the issue of anorexia nervosa: for critics like Susan Gubar and Sandra Gilbert anorexia expresses the sexual and cultural repression suffered by women, whereas for Cohen it is a disease of the entire family *carried by the daughter* who, in a sense, sounds the alarm through her illness. (In keeping with her notion that the ideology of the nuclear family began to crumble just after the mid-nineteenth century and that today we have gone beyond it to a freer configuration for daughters, she does distinguish between the anorexia of the nineteenth century that *disguised* the damaging logic of family ideologies and the anorexia of today that *betrays* and *exposes* that logic.)

The importance of the daughter in the history of the family can be observed, Cohen argues, in the prominence of father-daughter relationships in the fiction of the last century. The dyad of husband and wife, unable to withstand the strains attendant upon the fading of romantic love, requires the triangulation created by the daughter's presence in order to maintain its stability. Father and daughter, the argument continues, form a new dyad of complementary beings, the father raising the daughter so as to mold her to himself. Since it is this dynamic that keeps the family going, the father-daughter dyad dominates the domestic novel — or novels that "deal explicitly with family instability" (25) — and its dominance explains "the absence or thematic inconsequence of the mother in nineteenth-century literature" (23). Clearly those novels of family instability written by Dickens and Thackeray are not on Cohen's mind, nor is she even thinking of the novels of Elizabeth Gaskell, for whom the mothers of daughters in particular loom very large. She is thinking rather of the canon of motherless women novelists and feminocentric male writers represented in her book — Jane Austen, Emily Brontë, George

Eliot, Samuel Richardson, and Henry James — a canon deeply influenced by the tradition of feminist criticism from which Cohen claims to dissent.

The consonance between the evolution of the novel and what family systems theorists see as the evolution of the nuclear family becomes a tricky business here. The question of selectivity and of the burden of historical explanation that five novels are meant to bear in Cohen's book is never addressed. And the issue of gender, of the novelist's gender, is also elided when she generalizes from what is an unacknowledged tradition of women's fiction to apply to the whole of the nineteenth-century novel. The elision of gender is not altogether unintended on Cohen's part, for in her Conclusion she aligns herself with those critics whose interests transcend gender difference: men who write feminist criticism, critics who write about role reversal and transvestism, those who see that the "distinctions that have been made between male and female writing will become blurred" (185). It is after all a man, Henry James, who is the hero of Cohen's story, the writer who finally provided a "revolutionary vision" of family and fiction. Aware of this apparent irony, she offers the explanation that James and, to a lesser degree, Hardy, Meredith, and Gissing and *not their female contemporaries* achieved this vision because woman, as regulator and mediator, "could not be the one to imagine for herself a new creative role in culture" (185). What do we make then of Cohen's apparently contradictory claims for the progressively increasing power women were meant to gain over time by "passing through" the ideology of the family? A rather conventional celebration of the modern male novelist as social iconoclast is claimed here as critical gender-bending and defended on the grounds that women were too completely locked into their good-daughter roles to imagine transcending them. On the one hand, repression ultimately liberates the daughter and, on the other, it places blinders on her.

Already clear from my comments on Cohen's relationship to feminist criticism is the teleological nature of her thinking about history and about the evolution of the daughter's place in the family. Just as her book moves through five novels — *Clarissa, Mansfield Park, Wuthering Heights, The Mill on the Floss*, and *The Awkward Age* — toward the revolutionary achievement of James, she sees the nuclear family moving through a period of entrenchment and stability to a moment of ultimately liberating crisis, breakdown and revision. She regards the novelists in her study as cannily able to see the limits of their culture's ideology and, in some cases, to anticipate ruptures in the ideological underpinnings of family life. James, because of his "sensitivity . . . to emerging social trends," could see "around the ideology of the nuclear family in the 1890s" (15). There are two problems here: first, Cohen tries to see the movement of fiction and developments in the social history of the family in a consistent and always tightly connected pattern that, if it exists at all, would require a monumental study of family history as well as analysis of scores of novels. This effort leads her, for example, to explain the difference between Austen's and Brontë's representations of family life — stable in the first case and disintegrating in the second — in terms of their different chronological relationships to "the evolution of the ideology of the nuclear family" (110). This insistent teleology also accounts for statements about George Eliot's inhabiting a moment when the ideology of the "nuclear family" was "already in decline" and about her consequent role as "a point of transition" to James. This evocation of a tightly interlocking chain of novels, linked by their progressive distancing from a particular ideology of the family, seems finally unconvincing, itself a literary historical fiction.

The second difficulty of Cohen's historical vision is its ahistoricism. Did family structures during the time of Richardson's writing of *Clarissa* (1748), the novel that Cohen believes provided a "blueprint" for the nineteenth-century domestic novel, really bear so close a relationship to the kind of family Austen knew in 1814, when she published *Mansfield Park*? (Dates, by the way, are hard to come by in this book: it is perhaps my obsessiveness that makes me look for them, but I suspect that Cohen invites the search by making what is essentially an historical argument.) Does the term "nuclear family" suffice to describe social patterns and ideologies from 1748 to 1814 to 1847 to 1860? And did this ideology really begin to unravel as early as *1860*? I have difficulty enough seeing the breakdown in the ideology of the family that Cohen claims for the 1890s, a breakdown that emerges in the last pages of her book as virtually indistinguishable from that of the 1990s. It is striking, as well, that class, nationality, and historical movements (like suffrage, reform of marriage and divorce laws, or women's movements in general) that are intimately related to the fate of the family are ignored completely as elements that influence the story Cohen tells. Finally, when we are told that Freud gave "scientific form" to what Richardson described at least one hundred and fifty years earlier and that Gregory Bateson did the same for James (180), the legitimacy of the historical argument Cohen is making seems severely undermined.

The irony of this study — and perhaps of many such works of criticism that try to fit a few canonical works of literature into a sweeping vision of historical change — is that its local observations and interpretations are much richer than its analytical framework. In the case of *The Daughter's Dilemma*, the application of "family systems" analysis to individual texts — an enterprise that seemed to me questionable at first — yields some interesting and original readings. Most successful, to my mind, are the readings of *Mill on the Floss* and especially *Mansfield Park*. Maggie Tulliver's relationship to her father, her role in the dynamic of family survival, and the inextricability of her connections to men outside of her family from those to the men within her family all take on new meaning in the context of Cohen's theoretical perspective. With Austen, Cohen's interest in the daughter's role in sustaining familial equilibrium serves her well in analyzing Fanny Price's entry into the Bertram family, her important tie to Sir Thomas, and, indeed, the seeming weakness of her identity. Especially telling is Cohen's comparison of *Mansfield Park* with other Austen novels: *Mansfield Park*, with its idealized family and pale heroine, inverts the structure of works like *Pride and Prejudice* and *Emma* that contain unstable or "disequilibrated" families and dominant, idealized (if problematic) heroines. In all cases, Cohen argues, the essential dynamic between daughter and family remains constant. One wishes for an even fuller treatment of these observations about Austen's novels: comparative analysis of one author's works seems to illuminate more successfully the vision of the family Cohen wishes to evoke than the tracing of a trajectory over the space of some one hundred and fifty years.

Nancy Paxton's historical focus in *George Eliot and Herbert Spencer* is, by contrast, very precise. She reproduces and analyzes an ongoing textual dialogue between Eliot and the theorist of social evolution she once wished to marry, with particular emphasis on their views on the "woman question" and its relation to evolutionary theory. Paxton pairs novels by Eliot with works by Spencer — *Adam Bede* with the essay "Personal Beauty," *Silas Marner* with *First Principles*, *Middlemarch* with *The Study of Sociology*, and so forth — and argues thereby that Eliot wrote overtly in response, and increasingly in opposition, to Spencer's ideas about gender and femininity in her fiction. Spencer began with certain progressive ideas about women's education and, by virtue of his Individualism, supported the abolition of legal restrictions that kept women tied to the domestic sphere, but he grew increasingly conservative in his notions about the way woman's biology would determine and indeed limit her social role. He drew connections between physical beauty in women and their corresponding goodness, altruism, and maternal generosity; he developed biological, evolutionary justifications for women's inherent inferiority and subordinate position within the family.

Eliot, then, began by finding support for her own interests in the emancipation of women in Spencer's Individualist views but ended by writing more and more consistently against him, chafing at his belief in the destiny-determining role of biology. An important focus for understanding their differences and the ways they expressed them is the issue of maternity, about which Paxton is especially insightful (indeed she might have underscored the question of maternal love in their works as the dominant theme of her book). The "maternal" for Spencer lay inextricably with biologically determined instincts; for Eliot the "maternal" was wholly separable from the body, even from actual maternity. Paxton locates an important statement of Eliot's understanding of maternal "sensations and emotions" in her 1854 essay "Woman in France: Madame de Sablé" and argues that Eliot struggles to defend this understanding throughout her fiction (9). Examples of Eliot's resistance to a Spencerian notion of the maternal abound — from Hetty Sorrel's lack of maternal feeling for her own child to Dinah Morris's maternal love for Hetty herself, to Silas Marner's maternal love for Eppie and Eppie's mother's scant maternal concern for her child, to the Princess Halm-Eberstein's abnegation of moral responsibility toward her son Daniel Deronda. Eliot, herself a childless but maternal woman, repeatedly challenged Spencer's confusion between the biological and the moral dimensions of motherhood and regularly cast childless women as those with the strongest, most reliable maternal emotions.

The precise historical focus of Paxton's work helps to revive our sense of Spencer's enormous influence among his contemporaries. At times, in the course of reading this book, it becomes difficult to understand how and why Eliot could take seriously the theorizing of a man who believed in the "instinctive altruism of beautiful women" (177) and who proposed that education of certain kinds might sap women's vital energies and make them unfit to reproduce (143). But Paxton's convincing case for Eliot's ongoing involvement with Spencer's ideas, together with what we know of his importance to other nineteenth-century figures in England, America and on the Continent, reminds us of the potency of evolutionary theory in that century. This book vividly underscores the clash between evolutionism and movements for women's emancipation, the formidable intellectual obstacles to ideas of women's equality, and the currency among an intellectual elite of notions about things like sexual selection and the "laws of attraction" (Paxton has a very interesting reading of the Maggie Tulliver-Stephen Guest relationship as exposing the inadequacy of the "laws of attraction"). Paxton describes the formation in 1861 of the "X Club," a group of men, including Thomas Huxley, John Tyndall, and Sir John Lubbock, who met to discuss evolutionary ideas and, among other things, to formulate arguments "to counter the feminist challenges of the 1860s" (144). This overt and localized tension between evolutionism and feminism constituted an important element in the gender debates of the 1860s, the decade that saw the publication of Mill's *Subjection of Women* and Ruskin's *Sesame and Lilies*, as well as Eliot's *Mill on the Floss, Silas Marner, Romola*, and *Felix Holt, The Radical*.

Paxton's grounding in these debates enables her to enter interestingly into a dialogue with contemporary feminist critics about the nature of what she calls George Eliot's "feminism." For others Eliot has often seemed either a failed feminist or an anti-feminist intellectual, but Paxton finds those critics failing to distinguish between nineteenth-century and twentieth-century feminism and sees their judgments of Eliot as anachronistic. For Paxton, Eliot's feminism — and we must assume that she uses the term in this context to refer to a set of *nineteenth-century* beliefs — is not unambiguous: she refused to sign Barbara Bodichon's petition for women's suffrage in 1867, remained aloof from many of the women close to her who actively campaigned for women's rights, and imagined for many of her heroines a fate of absorption into husbands' lives and an ultimate relinquishing of ambitions in the public sphere. But Paxton locates Eliot's feminism not only in her continual engagement in and frequent support of many feminist causes but, more importantly and subtly, in her resistance to misogynistic evolutionism in her novels. Uniquely placed to participate in scientific and intellectual debate, Eliot exercised her right to take issue with male social thinkers on their own terms. It is also in Eliot's notions about the female sphere of maternality that Paxton finds the novelist's complicated but profound consciousness of women's rights and powers.

By pairing Eliot with Spencer, then, Paxton allows Eliot's feminism to become more apparent and less ambiguous than it might otherwise seem, particularly to the eyes of twentieth-century feminist critics. Paxton makes this point directly in discussing *Middlemarch*: "Eliot's stanch defense of Dorothea's special capacities for sympathy and imagination and her valorization of her acute consciousness of the ties that bind her to her family, her husband, and her community, appear suddenly more liberal and more feminist when they are compared with Spencer's misogynistic interpretation of the significance of women's physical, mental, and moral differences in *The Study of Sociology*" (183). This comparison provides a useful corrective to certain anachronistic — or perhaps merely partial — critiques of Eliot's position on the woman question, but it also makes inevitable its own kind of distortion, or incompleteness. Although Paxton includes accounts of Eliot's disagreements with Bodichon or Emily Davies, she does not approach Eliot's fiction from the perspective of a debate among the varieties of Victorian feminism. The issue of female suffrage, which comes up in connection with *Felix Holt*, is not, to my mind, the object of a sufficiently probing analysis. Eliot's resistance to extending the vote, not just to women but to unenfranchised men, places her closer to Spencer on this point than to many British feminists. Even a comparison with other literary women — Charlotte Brontë, for instance, or Elizabeth Gaskell — would shift or simply broaden our understanding of Eliot's position and prose. This was not, of course, the book that Paxton was writing, nor should it have been, but the reader does have the sense that while important pieces of the puzzle are being added, others are being somewhat obscured. Paxton lets an opportunity slip by, for example, when she mentions that by the time Eliot wrote *Silas Marner* she had dropped the "male persona" of *Adam Bede* (106). The implications of Eliot's use of male narrators in her early fiction seem worth exploring in the context of

Paxton's subject, and such an exploration might shed light on Eliot's complicated relationship to the woman question and, indeed, to her own sex and
sexuality.

The practice of understanding Eliot's positions and rhetoric primarily, if
not exclusively, in relation to Spencer's does show signs of strain in Paxton's
repeated efforts to argue against the notion of Eliot's conservatism. Not only
does this happen in the chapter on *Felix Holt*, where she makes claims for
Eliot's progressivism as against Spencer's more conservative views, but in
the section on *Middlemarch*, where the frequently used strategy of enhancing
Eliot's liberalism by showing her to be less extreme than Spencer begins to
wear thin. It is perhaps as much the need to answer certain modes of contemporary criticism as it is the decision to use Spencer as the point of reference
that accounts for this sometimes distracting pattern in Paxton's work.

The relationship between the authors of these two works and the larger
critical and theoretical communities of which they are a part is, in fact, the
subject on which I wish to end. In both of these books the authors include
what seem to be extraneous and, in some cases, misleading statements about
their theoretical filiations. In her Introduction Paxton mentions the closeness
of her method to "new historicism," a claim she never fully explains and
an estimation that seems off the mark. In any case, the injection of this
claim in the Introduction adds little to the merit of Paxton's book or to an
understanding of what she is after, but appears to satisfy a perceived need to
let us know "where she stands." Paula Cohen, whose proclaimed differences
with a certain kind of feminist criticism are in fact borne out in the course
of her study, ends her book with a statement of her debt to postmodernism
and deconstruction. I do not grasp the meaning or the truth of this claim —
the book seems to me to owe nothing at all to deconstruction — and I find
it wholly unnecessary, especially at that point in the book. Both of these
works of criticism, each in its own way, make very clear the critical and
theoretical assumptions that propel them: each has a clear, well-defined meth-
odology; each has a distinct perspective; each speaks quite eloquently for
itself and does not need the imprimatur of any doctrine or school.

Princeton University

"A TERRIBLE BEAUTY IS BORN": TEXTUAL SCHOLARSHIP IN THE 1990s

By Judith Kennedy

A DECADE AGO, critics of nineteenth-century literature tended to give polite nods of recognition to the work of textual scholars (theorists and editors alike) while for the most part accepting modern editions of nineteenth-century texts on trust. Editing was commonly viewed as the work of dry-as-dust scholars who dutifully and methodically researched the history of texts, cleaned up any transmissional "corruptions" that had inadvertently crept into subsequent publications of works, and aimed or claimed to produce "definitive" editions, ones that represented either the "best" texts or the authors' "final intentions." In the last few years, a revolution in textual studies has occurred that has parallels with the challenges to the tradition and its canons that have rocked other scholarly disciplines. And while Renaissance specialists contributed significantly to earlier developments in textual scholarship and still are heavily involved in the current debate (Steven Urkowitz, Gary Taylor, and John Dover Wilson, for instance), many of the central voices in the recent dialogues come from scholars who work primarily in nineteenth- and early twentieth-century British and American studies, such as Jerome J. McGann, Hershel Parker, Donald H. Reiman, Peter L. Schillingsburg, Donald Pizer, George Bornstein, and more recently, W. Speed Hill, Philip Cohen, and Allan Dooley, among others. The European school, led by such theorists and editors as Hans Zeller and Hans Walter Gabler, is similarly more interested in modern texts.

Because of the unsettling and certainly unsettled debates and the new, ever-evolving theories related to texts, a great number of literary scholars today have come to realize that there are, indeed, no definitive editions. Editions can "only ever be contingent and temporary" (Greetham, "Textual Scholarship," *MLA Introduction to Scholarship*, 105; see below). And there is a deepening awareness among literary critics that the texts they use and interpret depend to a great extent upon the critical judgment and theoretical orientation of the individual editors, who privilege particular versions and variants, who in short, in the words of George Bornstein, "set . . . the field of literary study" ("Introduction: Why Editing Matters," *Representing Modernist Texts*, 1–2; see below). While most Victorian scholars will probably continue to concentrate on the interpretation of texts, many of them also keep up with the current issues in textual scholarship to be informed about the construction of available editions and knowledgeable in selecting the particular texts upon which their own studies are based.

This essay will suggest some of the main venues for learning about the critical debate in textual editing and look broadly at that debate before focusing on three books about textual issues related specifically to Victorian literary works.

D. C. Greetham, an interpreter and analyst of textual scholarship in all its interdisciplinary aspects, founded the Society for Textual Scholarship in 1979. STS provides an ongoing forum for the discussion of contemporary textual work in its biennial conferences (most recently at the CUNY Graduate Center, April 1993) and through its journal *Text*, which Greetham publishes with his colleague, W. Speed Hill. *Text* has become a leading journal in the field because of the keen targeting of most of its essays on the current debates. As might be expected, papers presented at the STS conferences are frequently expanded for *Text*. Other important sources of current developments in the field are the Toronto Conferences on Editorial Problems, the meetings of the Association for Documentary Editing, or those run by the Bibliographical Society of America, all of which also publish their proceedings and other articles in their respective collections of essays or journals. At its annual convention, the Modern Language Association generally offers several sessions on textual scholarship, such as those regularly offered by the Discussion Group on Bibliographical and Textual Studies.

Greetham has commented that "textual scholarship is always querulous, interrogative, incredulous and dissatisfied," that "it is perhaps the exemplary discipline for today's 'hermeneutics of suspicion' " ("Textual Scholarship," 103). In such a charged atmosphere, Greetham's *Textual Criticism, An Introduction* (New York: Garland, 1992) provides a superbly sensible and encyclopedic overview. This dense introductory exploration emphasizes the continuities and reciprocations in the related textual practices of enumerative, systematic, and descriptive bibliography, paleography, typography, textual criticism and scholarly editing. Scholars who are new to these disciplines may prefer to begin with the last two chapters, using the beginning sections as reference tools when questions relating to these specialties arise, and play catch-up with these more technical chapters after reading Chapters 8 and 9, "Criticizing the Text: Textual Criticism" and "Editing the Text: Scholarly

Editing." Here is a straightforward and objective narrative that provides a history of various theories and their applications to texts, right into the midst of the major controversies of the early 1990s. Greetham has further condensed some of the information covered in these chapters in the section "Textual Scholarship" in the newly revised MLA publication edited by Joseph Gibaldi, *Introduction to Scholarship in the Modern Languages and Literatures*, 2nd ed. (New York: MLA, 1992).

Texts, of course, exist in many forms: drafts in the hand of an author (or anyone else who may have heard and copied down any of a number of oral renditions), "fair copies," typed manuscripts, printer's proofs, first editions, subsequent (censored, abridged, revised, or expanded) editions, pirated copies, translations, and today, even computer-generated versions. Feeling an intense sense of identification with Teufelsdröckh's editor in *Sartor Resartus*, the modern scholarly editor must figure out just how best to reproduce the "work" within all its available, disparate versions. Greetham's book traces the history of textual theory and practice through the recent challenges faced by the Anglo-American tradition. This tradition had developed along the lines of the carefully reasoned and evolving theories and practices of W. W. Greg, Fredson Bowers, and G. Thomas Tanselle and favors eclecticism or the mixing of early and late "witnesses" or versions as determined by an editor. He or she usually selects one version, a "copy-text" (frequently the author's manuscript or a first edition that best illustrates the writer's habits of spelling, punctuation, and other such original surface features), and then "emends" the copy-text with later changes made or authorized by the author and considered to be his or her "final intentions" for the work. Greetham finds that this dominant Anglo-American approach has been challenged on two fronts, and he perceptively ties them to parallel developments in literary criticism. The first challenge comes from structuralism: "On the one hand, the influence of structuralism has favored the production of 'genetic' editions in which all variants are listed in a continuous display of variation rather than in the eclectic or stemmatic privileging of one, originary moment." This genetic method, which shows the composition process, has become "virtually the norm in Franco-German editing" ("Textual Scholarship," 110). The most famous — to many, infamous — genetic edition is Hans Gabler's version of Joyce's *Ulysses*, which records in a "synthetic" or "synoptic" apparatus the variants of the work on one side of each page, with a clear reading text on its recto. But as Greetham notes, Gabler's procedures still assume "an authorial intention towards perfection" (111).

Perhaps the greater challenge to the tradition has been led by Jerome J. McGann, who argues that the author and the originary moment represent only one stage in a text's transmission. Greetham explains that McGann's "social textual criticism" (attacked in turn by T. H. Howard-Hill and others) "insists that all public appearances of a text — as revised and changed by authors, editors, readers, publishers, friends, and relations — have potentially equal textual significance and that the 'bibliographical code' (the various physical forms in which a text appears publicly) is just as much a part of its social meaning as the 'linguistic code' of its verbal content.'' Greetham ties McGann's theories to those of D. F. McKenzie, who has advanced a "similar position, one that treats all remains of a culture as 'text' and therefore withdraws some of the privilege traditionally accorded 'literature' '' (111–12).

Greetham reviews many of the derivations and variations in the ever-evolving theoretical metamorphosis that is shaking textual scholarship and scholarly editing today. His survey touches on some of the issues raised by the innovations in these disciplines, such as Peter Schillingsburg's vision of multiple computer-created texts of nineteenth-century novels (*Scholarly Editing in the Computer Age*, 1986); Donald H. Reiman's emphasis on "versioning" rather than final intentions in the editing of Romantic texts (*Romantic Texts and Contexts*, 1987); and Hershel Parker's "new scholarship" which "promises a 'full intentionality' drawn from multiple, and frequently contradictory, states of many nineteenth- and twentieth-century American authors" (*Flawed Texts and Verbal Icons: Literary Authority in American Fiction*, 1984, and '' 'The New Scholarship': Textual Evidence and Its Implications for Criticism, Literary Theory, and Aesthetics,'' 1984). These recent theories challenge the basic principles of final intentions and eclecticism that have dominated in the Anglo-American tradition. Instead of "postulating a single, consistent, authorially sponsored text as the purpose of the editorial enterprise, they suggest multiform, fragmentary, even contradictory texts as the aim of editing, sometimes to be constructed ad hoc by the reader.'' Since practical applications of some of these theories still need to be beaten out, "eclectic, intentionalist editions are still being produced more than any other form'' (112).

As the field of textual scholarship today is fraught not only with slippery terms, which shift slightly when used by different theorists, but also with nuances of theoretical change, Greetham's works are indispensible aids. Greetham consistently offers elucidation of terminology and shifts in theories and practices, as well as his own perceptive analysis of the philosophical and interdisciplinary underpinnings of recent theories of texts. Besides directing editors to the procedures outlined by the Center for Scholarly Editions and their consultation services, in Chapter 9 of *Textual Scholarship* Greetham traces the stages of preparing a version of a text for publication, pointing out the rationale, logic, or practicality of the various editorial decisions at each step. Excellent "apparatus" also accompanies this major work, including appendixes that illustrate different types of scholarly editions and finely selected bibliographies.

I have devoted so much of this essay to Greetham's work because his explications of "the state of textual studies at the present time" are so clear and useful and provide a solid grounding for the following briefer discussions of three collections of essays that jump right into the current theoretical fray. The first is a group of essays by one author, Jerome J. McGann, the Satanic Hero of textual scholarship in the late 1980s, who has been at the center of many of the controversial issues. He has drawn great heat in both the anathemas and cheers that have been flung his way by textual critics. Although he has responded to some of Howard-Hill's analyses about the nature and derivation of his theories (in a response to Howard-Hill's comments in *Text* 5), McGann's ideas have been criticized by others as well — either as being abstract and untenable, or as lost in lapses of circularity, redundancy, and esoteric ramblings. I believe part of the negative critical reaction is a result of McGann's courage in presenting some of his ideas in flux, as they were developing, with all their unresolved problems out front, not as his "final intentions" for his own theories. McGann's achievement is paramount in this field, not only because his views should ultimately lead to some new directions in the editing of texts but also because textual scholarship is a much more vital and responsible discipline today as a result of the catalyst of his work. His critics argue that practical applications of his theories still need refining and that models of editions of texts that follow along the lines of his positions still need to be done. Despite the problematic nature of his evolving textual rationale, McGann's latest work, *The Textual Condition* (Princeton: Princeton UP, 1991) is certainly one of the pre-eminent theoretical works in the field today, because it helps to clarify, develop, and illustrate with specific cases many of McGann's most important positions.

McGann explains in his introductory chapter "Texts and Textualities" that "Today, texts are largely imagined as scenes of reading rather than scenes of writing. This 'readerly' view of text has been most completely elaborated through the modern hermeneutical tradition in which text is not something we *make* but something we *interpret*" (4); and further, "Various readers and audiences are hidden in our texts, and the traces of their multiple presence are scripted at the most material levels" (10). In this book McGann means to change the focus of textual scholarship "by studying those structures of textual variability that display themselves across a much more extensive textual field. Most important, in our present historical situation, is to demonstrate the operation of these variables at the most material (and apparently least 'signifying' or significant) levels of the text: in the case of scripted texts, the physical forms of books and manuscripts (paper, ink, typefaces, layouts) or their prices, advertising mechanisms, and distribution venues" (12). McGann maintains that his work is not a theory of textuality but "a kind of anti-theory, a 'theory' that would refuse to attempt either a definition or even a comprehensive description of the essential features of text. What is textually possible cannot be theoretically established. What can be done is to sketch, through close and highly particular case studies, the general framework within which textuality is constrained to exhibit its transformations. . . . [This book] maps its particular investigations along the double helix of a work's reception history and its production history. . . . [The map needs to be] followed into the textual field, where 'the meaning of texts' will appear as a set of concrete and always changing conditions: because the meaning is in the use, and textuality is a social condition of various times, places, and persons'' (16). In ensuing chapters McGann gives numerous concrete examples of how one might deal with specific editorial decisions, including some that might occur in editing D. G. Rossetti, Byron, Swinburne, Yeats, and *The New Oxford Book of Verse of the Romantic Period*, while he more extensively discusses editing the works of William Blake and Ezra Pound. McGann includes an excellent, detailed model of projects, dealing specifically with Blake's *Songs*, to use in the classroom, in which students may ''engage with literary work through highly particular studies of the production, transmission, and reception histories of specific texts'' (46).

Another version of some of the ideas in McGann's new book appears in ''Literary Pragmatics and the Editorial Horizon,'' the first essay in *Devils and Angels: Textual Editing and Literary Theory*, edited by Philip Cohen (Charlottesville: UP of Virginia, 1991). Cohen's collection exhibits various dialogues that recast the assumptions and working methods of editorial scholarship, and three respondents comment on the various essays. Cohen's introductory essay provides a succinct and solid background for the following articles which, in addition to McGann's, include others by Peter Shillingsburg, T. H. Howard-Hill, Paul Eggert, D. C. Greetham, Philip Cohen and David H. Jackson, Steven Mailloux, James McLaverty, Hans Walter Gabler, Joseph Grigely, and William E. Cain.

All of these essays are accessible to the non-specialist and, in fact, provide exciting discussions of the theories and practices in the field. As convincing as one point of view may appear, different or even contradictory perspectives offered in the next article force the reader into involvement with the issues. Following McGann's essay is one by Peter Shillingsburg, who serves as the General Editor of *The Thackeray Edition Project*, which is a new series published by Garland that presents Thackeray's works in editions providing guidance to Thackeray's composition and revisions and preserving features of his punctuation. Peter Shillingsburg has also edited the second book published in this series, *Vanity Fair* (1989). In his essay in *Devils and Angels*, Shillingsburg states, ''The reader and the editor have a dual responsibility to authorial intention and to the social contract; both are operative'' and ''editions such as . . . my Thackeray edition are attempts in different ways to emphasize alternative texts, or multiple texts, or indeterminate texts, but all these editions are controversial'' (41). The essays in *Devils and Angels* by McGann and by Shillingsburg are followed by a response from T. H. Howard-Hill, who offers pointed reactions to various aspects of their respective arguments.

Another important collection of essays is *Representing Modernist Texts: Editing as Interpretation*, edited by George Bornstein (Ann Arbor: U of Michigan P, 1991). Although the articles focus on works by twentieth-century authors, the concerns they raise are relevant for nineteenth-century texts as well, and the essays by George Bornstein, Richard J. Finneran, and Michael Groden are of particular interest. In his ''Introduction: Why Editing Matters'' (1–16), Bornstein illustrates how literary interpretation is tied to editorial decisions. He notes, for example, that the publication of the *Waste Land* drafts in 1971 led to realization of Ezra Pound's editorial contribution toward its final shaping. But as Bornstein comments, ''Only recently have scholars begun to ponder the deeper implications of that edition: the arbitrariness of excluding all but the final published form of a work, the dissolution of the notion of a single author, and the role of social forces in the literal constitution of a text'' (2–3). In its entirety this collection seeks to explore the implications for literary critics and theorists of the challenges made to the concept of ''final authorial intentions'' (a term which Bornstein keenly dissects and analyzes), especially as offered by recent theories, such as Reiman's on ''versioning'' and multiple texts. Some of the articles subscribe to author-based theories and others to socially constituted views of texts; ''some may view texts as historically discrete entities to be reproduced in facsimile while others see no way of avoiding individual, aesthetic choices by editors.'' And few of the contributors exclusively favor any one approach (9).

In ''Text and Interpretation in the Poems of W. B. Yeats'' (17–48), Richard J. Finneran analyzes textual problems in dealing with Yeats's poems. After reviewing editorial decisions in three new versions of Yeats's poems (edited independently by Albright, Jeffares, and Martin), Finneran then discusses in detail how the changes he made to *The Poems* (1989) (in titles, punctuation, the order of the poems, and other textual revisions) affect interpretation.

And the concluding essay in Bornstein's collection, Michael Groden's ''Contemporary Textual and Literary Theory'' (259–86), once again reviews the major challenges to the tradition, especially as represented in the work of G. Thomas Tanselle, whom some textual scholars consider its strongest contemporary proponent. Many editors consider Tanselle's works, especially his latest books, *A Rationale of Textual Criticism* (1989) and *Textual Criticism and Scholarly Editing* (1990) classics in the field, while his recent article on ''Textual Criticism and Deconstruction,'' in *Studies in Bibliography* 43 offers a counter-assault on the deconstructionists whose positions challenge the bases of his work. Groden's essay also deals fully and incisively with the concepts of author/authorial intention, work/text, and many other important issues in textual and literary theory.

Three books that specifically illustrate new avenues of research in Victorian studies are *Author and Printer in Victorian England*, by Allan C. Dooley (Charlottesville: UP of Virginia, 1992); *The Victorian Serial*, by Linda K. Hughes and Michael Lund (Charlottesville: UP of Virginia, 1991); and *Victorian Authors and Their Works: Revision Motivations and Modes*, edited by Judith Kennedy (Athens: Ohio UP, 1991).

Dooley's book is an exploration of the ways in which several technical advances employed by Victorian printers significantly influenced the texts of classic works by authors such as Dickens, Browning, Arnold, Tennyson, Eliot, Hardy, and Trollope. As Dooley discovers, these authors seem to have been strikingly knowledgeable about and interested in the printing of their books; they understood the significance of technical advances and moved to exploit them. Dooley establishes the typical patterns of book production and textual change of literary works produced in Victorian England (1840–90), and he illustrates, through many specific cases, how the new technology multiplied the numbers of discrete stages a text went through during a span of time (the author's life or the use of a set of plates, for instance). The concluding chapter, "Textual Change and Textual Criticism," analyzes the work of modern editors of nineteenth-century texts, suggesting that "where the former aim of the scholar was to produce a relatively pristine, authoritative, single text of a given work, textual editors now are interested in presenting the growth, the life, the history of a text." After reviewing the problems of variants, errors, corrections, revisions, versions, and authorial control of textual change, Dooley proposes an approach to editing that aims at discovering the "fullest, most important, most valuable expression of authorial intention toward the text of a work. . . . This proposal sanctifies neither original intention nor final intention and does not dictate a uniform choice of preferred text" (173). Instead Dooley suggests that the textual critic seek that text which "most fully embodies the author's best, most complete, most successful effort to get the work right, even if that effort occurred years after the work was created; even if the author's taste and judgment differ from ours; even when the author revised further (if less successfully) in later editions" (174). Although Dooley acknowledges he is not fully considering alternate textual theories in his study, he probably anticipates hearing from other critics who espouse collaborative or social textual criticism or those who advocate genetic theories. They can certainly be expected to react to Dooley's proposals, which are basically author-centered and privilege "best" versions. Regardless of the reactions from those who adhere to competing textual orientations, Dooley's study represents an elucidating work on the history of Victorian printing and one of major interest to Victorianists who interpret the specific Victorian works he studies.

In contrast to Dooley's focus on techniques of production and their conse-quences, Hughes and Lund in *The Victorian Serial* are more interested in interpreting the Victorian audience that consumed the installment versions of literary texts. *The Victorian Serial* is, in a way, a testimony to the significance of textual study for literary interpretation and cultural studies. For as Hughes and Lund see it, Victorian readers who encountered stories a part at a time, frequently generated different interpretations from those made in the twentieth century based upon single-volume readings. They suggest that "publication format became an essential factor in creating meaning" and that "this reading process was entertwined [sic] with a vision of life no longer shared by the dominant literary culture of the twentieth century" (2). Central to the authors' concerns are the Victorians' views on time, history, family, politics, material-ism, and religion and on how these themes were reflected in the audience's reception of and relationship with serial productions. Because of its focus on audience, the book makes extensive use of reviews of installment numbers, which reveal the immediate reception history of texts as they developed in stages and, at least in part, the involvement of the audience who pleaded and suggested, or kicked and complained, about plots and characters. Some tex-tual critics will interpret this book mainly as evidence of the "collaboration" of the purchasing public, critics, editors, publishers, friends and relatives with the originary author in the creation of texts. But as Hughes and Lund use many models of works by Victorians that first appeared in installment issues (such as those by Dickens, Thackeray, Trollope, Patmore, Eliot, Brown-ing, Tennyson, and Morris), their book offers interpretations of texts as well. And in their concluding chapter, the authors suggest some pedagogical techniques for serial reading of the Victorians in classroom situations and some analyses of the adaptations of serial production in the twentieth century. *The Victorian Serial* has much to offer for textual, literary, and cultural studies and is a model of how the interfacing of these disciplines can lead to rich and deep interpretive insights.

Other models that illustrate how explorations in the history of texts can lead to new literary interpretations appear in the collection of essays edited by the present reviewer, *Victorian Authors and Their Works: Revision Motiva-tions and Modes* (Athens: Ohio UP, 1991). These essays address a broad variety of issues faced by editors, textual critics, literary scholars, composi-tion specialists, and others who are interested in the writing and revision processes involved in the development of Victorian texts. Chapters focus on the writing experiences of individual Victorian authors, such as Browning, Carlyle, Tennyson, Arnold, Henley, and Yeats; study the problems facing authors of texts that are transformed from serial-to-book versions, such as Conrad, Hardy, and Patmore; or explore the relationships between the composition and revision practices of artists who work in two modalities, the Pre-Raphaelites, Rossetti and Morris, as well as Beatrix Potter. Several of these articles also illustrate the problems involved in viewing a text as either a private or public work: they offer insights into individual authors' personal motivations or the influence of public forces at a particular moment in the continually adjusting interplay of all such possible sources of revision. The contributors include George Bornstein, Edward H. Cohen, Ashby Bland Crowder, Suzanne O. Edwards, Catherine Golden, David Leon Higdon, Linda K. Hughes, Fred Kaplan, Frederick Kirchhoff, Anne C. Pilgrim, John R. Reed, and Susan Shatto.

This review essay has sought to provide its readers with a map of recent sources to help them navigate through the current storm of controversy in textual scholarship and to suggest that, as the last three volumes illustrate, here is a rich, if highly controversial, field for new Victorian scholarship.

Kutztown University of Pennsylvania

INDEX

Acragas, 287n.14
Adams, J. F. A., 304
Adams, Sarah Flower, 260
Adl, Mohammed el, 271
All the Year Round, 70–71, 79, 84–86
Altick, Richard, 128, 134
Apostles, 283
Arbuthnot, John, 67
Arnold, Matthew, 6, 13, 287n.17
Athenaeum, 214
Auden, W. H., 329
Austen, Jane, 90–92, 95–97
Author, 230n.1
Aytoun, W. E., 236

Bain, George Grantham, 41–42, 45
Bakhtim, Mikhail, 112
Bancroft, Marie, 7
Barish, Jonas, 5–7
Barwell, Fredrick, 107n.6
Benjamin v. Madison, 48n.2
Bertillon, Alphonse, 45, 47, 48n.8
Besant, Annie, 211
Besant, Sir Walter, 211–31
Black's Law Dictionary, 20
Blackwood's Magazine, 74, 161
Bodichon, Barbara, 308, 377
Bodington, Alice, 302–04
Booth, Michael R., 5–6, 10, 14
Bornstein, George, 379, 385
Boucicault, Dion, 23–24
Bowes, Arthur, 28
Bridges, Yseult, 134
Brightwen, Eliza, 304
Brontë, Charlotte, 345–65
Browning, Elizabeth Barrett, 233–66
Browning, Robert, 242
Bryan, Margaret, 291
Bryce Commission, 305
Buckley, Arabella, 298–304

Bull, John, 67–87
Bulwer-Lytton, Edward, 148–51, 154
Burger, Gottfried, 235, 240, 242, 260
Burgh, A., 86n.4
Burton, Robert, 111–12, 120–23
Byrnes, Thomas, 33–34, 36, 41
Byron, George Gordon, Lord, 147–64,
    164n.4, 166n.10

Carlyle, Thomas, 77, 147–66
Carroll, Lewis. See Dodgson, Charles
    Luturidge
Charrington, Charles, 216
Chesterfield, Lord, 86n.3
Child, Francis J., 237
Chorley, Henry, 68
Clarke, Mary Cowden, 15–16
Cleopatra, 345–63, 364n.7, 364n.8,
    364n.9
Cobbe, Francis Power, 337–38
Cohen, Paula Marantz, 371–75, 378
Cohen, Philip, 379, 384
Coleridge, Samuel Taylor, 14–15, 233,
    241, 248, 260
Collins, Wilkie, 103–04, 127–44,
    169–70, 174, 179, 328
Connoisseur, 80
Contagious Diseases Act, 358
Cooper, Helen, 238, 244, 251, 256
Coser, Lewis A., 63n.5
Costello, Augustine E., 29, 36
Cowley V. People, 24
Craik, Dinah Maria, 64n.6
Craven, H. T., 6
Critic, The, 241
Curwen, John, 77

Darwin, Charles, 71, 291, 298–302
Darwin, Erasmus, 297–98
De Biefve, Edouard, 350, 354–55,

365n.11
Dibdin, Thomas John, 67
Dickens, Charles, 4, 7, 9–12, 16, 17n.3,
    68–70, 85, 102–03, 134, 169–89,
    294
Dodgson, Charles Lutwidge [pseud.
    Lewis Carroll], 111–25
Dooley, Allan, 379, 386–87
Douglas Jerrold's Shilling Magazine,
    69–71, 78, 84
Dramatic and Musical Review, The, 75,
    79

Echo, 215
Edinburgh Review, The, 152, 165n.4
Eliot, George, 1–7, 12, 17n.4, 89–108,
    226, 289, 371, 375–78
Ellis, Sarah, 127
English Review, The, 234
English Woman's Journal, 309–11, 313,
    317, 323n.2
Examiner, The, 73–74
Eyre, Governor, 186

Faithfull, Emily, 311
Fetis, F. J. 79
Finneran, Richard J., 385
Forster, E. M., 271–87
Forster, John, 170, 187n.4
Foucault, Michel, 22, 27, 191–92,
    196–99, 208, 263
Frank V. Chemical National Bank, 48n.6
Franklin V. State, 21
Fraser's Magazine, 148, 151–52,
    165n.5, 165n.7, 166n.11, 230n.1,
    337
Freud, Sigmund, 328, 364n.1
Frye, Northrop, 112, 120–22, 125n.3
Fuller, Margaret, 330
Furnivall, Fredrick J., 233

Galt, John, 151–52
Gardiner, William, 78
Gatty, Margaret, 297
Gilbert, William S., 85
Gloucester Journal, The, 78
Goethe, Johann Wolfgang von, 152,
    163–64, 260
Gosse, Edmund, 304
Gough, Elizabeth, 128–30, 134, 136,

138
Grand, Sarah, 223
Graneigen, Charles Lewis, 86n.2
Grannan, Joseph C., 32–3 Grant, Cary,
    8
Graves, Caroline, 143n.11
Graveson, Caroline, 283
Greetham, D. C., 379–83

Hales, John H., 233
Hallam, Arthur Henry, 282
Hapgood, Hutchins, 23
Hardy, Thomas, 191–208, 233–34,
    286n.1
Haweis, Hugh Reginald, 68, 73, 77,
    83–4
Hayman, Francis, 107n.6
Hazlitt, William, 14
Hemans Felicia, 252–53
Herridge, William, 243
Hodges, Edward, 80
Hogarth, George, 69, 77, 80, 82–83
Hogarth, William, 107n.6
Horace, 111–13
Hughes, Linda K., 386–87
Hughes, Thomas, 327–28, 331–41
Hunt, Leigh, 152, 165n.9

Ibsen, Henrik, 215–18
Indian Mutiny of 1857–58, 186, 187n.3,
    188n.15
Irving, Henry, 5, 7–8

James, Henry, 101, 307, 373
James, Thomas P., 187n.4
Jeffrey, Francis, 162
John Bull Magazine and Literary Re-
    corder, The, 68, 70, 86n.2

Kanin, Garson, 8
Kean, Edmund, 13
Kennedy, James, 151
Kent, Constance, 128–30, 136, 143n.17
Kent, Francis Savile, 128–29
Kingsley, Charles, 289, 294, 328,
    330–31, 337, 342n.10
Kingsley, Mary, 304
Korkowski, Bud, 125n.3

Labouchère Amendment, 283

Lady's Realm, 223
Lamb, Charles, 14, 69–70
Lane, Edward, 350, 354
Lefferts, William H., 29
Lewes, George Henry, 1, 6, 13, 289–290, 371
Lewis, Leopold, 5, 7
Liberal, 154
Lind, Jenny, 74
Linton, Eliza Lynn, 211, 222, 228, 230n.1
Lockhart, John Gibson, 165n.4, 166n.11
Loudon, Jane, 295–96
Lowry, Delvalle, 293
Luco v. United States, 24–25
Lund, Michael, 386–87
Lyell, Charles, 293

Macaulay, Thomas Babington, 152–54, 234
Maginn, William, 148–53, 164n.1, 165n.4
Mainzer, Joseph, 79
Marcet, Jane, 292–93
Marks, Harry H., 29, 41
Married Women's Property Act, The, 89, 99, 105n.1
Married Women's Property Bill, The, 98–99
Married Women's Property Committee, The, 308
Martin, Sir Theodore, 236
Martineau, Harriet, 239, 356–57, 363, 365n.17
Matrimonial Causes Act, 1857, 99
Maurice, F. D. 328
May, Rollo, 328–30
McGann, Jerome J. 379, 381, 383–84
Menippus, 111–124, 125n.3
Meredith, H. O., 271, 283
Mermin, Dorothy, 234–38, 249, 257, 261
Miall, Edward, 64n.9
Mill, John Stuart, 323n.3
Millais, John Everett, 108n.6
Miller, D. A. 14, 140–41, 141n.1, 312
Moore, Thomas, 148, 151–57, 159, 162, 165n.7
More, Hannah, 79, 86n.6
Morning Chronicle, The, 86

Morning Star, 75
Muenchener Morgenblatt, 28
Musical Herald, The, 69–71, 74–75, 78–80, 83–4
Musical Standard, The, 79, 80, 82
Musical World, The, 68–69, 71–72, 74–75, 77–80, 82

Napier, Macvey, 152
Nation, 214, 216
National Association for the Promotion of Social Science, 309
New Monthly Magazine, 241, 246–47, 265n.7
Newman, John Henry, 329
Nietzsche, Friedrich, 64n.5
Nightingale, Florence, 357
North British Review, 56

Observer, The, 74
Oliphant, Margaret, 133, 136
Orwell, George, 185

Paganini, Nicolò, 73–74
Paley, William, 291, 294, 301–02
Palmer, T. A., 11–12
Pater, Walter, 273
Paxton, Nancy, 371, 375–78
People V. Jennings, 19–22
Percy, Bishop, 233–34, 240, 250, 252, 260–61
Petronius Arbiter, 111–12, 114
Philadelphia Public Ledger, 28
Phillips, Patricia, 297
Pinero, Arthur Wing, 17n.2
Pinkerton, Allan, 27, 36
Plues, Margaret, 295
Poovey, Mary, 347–48
Porter v. Buckley, 21, 46

Quarterly Review, The, 165n.4
Queen, 217–18, 221–22, 227–28, 230n.8

Ramus, Peter, 122
Road Murder Case of 1860, 128–30, 133–34, 136, 138, 140–41
Robertson, Tom, 7
Robertson v. Rochester Folding Box Co., 22
Royal Aquarium Westminster, 82

Rubens, Peter Paul, 360–62
Rubinstein, Anton, 67–68
Rudd, Martha, 143n.11
Ruloff v. People, 25
Ruskin, John, 68, 131

Saintsbury, George, 221, 229
Saturday Review, 213, 221, 229, 230n.1
Scheler, Max, 54, 58, 64n.5
Scott, Charles C., 21–22, 25, 28, 47n.1, 48n.2
Scott, Sir Walter, 233–34, 240–42, 257–60
Seneca Falls Convention (1848), 330
Seymour, William, 32
Shakespeare, William, 7, 13–16, 355
Shaw, George Bernard, 77, 83, 216
Shillingsburg, Peter, 379, 384–85
Smith, Charlotte, 291–92
Spectator, 214, 216, 221, 226, 230n.6, 241
Spencer, Herbert, 371, 375–78
Somerset, Lady, 225
State v. Clark, 21, 46
Steffens, Lincoln, 36, 141
Sullivan, Arthur, 85
Symonds, Joseph Addington, 340
Symons, Arthur, 8

Taunton Commission, 305
Tennyson, Alfred Lord, 166n.12, 233–34, 165n.8, 247–48, 261, 265n.6, 265n.7, 282
Terry, Ellen, 8, 14
Thackeray, William Makepeace, 5, 264, 330
Times, The, 73, 75
Tissot, James, 108n.6
Tooley, Sarah A., 211–12, 229
Trimmer, Sara, 291, 297
Trodd, Anthea, 128–29, 134
Trollope, Anthony, 307–24
Twining, Elizabeth, 296

Udderzook v. Commonwealth, 26, 46

Wakefield, Priscilla, 290
Wallbridge, Arthur, 71
Walling, George W., 29, 33, 41
Webbe, Egerton, 72
Weeks, Caleb, 42
Westminster Review, The, 260
Whicher, Jonathan, 129, 140
Wilde, Oscar, 271, 273
Williams v. State, 48n.3
Wilson, John, 161, 164n.4
Woman/ For All Sorts and Conditions of Women, 229
Woman's Herald, 224–25
Woman's Labour Bureau, 229
Womankind, 223
Women's Suffrage Journal, 213
Wood, Ellen, 11–12
Wood, J. G., 303–04
Wordsworth, William, 233, 235, 241–48, 251

Yonge, Charlotte, 223

Zornlin, Rosina M., 296–97